THE MANAGEMENT OF SPORT

ITS FOUNDATION AND APPLICATION

THIRD EDITION

BONNIE L. PARKHOUSE, Ph.D.

Professor, Temple University
School of Tourism and Hospitality Management
Philadelphia, Pennsylvania

EDITOR

With the Endorsement of
The National Association for Sport and Physical Education (NASPE)
an association of the American Alliance for Health,
Physical Education, Recreation and Dance (AAHPERD)

National
Association
for Sport &
Physical Education

Boston   Burr Ridge, IL   Dubuque, IA   Madison, WI   New York   San Francisco   St. Louis
Bangkok   Bogotá   Caracas   Lisbon   London   Madrid
Mexico City   Milan   New Delhi   Seoul   Singapore   Sydney   Taipei   Toronto

McGraw-Hill Higher Education

*A Division of The **McGraw-Hill** Companies*

THE MANAGEMENT OF SPORT: ITS FOUNDATION AND APPLICATION, THIRD EDITION

Published by McGraw-Hill, an imprint of The McGraw-Hill Companies, Inc., 1221 Avenue of the Americas, New York, NY 10020. Copyright " 2001, 1996, 1991 by The McGraw-Hill Companies, Inc. All rights reserved. No part of this publication may be reproduced or distributed in any form or by any means, or stored in a database or retrieval system, without the prior written consent of The McGraw-Hill Companies, Inc., including, but not limited to, in any network or other electronic storage or transmission, or broadcast for distance learning.

Some ancillaries, including electronic and print components, may not be available to customers outside the United States.

This book is printed on acid-free paper.

1 2 3 4 5 6 7 8 9 0 QPF/QPF 0 9 8 7 6 5 4 3 2 1 0

ISBN 0–07–230032–9

Vice president and editor-in-chief: *Kevin T. Kane*
Executive editor: *Vicki Malinee*
Developmental editor: *Carlotta Seeley*
Senior marketing manager: *Pamela S. Cooper*
Media technology project manager: *Judi David*
Project manager: *Joyce Watters*
Senior production supervisor: *Sandra Hahn*
Coordinator of freelance design: *Rick D. Noel*
Cover designer: *Sheilah Barrett*
Interior designer: *Kathleen Theis*
Photo research coordinator: *John C. Leland*
Compositor: *Interactive Composition Corporation*
Typeface: *10/12 Palatino*
Printer: *Quebecor Printing Book Group/Fairfield, PA*

Library of Congress Cataloging-in-Publication Data

The management of sport : its foundation and application / [edited by] Bonnie L. Parkhouse. — 3rd ed.
   p. cm.
  Includes index.
  ISBN 0–07–230032–9 (alk. paper)
  1. Sports administration—Study and teaching—United States.   I. Parkhouse, Bonnie L.

GV713 .M35   2001
796'.06'9—dc21
                                     00–026077
                                     CIP

www.mhhe.com

Brief Table of Contents

Contents

Preface

This book represents a "labor of love" for me personally. Although it is virtually impossible to exhaustively describe the body of knowledge that constitutes a profession in one volume, *The Management of Sport: Its Foundation and Application,* third edition, reestablishes the precedent set by the previous edition, serving as the most comprehensive and current entry in its market. This edition is tailored around the informational needs of the sport manager and benefits from new contributors.

In the era of the fitness entrepreneur, sport has become even more significant (especially financially) and pervasive in our society. This multibillion-dollar industry places unique demands on its personnel and increasingly requires specialized training. Jobs in the sport industry involve myriad skills applicable to the sport setting and specific to the increasingly complex and multifaceted areas it represents. As a result, a new breed of specialists has emerged. Sport management is now recognized as a legitimate field of study in colleges and universities throughout the world. *The Management of Sport: Its Foundation and Application,* third edition, is the most comprehensive compilation of subject matter published to date for the sport management profession.

AUDIENCE
In increasing numbers, students with a wide variety of backgrounds are choosing a course of study in sport management. Our intention with this book is to cater to this changing and rapidly growing audience.

Also, although this book was primarily written for third- and fourth-year undergraduate and postgraduate students, instructors at other levels are encouraged to review its content for potential use as well. **Practitioners will also find it to be a valuable resource.**

FEATURES
Organization
This book uses a unique approach in addressing the substantive aspects of the profession by presenting both the theoretical foundations and subsequent application of these principles.

Content
This book is a compilation of great minds and talent from around the world. Over twenty contributors lent their expertise, providing credibility in regard to content and expanding the student's understanding of the concepts as applied worldwide. For example, there is a new chapter on sport governance, which addresses international, scholastic, collegiate, and professional sports. This chapter shows readers the importance of how sports organizations govern themselves. This topic and all of the other core topics integral to a career in sport management (e.g., finance, human resources, budgeting, and so on) are captured and bound in this book.

Current events in the field are also included, such as an updated history of employer-employee relationships in four professional team sports. It examines crisis situations, their influence on the industry, and how opposing sides worked through differences.

Pedagogy

This text uses many pedagogical features to aid students' comprehension of many diverse topics.

- Each author has indicated **key terms** with which the student will become familiar while reading the chapter. These terms are located at the beginning of each chapter, as well as in bold face type either in headings or text when they are discussed within the chapter.
- Each major section ends with a **Concept Check** that highlights the main discussion.
- A succinct, enumerated **Summary** emphasizes the key points in each chapter.
- Each chapter includes a complete list of **References.** It is recommended that students read these references carefully for supplemental information.
- **Review Questions and Issues and Case Studies** give students further insight into how to apply the theoretical principles.
- **Critical Thinking Exercises** ask readers to take what they've learned in each chapter and find the solution to a real-world problem facing sport management.
- Annotated **Web Sites** provide additional information not addressed in each chapter.

ACKNOWLEDGEMENTS

I would like to express my gratitude to all who contributed to *The Management of Sport: Its Foundation and Application,* 3d edition. Joyce Watters, project manager, Gary O'Brien and Tricia Musel, developmental editors, made an invaluable contribution to this work. Their tireless effort, expertise, and professionalism are greatly appreciated. They kept all of us on schedule under very challenging circumstances.

The ultimate success of a book is contingent on the quality of subject matter presented. Drawing on the expertise of a "Who's Who" list of contributors, this work—as forementioned—is the most comprehensive compilation of subject matter ever published for the sport management profession. Without question, the authors made a commitment to excellence and set other priorities aside to meet extremely demanding deadlines.

I am also grateful to Stan Brassie, University of Georgia, for significant input that enhanced the quality of several individual chapters.

A special thanks goes to the reviewers, who reviewed the current edition; their feedback was tremendously helpful in focusing the revision.

Ruth H. Alexander, University of Florida at
    Gainesville
David B. Carr, Ohio University
L. Marlene Mawson, Illinois State University
Anita M. Moorman, University of Louisville

Many thanks to everyone who contributed to this book. In my opinion, it's an accomplishment we can all be proud of.

                            Bonnie L. Parkhouse, Editor

Editor

BONNIE L. PARKHOUSE
Temple University

Bonnie L. Parkhouse, Professor, received a Ph.D. in Administration from the University of Minnesota. She is currently a member of the faculty in the School of Tourism and Hospitality Management. Previous faculty appointments include the University of Southern California and California State University, Fullerton. Eighteen of her studies have been published in distinguished refereed research journals. Numerous articles she has written have appeared in trade and commercial publications, and she is the senior author of previous books and the editor of the first and second editions of this revision.

Dr. Parkhouse is a former member of the editorial boards for the *Journal of Sport Management* and *Quest*. She is currently a member of the review board for the *International Journal of Sport Management*. She also served as one of seven members of the Sport Management Program Review Council (SMPRC), which acts as an entity for the purpose of reviewing sport management programs in the United States. On invitation, she has served as a consultant in sport management curricular matters at numerous institutions in the United States, as well as in England, Australia, and the Caribbean. Dr. Parkhouse is recognized as a progenitor of sport management curricula and theory; her publications are frequently cited by other authors.

Contributing Authors

JOHN AMIS
De Montfort University

John Amis is a doctoral student at the University of Alberta. He earned an undergraduate honors degree in mathematics and physical education from the University of Birmingham and a Master of Arts degree from Dalhousie University in Nova Scotia. John was the 1994 NASSM student essay award winner. He has published articles in *Leisure Studies* and the *Journal of Sport Management*.

ELIZABETH BARBER
Temple University

Betsy Barber, Academic Director for the School of Tourism and Hospitality Management, received her Ph.D. from the University of Iowa in 1987. Prior to teaching ten years at Temple University, Dr. Barber taught at Southern Connecticut State University. Her teaching experience is in recreation and leisure studies, commercial recreation, and tourism. She has given numerous presentations on customer service and she has published in a variety of research journals.

SCOTT BRANVOLD
Robert Morris College

Scott Branvold is an Associate Professor in the Management and Marketing Department at Robert Morris College in Pittsburgh, PA. His teaching experience at Robert Morris and the University of Oklahoma has involved both graduate and undergraduate programs and includes sport marketing, sport sociology, and legal issues in sport. He has been involved in sport as an athlete, coach, sports information director, and facility manager. A charter member in the North American Society for Sport Management (NASSM), he has presented several papers at NASSM, the American Alliance for Health, Physical Education, Recreation, and Dance (AAHPERD), and the International Sports Business Conference. He also has had articles published in the *Journal of Sport Management*, the *Journal of Sport Marketing*, and has written a chapter in *Sport Business: Operational and Theoretical Aspects*.

LAURENCE CHALIP
Griffith University

Laurence Chalip is a Senior Lecturer with the Faculty of Business and Hotel Management at Griffith University's Gold Coast Campus in Queensland, Australia. He has worked internationally in sport as an administrator, coach, and researcher, including working as an executive member of research teams at the Los Angeles and Seoul Olympics. He has held faculty positions at the University of Chicago, the University of Waikato, and the University of Maryland. He twice served as a lecturer for the International Olympic Academy in Greece. He earned his Ph.D. in policy analysis from the University of Chicago.

PACKIANATHAN CHELLADURAI
Ohio State University

Dr. Chelladurai is a recognized scholar of management science, specializing in organizational theory and organizational behavior in the context of sport. Dr. Chelladurai has authored four books and contributed over seventy articles to the sport management literature. He is the first recipient of the Earle F. Zeigler Award from the North American Society for Sport Management. He is the former editor of the *Journal of Sport Management* and current member of the editorial boards of the *Journal of Sport Management* and the *European Journal of Sport Management*. Dr. Chelladurai also serves as a guest reviewer for journals such as the *Journal of Sport and Exercise Psychology, Research Quarterly for Exercise and Sport,* and *Perceptual and Motor Skills*. He has been invited to lecture and/or teach in France, Finland, Greece, India, Japan, Korea, the Netherlands, Norway, Portugal, Scotland, and South Africa. He has participated in the formation of the North American Society for Sport Management, the European Association of Sport Management, and the Indian Association of Sport Management.

ANNIE CLEMENT
Florida State University

Annie Clement, Associate Professor, holds a Ph.D. from the University of Iowa and a J.D. from Cleveland State University. She is a member of the Ohio Bar and the United States District Court, Northern District of Ohio.

Dr. Clement is author of *Law in Sport and Physical Activity* and *Legal Responsibility in Aquatics* and ten book chapters, and coauthor of *Teaching Physical Skills* and *Equity in Physical Education*. A sought-after speaker and writer, she has over one hundred published works and has given two hundred presentations.

Annie Clement has received the American Alliance for Health, Physical Education, Recreation and Dance Honor Award and the Aquatic Council Award; the OAHPERD Merit Award; the Council for National Cooperation in Aquatics Merit Award; and the Tsunami Spirit Award from the Aquatic Therapy Institute. She has also received the NASPE Joy of Effort Award, the American Jurisprudence Award for Achievement in Business Associations, and was among the first twenty women selected by the American Council on Education in its Identification of Women Leaders in Higher Education. She is a Fellow of the American Bar Association Foundation, a research award given to only one-half of 1 percent of the ABA membership. Dr. Clement is a

past president of the National Association for Sport and Physical Education (NASPE) and the Ohio Teacher Educators.

PETER J. FARMER
Guilford College

Peter Farmer, Assistant Professor and Director of the Sport Management Studies program, Guilford College, holds a Ph.D. from the University of New Mexico, an M.B.A. from the University of Phoenix, and a M.Ed and B.S. from the University of Texas at El Paso. He currently teaches undergraduate sport management courses in the areas of sport marketing, sport and facility management. Dr. Farmer is currently completing a book on facility management and a publication on international sport policy. He has presented extensively in the areas of facility management and sport marketing. Dr. Farmer was a former Olympian for Australia.

HARMON GALLANT
Rice University

Harmon Gallant is currently the Director of the Sport Management Program, Department of Kinesiology, at Rice University in Houston. He received a B.A. in philosophy from Northwestern University and a J.D. from Illinois Institute of Technology/Chicago-Kent College of Law. He has been a member of the Illinois Bar since 1977. His recent publications include an essay on sports franchise relocations in the 1990's. Since 1993 he has authored a weekly column on legal issues in sports, and he is a regular contributor to *The Football Network* syndicated radio program. In 1998, Dr. Gallant was appointed to the Ethics Committee of the Houston 2012 Foundation, the city's Olympic bid Organization.

DIANNA P. GRAY
University of Northern Colorado

Dianna P. Gray, Associate Professor, received her Ph.D. from The Ohio State University, and has held faculty positions at Kent State and Indiana Universities. Her research and teaching areas include sport marketing, management, and media relations, and she has published in a variety of trade and scholarly journals. The Indiana Pacers, Cleveland Indians, Cleveland Force, Women's Basketball Coaches Association, and Gus Macker Basketball are among the various sport organizations for which she has served as a consultant. Dr. Gray is also on the Advisory Board of the Women's Sports Foundation and has served as a sport management curriculum consultant.

SUE INGLIS
McMaster University

Sue Inglis is an Associate Professor in the Department of Kinesiology. She earned her Ph.D. from The Ohio State University, and M.A. and B.P.E. from the University of Alberta. Sue's experience includes nine years varsity tennis coaching, seven years chair of McMaster's women's athletic program, leadership positions in NASSM (North American Society for Sport Management) including president 1993–94, member of the NASPE-NASSM Sport Management Task Force 1989–92 and the Sport Management Program Review Council 1992–95, and numerous years teaching and research in sport management. Dr. Inglis' interests and published work focuses on governance issues in sport and intercollegiate athletic environments and women's involvement in organizational life.

RICHARD IRWIN
University of Memphis

Dr. Irwin (Ed.D., 1990, University of Northern Colorado) is currently the Director of the University of Memphis Bureau of Sport & Leisure Commerce which is housed within the Department of Human Movement Sciences and Education. In addition to his university responsibilities Dr. Irwin has conducted extensive research in the area of sport marketing with specific foci on spectator assessments and the management of sponsorship and licensing programs. Dr. Irwin is also a market research consultant for several major sport organizations and a member of the *Sport Marketing Quarterly* Editorial Board.

BETTE B. KEYSER
Illinois State University

Bette B. Keyser, Assistant Professor in the Department of Health Sciences, received an Ed.D. in Curriculum and Instruction from Illinois State University. As Coordinator of Clinical Experiences in Health Education, she supervises both health education interns and student teachers. She has provided guidance to undergraduate students in portfolio development and to faculty interested in integrating student portfolios into professional preparation programs. Her publications and presentations have been in the area of student portfolios, pedagogy, inservice design, and critical thinking.

MICHAEL LEEDS
Temple University

Michael Leeds, Associate Professor, earned his Ph.D. in Economics from Princeton University in 1983. He earned a B.A. in Economics in 1977 from Haverford College. He has been a member of the Economics Department at Temple University since 1982. He has published articles in the areas of labor economics, applied microeconomics, and the economics of sports. Since 1994 he has been Director of the Honors Program in the Fox School of Business at Temple.

FRANK LINNEHAN
Drexel University

Dr. Frank Linnehan, Assistant Professor of Human Resources at Drexel University, received his Ph.D. in Human Resource Administration from Temple University. Dr. Linnehan's research interests include affirmative action, equal employment and workforce diversity initiatives, along with school-to-work transitions for high school students. He has authored or coauthored papers that have appeared in the *Academy of Management Journal, Group and Organization Management, Applied Psychology: An International Journal* and *Educational Evaluation and Policy Analysis.*

Prior to receiving his Ph.D., Dr. Linnehan worked for seventeen years in both line and human resource management in the financial services industry. He has held positions as a training and development specialist, HR generalist, human resources manager, and VP–Human Resources.

MIREIA LIZANDRA

Mireia Lizandra attended the University of Barcelona, Spain, where she received her degree in physical education as well as her J.D. from the same university. In the United States, she received her master's and doctorate degrees in sport administration from Temple University, Philadelphia, PA. While in Philadelphia, she worked with the Philadelphia Eagles Football Club. In 1990, she began working for the United States Olympic Committee in Colorado Springs, CO as an International Relations Coordinator. In that position, she was involved with the 1991

Pan American Games in Cuba, the 1992 Winter Olympic Games in Albertville, and the 1992 Summer Olympic Games in Barcelona. Later on, she took a position with the Atlanta Committee for the Olympic Games (ACOG) as the Director of the National Olympic Committee Relations Department. In that capacity, she orchestrated the communications between ACOG and the 197 National Olympic Committees. After the 1996 Summer Olympic Games, Mireia worked as a freelance consultant conducting and developing different national and international projects for several clients. In 1998, she took a position with The Marquee Group as Managing Director for Olympic and Pan American Projects. She has combined her jobs with teaching at the graduate level at Georgia State University, Georgia Institute of Technology and Temple University.

MARILYN MORROW
Illinois State University

Marilyn Morrow, Associate Professor and Chairperson in the Department of Health Sciences, holds a Ph.D. from Southern Illinois University at Carbondale and an M.A. and B.S. from Eastern Illinois University. Her teaching and research interests include publications and presentations in the area of professional preparation issues, including program assessment and portfolio development. She has coauthored a book designed to help students practice and build competency in a number of essential professional skills.

AARON MULROONEY
Kent State University

Aaron L. Mulrooney is currently an Associate Professor in the School of Exercise, Leisure and Sport. He holds an M.B.A. in Finance and a J.D. from the University of Akron and currently teaches graduate courses in sport law, finance, and facility management as well as coordinating the sport administration program at Kent. His primary publications have been in facility management and law, and he has developed presentations for various audiences at state, national, and international conferences. Along with Peter Farmer and Rob Ammon, he is currently completing a text specifically devoted to the topic of facility planning and management.

DANNY O'BRIEN
De Montfort University

Danny O'Brien is a doctoral student at De Montfort University, Bedford, England. He earned an undergraduate degree in physical education at California State University, Long Beach, and a Diploma of Teaching (Physical Education) from Australian Catholic University, Sydney. Danny is a former professional rugby league player and was the 1997 NASSM student essay award winner. His research focuses on organizational change and strategic decision making.

DR. BRENDA G. PITTS
Florida State University

Dr. Pitts is a Professor in Sport Management at Florida State University. She is the recipient of the year 2000 Dr. Earle F. Zeigler Award—the top award for scholars in sport management. Although Dr. Pitts is the youngest scholar to receive the award, her accomplishments are numerous in the award's recognized areas of student development, leadership, and scholarship. She is author/co-author of numerous publications and presentations primarily in the area of sport marketing, and is co-author of two sport marketing textbooks and a third forthcoming text. She is sought after for consulting in sport marketing, reviewing materials, and speaking at conferences. Her international stops have included South Africa, Hong Kong, Singapore, Malaysia, France, Germany, Hungary, England, The Netherlands, Scotland, and France. Dr. Pitts works with the Sport Management Library project—a project which has produced 8 textbooks and another 9 books are in development.

In addition, Dr. Pitts is recognized as one of the leading scholars on lesbian and gay sports. Her research is among the first of its kind and serves as the foundation for future research. She has produced several publications, given numerous presentations, and teaches a course titled 'Lesbian and Gay Sport Studies'. She works with the Federation of Gay Games—the international governing body of the Gay Games—conducting research, helping with the archives, and organizing and managing the Gay Games Conference. She is currently working on a book on the history and story of the Gay Games.

THOMAS H. REGAN
University of South Carolina

Tom H. Regan is an Associate Professor and Chairman of Sports Business at the University of South Carolina in the College of Professional Sciences. He brings with him a wealth of experience in the areas of regional economic impact analysis and event development in sports and entertainment. His research emphasis is regional economics and sports and entertainment event development. His recent accomplishments include a leading research study on the "Economic Impact of the Denver Broncos on the Denver Colorado Metropolitan Area," and a business/marketing plan proposed for luxury box seating at Notre Dame Stadium in South Bend, Indiana. Dr. Regan recently completed a comprehensive economic impact study on Golf Course Operations in the State of South Carolina. His work experience includes working as a staff accountant for Fox & Co., CPAs, and eight years as a comptroller for a fully integrated oil and gas company. He is currently working on a text book relative to "Managing Sport and Special Events." He holds bachelor and master of Accounting degrees from the University of Wyoming and a Doctorate degree in Sports Administration from the University of Northern Colorado.

MATTHEW J. ROBINSON
York College of Pennsylvania

Matthew J. Robinson, Associate Professor of Sport Management, received his Ed.D. in sport management from Temple University in 1995, held a faculty position at Allentown College of St. Francis de Sales and served as Head Men's Soccer Coach at Western Maryland College before coming to York College of Pennsylvania in 1998 to initiate the institution's sport management program. Robinson's teaching areas include sport marketing, media relations in sport, sport finance, sport ethics and legal aspects of sport. He has conducted research in the areas of job satisfaction of intercollegiate athletic directors, and athletic fundraising. He has also conducted marketing research for LPGA events, intercollegiate athletic programs and professional indoor soccer teams. Robinson has over 15 articles published and has made over 20 international and national presentations. He serves on the editorial boards of *Athletic Management* magazine and the *National Soccer Coaches Association of America Soccer Journal*. Robinson is a co-author for the book *Making the Games Happen: Profiles of Sport Management Professionals*.

LINDA A. SHARP
University of Northern Colorado

Linda A. Sharp received her B.A. from Baldwin-Wallace College and her J.D. from Cleveland-Marshall College of Law. Currently, she is a faculty member in the Sport Administration graduate program at the University of Northern Colorado. She is also an author and consultant in the areas of sport law and higher education law. She has presented at six Education Law Association National Conventions and for the last seven years, has spoken at the Stetson University College of Law Conference on Law and Higher Education. Professor Sharp has coauthored a monograph on *Camps on Campus* which was published by United Educators Insurance Risk Retention Group, Inc. and has written a monograph entitled *Sport Law* for ELA. For the years 1989–1999, Professor Sharp has written the chapter on "Sport Law" for ELA's *Yearbook of Education Law*. She has also prepared the last four supplements for the chapter on Tort Liability found in the *Legal Deskbook for Administrators of Independent Colleges and Universities* (2nd Edition). Professor Sharp is a past president of the Society for the Study of Legal Aspects of Sport and Physical Activity.

DAVID K. STOTLAR
University of Northern Colorado

Dr. David K. Stotlar has a Doctor of Education degree from the University of Utah and serves as Professor in the School of Kinesiology & Physical Education at the University of Northern Colorado. He teaches on the faculty in the areas of sport management and sport law. He has had more than forty articles published in professional journals and has written several textbooks and book chapters in sport, fitness, and physical education. He has made numerous presentations at national and international professional conferences. On several occasions, he has served as a consultant to fitness and sport professionals. He was selected by the USOC as a delegate to the International Olympic Academy in Greece and the World University Games Forum in Italy. He has conducted international seminars in sport management for the Hong Kong Olympic Committee, the National Sports Council of Malaysia, Mauritius National Sports Council, the National Sports Council of Zimbabwe, the Singapore Sports Council, the Chinese Taipei University Sport Federation, the Bahrain Sport Institute, the government of Saudi Arabia, the South African National Sports Congress, and the Association of Sport Sciences in South Africa. Dr. Stotlar's contribution to the profession includes having served as President of the North American Society for Sport Management.

SUE VAIL
York University

Dr. Vail holds an Associate Professor position at York University and is the Director of the Sport Administration Program within the School of Physical Education. Her doctoral research, at the University of Ottawa, investigated the organizational effectiveness of National Sport Organizations. Over the past several years, Dr. Vail's research has focused on ways to develop collaborative partnerships among community sport, recreation and education leaders.

Prior to accepting her position with York University, Susan was a consultant with the (then) Fitness and Amateur Sport Branch for eight years. Her responsibilities included working with a portfolio of National Sport and Recreation Organizations to assist them with issues of organizational development and leadership. Her knowledge of the national and provincial sport system in Canada is extensive.

More recently, she has done work with the Canadian Figure Skating Association, Tennis Canada, Calgary Olympic Development Association, ParticipACTION, Parks and Recreation Ontario, Ontario Physical and Health Education Association, Ontario Hockey Federation and the Ontario Ministry of Citizenship, Culture and Recreation.

BETTY VAN DER SMISSEN
Michigan State University

Dr. van der Smissen has the unique background of holding a doctorate in recreation, as well as a law degree. She is a member of the bar. Professionally, she has combined her legal and sport/physical activity interests in both her teaching and research, as well as organizational involvements. Dr. van der Smissen has taught both undergraduate- and graduate-level courses in the Legal Aspects of Sport and Leisure Services. For close to ten years she was Director of the School of Health, Physical Education, and Recreation at Bowling Green State University, with its extensive Sport Management program.

Her research is in the legal field. She has authored a three-volume reference on Legal Liability and Risk Management for Public and Private Entities.

M. ELIZABETH VERNER
Illinois State University

M. Elizabeth (Beth) Verner, Professor in the Department of Health, Physical Education and Recreation at Illinois State University, teaches fitness management at the undergraduate level, athletic administration at the graduate level, and coordinates the professional practice (senior field experience) program for undergraduate exercise science and athletic training students. She has authored articles and given presentations related to experiential learning, curriculum design, administration, and gender equity in sport. Dr. Verner is currently exploring a model based on social cognitive theory to study factors which influence the contribution patterns and preferences of those who financially donate to intercollegiate athletics.

PART I

Fundamentals

CHAPTER 1

Definition, Evolution, and Curriculum

Bonnie L. Parkhouse and Brenda G. Pitts

In this chapter, you will become familiar with the following terms:

Sport management
Sport administration

Sport Management Program
Review Council

Overview

Sport is a dominant influence in American society. No single aspect of our culture receives the media attention given to sport. The sport business industry, consisting of such business segments as sporting goods, sport marketing firms, sport sponsorship companies, professional sports, sports apparel, sports media, and recreational sports, is estimated to be the eleventh largest industry (Meek, 1997) and grows every year. According to *SportsBusiness Journal* (1998), the sport business industry is worth $324 billion dollars. Indeed, it is perhaps larger than any single estimate if one considers estimates of its many segments, some of which are shown in table 1-1.

Spectator sport, often professional sports, receives an unparalleled amount of media attention. There are sports media businesses and industries whose sole product is producing, televising, broadcasting, and printing information about spectator-driven sports events. Some of the largest events, often called sports mega-events, include football's Super Bowl, soccer's Women's and Men's World Cup, the Olympic Games, and basketball's NCAA Women's and Men's Final

Four. Not limited by individual sports, there are many new amateur and/or recreational sports events rivaling the traditional ones, such as the X-Games. The sports media industry includes newspapers, magazines, radio, and several sports channels.

The largest segment of sports, however, is not professional sports. It is participation sports. This consists of the thousands of sports, recreational, sports tourism, leisure, and fitness activities that millions of us participate in every day. The softball leagues, bowling leagues, hiking clubs, snow ski packages, fitness clubs, biking clubs, running groups, walking clubs, scuba trips, yachting and sailing regattas, in-line skating outings, marathons, and hundreds of other activities in which we participate make up the largest segment of the sport business industry. Everywhere one looks or participates in life, there is sport. There are even sports events for the amateur level that have grown to be sports mega-events. As you can see in the information provided in table 1-2, you will find sports organized in politics, at your workplace, and even through your religious affiliation.

TABLE 1-1   *Some numbers of the sport business industry*

Sports tourism (1998)	$111.8 billion
Sporting goods sales (1998)	$45.6 billion
Sports sponsorship expenditures (1998)	$13.2 billion
NASCAR (1998)	$2 billion
The Gay Games V economic impact (1998)	$350 million
Billiards products market (1998)	$235 million
Leading women's professional sports prize money (beach volleyball, bowling, downhill skiing, golf and tennis in 1996)	$65.4 million

Source: Pitts and Stotlar (in press). *Fundamentals of sport marketing.* Morgantown, WV: Fitness Information Technology.

TABLE 1-2   *Some categories of sports mega-events*

Geographical regions	African Games
	Asian Games
	Pan American Games
Disabilities	Special Olympics
	Paralympics
Religious affiliation	Maccabiah Games
Career/profession	Police Games
	World Student Games
	Corporate Games
Sexual orientation	The Gay Games
	EuroGames
Political affiliation	Commonwealth Games

Sources: (Preston, 1990; Pitts and Ayers, 1999).

Moreover, the sport industry is expanding and growing in many other countries. As the world becomes a smaller place and cultures and people mix, sports that once were unique to certain regions are making their way around the globe.

This multibillion-dollar industry also places unique demands on its management personnel. Management positions require management, marketing, communications, accounting, finance and economics, and legal skills applicable to the sport setting and specific to the increasingly complex and multifaceted areas it represents. There are millions of companies within the sport business industry and thus millions of jobs and careers requiring a specialized knowledge of the industry and its unique products. Because of this and the growing complexity of the industry, an academic field—sport management—emerged in the 1980s and 1990s to meet the need of those going into careers in the sport business industry. This new field is one of the fastest-growing areas on many college campuses.

SPORT MANAGEMENT DEFINED

From an *applied* perspective, sport management has existed since the time of the ancient Greeks, when combat among gladiators or animals attracted crowds of spectators. Herod, king of Judaea, was honorary president of the eleventh-century Olympics. A magnificent ceremony opened the Games, followed by athletic competition where thousands of spectators were entertained lavishly (Frank, 1984). According to Parks and Olafson (1987), given the magnitude of such events, there must have been purveyors of food and drink, promoters, purchasing agents, marketing personnel, and management directors. Sport management has emerged both as an academic discipline and a professional occupation. It is the main source of income and a full-time job for a significant number of people (Soucie and Doherty, 1996). Today, all of these individuals are known as *practitioners*; this term includes all persons employed in the applied field of sport management.

Although the terms **sport(s) management** and **sport(s) administration,** are often used interchangeably, the first most accurately describes this field from a universal, or global, perspective. That is, *management* is all-encompassing and represents the myriad sport-related areas identified by De-Sensi et al. (1990), including facilities, hotels and resorts, public and private fitness and racquet clubs, merchandizing, and collegiate and professional sports. They defined sport management as "any combination of skills related to planning, organizing, directing, controlling budgeting, leading and evaluating within the context of an organization or department whose primary product or service is related to sport" (p. 33).

Although some scholars have made the distinction that the function of administration is to set goals and policies and management executes those policies, it is an accepted practice to use these two terms synonymously. The term *management* is most commonly used in the field of sport management. For example, our professional organization is the North American Society for Sport Management (NASSM). The *Journal of Sport Management (JSM)*, which has garnered a high standard of scholarship in a relatively short time (Weese, 1995), has become a major resource for disseminating significant knowledge in sport management (Parkhouse, 1996).

The terms *sport* and *sports* are also used interchangeably. According to Parks, Zanger, and Quarterman (1998), sports is singular in nature, whereas sport is a more all-encompassing term. The North American Society for Sport Management (NASSM) has elected to use the collective noun "sport" and encourages its use. Refer to chapter 2 for a definition of the sport industry.

As previously mentioned, *sport* has several definitions (Loy, 1968; Snyder and Spreitzer, 1989; vander Zwaag, 1988). For contemporary sport management as an academic field of study, the term *sport* must now be more broadly defined. Because sport management is the academic area that encompasses the study of the sport business industry, the word *sport* must encompass all of the segments of the industry, such as sporting goods, sports tourism, and other previously mentioned. It is necessary to develop a more contemporary definition of sport management as it relates to the academic field. A review of the current sport management literature revealed different definitions for sport management. However, the one chosen for this textbook that we believe reflects the contemporary broad concept of the sport business industry is the following:

Sport management is the study and practice involved in relation to all people, activities, organizations, and businesses involved in producing, facilitating, promoting, or organizing any product that is sport, fitness, and recreation related; and, sport products can be goods, services, people, places, or ideas (Parks, Zanger, and Quarterman, 1998; Pitts, Fielding, and Miller, 1994; Pitts and Stotlar, 1996).

The NASPE-NASSM Joint Task Force on Sport Management Curriculum and Accreditation (1993) defined sport management as "the field of study offering the specialized training and education necessary for individuals seeking careers in any of the many segments of the industry."

CONCEPT CHECK

From an applied perspective, sport management has been in existence for centuries. Only recently, however, has sport management been acknowledged as an academic pursuit. This field shares two basic elements—sport and business administration, or management. The business component includes not only such management functions as planning, organizing, directing, and controlling, but also such areas as accounting, marketing, economics and finance, and law. From a sport management perspective, the term sport includes the spectator sport industry, which focuses on consumer entertainment, and the fitness industry, which concentrates on consumer participation in fitness-related activities. Although the terms sport management, sport administration, and athletic administration are often used interchangeably, the first most accurately describes this field from a universal, or global, perspective.

THE EVOLUTION OF SPORT MANAGEMENT

Although sport management is indeed a relatively new concept in academe, its acceptance as a legitimate area of study is well documented in the literature (Crosset et al., 1998; Parkhouse and Ulrich, 1979; Parkhouse, 1987; Parks et al., 1998; Soucie and Doherty, 1996). It is also the topic of numerous trade articles and several published textbooks and journals, and has been featured in such popular publications as *USA Today* and *Time*.

Although there has been no historical study to determine the history of sport management as a university program, Ohio University claims to have had the first in 1966. However, two decades earlier, between 1949 and 1959, Florida Southern University offered a sport management curriculum approved by the State Department of Education of Florida and was titled "Baseball Business Administration" (Isaacs, 1964). Considered to be the first and only of its kind, the curriculum consisted of nine content areas, some of which were similar to those content areas required in today's Sport Management Curriculum Standards. Some of them were Tickets and Tax Laws, Legal Responsibility and Insurance, Promotion and Public Relations, Park Maintenance, and Finances, Accounting, and Payroll Systems.

Perhaps the first time sport management jobs and careers were mentioned was in 1964 in a book titled *"Careers and Opportunities in Sports"* (Isaacs, 1964). Throughout the book, a variety of jobs are presented, such as working in sports trading cards, sports art, merchandising, sports journalism, and sporting goods. Many others are presented in table 1-3. Although Isaacs presents several sport management jobs and careers, in one chapter titled "Careers in Sports Administration" Isaacs describes sports administration as jobs that fall into one of two categories: (1) the executive offices of the ruling bodies of sport; and (2) the administrative bodies of competitive athletics teams. The Sports Administration Program at Ohio University was a master's offering that actually had its roots at the University of Miami in Coral Gables, Florida. James G. Mason, a physical education professor there, prepared a curriculum for a proposed program in sport management at the encouragement of Walter O'Malley, then president of the Brooklyn (soon to become Los Angeles) Dodgers. O'Malley first approached Mason in 1957 with the idea. Although it was never implemented, this curriculum became the basis of the Ohio University program (Mason et al., 1981). A few years later, Biscayne College (now St. Thomas University) and St. John's University became the first institutions granting baccalaureate degrees in sport management. The second master's program was established in 1971 at the University of Massachusetts.

In 1980, 20 colleges and universities in the United States offered graduate programs in sport management. By 1985, this number had grown to 83 programs in the United States (40 undergraduate, 32 graduate, and 11 at both levels), as identified by the National Association for Sport and Physical Education (NASPE). The May 23, 1988, issue of *Sports, Inc.* published a compendium of 109 colleges and universities with programs in sport management. Of the 109 institutions identified, 51 offered undergraduate degrees, 33 were at the master's level, and 25 sponsored both undergraduate and master's programs (Brassie, 1989). A follow-up survey of colleges and universities in the United States conducted by NASPE in 1993 identified 201 sport management programs, including six doctoral programs.

More recent surveys indicate that more than 200 programs existed at the end of the millennium in the United States. That's a growth of 5,000 percent over thirty years. According to the Sport Management Program Review Registry, fifty of those institutions either have approved programs, are currently in folio review, or have completed the Sport Management Registry Process. (See table 1-4.)

Although the first sport management programs were established between the 1940s and 1970s, the significant proliferation in curricular development was not observed until the mid-1980s. As a result, by 1988 only 10 percent of the programs had been in existence for more than five years.

Unlike the United States, the number of programs in Canada has not changed significantly in the past twenty years. In 1980 Bedecki and Soucie reported that ten undergraduate, nine master's, and two doctoral programs existed there. Eight years later, Soucie (1988) reported six undergraduate, nine master's and two doctoral programs. Today, ten undergraduate, seven master's, and two doctoral programs exist. Most Canadian campuses offer a course or two in sport management.

Present programs in the United States are more applied in nature, focusing on such areas as collegiate and professional sports, facility management, and health and fitness club management, whereas those in Canada are more theoretical. That is, the focus is on such subdisciplines as historical and cultural perspectives of sport and physical activity, psychological and sociological dimensions, and physiological and biomechanical aspects.

Sport management also has international appeal. In addition to Canada, Japan, Australia, New Zealand,

---

TABLE 1-3   *Sport administration jobs and careers presented in Stan Isaacs 1964 book "Careers and Opportunities in Sports"*

sports trading cards	sports themed restaurants
sports art	sports agent
sports merchandising	sports journalism
sports reporter	sports photographer
sports TV	sports radio
sports books	sports concessions
sports promoter	sports statistics organization
sporting goods	sports lawyers
sports accountant	

TABLE 1-4   *Current sport management program review registry*

Approved programs	Institutions currently in folio review	Institutions having completed the registry
Undergraduate 16	Undergraduate 12	Undergraduate 12
Master's 12	Master's 10	Master's 8
Doctorate 2	Doctorate 0	Doctorate 2
Total: 30	22	22

China, Greece, Italy, South Africa, France, and the United Kingdom have all implemented programs. In 1990 the Bowater Faculty of Business at Victoria College established Australia's first bachelor of business program in sport management. This specialization consists of a core of business courses, a required core of sport studies, and offerings that combine the concepts of sport and management, such as sport marketing and sport law. *The Guidelines for Programs Preparing Undergraduate and Graduate Studies for Careers in Sport Management,* published by NASPE in 1987, were especially instrumental in the development of the Australian model.

The National College of Physical Education and Sports in the Republic of China (Taiwan) also has established a curriculum in sport management. As of 1992, graduates of this program are prepared to assume leadership roles in sport management in Taiwan. Again, the U.S. model was influential in shaping this program, although other Asian models—notably that found in Korea—were also examined. The curriculum in Taiwan includes a business core, a sport studies core, an integrated core, and a variety of field experiences.

Recently the Japanese physical education curriculum has also undergone a significant transformation. The major reason is the decreasing demand for physical education teachers and the increasing need for personnel in the commercial sport sector. Specifically, the demand in the driving range industry is unique to Japan. Unlike the United States and other European countries, Japan has had tremendous growth in this area; more than 100 million people use driving range facilities

there each year. These facilities require personnel that have exceptional management skills. Management of spectator sports has also become increasingly important because this industry continues to grow rapidly not only in Japan, but worldwide as well. The curricular standards (discussed in the curriculum section) that were developed for the preparation of students for the sport management profession serve as an American model for curriculum development. As sport management becomes more global in nature, country-specific curricula will serve the same purpose (Crosset, Bromage, & Hums, 1998).

Sport management as an academic profession is also developing in these countries. For example, the European Association for Sport Management (EASM) is similar to the North American Society for Sport Management (NASSM). Its membership is primarily university professors in sport management. There is an annual academic conference, and there is a journal, the *European Journal for Sport Management (EJSM).* The EASM primarily serves countries in Europe, although many members are from other countries from around the globe.

In Australia, sport management academic professionals have also started an academic society, the Sport Management Association of Australia and New Zealand (SMAANZ). The SMAANZ hosts an academic conference and publishes a journal, the *Sport Management Review.*

Two professional associations in North America serve the sport management profession. The North American Society for Sport Management (NASSM) and the National Association for Sport and Physical

Education (NASPE) have monitored the rapid growth in this profession.

In 1985 NASSM was established to promote, stimulate, and encourage study, research, scholarly writing, and professional development in sport management (Zeigler, 1987). NASSM is the successor of the Sport Management Arts and Science Society (SMARTS), which was conceived in the 1970s by faculty at the University of Massachusetts. Like the members of SMARTS, those of NASSM focus on the theory, applications, and practice of management specifically related to sport, exercise (fitness), dance, and play. In addition to an annual conference, NASSM sponsors the *Journal of Sport Management* (JSM). JSM publishes refereed articles relative to the theory and applications of sport management. Published since January 1987, this journal has become the major resource for disseminating significant knowledge in the field.

NASPE, an association of the American Alliance for Health, Physical Education, Recreation, and Dance (AAHPERD), approved a sport management task force in 1986 to meet the needs of its members who were involved in sport management curricula. The NASPE task force included five professors and four practitioners. In an attempt to avoid duplication of the services offered by NASSM, the task force identified three agenda items: (1) curricular guidelines, (2) student guidelines for selecting programs, and (3) a directory of college programs preparing professionals in sport management. The task force drafted curricular guidelines and disseminated them to those directors of sport management programs identified by NASPE for input. Suggestions were then incorporated into the final document. In the fall of 1987, the NASPE Cabinet approved this document as NASPE's official curricular guidelines and published it as *Guidelines for Programs Preparing Undergraduate and Graduate Students for Careers in Sport Management* (Brassie, 1989a).

When NASPE published its 1987 guidelines for programs preparing undergraduate and graduate students for careers in sport management, NASSM was invited to endorse the guidelines. Many members of NASSM believed the NASPE guidelines were too limited, which led to a discussion of developing curricular standards endorsed jointly by NASPE and NASSM. A joint task force of five NASPE and five NASSM members was appointed by the respective associations to develop standards that could shape the preparation of prospective sport management students. The joint task force was also mandated to investigate the feasibility of accrediting sport management curricula as a means to provide an incentive for institutions to upgrade their respective programs. The members of the task force agreed that program review and approval was an approach that could help assure students and potential employers that graduates of an approved program had been prepared in content areas that would result in the development of appropriate knowledge and skills required of an effective professional. The joint task force convened in 1989 to begin identifying the essential curricular content areas, establishing standards, and developing a program approval protocol that could evaluate programs for compliance with the standards.

The curricular standards were approved by the NASSM Board of Directors in 1990 after discussion by the entire membership in attendance at both its 1989 and 1990 conferences. NASPE conducted presentations at its conventions in 1990 and 1991. After the presentation at the 1991 convention, a referendum card and descriptive documents were sent to the 181 institutions with sport management programs, and a vote was taken. The NASPE Cabinet, as a result of the positive vote, approved the standards in 1992.

After the adoption of the standards, the joint task force continued working on a protocol that could be used to evaluate an institution's sport management program. Both associations agreed on a protocol and decided to adopt a voluntary "program review" procedure rather than an "accreditation process" so that the evaluation would be viewed more positively and less threateningly by an institution. In May 1993, the first NASPE-NASSM Sport Management Curriculum Standards and Program Review Process was published. The **Sport Management Program Review Council** (SMPRC) was created to govern the review process, which officially began in 1994.

As stated earlier, as of late 1999, fifty institutions having academic programs in sport management are listed as having been through or are going through the program review process. For information about the content (curricular) standards, call 1-800-321-0789.

SPORT MANAGEMENT TODAY AND IN THE FUTURE

Sport management has grown tremendously as an academic field of study in a short period of time. The number of journals, for example, has grown

---

TABLE 1-5. *Some sport management and related journals*

Journal of Sport Management
European Journal for Sport Management
International Journal of Sport Management
Sport Management Review
Sport Marketing Quarterly
Cyber Journal of Sport Marketing
Legal Aspects of Sport and Physical Activity Journal
Marquette Journal of Sports Law
Seton Hall Journal of Sports Law

---

in number and content just within a decade (see table 1-5). The number of programs, students, and faculty continue to grow. Most programs today have an average of two full-time sport management faculty, while a few have five or more. As you will learn in the next section, there are primarily ten, nine, and five content areas required as a base of knowledge across the undergraduate, master's and doctoral curricula: management in sport, ethics in sport, marketing in sport, legal aspects of sport, social and behavioral dimensions in sport, and finance in sport. These areas are growing as areas of specialization as the number of faculty increases and develops specialized areas of research. Recently, Mahony and Pitts (1998) called for increased attention to developing areas of specialization in sport management. They believe and state the following:

It is critical for the future of the field that sport management researchers produce strong, theoretically grounded research that will be respected by colleagues in other fields and by the universities that employ sport management faculty. While publishing articles geared to practitioners is good for the field, a decision to focus the efforts of researchers too much on the needs of current practitioners could prevent the field's young professionals from developing a strong theoretical research agenda. This may not always affect practitioners today but will affect their efforts in the future. . . . We expect to see increased specialization in a number of sport management content areas. As programs expand, add more faculty, and broaden their course offerings, specialization is imminent. Specialization is critical for developing a unique body of knowledge . . . the more focused sport management faculty become in their research, the better their production will be as scholars. (pp. 262–63, 269–70)

Perhaps the field will grow to the extent that one day there will be colleges of sport management. Currently, there is a school of Tourism and Hospitality management in the United States with programs in sport, recreation, tourism, and hospitality management. Within a college there will be departments that focus on the different areas, such as a department of sport marketing and a department of sport finance, with large numbers of faculty who specialize in that area and students who want their sport management education focused on that area.

Today, one out of every ten people in the United States is working in the leisure industry. In addition, one-third of the nation's land is devoted to leisure, and Americans spend approximately one-third of their time and income on leisure pursuits. Tourism is the world's number one industry and one of four "markets" driving our economic future (AALR, 1994). Given these facts, it is probable that a significant number of sport management programs will expand to include such areas as tourism, sport tourism, gaming, and hospitality.

CONCEPT CHECK

Although the number of programs in Canada has not changed much in the past fifteen years, a significant proliferation in sport management curricula has occurred since the mid-1980s in the United States. Several other countries have also begun offering academic programs in sport management.

CURRICULUM

Curriculum in sport management has changed dramatically over the past thirty years. Historically, sport management has had a strong physical education orientation. Required courses for the sport management student twenty years ago typically included physiology of exercise, motor learning, and measurement in physical education. Electives often included sociology or psychology of sport and perhaps a course in the history or philosophy of physical education and sport. A course in the organization and administration of physical education and sport was about the only course with a managerial focus available. Sometimes electives were available in business or journalism, and the more sophisticated programs may have created internship opportunities. Sport management was often promoted as a nonteaching option in physical education, which physical education faculty tolerated primarily to offset the declining enrollment in teaching and coaching.

Unfortunately, many schools during this early period merely repackaged an existing physical education curriculum and added some catchy course titles to create a sport management curriculum (Berg, 1989). Parkhouse (1987) reported that a significant number of sport management programs still included physical education–related course-work that is questionable in meeting the educational or job-related needs of this industry. In 1989 Berg reported that only a handful of programs were sufficiently developed in terms of faculty and curriculum to produce qualified graduates.

In 1989 NASPE and NASSM created a joint task force to further develop curricular standards for the preparation of students for the sport management profession. The approach differed from the NASPE Guidelines approved in 1987. Rather than identifying specific courses, content areas were developed that could be met in a single course or in multiple courses in the curriculum. Rather than identifying foundational and applied areas of the curriculum, each content area included a body of knowledge needed by those preparing for careers in sport management. The standards were divided into the core content required at the baccalaureate, master's, and doctoral levels.

Today, the NASPE-NASSM Sport Management Curriculum Standards outline the minimum body of knowledge that a sport management program should offer at the undergraduate, master's, and doctoral levels. The Content Areas for Curriculum are presented in tables 1-6 to 1-8 (NASPE-NASSM, 2000).

FUTURE OF SPORT MANAGEMENT AS AN ACADEMIC PROGRAM OF STUDY

The future of sport management has great potential, although major hurdles must be confronted. First, although sport management is becoming increasingly more accepted as a profession—an appropriate prerequisite for employment in the sport

TABLE 1-6   *Sport management curriculum standards: undergraduate content areas*

Content Area 1—Sociocultural dimensions
Content Area 2—Management and leadership in sport
Content Area 3—Ethics in sport management
Content Area 4—Marketing in sport
Content Area 5—Communication in sport
Content Area 6—Budget and finance in sport
Content Area 7—Legal aspects of sport
Content Area 8—Economics in sport
Content Area 9—Governance in sport
Content Area 10—Field experience in sport management

TABLE 1-7   *Sport management curriculum standards: master's program content areas*

Content Area 1—Sociocultural context of sport
Content Area 2—Management and leadership in sport
Content Area 3—Ethics in sport management
Content Area 4—Marketing in sport
Content Area 5—Public relations in sport
Content Area 6—Financial management in sport
Content Area 7—Legal aspects of sport
Content Area 8—Research in sport
Content Area 9—Field experience in sport management

TABLE 1-8   *Sport management curriculum standards: doctoral program*

Content Area 1—Background requirements
Content Area 2—Research foundations
Content Area 3—Sport management theory in an area of specialization
Content Area 4—Advanced cognate consisting of a minimum of two courses outside the department that support the specializations cited in content area 3.
Content Area 5—Field experience

industry—it will become legitimate only when graduates of sport management programs are able to demonstrate that they have the knowledge necessary to be successful in the marketplace, are able to perform the functions expected of a manager, and qualify for advancement through the ranks of the organization. NASPE and NASSM are working collectively to encourage all sport management programs to submit their curricula for evaluation through the program review process so that every sport management student is subjected to the rigor of those content areas that are necessary for successful management.

Second, the potential of sport management will be influenced by the quality of its faculties. The new doctoral graduates of sport management programs compose the faculties of tomorrow. Many more talented and energetic students are needed in our doctoral programs to supply these faculty with quality pedagogy and scholarship, which is imperative for the growing number of programs in this profession.

Lastly, sport management must continue its development as an area of scholarship. Considerable research predicated on management theories that are specific to sport need to be developed. The extent to which the latter is accomplished will largely determine whether sport management will take its place among the widely accepted professions or decline as an area with little substance.

CONCEPT CHECK

Historically, sport management has had a strong physical education orientation. Today the focus is on foundation areas of study, with a strong emphasis on sport management courses, application areas of study that build on foundation subject matter and are specific to the sport industry, and field experiences. Given its nature, sport management is a multidisciplinary field of study. It requires the cooperation of several disciplines, especially business administration (management) and physical education (now commonly referred to as "sport studies," "exercise and sport sciences," or similar titles that more accurately describe the academic components of physical education).

SOME THOUGHTS ON THE GROWTH OF THE FIELD OF SPORT MANAGEMENT

The sport management discipline has come a long way since Earle F. Zeigler planted its first seed when he introduced, approximately forty years ago, the first major textbook on the administration of physical education and athletics. In that relatively short period of time, sport management has created a solid niche for itself. It now has a clear social identity, and it is fully integrated within the broader academic sector of sport and business sciences and physical education.

From a professional practice perspective, administrators in sport have evolved from being volunteer and part-time administrators to full-time university-trained professionals. All over the world, sport management university graduates are now at work managing the sport sector. Over the years, academic programs have mushroomed in order to meet the increasing demand for competent graduates for this new industry. Furthermore, the quality of academic programs has also increased as curriculum standards for the discipline were developed and implemented. Hence, not only is sport management now recognized as a unique professional occupation, but also practitioners with proper academic credentials have taken over this field of practice.

From a disciplinary perspective, sport management has been embraced as a distinct academic subject, and it is now accepted as a legitimate and unique field of inquiry. Such rapid progress is largely due to the emergence of continental and international organizations and societies like NASSM, EASM, and SMAANZ. These organizations, particularly through their publications and annual conferences, have considerably enhanced the credibility of the discipline. Past and present academic leaders behind these organizations deserve a lot of credit as they have contributed a lot to the construction and advancement of the field.

From a research perspective, excellent sport management journals are now published regularly by these organizations. As a consequence, the quantity of published research has clearly increased as more avenues for publication emerged, and as doctoral students joined the ranks of active sport management scholars. Still, sport management research is in its infancy, and there remains a vast research agenda. Also, in comparison with other sport science disciplines, there are still relatively few active researchers in sport management. The development of more scholars needs to be an area of focus in the new millennium. Nevertheless, it appears that the initial call by early pioneers for a more solid theoretical foundation has been heard. In less than half a century, sport management has clearly matured and become a respected discipline in the sport sciences.

Dan Soucie, Ph.D.
Nanyang Technological University
Singapore

As the numbers of sport management programs have increased, I have seen both positive and negative results. The negative is that the supply of graduates in sport management has exceeded demand. This has had a tendency to depress salaries and increase the competition for the positions that are available. However, the positive is that only the most qualified students are hired. Colleges and universities have upgraded the curricula and the experiences they provide for their students to enable their students to be competitive in the job market. As a result, sport management programs today are much stronger and the quality of graduating students is much higher.

Another positive today is that sport management degrees have much higher visibility and acceptance in the sport industry. As administrators with sport management degrees climb the career ladder, they will be in a position to hire graduates of sport management programs.

In summary, the growth of sport management as a profession is still in its infancy, but only those students who are bright and well prepared will enjoy a rewarding career. Students who are non-committed and not well prepared need not apply!

Stan Brassie, Ph.D.
The University of Georgia
Athens, GA

When I entered the academic field of sport management in 1981, most sport management curricula were specializations within physical education programs, most faculty were physical educators, there were no sport management textbooks, and there were no scholarly associations or journals. Moreover, many sport management programs had only one or two faculty members, and most curricula still included physical education courses. It has been most gratifying for me to witness and to participate in the evolution of sport management from its humble beginnings to its current position as a respected entity in the academy. An essential feature of this evolution has been the large number of people involved in the process and their selfless commitment to the development of our field. Sport management has clearly been a team effort!

Sport management has made many advances, but there are challenges yet to be addressed. Three actions I believe would enhance the quality of sport management as an area of academic study are (a) a greater emphasis on the sport studies component of the curriculum; (b) an increase in the number of qualified faculty required to constitute a critical mass in NASPE-NASSM approved programs; and (c) the continuation of our quest to establish a unique body of knowledge.

Much of the responsibility for the future of sport management rests with the individuals who are reading this chapter. I encourage each of you to learn about the history of the field through the many publications available to you, to determine to have a positive impact on the continued development of sport management, and to dedicate your intellect and energy toward that objective. Your lives as well as sport management will be all the richer for your efforts!

Janet Parks, DA
Bowling Green University
Bowling Green, OH

As we move into the new millennium there are over a hundred books in sport law, and courses in sport law are found in over half of the law schools in the United States and in over 80 percent of the sport management curricula. Today, most sport law authors specialize in one or more areas of law.

The American Bar Association (ABA) has an Entertainment and Sport Law Section and a Committee on Sport in the Section of Business.

As society develops an appetite for risk management, supervision, and compliance in the workplace, a need for persons knowledgeable in law is a must. When the workplace is sport with its inherent risks, the need for an expert in sport law is a must. The sport lawyer will be a multidisciplinary specialist with skills appropriate to teach, advise, and practice in both law and in sport.

Annie Clement, Ph.D., J.D.
Florida State University
Tallahassee, FL

In the second half of the twentieth century, sport management "came on like gangbusters." By that statement I am simply affirming the tremendous interest in this area of endeavor that has resulted in the establishment of several hundred professional training programs in North America alone. Yet at the moment, I am finding it necessary to analyze philosophically what I anachronistically am calling the "plight" of sport management as the profession strives to cross the so-called postmodern divide from one epoch to another.

It can be argued that indeed the world is moving into a new epoch as the proponents of postmodernism have been affirming over recent decades. An epoch approaches closure when many of the fundamental convictions of its advocates are challenged by a substantive minority of the populace. Within such a milieu there are strong indications that sport management is going to have great difficulty crossing this postmodern chasm.

Scholars argue that many in democracies, undergirded by the relative achievement of various rights being propounded (e.g., individual freedom, privacy), have come to believe that they require a supportive "liberal consensus" within their respective societies. Conversely, conservative, essentialist elements functioning in such political systems feel that the deeper foundation justifying this claim of a (required) liberal consensus has never been fully rationalized (keeping their more authoritative orientation in mind, of course).

However, postmodernists form a growing, substantive minority that supports a more humanistic, pragmatic, liberal consensus. Within such a milieu there are strong indications that present sport management is going to have difficulty crossing the postmodern divide. I say this because at present competitive sport appears to be a social institution with an implied theory that daily gives indications of not being able to live up to its assertive, yet vague proclamations.

There is a need to answer such questions as (1) where sport *has been,* (2) where it *is now,* (3) where it *is heading,* and (4) where it *should be heading.* Further questions that should be considered are (5) what competitive sport's prevailing drift is, (6) what various kinds of sport forms are available today, (7) what the advantages and disadvantages of sport involvement in life are, and (8) what sport's residual impact is.

In response to these questions, sport may be postulated as "the destroyer," "the redeemer," the institution being tempted by "technology and science," the social phenomenon where heroes and villains are created, and, finally, the institution surviving within an era characterized by a vacuum of belief. I firmly believe that the sport manager of the twenty-first century needs to understand competitive sport's dilemma fully, since he or she will be confronted inevitably by the postmodern divide.

In crossing this frontier, many troubling and difficult decisions, often ethical in nature as well, will have to be made as the sport management profession seeks to prepare prospective professionals capable of guiding sport into becoming a truly responsible social institution.

Earle F. Zeigler, Ph.D.
The University of Western Ontario
Emeritus Graduate Faculty
Oregon State University

CRITICAL THINKING EXERCISE

You are a first-year college professor of sport management with a personal interest in major league baseball and other men's professional sports. You would love to focus on these for case studies and examples in class, even though you know that there is much more to the sport business industry. Should you compromise your personal interests in a couple of sports to be sure you teach your students about the true breadth and depth of the sport business industry? Why or why not? What is your responsibility to the students, to the program, and to the growth of sport management as a field of study? What material

exists in the literature that will help you determine the content of your sport management curriculum, courses, and lectures?

SUMMARY

1. Although sport management is relatively new to academia, its acceptance as a legitimate area of study is well documented in the literature.
2. Although the terms *sport management* and *sport administration* are often used interchangeably, the first most accurately describes this field from a universal, or global perspective.
3. In 1993, the NASPE-NASSM Sport Management Curriculum Standards were initially published and again in 2000 with minor changes. Sport management programs should use the standards to develop curricula.
4. The North American Society for Sport Management (NASSM) and the National Association for Sport and Physical Education (NASPE) Task Force on Sport Management corroborate a rapid growth in this profession. NASSM was established to promote, stimulate, and encourage research, scholarly writing, and professional development in the area of sport management. The Task Force focuses on curricular needs. The *Journal of Sport Management* is the major resource for disseminating significant knowledge in this field.
5. This relatively new field has great potential, but its destiny is still in question. It is imperative that those responsible for the curricular development of sport management programs at both the national and institutional levels accept this responsibility for ensuring quality professional preparation. At the institutional level, proliferation in the interest of increasing student enrollment must give way to a commitment to excellence.
6. Quality control is currently a major concern of academicians and practitioners in this field. In this endeavor, an "accrediting" agency comparable to those in business administration and communications is now being operationalized in sport management.

REVIEW QUESTIONS AND ISSUES

1. What is sport management? What is the sport business industry?
2. What is the purpose of accreditation? What is the difference between accreditation and

program approval? How can program approval resolve the quality control problem that currently exists in sport management programs? Why have some academicians been reluctant to support accreditation?

3. Why does the term *sport management* more accurately describe this field than *sport administration*.

4. How has the sport management curriculum changed over the past twenty-five years?

SOLUTION TO CRITICAL THINKING EXERCISE

Help in solving this dilemma: The majority of students in sport management do not go into jobs and careers with the few large men's professional sports, such as MLB, the NBA, and the NFL. Therefore, your first consideration is the depth and breadth of the sport business industry and the enormous variety of jobs and careers into which sport management students will be going. The sport management curriculum standards will guide you in the development of content for programs and courses. The curriculum standards provide the base knowledge, applicable to any sport business job or career, that every sport management student should know. Current textbooks and academic journals will help in developing courses and lecture material. You will discover, however, that there is an overemphasis on men's professional sports and college athletics in many of these materials. Therefore, use a variety of materials and books from a variety of sources. For example, for every industry segment, there are trade journals and magazines to which you could subscribe that would help with disseminating information on those segments. The Sporting Goods Manufacturers Association publishes several newsletters, magazines, and reports. They also have a web site and stage annual meetings and conventions. As another source for another type of industry segment, the Snow Sports Industries of America is an umbrella organization for many different sport businesses, such as equipment, marketing, financial, facilities, and clothing, relating to a variety of snow sports. The SIA also publishes several newsletters, magazines, and reports. Moreover, you could assign the students to seek information on different industries, bring the materials to class, and use the materials to share with the class to keep for future classes.

REFERENCES

American Association for Leisure and Recreation (AALR) (1994). *Guide for Department Chairs of Leisure, Parks, & Recreation Curricula.* Reston, VA.

Bedecki, T., and Soucie, D. (1980). Trends in physical education, sport, and athletic administration in Canadian universities and colleges. Paper presented at the 26th Annual Conference of the Canadian Association for Health, Physical Education, and Recreation. St. John's, Newfoundland.

Berg, R. (1989). The quest for credibility. *Athletic Business,* 13(11), 44–48.

Brassie, S. (1989a). Guidelines for programs preparing undergraduate and graduate students for careers in sport management. *Journal of Sport Management,* 3(2), 158–64.

Crosset, T. W., Bromage, S., and Hums, M. A. (1998). History of sport management. In L. P. Masteralexis, C. A. Barr, and M. A. Hums (eds.), *Principles and Practice of sport management.* Gaithersburg, MD: Aspen Publishers.

DeSensi, J., Kelley, D., Blanton, M., and Beitel, P. (1990). Sport management curricular evaluation and needs assessment: A multifaceted approach. *Journal of Sport Management,* 4(1), 31–58.

Frank, R. (1984). Olympic myths and realities. *Arete: The Journal of Sport Literature,* 1(2), 155–61.

Isaacs, S. (1964). *Careers and opportunities in sports.* New York: E. P. Dutton & Co.

Loy, J. (1968). The nature of sport: A definitional effort. *Quest,* 10, 1–15.

Mahony, D., and Pitts, B. G. (1998). Research outlets in sport marketing: The need for increased specialization. *Journal of Sport Management,* 12, 259–272.

Mason, J., Higgins, C., and Owen, J. (1981). Sport administration education 15 years later. *Athletic Purchasing and Facilities* (January), 44, 45.

Meek, A. (1997). An estimate of the size and supported economic activity of the sports industry in the United States. *Sport Marketing Quarterly,* 6(4), 15–21.

NASPE-NASSM. (2000). *NASPE-NASSM Sport Management curriculum standards and program review.* Reston, VA: AAHPERD Publications. (www.aahperd.org/naspe)

Parkhouse, B. L. (1987). Sport management curricula: Current status and design implications for future development. *Journal of Sport Management,* 1(2), 93–115.

Parkhouse, B. L., and Ulrich, D. (1979). Sport management as a potential cross-discipline: A paradigm for theoretical application. *Quest,* 31(2), 264–76.

Parkhouse, B. L. (1996). Definition, evolution, and curriculum. In *The Management of Sport: Its Foundation and Application* 2nd Edition. B. L. Parkhouse, (ed.), Mosby: St. Louis. pp. 3–12.

Parks, J., and Olafson, G. (1987). Sport management and a new journal. *Journal of Sport Management,* 1(1), 1–3.

Parks, J., and Quain, R. (1986). Curriculum perspectives. *Journal of Physical Education, Recreation and Dance,* 57(4), 22–26.

Parks, J. B., Zanger, B., and Quarterman, J. (1998). *Contemporary sport management.* Champaign, IL: Human Kinetics.

Parks, J., Zanger, B., and Quarterman, J. (1998). Introduction to sport management. In J. Parks, B. Zanger and J. Quarterman (eds.), *Contemporary sport management.* Champaign, IL: Human Kinetics.

Pitts, B. G., Fielding, L. W., and Miller, L. K. (1994). Industry segmentation theory and the sport industry: Developing a sport industry segmentation model. *Sport Marketing Quarterly,* 3(1), 15–24.

Pitts, B. G., and Stotlar, D. K. (1996). *Fundamentals of sport* marketing. Morgantown, WV: Fitness Information Technology.

Sandomir, R. (1988). The $50 billion sport industry. *Sports Inc.* (November 14).

Snyder, E., and Spreitzer, E. (1989). *Social aspects of sport.* Englewood Cliffs, NJ: Prentice-Hall.

Soucie, D. (1988). Promotion of sport management programs in Canada. Paper presented to the North American Society for Sport Management. Champaign, Illinois.

Soucie, D., and Doherty, A. (1996). Past endeavors and future perspectives for sport management research. *Quest, 48,* 486–500.

Street & Smith's *SportBusiness Journal* (1999) Research Department.

vander Zwaag, H. (1988). *Policy development in sport management.* Indianapolis: Benchmark Press.

Weese, W. J. (1995). If we are not serving practioners, then we're not serving sport management. *Journal of Sport Management, 9,* 237–243.

Zeigler, E. (1987). Sport management: Past, present, future. *Journal of Sport Management,* 1(1), 4–24.

WEBSITES

www.unb.ca/web/sportmanagement

This site contains information on various sport management organizations/conferences and links to such sites as Pro Sport Web Sites.

www.sportsjobs.com

www.sportscareers.com

www.sportlink.com/employment/jobs

These sites contain information about jobs and job openings in the sport, recreation, and fitness industries.

www.unb.ca/sportmanagement/

Home site for the North American Society for Sport Management (NASSM) with many links to other sport-related sites.

CHAPTER 2

Sport Management: Scope and Career Opportunities

Packianathan Chelladurai

In this chapter, you will become familiar with the following terms:

Sport industry
Sport products and services
Participant services
Spectator services and
sponsorship services

Consumer services and human
services
Human resources
Technologies
Support units

Context, or situational
contingencies
Job dimensions

Overview

Most of the students in sport management degree programs have a professional career in mind just like students in accounting, engineering, and nursing. Although the career options in other professional preparation programs are clearly defined, that is not the case with sport management. This should not be surprising, because the field of sport management is relatively new compared with other fields. It is an offshoot of the older field called *physical education.* In earlier days, a specialized field within physical education called *administration of physical education* was concerned with management of physical education and sport in educational institutions. Subsequently, as the intercollegiate athletic programs and intramural programs grew in size and stature, specializations were developed to address the concerns of these programs.

Sport management, as it is taught and practiced, now encompasses all of these focuses, and, in addition, has been expanded to include professional sports. On a different level, sport management has been broadened to emphasize specialties within management such as facility management, event management, marketing, sponsorship, and sport law. The growth of sport management has been impressive indeed.

In an attempt to define the career opportunities within sport management, the scope of sport management as practiced today is first described. After this description, the organizational contexts in which sport management is practiced are presented. Finally, some guidelines for students who seek a career in sport management are outlined.

SCOPE OF SPORT MANAGEMENT

Many students are likely to be bewildered by the various terms used to describe the field of sport management. First, the use of the term *sport* engenders some confusion. The term has been used

15

in a generic sense to denote those kinds of physical activities that concern those of us in the field, including competitive sports, recreational sports, exercise, and dance. For instance, the constitution of the North American Society for Sport Management (NASSM) defines the field as "the theoretical and applied aspects of management theory and practice specifically related to sport, exercise, dance, and play as these enterprises are pursued by all sectors of the population." Others use the term to refer to a specific form of physical activity. For instance, Snyder and Spreitzer (1989) implicitly distinguish between sport and other forms of physical activity when they state:

We define sport as (1) a competitive, (2) human physical activity that requires skill and exertion, (3) governed by institutionalized rules. With this definition in mind, it is clear that some activities can be classified as sport under some conditions but not under others.

In our own field, Mullin's (1980) view of sport management is confined to an activity that "is play-like in nature, is based on physical prowess, involves physical skill, strategy or chance, is uncertain of outcome, is governed by rules and has specialized equipment and facilities." From this perspective, although sport is a form of physical activity, not all physical activities are sport. For the purpose of this text, I will follow the lead of NASSM and use the term *sport* in a global sense covering various forms of physical activities.

Yet another term that might confuse the reader is **sport industry.** Many scholars and practitioners tend to use the term in its singular form. Considering that an industry is a group of organizations that produce the same or similar products that are substitutable for each other, the question arises whether we are indeed a single industry. From this perspective, Mullin (1980) noted that "we have a collection of sport management occupations. The sports industry is fragmented. It is in fact a number of sports industries."

CONCEPT CHECK

The term **sport** *is used to refer to all recreational and competitive sports, exercise and fitness activities, and dance. Management encompasses the activities associated with administration, supervision, and leadership.*

The view of sport management as dealing with different products and different industries suggests that the best way to define the field is to catalogue and describe its various products. This approach is consistent with the modern view that (1) all organizations are mechanisms that have evolved to facilitate the process of exchange of products, and (2) the types of organizational arrangements needed to support any particular exchange will depend on the inherent characteristics of the exchange (Hesterly et al., 1990). As noted elsewhere, "if we can define, describe, and classify the products of exchange within the context of sport, then we should be able to capture the essential nature of the field and its boundaries" (Chelladurai, 1994). Based on this view, Chelladurai (1994) defined sport management as "a field concerned with the coordination of limited human and material resources, relevant technologies, and situational contingencies for the efficient production and exchange of sport services." This definition incorporates the notions of (1) **sport products (services),** (2) the production and exchange of those products, and (3) the coordination of the processes of such production and exchange. (Also refer to the definition of sport in chapter 1.)

SPORT PRODUCTS AND SERVICES

Products can be either goods or services. Goods within the context of sport are tangible things such as golf clubs, tennis balls, soccer shoes, weight training sets, basketball boards, and volleyball uprights. In many instances, sports equipment is needed to engage in sporting activities. Typically, however, sport management has not been concerned with goods per se except in their purchase, care, and maintenance. The production of these goods has been left to conventional manufacturing industries. On the other hand, most products are services, which are intangible, perishable, heterogeneous, and simultaneous (see table 2-1 for a description of these characteristics).

An earlier elaborate classification of sport products (Chelladurai, 1992, 1994) can be meaningfully collapsed into fewer classes as shown in figure 2–1. The major classes of sport products and services are **participant services, spectator services,** and **sponsorship services.** These services can be broken down into smaller categories as follows.

TABLE 2-1 *Characteristics of a service*

Characteristic	Service
Intangibility	A service is intangible because the client or customer cannot judge its quality before experiencing it. Also, because the sensual and psychological benefits (feelings such as comfort, status, and a sense of well-being) are individualistic, the services offered will remain intangible.
Perishability	A fitness consultant cannot produce service without customers, nor can services be stored for future use. In contrast, a manufacturer can continue to produce fitness equipment and inventory it for future sales.
Heterogeneity	Services are likely to be heterogeneous because (1) two clients with different psyches may perceive the quality of the service and the same fitness instructor differently, (2) one client may perceive the service differently at different times because of changes in frame of mind or mood, (3) two fitness instructors with different education, experience, expertise, and leadership style may not provide the same quality of service, and (4) the same instructor may not provide the same quality services at different times. Students should be familiar with variations of the quality of lectures by different professors or by the same professor at different times.
Simultaneity	Because a service is perishable, it has to be used as it is produced, and because of this simultaneity of production and usage, the interface between the employee (the producer) and the client (the consumer) becomes critical. In contrast, a tennis racket is produced at one point and sold to a customer at another.

From Chelladurai, P. (1992). A classification of sport and physical activity services: Implications for sport management. *Journal of Sport Management, 6,* 38–51.

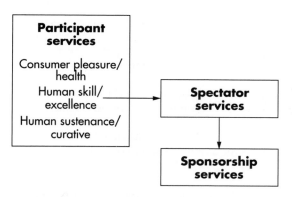

FIGURE 2–1   A classification of sport products.

Participant services

Participant services are broken down on the basis of two criteria: (1) the distinctions among **consumer, professional,** and **human services** (table 2-2), and (2) the client motives for participation in sport and physical activity (table 2-3).

Consumer-pleasure and health services. Consumer-pleasure and health services involve scheduling or reserving facilities and/or equipment as requested by clients who seek pleasure in physical activity. This class of service includes organizing and conducting different kinds of competitions for clients. Bowling alleys are prime examples of this service. The same type of service also can be provided to those who engage in physical activity for fitness and health reasons. For example, an enterprise may allow clients to use its fitness equipment and facilities for a membership or user fee.

Human skills and excellence. This class of service requires the expert application of teaching technology and leadership in developing the skills (including techniques and strategies) of clients in various forms of sport and physical activity. Clients may be satisfied with developing their skills to a level where they enjoy the activity. When clients want to excel in an activity, expert guidance and coaching need to be provided. In our culture, the pursuit of excellence in sports is highly valued and practiced, thus the

TABLE 2-2 *Description of consumer, professional, and human services*

Service	Description
Consumer	Consumer services are largely based on renting facilities or retailing goods. For example, when a university permits its students to use its gymnasia and playing fields on a drop-in basis, it is offering a consumer service. A racquetball club may restrict its operations to renting its courts and selling sporting goods. Such services require very little expertise on the part of the first-line operators. For instance, the clerk in the front office need only to know the appropriate reservation procedures for the facilities or equipment and guidelines for their use.
Professional	Professional services are largely based on knowledge, expertise, and special competencies of the employee, the service provider (e.g., lawyer, accountant, architect). Direct and active leadership is provided by the service worker in assessing clients' needs and making appropriate decisions.
Human	Application of knowledge can transform *people's* view to enhance personal well-being (e.g., educating the child, coaching the athletes, and enhancing the spiritual life). The input in these services are people; the output are people whose attributes have been changed in a predetermined manner.

From Chelladurai, P. (1992). A classification of sport and physical activity services: Implications for sport management. *Journal of Sport Management, 6,* 38–51.

TABLE 2-3 *Client motives for participation in physical activity*

Motive	Description
Pursuit of pleasure	People may participate to enjoy the kinesthetic sensations experienced in a physical activity or the competition posed by certain activities (e.g., a game of squash). The pleasures they seek can be enjoyed only during participation.
Pursuit of skill	The desire to acquire physical skills may compel people to participate in physical activity. That is, individuals may focus on perfecting their skills through continued vigorous physical activity.
Pursuit of excellence	People may participate in a form of physical activity with a desire to excel in that or another activity. A basketball player and a discus thrower may train with weights to enhance performance capability in their sports.
Pursuit of health and fitness	People may participate in vigorous physical activity mainly for health-related benefits (e.g., fitness, stress reduction, longevity) that accrue as a consequence of such participation.

From Chelladurai, P. (1992). A classification of sport and physical activity services: Implications for sport management. *Journal of Sport Management, 6,* 38–51.

importance attached to coaching various age groups at various educational and professional levels.

Human sustenance and curative. Human sustenance and curative services require organizing and conducting exercise and fitness programs on a regular basis under the guidance and supervision of experts. When healthy individuals want to participate in this class of service, their intention is to maintain and sustain present levels of fitness and health. This form of service also can be extended to rehabilitate those deficient in fitness, health, and/or physical appearance (e.g., cardiac rehabilitation, relaxation and stress reduction, and weight loss programs). This latter form of service is more curative and requires careful attention to scientific knowledge relevant to these clients.

This classification covers only those services in which clients actively participate in an activity. Sport management is concerned with much more than these participant services. We need to consider spectator services, sponsorship services, donor services, and social ideas to more clearly delineate the boundaries of sport management (Chelladurai, 1994).

Spectator services

First note that spectator services are fundamentally an offshoot of the pursuit of excellence, a participant service as described earlier. The second caveat is that spectator services also entail entertainment. These spectator/entertainment services are based on (1) the contest, (2) the spectacle, and (3) the notion of third place.

A contest exists when two opponents (individuals or teams) strive to demonstrate excellence by winning an event. The excitement and entertainment generated by a contest are derived from the excellence of the contestants; the unpredictability of the outcome; and fans' loyalty to the sport, team, and/or athlete.

Spectacle refers to the sight and splendor of opening parades, halftime shows, and closing ceremonies provided by the organization presenting the contest. These may be considered product extensions of the contest itself. Spectacle also includes the grandeur and vastness of the stadium, gymnasium, or playing surface; the ambience of the total setting—the large number of spectators, their colorful outfits, and their antics.

The concept of third place in the context of a sport contest was highlighted by Melnick (1993), who argued that modern life, both at home and at work, is characterized by reduced and tenuous primary social ties with family and friends. Therefore individuals seek the satisfaction of their social needs in less personal ways in "casual encounters with strangers of a quasi-primary kind" (Melnick, 1993). And the places where such casual encounters can take place are called *third places* (in contrast to the home and workplace).

Although there are several examples of third places (e.g., bars), "sports spectating has emerged as a major urban structure where spectators come together not only to be entertained [by the contest] but to enrich their social psychological lives through the sociable, quasi-intimate relationships available" (Melnick, 1993). In essence, spectator services include the excitement of a contest and the offering of the stadium or gymnasium as third place for the spectator.

The third place as just defined also serves as a forum for BIRGing—*basking in reflected glory* (Cialdini et al., 1976; Wann and Branscombe, 1990)—and CORFing—*cutting off reflected failure* (Snyder et al., 1986; Wann and Branscombe, 1990). It is argued here that the presence of quasi-intimate relationships in a third place permits unmitigated expression of reflected glory and distancing from reflected failure.

Sponsorship services

There are two elements in the sponsorship services. First is the market access. The organization that seeks sponsorship offers the sponsor, in return, access to a market of its own; that is, the access to communication with the direct and indirect consumers of a sport. For example, for those who sponsor the Olympic Games, the payoff is access to the billions of people who watch the event. In some cases the sponsor seeks association with excellence related to an athlete, team, or event. Sponsors of the Olympic Games emphasize their association with the best and biggest sporting event in the world. Similarly, for those who sponsor Michael Jordan or seek his endorsements, the return is association with perhaps the most talented and accomplished basketball player of all time. In these cases, such association projects the sponsoring organization as excellent in its own right.

From a different perspective, some sponsors may wish to be associated with a worthy cause such as special sports events organized by community and charitable organizations. In this case, the sponsor is projected as a socially responsible enterprise.

The emphasis on the services produced is just one way to describe the sport management field. As the definitions by different authors suggest, there are other ways of describing the field. For instance, Parks and Zanger (1990) and Parks, Zanger, and Quarterman (1998) have listed as segments of the sport industry the following areas: intercollegiate athletics, professional sports, international sport, campus recreation, community-based sport, physical fitness industry, facility management, event management, sport marketing, sports information, sports communication, sports journalism, athletic training, sports medicine, health promotion, sport tourism, health promotion, sports club management, aquatic management, sport tourism, sport management and marketing agencies, and consulting and entrepreneurship. Similarly, Masteralexis, Barr, and Hums (1998) divide the sport industry into (a) amateur sport industry, including high school and youth sports, collegiate sport, the European sport club system, and international sport; (b) professional sport industry, including sport agency and professional sport; (c) sport industry support segments, including facility management, event management, media relations, sport broadcasting, sporting goods industry, and sale of licensed products; and (d) lifestyle sports, including health and fitness industry and recreational sport.

CONCEPT CHECK

The services in sport management include participant services (consumer-pleasure and health, human skill and excellence, and human-sustenance and curative services), spectator and entertainment services, and sponsorship services.

PRODUCTION AND MARKETING

The next essential thrust in the definition of sport management is the inclusion of both the production and marketing of services. That is, management is seen as the coordination of the factors and processes of both production and exchange—that is, marketing is seen as one, albeit a major, function of management.

The distinction between the production of a service and the marketing of that service is clearly evidenced in the case of certain services. Take, for example, the spectator services where the production of entertainment largely rests with the players and the coaches of both contesting teams. The marketing of the players, the teams, and the contests can be carried out by others independent of the production of that entertainment. Similarly, sponsorship services can be independent of a team cultivating its fans and its own market. Along the same vein, it can be argued that the consumer-pleasure and health services, which involve only the renting of facilities and/or equipment, can be marketed independently of the production of these services.

In this case, the producers of the service are separated from the consumers of the service.

On the other hand, the distinction between production and marketing is not so clear in the case of human services. This is because the production of human services requires the simultaneous involvement of the client and the service provider. Moreover, client involvement in the production of human services is physical and at times agonistic, as in the case of human-excellence services. In other words, the client is at least partially responsible for the production of that service. The interface between the employee and the client in a human service is the forum for both the production and the exchange of a service—that is, the service provider is simultaneously the producer and marketeer of that service. Even in these cases, it is useful to keep the distinction between production and marketing in mind for analytical purposes.

CONCEPT CHECK

Although most services are produced and consumed simultaneously, the marketing of some services can be separated from the production of them, as in the case of spectator services.

MANAGEMENT AS COORDINATION

The third significant element in the definition is coordination of those factors associated with the production and marketing of products. Management has been described from various perspectives, e.g., the functions a manager has to carry out (Fayol, 1949), the skills a manager has to have (Katz, 1974), and/or the roles one has to play as a manager (Mintzberg, 1975). When these descriptions are analyzed, we notice that the central thrust of each of them is the idea of coordinating the activities of individuals and groups toward the attainment of organizational goals with limited resources. For example, the managerial functions of planning, organizing, leading, and evaluating are all focused on the coordination of human and material resources. In summary, coordination is the name of the game managers play.

The significant factors that need coordination for the production of sport services can be grouped

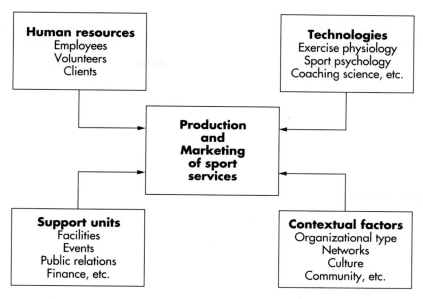

FIGURE 2–2 Factors of coordination in sport management.

into (1) **human resources** (e.g., paid employees, volunteer workers, and the clients themselves), (2) **technologies** (e.g., exercise physiology, sport psychology, pedagogy, coach education, and sport nutrition), (3) **support units** (e.g., the units dealing with facilities, events, ticket sales, legal affairs, finance, public relations), and (4) **context or situational contingencies** (e.g., organizational types, interorganizational networks, government regulations, cultural norms, and community expectations). The various factors that need to be coordinated in sport management are illustrated in figure 2–2.

HUMAN RESOURCES

Although human resources management is a fundamental task in every organization producing any form of product, the task is made onerous in the case of human services, where clients also must be managed. The human resources of any venture offering sport and physical activity service should involve the clients of that service, since service cannot be produced without active client participation (Chelladurai, 1992). Clients may vary in their orientation toward sport and physical activity (pursuit of pleasure, health, and/or excellence) and in the degree of commitment to such programs. Motivating clients and gaining their compliance is a challenge to service providers.

Paid employees may be further classified into consumer service or professional service employees. Consumer service employees engage in simple, routine activities requiring little training, whereas professional service employees provide complex, knowledge-based, and individualized service to clients.

Sport organizations also are characterized by heavy involvement of volunteers. These volunteers are the mainstay of projects such as the Special Olympics and youth sport organized by city recreation departments. The conventional approaches to managing paid workers have to be considerably modified in the case of volunteers. The coordination of volunteer contributions with those of paid employees is a critical area of sport management. In summary, motivating these different types of employees and coordinating their activities is a highly significant component of sport management, which offers both challenge and opportunity for sport managers.

TECHNOLOGIES

Technology refers to *the processes that transform orga-nizational inputs into desired outputs* (Pierce and Dunham, 1990). Technology includes all equipment used, techniques employed, and knowledge units derived from different subject areas. For example, fitness assessment and exercise prescription involve sophisticated equipment, specific organizational arrangements for the production of this service, and the knowledge derived from physiology, nutrition, and psychology. Coaching a high school pole vaulter would entail the modern fiberglass poles, and the knowledge units derived from biomechanics, sports medicine, and coaching science, for example. The more critical component of technology as defined here is the knowledge units that are generated in other allied fields. Those who use these knowledge units are professional people. Coordinating their activities with those of other organizational activities is the essence of sport management.

The relative significance of these technologies obviously varies from service to service (and with quality levels expected of a service). For example, human services aimed at enhancing excellence and/or health entails greater application of relevant knowledge as compared with consumer services. Following this argument, we can expect a high school coach to be more highly trained in the application of knowledge than a volunteer youth coach.

SUPPORT UNITS

In a small enterprise, all of the necessary activities can be carried out by a few individuals. For example, there may be only one physical educator or coach in a small rural school. That person, apart from coaching the school team, may also carry out all arrangements for a game to be played on Saturday afternoon. Of course, a coach may recruit some students to assist in the process. However, as the organization grows in size and scope, several subunits may have to be created. Take the case of a Division I university athletic department. In this case, the coaches are assigned only coaching duties. All other necessary activities are assigned to specialized units. Thus we are likely to find separate units for facility management, event management, ticket sales, media relations, legal affairs, compliance to rules, etc. Coordinating the activities of these units is the responsibility of the top manager, the athletic director.

The term *support units* may be misleading. It is used here to emphasize that these units do support the fundamental purpose and activities of the department, that is, to provide student athletes the opportunity to pursue excellence. However, the term does not minimize their importance. That is why nearly every sport management degree program includes specialized courses in these areas.

CONTEXT

No organization operates in a vacuum. A host of environmental factors have an impact on the organization and its activities. These external forces may facilitate or constrain the organization in the production and marketing of its services. A successful sport manager would effectively coordinate the activities of the organization with the demands and constraints of these external factors. These factors may be classified as organizational types, interorganizational networks, market conditions, government, culture, and community.

Sport organizations differ in their profit orientation (e.g., a high school athletic department vs. a professional sport franchise). The emphasis on profit orientation imposes a different set of demands and constraints on managers of professional sports than it does on a high school athletic director.

A funding source is another factor that may affect the coordination process. In private organizations, which are sustained by membership fees, donations, and/or shares, the manager will be more influenced by the needs and desires of the members, clients, and donors. In contrast, the manager in a public organization such as the city recreation department will have to coordinate the department's activities with not only the preferences of taxpayers but also the pressures exerted by city politicians.

Interorganizational networks such as the National Collegiate Athletic Association (NCAA) and the U.S. Olympic Committee link those organizations producing the same services. Other examples are the professional leagues, such as the National Football League (NFL) and the National Hockey League, national and international sports federations such as the U.S. Tennis Association (USTA) and the International Federation of Basketball Associations (FIBA), and industry associations such as the Aerobic and Fitness Association of America (AFAA) and Club Managers Association of

America (CMAA). These networks, or governing bodies, control member organizations and their operations to varying degrees.

The context would also include market conditions such as the rise and decline in the demand for services, and the organizations competing for clients and customers and resources. Thus a professional sport franchise has to coordinate its own activities, tactics, and strategies to counteract those of the competitors, which provide the same or similar services.

By the same token, operations should be consistent with government regulations, cultural norms, and societal expectations. For instance, the recent societal thrusts in favor of diversity and gender equity have affected the practice of management in general, and sport management in particular. The growing sport management literature on considerations of gender equity is a case in point, emphasizing the need for sport managers to alter their employment practices.

The need to coordinate the operations of a sport organization with a local community's interests and desires is best illustrated by the influence exerted by alumni associations in intercollegiate athletics. Similarly, professional sport franchises depend on local governments for building and/or renting stadiums and arenas (Johnson, 1993). Even smaller sport organizations look up to local communities for concessions and tax exemptions.

CONCEPT CHECK

Sport management is concerned with the coordination of material and human resources (clients, paid and volunteer workers); technologies (facilities, equipment, process, and knowledge units underlying the production process); support units dealing with (facilities, events, legal affairs, etc.; and contextual factors such as organizational type, interorganizational networks, government regulations and community expectations).

CAREER PLANNING

Many who read this text will step into the world of organizations and work related to sport and physical activity. Career opportunities in this field are well described in Parks and Zanger's (1990) *Sport and Fitness Management: Career Strategies and Professional Content.* Several authors contributing to this text have discussed careers in intercollegiate athletics and professional sport, facility management, campus recreation programs, community-based sport, sports information, sport marketing, sports journalism, sports club management, the physical fitness industry, athletic training and sports medicine, and consulting and entrepreneurship. Kelley et al. (1991) have elaborated on sport and fitness management careers clustered according to similarity of objectives and profit orientation. In addition, other authors have discussed issues of career patterns in sport management (Fitzgerald et al., 1994); gender and careers in sport management (Cuneen and Sidwell, 1993; Inglis, 1988; Lovett and Lowry, 1988, 1994; Pastore, 1991, 1992; Pastore and Meacci, 1994); roles, responsibilities, and stress associated with jobs in sport and recreation (Cuskelly and Auld, 1991; Danylchuk, 1993; Hatfield et al., 1987; Quarterman, 1994); and the employment status of sport management graduates (Kjeldsen, 1990; Parks, 1991; Parks and Parra, 1994). This list does not exhaust all relevant information about careers in sport management. Students should consult other sources including trade journals. The following sections outline some general concerns in selecting a job or career.

Once students enter the work world, they are likely to move from one job to another. This movement may be vertical in the sense that they get promoted to higher level jobs in the same line of work. Consider the careers of May and June reported in the case study at the end of this chapter. Both women joined an intercollegiate athletic program as clerks. In time, May was promoted to the position of assistant director of the ticket office. In contrast, June left that athletic department to become a coach in a smaller four-year college. This progression through various jobs in one or several organizations is known as *one's career.* But every career begins with a first job, which is where our interests lie at the moment.

The descriptions of the jobs in these two organizational contexts contain information available to everyone. Also, the progression through various jobs to higher positions in each organization is known to everybody (or can be gleaned from the records). This aspect of one's career is rightfully known as the *objective* or *external career* (Johns, 1988).

What is not evident to observers is the personal experiences and reactions felt by two individuals in their career tracks. It is not clear to others why Person Y chose to leave athletics altogether and enter the field of parks and recreation. It may be presumed that Person Y did not like the experiences with the athletic program, and therefore preferred to move to another field where the experiences were more acceptable. However, the meanings Person Y had attached to the experiences in the two fields, and the reactions to those experiences were personal, and imperceptible or misunderstood by others. This aspect is called *subjective* or *internal career*.

CONCEPT CHECK

Career refers to one's progress from the first job to the final job before retirement. Such jobs may involve the same or different organizations. The objective aspect of the career is what external observers gather from written job descriptions, whereas the subjective career is what the incumbent of a job internally experiences.

Focus on external career

In making decisions about a job in sport management, the graduate has to consider several factors. Some of them, as noted earlier, would be objective factors such as job description, organizational type, and geographical location. Many questions related to these factors can be verified through objective analysis.

Job descriptions should contain information on organizational philosophy and policies; organizational type and size; tasks and activities associated with the job, working conditions, including supervision, salary, and fringe benefits; and promotional opportunities. The prospective applicant should carefully peruse all of this information. If necessary, the student may write or call the prospective employer for more information.

Although written job descriptions are useful, a one- or two-day visit to the organization may provide additional information. It may also be useful to interview one or more employees of the organization to get their personal feelings about the organization and their jobs. Such visits and interviews will help the applicant to verify the job description and assess the mood and spirit of the organization. An institution may advertise its employment practices as equal opportunity, but the student may find that all employees of the organization are of one race or gender. Again, the working conditions such as room size, lighting, ventilation, seating arrangements, and parking facilities may not be as good as advertized. In summary, a thorough analysis of the job description and the organization would be worthwhile.

Organizational type. Consider that you are contemplating a job as manager of a racquetball club. Such a club may be operated by a branch of the YMCA; a city recreation department; a university intramural department; a private, exclusive nonprofit organization; or a private profit-oriented commercial firm. Although the same tasks need to be carried out in all of these settings, there are other factors that affect the employees.

Some differences among organizations were discussed earlier. To extend that discussion, city recreation department personnel are likely to enjoy relatively greater job security and higher salaries than those in a private, profit-oriented commercial club. On the other hand, there are probably many levels of hierarchy through which a proposal has to be processed, which may impede the decision-making process. This is known as *red tape* in governments.

As another example, personnel working in a university intramural department may have higher social status than those carrying out the same activities in a commercial club. After all, the university is the ivory tower! Also, the university department personnel are exposed to students' youthful, energetic, and carefree lifestyles. Some may feel that is a reward in itself. Similarly, those who work in a Division I university athletic department or a professional club may gain satisfaction from the association with excellence in sport irrespective of the nature of their jobs or their remunerations.

Geographical location. People have preferences for particular geographic locations. Preferences may be based on the proximity of family and friends, or even health. Some may prefer an urban center, whereas others may enjoy life in a less thickly populated locale. These are important considerations inasmuch as they will enhance one's quality of life. After all, a job is only a tool to enjoy one's life.

Focus on internal career

The internal career simply implies a fit between the job and its context, and the personal characteristics of the individual. The job and the context refer to what the individual is required to do in a job and the parameters of a particular organization, including its policies, procedures, working conditions, supervision, and work group. The personal characteristics include the person's personality, needs, values, beliefs, and preferences, along with abilities, skills, and talents. Abilities, skills, and specialized knowledge required for a successful job performance can be increased through general education and specialized professional preparation programs. Personality, needs, values, and preferences are relatively more stable.

The central issue for people who desire a job in sport management is to assess the fit between their personal characteristics and the characteristics of the job as well as those of the organization offering the job. Let us consider job characteristics. Obviously, salary, fringe benefits, the chance for advancement, and the location are important considerations. Salary may be the primary consideration for a student who has incurred enormous debt while in college. If only one job were available, such a student might be forced to take it without any consideration of the other job characteristics. On the other hand, if more than one job were available, the applicant should evaluate the jobs in terms of their characteristics and choose the one that offered the best fit.

It is not our intent to discuss the ways in which people differ. It will be useful, however, to point out some ways in which jobs differ. Consider the differences and decide whether those **job dimensions** are consistent with personal needs, values, and preferences.

Job dimensions. There are several schemes to define and describe the attributes of job dimensions (Campion and Thayer, 1985; Hackman and Oldham, 1980; Stone and Gueutal, 1985). This section

outlines some of the more significant dimensions of a job.

In discussing the differences between consumer services and the professional and human services (see table 2-2), I alluded to the differences in the degree to which jobs may be simple or complex. The complexity of a job increases as the variety of activities increases. For example, a secretary in an athletic department may be assigned only the task of typing, whereas another secretary may be involved in typing, answering telephones, and taking notes in departmental meetings. The latter person enjoys a variety of tasks, and, therefore, a relatively more complex job. The more important element in complexity is the variability of the tasks, that is, an employee is required to make different decisions based on different pieces of information. A coach may use different techniques to motivate athletes based on individual differences among those athletes. Similarly, the director of a city recreation department may use varying approaches when dealing with politicians, taxpayers, or participants. In contrast, the job of locker room attendant is not as complex as that of a coach. Consider a racquetball club that simply rents its premises and equipment to its clients. The necessary tasks in such a club may relate to keeping the courts and equipment in good repair, reserving the courts according to some specified criteria, budgeting and accounting, legal affairs, and marketing the club and its activities. As you can see, the activities in the first two tasks can be clearly specified and made routine.

From a different perspective, simpler jobs can be made routine and standardized. Everything required of the job may be specified by rules and regulations. What is to be done, when it is to be done, how should it be done, and who should do it can be stated in advance in the first two tasks. Also, monitoring and controlling these activities are easily carried out. On the other hand, the activities in the next three tasks are more complex in that every situation may entail different information, and therefore different decisions.

It must be noted that a job may contain some tasks that are routine and others that are more complex. Therefore the prospective applicant would do well to verify if the degree of simplicity or complexity in the job is consistent with personal preferences. There are those who prefer a structured and orderly setting. Others may feel restricted in such jobs, and prefer more flexibility, autonomy, and challenge of deciding how the job should be carried out.

The degree of interaction with other people required may vary from job to job. Take two individuals in the athletic department's public relations office. One may be involved in collating all the department's media coverage. The same person may also engage in preparing advance material for the media. In all these activities, he or she may not be required to interact with the media people or other clients to any great extent. On the other hand, the second person's job may require both contact with the media and response to queries on a regular basis. Some people would like a job that requires interaction with people, whereas others may be uncomfortable in that position.

There is also the question of feedback. Some jobs provide clear and immediate feedback, and others delayed feedback. For example, when a fitness club employee sets out to recruit more members, feedback is likely on a daily, weekly, or monthly basis relative to the success rate. It is immediate and clear in terms of the exact number of new members recruited. Consider the same individual who is also in charge of a program of weight loss through physical activity. Feedback is going to be delayed because weight loss takes time. Also, feedback may not be clear-cut in the sense that some of the clients may lose weight, others may not. In addition, the weight one loses or gains is a function of many other factors such as diet and activity patterns away from the club.

In some jobs, one can identify the outcome of his or her efforts. If a marketing specialist in a university athletic department garners a few rich sponsorships, that particular outcome is attributable to that individual's efforts. On the other hand, if a person is one of several employees in charge of crowd control in a game, personal contribution to the total effort cannot be identified easily.

In the previous example, those in charge of crowd control realize and enjoy the significance of their jobs. Can you imagine what would happen if their collective responsibility falters in a game with 80,000 or so spectators? Some of you might have heard some of the gruesome tales of tragedies during sporting events in other parts of the world. Their job is so significant because peoples' welfare

and lives are at stake. From this perspective, other jobs may not be so significant.

CONCEPT CHECK

A job can be evaluated on its relative complexity, requirement of interaction with other people, feedback available from the job itself, the possibility of identifying one's own contribution, and its significance.

After careful analysis of the job and the organization that offers the job, the student has to evaluate the extent to which the characteristics of the job and the organization match his or her personal skills and abilities, needs, and values. In this assessment the student should consider the various higher level jobs one may move through in one's career. It is conceivable that the first job may be quite routine and devoid of any autonomy. Although this situation may not be acceptable immediately, subsequent promotions may land that person in a more complex and autonomous job. For example, the first job in a professional sport club may involve simply selling tickets at the counter. Although this may not be very appealing, the opportunity exists for that person to move up in the hierarchy to a job such as the marketing director. That position may offer considerable flexibility and freedom of operation for the incumbent. Therefore students are well advised to consider not only the immediate job that is offered but also the other jobs that the present one may lead to.

Students should also note what Hums and Goldsbury (1998) identify as myths surrounding careers in sport management. Three of them serve as reality checks for those aspiring to enter sport management. In dispelling the myth that "most employment opportunities are in professional or college sport," these authors note that the job opportunities in professional or collegiate sport are limited because only a few organizations deal with this segment of sport. Another myth is that "sport management jobs are glamorous and exciting." Hums and Goldsbury (1998) note that "sport managers labor in the background so others can enjoy the spotlight. A typical work week for that event coordinator is fifty to sixty hours per week, including lots of late nights and long weekends" (pp. 479–80). Yet another myth is that "sport management jobs pay well." As Hums and Goldsbury note, because of the high number of applicants for jobs in sport management, the salaries tend to be low for most jobs in sport management. It must also be noted that with necessary ability and perseverance, some people rise to the top positions that pay high salaries.

CRITICAL THINKING EXERCISES

1. You have the good fortune to get two job offers. The first job is that of a supervisor of ticketing operations in an athletic department of a Division I institution. The second job is that of a coordinator of youth sport programs in the recreation department of a mid-sized city. Which one would you take? And why?
2. Imagine that you are the assistant to the event manager of a large athletic department. What kinds of tasks would you be involved in? Who are the people you are most likely to interact with in performing your duties?

SUMMARY

1. The products (i.e., the services) with which sport management is concerned are varied. Some of them are *participant services* wherein clients participate vigorously in some form of sport and physical activity. The other services labeled *spectator* and *sponsorship services* are nonparticipant services.
2. Sport management was defined as "a field concerned with the coordination of limited human and material resources, relevant technologies, and situational contingencies for the efficient production and exchange of sport services" (Chelladurai, 1994).
3. The coordination was said to involve human resources (clients, paid employees, and volunteer workers), technologies (the processes and knowledge units employed in the production of a service), support units (dealing with facility management, event management, legal affairs, public relations), and contextual factors (organizational type, interorganizational networks, government rules and regulations, community expectations, and social norms).
4. The objective and subjective aspects of a career were described. It was emphasized that a match between one's personal characteristics

and the characteristics of the job and the organization is the critical factor that a student should consider before accepting a job. In this regard some of the job and organizational characteristics were outlined.

CASE STUDY

May Baxter and June Armstrong were good friends. They both went to the same school in a rural setting and graduated with good standing. Both played on the high school basketball team and were members of the school track team. They went to the same university and graduated with degrees in sport management. They were lucky to get jobs in the athletic department of a neighboring university.

May's first job was as a ticket office clerk. Her superiors, noting her diligent work and her interpersonal skills, promoted her to the position of supervisor of clerks. The same hard work and positive attitude in successive jobs facilitated her promotion to the position of assistant director of the ticket office within six years. She enjoyed her work very much and took great pride in being associated with an organization that had a high profile within the university and the community. She looked forward to possible promotions such as the assistant or associate athletic director either in the same university or in another. To equip herself better for the future, she enrolled part time in an MBA program.

June's first job was as a clerk in the media relations office. Like May, June impressed her bosses with her work effectiveness and pleasant manner. She was promoted to a supervisory position within her department. Everybody assumed she was happy in her job and had expectations that she would quickly move up in her career. However, June was becoming restless with her current job and future prospects. She felt that she was removed from where the action was, that is, she realized that she was not directly involved in the production of the fundamental service of the department—the production of excellence in sports. She perceived her own job and those in her department as only supplementary to that fundamental task. In short, she felt that her own abilities, interests, needs, and values would be best served if she were to become a coach. With this in mind, she volunteered to assist the coach of the women's basketball team. In that role, she assiduously learned everything she could from the coach. In addition, she began taking courses such as sport psychology and coaching science. Subsequently, she applied for and got a job coaching the women's basketball team at a four-year college. She soon proved to be an effective coach with a winning tradition. She enjoyed her present status and was looking forward to being a coach at a big university. The media and the community began noticing her achievements and winning ways.

1. *Compare and contrast the careers of May Baxter and June Armstrong.*
2. *What are the differences between the first job of May (ticket office clerk) and June (media relations clerk)?*
3. *How would you distinguish between May's present job (assistant director of the ticket office) and June's present job (coach in a four-year college)?*
4. *In this chapter, sport management was defined in terms of various services. Discuss the services in which May and June are currently engaged.*

REVIEW QUESTIONS AND ISSUES

1. Define the field of sport management. Describe the various categories of services produced and marketed in the field. Explain the significance of defining the field from the perspective of its products.
2. Select a service (e.g., fitness service, youth soccer) offered by an organization (e.g., commercial fitness club, local YMCA, city recreation department). Describe the human resources, technologies, support units, and contextual factors associated with the production and marketing of the chosen service.
3. Distinguish between objective and subjective careers.
4. Consider any sport-related job. Describe it in terms of the job dimensions referred to in the chapter.
5. Evaluate the job in terms of how it matches your abilities, education, needs, and values.

SOLUTIONS TO CRITICAL THINKING EXERCISES

1. The choice of one of those jobs will be based on your personal orientation and your assessment of the job. The factors that could influence your choice would include the geographical location (e.g., large and crowded city), the reputation of the organization (e.g., treatment of employees), opportunities for advancement

to higher-level positions, and similar considerations. One other difference between the two jobs is that the ticketing operations may be limited to supervising the employees of the unit who are involved with routine tasks. On the other hand, the coordinator of youth programs is likely to be more involved with participants, coaches, parents, and volunteer workers. This aspect of the job may be more appealing to some.

2. Obviously, as an assistant to the event manager, you will do everything the manager assigns or delegates to you. Some of those tasks may be routine, such as checking the media booths and/or concessions for cleanliness and necessary supplies, assigning paid and volunteer workers to different gates of entry, and verifying the arrangements for the arrival of dignitaries. While these tasks are routine, your interactions with other workers (e.g., volunteers), other units (e.g., facility management or security), and the patrons themselves could be exciting. As noted in the chapter, event managers and their assistants are responsible for the safety of the spectators and their enjoyment of the event.

REFERENCES

Campion, M. A., and Thayer, P. W. (1985). Development and field evaluation of an interdisciplinary measure of job design. *Journal of Applied Psychology, 70,* 29–43.

Chelladurai, P. (1992). A classification of sport and physical activity services: Implications for sport management. *Journal of Sport Management, 6,* 38–51.

Chelladurai, P. (1994). Sport management: Defining the field. *European Journal for Sport Management, 1,* 7–21.

Cialdini, R. B., Borden, R. J., Thorne, A., Walker, M. R., Freeman, S., and Sloan, L. R. (1976). Basking in reflected glory: Three (football) field studies. *Journal of Personality and Social Psychology, 34,* 366–75.

Cuneen, J., and Sidwell, M. J. (1993). Effect of applicant gender on rating and selection of undergraduate sport management interns. *Journal of Sport Management, 7,* 216–27.

Cuskelly, G., and Auld, C. J. (1991). Perceived importance of selected job responsibilities of sport and recreation managers: An Australian perspective. *Journal of Sport Management, 5,* 34–46.

Danylchuk, K. E. (1993). Occupational stressors in physical education faculties. *Journal of Sport Management, 7,* 7–24.

Fayol, H. (1949). *General and industrial management.* London: Pitman. First published in French in 1916.

Fitzgerald, M. P., Sagaria, M. A. D., and Nelson, B. (1994). Career patterns of athletic directors: Challenging the conventional wisdom. *Journal of Sport Management, 8,* 14–26.

Hackman, J. R., and Oldham, G. R. (1980). *Work designed.* Reading, MA: Addison-Wesley.

Hatfield, B. D., Wrenn, J. P., and Bretting, M. M. (1987). Comparison of job responsibilities of intercollegiate athletic directors and professional sport general managers. *Journal of Sport Management, 1,* 129–45.

Hesterly, W. S., Liebeskind, J., and Zenger T. R. (1990). Organizational economics: An impending revolution in organization theory? *Academy of Management Review, 15* (3), 402–20.

Hums, M. A. Q., and Goldsbury, V. R. (1998). Strategies for career success. In L. P. Masteralexis, C. A. Barr, and M. A. Hums (eds.), *Principles and practice of sport management* (pp. 476–96). Gaithersburg, MD: Aspen Publishers.

Inglis, S. E. (1988). The representation of women in university athletic programs. *Journal of Sport Management, 2,* 14–25.

Johns, G. (1988). *Organizational behavior: Understanding life at work.* 2d ed. Glenview, IL: Scott, Foresman.

Johnson, A. T. (1993). Rethinking the sport-city relationship: In search of partnership. *Journal of Sport Management, 7,* 61–70.

Katz, R. L. (1974). Skills of an effective administrator. *Harvard Business Review, 52,* 90–102.

Kelley, D. R., Beitel, P. A., DeSensi, J. T., and Blanton, M. D. (1991). In B. L. Parkhouse (ed.), *The management of sport* (pp. 12–26). St. Louis: Mosby.

Kjeldsen, E. K. M. (1990). Sport management careers: A descriptive analysis. *Journal of Sport Management, 4,* 121–32.

Lovett, D. J., and Lowry, C. D. (1994). "Good old boys" and "good old girls" clubs: Myth or reality. *Journal of Sport Management, 8,* 27–35.

Lovett, D. J., and Lowry, C. D. (1988). The role of gender in leadership positions in female sport programs in Texas college. *Journal of Sport Management, 2,* 106–17.

Masteralexis, L. P., Barr, C. A., and Hums, M. A. (1998). *Principles and practice of sport management.* Gaithersburg, MD: Aspen Publishers.

Melnick, M. J. (1993). Searching for sociability in the stands: A theory of sport spectating. *Journal of Sport Management, 7* (1), 44–60.

Mintzberg, H. (1975). The manager's job: Folklore and fact. *Harvard Business Review, 53,* 49–61.

Mullin, B. J. (1980). Sport management: The nature and utility of the concept. *Arena Review, 4* (3), 1–11.

Parks, J. B. (1991). Employment status of alumni of an undergraduate sport management program. *Journal of Sport Management, 5,* 100–110.

Parks, J. B., and Parra, L. F. (1994). Job satisfaction of sport management alumni. *Journal of Sport Management, 8,* 49–56.

Parks, J. B., and Zanger, B. R. K. (1990). Definition and direction. In J. B. Parks and B. R. K. Zanger (eds.), *Sport and fitness management: Career strategies and professional content* (pp. 1–4). Champaign, IL: Human Kinetics.

Parks, J. B., Zanger, B. R. K., and Quarterman, J. (1998). *Contemporary sport management.* Champaign, IL: Human Kinetics.

Pastore, D. L. (1991). Male and female coaches of women's athletic teams: Reasons for entering and leaving the profession. *Journal of Sport Management, 5,* 128–43.

Pastore, D. L. (1992). Two-year college coaches of women's teams: Gender differences in coaching career selections. *Journal of Sport Management, 6,* 179–90.

Pastore, D. L., and Meacci, W. G. (1994). Employment process for NCAA female coaches. *Journal of Sport Management, 8,* 115–28.

Pierce, J. L., and Dunham, R. B. (1990). *Managing.* Glenview, IL: Scott, Foresman/Little, Brown Higher Education.

Quarterman, J. (1994). Managerial role profiles of intercollegiate athletic conference commissioners. *Journal of Sport Management, 8,* 129–39.

Snyder, C. R., Lassegard, M. A., and Ford, C. E. (1986). Distancing after group success and failure: Basking in reflected glory and cutting off reflected failure. *Journal of Personality and Social Psychology, 51,* 382–88.

Snyder, E. E., and Spreitzer, E. A. (1989). *Sociological aspects of sport.* 3d ed. Englewood Cliffs, NJ: Prentice-Hall.

Stone, E. E., and Gueutal, H. G. (1985). An empirical derivation of the dimensions along which characteristics of jobs are perceived. *Academy of Management Journal, 28,* 376–96.

Wann, D. L., and Branscombe, N. R. (1990). Die-hard and fair weather fans: Effects of identification on BIRGing and CORFing tendencies. *Journal of Sport and Social Issues, 14* (2), 103–17.

WEBSITES

www.ncaa.org/market/ads/
www.ncaa.org/human-resources/
These two sites contain information on jobs within the NCAA and links to jobs in the field at their member institutions. Organized by category, such as coaching, administration, marketing, etc.

www.coolworks.com/showme/
coolworks has a site featuring seasonal jobs at ski areas, resorts, national parks, cruises, and camps.

www.sponsorship.com/jobBank/jobBank.html
IEG jobBank has a place for resumes. It also lists executive-level jobs available in event and sports marketing.

www.onlinesports.com/pages/Resumes.html
Online Sports Career Center has a place to post brief resumes.

www.sportlink.com/employment/jobs/index.html
This is the website of the Sporting Goods Manufacturers Association Career Center, which provides a list of jobs available in the sporting goods industry.

CHAPTER 3

Experiential Learning Through Field Experiences: Internships and Practica

M. Elizabeth Verner, Bette B. Keyser, and Marilyn J. Morrow

In this chapter, you will become familiar with the following terms:

Experiential learning
Experiential education
Discrete experiential education
Nondiscrete experiential
 education
Field experience
Internship
Practicum/Practica

Cooperative education
Alternating cooperative
 education
Parallel/extended day
 cooperative education
Service-learning
Academic service-learning
Pedagogical approach

Vocational self-concept
Formal sources
Informal sources
Working portfolio
Showcase portfolio
Reflective statement

Overview

As students reach the point in their plan of study where they begin to consider a field experience, it is helpful for them to think about *how* they learn through an understanding of the learning process and the relationship between theoretical and experiential learning. An overview of the historical development of experiential education provides students with an awareness of why field experiences are important and how they have become an integral part of the curriculum designed to prepare professionals in various walks of life. Likewise, recognition of the importance of internships and practica in the sport management curriculum is beneficial to students when they contemplate the value of experiential learning as a component of their own professional preparation.

This chapter provides information about the value of field experiences for the student, the sponsoring agency, and the university. Research pertaining to desirable intern characteristics is summarized to guide students in assessing their potential *fit* for a sport management internship. The preparation and utilization of career advancement materials is discussed to help students to market themselves. Practical suggestions are offered on how to secure an internship. Additionally, a case study, written by a successful intern willing to share his experience with other students is included to encourage students to consider developing a portfolio to gain an additional competitive edge.

CONCEPTUAL BACKGROUND
Learning theory
In her keynote address during the 22nd annual National Society for Experiential Education Conference in the fall of 1993, Dr. K. Patricia Cross described learning as an active, dynamic process in which new material interacts with what is already known to transform and deepen meaning. New information results in meaningful learning when it connects with what already exists in the mind of the learner. Therefore learning is transformational rather than additive. This assumption promotes the concept of mental structures that store and organize learned material in the schema of a multidimensional map of interrelated ideas, with all sorts of connections among stored material. "The excitement of learning comes when new connections are made, sometimes transforming the structure, pulling apart some connections and making new ones" (Cross, 1994).

Experiential and academic approaches to learning become natural allies in the process of constantly changing and reformatting thought structures. For example, enlightenment occurs when something read in a textbook comes to life as the learner makes the connection between the idea and its execution. Likewise, revelation is apparent when the learner comprehends the textbook explanation for phenomena previously observed but never understood (Cross, 1994).

One of the most sophisticated combinations of learning theory and learning styles research is authored by Dr. David Kolb. He posits that learning is a social process based on experience and defines learning as "the process whereby knowledge is created through the transformation of experience" (Kolb, 1984). Kolb's learning theory synthesizes the work of Dewey, Lewin, and Piaget; it emphasizes adapting, creating, and re-creating, as well as insight and application (Hesser, 1990).

Experiential learning is frequently explained by reference to Kolb's experiential learning cycle (see figure 3–1 for a graphic representation). According to this model, the learner proceeds from the actual experience itself through a process of reflection about the experience; conceptualization or generalization that relates the experience to theories and to other experiences; and active experimentation with changed practice, based on these considerations.

Kolb's perspective on learning is called "experiential" because it "differentiates experiential learning theory from rationalist and other cognitive theories of learning that tend to give primary emphasis

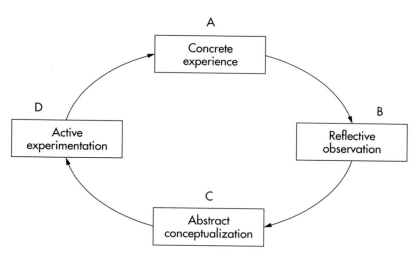

FIGURE 3–1   Kolb's experiential learning cycle.
From Kolb, D.A. (1976). *Learning style inventory technical manual.*

to acquisition, manipulation, and recall of abstract symbols and from behavioral learning theories that deny any role for consciousness and subjective experience in the learning process" (Kolb, 1984). The intent of Kolb's work "is not to pose experiential learning theory as a third alternative to behavioral and cognitive learning theories, but rather to suggest through experiential learning theory, a holistic, integrative perspective on learning that combines experience, perception, cognition, and behavior" (Kolb, 1984).

Experiential learning and experiential education

Experiential learning refers to learning in which the learner is directly in touch with the realities being studied. It is contrasted with learning in which the learner only reads about, hears about, talks about, or writes about these realities, but never comes into contact with them as part of the learning process (Keeton & Tate, 1978).

Experiential education is a form of pedagogy, or teaching methodology, employed to facilitate experiential learning. Therefore " 'Experiential education' refers to learning activities that engage the learner directly in the phenomena being studied. This learning can be in all types of work or service settings by undergraduate and graduate students of all ages. . . [Experiential education is] carefully monitored, experience-based learning" (Kendall et al., 1986).

There are two basic categories of **experiential education activities: discrete and nondiscrete**. Discrete activities are those that are self-contained and constitute a separate entity. Examples of discrete experiential education activities include field study, internships, practica, student teaching, clinical experiences, cooperative education, and service-learning.

Nondiscrete experiential education activities are more often than not extensions or components of a course or program. As such they are not self-contained, separate entities. Many of the nondiscrete experiential education activities are considered to be innovative classroom instruction techniques. Examples of nondiscrete experiential education activities include: field trips, simulation/games, group process, role play, laboratory work, oral interviews, and participatory observations. Table 3-1 provides a more complete list of the most common types of experiential education activities.

No matter which activity becomes the vehicle, experiential learning is that transformation which "occurs when changes in judgments, feelings, knowledge, or skills result for a particular person from living through an event or events"

TABLE 3-1 *Types and forms of experiential education*

1. Discrete experiential education courses or programs	2. Experiential education as one or more components of a course or program	3. Other experiential techniques incorporated into a course or program
Cooperative education	Field projects	Role playing
Field study, fieldwork, field research	Field trips	Laboratory work
Independent study	Participatory observations	Simulation games and exercises
Internships	Oral interviews	Student-led class sessions
Practica	Site visits/field observations	(presentations or discussions)
Service-learning	Use of primary source or raw	Group learning activities
Work-learn	data	Other active forms of learning
Others	Others	

From *Strengthening Experiential Education Within Your Institution* by Kendall, J. C., Duley, J. S., Little, T. C., Permal, J. S., Rubin, S. National Society for Experiential Education, 3509 Haworth Drive, Suite 207, Raleigh, North Carolina 27609, 1986, page 31.

(Chickering, 1976). The value inherent in learning through experience is amply expressed in the adages: "No man's knowledge here can go beyond his experience" (John Locke, 1690, *Essay Concerning Human Understanding*), and "The great difficulty in education is to get experience out of ideas" (George Santayana, 1863–1952).

Field experiences, internships, practica, cooperative education, service-learning, and academic service-learning

Experiential learning in the form of field experiences, defined more specifically as practica and internships, are the types of experiential education activities that will be discussed in this chapter. **Field experience** is "an off campus learning activity, generally for credit, in which a student accepts a large share of the responsibility for his/her own learning" (Davis et al., 1978).

Internships are a type of field experience. They are "structured and career-relevant work experiences obtained by students prior to graduation from an academic program" (Taylor, 1988). Because they are most often pursued during the later stages of an academic degree program, internships are frequently the culminating experience for the plan of study. As such, they provide the student with an opportunity to experience the fusion of principles and theories with the solution of practical problems (Hoekstra, 1975; Rex, 1961). Because each should inform the other, the relationship between theory and practice can be realized as a result of participating in an internship (Sweitzer and King, 1999).

Similar to internships, **practica** are "academically credited field experiences designed to meet specific academic objectives. They may be general and interdisciplinary in nature or oriented toward specific preprofessional training. These experiences are often degree requirements" (Stanton and Ali, 1987). Practica, however, are typically shorter than internships and frequently occur earlier in the academic degree plan of study.

On occasion, internships, and to an even lesser degree practica, are sometimes classified as **cooperative education** (co-op) experiences. To qualify as cooperative education, the field experiences must be "paid work experiences closely related to [the student's] academic and career pursuits" (U.S. Department of Education, 1991).

Cooperative education typically subscribes to one of two basic formats. The first is **alternating cooperative education,** which is a "plan of providing full-time, paid periods of work, balanced with full-time periods of study in institutions of higher education" (Gould, 1987). The second is **parallel or extended-day cooperative education,** which is a pattern allowing "attendance in classes, day or night, concurrent to a co-op placement" (Sheppard, 1987). Whether or not the experience is alternating or parallel/extended-day, receipt of payment in some form is usually necessary for the endeavor to be considered a cooperative education experience.

A concept that has evolved since the late 1960s, **service-learning** as defined by Jacoby (1996, p. 5), "is a form of experiential education in which students engage in activities that address human and community needs together with structured opportunities intentionally designed to promote student learning and development. Reflection and reciprocity are key . . . to service-learning." Due to its "commitment to social justice" (p. 10), service-learning could be confused with volunteer or community service programs. A striking difference is that service-learning includes intentional goals for student learning and development. Volunteer or community service programs, on the other hand, may lack the reflective component and intentional learning goals inherent in service-learning. (Jacoby, 1996).

"**Academic service-learning** is a pedagogical model that intentionally integrates academic learning and relevant community service" (Howard, 1998, p. 22). Within this context, service-learning is a teaching methodology more than a values model, leadership development model, or a social responsibility model. There is an *intentional* effort made to utilize community-based learning to enhance academic learning, and to utilize academic learning to inform community service. There is an *integration* of the two kinds of learning, experiential and academic; each works to strengthen the other. Additionally, the community service experiences must be *relevant* to the academic course of study (Howard, 1998). In short, academic service-learning is a teaching methodology whereby "service is integrated into the course by means of an assignment (or assignments) that requires some form of reflection on the service in light of course objectives (Weigert, 1998, p. 7).

CONCEPT CHECK

*Both contexts, experiential and academic, are important as allies in the cyclic process whereby knowledge is created through the transformation of experience. Experiential education as a **pedagogical approach** refers to learning activities that engage the learner directly in the phenomena being studied. Field experiences are a type of experiential education and are often defined in terms of internships and practica. For a field experience to qualify as a co-op experience, the intern is typically paid. In an effort to link service-learning and academic study, academic service-learning is a field experience that provides community service through the achievement of course/curriculum objectives.*

Application to sport management curriculum

Within the context of sport management, experiential learning is broadly interpreted as field experience. This concept is then more narrowly defined in terms of internships and practica in an attempt to operationalize curricular expectations. For example:

Internships are self-contained for academic credit. They involve actual work in a sport management setting subsequent to the junior year, in which management practices are applied. Final arrangement(s) for the internship are completed by a member of the faculty. The internship is a full-time (40 hr/week) work experience for a minimum of 400 hr. It must be directed and evaluated by a qualified faculty member with appropriate supervision by an on-site professional (NASPE-NASSM, 1993).

Practica are similar to internships in terms of direction, evaluation, supervision, and the intent that they be career-relevant. Practica differ from internships in that they are not necessarily self-contained or offered for academic credit. Practica may assume various forms and may be extensions of a course. They are frequently pursued along with other course work, close to campus, and on a part-time basis, since they are less time-consuming than internships. Some practica yield academic credit, whereas others may not (NASPE-NASSM, 1993).

A practicum and an internship are required by the "Standards for Curriculum and Voluntary Accreditation of Sport Management Education Programs" (NASPE-NASSM, 1993). The internship is a core component and the most commonly found element among undergraduate sport management programs in the United States (Parkhouse, 1987). Field experience plays an essential role and is highly valued in the preparation of both graduate and undergraduate sport management students (Brassie, 1989; Cuneen, 1992; Cuneen and Sidwell, 1993; DeSensi et al., 1990; Li et al., 1994; Parks and Quain, 1986; Sutton, 1989; Ulrich and Parkhouse, 1982).

As cornerstones of the curriculum, practica and internships take students beyond the classroom by placing them in a real work environment, thus providing the opportunity to bridge theory and practice. Participation in these activities helps students to develop professional attitudes, behaviors, and values while providing the opportunity to problem solve and link theory with actuality. At the heart of these activities is *learning by doing*. Because they take place in the "real" workplace, practica and internships ensure opportunities to "practice the profession" while being immersed in the work behaviors and social culture of the host organization (Verner, 1993).

In their book, *Sport Management Field Experiences,* Cuneen and Sidwell (1994) answer questions often asked by sport management students, their families, friends, and support groups. Intended to be an introduction to the purposes of field experiences, site search methods, credentials preparation, interview processes, conduct of field experiences and appropriate academic exercises, Cuneen and Sidwell's work is a key resource that should be consulted by sport management students seeking practica and internships.

HISTORICAL OVERVIEW
From on-campus laboratories to off-campus work experiences

Learning experiences that take place outside the traditional classroom have not always been endorsed as a part of college and university study. Acceptance of experiential learning, and thus internships, as a part of higher education curricula has evolved in recent years.

According to Keeton and Tate (1978), experiential learning has been documented in American higher education as far back as the 1830s, when skepticism and serious debate preceded the introduction of laboratory sciences at Yale University. Not until the late nineteenth century did laboratory sciences gain respectability as collegiate courses. Applied studies became an accepted part of the curriculum in land-grant institutions after the Civil War. Medical students at Johns Hopkins University began to engage in clinical experiences during the 1870s, when performing autopsies and visiting hospital wards became a part of their training (Houle, 1976).

Cooperative education became a component in the plan of study for many technically oriented programs in the early twentieth century. More recently, studio arts have become recognized as credit-bearing activities in many higher education institutions. Field studies are now commonplace in the sciences of botany, anthropology, and archaeology. Several "professional and applied fields—medicine, architecture, clinical and counseling psychology, social work, and elementary and secondary education—have accepted experiential learning as a regular part of professional preparation" (Kendall et al., 1986). Therefore it is from well-established precedents that field experience in the form of a practicum and an internship be endorsed as experiential learning components by the NASPE-NASSM Joint Task Force, which developed the sport management curricular guidelines.

CONCEPT CHECK

American institutions of higher learning have not historically endorsed experiential learning as an accepted element of the credit-bearing curriculum. However, throughout the last century, experiential education as a pedagogical approach that directly engages the student in learning by doing has increasingly become a requirement in a number of professional preparation programs. Following this trend, the NASPE-NASSM Curricular Standards require a practicum and an internship in the professional preparation of sport managers.

BENEFITS OF THE INTERNSHIP EXPERIENCE

The internship is a triangular relationship entered into by three principal parties. These include the student, university, and sponsoring organization.

Each one of the three helps to define the internship expectations. As a result, each has the potential to benefit from the unique educational opportunity that can develop. Students most notably desire to accomplish academic, personal, and career-related goals. The university and sponsoring organization desire to provide practical, on-the-job experience for students to help them meet their goals (Lanese and Fitch, 1983). Additionally, the university can help students reinforce the connection between theory and practice. Further, the sponsoring organization can help to strengthen the profession by enhancing the work force through the development of more capable entry-level employees. Following are benefits of specific value to the student, university, and sponsoring organization that can evolve from the internship relationship.

Value for students

Inherent in an internship experience for students is the opportunity to function as a professional and to become a part of the organization's culture through experiential awareness not only of its structure, resources, and purpose, but also the other internal and external factors that shape the organization (see Chapters 5–7). This includes becoming immersed in the behaviors, attitudes, beliefs, and values of the organization, an occurrence that can happen only when the internship experience duplicates or approximates that which is experienced by a full-time employee. Therefore, outside commitments such as coursework or other employment should not be pursued during the internship (Sutton, 1989). Interns should expect to follow all rules, regulations, and policies of the sponsoring organization to acquire the values, behaviors, and attitudes that constitute the culture of a professional in the organization. Granted, students pursuing full-time internships who are totally involved with the host organization may be making a considerable sacrifice. However, tremendous benefits can be realized by those who accept the challenge (Verner, 1993). Following are some of the benefits that may be realized by students.

A new learning environment. Knowledge and skills are acquired in different ways by different people. The practical settings that internships offer may be more effective learning environments for some students than the traditional classroom. Problem solving associated with an internship occurs in the "real world." The circumstances are not fictitious or contrived. Therefore lessons learned from the decision process can have a greater impact when experienced during an internship. For many students, the implications of problem solving and decision making have greater meaning and are longer lasting when associated with an internship rather than a simulated situation within the classroom.

Realization of the meaning of professional commitment. Misconceptions often exist related to the totality of a career. It is not uncommon for the enjoyable and interesting parts of the job to be amplified at the expense of diminishing the less desirable tasks. A full-time internship places students in organizations where they are confronted daily with both the positive and negative sides of their career choice.

Assessment of skills and abilities by practitioners. Because of the environment in which they function, practicing professionals often view things from a more pragmatic and realistic perspective than college professors do. As a result, practitioners' assessment of interns' strengths and weaknesses can provide additional insight into the interns' potential for that particular career. This may help students progress toward greater crystallization of **vocational self-concept** and work values by facilitating the identification of vocationally relevant abilities, interests, and values (Taylor, 1988).

"Experience" as a category on the résumé. One of the most frustrating obstacles for neophyte professionals to overcome is lack of experience. Internships provide the opportunity to gain invaluable work experience and as a result create another entry on the résumé. Researchers have documented the value of work experience and internships in securing a job. Evaluation of résumés, including background as well as presence or absence of an internship for six college women graduates, indicated that the most common reasons for success in being selected for a job was relevant work experience and completion of an internship related to the job (Avis and Trice, 1991).

Two-way screening process. Students can determine whether they feel suited for the career choice during the internship, and those with whom they work can evaluate the performance of interns within the context of the real work environment. This is not to say that interns should expect to be hired by the host organization, although this does happen on occasion. Evaluation of an intern's potential is more valuable when based on how the student performed on the job rather than on the evaluator's perceptions of how the student *may* function on the job.

New mentor/mentee relationships. New relationships develop as a result of contact with people encountered during the internship. These new relationships can help interns learn more about themselves, both professionally and personally. Through guidance, direction, and suggestion, mentors can help interns develop attitudes and behaviors necessary for success in their career. Many insights can be gained when interns learn from the mistakes and successes of those who have preceded them. Administrators advocate that all young professionals seek to establish mentor/mentee relationships (Young, 1990). Quality internships in sport management provide a forum for the development of strong mentor/mentee relationships (Brassie, 1989; Parks and Quain, 1986).

Networking. Being on the inside of the organization allows interns to be a part of the informal employee network. Students can learn of potential job openings before they are advertised, and they can develop important contacts as well as possible references for future career opportunities. Young (1990) found "administrators agreed that recommendations by network contacts often take precedence over a candidate's experience in a job search [which] reinforces the adage 'it's *who* you know that counts.' "

Information regarding vacancies or job availability can be from formal or informal sources. **Formal sources** are the traditional mechanisms for attaining job information, such as placement office bulletins and employment ads. **Informal sources** include friends and professional contacts. Greater access to informal sources of information regarding the job search is available to students who complete an internship (Parks, 1991; Taylor, 1988). According to Taylor (1984), the use of informal, as opposed to formal, sources of job information produces more satisfying job opportunities. Parks (1991) found the job placement strategy most frequently used by sport management majors was personal contact.

Mirror feedback and evaluation. Internships offer students the chance to discover whether theoretical ideas and textbook principles work in actual situations. The resulting successes and failures help establish a personal, critical assessment of how effective different strategies may be in a realistic environment.

Dealing with crises and critical decisions. In the real work world, daily incidences are not always predictable, and some situations may occur in which interns have had no experience. The conditions of the moment may not allow for consultation with mentors, the university supervisor, or textbooks. Action and decision making in such realistic dilemmas can accelerate the maturation process. Professional growth and development become evident as interns move away from reacting as students and assume the posture of young professionals.

Springboard for a career. An internship is the intermediate step between being a student and being a full-time professional. Depending on what the intern makes of the opportunity, it can be either a springboard or a barrier to a valued career position. A successful internship experience provides the basis for an excellent reference for future employment.

Value to university

Keeping in touch with the "real world." As new techniques and technology are developed and incorporated into the profession, it is helpful for university faculty to have exposure to what is and is not working in real-life situations. As visits and contacts are made with professionals who supervise student interns, faculty have the opportunity to discuss and witness both the effective and the ineffective procedures, equipment, and methodologies. This allows faculty to remain closer to the cutting edge of the profession (Verner, 1990).

Updating curriculum. Sport management educators believe one of the most valued characteristics of an effective graduate program is that the program is "updated to include current areas of subject matter in sport management" (Li et al., 1994). The university may improve its educational programs and test "its curricula through feedback" associated with the internship (McCaffrey, 1979).

Faculty who supervise interns have tremendous opportunity to remain abreast of current developments in the profession. Additionally, feedback can be gained not only from student interns but also from sponsoring organization supervisors. Based on their exposure during the field experience, interns can inform faculty of the strengths and weaknesses of the curriculum. Likewise, feedback can be provided by supervisors in sponsoring organizations regarding how well prepared the intern was to accept responsibility and function in the organization (Konsky, 1976). Information from all of these sources can be useful to faculty as they update their lectures and revise the curriculum. Enriched by feedback from the field and subsequent reformulation of the curriculum, professional preparation programs will remain in step with the industry, and better prepared students will emerge to join the work force.

Exposing students to new equipment. Even though it is relatively inexpensive to update the curriculum based on various forms of feedback, at a time when technology is changing so rapidly, it is quite expensive to keep college/university teaching laboratories up to date. Higher education institutions often experience financial limitations, prohibiting replacement or addition of new equipment so that students can be exposed to the latest available. It is particularly difficult to remain current with the most advanced equipment in the fitness industry because manufacturers are constantly designing and producing updated cardiovascular and resistive weight training apparatus. Internship experiences can provide students with the opportunity to work with equipment that may not be available on the campus.

Enriching classroom instruction. Classroom instruction can be enriched through the process of students relating their field experiences to the content being discussed (Gryski et al., 1992). Because they have been a part of the organization and have experienced what happens there on a day-to-day basis, the relationship between theory and practice may be more apparent for a student who has completed or is enrolled in a practicum or internship. Students who have not yet completed a field experience can become enlightened when fellow students who have completed an internship share their experiences and relate them to topics of instruction.

Developing research contacts. Faculty who supervise interns network with professionals in the field. Extensions of these relationships may lead to developing new ideas or strategies for research, as well as solidifying contacts that may be valuable in other endeavors (Cottrell and Wagner, 1990). Particularly enhanced through these faculty/practitioner relationships are opportunities related to applied research. Interaction with practicing professionals can provide faculty the opportunity to engage in research, possibly using the organization, its clients, or employees as the population to be studied. A few examples of applied research opportunities that may promote collaboration among the intern, faculty advisor, and sponsoring organization supervisor include study related to the following: (1) fan recognition of identified advertising displays in a sports venue, which may influence an advertiser's marketing approach; (2) client preference for cardiovascular equipment in a fitness environment, which may influence management's purchasing pattern; (3) donor motivation characteristics of those who, through gift-giving, financially support the organization, which may help the fundraiser better relate to current donors as well as know how to approach new donors.

Enhancing public relations. Through interaction with sponsoring organizations, universities can disseminate information about the strength of their programs and the capabilities of their graduates (Gryski et al., 1992). This interaction provides a valuable basis upon which to build relationships between the university and potential employers for graduates. It may also increase the likelihood that future interns may be placed with the sponsoring organization (Sink and Sari, 1984).

Value to sponsoring organization

Expanding the available work force. It should not be expected that motivation on the part of an organization for hosting an intern is completely altruistic. In return for the time and energy invested in helping students advance their knowledge, skill, and ability, sponsoring organizations with an effective intern will gain an additional staff member. This aspect can be particularly appealing when budget constraints have inhibited hiring practices (Bjorklund, 1974; Conklin-Fread, 1990).

Even in the beginning of the experience, when interns would not be expected to be full contributors, simple tasks and responsibilities can be assigned, thus allowing regular employees to direct their attention to higher-order tasks. As the interns become acclimated to the agency, greater responsibility can be assumed (Verner, 1990).

Bringing new ideas into the organization. Periodically introducing new ideas into the organization promotes variety and vitality. With each change in staff, new ideas are introduced to the agency. Such is also the case when hosting interns. "Students may sometimes serve as agents of change as they bring some of the latest information and innovation from the academic world into the field" (Gryski et al., 1992). Though they often have not had the opportunity to try many of their ideas, interns can offer a new perspective and a fresh outlook on tradition-laden policies and procedures. Because of their recent classroom exposure to literature and theories, interns are an excellent source of creative ideas (Verner, 1990).

Evaluating potential employees. Throughout the internship experience, personnel within the agency have the opportunity to evaluate the intern's capability to become a regular employee. Agency personnel can preview, with "no strings attached," preprofessionals who may be candidates for future job vacancies. Thus the internship can provide assistance in identifying talent among potential employees.

Assisting higher education to develop more-qualified employees. Through the sponsorship of internship opportunities, organizations blend their efforts with those of academic institutions to develop a more qualified work force. The value of field experiences in accomplishing this goal was substantiated by DeSensi et al. (1990) when business or agency personnel in sport management organizations "indicated that both practica and internship experiences were very important" (p. 49). No doubt sport management curricular improvements since the late 1970s have narrowed the gap between employer expectations and entry-level employee abilities, but at that time Parkhouse and Ulrich (1979) found employers believed that "on-the-job training rather than formal preparation, better serves the organization's needs."

CONCEPT CHECK

Internships and practica can benefit everyone involved in the triangular relationship—the student, university, and sponsoring organization. However, the student probably gains the most.

POTENTIAL INTERNSHIP INVOLVEMENT FOR SPORT MANAGEMENT STUDENTS

Before evaluating and selecting an internship site, students can narrow the search by creating a list of objectives they hope to accomplish during the internship experience. This process will enhance self-direction, which, according to Shipton and Steltenpohl (1980), promotes higher quality in experiential learning endeavors. By clarifying goals and planning a program to attain those goals, essential skills in self-direction are developed. Becoming self-directed related to one's education requires the following: (1) "learning how to plan"; (2) "learning how to assess personal values, interests, skills, aptitudes, and developmental needs [that contribute] to goal setting"; and (3) "knowing how to identify alternative learning activities and resources in relation to purposes." Having an environment in which to practice what is expected to be learned is requisite to developing ability in self-direction. Determining the most appropriate environment can be accomplished, in part, by subscribing to sound evaluation and selection criteria.

When considering potential organizations, it is helpful to be both creative and futuristic. Rather than being restrained by considering only typical placement sites, students should also look for organizations that could benefit from the knowledge, skill, and experience the intern could provide. Conversely, interns should evaluate whether potential organizations offer appropriate opportunities to fulfill their internship objectives. The following possibilities may meet the objectives of interns in fitness, leisure, and sport management:

1. Fitness
   a. Corporate fitness/wellness programs
   b. Hospital fitness/wellness programs—both for rehabilitation and for apparently healthy populations
   c. YMCA/YWCA and park district fitness/wellness programs for community residents
   d. Resort and cruise ship fitness/wellness programs
2. Leisure
   a. Park districts and YMCA/YWCAs
   b. Cruise ships, resorts, and hotels
   c. National parks, amusement and theme parks
   d. Hospitals and rehabilitation clinics for therapeutic populations
3. Sport Management
   a. Collegiate athletic departments
   b. Professional sport organizations
   c. Youth sport associations
   d. Governing organizations for all levels of sport

CONCEPT CHECK

Prospective interns should create a list of objectives to help define what they hope to accomplish during the internship. The process of developing objectives will assist in self-direction by clarifying goals and assist in planning to accomplish those goals. As a result, prospective interns should not be hesitant to make known their desires related to the type of internship placement.

COMPETENCIES DESIRED OF INTERNS

Two recent research studies documented potential employers' perceptions of desired competencies for sport management interns. Cuneen and Sidwell (1993) surveyed personnel who interview and select interns in major and minor league professional sports, college and university athletics, associations and conferences, resorts and clubs, event management, and the media. The respondents ($N = 215$) reacted to six fictitious potential intern résumés providing a rank order and identifying the one they would select for placement in their organization. From this assessment, nine intern qualifications emerged as the most desirable. In order of preference, the desired competencies were "(1) marketing/promotion experience, (2) evidence of computer skills, (3) evidence of writing skills, (4) sales experience, (5) internship goal, (6) practical/work experience, (7) athletic/sport background, (8) well-rounded, and (9) sports reporting experience."

Klein (1994) completed doctoral dissertation research, which led to the development of a "top ten" list of criteria for sport management interns as perceived by college athletic internship supervisors, nonprofit organization internship site supervisors, and sport management faculty advisors ($N = 143$). From an initial group of twenty knowledge competencies, eight technical skills, seventeen personal qualities, and seven selection criteria (fifty-two possible qualifications), the "top ten" list evolved and included seven personal qualities, two knowledge competencies, and one technical skill. The "top ten" criteria (actually there were eleven because of a tie for tenth place) for sport management interns emerging from this study in rank order were (1) reliable, (2) responsible, (3) willing to learn, (4) positive attitude, (5) verbal skills, (6) ethics, (7) communications, (8) cooperative, (9) adaptable to situations, (10) attention to detail, and (11) demonstrates initiative.

The two lists of competencies differ considerably in the items identified, most likely because of the differences in populations surveyed and the methodologies employed for the studies. Nonetheless, the results provide a point of departure for determining desirable intern characteristics.

Concept Check

Sport management intern competencies have been identified in recent research and include as the top three work-related skills: marketing/promotion experience, computer skills, and writing skills. The top three personal qualities include reliability, responsibility, and willingness to learn.

UTILIZING CAREER ADVANCEMENT MATERIALS TO MARKET ONESELF

With consideration given to desirable intern characteristics and after spending introspective time to assess personal and professional strengths and weaknesses, students should develop materials to market themselves. Three pieces of marketing material are often used to kick off this million-dollar marketing campaign: cover letter, résumé, and student portfolio. (Consider this a million-dollar marketing campaign because today's graduates may expect to make a million dollars or more in a lifetime of work.)

Cover letter and résumé preparation is briefly discussed in the following section, while considerably more space is dedicated to the development and use of a student portfolio. Excellent resources on career advancement are noted at the end of this chapter.

Cover letter and résumé

Prospective interns should design a résumé and prepare a cover letter that connects their professional skills and personal abilities with the tasks believed to be important to successful completion of the internship in question. The cover letter and résumé should look professional because they are the first impression given by the potential intern. Make the cover letter concise and well constructed with correct grammar, punctuation, spelling, and appropriate word choice. The résumé should provide all information that will help the agency staff become familiar with the candidate, including contact information, educational background, experiences related to the internship, and previous employment and volunteer experiences. According to Cuneen and Sidwell (1993), specificity regarding work-related skills is of tremendous value. For example, it is preferable for the résumé to identify the type of computer hardware and software used rather than simply indicating that the candidate is computer literate. Professional organization memberships, as well as school affiliations, should be listed. Leadership positions held in professional organizations and school affiliations should be highlighted. Refer to web sites describing career advancement materials at the end of the chapter for examples of résumés and cover letters.

Student portfolio

Recently, faculty from several fields of study have suggested that student portfolios are beneficial in assisting students in their preparation for internships and job interviews, as well as their entry into chosen careers. Professions where student portfolio development have been recommended include business, teacher education, health education, and applied health professions. Faculty from several fields of study have stated that student portfolio development contributes in a positive manner to success in undergraduate coursework as well.

Portfolio definitions and purposes. Although the definition and purpose of the student portfolio are often described differently by those representing various fields of study, it is agreed by most writers that a portfolio is a collection of student work gathered over time. In the early 1990s, researchers at the Northwest Regional Educational Laboratory in Oregon defined the student portfolio as "a purposeful collection of student work that tells a story of the student's efforts, progress, or achievement in a given area (Arter & Spandel, 1992, p. 36). The student portfolio has been described as having many purposes. "Why develop a student portfolio?" is a fair question to ask. One purpose is to document one's learning and growth during the undergraduate professional preparation program (Stone, 1998). Stone describes such a portfolio as the best work that a student can show others to demonstrate accomplishments over time and across a variety of contexts. Second, a portfolio may be a means for a student to reflect upon the successes and failures during experiences of applying knowledge and skills in classroom simulations or practica. For example, Stone suggests that logs, journals, self-evaluations, and reflective captions on items selected for portfolio inclusion can provide a student an opportunity for introspection and reflection. A third purpose of a portfolio is for showcasing to prospective internship supervisors and employers what a student knows and can do. Prospective employers find that this collection of work provides much more information than is given on a résumé, and thus it is seen as an important marketing tool that accompanies the résumé (Ellery & Rauschenbach, 1997).

Typically, interest by faculty has been increasing to use the student portfolio in yet another manner. It is seen as a tool for assessing and evaluating what a student knows and can do, and how well a student is progressing. Because this latter purpose involves controversy, especially within the field of education, research and development projects have been ongoing to determine the reliability and validity of the portfolio in assessing student achievement (Storms, Nunez, and Thomas, 1996).

Student portfolio types. The type of portfolio to be developed is determined by the audience for which it is intended. One type of portfolio is the **working portfolio** that contains cumulative work collected by the student in a purposeful manner according to stated guidelines or criteria. Selected work accumulated during enrollment in a single course and from many courses over a period of time shows one's efforts and progress toward the achievement of specific goals or standards. For example, the NASPE-NASSM Sport Management Program Standards provide specific areas of knowledge requisite for a student to enter into a career in sport management. The sport management working portfolio would contain samples of work selected by the student from undergraduate courses with the inclusion of the following areas: behavioral dimensions of sport; management and organizational skills in sport; ethics in sport management; marketing in sport; communication in sport; finance in sport; economics in sport; legal aspects of sport; governance in sport; and field experiences in sport management (NASPE-NASSM Joint Task Force on Sport Management Curriculum and Accreditation, 1993). This type of portfolio often includes student reflections and is most likely intended for the student, classmates, and course instructors.

A second type of student portfolio is the **showcase portfolio,** a purposeful collection of the student's best works as documentation of mastery of content and skills standards. A portfolio of this type provides evidence that links coursework to skills directly related to core competencies defined by a discipline (Waishwell et al., 1996). Such a portfolio can be presented to prospective practicum or internship supervisors and employers as evidence clearly documenting a student's readiness to enter the profession.

Selecting items for the portfolio. A wide variety of materials should be gathered for a portfolio (Hansen, 1992; Cleary, 1993). Suggested items include videotapes, writing samples, presentations and performances, individual and group projects, and career goal statements. Specific examples from the field of sport management might include marketing plans, budgets, and evidence of web site development. The student may wish to include a **reflective statement,** which is an introspective process of describing one's philosophy, values, or beliefs to others. For example, the sport management student might develop a reflective statement describing his or her personal leadership style.

In developing a showcase portfolio for either an internship or the employment interview, the student should select documents that demonstrate the link between classroom experiences and the knowledge and skills required for an internship or professional position. Products should be selected that demonstrate the ability to apply the theory and content of academic coursework to the "real life" skills needed by a sport management professional. Throughout the process of developing the showcase portfolio, it is important to remember that each portfolio is a unique effort, a tool designed to help students to market themselves. Although guidelines for portfolio development are often suggested, each student, with guidance from faculty members, should carefully select the documents to be included.

Items that demonstrate the student's acquisition of sport management content and skills should also be incorporated. Although any item can be included, a student might utilize the NASPE-NASSM Sport Management Program Standards during the selection process. Class projects and assignments that document the acquisition of knowledge and skills in one or more core content areas of the Program Standards would be especially relevant and appropriate. For example, a student might select an item that demonstrates competence in finance in sport or legal aspects of sport.

A recent survey of sport management professionals provides additional direction for the selection of portfolio items. In a study by Kadlecek and Thoma (1999), 186 sport management professionals were asked to identify the essential components of a portfolio. The five items that were identified as being most important for a portfolio included a marketing plan, a budget project, a sponsorship proposal, an ad media campaign, and a ticket sales campaign. Other items identified as important included evidence of web page development, an

event bid, a risk management assessment, and a press release.

Organizing the showcase portfolio. The keys to a successful showcase portfolio are the types of documents included and the way in which they are presented, not the amount of material accumulated (Ellery & Rauschenbach, 1997). In fact, a portfolio that is too bulky or not carefully organized may be counterproductive. It is important to remember that a person who is conducting interviews to choose the best candidate for an internship or employment may be pressed for time. Few will have the time to review a lengthy portfolio, especially if there are a number of applicants.

Figure 3–2 provides an example of how a student portfolio for sport management might be organized and the types of documents that could be included. One technique to begin the portfolio is to start with a current one-page résumé. This reminds the interviewer of important information about the candidate, including academic preparation, relevant work experiences, and appropriate certifications and volunteer experiences. A table of contents is often then presented. Listing all portfolio items with page numbers can serve as an important organizational tool. This organization will help someone to easily locate a relevant document as opposed to searching needlessly through all documents. Several portfolio experts suggest that a brief reflective statement be included next (Montgomery, 1997; Ellery & Rauschenbach, 1997). This statement should be limited to one or two pages and should describe one's

---

I. One-Page Résumé
II. Table of Contents (listing page numbers)
III. One- to Two-Page Reflective Statement
IV. Documentation of Content and Skills
   Acquisition
   a. Budget Project
   b. Marketing Plan
   c. Sponsorship Proposal
   d. Ad and Media Campaign
   e. Ticket Sales Campaign
   f. Press Release
   g. Legal Aspects of Sport Management
      Issue Presentation

FIGURE 3–2 Sport management student portfolio.

strengths as a sport management professional and one's leadership/management style.

Incorporating the portfolio during an interview. Following the development of an organized, quality portfolio documenting that one has the skills and knowledge essential for entry into sport management, the student faces yet another challenge. This challenge is to successfully integrate the portfolio into the interview process. In addition to getting the portfolio into the interviewer's hands, the student must also draw the attention of the interviewer to those items that best market the interviewee as the best candidate. During the interview, the student should listen very carefully to identify an early question that provides the opportune moment to hand the portfolio to the interviewer. Before offering the portfolio, the student needs to open it without difficulty to the specific section or item that contains evidence of the professional quality or skill, knowledge, or experience the interviewer asked about. Throughout the rest of the interview, the interviewee should continue to make references to documented work in the portfolio while encouraging the reader to take time to view it. It takes forethought and planning to be prepared to then elaborate on how and why the piece of work being viewed is important to one's future performance in sport management. Helping the interviewer see the value and worth of one's portfolio can enhance the overall interview experience and the impending outcome.

Concept ✓ Check

In the past ten years, the student portfolio has emerged as a method to document the acquisition of specific skills that are essential to entering the profession. The working portfolio combines many examples of student work that are completed during the undergraduate or graduate experience. As the student prepares for the internship or practicum, he or she will develop a showcase portfolio that contains the best work and documents essential skills needed in sport management. The portfolio can be continued throughout the internship/practicum, adding new work from that experience. More and more employers regard the portfolio as a useful supplement to the interviewing and hiring of a sport management professional.

SECURING AN INTERNSHIP

There are four basic steps to securing an internship: (1) identifying potential internship organizations; (2) contacting those of greatest interest; (3) interviewing with several organizations to find out more about their offerings; and (4) selecting the organization best suited for personal objectives. Before embarking on the process of securing an internship, students should become familiar with the expectations, resources, and requirements at their universities. By working closely with a university adviser or internship coordinator, the student will benefit by suggestions and become aware of approved university procedures.

Awareness of potential sites

Internship opportunities are advertised in many ways, most commonly in publications distributed to professionals in the field. Refer to the Web Sites at the end of this chapter that describe sport management internship opportunities. Following are additional internship resources categorized by career option.

1. Fitness
   a. Association for Worksite Health Promotion *Who's Who in Employee Health and Fitness*
   b. American College of Sports Medicine *Career Services Bulletin*
   c. University Internship Services *Directory of Internships*
2. Leisure
   a. National Recreation and Park Association *Park and Recreation Opportunities Bulletin*
   b. Resort and Commercial Recreation Association *Internship Directory*
   c. *Resource Sharing: Recreation Intern Programs within the Armed Forces*
   d. *YMCA Directory*
3. Sport Management
   a. National Collegiate Athletic Association's *The NCAA News*
   b. University Internship Services *Internship Directory* (available from University Internship Services, 2609 West 49½ St., Suite 100, Austin, TX 38731)
   c. *Sports Fan's Connection*

Initial contact

Initial contact should be made by sending the cover letter and résumé to preferred organizations. Allow approximately ten working days to receive a response. If no response is received, follow up the initial contact with a phone call. During this conversation, students can provide additional information or arrange to meet with someone from the agency to discuss the possibility of an internship.

Interview

The purpose of the initial contact is to arrange for an interview or to discuss the possibility for an internship. Try to obtain interviews with different agencies to compare the various opportunities. When visiting these organizations, tour the facilities and meet as many staff members as possible to evaluate the organizational culture and climate. Questions should be asked by both the interviewer and the interviewee to provide the information needed to help each make the appropriate choice to facilitate a good fit between the intern and the agency. Expectations held by the student, the agency, and the university should be discussed.

Selection

An internship site selection should occur only after the student has given considerable thought to the information collected during the interview, as well as from conversations with previous interns and the university internship supervisor. Information from these sources should be balanced against the student's objectives for the internship experience. Factors to consider when making the selection should include the following:

Position identity. The agency selected for the internship should be similar to that desired for an entry-level position. If that is not possible, the agency should be one that will provide the experience needed to be competitive for the desired entry-level position. The anticipated tasks and responsibilities should be transferable. At a minimum, the skills used in the internship should be similar to those required by the desired entry-level position (Sutton, 1989).

Compensation. Remuneration, or the lack thereof, should be the pivotal point for site selection only if financial compensation is absolutely required to be able to pursue the internship. However, significant financial compensation is not typical; in most internship situations, there is no remuneration.

Time span. The length of the internship will be determined in part by university and organizational requirements. Typically, internships occur within the semester; however, some are six months to one year in duration. The time of year should be considered, since organizations may be involved in cyclic work patterns and may only accept interns during specific times of the year.

Location. Students seeking permanent residence in particular parts of the country may want to consider obtaining internships in the desired regions. This not only provides the opportunity to learn more about a selected area but also can help students make professional contacts with knowledge of future job opportunities.

New experience. Internships are perfect times to try something unfamiliar and challenging. During this period, experiment and explore new aspects of the profession. There is little risk on the part of either the intern or the host organization in terms of an extended commitment or obligation.

Compatibility. By taking initiative and being proactive, students can assume responsibility for making the internship experience happen "for" them, not "to" them. Prospective interns should define the parameters that are acceptable to them and identify their needs and desires, thus taking an active role in shaping the experience. An internship is a three-way agreement, with the student's part being most important. While students need to be aware of the constraints of the agency and its bottom-line necessity to serve clientele, within those parameters students should be articulate in defining what they would like the experience to include (Verner, 1993).

CONCEPT CHECK

There are recommended steps to be followed in seeking an internship placement. However, before embarking on the search process, potential interns should contact the university internship coordinator or academic adviser who coordinates the internship program to become familiar with university policies, procedures, expectations, and resources.

SOLIDIFYING INTERNSHIP EXPECTATIONS

After the intern, university representative, and supervisor from the sponsoring organization have concurred that the internship can take place, an agreement should be developed to solidify the parameters and expectations of the internship experience. A document signed by the three parties is often used for this purpose. Although many universities and sponsoring organizations have used the term *learning contract* to refer to this document, there is reason to believe that *learning agreement* or other terminology that excludes the term *contract* might be a better choice. The preference for refraining from using *contract* is to avoid any legal implications that may be inherent in the term. The intent to identify expectations related to the internship can be accomplished without using the term *contract*; so as a measure of caution, the document specifying these conditions should not include this term.

Items covered by the learning agreement include anything that aids in clarifying the intentions and expectations of the student, university, and sponsoring organization supervisor. These include, but are not limited to, criteria related to educational goals, work-related objectives, learning activities, evaluation and grading techniques, academic credit, supervision support, and insurance coverage. Often, organizations that sponsor internship programs require some type of learning agreement before the experience can begin. This ensures that all parties clearly understand and agree to the role each will play in the internship relationship (Stanton and Ali, 1987). (Figure 3–3 provides an example of a learning agreement.)

STAGES OF AN INTERNSHIP

While each intern's experience subscribes to a certain element of uniqueness, some faculty who have supervised internships over a period of many years believe threads of similarity exist among most internship experiences. Some of the concerns and challenges that confront interns seem to occur in a predictable order. One of the similarities that cuts across various internship experiences is the phases students progress through as the internship unfolds. Sweitzer and King (1999) typify the five stages of an internship and call the stages anticipation, disillusionment, confrontation, competence, and culmination. The timing of migrating through the stages differs considerably from intern to intern. Additionally,

the end of one stage and the beginning of the next are not completely separate. Overlap often exists from one stage to the other. Sweitzer and King's explanation of what to expect during the course of an internship may be helpful as the interns prepare for and progress through the internship experience: (1) *anticipation:* looking forward to the internship and dealing with the accompanying anxiety; (2) *disillusionment:* a sense of despair when reality falls short of desire, a lack of certainty or affirmation about the experience; (3) *confrontation:* dealing with issues that are causing disillusionment, working through the difficulties; (4) *competence:* increased confidence resulting from successfully confronting and dealing with issues; (5) *culmination:* a sense of uneasiness that surfaces near the end of the experience as reflection clarifies what has transpired and anticipation seeks what the future may hold.

CRITICAL THINKING EXERCISES

1. On your résumé you indicate the availability of both references and a portfolio. An employer calls you to set up an interview, and during the conversation asks you to explain the portfolio and its purpose. In a paragraph, provide your response to the prospective employer.

2. Question: During the new millennium, many undergraduate and graduate sport management programs will begin to require student portfolios. What might be the impact of this practice from the perspective of the student? internship supervisor? prospective employer? the sport management profession?

SUMMARY

1. Historically, experiential learning endeavors have not been considered viable educational activities worthy of academic credit in American colleges and universities. However, over the last few decades, there has been considerable growth in the endorsement of field experiences as valuable components in the academic degree preparation for a number of professions. Curricular standards developed by the NASPE-NASSM Task Force require both a practicum and an internship experience in the preparation of sport managers.

2. The internship represents a three-way agreement. Tremendous benefits can be gained by

Illinois State University Department of Health, Physical Education, and Recreation Professional Practice – Cooperative Education & Internship **LEARNING AGREEMENT**		

PART I

A. NAME	SOCIAL SECURITY NO.

CAMPUS ADDRESS *Street*	HOME ADDRESS *Street*

City	*State*	*Zip*	*City*	*State*	*Zip*

PHONE	PHONE

ADDRESS WHILE DOING CO-OP/INTERNSHIP *Street*		

City	*State*	*Zip*	PHONE *(include area code)*

DATE CO-OP/INTERNSHIP COMMENCES	*DATE CO-OP/INTERNSHIP TERMINATES*

B. CO-OP/INTERNSHIP ORGANIZATION

ADDRESS   *Street*

City	*State*	*Zip*	PHONE *(include area code)*

NAME OF AGENCY SUPERVISOR

STUDENT POSITION

STUDENT POSITION IS – ☐ Paid *or* ☐ Unpaid

C. FACULTY SPONSOR/ADVISER

PROGRAM

ADDRESS   *Street*

City	*State*	*Zip*	PHONE *(include area code)*

CREDITS TO BE AWARDED		
PROGRAM	COURSE NO.	NO. OF CREDITS

Copies: White - *Faculty Adviser* Canary - *Agency Supervisor* Pink - *Dept. P.P. Coordinator* Gold - *Student*	**For Graduate Use:** Green - *Coordinator*

FIGURE 3–3   Sample learning agreement.

Adapted by Illinois State University from Stanton, T., and Ali, K.: *The experienced hand: a student manual for making the most of an internship.* National Society for Experiential Education, 3509 Haworth Drive, Suite 207, Raleigh, North Carolina 27609, 1987, p. 63–65. Reprinted with permission.

Professional Practice Learning Agreement

PART II. The Professional Practice Co-op/ Internship Experience

A. Job Description: Describe in as much detail as possible your role and responsibilities while on your internship or co-op. List duties, projects to be completed, deadlines, etc., if relevant.

B. Supervision: Describe in as much detail as possible the supervision to be provided. What kind of instruction, assistance, consultation, etc., you will receive from whom, etc.

C. Evaluation: How will your work performance be evaluated? By whom? When?

PART III. Learning Objectives/ Learning Activities/ Evaluation

A. Learning Objectives: What do you intend to learn through this experience? Be specific. Try to use concrete, measurable terms.

FIGURE 3–3   (cont.) Sample learning agreement.

B. Learning Activities

(1) On-the-Job: Describe how your internship/co-op activities will enable you to meet your learning objectives. Include projects, research, report writing, conversation, etc., which you will do while working, relating them to what you intend to learn.

(2) Off-the-Job: List reading, writing, contact with faculty sponsor, peer group, discussion, field trips, observations, etc., you will make and carry out that will help you meet your learning objectives.

C. Evaluation: How will you know what you have learned, or that you have achieved your learning objectives? How do you wish to evaluate your progress toward meeting these objectives? Who will evaluate? When? How will a grade be determined? By whom? When?

PART IV. Agreement

This agreement may be terminated or amended by student, faculty supervisor, or worksite supervisor at any time upon written notice which is received and agreed to by the other two parties.

STUDENT SIGNATURE		DATE
FACULTY ADVISER		DATE
AGENCY SUPERVISOR		DATE

FIGURE 3–3   (cont.) Sample learning agreement.

each of the three principal parties involved in the internship experience—the intern, university, and sponsoring organization.

3. Desirable competencies of sport management interns have been identified in recent research. After considering these competencies, prospective interns should consult with their university internship program coordinator, and begin the process of preparing career advancement materials and selecting an internship site. There are recommended ways to market oneself as well as search for, select, and solidify an internship placement.

4. When an organization decides to offer an internship, it should specify in writing the expectations and intent for the internship. It is advisable that this document not be called a "learning contract"; a better title may be "learning agreement."

The following case study was written by a student during the final few weeks of his internship experience. It is offered as a testimonial to the value of developing and using a student portfolio. As you become aware of this student's perspective, consider the suggestions he offers as a seasoned intern.

CASE STUDY

Each year, thousands of graduates enter the job market to compete for employment. These students have completed their degrees in hopes of attaining a job related to their field of expertise. Unfortunately for these students, there are fewer jobs than there are students. Students must find ways to present themselves to the employers using as many techniques as possible. One such approach that is currently being used on college campuses is student portfolios.

As a college freshman, I spent most of my time taking courses to satisfy university requirements and practicing poor study habits. I had no real idea what I wanted to do after graduation, and after all, it seemed so far away. I remember thinking to myself; "I will have no problem getting a job because I will have a college degree." To say I was a bit naive would be completely accurate. However, time passed and before I knew it, I was a sophomore.

As a sophomore, I chose the sport management major, as it seemed the right fit for my interests. So I began taking sport management courses, not

knowing what to expect or even what was ahead for me. I remember being in my major class thinking, "is this the area I really want to be involved with for the rest of my life?" At the completion of the class, my instructor advised us to update four specific items for our "portfolios." I, like many others, thought the idea was just another assignment and nothing to be too concerned about. The portfolio I developed lacked effort and importance. My classmates and I felt if we "just got it done," it would not be an issue anymore and we could move on.

My junior year rolled around and I continued taking the sequences of courses, studying and learning more about the field of sport management. I completed projects and kept them filed away for some reason. Like the previous semesters, there was some importance placed on the portfolio, but nothing to prepare us for the future.

My senior year came and with it a new outlook on school and life. I was finally realizing it was about time to step out into the real world. I thought continuously about being out there and not being prepared or not having the knowledge necessary for employment, so I can honestly say that I applied myself 100 percent. As part of this experience of being a senior who would be graduating in just two short semesters, I took great pride in doing everything that I could do to prepare for the future. One such preparation was the development of my personal portfolio. I am not speaking of the portfolio required by the professors early on in the program, but a product of my work and success as a college student.

I was introduced to the concept of portfolios by one of my instructors, who provided suggestions on developing a showcase portfolio. She provided the class with a handout to help us to structure and organize our portfolios. As students we were responsible for meeting certain criteria for the portfolio, but at the same time we had great liberty to use creativity to tailor our portfolios to our personalities.

As I began to develop my portfolio, I reevaluated all of my projects, papers, and assignments from courses throughout the program. As I looked through these items, I took time to correct and modify them for accuracy, currency, and thoroughness. Next, I decided to organize the portfolio based on the NASPE-NASSM Sport Management Program Standards. I felt this was the best way for the items to be organized for both me and for employers. A key to successful portfolio design is ease of reading. You want to catch the viewer's attention by selecting content that is meaningful and providing relevant evidence of your acquired knowledge, skills, and experiences. I also wanted the portfolio to be professional, yet exciting. I completed this task by placing a fair amount of color in the portfolio, using protector sheets, and organizing it with divider sheets and tabs in a leather binder. The items I included were as follows: projects, assignments, papers, certifications, reflective statement, volunteer work résumé, table of contents, and presentations. Throughout the process I kept in mind my own personality and my intended viewer/reader.

When it came time to use my portfolio, I was thankful for all the time and effort I put into developing the total package. It definitely has proven to be an asset to my career opportunities thus far. For example, as part of the final requirement for my undergraduate degree, I was to complete a sport management internship. The process required me to schedule and complete an interview with my site supervisor. At this time we discussed one another's expectations during my internship, my strengths and weaknesses, and specifics about the site. For the interview, I brought my portfolio that I had developed throughout my college career. As we talked and time went on, I realized that I had to incorporate my portfolio into the interview. The most difficult task is not developing the portfolio but finding a smooth transition to using it in an interview. The answer to this problem is, "there is no perfect time!" You must just have a feel for the interview and the conversation to determine when to share your portfolio with the interviewer.

Currently, I use my portfolio to support my work in my internship. It is nice to have a handy reference on my desk to help me navigate my way through problems. Also, I have used my portfolio to help me generate ideas for new projects.

As I move on in my professional career, I plan to continue adding to and replacing materials in my portfolio. By this I mean I will add new project materials that I am especially proud of and feel would be beneficial to a future employer as well as me. Second, I will replace dated work with current work that could aid me in future projects. Finally, I would like to keep my portfolio updated as evidence of personal achievement.

For those of you contemplating a portfolio, I would without a doubt recommend developing one. I have gained much from developing my portfolio, and I offer you the following suggestions when beginning your own professional portfolio:

- *Seek the assistance of a professor for support.*
- *Organize your portfolio so it is easy for the viewer to read.*
- *Develop your portfolio to represent you and your personality.*
- *Use your creativity to gain interest and maintain the viewer's attention.*
- *Use materials that will be beneficial for an employer to see.*
- *Start development of the portfolio EARLY in your program.*
- *Keep all materials from each class in your program and any other course material you feel would be appropriate.*
- *Update your materials as you go through the program; DO NOT wait until you begin to use your portfolio.*
- *Seek ideas by browsing through former students' portfolios.*
- *Do your very best to make it what you want it to be.*
- *And . . . good luck!*

Your future is not going to rest on your decision to not develop a portfolio. However, the job market continues to be saturated with college graduates. As this happens, employers can continue to be more selective in who they choose to hire. A portfolio is an excellent way to market yourself and place yourself a step higher on the employer's candidate list. As a college student, you have all that is needed to develop a quality portfolio, but you must provide the effort and determination to make it useful and complete. The portfolio is an excellent tool for graduates entering the job market to showcase their abilities and to seek promotion or career advancements.

REVIEW QUESTIONS AND ISSUES

1. What role do experiential and academic learning play in the process of creating knowledge through transformation?
2. Describe Kolb's experiential learning theory in terms of its structure and relate the four components to one another.

3. What are the two field experience components required by the NASPE-NASSM curriculum standards? How do they differ and how are they similar?

4. Identify and describe three possible benefits for the intern that can result from an internship experience.

5. What are three university/faculty benefits that can be realized from an internship experience? Name and describe them.

6. An organization that sponsors internship opportunities can benefit in numerous ways. List and describe three possible benefits that can result from hosting an intern.

7. Competencies desired by sport management interns have been documented in two research studies (Cuneen and Sidwell, 1993; Klein, 1994). Name any six of the desired competencies identified among the top five on either of the two lists generated by these two studies.

8. Describe the major differences between a working and a showcase portfolio. What are the benefits of each type?

9. Identify the three purposes of a student portfolio. Which of the three is the most important to you as a student? Explain why.

10. What term is *not* recommended for use in the document that specifies arrangements and expectations for the internship? Why should this term not be associated with the document that solidifies the internship relationship?

SOLUTIONS TO CRITICAL THINKING EXERCISES

1. Sample answer: The portfolio is a representative collection of my best work from all sport management classes. It provides evidence of my sport management skills, writing style and problem-solving abilities. The reason why I would like you to review it is that it demonstrates my professional skills as well as my commitment to high-quality work.

2. Sample answer: The student feels prepared for the entry-level job, the internship supervisor confirms the skills of the new intern, the prospective employer can better compare two job applicants, and the sport management profession supports common entry-level skills through student documentation.

REFERENCES

Arter, J. A., and Spandel, V. (1992). Using portfolios of student work in instruction and assessment. *Educational Measurement: Issues and Practice, 11* (1), 36–44.

Avis, R. K., and Trice, A. D. (1991). The influence of major and internship on the evaluation of undergraduate women's résumés. *College Student Journal, 25,* 536–38.

Bjorklund, C. (1974). *A feasibility study of internships in educational management and innovation.* Boulder, Co: Western Interstate Commission for Higher Education.

Brassie, P. S. (1989). Guidelines for programs preparing undergraduate and graduate students for careers in sport management. *Journal of Sport Management, 3* (2), 158–64.

Chickering, A. W. (1976). Developmental change as a major outcome. In M. T. Keeton (ed.), *Experiential learning: Rationale, characteristics, and assessment* (pp. 62–109). San Francisco: Jossey-Bass.

Cleary, M. J. (1993). Portfolio development for health education students. Paper presented at annual convention of American Alliance for Health, Physical Education, Recreation, and Dance, Washington, D.C.

Conklin-Fread, M. T. (1990). An investigation of the direct, indirect, and intangible benefits which accrued to hospital dietetic departments sponsoring an internship for student dietitians (Doctoral dissertation, New York University, 1990). *Dissertation Abstracts International, 51/08B, 3785.*

Cottrell, R. R., and Wagner, D. I. (1990). Internships in community health education/promotion professional preparation programs. *Health Education, 21* (1), 30–33.

Cross, K. P. (1994). The coming of age of experiential education. *NSEE Quarterly, 19* (3), 1, 22–24.

Cuneen, J. (1992). Graduate level professional preparation for athletic directors. *Journal of Sport Management, 6* (1), 15–26.

Cuneen, J., and Sidwell, M. J. (1994). *Sport management field experiences.* Morgantown, WV: Fitness Information Technology.

Cuneen, J., and Sidwell, M. J. (1993). Sport management interns: Selection qualifications. *Journal of Physical Education, Recreation and Dance, 64* (1), 91–95.

Davis, R. H., Duley, J. S., and Alexander, L. T. (1978). *Field experience.* East Lansing, MI: Instructional Media Center.

DeSensi, J. T., Kelley, D. R., Blanton, M. D., and Beitel, P. A. (1990). Sport management curricular evaluation and needs assessment: A multifaceted approach. *Journal of Sport Management, 5,* 31–58.

Ellery, P. J., and Rauschenbach, J. (1997). Developing a professional portfolio. *Strategies, 11* (2), 10–12.

Gould, P. (1987). Alternating cooperative education programs. In D. C. Hunt (ed.), *Fifty views of cooperative education* (5th ed.). Detroit: University of Detroit.

Gryski, G. S., Johnson, G. W., and O'Toole, L. J. (1992). Undergraduate internships: An empirical review. In A. Ciofalo (ed.), *Internships: Perspectives in experiential learning (pp. 195–210).* Malabar, FL: Krieger Publishing.

Hansen, J. (1992). Literacy portfolios: Helping students know themselves. *Educational Leadership, 49* (8), 66–68.

Hesser, G. (1990). *Experiential education as a liberating art.* Raleigh, NC: National Society for Experiential Education.

Hoekstra, R. B. (1975). *Internships as a means of training educational leaders: An historical and contextural perspective.* (ERIC Document Reproduction Service No. ED 103 999).

Houle, C. O. (1976). Deep traditions of experiential learning. In M. T. Keeton (ed.), *Experiential learning: Rationale, characteristics, and assessment* (pp. 19–33). San Francisco: Jossey-Bass.

Howard, J. P. F. (1998). Academic service learning: A counternormative pedagogy. In R. A. Rhoads and J. P. F. Howard (eds.), *Academic service learning: A pedagogy of action and reflection* (pp. 21–29). San Francisco: Jossey-Bass.

Jackowski, M., and Gullion, L. (1998). Teaching sport management through service-learning: An undergraduate case study. *QUEST, 50,* 251–65.

Jacoby, B. (1996). Service-learning in today's higher education. In B. Jacoby and associates (eds.), *Service-learning in higher education: Concepts and practices* (pp. 5–25). San Francisco: Jossey-Bass.

Kadlecek, J., and Thoma, J. E. (1999). Sport management student portfolios: What practitioners want included. Paper presented at the annual conference of the National American Society for Sport Management, Vancouver, Canada.

Keeton, M. T., and Tate, P. J. (1978). *Editor's notes:* The bloom in experiential learning. In M. T. Keeton and P. J. Tate (eds.), *New directions for experiential learning: Learning by experience—what, why, how* (pp. 1–8). San Francisco: Jossey-Bass.

Kendall, J. C., Duley, J. S., Little, T. C., Permaul, J. S., and Rubin, S. (1986). *Strengthening experiential education within your institution.* Raleigh, NC: National Society for Experiential Education.

Klein, D. C. (1994). *Knowledge, technical skills, personal qualities, and related selection criteria for sport management internships* (Doctoral dissertation, University of New Mexico).

Kolb, D. A. (1984). *Experiential education: Experience as the source of learning and development.* Englewood Cliffs, NJ: Prentice-Hall.

Konsky, C. (1976). Practical guide to development and administration of an internship program: Issues, procedures, and forms. Normal, IL: Illinois State University. (ERIC Document Reproduction Service No. ED 249–539).

Lanese, L. D., and Fitch, W. C. (1983). How to get an intern off and running: A model. *Performance and Instruction Journal, 22,* (1), 30–32.

Li, M., Cobb, P., and Sawyer, L. (1994). Sport management graduate programs: Characteristics of effectiveness. *Journal of Physical Education, Recreation and Dance, 65* (5), 57–61.

McCaffrey, J. T. (1979). Perceptions of satisfaction and dissatisfaction in the internship experience. *Public Administration Review, 39,* 241–44.

Montgomery, K. K. (1997). Student teacher portfolios: A portrait of the beginning teacher. *The Teacher Educator, 32,* 216–25.

NASPE-NASSM Joint Task Force on Sport Management Curriculum and Accreditation. (1993). Standards for curriculum and voluntary accreditation of sport management education programs. *Journal of Sport Management, 7,* 159–70.

Parks, J. B. (1991). Employment status of alumni of an undergraduate sport management program. *Journal of Sport Management, 5* (2), 100–110.

Parks, J. B., and Quain, R. J. (1986). Sport management survey: Employment perspectives. *Journal of Physical Education, Recreation and Dance, 57* (4), 22–26.

Parkhouse, B. L. (1987). Sport management curricula: Current status and design implications for future development. *Journal of Sport Management, 1* (2), 93–115.

Parkhouse, B. L., and Ulrich, D. O. (1979). Sport management as a potential cross-discipline: A paradigm for theoretical development, scientific inquiry, and professional application. *Quest, 31* (2), 264–76.

Rex, R. G. (1961). A theory of the internship in professional training. (Doctoral dissertation, Michigan State University, 1961). *Dissertation Abstracts International,* 23/02.

Sheppard, J. (1987). Parallel and extended-day cooperative education programs. In D. C. Hunt (ed.), *Fifty views of cooperative education* (5th ed.). Detroit: University of Detroit.

Shipton, J., and Steltenpohl, E. (1980). Self-directedness of the learner as a key to quality assurance. In M. T. Keeton (ed.), *New directions for experiential learning: Defining and assuring quality in experiential learning* (pp. 11–27). San Francisco: Jossey-Bass.

Sink, K. E., and Sari, I. F. (1984). Internships: A mutually beneficial relationship. *Performance and Instruction Journal, 23* (10), 23–25.

Stanton, T., and Ali, K. (1987). *The experienced hand: A student manual for making the most of an internship.* (2d ed.) Cranston, RI: Carroll Press.

Stone, B. (1998). Problems, pitfalls, and benefits of portfolios. *Teacher Education Quarterly, 25,* 105–14.

Storms, B. A., Nunez, A. M., and Thomas, W. H. (1996). Using portfolios to demonstrate student skills. *Thrust for Educational Leadership, 25,* 6–9.

Sutton, W. A. (1989). The role of internships in sport management curricula: A model for development. *Journal of Physical Education, Recreation and Dance, 60* (7), 20–24.

Sweitzer, H. F., and King, M. A. (1999). *The successful internship: Transformation and empowerment.* Pacific Grove, CA: Brooks/Cole.

Taylor, M. S. (1988). Effects of college internships on individual participants. *Journal of Applied Psychology, 73* (3), 393–401.

Taylor, M. S. (1984). Strategies and sources in the student job search. *Journal of College Placement, 45* (1), 40–45.

Ulrich, D., and Parkhouse, B. L. (1982). An alumni-oriented approach to sport management curriculum design using performance ratings and a regression model. *Research Quarterly, 53* (1), 64–72.

U.S. Department of Education. (1991). *Cooperative education program: Guide for the preparation of applications fiscal year 1992.* Washington, DC: U.S. Department of Education.

Verner, M. E. (1993). Developing professionalism through experiential learning. *Journal of Physical Education, Recreation and Dance, 64* (7), 45–52.

Verner, M. E. (1990, September). The internship advantage. *Fitness Management,* pp. 34–35.

Waishwell, L., Morrow, M., Micke, M., and Keyser, B. (1996). Utilization of the student portfolio to link professional preparation to the responsibilities and competencies of the entry level health educator. *Journal of Health Education, 27* (1), 4–9.

Weigert, K. M. (1998). Academic service learning: Its meaning and relevance. In R. A. Rhoads and J. P. F. Howard (eds.), *Academic service learning: A pedagogy of action and reflection* (pp. 3–10). San Francisco: Jossey-Bass.

Young, D. (1990). Mentoring and networking: Perceptions by athletic administrators. *Journal of Sport Management, 4,* 71–79.

WEBSITES

Sport management internship opportunities

Adidas

www.adidas.com/

Adidas home page, which links to the Adidas Career Center, where internship and job opportunities within the Adidas Corporation are described.

HPCAREERNET

www.hpcareer.net

Internships and jobs in health promotion

International Association of Assembly Managers

www.iaam.org

Describes the IAAM Foundation Internship Program, which is designed to place students at participating public assembly facilities that agree to give the student a structured, well-supervised job (in a full-time position) that exposes him or her to a wide range of facility activities.

Northeast Athletic Job Link

www.bright.net/~joblink/

Vacancies in Northeastern U.S. elementary, junior high, and high schools as well as colleges and universities including: physical education, head and assistant coaches, coaching/teaching at public and private schools, health education, recreation, athletic directors, athletic training, sports information, graduate assistantships, and internships.

Team Marketing Report, Inc. (TMR)

www.teammarketing.com/

Describes the Team Marketing Report, Inc. Editorial Intern Position as well as other sport management job opportunities and links advertising other sports-related job opportunities.

University Internship Services

www.internsearch.com

University Internship Services Directory of Internships

WellTech International

www.welltech.com

The Career Center link provides health promotion, recreation and fitness internship listings, employment listings and résumé center.

Women's Sports Foundation

www.WomensSportsFoundation.org

Several internship opportunities within WSF are described along with the application process.

Career advancement materials

Plattsburgh State University, Career and Placement Center: Résumé and Cover Letter Writing Resources

www.plattsburgh.edu/stuvp/careerplacement/students/résumé.html

This career placement center maintains an extensive list of Internet sites that will serve as good resources for sport management students as they develop résumés/cover letters.

National Association of Colleges and Employers

www.jobweb.org/catapult/guenov/restips.html

Combining the interests of higher education and business, this site provides students with résumé development information, including samples of excellent résumés.

College of William and Mary

www.wm.edu/csrv/career/stualum/resmdir/contents.html

Students are provided a detailed description of each section of an effective résumé in addition to several examples of good résumés.

Worchester Polytechnic Institute

www.wpi.edu/Admin/Depts/CDC/Résumé/index.html

In addition to providing information about résumé development, this site also addresses the use of electronic résumés and includes a helpful list of action verbs.

CHAPTER 4

Research and Inquiry

Sue Inglis

In this chapter, you will become familiar with the following terms:

Organizational behavior	Deductive reasoning	Triangulation
Organizational theory	Inductive reasoning	Quantitative
Organizational science	Validity	Survey research
Work-related functions	Reliability	Peer review
Inquiry	Paradigm	Human ethics
Theory	Qualitative	

Overview

Managing sport is full of challenges and complexities! In this chapter we take a look at the importance research and inquiry play in advancing our understanding of the management of sport. Research and inquiry represent our curiosity about how sport is managed and how management practices can be improved by asking good questions and seeking new information that will ensure that sport is effectively managed within society.

Learning about key concepts of research and inquiry sharpens critical thinking skills and makes us better students, practitioners, and scholars of management, thus enhancing our potential to understand and anticipate organizational life, and work effectively toward desired change. There is a certain air of excitement associated with research; this chapter is written in the hope that the reader catches a bit of it!

As long as sport has existed, so has its management. The citizens of Elis, Greece, for example, managed the ancient Olympic Games (Harris, 1967; Kyle, 1987). In the nineteenth and twentieth centuries professional organizations emerged to manage amateur and professional sport (Hardy, 1986; Hardy and Berryman, 1983). The study of sport and its management, however, is a relatively new field in contemporary society and is characterized by emerging specializations and refined ways of conducting inquiry and research. The purpose of inquiry and research is to understand sport management and to allow for a meaningful contribution to the practical side or "the doing" of the management of sport.

This chapter begins with an organizational behavior and theory and work-related functions framework that is helpful in understanding relevant topics within sport management. A major portion of the chapter is concerned with knowledge development in the field of sport management. Within knowledge development, the concepts of theory and deductive and inductive reasoning are pertinent. Also introduced are the foundations of sport management, including sport and business administration and areas such as sociology and psychology from which theory can be derived. The importance of working with theory as the field of sport management develops is a theme stressed throughout the chapter.

Various types of validity and reliability are introduced as important concepts in conducting research and in evaluating published research. Next, key steps involved in the research process and qualitative and quantitative approaches to research design are outlined. Within the qualitative approach, direct and participant observation, focus group and social action research, and within the quantitative approach survey research (the most popular design used in sport management research) and experimental designs are presented.

Guidelines for evaluating various types of published research are included. These should be helpful in identifying a variety of sources, including books and peer-reviewed journal articles, as well as understanding key questions to ask in assessing published work.

Individuals engaged in research have an obligation to adhere to ethical guidelines. The reader is introduced to some of the ethical areas through practical examples of communication between the researcher and respondents. The final section provides ideas on new directions for research in sport management.

Although the topics and concepts cannot be fully explored in one chapter, hopefully the chapter will serve as an introduction for the reader and inspire more reading and application of sound research in this field of study.

FRAMEWORK FOR SPORT MANAGEMENT

A useful way of depicting some of the topics in sport management follows the organizational behavior and organizational theory framework used in the management literature (Daft, 1995; Johns, 1992; Steers, et al., 1996). Recently, scholars in sport management have published textbooks using this framework. See Slack (1997) and Chelladurai (1999) for two excellent examples. **Organizational behavior** includes areas such as individual perceptions, individual differences,

learning styles, motivation, communication, leadership, decision making, conflict, and work group behavior. Organizational behavior helps us understand why people behave the way they do in their organizational lives and is thought of as taking a micro perspective, that is, a concern with individuals and groups as basic components for the analysis of work behavior. Questions such as "How do individual differences affect the way we perceive others?" "What factors are involved with motivating individuals to perform on the job?" "How do group norms affect work behavior?" "What leadership styles are most prominent in the managing of change?" and "How do conflict management strategies apply to sport management?" are the types of questions typical of the organizational behavior perspective.

Organizational theory includes the study of areas such as the design, technology, and environment of organizations. Organizational theory takes a macro perspective, with the organization as the unit of analysis. Questions and areas include "What are useful ways of describing the structures of our sport organizations?" "What effect does size have on the design and function of the organization?" "What role does a turbulent environment have on the design and operations of our work sites?" and "How do similar organizations compete for scarce resources?"

Organizational behavior and organizational theory fit under the umbrella term of **organizational science.** Organizational behavior and theory provide a useful way of understanding organizational life. Introductions to a number of organizational behavior and theory topics are provided in this textbook. The other range of topics actively pursued by researchers and writers of sport management include **work-related functions** of marketing (including advertising, sponsorship, and promotions), facility management, finance, computer application in sport environments, product development, and case law and its application to sport environments. These are just a few examples of the range of topics of interest to scholars in sport management. The inquiry and research into these topics will advance the understanding of how sport is managed and can be most effectively delivered to the benefit of the participants, spectators and communities. How knowledge is acquired and the meaning of theory are also important to understand, and they are the focus of the next section.

CONCEPT CHECK ✓

An organizational science framework for understanding specializations within sport management includes organizational behavior with an emphasis on the individual and group, and organizational theory with an emphasis on the organization as the unit of analysis. A number of work-related functions (e.g., marketing, legal liability, and facility management) are also important areas within sport management.

INQUIRY AND DEVELOPING KNOWLEDGE

Inquiry is the art and skill of arriving at new understandings about a problem, issue, or phenomenon through the process of asking good questions, identifying and evaluating good sources of information, drawing reasoned conclusions and emergent questions and communicating to others.

Developing knowledge through research and inquiry in the field of sport management involves creating theory and testing theory. In simple terms, a **theory** is an explanation of how concepts are related. For researchers, a theory will be a series of statements that capture what is currently known about related concepts and assumptions about the concepts. Assumptions represent the ideas and views we think are true about particular issues without knowing for sure. Often, assumptions are the answers to our research questions we have before we begin the research (Hubbuch, 1996). The theory may be derived from the "field," that is, where the theory is played out in practice and may be tested and explored in various types of studies. Managers use theories, too. Although managers may not formally write down their ideas about particular concepts, their behavior at work often reflects trial-and-error attempts related to different theories they hold.

Using theories in research helps in three important ways (Hamner and Organ, 1978). First, theories provide a practical way of organizing knowledge and therefore provide a structure for understanding. Second, a good theory will summarize or capture a great deal of information in a few critical propositions. Third, theories help direct future study and practice. Good theories help to explain real behavior in real organizational settings, thus good theory development is inextricably linked to practice. Daft and Steers (1986) offer the well-known quote of Kurt Lewin, "There is nothing so practical as a good theory." This is true for sport management.

To evaluate what makes a good theory, Kaplan's (1964) framework can be used.

1. *Internal consistency.* Are the concepts and relationships between the concepts in the theory free from contradiction? Do the concepts and relationships make sense?
2. *External consistency.* Does the theory seem to make sense when viewed in relation to real life examples?
3. *Scientific parsimony.* Is the theory simple? Does the theory include only the main concepts that explain a phenomenon?
4. *Generalizability.* Does the theory apply to a variety of situations? For example, if we have a theory about why there are so few women in management positions within those organizations, does the theory hold true for other situations of few women in management?
5. *Verification.* Can we test the theory? For the theory to be useful, it would need to be tested or explored in a research setting.

When a theory satisfies these characteristics, it has greater meaning and usefulness to both researchers and managers.

The work of Thibault et al. (1993) is a good example of a research program reflecting Kaplan's framework for good theory. These authors were interested in understanding how sport organizations develop strategies to anticipate change and environmental challenges. They developed a relatively simple and meaningful theory, of value to sport managers and theorists, that explains how different nonprofit amateur sport organizations develop different strategies and plans for their organizations. Their framework (theory) incorporated the two main dimensions of program attractiveness and competitive position with a number of imperatives in both dimensions. The imperatives for program attractiveness were "fundability," size of client base, volunteer appeal, and support group appeal. For competitive positions the imperatives were equipment costs and affiliation fees. When plotted on a matrix, these two dimensions produced four strategic types called *enhancers, innovators, refiners,* and *explorers.* In a subsequent study (Thibault et al., 1994), the theory was tested on a sample of thirty-two national sport organizations. The findings supported the theory and, most importantly, provided a contingency framework for understanding how different sport organizations employ differing strategies to cope with environmental variances.

DEDUCTIVE AND INDUCTIVE REASONING

Deductive and inductive reasoning are two ways of working with theories and knowledge development. They are illustrated in figure 4–1. **Deductive reasoning** is a process of inquiry in which one works from general principles to specific instances or observations. For e1xample, if a study worked from the principle that involving employees in

decisions concerning scheduling of work will lead to lower absenteeism, then the study would be designed or a situation found in which employees are involved in these scheduling decisions. Ways of assessing and measuring whether the reality of the employee involvement did in fact fit with the initial theory or principle would be developed. **Inductive reasoning** works the other way. Inquiry from a number of observations and situations leads to a general theory or principle. What principle is captured in the reality of the observations?

USING FOUNDATIONS AND THEORY IN SPORT MANAGEMENT

Good researchers have substantive knowledge in the area they are studying. Moving to more theoretical-based research in sport management implies that for the phenomena under study, the foundations and frameworks informing the research area will be used. Lambrecht (1991), drawing on Parkhouse's 1987 work, depicted sport management as originating from the two primary disciplines of sport studies and business administration. We can add to this depiction the parent disciplines such as anthropology, economics, sociology, political science, and psychology that inform sport studies and business administration. This is an important message within sport management. To develop substantive knowledge and theory in sport management, exposure to other areas and parent disciplines, such as labor studies and women's studies, is necessary. From new insights and knowledges, combined with working knowledge and experience in sport management, greater understanding will be possible.

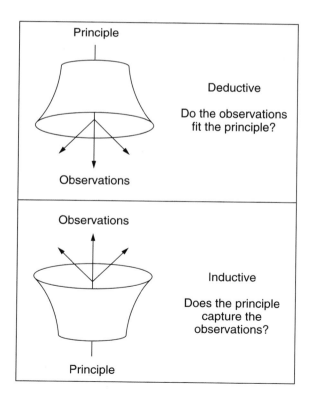

FIGURE 4–1   Deductive and inductive reasoning.

> ## CONCEPT CHECK
>
> *Understanding theory is important in developing new knowledge that will be useful to the practice of sport management. Deductive and inductive reasoning represent ways we work with theory. The two major academic disciplines of sport studies and business administration inform sport management. Additional disciplines (psychology and sociology as examples) also inform the field. New interdisciplinary alliances with areas like labor studies and women's studies are encouraged.*

VALIDITY AND RELIABILITY

An understanding of the concepts of validity and reliability are important in developing knowledge and theory about sport management. **Validity** addresses the question, "To what degree does this measure or capture what it is intended to measure or capture?" A number of types of validity help the researcher and reviewer of published work to determine how accurately the measure reflects reality. Researchers working in qualitative and quantitative designs approach validity from distinct perspectives (Lather, 1986). Five types of validity (there are more!) defined here help in constructing research designs that validate social knowledge and give confidence to the trustworthiness of the data.

Face validity is the most basic and answers the question, "does the indicator measure the concept?" (Neuman, 1997). This can be asked of the scientific community or the research participants. Fletcher and Bowers (1991) use face validity in advertising research to assess whether the results seem logical or predictable. In qualitative designs, member checks (Guba and Lincoln, 1981; Reason and Rowan, 1981) are used. Member checks involve the participants of the research reviewing the tentative results, with subsequent refinements made in light of these reactions.

Content validity is the extent to which the items/variables most fully represent the theoretical construct under study (Neuman, 1997). In survey research, a "panel of experts" is often used during the development of the questionnaire to ensure that the concept under study is being fully captured.

Construct validity refers to situations in which multiple indicators of a concept must be measured. It is concerned with assessing the consistency with which the different indicators operate (Neuman, 1997). Similar to content validity, experts may be used to assess the conceptual appropriateness of measures. Statistical analysis is also used.

Predictive validity suggests that results from one measure can be verified by comparing them with another (Fletcher and Bowers, 1991). For example, if an advertising campaign designed to solicit inquiries about season ticket sales does in fact generate a high number of inquiries, the advertising campaign could be considered to have high predictive validity.

Catalytic validity as described by Lather (1986) is that in which individuals who have been part of the research develop self-understanding and self-determination through the research process. This is a term specific to qualitative methodology.

Reliability addresses the question, "To what degree will the measure be consistent over time?" Reliability in research can be improved by taking care in developing questions and instructions that will be used in interviews, focus groups, surveys, or experiments. Questions need to be pretested with a small group before the actual research is conducted. Interviewers must be well trained. A common measure of estimating internal consistency reliability used in survey research is on the basis of a coefficient alpha (Mueller, 1986; Nunnally, 1970). Nunnally stresses the importance of assessing reliability and outlines various ways reliability can be assessed. Reliability coefficients of 0.70 or higher for subscale or item measures are considered satisfactory; if, however, decisions are to be made with respect to specific scores, a reliability of 0.90 is considered minimal and 0.95, desirable (Nunnally, 1978).

The analogy of a target to measures of validity and reliability from Babbie (1995) is helpful in understanding these important concepts (figure 4–2).

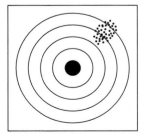
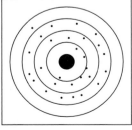
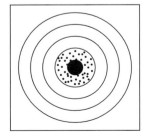

Reliable but not valid   Valid but not reliable   Valid *and* reliable

FIGURE 4–2   Measures of validity and reliability.
From Babbie, E. R. (1995). *The practice of social research* (7th ed). Belmont, California: Wadsworth.

In the first square the results are reliable because they hit the target in the same place. The problem is, the results are off the mark and therefore not valid. The second square is valid because the target is being hit closer to the center, but it lacks consistency. Finally, the ideal situation of validity and reliability—on the mark—is shown in the third square.

A research study by Hums and Chelladurai (1994), which examined fairness around the allocation of resources in intercollegiate athletics, was "on the mark" in terms of its reported validity and reliability. The face and construct validity of the instrument, which was developed to assess distributive justice, was based on a panel of experts' feedback on the instrument's relevance, clarity, and conciseness in measuring distributive justice. Additionally, the internal consistency estimates and test, retest reliability estimates were substantial and added empirical support to the instrument.

QUALITATIVE AND QUANTITATIVE PARADIGMS

In their simplest form, our "ways of knowing" by inquiry through research can be thought of as qualitative and quantitative paradigms. The term **paradigm** refers to a way of conceptualizing the theoretical perspective in which we look at the world (Bogdan and Biklen, 1992). Table 4-1 presents selected characteristics of qualitative and quantitative paradigms. Table 4-1 is useful in acquiring an initial understanding of some of the differences between the two perspectives. The qualitative-quantitative perspective is a useful way of introducing readers to designs and underlying philosophies.

Qualitative

Qualitative methodologies involve the exploration of situations that are lived or observed in everyday life. Interaction with people who are closely connected to the phenomena under study provide rich insights into peoples' conditions, behavior, and perceptions. Qualitative data provide the basis for developing theory.

Morse (1994) describes qualitative processes as following an analytical scheme that includes *comprehending* what is being observed or talked about, *synthesizing* to make generalized statements about the individuals or things, *theorizing* by offering explanations that connect the data to real-world experiences, and *recontextualizing* by thinking about the theory in different settings.

Included in the qualitative paradigm are the research designs of participant observation and direct observation. As outlined by Johns (1992), in *participant observation* the researcher is a functioning member of the group being studied. When the researcher observes, but is not actually involved in the activity, it is called *direct observation*. Mintzberg's classic study of the 1970s, in which he spent a week with each of five male executives assessing what types of activities and roles the managers were actually involved in, is a good example of direct observation. The results of this direct observational method helped to dispel some of the myths of what managers' activities were thought to be like (Mintzberg, 1975).

A more recent example of direct observation of leaders and work is found in the diary studies of Helgesen (1990) in which, like Mintzberg, she spent time with four top executives. Through this research an exploration of how female leaders make decisions, structure their companies, and work with employees and communities was revealed. Both examples, in their own right, have provided rich information about leaders at work.

Focus groups are another example of qualitative research design for use in sport management (Inglis, 1992). *Focus groups* are moderated discussion groups of five to ten people who are brought together on the basis of some important interest or similarity. Focus groups can be used in a variety of ways. These groups are useful to the research process when developing survey or interview questions (Morgan, 1988), as well as in assisting with the interpretation of survey results. In advertising planning cycles, Fletcher and Bowers (1991) suggest focus group research is important in the stages of the research that ask the questions, "Where could we be?" and "How could we get there?" In-depth input from potential consumers is important.

As the qualitative paradigm seeks to work with people to reach new meanings, social action and change can be a desired outcome. This critical social action seeks to empower the participants. Lather (1986) wrote of "research as praxis," that is, research that is committed to building a more just society by altering maldistribution of power, resources, and services. Within sport management research, aspects of Vail's (1992) work on community delivery

TABLE 4-1 *Selected characteristics of qualitative and quantitative paradigms*

Selected characteristics	Qualitative	Quantitative	
		Survey research	Experimental
Goal	Discovering the experience Developing theory	Show relationships Hypothesis testing	Hypothesis testing Prediction
Research site	Participants' locale, close to natural location as possible	Mail	Researchers' locale Laboratory or other experiment setup
Data Collection method	Observation, interviewing	Participant responses	Experiments using scientific method
Using	Interview guides, probes	Surveys	
From Sources	Informants, participants Field notes, personal documents, official documents, photographs	Respondents	Testing protocol Subjects
Variables Empiricism	Not controlled Words as the information	Controlled	Controlled Numbers as the information
Analysis	Content of the experience	Descriptive and/or predictive statistics Bounded by study	
Findings based on	Inference as results emerge from coherent whole, insight, intuition	Survey results	Direct product of observable processes
Theory	Emerges from data to support previous theory or to build new theory	Supported or not supported by data, based on probabilistic model, a prior set alpha level of significance	
Phrases and designs associated with approach	Action research, grounded theory, fieldwork, focus groups, case studies, participant observation, naturalistic	Social survey, descriptive, correlational	Experiment, positivist, statistical

Modified from Bogdan and Biklen (1992). *Qualitative research for education: An introduction to theory and methods.* Boston: Allyn and Bacon, Inc. and Morse, J. M. (ed). (1994). *Critical issues in qualitative research methods.* Thousand Oaks, CA: Sage.

systems reflects a social action perspective. In this research, a partnership involving a university researcher and a parks and recreation employee brought representatives of various community sport organizations together to assess the community's sport needs, solutions, roles various partners could play, and structures to facilitate desired change. Background data were collected by means of a survey mailed to 400 individuals and groups in the community. This was followed by focus groups, extensive retreat workshops, and planning sessions, which resulted in a collective vision and structure to more effectively deliver community sport. Change in how sport is delivered and how the sport-related resources are used is occurring in this community (Vail, 1992). This research is also a good example of how research designs from qualitative and quantitative paradigms can be effectively used together as multiple data collection techniques to address research questions. This **triangulation** includes multiple data sources, methods, and theoretical schemes (Lather, 1986), and can move the researcher closer to establishing the trustworthiness of the data. Triangulation can be extremely beneficial if the designs are well suited to the questions being raised and the outcomes desired.

Quantitative

Quantitative methodologies involve specifically identified variables that are studied under rigorous test conditions. Quantitative data are objective measures. Survey research and experimental designs are the two most common types of quantitative research.

Survey research has as its goal the describing and exploring of variables, relationships between variables, and perceptions as offered by individuals through the completion of questionnaires. These goals and other characteristics place survey research primarily within the quantitative paradigm. Survey research is the most extensive research design used in sport management (Olafson, 1990; Paton, 1987). When relationships between variables are studied, we must be careful to note that the correlation that may be found does not imply causation. For example, arena managers may be found to be satisfied with their work and may be found to be in good health. It cannot be suggested from these results that satisfaction causes good health.

Conducting good survey research, like other types of research, requires knowledge of the subject matter and theoretical foundations, as well as knowledge about the design and conduct of the survey, coding of the survey, and analysis. The analysis often requires computers. The type of statistical analysis required will depend on the research question, the design, and the response format of the survey. Some research questions involve simple yet meaningful analysis, whereas others involve more complex analysis. Survey research should not be conducted unless the individuals involved have the knowledge, expertise, and time, and the research question has been carefully developed.

Experimental designs are placed in the quantitative paradigm. Experimental designs allow for the manipulation of variables under closely controlled, laboratory-like settings. In these settings, issues of causation and prediction can be addressed. Although experimental research is conducted in many management environments, sport management has not, to any great extent, utilized this research design. Hopefully this will soon change, because there are appropriate areas in which experimental research designs would make a meaningful contribution to the understanding and practice of sport management.

For example, consider a closely controlled laboratory setting in which sport managers are engaged with consumers in simulated decision-making activities involving event ticket pricing, augmented product pricing, and consumer behavior. Similarly, consider the use of a computer program and conditions in which individuals (subjects) are involved in decisions about strategies, expenditures, or organizational crises. These testing conditions would allow the researcher to replicate an organization's environment while controlling for time and access to information factors. Results of these types of experiments would provide valuable information to sport managers and contribute to the theoretical understanding of the concepts under study.

CONCEPT CHECK

The challenge to sport management researchers is to understand qualitative and quantitative research designs. Knowledge derived from qualitative and quantitative inquiry and designs needs to be conveyed in useful ways to practitioners in sport management environments.

Steps in the research process

Both qualitative and quantitative research involve a number of steps. While the seven steps outlined here are a very simplified representation of the rigors of good research (Neuman, 1997) and inquiry, they help to show the ongoing nature and key components.

1. *Choosing a General Topic.* This should be based on a strong need within sport management to know more about the topic. The topic should be of great interest to the researcher, and it is highly desirable that the topic be socially significant to improving sport and its place within society.
2. *Developing a Research Question within Related Theoretical Framework.* After much background reading and narrowing of the topic, the researcher should have a good understanding of the research question, related theory, and how the question fits with past research and will contribute to new insights.
3. *Designing the Study.* After considering the various ways the study could be conducted, the researcher will decide on a design and the details of the study. This might include the design of questionnaires, the plan for interviewing research participants, participant observation, archival searches, or the design of a controlled experiment. Ethics approval will be obtained at this stage.
4. *Collecting the Data.* The researcher collects the data, paying particular attention to appropriate protocols.
5. *Analyzing the Data.* The researcher analyzes the data, looking for patterns, significant findings, and new understandings.
6. *Interpreting Findings, Drawing Conclusions.* The results are interpreted with reasoned conclusions drawn, new questions identified, implications for future research, and changes to the management of sport, which might include new policy development or new practices.
7. *Communicating Results.* The results are shared with others in a variety of forums ranging from workshops with practitioners and scholarly conference presentations to published reports, journal articles, and books.

EVALUATING PUBLISHED RESEARCH

Good research and inquiry in sport management require accessing relevant literature. Where to locate and how to evaluate the literature are two very important aspects. Published research takes a variety of forms, including the following:

- Books written by one or more authors
- Books edited by one or more individuals, which include chapters written by a variety of contributors (of which this textbook is an example)
- Peer-reviewed journal articles by one or more authors
- Nonpeer-reviewed journal articles by one or more authors
- Abstracts and proceedings of conferences
- Occasional paper series published or circulated by the agencies involved in the production, including government documents and papers from a university
- Popular magazines

There is no definitive order to this list in terms of quality of writing, scholarly rigor, or ability to make a useful contribution to the knowledge base, or to communicate to selected audiences. **Peer-reviewed** journal articles are generally considered to be regarded with greater credence in terms of scholarly writing and research. A brief description of the process by which an article is published demonstrates the nature of the peer-review process. Manuscripts submitted to the editor of the *Journal of Sport Management*, for instance, are sent to three reviewers who remain anonymous. These reviewers are from an editorial board, selected for their proven ability in research and writing, to critically yet fairly evaluate the work of their peers. It is not unusual for manuscripts to be rejected for publication (often the acceptance rate is approximately 40 percent of all manuscripts submitted for review) or to be accepted with major or minor revisions. Once manuscripts are accepted for publication, they appear as articles in the journal. The time frame for a manuscript from time of submission to a journal to its publication is often one to two years. Nonpeer-reviewed writings, such as books, do not go through the same process. The difference between the rigor exposed to manuscripts submitted to peer-reviewed journals and other journals and books should be clear. Even though not anyone can write a book, it is often easier to publish a nonpeer-reviewed abstract, manuscript, or book than a peer-reviewed manuscript.

EVALUATING INTERNET SOURCES

Many types of published sources, including peer-reviewed journals, can now be found on the Internet. Given the growth of technology and the open access that allows more people to post items online without evaluation by professional experts, great care must be taken in critically evaluating the sources found.

Some questions to keep in mind when evaluating published research (including sources found on the Internet) are "What is the source of the information?" "Have the possibilities of where good information may be found been exhausted?" and "Have a variety of sources been used?"

What follows are some guiding questions that need to be answered as published research is reviewed. The published research is classified under research studies, concept pieces, and prescriptive writings.

If the work is the result of a research study:

What research question was addressed? What theoretical perspectives inform the work? Who were the subjects/respondents? How was the sample drawn and described? How were the data collected? What methodology(ies) were employed? What type of analysis was included? Were appropriate statistical applications used to analyze the data? What key results were reported? How were the results linked to previous studies or theory? Were there recommendations for future research? Were there recommendations for program change or policy development?

If the work is a "concept piece," that is, outlining a concept that is new or derived from another field of study that could be applied to sport management environments:

What issue was addressed? What theoretical perspectives informed the work? What links to sport management were made? Was there a clear indication of how the concept is relevant to sport management and how it could be of value to the field?

If the work is prescriptive, that is, suggesting how a particular function or area of sport management should be conducted:

What was the topic under discussion? Was there support from other areas for this proposed application or use in sport management environments? Was it communicated clearly?

Questions applicable to all three types of work within inquiry and research in sport management (research studies, conceptual writing, and prescriptive) include:

Were assessments and measures of validity and reliability indicated? What is the contribution of this work to the study and understanding of sport management? Does the work make a contribution to your topic of inquiry, your position, or your line of thinking?

ETHICS IN INQUIRY AND RESEARCH

Individuals engaged in research have an obligation to conduct the research within ethical guidelines and to report the research accurately. Most institutions have human ethics committees in place that review all research proposals. Application for **human ethics** approval generally involves assurance that the project is well planned, the purpose of the research is clear, and the involvement level of subjects or respondents is detailed. How subjects or respondents are told about their involvement with the research, how they will be treated throughout the duration of their involvement with the research, and how they will be told of their right to withdraw at any time is all part of the proposal for ethics approval. The experience level of the researcher(s) is often included in submissions.

Ethics review committees work to ensure the following:

1. Subjects or respondents enter research projects voluntarily and understand the nature of the risks involved.

2. A plan for obtaining informed consent is in place.

3. If necessary, subjects or respondents will be debriefed at the end of the research project.

Cover letters for surveys and consent forms for participants in focus group research are two common areas within sport management research where good communication between the researcher and respondents or subjects is important. Johns (1992) reminds us that ethical research has a practical side as well. For good research, cooperation between the researcher and subject is necessary. Cooperation is easier to achieve and maintain when people feel ethical questions are being addressed.

The box on the next page shows two examples of how researchers communicate with subjects as respondents in survey research (*1a*) and as key informants in focus group research (*1b*).

The interaction between researcher and respondent is much greater with qualitative methodologies. As such, it is important to ensure that the

Examples of 1(a) informing subjects in survey research and 1(b) as key informants in focus group research

1(a) Excerpts from cover letters in survey research

You may be assured of complete confidentiality. Your name will not be placed on the survey. Published and reported results will not identify individuals or organizations, and any discussion will be based on group data.

All individual results are confidential and will only be examined by the researchers. Your survey has an identification number for mailing purposes only so your name can be checked off the mailing list when your questionnaire is returned. Your name will not be placed on the survey.

Please do not hesitate to contact us if you have any questions. Thank you for your assistance.

1(b) Excerpt from key informant consent form in focus group research

This session is part of a research project and information will be used to help interpret results of the survey you previously completed. Tape recorders and flip charts will be used. Excerpts from the session will be used for teaching and research presentations and publications. Individual names will *NOT* be directly associated with any statements. We respect that participants have the right to withdraw at any time during the session.

Your feedback on this session, or additional comments you wish to make, are welcome. Please write. Thank you for helping.

Release and agreement by participant

I, _____, have read the above, and I am willing to participate in the session and permit use of the information gathered during the session for the purposes outlined.

Signed: _____ Date: _____

Inglis, Danylchuk and Pastore, 1996.

Based on research by Sue Inglis, 1993.

---

respondent feels comfortable disengaging at any time during the research and that time is taken to properly debrief after individual sessions and at the completion of the project.

The close interaction between researcher and participant often requires multiple ways of disengaging from the research process. For example, debriefing sessions involving individual and group members and continued access by the participant to the researcher are commonly used to assist both parties in moving away from the project. These are some of the challenges unique to qualitative methodologies in sport management research.

Ethical considerations in the publication and presentation of research include ensuring that a manuscript is submitted and under review to only one journal, identifying multiple authors in descending order based on the quality and quantity of their contribution to the research (unless noted otherwise), clearly communicating the roles of editor and contributing author to work, and providing accurate references in the writing.

NEW DIRECTIONS

In developing this section a number of scholars in sport management were contacted.* The purpose was to tap the expertise of others so their ideas on future directions and skills needed could be

*Recognition and appreciation are extended to the following sport management scholars who contributed to the ideas expressed in this section: Dr. Bob Boucher, University of Windsor; Dr. Laurence Chalip, Griffith University; Dr. Wendy Frisby, University of British Columbia; Dr. Janet Parks, Bowling Green State University; Dr. Trevor Slack, De Montfort University; Dr. Dave Stotlar, University of Northern Colorado; Dr. Jim Weese, University of Windsor; and Dr. Earle F. Zeigler, Professor Emeritus, University of Western Ontario.
Soucie (1994) provides a current overview of the types of doctoral dissertation topics in administration 1949–1993 as well as the types of articles published in the *Journal of Sport Management* 1987–1993.

incorporated in this section. The first question was, "What are some of the areas for research in sport management that should be explored?" The responses offer readers a sense of the scope for future directions. A number of individuals responded, "The field is wide open—there are so many areas and topics to be studied!" Looking at these ideas for future research reinforces the idea that bringing in ideas from other disciplines and experiences opens up tremendous opportunities for study. In doing so, a leadership role is taken in studying sport management in such a way as to link sport in a meaningful way to changing society.

New directions in sport management need to delve into a variety of sport-related environments. Such settings could include sporting good retailers and manufacturers, major corporations that are involved in the sport industry, single and multisport community sport, and amateur and professional sport organizations. Traditionally, sport management research has clustered around intercollegiate athletics. Although intercollegiate athletics play important roles and are of obvious interest to researchers (Paton, 1987), there are important issues in all sport-related environments that could benefit from researchers' attention.

With the call made for sport management to work from theoretical perspectives (Olafson, 1990, 1995; Paton, 1987; Slack, 1993, 1996), we can look to the areas of business administration, higher education, and public policy as examples of areas that have advanced. These areas, like sport management, are informed by parent disciplines such as sociology, anthropology, economics, political science, and psychology. Using the framework of organizational behavior and organizational theory and work-related functions introduced earlier in the chapter, a selection of topic areas provided by individuals currently contributing to sport management includes:

Organizational behavior

Policy as it affects people
Leadership—transformational, gender, and management
Ethics and values
Decision-making theory
Conflict management
Consumer behavior

Cultural analysis of people and work
Human resource management
Impact of sport on community well-being
Team building
Empowerment
Power and politics
Accountability in sport delivery systems
Volunteer management

Organizational theory

Community sport delivery models
Interorganizational links
Economic impact of participation and entertainment sport
Organizational strategy
Structure and design of sport organizations
Policy as it affects structures and products
Comparative studies of sport organizations and other organizations
Organizational technology

Work-related functions/issues

International legal issues
Effects of advertising in sport
International comparative marketing mixes
Increasing attendance at games
Integration of all in sport, inclusive of gender, race, ability, and sexual orientation
Increasing job satisfaction

Additional ideas for future research in sport management are found in the Dr. Earle F. Zeigler addresses given at the annual North American Society for Sport Management conference. A few ideas from recent lectures are noted here. The importance of scholars in sport management working with the practitioner is a recurring theme (e.g., Chelladurai, 1992; Parks, 1992; DeSensi, 1994; Slack, 1996; Boucher, 1998). Chelladurai (1992) emphasized the need for those in academia and practice to work together so that what is studied makes a contribution to practice. Parks (1992) stressed the importance of bridging the gap between the scholar and the practitioner. Frameworks, she argued, like Boyer's discovery, integration, teaching, and application help us to understand the practical. In a similar vein, Boucher (1998) called for research of a more practical nature to help bridge the gap between theory and practice.

DeSensi (1994) emphasized and provided a way of understanding and moving from a monocultural to a multicultural organization that would be respectful of full integration of individual and cultural diversity. Understanding and moving toward multicultural organizations involves social action. These, she suggests, are important directions for sport management. Boucher (1998) was in agreement with DeSensi when he called for a more theoretical curriculum to help understand social issues affecting sport.

Olafson's (1995) call for new directions in sport management research emphasized contributions that address sound theoretical bases, research centers of excellence, the use of a variety of research designs, and the exploration of new issues in new ways.

Chelladurai (1992) stressed the importance of considering a broad definition of sport that involves the aspects of providing human services as well as entertainment. This broadening of our understanding of what constitutes the sport industry (Slack, 1996) will help us to conduct meaningful research in a wide variety of sport organizations, including organizations that exert major influence on sporting events as major sponsors and partners. Slack (1996) also outlined the importance of knowing and understanding current concepts in the management literature, incorporating new approaches to conducting sport management research, and developing two-way linkages between faculty and students in teaching and research with business academic units.

The second question asked of scholars in the field was "What are the skills and abilities necessary for students (and scholars) to acquire for competence in conducting research in sport management?" It is important to understand previous trails of research and how we would proceed to discover new pathways. The ideas expressed in this section serve as a self-check to see where efforts need to be made to acquire new skills.

Reading, reading, and more reading is basic to conducting good research. Reading of field-related journals as well as journals from other disciplines is essential. Reading about previous research and reading to understand methodologies that will be most appropriate to the research being conducted, and reading from sources outside of North America is important to develop our understandings and knowledge bases from broad perspectives.

Related to reading are problem-solving skills. Integration and imagination are important to extend research agendas beyond the obvious. Our present, obvious way of conducting research in sport management is to use survey design and offer a description of some phenomena. These types of scholarly activity are important, but they are not enough. There is a need to understand what sport managers identify as critical management problems, and there is a need to develop theory-based understandings to these problems. Returning for example, to Thibault et al. (1993, 1994) we see important insight about how sport organizations develop strategies through the development of the theory and testing of the theory. The conceptual framework will have important implications for sport managers who need to understand why, given particular environmental and organizational characteristics, various types of strategies are employed. The framework is also applicable to other types of sport organizations.

We need to be able to find the links and to access various information sources to learn to make decisions about critical concepts and what is worth knowing. Included in this would be the ability to draw from a variety of literature sources and to take meaningful directions for new research that could make a contribution to sport management as well as to the parent disciplines. The research questions must, where appropriate, have relevance to the practice of management. Learning to formulate realistic research questions is a skill that requires constant refining.

Access to databases including sport management and databases from related fields and knowing how to conduct computerized searches is critical. These skills are related to other computer skills that aid the research process tremendously. Both qualitative and quantitative paradigms utilize computers in data entry and analysis.*

Communication skills include good writing as well as the ability to identify and deliver messages in the most effective ways. The results of our work should be communicated in ways that satisfy not only the academic journals, but also other

---

*For example, the SPSS/PC+ (Statistical Package for the Social Science/Personal Computer enhanced edition) is a commonly used statistical package for quantitative analysis, and the NUDIST (Nonnumerical, Unstructured Data Indexing, Searching and Theorizing) software is available for qualitative analysis.

audiences, including classroom situations and practitioners. Some of the results of our work can lead to policy development and program change.

To summarize, the skills needed to conduct and evaluate good research in sport management that have been introduced in this chapter are understanding theory development and methodologies, the ability to evaluate published research, the ability to read and develop meaningful research questions, computer skills, the ability to conduct the research, and the ability to impart new knowledge to both scholars and sport managers.

CONCEPT CHECK

A variety of sources of published research on sport management are available. Questions to evaluate the written work are helpful in assessing the merits of the work and the meaning to the individual. Individuals conducting sport management research must adhere to ethical guidelines. New directions for research and inquiry in sport management include a variety of areas, and a number of skills are necessary to conduct good research.

CRITICAL THINKING EXERCISES

1. Outline a new sport management research study that would use both qualitative and quantitative methodologies. What methods would be appropriate and why? What would the time frame for conducting the research be?
2. A sport management researcher at a highly respected university is conducting survey research involving the marketing directors of the corporations involved in the sponsorship of a major sporting event. Why would the study need to have human ethics approval? What ethical considerations should be communicated to the research participants?

SUMMARY

1. A framework that helps us think about sport management includes organizational behavior, organizational theory, and work-related functions such as marketing and legal issues.
2. Inquiry and research in sport management are based on theory development and testing.
3. Deductive and inductive reasoning are used in knowledge development.
4. The foundations of sport management include sport studies and business administration. The foundation is further informed by parent disciplines such as psychology and sociology.
5. Validity and reliability are important concepts in conducting research.
6. Research can be viewed from qualitative and quantitative approaches. Examples of a qualitative approach include focus groups, participant observation, and social action research. Examples of a quantitative approach include survey research, which is the most common design used in sport management research, and experimental designs.
7. Of the number of published sources of sport management writing, peer-review journal articles have the most rigorous review process.
8. Ethical considerations are important in conducting research.
9. The topics for future research are endless. The researcher must possess a number of important skills to conduct meaningful research.
10. Where appropriate, the research should be informed by theory.
11. The research conducted in sport management should make a valuable contribution to understanding and improving the practice of sport management.

CASE STUDY

The marketing department of a semiprofessional baseball club approaches a sport management program. The club is interested in having research conducted to answer the following questions:

1. *Who is coming to the games?*
2. *What are the reasons the fans are coming to the games?*
3. *What aspects of the game could be changed to make the game more attractive for the fans?*

The marketing director is interested in other questions that may provide useful information. She is also interested in the various designs and research considerations that would be used to address the questions. Before contracting for this research, the baseball club needs a two-page statement by interested individuals or groups. Considering the information contained in this chapter, what would some of the important parts of the statement for the submission to the marketing director be?

REVIEW QUESTIONS AND ISSUES

1. Outline and discuss an example of Kurt Lewin's statement, "There is nothing so practical as a good theory." The example should be from a sport management environment.
2. Select an article from the *Journal of Sport Management*. Decide if the article represents a research study or a concept piece. Use the guide questions from the section in this chapter on evaluating published research on p. 63 to guide discussion of the article.
3. Outline an experiment that could be designed to test the hypothesis that attention to customer service factors will have an effect on customer satisfaction.
4. An athletic director at University X complains, "Every year I get requests from across the country to complete surveys. Although I am sure they are well-meaning studies, I never see any changes to the problems facing intercollegiate athletics." Discuss.

SOLUTIONS TO CRITICAL THINKING EXERCISES

1. Have you explained the ways in which your research example is well suited to both objective (quantitative) and subjective (qualitative) measures? Is your time frame for the research reasonable?
2. Have you addressed the key considerations related to: (a) why ethics approval is important, (b) how the nature of the research would be communicated with the research participants, and (c) how confidentiality of responses would be ensured.

REFERENCES

Babbie, E. R. (1995). *The practice of social research.* 7th ed. Belmont, CA: Wadsworth.

Bogdan, R. C., and Biklen, S. (1992). *Qualitative research for education: An introduction to theory and methods.* 2d ed. Boston: Allyn and Bacon.

Boucher, R. L. (1998). Toward achieving a focal point for sport management: A binocular perspective. *Journal of Sport Management, 12* (1), 76–87.

Chelladurai, P. (1999). *Human resource management in sport and recreation.* Champaign, IL: Human Kinetics.

Chelladurai, P. (1992). Sport management: Opportunities and obstacles. *Journal of Sport Management. 6* (3), 215–19.

Daft, R. L. (1995). *Organization theory and design.* 5th ed. New York: West.

Daft, R. C. and Steers, R. M. (1986). *Organizations: A micro/macro approach.* Glenview, IL: Scott, Foresman.

DeSensi, J. (1994). Multiculturalism as an issue in sport management. *Journal of Sport Management. 8* (1) 63–74.

Fletcher, A. D., and Bowers, T. A. (1991). *Fundamentals of advertising research.* 4th ed. Belmont, CA: Wadsworth.

Guba, E. G., and Lincoln, Y. (1981). *Effective evaluation.* San Francisco: Jossey-Bass.

Hamner, W. C., and Organ, D. (1978). *Organizational behavior: An applied psychological approach.* Dallas: BPI.

Hardy, S. (1986). Entrepreneurs, organizations, and the sport marketplace: Subjects in search of historians. *Journal of Sport History, 13* (1), 14–33.

Hardy, S. H., and Berryman, J. W. (1983). A historical view of the governance issue. In J. Frey (ed.), *The governance of intercollegiate athletics* (pp. 15–28). New York: Leisure Press.

Harris, H. A. (1967). *Greek athletes and athletics.* Bloomington, IN: Indiana University Press.

Helgesen, S. (1990). *The female advantage: Women's ways of leadership.* New York: Doubleday.

Hubbuch, S. M. (1996). *Writing research papers across the curriculum.* 4th ed. New York: Harcourt Brace.

Hums, M. A., and Chelladurai, P. (1994). Distributive justice in intercollegiate athletics: Development of an instrument. *Journal of Sport Management, 8* (3), 190–99.

Inglis, S. (1992). Focus groups as a useful qualitative methodology in sport management. *Journal of Sport Management, 6* (3), 173–78.

Inglis, S., Danylchuk, K. E., and Pastore, D. (1996). Understanding retention factors in coaching and athletic management positions. *Journal of Sport Management, 10,* 237–49.

Johns, G. (1992). *Organizational behavior: Understanding life at work* (3d ed.) New York: HarperCollins.

Kaplan, A. (1964). *The conduct of inquiry.* San Francisco: Chandler.

Kyle, D. G. (1987). *Athletics in ancient Athens.* Leiden: E. J. Brill.

Lambrecht, K. (1991). Research, theory and practice. In B. Parkhouse (ed.), *The management of sport: Its foundation and application* (pp. 28–29). St. Louis: Mosby.

Lather, P. (1986). Issues of validity in openly ideological research: Between a rock and a soft place. *Interchange, 17* (4), 63–84.

Mintzberg, H. (1975). The manager's job: Folklore and fact. *Harvard Business Review, 53* (4), 49–61.

Morgan, D. L. (1988). *Focus groups as qualitative research.* Newbury Park, CA: Sage Publications.

Morse, J. M. (ed.). (1994). *Critical issues in qualitative research methods.* Thousand Oaks, CA: Sage Publications.

Mueller, D. J. (1986). *Measuring social attitudes: A handbook for researchers and practitioners.* New York: Columbia University Teachers' College Press.

Neuman, W. L. (1997). *Social research methods: Qualitative and quantitative approaches.* 3d ed. Boston: Allyn and Bacon.

Nunnally, J. C. (1970). *Introduction to psychological measurement.* New York: McGraw-Hill.

Nunnally, J. C. (1978). *Psychometric theory.* 2d ed. New York: McGraw-Hill.

Olafson, G. (1990). Research design in sport management: What's missing, what's needed? *Journal of Sport Management, 4* (2), 102–20.

Olafson, G. A. (1995). Sport management research: Ordered change. *Journal of Sport Management, 9* (3), 338–45.

Paton, G. (1987). Sport management research—what progress has been made? *Journal of Sport Management, 1* (1), 25–31.

Parkhouse, B. (1987). Sport management curricula: Current status and design implications for future development. *Journal of Sport Management, 1* (2), 93–115.

Parks, J. B. (1992). The other "bottom line" in sport management. *Journal of Sport Management, 6* (3), 220–29.

Reason, P., and Rowan, J. (1981). Issues of validity in new paradigm research. In P. Reason and J. Rowan (eds.), *Human inquiry: A sourcebook of new paradigm research* (pp. 239–62). New York: Wiley.

Slack, T. (1993). Morgan and the metaphors: Implications for sport management research. *Journal of Sport Management, 7* (3), 189–93.

Slack, T. (1996). From the locker room to the board room: Changing the domain of sport. *Journal of Sport Management, 10* (1), 97–105.

Slack, T. (1997). *Understanding sport organizations: The application of organization theory.* Champaign, IL: Human Kinetics.

Soucie, D. (1994). Management theory and practice. In E. F. Zeigler (ed.), *Physical education and kinesiology in North America professional and scholarly foundations* (279–313). Champaign, IL: Stipes.

Steers, R. M., Porter, L. W., and Bigley, B. A. (1996). *Motivation and leadership at work.* 6th ed. New York: McGraw-Hill.

Thibault, L., Slack, T., and Hinings, B. (1993). A framework for the analysis of strategy in nonprofit sport organizations. *Journal of Sport Management, 7* (1), 25–43.

Thibault, L., Slack, T., and Hinings, B. (1994). Strategic planning for nonprofit sport organizations: Empirical verification of a framework. *Journal of Sport Management, 8* (3), 218-33.

Vail, S. (1992). Toward improving sport delivery: A community perspective. *Journal of Applied Recreation Research, 17* (3), 217–33.

RELATED JOURNALS

Administrative Science Quarterly
Cyber-Journal of Sport Marketing
European Journal for Sport Management
Festival Management and Event Tourism
The Academy of Management Review
International Journal of Sport Management
International Studies of Management and Organization
Journal of Business Communications
Journal of Business Research
Journal of Business Strategy
Journal of Consumer Research
Journal of Legal Aspects of Sport
Journal of Management Studies
Journal of Marketing
Journal of Marketing Research
Journal of Organizational Behavior
Journal of Sport Management
Journal of Sports Marketing Sponsorship
Managing Leisure
Organizational Behavior and Human Decision Processes
Organizational Studies
Quest
Sport Management Review
Sport Marketing Quarterly

WEBSITES

Arnova

www.arnova.org

"The Association for Research on Nonprofit Organizations and Voluntary Action (ARNOVA) is an international, interdisciplinary network of scholars and nonprofit leaders committed to strengthening the research community in the emerging field of nonprofit and philanthropic studies."

Associated with ARNOVA is an electronic forum (can be accessed through the website) to facilitate the sharing of concerns, interests, and solutions among scholars and practitioners.

Nassm

www.nassm.org

This is the official website for the North American Society for Sport Management (NASSM).

The website includes information concerning the membership, history and publications of NASSM, the scope of sport management, conferences, universities offering sport management programs, program review, and NASSM initiatives.

PART II

Human Resource Management

CHAPTER 5

Organizational Theory and the Study of Sport

John Amis and Danny O'Brien

In this chapter, you will become familiar with the following terms:

Organizational effectiveness	Resource-based approach	Organizational size
Organizational structure	Competitive advantage	Power
Complexity	Distinctive competence	Political activity
Formalization	General environment	Decision-making
Centralization	Task environment	Bounded rationality
Configurations	Domain	Organizational change
Strategy	Technology	
Diversification	Interdependence	
Integration	Differentiation	

Overview

The global sport industry is made up of a wide variety of organizations. There are those such as Reebok and the Atlanta Falcons, whose main purpose is to make a profit for their owners and shareholders. There are others, such as Surfrider Foundation and Basketball Canada, that are referred to as not-for-profit or voluntary organizations, whose purpose is to provide a service to their members. Any money generated is used to further the goals of the organization. There are also quasi-nongovernment organizations, such as Sport England or Sport Canada, that are federally funded and play leadership, advisory, and distributive roles within the sport field.

In some cases a sport organization may be a part of a larger body, such as a state or municipal

government. Its actions are, in part, established and controlled by the larger agency. Other organizations, such as the International Olympic Committee (IOC) and the National Collegiate Athletic Association (NCAA), operate in a highly autonomous manner. Sport organizations such as Nike, the athletic footwear, equipment, and clothing company, or Brunswick, which is involved in operating bowling alleys and power boat manufacturing, employ thousands of people and operate with detailed policies and procedures. By contrast, a local sporting goods store or municipal swimming pool has few employees and operates rather informally. Some organizations in the sport industry use advanced microelectronic technology such as computer-assisted manufacturing (CAM) or advanced information technology (AIT). Huffy, for example, uses CAM in the manufacture of its bicycles. On the other hand, in organizations that build custom-designed sports equipment, such as handmade skates or specialized skis, workers use the skills they have acquired over years.

Organization theory is a discipline that helps us to understand why sport organizations such as those just mentioned are structured and operated in different ways. It helps us to understand why large sport organizations have different structures than small ones; why sport manufacturing organizations operate in a different way from those in the service sector; and why voluntary sport organizations may pursue different strategies from those that are designed to make a profit. Organization theory also helps us understand how processes such as change and decision making can be managed. In short, organization theory can make us better managers by providing an understanding of the way sport organizations are structured and operated.

In this chapter we explore some of the central issues in organization theory. We begin by looking at what many sport managers consider the most important issue to address—effectiveness. We look at what constitutes an effective organization and discuss the different models that have been used to explain **organizational effectiveness.** One of the key factors that influences the effectiveness of a sport organization is whether it has an appropriate structure and design. In the next two sections of the chapter we discuss these issues. We examine major concepts used to explain **organizational structure** and look at how these concepts can be used to understand the different designs we see in sport industry organizations.

One main premise of organization theory is that the structure of an organization is influenced by the context in which it operates. To be effective there must be a fit between the structure of a sport organization and the pressures placed on it by contextual factors such as *strategy, environment, technology, and size.* Consequently, the impact that each of these factors, or contingencies as they are sometimes called, can have on a sport organization's structure are examined. We then move on to examine the impact of *power and politics* before finally looking at two of the more common organizational processes, decision-making and change.

EFFECTIVENESS IN SPORT ORGANIZATIONS

All organizations exist to achieve a goal or set of goals. It may be pursuing a national championship, making a profit, or developing young athletes. The ultimate goal of most professional sport organizations is to win the major championship in their sport. Yet each season, only one team can achieve this goal. Does this mean that all the other clubs are ineffective? The Kansas State University Wildcats football program did not play for the national championship in 1998, yet season ticket and television revenues increased 249 percent from 1990 to 1998 (Meninger, 1999). Was the franchise effective? Effectiveness, quite clearly, is a difficult concept to define and measure. As a result, researchers have come up with various approaches in an attempt to explain this aspect of organizations. Four of these, the goal attainment, systems resource, internal process, and strategic constituents approaches, are now briefly outlined.

Goal attainment approach

The goal attainment approach is based on the identification of primary goals and how well an organization attains or makes progress toward them (Etzioni, 1964). An organization that achieves its goals is seen as being more effective than one that does not. It is this approach that has been used most extensively in evaluating the effectiveness of sport organizations (see Frisby, 1986; Chelladurai, 1987). For this approach to be workable there must be a consensus among members of the organization on the goals that are to be pursued. In addition, there must be a small enough number of goals to be manageable.

Despite its simplicity as an easy-to-implement measure of organizational effectiveness, the goal attainment approach is, in a number of ways, problematic. First, in any sport organization, there are often multiple and conflicting goals being pursued. For example, the decision by the Florida Marlins to "sell off" many of their highly rated players at the end of the 1997 World Series–winning season was motivated by the goal of improving financial performance rather than of giving the club the best possible chance of retaining its title. A second problem concerns the vagueness of some of a sport organization's goals. For example, objectives related to job satisfaction or player development are difficult to quantify and difficult to use in the goal attainment approach. Finally, there is a problem of which goals take precedence within a sport organization, and whether the sport organization should focus on long- or short-term priorities.

Systems resource approach

Rather than focusing on organizational outputs, as the goal attainment approach does, the systems resource approach to organizational effectiveness focuses on the inputs of an organization, specifically its ability to attract scarce or valued resources (Yuchtman and Seashore, 1967). These resources may include members, the fans attending a game, or the income generated from sales of licensed merchandise. Although securing resources is vital to the survival of a sport organization, and survival is *the* overriding measure of effectiveness, there are several problems with the systems resource approach.

First, care must be taken when using this approach with public sector sport organizations. Because much of the funding distributed to these organizations is often guaranteed, or at least subject to only minor yearly fluctuations, the securing of these types of resources is not an appropriate measure of effectiveness. Second, an organization can be effective even when it does not obtain the most desirable resources. Cameron (1980) cites the example of the Seattle Supersonics who, despite being unable to attract any superstars to the team, and with a rookie coach, reached the National Basketball Association (NBA) finals in 1978 and won the 1979 championship. Finally, there is a difficulty in determining the differences between inputs and outputs. For example, a sport club may increase the size of its membership in a particular year, an increase in inputs. However, it might be that one of the club's goals was to increase its membership. In this case, the number of members is an output. The systems resource approach is most applicable to understanding sport organizations in situations where outputs cannot be objectively measured, where there is a clear connection between the resources obtained and the final product, and when the supply of resources is not formally guaranteed by another organization.

Internal process approach

As opposed to outputs (goal attainment), or inputs (systems resource), the internal process approach focuses on throughputs, the internal activities by which inputs are converted into outputs. Here, indicators of effectiveness can include things such as a supervisor's concern for her or his workers, feelings of group loyalty, good communications, and the personal development of subordinates (Daft, 1992). Some writers propose that the internal process approach should focus on fiscal efficiency (Evans, 1976). Here, measures such as inventory turnover and changes in sales volume are used as criteria for assessing effectiveness.

Although the internal process approach is useful in comparing organizations with different outputs, it does have its shortcomings. First, it is often difficult to quantifiably measure criteria such as group loyalty or good communications, which, from this perspective, are indicators of effective performance. Second, this approach takes no account of the notion of equifinality, the means by which two organizations with different internal processes could be equally effective in reaching the same end point. Third, the approach is deficient in that a sport organization can have poor communication and low morale and yet still be considered successful.

Strategic constituents approach

The strategic constituents model (Connolly et al., 1980) is a more current means of understanding organizational effectiveness. It provides an integrative approach that takes into account the political nature of organizations. It also acknowledges the fact that organizations consist of a number of constituents, which often have differing goals and priorities. For example, in a professional sport organization, owners often have different goals than players. Although both want to win games, owners want to make a profit, while players want larger salaries. As a result, the organization's general manager has to work toward a compromise to ensure the future effectiveness of the organization. A major strength of the strategic constituencies approach is that it acknowledges that effectiveness is a complex and multidimensional concept that is affected by pressures internal and external to the organization. As a result, it takes into account the political nature of organizations and the fact that managers have to consider all groups that have an interest in the organization.

The fundamental problem with this approach is the difficulty associated with identifying the relative importance of the different constituents.

Individuals and groups within the organization will view various constituents differently. Also, the relative importance of these groups may change over time. Still, by offering a more holistic approach than the previously discussed models, and considering an organization as a political system, the strategic constituents approach provides one of the better ways of determining effectiveness.

THE STRUCTURE OF SPORT ORGANIZATIONS

To be effective, a sport organization must be structured to respond to the contextual situation in which it operates. Consequently, an understanding of the different elements of structure is one of the basic tenets of organization theory. The structure of an organization is also important because, as Miller (1987) has pointed out, it influences the flow of information and affects collaboration, modes of coordination, allocations of power and responsibility, and levels of formality and *complexity*. Although organizational theorists have identified many different dimensions of organizational structure (cf. Miller and Droge, 1986; Pugh et al., 1969) the three most commonly found in the literature are *complexity, formalization*, and *centralization*. These three variables have also been shown to be theoretically and empirically applicable to the study of sport organizations (Frisby, 1986; Kikulis, Slack, and Hinings, 1992, 1995; Slack and Hinings, 1987, 1992). Each of these dimensions is briefly discussed in the following paragraphs.

Complexity

Complexity refers to the extent to which an organization is differentiated, that is, the way in which the organization is divided into different divisions, departments, groups, or individual roles, each with its own tasks and responsibilities. This differentiation may occur either horizontally, vertically, or spatially.

Horizontal differentiation occurs as a result of the different parts of the organization becoming specialized in different activities. This specialization is carried out in an attempt to increase organization efficiency and can occur in two ways. First, the total work to be performed in the organization may be divided into separate, discrete, and narrow tasks. Second, the employment of specialists to perform a range of organizational activities can result in

diversely trained individuals bringing different approaches, goals, and terminology to the organization. This can present communication and coordination problems, which can, in turn, increase complexity. For example, in putting together its made-for-television documentaries on each of the twelve Association of Surfing Professionals (ASP) World Championship Tour (WCT) events each year, the broadcast production company Online Sports must coordinate interactions between professional surfers, television producers, event managers, marketing managers, sponsors, and various lawyers. Despite Online Sports employing specialists to deal with these different groups, each will have different objectives, jargon, and time frames, thus increasing the complexity of the organization.

Vertical differentiation refers to the number of hierarchical levels in a sport organization. The more levels there are, the greater become the problems of communication, coordination, and supervision, hence the more complex becomes the organization. Vertical differentiation is often directly proportional to the size of the organization (Blau and Schoenherr, 1971) and also to the degree of horizontal differentiation. When a job is highly specialized, it is difficult for the worker to relate his or her work to that of others, so control of the work is often passed to the manager. This has the effect of increasing the number of vertical levels in the organization. The number of workers that a manager can viably supervise is referred to as the *span-of-control*.

Spatial differentiation refers to the degree of geographical separation of the various divisions of the same organization. Thus, an organization based entirely on one site, such as a single-outlet sports shop, has a very low degree of spatial differentiation. On the other hand, a large organization such as the National Football League (NFL) can be considered highly spatially differentiated because its franchises are distributed throughout the United States. In addition, the NFL has part ownership of the European-based World League of American Football. This makes the NFL's operation much more difficult to coordinate and much more complex than the sports shop.

The more horizontally, vertically, and spatially differentiated an organization is, the more complex it becomes. Increased complexity results in an organization in which coordination and communication are more difficult and management more demanding.

Formalization

One of the ways of managing complexity is through the use of **formalization.** Formalization refers to the extent to which rules, regulations, job descriptions, policies, and procedures govern the operation of an organization. In a highly formalized organization, such as one that uses production-line techniques to manufacture sports equipment, employees will have little discretion over how and when they carry out their tasks. The head coach of a Women's National Basketball Association (WNBA) team will, by contrast, find her or his job far less formalized, with the freedom to set day-to-day activities (provided the team is winning!).

Formalization may vary not just among organizations, but also among departments and hierarchical levels within the same organization. For example, adidas's research and development department will operate under much less formalized conditions than will its manufacturing plants. This is a direct result of the research and development department employing highly trained professionals who require a far greater degree of flexibility in their *modus operandi* than do the less-skilled production line workers. Likewise, because of their need to operate quickly and in the best interests of the entire organization, senior managers are usually subject to less formalization than are lower-level managers.

Formalization allows strict worker control without the necessity for expensive close supervision. It also permits the standardization of outputs, allowing items such as athletic shoes to be designed on one continent, manufactured on another, and sold on a third.

Centralization

Centralization refers to the hierarchical level of the organization at which decisions are made. In centralized organizations, decisions tend to be made by upper levels of management; in more decentralized organizations, similar decisions would be delegated to a lower hierarchical level. As an organization grows, it quickly reaches a point whereby it becomes impossible for a single person to make all decisions necessary for day-to-day operation. In addition to not possessing sufficient expertise in all areas of the operation (e.g., research, manufacturing, marketing, and finance), if one person were to try to take responsibility for all decisions, it would take an intolerably long time to make even minor

decisions. Consequently, decisions that are regarded as less crucial are delegated to lower levels, allowing senior management to concentrate on strategic decisions affecting the entire organization. In a large university athletic department, for example, there will normally be different individuals or even departments concerned with marketing, publicity, media information, and scheduling. The athletic director (AD), while overseeing all departments, will not be involved with minor details, such as ensuring that every local newspaper has the statistics on the men's basketball team, or that the women's soccer team has a balance of home and away fixtures. The AD will more likely be concerned with securing corporate sponsorship agreements, arranging with television companies to broadcast certain home games, and changes to conference regulations. By delegating authority, the AD can maintain control of the athletic department while ensuring that it functions effectively.

Organizations that are highly decentralized are often highly formalized. This allows decisions to be made quickly while maintaining top management control of the organization. This, in fact, brings into question exactly how decentralized such organizations are, because even though decisions are made at lower levels, the range of choice in decision making is controlled at an upper level.

THE DESIGN OF SPORT ORGANIZATIONS

It is something of a truism to say that all sport organizations are different. It has been claimed that there are as many different classes of organizations as there are people who wish to classify them (Carper and Snizek, 1980). Organizations do, however, exhibit various common characteristics. For example, sport organizations may be complex or simple, they may be highly formalized or flexible, they may have centralized or decentralized decision-making mechanisms. When organizations are objectively regarded along such dimensions, it becomes possible to classify various combinations of these characteristics to produce design types or **configurations.** A design type is, quite simply, a particular patterning of structural variables. Various researchers have used different characteristics to classify organizations. In one of the more popular classifications, Mintzberg (1979) used design parameters such as complexity, formalization, training of members, and centralization, along with contingency factors such as age, size, and environment, to produce five design types. He termed these the simple structure, the machine bureaucracy, the professional bureaucracy, the divisionalized form, and the adhocracy.

No matter which configuration an organization fits into, it is made up, Mintzberg argues, of five different parts. The operating core consists of those individuals responsible for the basic work required to produce the final product. In the International Lifesaving Federation (ILF) for example, the world governing body for surf lifesaving competition, the operating core consists of the surf lifesaving clubs and their athletes who compete in the surf lifesaving events, both professional and amateur. The strategic apex would be the president of the ILF, Derek Whitting, and the organization's board of directors. The middle line comprises those organizational parts that link the operating core to the strategic apex. In the ILF, this would consist of the surf lifesaving national governing bodies, which link the regional and state associations, located in countries throughout the world, to the world governing body situated in Leuven, Belgium. The technostructure includes the specialists responsible for designing the procedures, competitions, and equipment that must be standardized in all participant countries. In the ILF, this includes past and present competitors, medical and first aid professionals, textiles specialists, and also specialists in areas such as event coordination and management. Finally, the support staff consists of the people who provide some kind of support to the rest of the organization. In the ILF, these include secretarial staff, maintenance engineers, and canteen operators.

In addition to the five configurations and the five different parts of the organization, Mintzberg proposed five ways in which coordination can be achieved in an organization. Direct supervision is the most basic type and consists of one individual giving instruction to others. An executive director, who manages a small national sport organization's head office, will generally operate in this manner, directly supervising all others in the office, such as the technical director, the marketing director, the secretary, and the receptionist.

Standardization of work occurs when the way work is to be carried out is determined by someone other than the person doing the actual work. At Nike's athletic shoe division, the standardization of work is the role of the design specialists and production engineers; the actual work of making the shoe is done by unskilled production workers. The standardization of outputs occurs when it is the results of the work that are specified, not the way in which these results are to be achieved. For example, the owner of a professional football franchise may instruct the marketing manager to increase average attendance for each of the first five home games by ten percent of the previous season's average. However, he or she will leave exactly how this is carried out to the marketing manager.

The fourth way in which coordination can be achieved is through the standardization of skills. Sport medicine personnel and sport lawyers operate with skills that have been standardized through training programs. These skills are further regulated by the professional organizations to which these people must belong. Finally, coordination can be achieved through mutual adjustment, whereby processes and procedures are modified through informal communication among parties. An example of this would be a group of people who come together for a limited period and work together to stage a basketball tournament or other similar sporting event.

In each of the configurations described by Mintzberg, one part of the organization and one method of coordination predominates. A small, entrepreneurial business, such as an owner-operated sports store, will be dominated by the owner of the organization, the strategic apex. Because the operation has few employees, coordination is carried out by direct supervision. The result of this is what Mintzberg refers to as a simple structure.

A sport organization that mass-produces a standard output, such as a baseball bat, will have the technostructure as its dominant part. The stable nature of the production process, whereby thousands of bats are built to the same specification, is established by designers and engineers. This results in the standardization of work processes being the primary means of coordination. The operation will be highly formalized, with each stage precisely detailed to ensure the constant nature of the end product. The appropriate configuration is therefore the machine bureaucracy.

The rise of professionalism in many industries, sport included, has led to the creation of a configuration known as the professional bureaucracy.

A professional bureaucracy combines the standardization of the machine bureaucracy with the decentralization that stems from the professional's need for autonomy. Therefore, although an end product might be narrowly defined, the professional operator has the freedom, within certain guidelines (such as a medical code of ethics), to decide exactly how this end point is reached. In this design type, it is the workers of the operating core that take precedence, with coordination achieved by the standardization of skills. A good example of a professional bureaucracy is a sport medicine clinic.

The fourth of Mintzberg's configurations, the divisionalized form, arises when an organization becomes large and diversifies into other industries, some of which may be outside the area of sport. Brunswick is a good example of a divisionalized form, with involvement in power boats, bowling alleys, and defense products. The creation of divisions, which operate with relative autonomy, makes midline managers as key players in this type of configuration. These are the people who provide the link between the various divisions and the head offices.

When environmental uncertainty is high and flexibility is a valued organizational characteristic, the appropriate design type may be an adhocracy. In this configuration, collaboration among various support staff and operators is favored. Cross-functional groups are created with tasks coordinated by mutual adjustment. The selective *decentralization* that results creates a highly responsive design type. An example might be an investigative reporting team from a television company assigned to a major sporting event such as the 1999 Rugby World Cup finals in Wales. Consisting of a reporter, a cameraperson, and a producer, this team is put on location to report interesting stories as they happen. The team must operate independently as a semiautonomous group and make quick decisions regarding what to cover.

It is important to note that the configurations described here are ideal types. It is highly unlikely that organizations that exhibit pure forms of these design types could be found. Indeed, the examples just cited, although predominantly exhibiting characteristics of the design type that they are used to illustrate, all exhibit characteristics of other designs. What these configurations allow, however, is a comparison and contrast of sport organizations along a number of dimensions. In addition to providing information about what type of sport organization design works best in different situations, these design types also provide a frame of reference for examining other organizational phenomena. For example, do adhocracies and divisionalized forms formulate strategies in different ways? What about the way in which decision making is carried out? It is this type of insight that increases our theoretical understanding of sport organizations and improves the practical performance of sport managers.

CONCEPT CHECK

There are three primary concepts used to examine the structure of an organization: complexity, formalization, and centralization. Organizational design refers to the patterning of structural dimensions.

STRATEGY AND SPORT ORGANIZATIONS

All sport organizations are subject to constant changes in their contextual situations. New competitors enter the marketplace, government legislation that affects business practices changes, and employment equity programs are stressed. To successfully respond to these and other types of change, sport managers need to formulate a **strategy** for their organizations. This strategy will require changes in the structure of a sport organization. To be effective, there must be a fit between an organization's strategy and its structure. Strategy is essentially like a coach's game plan. It is designed to help a sport organization achieve its objectives by addressing such issues as what products and/or market segments to compete in; how to best allocate resources; and whether to diversify, expand, or even shut down certain aspects of the organization.

There are four basic types of strategy that a sport organization can follow: a growth strategy, a defensive strategy, a stability strategy, or a combination strategy. Growth strategies are pursued through either **diversification** or **integration.** Diversification occurs when a sport organization moves into new products or markets. These may be related or unrelated to the organization's existing business. Reebok's decision in 1986 to buy Rockport, a casual and dress shoe manufacturer, is an example of related diversification. Integration can occur either horizontally or vertically. Horizontal integration involves a sport organization buying another organization, usually a competitor in the same business. Vertical integration occurs when a supplier (backward integration) or a distributor (forward integration) is acquired. In the early 1990s, for example, Nike bought out a number of its distribution operations.

Defensive strategies, used if there is a decreased demand for a sport organization's products or services, may take one of three forms. A turnaround strategy is used to counter decreasing revenues or rising costs. It may involve cost-cutting measures, layoffs, or a change in the markets in which the company operates. Divestiture involves selling the business or part of a business. Liquidation occurs when a company or part of a company is shut down and sold to obtain capital.

Stability strategies occur when a sport organization maintains its current level of activity with no intent to grow. The organization strives to maintain its market share and/or provide the same level of service as in the past. A combination strategy simply involves a sport organization using the strategies previously outlined in some combination. The type of strategy a sport organization chooses will influence its structure. Sport organizations, which seek growth in new markets, will require a flexible structure such as a professional bureaucracy or an adhocracy. A sport organization that adopts a more defensive strategy will most likely exhibit a more bureaucratic type of structure.

Recently, there has been an emphasis on viewing organizations as bundles of resources that can be used to provide a position of sustainable competitive advantage. Adopting this **resource-based approach,** Amis et al. (1997) showed how sponsorship agreements need to be considered as strategic investments, and as such, should be tested against certain preconditions. First, the value of different sponsorships should be distributed unevenly, or heterogeneously, across the industry. This is of overriding importance: if all firms have access to equivalent resources, in this case sponsorship agreements, then no advantage can accrue to any individual organization. Second, any sponsorship that is capable of providing a competitive advantage must be imperfectly imitable. That is, there should be no ready substitute available that a rival

firm can use to nullify the advantage. Third, the resource, once secured, should be imperfectly mobile: it should not be possible for a competitor to simply acquire the sponsorship once it is seen as valuable. This is achieved in the first instance by the use of contracts, but over time, an image builds up that ties the sponsor and the sport together, thus reducing the effectiveness of the sponsorship elsewhere. Finally, there must be ex ante limits to competition—there must be some risk in entering into any sponsorship agreement. If such an investment was risk free, in other words if its true value was clearly apparent in advance to all firms, there would be no opportunity for accruing any **competitive advantage.** Amis, Slack, and Berrett (1999) developed this framework further, suggesting that the best sponsorship deals are those that can be strategically refined into an area of **distinctive competence.** They argued that the best sponsorship agreements clearly differentiate a firm from its rivals, add perceived customer value to a product or service, and are capable of being used across the firm in a variety of ways (for example, in advertisements, entertaining clients, developing corporate culture, and in point-of-purchase marketing).

ENVIRONMENT OF SPORT ORGANIZATIONS

Another factor that influences the structure and operation of a sport organization is the environment in which it operates. Although we can think of the environment as including everything external to the organization, this is of little practical or theoretical use. A more relevant approach is to think of the environment as consisting of two parts, the general (or distal) and the task (proximal).

The **general environment** consists of various influences that although not directly affecting the organization, affect the industry as a whole. These influences can be divided into a number of different sectors (Daft, 1992). Some of the more common are briefly explained here.

The economic environment includes elements that will indirectly affect the sport organization, including the general economic climate, the system of banking being used in the country in which the organization exists, and patterns of consumer consumption. For example, in times of economic recession, most people have less money to spend on leisure activities, such as attending sporting events. This may force professional sport franchises to reduce the price of admission, which may adversely affect profit margins. Sociocultural factors include the class structure of the social system within which the sport organization operates, the culture in which it exists, trends in consumer taste, and the sporting tradition of the locale. For example, the demise of the North American Soccer League in the 1980s was in large part brought about by sociocultural factors, specifically the failure of North American fans to take to the sport. With the recent rise of Major League Soccer, and the successes of the men's and more notably the women's national teams, there are signs that this trend is changing and that professional soccer may be starting to build on its popularity as the most widely played sport in North America.

Legal regulations regarding such things as taxation, unionization, and gender equity can all have a dramatic effect on sport organizations. After a succession of fatalities at English professional soccer matches, notably the 1989 disaster at Hillsborough in Sheffield, England, where ninety-six people died, tough regulations were introduced regarding obligatory ground safety standards. Because they could not meet these legislated standards, several clubs have in recent years had their applications to join the professional Football League denied. Ecological issues regarding physical surroundings can play an important role in a sport organization's success. For example, many ski resorts in Europe were diastrously affected by the brutal avalanches in the devastating winter of 1998–99. Technological advancements must be constantly monitored because they may change the nature of the industry in which the sport organization operates. The use of carbon fiber composites in the manufacture of tennis rackets immediately rendered wooden rackets obsolete and hence revolutionized the industry.

The **task environment** is made up of those aspects that directly impinge on the operating procedures of an organization. It is these influences that are characteristically given the most attention by sport organization managers because it is these over which they can exert the most direct leverage. Typically included would be groups such as suppliers, customers, competitors, members, shareholders, and regulatory agencies. Each sport organization's task environment is unique, with its constituent influences changing over time.

The **domain** of a sport organization denotes the territory in which it chooses to operate and will consequently delineate the organization's task environment. Different sport organizations, ostensibly within the same area, may have different domains and therefore different task environments. Ping (expensive) and Northwestern (inexpensive), both makers of golf clubs, have identified different domains, based on price, in which to operate. As a result, they have come into contact with different suppliers, customers, and competitors.

Environmental uncertainty

The degree of uncertainty a sport organization faces determines the extent to which its environment may be deemed dynamic or stable. An organization facing a regular set of demands from an unchanging environment—for example, a tennis ball manufacturer such as Wilson—may face stable conditions (Litterer, 1973). By contrast, dynamic environments are characterized by rapid change and much uncertainty. These conditions may be caused by an increased number of competitors, a declining market, legal changes, or the availability of substitute products. Athletic footwear companies, because of the constant battle among competitors to introduce new features and styles, operate in a highly dynamic environment.

All sport organizations try to limit the uncertainties they face. They can try to do this either by altering their internal structure, processes and behaviors; by modifying their external environmental characteristics through such things as long-term contractual arrangements with suppliers and customers; or by creating a joint venture with another organization to meet objectives that neither organization could attain on its own.

Relationship between environment and organizational structure

Environmental uncertainty directly affects organization structure, specifically the aspects of complexity, formalization, and centralization. A sport organization faced with an uncertain environment will have to increase the number of departments and specialized personnel required to buffer the organization from environmental disruption. This is most often achieved by assigning staff to boundary-spanning roles to secure and evaluate relevant environmental information (Child, 1984). For example, the managers of a fitness center may see a societal interest in the relationship between diet and fitness. They may hire a dietitian to counsel clients on eating habits and to keep other members of staff who are involved in prescribing fitness programs abreast of subsequent nutritional developments related to fitness. As a result of such a change, the complexity of the organization is increased.

Increased levels of complexity require an appropriate means of integrating different individuals and departments. In uncertain environments, flexible rather than highly formalized hierarchical methods of coordination are most effective, resulting in a decrease in formalization. This type of arrangement can be seen in a sport law practice. Because of the need to adapt to the requirements of different cases, experts in various aspects of law may be required to work on a particular project. Consequently, the flexibility to move from one case to the next is important. In contrast, in stable environments, sport organizations can capitalize on the economies that result from the use of formalized procedures. Many government agencies involved with the provision of sport services operate in this way. Because of the need to treat all clients equally and the relatively unchanging nature of the services provided, a relatively unchanging organizational design is most appropriate.

The more complex an organization's environment, the greater the amount of information that must be assimilated to make accurate decisions (Mintzberg, 1979). If the complex environment is perceived as hostile, however, there may be a move to, at least temporarily, centralize the decision-making structure. This ensures that everyone is aware of who is in control and allows important decisions to be made quickly. For example, in September 1984, when Nike found itself having problems because of Reebok's success in aerobics, Phillip Knight returned to the presidency of the company, a position he had relinquished only a year earlier (Dodds, 1985).

SPORT ORGANIZATIONS AND TECHNOLOGY

Technology has fundamentally altered the way in which virtually all sport organizations operate. From the use of *computer-aided design* (CAD) by large manufacturing companies, to the installation of a personal computer and facsimile machine at a local sports club, technology has significantly affected the structure and processes of sport organizations. Although there has been considerable variation in the way researchers have defined technology, it is generally accepted as constituting the materials, knowledge, and equipment, and processes required to produce a desired good or service (Perrow, 1967). Although different studies have focused on various facets of technology, in this chapter we concentrate on organizational-level technology and the seminal works of Joan Woodward, Charles Perrow, and J. D. Thompson. We look at the use of microelectronic technologies in sport organizations, and finally we examine the relationship between technology and organization structure.

Research on technology and organizations

During the 1950s, Joan Woodward studied 100 manufacturing organizations operating in the south of England. She grouped the organizations in her study into three major categories: unit, or small-batch production; mass, or large-batch production; and continuous process production. Organizations involved in unit production were seen as exhibiting the least amount of technological complexity. They were less structured than those in other categories, tended to have a smaller number of hierarchical levels, exhibited lower levels of formalization, and employed a more decentralized decision-making structure. An example of such a sport organization would be a custom bike manufacturer who produces a different bike for each customer. Mass production organizations manufacture large quantities of the same product, often using assembly lines. The process is repetitive and routine, with few skilled workers and a high level of formalization. Organizations such as Reebok use this type of mass production to manufacture their athletic footwear. Organizations that use continuous process production are highly mechanized so that the production process does not stop. This type of production is associated more with businesses such as oil refineries than sport organizations.

The work of Charles Perrow is more generalizable than that of Woodward, being applicable to both manufacturing and service organizations. During the 1960s, Perrow identified four main technologies, each associated with a different type of organization structure. *Routine technology* is found in bureaucratic types of organizations with control of generally unskilled workers achieved through high levels of formalization and centralized decision making. *Craft technology* requires a more flexible structure and is hence characterized by less formalization and centralization, with coordination achieved through mutual adjustment and the past experience of staff. *Engineering technologies* are analogous to Mintzberg's professional bureaucracies, with the professional staff accorded a certain amount of decision-making autonomy to go along with the moderate levels of formalization and centralization. *Nonroutine technology* requires a very flexible structure with low levels of formalization, professionally trained operatives, and decision making by means of mutual adjustment. Often more than one type of technology will exist in an organization. For example, Reebok will employ routine technology to manufacture its running shoes, but nonroutine technology to design and develop them.

J. D. Thompson's (1967) approach to technology focuses on **interdependence** among different organization subunits. Different degrees of interdependence require different types of technology. *Pooled interdependence* requires a mediating technology to link together independently operating organizations. For example, each branch of "Club Fit," a Canadian chain of fitness centers, operates independently, yet each contributes to the overall profit or loss of the organization. As such, the different branches exhibit a pooled interdependence. Complexity is low, with coordination achieved through a highly formalized mechanism detailing appropriate policies and procedures for each branch. *Sequential interdependence* is found in a sport organization when the output of subunit A forms the input of subunit B. This is most often found in assembly line production, such as in the manufacture of tennis balls, where a standard product is produced repetitively at a standard rate. This type of interdependence requires higher levels of coordination than pooled interdependence because of the need to coordinate the various units involved in the production process. Levels of complexity and formalization are therefore high, with decision making centralized.

Reciprocal interdependence is the highest form of interdependence and is associated with what Thompson called "intensive technology." The various units involved in this type of interdependent

relationship all depend on each other for their inputs. For example, in a voluntary sport organization, volunteer workers, professional staff, administrators, coaches, sponsors, and athletes all need to interact to put on a successful sporting event. Complexity is very high, formalization low, and decision making decentralized. Coordination in such situations is achieved through frequent communication. The people involved are usually highly skilled and hence able to call on their experience and training to make situations workable.

It is also important for managers to appreciate that when clearly differentiated subunits are interdependent, there is a propensity for conflict to develop. In fact the greater the degree of **differentiation** and interdependence, the greater is the likelihood of conflict developing (Amis, Slack, and Berrett, 1995). Thus subunits that are reciprocally interdependent are more likely to enter into conflict than those that are sequentially interdependent, and those that are sequentially interdependent are more likely to enter into conflict than those that have pooled interdependence.

Microelectronic technologies

Over the last fifteen years, many traditional manufacturing and service technologies have been replaced or augmented with microelectronic technologies, most of which are computer related. There are two major facets of microelectronic technology that affect the structure and operation of sport organizations, computer integrated manufacturing (CIM) and advanced information technologies. CIM refers to the linking together of different parts of the manufacturing process with computers. This includes everything from computer-aided design and computer-aided manufacturing (CAM) to the warehousing, shipping, and servicing of finished products. These techniques are commonly used to design, produce, and distribute a wide variety of sports equipment, from running shoes to tennis rackets.

Advanced information technology involves the linking together of computers through telecommunications systems, thus allowing virtually anyone with a personal computer and modem to send information to, and receive information from, any part of the world. This allows for prompt identification of key issues and potential problems, as well as a broader participation in decision making.

In recent years, this type of technology, primarily through the Internet, has had a huge impact on sport organizations. The Internet has been a catalyst for the convergence of the sports, entertainment, and computer technology industries, seemingly without boundaries. While there have been concerns about gambling, fraud, and ethical questions to do with intellectual property rights, the Internet has become an important marketing tool. Electronic commerce has allowed organizations to target individuals who may be geographically dispersed and located far away from any traditional purchasing outlet. Furthermore, technological improvements have allowed radio broadcasts of sporting events to become commonplace with live video coverage almost available. These developments present significant opportunities not only to develop new streams of revenue, but also to build brand awareness and sponsorship opportunities.

Relationship between technology and organizational structure

The multidimensional nature of technology and complexity render clear relationships difficult to find. Technologies such as Woodward's mass production, Perrow's routine, and Thompson's sequential are generally associated with bureaucratic types of structures, suggesting high levels of task specialization and vertical differentiation, and hence complexity. However, specialization, as measured by the amount of professional training of the workforce, is likely to be low (Hage and Aiken, 1969). When technology is nonroutine, or of unit production, task specialization and the number of hierarchical levels will be low, but complexity as measured by the amount of the staff's professional training will be high. There is a clearer relationship between technology and formalization. Generally, the more routine technologies are associated with the greater presence of rules, regulations, and job descriptions (Hage and Aiken, 1969; Gerwin, 1979). Although there are exceptions (e.g., Hinings and Lee, 1971), most studies show at least a slight relationship between the level of technology and the degree to which decision making is decentralized (Child and Mansfield, 1972; Khandwalla, 1974; Hage and Aiken, 1969). Generally speaking, organizations that employ routine technology will be more centralized than those employing nonroutine technology.

SIZE AND SPORT ORGANIZATIONS

Intuitively, we all know that large sport organizations operate and are structured differently from small ones. Size is, for many organization theorists, the most important influence on the structure and processes of an organization. In this section, we look at the various ways of assessing **organizational size,** and we also examine the ways in which size affects a sport organization's structure.

There are many ways to assess the size of a sport organization: the number of employees, market share, number of fans, return on investment, and number of members are all possible measures. In the most detailed analysis of the concept of size, Kimberly (1976) suggested that there are four aspects of the concept that can be found within the literature. The first of these is the physical capacity of an organization (e.g., the physical capacity of a professional baseball organization could be measured by the number of fans its stadium can hold). Organizations with stadiums that will hold more fans are seen as being bigger than those with a smaller capacity. A second measure is the volume of organizational inputs or outputs (Kimberly, 1976). Organizational inputs could refer to the amount of money a voluntary sports club is able to generate. A club with a lot of money would be described as larger than one with less money. In a similar vein, a fitness center with a lot of members (inputs), would be seen as bigger than one with fewer members. If applied to a retail sporting goods store, organizational outputs could be measured by the number of units of an item sold (e.g., athletic shoes). If used to assess the size of a department of sport studies, outputs could be the number of graduates per year. The third measure of size is the amount of discretionary resources available to an organization. This could include measures such as the wealth of an organization or the size of its net assets; the bigger the net assets, the larger the organization. The final measure that Kimberly suggested can be used to measure size involves the personnel available to an organization, for example, the number of employees or the number of members. This is the most common measure of size, used in more than 80 percent of studies on this topic (Kimberly, 1976). There is, however, a problem applying this measure to some types of sport organizations. A ski resort would, for instance, have more employees in winter than in summer. There is also a question with how to classify part-time employees. For example, a sporting goods store may hire part-time sales clerks. How are these people measured when recording the size of an organization? Notwithstanding these problems, it is primarily people who have to be managed in any organization and, as such, available personnel is the most widely used and accepted measure of organizational size (Child, 1973). Amis and Slack (1996), in their study investigating the relationship between the size and structure of voluntary sport organizations, overcame these problems by using the number of members registered within the organization, and the organization's annual income.

Within the organization theory literature, there has been considerable debate about the impact that size has on the structure of an organization. Despite this debate, the majority of studies acknowledge that size influences the structure of an organization. Most researchers (Khandwalla, 1977; Mintzberg, 1979) have suggested that large organizations are more complex than small ones. This increased complexity arises for several reasons. First, as organizations grow, it becomes economically feasible to add specialists. For example, a small sporting goods store will not be able to afford its own lawyer and accountant, whereas a large sports equipment manufacturer will have the necessary resources to employ these types of specialists. Increased size also contributes to complexity in that, as sport organizations grow, they tend to diversify. The NBA, for example, capitalized on core competencies developed through organizing men's professional basketball when it diversified into a professional women's league with the WNBA. This increase in specialists and/or product diversification requires managing. This is usually accomplished by introducing new levels of management into the organization, which also serves to increase complexity.

With this increase in complexity comes a concomitant need for coordination and control. This can be achieved through direct supervision or the formalization of modes of operation. Because direct supervision is expensive, formalization, through the use of rules, regulations, policies, and procedures, is the most frequently used method of integrating the functions of an organization. It should be noted that the industry in which the organization is operating may also affect the size-formalization relationship. In organizations where work is relatively repetitive and unskilled, such as a sport

equipment manufacturer, formalization is likely to be high. However, in a professional-based structure—for example, a large sport medicine clinic that employs professionally trained staff such as doctors, physiotherapists, and x-ray technicians—formalization is low. The reason for this is that professional training is designed to accomplish the same goals as formalization, that is, the organization and regulation of members (Hall, 1982).

The relationship between size and centralization is somewhat paradoxical. As Blau and Schoenherr (1971) point out, a large organization places conflicting pressures on its senior managers. This is because size raises the importance of managerial decisions, thus discouraging delegation, while simultaneously expanding the volume of managerial responsibilities, which exerts pressure to delegate. Despite this paradox, most research has shown that as an organization gets larger, decision making is decentralized. There is, however, a caveat in that, as noted earlier, if decentralization is accompanied by increasing levels of formalization pertaining to how, when, and by whom decisions should be made, it is questionable if *decentralization* has in fact taken place. Amis and Slack's (1996) results, while supportive of the wider literature, also found that the relationship between size and centralization was somewhat ambiguous. This they attributed to the reluctance of volunteers to cede authority to professional staff, even in the larger, more complex organizations.

POWER AND POLITICS

In the previous four sections of this chapter, we have looked at how an organization's strategy, environment, technology, and size can influence its structure. However, despite the explanatory **power** of these variables in helping to understand organizational structure, there is much that remains unexplained. Some organization theorists have suggested that a focus on the power and politics of organization life can explain much of what the so-called contingency variables leave unexplained. The argument presented by those who subscribe to this viewpoint is that those people who hold power in an organization will adopt the type of structure that will help maintain or increase their power. One way of doing this is to engage in **political activity**.

The power to make choices about the way a sport organization should be structured and operated can arise from a number of sources. A sport manager can exhibit *legitimate power* because of his or her position in the organization. For example, the manager of a baseball team can pick any lineup or batting order that he chooses because of the formal position of authority that he holds. He is not required to discuss the decision with his players, although he may wish to do so. Often with legitimate power comes *reward power,* the power to allocate benefits and favors to those who conform to the power holder's demands. The decision of a newly appointed chief executive officer of a ski hill to promote those who have loyally supported his or her rise to the top is a clear example of reward power. *Coercive power* is in some ways the opposite of reward power and can be employed by those who have the power to punish or impose sanctions on others. A coach may use coercive power to "sit out" a player who did not work hard in practice. *Referent power* is the type of power that a person has because people look up to them. College football and basketball coaches may win the respect of alumni and/or players because of the values they espouse. They also may obtain power because of their vast knowledge of the sport: this is termed *expert power*. None of these types of power is discrete and they may even overlap, but either individually or in combination, they can be used to influence the structure and operation of a sport organization.

Political behavior involves the effective use of different bases of power (Mintzberg, 1983). Gandz and Murray (1980) found that the use of political power was a common feature of organization life, particularly at its higher levels. By using political power, sport managers can shape the structure of the organizations in which they work. Political power can come through four main activities: building coalitions, using outside experts, building a network of contacts, and controlling information. We will now look briefly at each of these.

Coalitions are built when sport managers spend their time communicating their views to others, building up trust relationships, and building mutual respect with others, both inside and outside the organization. Coalition building occurs in many sport organizations, and it is often carried out outside the work environment in places like bars, restaurants, and golf courses. Using outside experts or consultants enables sport managers to legitimize their own views about the structure and process of an organization. Frequently, hiring an outside expert is seen as a means of gaining an objective view. However, managers rarely hire individuals whose views are opposed to their own.

All managers develop political power by establishing a network of contacts both inside and outside their organizations. We often see this type of activity when cities are bidding to host major sporting events such as the Olympic Games. Managers from the bidding committee try to build up contacts with IOC members, politicians, and diplomats who can influence the decision process. Finally, controlling information is a form of political activity that can be used to influence the outcome of decision making. Sport managers, by emphasizing facts that support their position and ignoring or de-emphasizing other managers' positions, can promote their own ideas and how their organization should be structured and operated. This type of tactic is frequently used by the owners of professional sport franchises when looking for public subsidies for a stadium or arena. Positive facts about the economic benefits of the facility to the community are emphasized, while counter views are suppressed. For example, on May 18, 1999, voters in the city of Mesa, Arizona voted on whether local and state sales taxes should be used for a proposed $1.8 billion dollar development that included a new stadium for the Arizona Cardinals football team. Proponents for the project tried to convince voters of the economic benefits that would accrue from the investment, notably job creation, while those opposed pointed out to voters their belief that such vast sums of public money should not be spent on football stadiums, and were unlikely to be repaid to the city.

CONCEPT CHECK

Strategy, environment, technology, and size are contingency factors that affect the structure of an organization. Sport managers may also exercise the power they have and engage in political activity to influence the structure of the organization.

DECISION MAKING IN SPORT ORGANIZATIONS

In addition to understanding the structure and design of sport organizations and the contingencies that influence them, sport managers also must develop an understanding of the many processes that take place in sport organizations. **Decision making** and change are two of the most important of these. Whether it involves deciding on the color of the company letterhead or pursuing a multimillion-dollar takeover bid, decision making centers on making a choice between different alternatives (Drucker, 1966). Sport managers must use their judgment to make decisions about such things as hiring and firing employees, the addition of new products or programs, and the divestment of divisions that are making a loss.

The decisions that a sport manager has to make can be categorized into two types (Simon, 1960). *Programmed decisions* are repetitive and routine and are based on clearly defined policies, procedures, and/or past experiences. Such decisions may include the number of coaches to hire for a certain number of participants in a children's sport camp, or whether to pass or fail a student in a sport management course. *Nonprogrammed decisions* involve unique situations with few or no established guidelines or procedures to direct the way in which they should be handled. Decisions being made by the Sydney Organizing Committee for the Olympic Games (SOCOG) as to what new infrastructure to build and where to build it in order to have the most beneficial long-term impact on the city would fall into this category.

There are three types of conditions under which decisions are made. Each is based on the extent to which the outcome of a particular decision can be predicted. A decision is made under conditions of certainty when the costs and benefits of all available alternatives are completely understood. Because of the constantly changing nature of sport organizations, this is an ideal situation that is rarely, if ever, realized. More common are decisions taken with a degree of risk. Here, there is a basic understanding of the available alternatives, but the potential cost and benefits of each are not 100 percent known. Decisions made by the coach of a college basketball team regarding potential sponsorship opportunities may enter into this category. For example, if one shoe company is offering a deal for five years at $1,000,000 per year, and another is offering a ten-year deal at $750,000 per year, which is better? Much will depend on changes in the economy and the future willingness of shoe companies to pay college coaches to have their players endorse products.

The decision-maker must therefore assign probabilities to possible outcomes and determine the most attractive alternative. Under conditions of uncertainty, the decision alternatives and their potential outcomes are both unknown, because there are no data or past experiences upon which to base the decision. Decisions such as whether to expand a sport equipment manufacturing company into one of the former Soviet bloc countries, which may offer cheap labor but carries a long history of political instability, would fall into this category.

Although there are various models to explain the process of decision making, in this chapter we briefly outline the two commonly associated with individual decision making. The *rational model* is an ideal description of how decisions should be made through a linear analysis of the problem and the rational identification of solutions. The implicit assumption in this model is that decision making is carried out, as proposed by classical management theorists, to maximize the potential for the attainment of organizational goals. The decision process is seen as a process of linear steps. First, it is determined that a problem exists; the decision criteria are then identified and weighed based on the interests of the organization; all possible alternatives that might solve the problem and meet the criteria are then listed; these alternatives are evaluated against prespecified criteria; finally, the best alternative is chosen (Robbins, 1990). The various assumptions that are made by adherents of this approach are, as Pfeffer and Salancik (1977) noted, so much a part of the ideology of how management is practiced as to be virtually taken for granted. However, they go on to add that these assumptions are less than completely persuasive.

Much of the criticism of the rational model emanates from the work of Herbert Simon (1945) and his concept of **bounded rationality.** Simon suggested that rather then being a completely rational process, organization decision making is bounded by the emotions and limited cognitive ability of managers to process information, by factors such as constraints on the time and money available, and by imperfect information that is available. Because of this, managers "satisfice." A limited number of decision alternatives and outcomes are considered, with the manager searching for the first acceptable solution. For example, the owner of a sporting goods store wishing to hire a new employee will hold the position open only until he or she has found a satisfactory applicant. The process will not be extended indefinitely until the ideal candidate has been found. As much as the rational model intuitively appeals to a manager's sense of order, the bounded rationality approach provides a much more realistic account of how decisions are actually made. It also draws attention to the political nature of decision making.

CHANGE IN SPORT ORGANIZATIONS

Sport organizations are in a constant state of transition, and so change is another important process that managers need to understand. To survive and grow, a sport organization must be able to adapt to changes in environment, size, strategy, and technology. New people enter the organization, others leave, physical layout is reorganized, and new products and programs are developed. The changes that are being discussed are not the day-to-day fluctuations evident in all organizations but those that are systematically planned and implemented in an attempt to retain or confer a sustainable competitive advantage.

Organizational change can occur in the following four areas: technology, products and services, structure and systems, and personnel (Leavitt, 1964; McCann, 1991). Technological change refers to the changes that occur in production processes, skills and methods used to deliver services, or knowledge base. Tennis racquet manufacturer Dunlop has, for example, undergone profound changes in how it designs, manufactures, and sells tennis racquets as a result of technological advances that have seen racquets designed by computers and made from increasingly sophisticated materials such as carbon fiber. A change in products or services may involve the deletion, addition, or modification of the sport organization's various offerings. Structural and systemic changes include modifications to areas such as the sport organization's division of labor, authority structure, or control systems. This is particularly evident when a company such as Mark McCormack's International Management Group (IMG) undergoes rapid expansion. When IMG was a small entrepreneurial company, McCormack took responsibility for virtually all operations. As the company grew, responsibilities had to be delegated, which, in turn, required the implementation of a suitable control system and authority structure.

Personnel changes involve altering the ways in which people think, act, and relate to each other.

A sport organization's output, costs, and work force must remain relatively fixed if the organization is to be successful. This complements managerial preferences for stability and predictability. At the same time, there is a need to look for new markets, new technologies, and new methods of service delivery. Therefore, what is required is an almost paradoxical balancing between change and stability. If incorrectly managed, organization performance can rapidly deteriorate. Productive attention to detail can become an obsession with trivia, rewarding innovation can escalate into superfluous invention, and measured growth can lead to unsuppressed expansion (Miller, 1990).

The impetus for change may arise externally from the environment of the sport organization or from inside the organization itself. There are perspectives that attempt to explain both. For example, contingency theorists (Burns and Stalker, 1961; Lawrence and Lorsch, 1967) and population ecologists (Carroll and Hannan, 1989) focus on exogenous sources of change. On the other hand, resource dependence theorists (Pfeffer and Salancik, 1978) and those who adopt a contextual approach (Pettigrew, 1985; 1987), stress the interaction of internal and external factors.

The pervasive necessity for change in sport organizations is matched only by the equally ubiquitous resistance to it. This resistance may emanate from the organization itself, or from environmental constituents. Organization members may resist in an attempt to protect their self-interests, particularly if goals relating to power, money, prestige, job security, or professional competence are threatened as a result of the change (Patti, 1974). Resistance may arise as a direct result of the uncertainty that accompanies change, especially in situations where there is a lack of trust between those initiating the change and those it will affect. Change may also be resisted if different organization stakeholders have differing opinions of the costs and benefits of the proposed change. Finally, change may be resisted because of costs in time, effort, and money that are incurred. Different parties may not feel that the benefits of change outweigh the associated costs. This has become particularly apparent in Canadian national sport organizations with the pressure the government has placed on these organizations to change and adopt a more professional and bureaucratic structure. Despite increases in funding for those organizations that adopted this type of design, the many volunteers who have traditionally controlled them have often refused to accept the loss of power that would result from a move to this type of structural arrangement.

There are various means by which sport organization managers can deal with resistance and implement change. These are not mutually exclusive and often are used in conjunction with one another. Educating organization members about the necessity for change and using communication techniques to keep them informed of how the change is progressing can help reduce resistance. Gaining the participation and involvement of those change-resistant groups through mechanisms such as change teams can ease the planning and implementation process. Providing facilitation and support, through devices such as career counseling, job training, and therapy, to those adversely affected by the change can address some of the fear, anxiety, and uncertainty that the change process creates. As a last resort, the process can be somewhat smoothed by techniques of negotiation, manipulation, co-optation, or even coercion, in an attempt to pressure opposition groups into accepting the desired changes.

CONCEPT CHECK

There are many processes that take place in sport organizations. Because of space we have only looked at two of the most important, the process of decision making and the process of change. Others include the process of human resources management, the process of managing organizational culture, and the process of leadership.

CRITICAL THINKING EXERCISES

1. The Association of Surfing Professionals (ASP) runs a twelve-event World Championship Tour (WCT). Most of the WCT events, and almost all of the surfers, are sponsored by either Billabong, Quiksilver, Gotcha, Rip Curl, O'Neill, or one of a dozen or so smaller companies involved in the surf industry. To date,

and despite approaches in 1998 from the biggest sport management group in the world, International Management Group (IMG), the ASP has actively avoided involvement with any of the large international television networks. Instead, they employ a relatively small company called Online Sports to produce one-hour documentaries on each WCT event, plus short news clips for satellite pickup, which is subscribed to by many of the television networks. Why would the ASP actively avoid aligning themselves with any of the big international TV sport networks?

2. In the late 1980s, a multinational consumer electronics firm was trying to establish itself across North America. Prior to June 1991, the firm annually committed about 20 percent of its marketing budget to sponsoring a wide range of sporting events, teams, and individuals. Over a short period of time, money was invested in sponsoring Indy Car racing, golf tournaments, tennis competitions, an NFL quarterback, and various Canadian Olympic athletes. However, by 1994, a rigid policy of not pursuing any new sponsorship agreements was in place. Why do you think that the firm had this sudden change in strategy?

SUMMARY

1. For most sport managers, the main objective is to develop an effective sport organization. Effectiveness can be looked at from a number of different perspectives. The strategic constituents approach, which takes into account the political nature of organizations and the influence this has on effectiveness, is the most useful of these perspectives.

2. To be effective, a sport organization must be structured to fit with the demands of the contextual situation within which it operates. The three most common dimensions used to describe the structure of a sport organization are complexity, formalization, and centralization. The way in which the dimensions of organizational structure are patterned is referred to as the design of the organization. There are many different organizational design types that sport organizations may exhibit. Mintzberg (1979) identified five design types, or what he

termed *configurations*: simple structure, machine bureaucracy, professional bureaucracy, divisionalized form, and adhocracy. Examples of each of these design types can be found in the organizations that make up the sport industry.

3. A sport organization's strategy, environment, technology, and size will all influence the type of structure it exhibits. These variables are called *contingencies* because a sport organization's structure is contingent upon them.

4. Structure may also be a product of power and politics. Senior individuals and the members of dominant coalitions within a sport organization may attempt to preserve the structure of an organization to preserve power and privileged position. The emphasis that some organizational theorists place on power and politics stands in contrast to the rationality of the contingency approach.

5. There are many different processes that occur within a sport organization. We looked briefly at two of these, the process of decision making and that of change. Some people see decision making as a rational process, but many organization theorists challenge this position and suggest that decision makers operate with bounded rationality. That is to say that decision choices are limited by factors such as expertise, organizational politics, and time. Change is also an important process in sport organizations. It is somewhat paradoxical because although sport managers seek stability and predictability, if the organizations they manage are to remain competitive, they must change to meet the demands of their respective markets.

CASE STUDY

In the late 1960s, a young blacksmith and rock climber, Yvon Chouinard, noticed while climbing on the big walls of Yosemite and the spires of Wyoming's Grand Tetons, the damage that was being caused by the equipment that climbers were using. Using his skill as a blacksmith, he designed a piece of hardware that provided the same kind of protection on the rock face, but could be removed with no damage to the wall. It was a durable, high-quality piece of equipment that could be used repeatedly with no unnecessary harm to the environment.

Yvon's interest in climbing and the environment, and also in function and quality, led him to research the clothing people used while climbing. He was intrigued by the heavy canvas shorts and pants he saw in Europe, and the thick cotton rugby shirts from Scotland. Calling his business The Chouinard Equipment Co., Yvon brought the clothes back from Europe and sold those and his climbing hardware out of the trunk of his car in the parking lots of Yosemite National Park. The quality of Yvon's products was of paramount importance, since his life was on the line just like his customers'. As the business grew, Yvon changed its name to Patagonia, and he became an early advocate and a manufacturer of innovative products for "clean climbing," a style of climbing that did not deface the rock. By the early 1980s, the company was becoming financially successful, and Yvon immediately began giving money to environmental activists. He also adopted the mission statement: "to make the best quality products with no unnecessary harm." The natural progression from there was to look at the environmental impacts of Patagonia's products and corporate activities.

In the late 1980s, Yvon thought that Patagonia had achieved a breakthrough by using the tagua nut to make buttons, thus replacing a plastic resin-based material with one that was sustainably harvested from the Brazilian rainforest. To his horror, however, he discovered that the tagua nut buttons, after several washings, began to break by the thousands. As all Patagonia products come with a lifetime guarantee, they were forced to sew new buttons onto all shirts returned to them. As Jill Zilligen, Patagonia Director of Environmental Programs stated, "we learned that, in a business built on quality and environmental ethic, we had to be strategic in our environmental improvements" (Zilligen, 1996, p. 2).

So in 1991, the company turned their attention inward, and set about research and development to learn more about the impacts their products had on the environment. They commissioned a study on the four main fibers used in their lines: polyester, nylon, cotton, and wool. They studied the full life cycle of the products and concluded that there were parts of the process they could control and change, and others that they could not immediately affect. Out of this, they were able to introduce a line of products made from recycled polyester and soda bottles—a warm, quick-drying fleecy fabric called PCR (post consumer recycled) Synchilla. They also concluded that, due to the insecticides used in its production, the most environmentally harmful fiber used in their clothing was in fact cotton. This led to Patagonia's spring 1996 commitment to using only organically produced cotton in its products.

To make such a radical change in production processes involved every member of the company. Senior management took employees on trips through the Californian Central Valley cotton fields and sent out educational materials to their associates around the world. They also directly sourced their own raw materials, and then worked at educating their distributors to make sure that the products actually sold. In addition, they changed their organization from functional work groups to product development teams, and held conferences to bring vendors, contractor, and Patagonia staff together to explore new ways of improving quality and environmental performance. Finally, all staff were given paid time off to field-test new products.

Yvon Chouinard's company today makes in excess of three hundred pieces of clothing and accessories each season, with sales in excess of $150 million. Patagonia has also recently diversified into the surfboard and surfwear industry, applying the same principles of quality and environmental awareness in their production methods. Now sold in specialty stores throughout the world, the firm has come a long way since Chouinard's days of selling products from the trunk of his car.

REVIEW QUESTIONS AND ISSUES

1. Describe the changes in strategy, size, environment, and technology that Patagonia has experienced over the last twenty-five years.
2. What changes do you think have taken place in Patagonia's structure since the tagua nut problem?
3. With wholesale changes to production processes, and a strong emphasis on research and development, what implications would this have for the division of labor, authority structure, and control systems at Patagonia?
4. A possible source of resistance to the changes stemming from Patagonia's environmental initiatives is the increased cost of organic and heavily researched raw materials. What steps has the company taken to reduce this resistance? What other problems might there be for

companies taking an environmental stance in their product development?

SOLUTIONS TO CRITICAL THINKING EXERCISES

1. The ASP has, to date, actively avoided serious involvement with any of the major television sports networks because they are almost solely reliant on the surfing industry for support. Most contests and almost all of the surfers are sponsored by either Quiksilver, Billabong, Gotcha, Rusty, Rip Curl, O'Neill, or one of about a dozen smaller companies. These companies have significant vested interests in maintaining the status quo, in using their sponsored surfers and events to leverage their influence within the surfing community. In so doing, they have successfully used their coercive power to discourage the ASP from signing on with a large television network that could potentially take their primary promotional tools away from them. From the ASP's perspective, they see the current arrangement as spreading their risk, rather than being reliant on one or a few key sponsors.

2. Although initially viewed as a useful marketing technique, the sponsorships that the firm was involved in lacked any strategic coherence. All of the agreements had been initiated by groups looking for support. There was no attempt to secure sponsorship agreements as part of a preconceived marketing strategy. Consequently, the agreements did little to help the firm build a recognizable marketing presence. Further, because of the rapidity with which new agreements were entered into, there is little likelihood that any of the agreements across the firm were leveraged to, for example, help build corporate culture, further relationships with key clients, or help in brand development. Sponsorship investments were simply viewed as securing walking billboards, and thus were the first things to be curtailed when funds became less available.

REFERENCES

Amis, J., Pant, N., and Slack, T. (1997). Achieving a sustainable competitive advantage: A resource-based view of sport sponsorship. *Journal of Sport Management, 11*, 80–96.

Amis, J., and Slack, T. (1996). The size-structure relationship in voluntary sport organizations. *Journal of Sport Management, 10,* 76–86.

Amis, J., Slack, T., and Berrett, T. (1995). The structural antecedents of conflict in voluntary sport organizations. *Leisure Studies, 14,* 1–16.

Amis, J., Slack, T., and Berrett, T. (1999). Sport sponsorship as distinctive competence. *European Journal of Marketing, 33,* 250–73.

Blau, P. M., and Schoenherr, R. A. (1971). *The structure of organizations.* New York: Basic Books.

Burns, T., and Stalker, G. M. (1961). *The management of innovation.* London: Tavistock.

Cameron, K. S. (1980). Critical questions in assessing organizational effectiveness. *Organizational Dynamics, 9,* 66–80.

Carper, W. B., and Snizek, W. E. (1980). The nature and types of organizational taxonomies: An overview. *Academy of Management Review, 5,* 65–75.

Carroll, G. R., and Hannan, M. T. (1989). Density dependence in the evolution of populations of newspaper organizations. *American Sociological Review, 54,* 524–41.

Chelladurai, P. (1987). Multidimensionality and multiple perspectives of organizational effectiveness. *Journal of Sport Management, 1,* 37–47.

Child, J. (1973). Parkinson's progress: Accounting for the number of specialists in organizations. *Administrative Science Quarterly, 18,* 328–46.

Child, J. (1984). *Organization: A guide to problems and practice.* 2d ed. London: Paul Chapman Publishing Ltd.

Child, J., and Mansfield, R. (1972). Technology, size, and organization structure. *Sociology, 6,* 369–93.

Connolly, T., Conlon, E. M., and Deutsch, S. J. (1980). Organizational effectiveness: A multiple constituency approach. *Academy of Management Review, 5,* 211–18.

Daft, R. L. (1992). *Organizational theory and design.* 4th ed. St. Paul, MN: West.

Dodds, L. (1985, August 21–September 3). Heading back on the fast track. *Financial World,* 90–91.

Drucker, P. (1966). *The effective executive.* New York: Harper and Row.

Etzioni, A. (1964). *Modern organizations.* Englewood Cliffs, NJ: Prentice-Hall.

Evans, W. M. (1976). Organizational theory and organizational effectiveness: An exploratory analysis. In S. L. Spray (ed.), *Organizational effectiveness: Theory, research utilization* (pp. 15–21). Kent, OH: Kent State University Press.

Frisby, W. (1986). Measuring the organizational effectiveness of national sport governing bodies. *Canadian Journal of Applied Sport Science, 11,* 94–99.

Gandz, J., and Murray, V. V. (1980). The experience of workplace politics. *Academy of Management Journal, 23,* 237–51.

Gerwin, D. (1979). Relationship between structure and technology at the organizational and job levels. *Journal of Management, 16,* 70–79.

Hage, J., and Aiken, M. (1969). Routine technology, social structure, and organizational goals. *Administrative Science Quarterly, 14,* 366–76.

Hall, R. H. (1982). *Organizations: Structure and process.* 3d ed. Englewood Cliffs, NJ: Prentice-Hall.

Hinings, C. R., and Lee, G. L. (1971). Dimensions of organization structure and their context: A replication. *Sociology, 5,* 83–93.

Khandwalla, P. N. (1974). Mass output of operations technology and organizational structure. *Administrative Science Quarterly, 19,* 74–97.

Khandwalla, P. N. (1977). *The design of organizations.* New York: Harcourt Brace Jovanovich.

Kikulis, L. M., Slack, T., and Hinings, B. (1992). Institutionally specific design archetypes: A framework for understanding change in national sport organizations. *International Review for the Sociology of Sport, 27,* 343–70.

Kikulis, L. M., Slack, T., and Hinings, C. R. (1995). Sector-specific patterns of organizational design change. *Journal of Management Studies, 32,* 67–100.

Kimberly, J. R. (1976). Organizational size and the structuralist perspective: A review critique and proposal. *Administrative Science Quarterly, 21,* 571–97.

Lawrence, P. R., and Lorsch, J. (1967). *Organization and environment.* Boston: Harvard Graduate School of Business Administration.

Leavitt, H. J. (1964). Applied organizational change in industry: Technical and human approaches. In W. W. Cooper, H. J. Leavitt, and M. W. Shelly (eds.), *New perspectives in organizational research* (pp. 55–71). New York: Wiley.

Litterer, A. J. (1973). *The analysis of organizations.* 2d ed. New York: Wiley.

McCann, J. E. (1991). Design principles for an innovating company. *Academy of Management Executive, 5,* 76–93.

Meninger, B. (May 3–9, 1999). Byproduct of success: Money. *Street & Smith's SportBusiness Journal, 2* (2), 30–31.

Miller, D. (1987). Strategy making and structure: Analysis and implications for performance. *Academy of Management Journal, 30,* 7–32.

Miller, D. (1990). *The Icarus paradox: How exceptional companies bring about their own downfall.* New York: HarperCollins.

Miller, D., and Droge, C. (1986). Psychological and traditional determinants of structure. *Administrative Science Quarterly, 31,* 539–60.

Mintzberg, H. (1979). *The structuring of organizations.* Englewood Cliffs, NJ: Prentice-Hall.

Mintzberg, H. (1983). *Power in and around organizations.* Englewood Cliffs, NJ: Prentice-Hall.

Patti, R. J. (1974). Organizational resistance and change: The view from below. *Social Service Review, 48,* 367–83.

Perrow, C. (1967). A framework for the comparative analysis of organizations. *American Sociological Review, 32,* 194–208.

Pettigrew, A. (1987). Context and action in the transformation of the firm. *Journal of Management Studies, 24,* 649–70.

Pettigrew, A. M. (1985). *The awakening giant.* Oxford: Basil Blackwell.

Pfeffer, J., and Salancik, G. (1977). Organizational design: The case for a coalition model of organizations. *Organizational Dynamics, 6,* 15–29.

Pfeffer, J., and Salancik, G. (1978). *The external control of organizations: A resource dependence perspective.* New York: HarperCollins.

Pugh, D. S., Hickson, D. J., and Hinings, C. R. (1969). An empirical taxonomy of work organizations. *Administrative Science Quarterly, 14,* 115–26.

Robbins, S. P. (1990). *Organization theory: Structure, design and applications.* 3d ed. Englewood Cliffs, NJ: Prentice-Hall.

Simon, H. A. (1945). *Administrative behavior.* New York: Macmillan.

Simon, H. A. (1960). *The new science of management decision.* Englewood Cliffs, NJ: Prentice-Hall.

Slack, T., and Hinings, C. R. (1987). Planning and organizational change: A conceptual framework for the analysis of amateur sport organizations. *Canadian Journal of Sport Sciences, 12,* 185–93.

Slack, T., and Hinings, C. R. (1992). Understanding change in national sport organizations: An integration of theoretical perspectives. *Journal of Sport Management, 6,* 114–32.

Thompson, J. D. (1967). *Organizations in action.* New York: McGraw-Hill.

Yuchtman, E., and Seashore, S. E. (1967). A systems resource approach to organizational effectiveness. *American Sociological Review, 32,* 891–903.

Zilligen, J. (1996). The role of business organizations on ecological sustainability: A reality check. Speech given at Academy of Management Conference, Cincinnati, Ohio, August 11, 1996.

WEBSITES

www.patagonia.com

Students interested in how organizations in the sport industry can integrate values such as environmental awareness into their structure and operation can review the evolution and efforts of this manufacturer of climbing, hiking, and surfing equipment.

www.sydney.olympic.org.au/index.html

Following the theme from the Patagonia site, students can see how environmental issues are being addressed in the staging of major sporting events, in this case, the Sydney 2000 Olympic Games. Areas addressed include materials used in the design and construction of facilities, transport to and within venues, merchandizing, catering, and waste management. The site includes a plan that lists the Sydney Organizing Committee for the Olympic Games' (SOCOG) environmental commitments that they claim exceed the standards established by the IOC in response to its incorporation of environment as the third dimension of Olympism.

CHAPTER 6

Group Decision Making
and Problem Solving

Laurence Chalip

In this chapter, you will become familiar with the following terms:

Groupthink
Group polarization
Social loafing
Free rider problem
Status influence
Limited creative flexibility
Divergent thinking

Convergent thinking
Plunging in
Brainstorming
Nominal group technique
Synectics
Role plays
Decision pitfalls

Crawford slip method
Dialectical decision making
Delphi technique
Delphi panel
Facilitator
Decision support systems

Overview

Group decision making and problem solving are pivotal tasks for sports managers. This chapter describes occasions when sport managers use group decision making and problem solving.

The chapter describes how to determine whether or not to use a group when solving a problem or making a decision. It goes on to explain the criteria that should be applied to select group members.

Seven techniques that have been prescribed for group decision making and problem solving are reviewed. The techniques are brainstorming, the nominal group technique, synectics, ideawriting, the Crawford slip method, dialectical decision making, and the Delphi technique. It is pointed out that each method may be appropriate under specific circumstances, and it is noted that the methods can be modified or combined to fit specific needs.

Procedures for facilitating group decision making and problem solving sessions are then described. Methods for sequencing the process, assuring balanced participation, and maintaining a task-oriented climate are outlined.

The chapter concludes with a discussion of group decision support systems. It is noted that sports organizations are making increasing use of decision support technologies.

THE SCOPE OF GROUP DECISION MAKING AND PROBLEM SOLVING

Whether managing a unit, a task force, or an entire organization, managers work with and through groups. During the course of a career, groups may help the manager to create plans, generate ideas, solve problems, make decisions, set agendas, establish policies, and govern. Consider the following examples.

Planning

Organizers of the Sydney Olympic Games in 2000 needed to develop plans to enhance the tourism that would be generated by the Games. The degree to which the Games would foster tourism into Australia and beyond Sydney would depend on what various tourism managers did to leverage the Olympic Games. In order to begin a coordinated planning process, consultants to the Tourism Forecasting Council (of Australia) convened groups of tourism managers and policy makers from throughout Australia to discuss possible strategies and potential outcomes that might be associated with Olympic tourism. The ideas that were generated in these discussions were then fed back to the managers and policy makers for comment and further consideration. Finally, the comments of the group were used as a basis for planning the tourism development component of the 2000 Olympic Games. (The outcomes of this work are discussed in Tourism Forecasting Council, 1998.)

Generating ideas

Early in 1994, a company, Playmakers, was created to provide sport services to organizations in Maryland, Virginia, and Washington, D.C. Playmakers's services were based on ideas generated during day-long creative sessions several months before. At those sessions, four managers with experience in the sports industry met to discuss new services that might be well received by athletes, parents, coaches, and administrators. Problems with existing sports programs were discussed, and successful nonsport businesses were scrutinized for concepts that might be applicable to the sports industry. The resulting ideas for solving problems and borrowing concepts were then aggregated into a comprehensive service plan. That plan established the conceptual foundation for the new sports enterprise.

Problem solving

Problems crop up throughout the normal course of doing business. Solutions to these problems may require input from several departments or experts. For example, in the university's athletic department, concerns about athlete eligibility can precipitate meetings among representatives from the compliance, coaching, and academic support units.

Similarly, problems that might accrue when moving a team franchise from one city to another might need to be identified and resolved through meetings of various front-office staff.

Decision making

Each year, athletes leaving college sport are drafted onto professional teams. The process requires that decisions be made about who should be drafted and in what order. Those decisions require input from scouts, coaches, and management. These are not individual decisions: they are group decisions (cf. Whittingham, 1992). Similarly, when designing or redesigning a sport facility, architects often like to meet with groups of future users in order to determine core needs and design criteria that must be taken into account in facility design.

Agenda setting

When the Clinton administration took office in 1993, it made health care reform a leading priority. Since the health benefits of regular exercise are well established, it concerned some sports leaders that sport was not incorporated into the Clinton health agenda. In response, the President's Council on Physical Fitness and Sports called a two-day "strategic planning forum" in November 1993. Experts from government, medicine, recreation, sport service organizations, and the sporting goods industry were brought together to discuss ways in which to add sport to the national health agenda.

Policy making

In 1974, President Ford created the President's Commission on Olympic Sports. That commission formulated the recommendations that served as the basis for the Amateur Sports Act. As part of the commission's work, it formed groups of experts, one for each Olympic sport. Each group met to discuss the needs for its sport and policies that might address those needs.

Governance

Many sports organizations are responsible to boards or committees elected from the membership or assigned to represent specific constituencies. Local recreation leagues, regional sports associations, and the United States Olympic Committee are all governed on the basis of decisions made by groups.

We see that *group decision making* and *problem solving* can become significant elements of the sports manager's work. A substantial body of research has been devoted to understanding the methods and pitfalls of group decision making (e.g., Davis, 1992; Goodwin and Wright, 1998, pp. 295–314; Hollenbeck et al., 1998). To be effective, the manager must address three issues (1) When should a group be used? (2) Who should be included? (3) What methods will optimize the group's efforts and provide appropriate decision support? Each of these tasks is discussed in the next section.

CONCEPT CHECK

Sport managers at all levels of an organization work with and through groups. Groups aid the manager in planning, generating ideas, problem solving, decision making, agenda setting, policy making, and governance.

WHEN TO USE A GROUP

Groups can be advantageous when solving problems or making decisions (Kerr et al., 1996; Koopman and Pool, 1991). Consider the following four benefits:

1. More ideas are possible as increasing numbers of persons are included. For example, the four sport managers who met to plan Playmakers were able to identify more existing problems, more potential solutions, and more useful concepts than any one, two, or three of them could have generated alone.
2. More information is available. For example, at successive stages of developing the analysis of tourism strategies for the 2000 Olympic Games, the many tourism managers and policy makers were able to share their experiences, as well as results from consultations and marketing research already carried out. Consequently, a more complete analysis was obtained, and better planning was enabled.
3. Alternative perspectives become accessible. For example, coaches, compliance officers, and academic support personnel can each contribute different reflections about athlete eligibility and the resources available to address athletes' needs.
4. The fairness of a decision is judged, in part, by who had input. Thus the President's

Commission on Olympic Sports in the United States and the Sport Development Inquiry Committee in New Zealand each sought legitimacy for their recommendations by obtaining testimony from representatives of as many sport organizations as could be invited to the many hearings that were held (Chalip, 1995, 1996).

However, these benefits are not without cost. It is more time-consuming to engage in group decisions than to simply make a decision independently. This is particularly true if the matter to be addressed is one over which there is likely to be some conflict (Janis and Mann, 1977). Yet conflict can be beneficial. Although conflict over sensitive decisions can challenge group cohesion, conflict can also aid decision making, by prompting the search for information and requiring consideration of alternative views (Dooley and Fryxell, 1999; Putnam, 1986).

These factors suggest the following three criteria for determining whether or not to seek group input into a decision: (1) How important is the quality of the decision? (2) How much do others have to accept or commit to the decision for it to be implemented? (3) How much time is reasonable to make the decision?

Logical analysis suggests that the manager has five alternatives (Vroom and Yetton, 1973): (1) Solve the problem independently, using information available at the time; (2) obtain information from others, but make the decision independently; (3) collect suggestions (as well as information) from others individually, then make the decision independently; (4) collect suggestions and information from others as a group, but make the decision independently; or (5) meet with the group to formulate alternatives, and make the final decision as a group.

Which of these five alternatives the manager should choose depends on the requisite quality, commitment, and time for decision. The first alternative should be chosen in cases when the decision is relatively trivial (i.e., the concern for quality is negligible), particularly if subordinates are likely to accept the decision. It is also chosen when urgency prohibits consultation with others. The second alternative is appropriate when decision quality is important, but subordinates are likely to accept the decision. As the need for information and

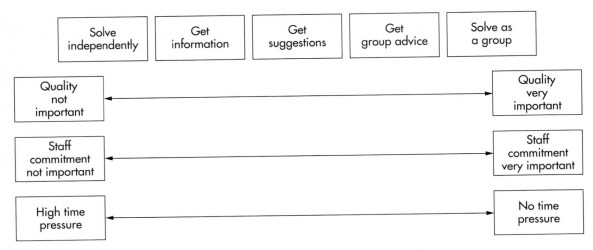

FIGURE 6–1   The relationship between situational factors and choice of decision strategy.

subordinate support rises, the manager will move to the third and fourth alternatives. Finally, when decision quality is important and subordinate support is critical, alternative five is appropriate.

Figure 6–1 illustrates the relationship between situational factors and the choice of decision strategy.

> **CONCEPT CHECK**
>
> *The advantages of group problem solving and decision making include more available ideas, more available information, alternative perspectives, and enhanced fairness. Disadvantages of working with a group are time consumption and potential for conflict. However, conflict can also be beneficial if it furthers the group's exploration of ideas. Decision quality, support, and time constraints determine whether or not a manager should seek group input into a decision.*

WHOM TO INCLUDE

Groups tend to be most effective when they include from five to twelve members (cf. Moore, 1987). The preceding discussion suggests two criteria for selecting group members: (1) persons who have requisite information, and (2) persons affected by the decision or who may have to cooperate in implementing the group's decision. Research into effective group decision making also suggests the value of including persons simply because they add

diverse viewpoints, beliefs, or inclinations (Janis, 1982; Lamm, 1988). This can be particularly important if the decision is relatively risky.

Janis (1982) studied decision processes in four policy failures (the Bay of Pigs invasion, the invasion of North Korea, Pearl Harbor, and the Vietnam War) and two policy successes (the Cuban missile crisis and the Marshall Plan). He concludes that groups whose members readily agree make poorer policy choices than do groups whose members dispute options and values. The problem, he argues, is that groups prizing harmony will avoid contentious evaluation of policy alternatives. Consequently, the group will censor the input of information or values that are inconsistent with dominant preferences. Since this prevents the group from learning from its decision failures, it can cause the group to persist with policies even after they have become overtly detrimental. Janis calls these phenomena **groupthink.** He describes them this way:

> The more amiability and esprit de corps among the members of a policy-making in-group, the greater is the danger that independent critical thinking will be replaced by groupthink, which is likely to result in irrational and dehumanizing actions directed against out-groups.

The groupthink formulation has generated substantial research. Findings from field studies and laboratory experiments are generally supportive (e.g., Choi and Kim, 1999; Mulcahy, 1995; Schafer and Crichlow, 1996).

Lamm and Myers (1978) describe a related phenomenon that they call **group polarization.** Group polarization refers to the tendency of groups to develop positions and attitudes that are more extreme than those held by individual group members before participating in group decision making. First, group members are reinforced for taking positions that support the direction of group sentiment. This causes members to reinforce gradual shifts in attitude that are more extreme than any individual member's initial sentiment. Second, the group elaborates information and arguments that support its biases. This, in turn, supports the group's continued drift by engendering the impression that evidence is accumulating in support of more extreme positions. The formulation is supported by a substantial volume of research (Lamm, 1988).

Group polarization is a matter of particular concern when a decision involves risk, because it can cause groups to choose options that are unnecessarily risky or overly cautious. Groups that begin with a risky bias are likely to become more risky; groups that begin with a conservative bias are likely to become more conservative. For example, when considering the feasibility of a new tournament, a group whose members were all fiscally conservative would be likely to reject the tournament. Conversely, a group whose members favored risky initiatives would be likely to approve the tournament.

Research suggests that the following three selection procedures can reduce a group's vulnerability to groupthink or group polarization (Dooley and Fryxell, 1999; Neck and Moorhead, 1995; Schweiger et al., 1986): (1) New perspectives can be obtained by rotating outside experts onto the group temporarily. (2) Critical evaluators can be incorporated to monitor and review the group's reasoning. (3) One or more group members can be assigned the role of devil's advocate.

CONCEPT CHECK

Persons should be selected for a group because they have needed information, will be affected by the implementation of the decision, or will bring a distinctive perspective to the group. Groups lacking diversity can succumb to groupthink or group polarization. Critical perspectives, such as a designated devil's advocate, can be incorporated to inject useful conflict and avoid early consensus.

TECHNIQUES FOR GROUP DECISION

Even if the manager is careful to minimize group vulnerability to polarization or groupthink, other pitfalls endanger the efficacy of group decision. Four of these are particularly important: *social loafing, status influence, limited creative flexibility,* and *plunging in.* A number of techniques for group decision making have been reported to aid groups in circumventing these pitfalls. To clarify the circumstances under which each technique becomes advantageous, it is first necessary to describe the four pitfalls.

Since the product of a group's activities is typically a joint product, the rewards to individual group members are rarely contingent on their individual performance in the group. If the decision or problem solution is truly a result of group interaction, it becomes impossible to specify accurately what percentage of the outcome is attributable to each member. In the best group decisions, the products of interaction among group members may be more significant than the discrete bits contributed by individual members. Consequently, it is rarely possible to apportion credit or benefits to each member in proportion to the member's unique contribution. This makes it possible for group members to reduce their individual efforts, allowing others to sustain the group's work. This problem of **social loafing,** sometimes called the **free rider problem,** can impede the group's performance (Hardin, 1982).

Social loafing is not the sole cause of differences in individual contributions to the group's activity. Higher-status individuals are likely to wield more influence than persons of lower status (Hollander, 1964). **Status influence** manifests itself both in terms of group process and the outcome of the group's work. Higher-status individuals are more likely to speak and be spoken to. Their input is likely to be deemed more credible. The group is most likely to choose an alternative preferred by high-status members.

The search for alternatives is itself guided by the *mental models* of group members (Cannon-Bowers et al., 1993; Carroll et al., 1998). Each member of the group understands the problem on which the group is working by constructing working models of it in their minds (Johnson-Laird, 1983). A substantial body of work has shown that members will make considerable use of *analogies* to construct their mental models. Collins and Gentner (1987) describe the phenomenon this way:

Analogies are powerful ways to understand how things work in a new domain. We think this is because they enable people to construct a structure mapping that carries across the way the components in a system interact. This allows people to create new mental models that they can run to generate predictions about what should happen in various situations in the real world.

There is, however, a limitation that can become particularly acute as the group works together. Research shows that people often fail to search through an adequate array of analogies when problem solving (Gick and Holyoak, 1980; 1983). This **limited creative flexibility** may be exacerbated in the group situation because the group will communicate most effectively if members share a common mental model (Cannon-Bowers et al., 1993; Carroll et al., 1998). The utility of a common mental model may cause the group to anchor on a single model or a limited subset of analogies. In so doing, the group loses a proportion of its creative flexibility.

Creative flexibility requires a balance of two kinds of thinking: **divergent thinking** and **convergent thinking.** These are separate processes. During divergent thinking, there is an active search for ideas. Ideas are generated, explored, expanded, and recombined. During convergent thinking, on the other hand, ideas are evaluated and compared. Whereas divergent thinking enlarges and elaborates the range of ideas, convergent thinking winnows ideas by evaluating, synthesizing, and selecting. Research on group problem solving shows that groups often **plunge in** to make a decision before they have adequately probed their problem or elaborated a sufficient array of alternatives (Scheidel and Crowell, 1979). In other words, groups too often begin convergent thinking without first having engaged in enough divergent thinking.

CONCEPT CHECK

Common pitfalls in group decision making include social loafing, status influence, limited creative flexibility, and plunging in. Creativity can be enhanced by first using divergent thinking to generate and expand ideas, and then using convergent thinking to synthesize ideas and select among alternatives.

An entire consulting industry has grown to "facilitate" group decisions using techniques originally designed to circumvent one or more of the pitfalls discussed so far. The consulting organization's preferred technique is typically marketed as a magic bullet, capable of enhancing any group process. It is usually offered as a fixed formula whose efficacy depends on precise adherence to sequential steps and specific rules (with which the consulting organization is fully familiar). Alas, no single technique or process is appropriate to all groups or decision situations. However, specialized techniques can prove useful if the manager applies each to circumvent the pitfall it is designed to circumvent. In fact, the methods can often be tailored to specific situations through combination or modification. This point is illustrated in the following description of seven techniques for group decision making and problem solving: brainstorming, the nominal group technique, synectics, ideawriting, the Crawford slip method, dialectical decision making, and the Delphi technique.

Brainstorming

The technique of **brainstorming** was originally developed by the advertising executive Alex Osborn (1948) as a means to elevate the flow of ideas during meetings. It has since enjoyed substantial popularity as a method for assembling a volume of ideas about management problems that can be readily expressed as simple, discussable questions. For example, during the planning phases of Playmakers, brainstorming was used to develop ideas in response to the question, "What activities could a sports camp offer as selling features to parents?" Brainstorming has also been used to collect ideas for questions like, "How can we promote more attendance for this event?" and "How can we reduce our dropout rate?"

The key principle of brainstorming is to separate the phase of divergent thinking from the phase of convergent thinking. The process begins with *idea generation* (i.e., divergent thinking), during which all judgment and criticism (i.e., convergent thinking) are disallowed. There are four rules during the idea generation phase:

1. Every idea is welcomed, no matter how wild or silly.
2. No criticism or judgment of any kind is permitted.

3. Produce as many ideas as possible; the goal is quantity, not quality.
4. Combine ideas or piggyback onto an idea wherever possible.

During a brainstorming session, bursts of ideas are often followed by quiet periods. When everyone becomes quiet, it is sometimes assumed that the group has listed its full complement of possibilities, and the idea generation phase is called to an end. However, quiet periods can precede a new flurry of ideas. For this reason, it is usually better to set time boundaries in advance, rather than simply to stop when there seems to be a lull.

The idea generation phase requires a leader who will enforce the rules and encourage participation. It also requires a recorder to keep track of the ideas. Neither the leader nor the recorder should participate in idea generation. However, the leader should be prepared to offer an idea to prompt further thinking if there is a substantial lull during the meeting. For the group to combine ideas, it is preferable to have the recorder write each idea where it can be seen, such as on a blackboard or flip chart.

Once the idea generation phase is completed, the group begins *idea evaluation.* Now judgment and critical appraisal are permitted. Ideas can be eliminated, modified, or further combined.

Group members sometimes become impatient with the rigid separation of divergent thinking from convergent thinking. However, research shows that the technique is effective. In particular, groups using brainstorming produce more ideas and more high-quality ideas than do individuals or groups that generate and evaluate ideas simultaneously (Nijstad et al., 1999; Stein, 1975).

Nominal group technique

The **nominal group technique** (Delbecq et al., 1975) provides a useful variation on brainstorming. It is particularly useful if the time available to meet is too short for a full brainstorming session. Since it begins the group's activities with a period of individual work, it can also reduce the impact of social loafing, status influence, and group polarization. For these reasons, the technique is often used as a lead-in to other decision methods, such as brainstorming (cf. Madsen and Finger, 1978).

As with brainstorming, the nominal group technique begins with a *stimulus question.* Like brainstorming, it also requires a leader and a recorder.

There are typically four steps for generating a group decision:

1. Each group member silently writes as many responses to the stimulus question as possible. This period of written response could be at the beginning of the meeting, or group members could be required to come to the meeting with written responses already prepared. It is expected that group members will not have discussed their individual ideas in advance.
2. Each member contributes one idea. The idea is recorded onto a blackboard or flip chart. There is no discussion of ideas. Rather, the leader calls on each member in turn until all ideas are recorded or until the group determines that a sufficient number of ideas have been collected.
3. The group discusses each idea on the list. Each idea is discussed separately. Discussion of each idea continues until members are clear about its meaning.
4. The group ranks the ideas and discusses its rankings. A final choice may be made by majority vote.

Research confirms that in most circumstances the nominal group technique is superior to informal methods of group problem solving (Fox, 1987; Hornsby et al., 1994). It generates a larger number of high-quality ideas and a more even distribution of contributions from members. It is also rated favorably by most participants.

Synectics

There is substantial evidence that people fail to adequately explore the problem domain when problem solving (Bereiter and Scardamalia, 1985; Hollenbeck et al., 1998). This impediment can be exacerbated in group situations when there is inadequate development of alternative problem representations. **Synectics** (Gordon, 1961) is intended to stimulate original group thinking by formalizing the development of analogies.

The technique requires a diverse group of specialists to share information via metaphor and analogy. Once the group is familiar with the problem to be solved, the group leader selects from one of the following four analogy types: personal, direct, symbolic, and fantasy. To understand how each of these works, consider the problem of crowd control at a motorcycle rally (cf. Veno and Veno, 1996). Using a personal analogy, group members might imagine themselves as spectators at the rally. Using a direct analogy they would explore situations where a comparable function is accomplished, such as a cattle drive. To use a symbolic analogy, the group might compare the role of police officer with that of a parent. This analogy would direct the group's attention to such factors as anticipating the needs of spectators and developing a trusting relationship with them. Finally, when using fantasy, anything goes, even magic or science fiction. For example, the group might imagine personal antigravity machines that would allow each spectator to float above the rally.

As each new analogy is introduced, it is the leader's job to steer participants into a detailed analysis. The purpose is to use the analogies to direct participants' minds away from traditional solutions to new insights. To facilitate the process, the group might go beyond discussion to **role plays** or to collecting information and the analogy. For example in the case of the motorcycle rally, a synectics group might role-play the parts of spectator and rally official, or the group might decide to learn more about how cattle are herded.

There is scant experimental evidence for the effectiveness of synectics, although the technique receives substantial favorable comment from users in industry (Stein, 1975). One problem may be that users have trouble applying analogies effectively (cf. Reed et al., 1985; Catrambone and Holyoak, 1987). As the group works with an analogy, it may be necessary for members to seek as many features as possible that are analogous to the group's problem (Holyoak and Koh, 1987). The specification of analogical similarity may further the group's insight.

Combining synectics with other methods. Synectics is intended to help groups extend their thinking by expanding the range of analogies from which they work. This can make it a useful tool in brainstorming or nominal group sessions. For example, it can generate new creative flurries during brainstorming by directing thinking onto new avenues. Similarly, synectics can be combined with the nominal group technique by requiring members to silently prepare a list of analogies for subsequent

discussion and exploration. During the initial meetings to design Playmakers, the four managers made explicit use of analogous situations (e.g., youth tour groups) to facilitate their brainstorming about new sport service opportunities. In some instances the analogous situations were researched in advance of the meeting. Elements of synectics, brainstorming, and the nominal group technique were modified and combined to meet the needs of the planning session.

This example illustrates the key point well—the technique itself is less important than the **decision pitfalls** its methods allow the group to circumvent. The effective manager first determines which pitfalls need to be circumvented, and then uses, modifies, or combines techniques as prescribed by the anticipated pitfall.

Ideawriting

Ideawriting (Thissen et al., 1980) reduces social loafing, status influence, and group polarization by extending independent work into the phase of idea analysis and evaluation. The procedures for ideawriting are relatively simple. Each participant responds to the stimulus question by writing his or her ideas on a pad. The pad is then placed in the middle of the group. Each person takes each other person's pad and writes a response, analysis, evaluation, and/or extension. The original writer then reads the responses. Finally ideas and principles are discussed and summarized.

Although ideawriting does not promote the breadth of creativity fostered by brainstorming or synectics, it enjoys the unique advantage that it can be used with very large groups. Moore (1987) describes an application of ideawriting with 700 participants at an international conference. The participants were divided into small groups of between four and five persons each. Each group worked to identify community needs, such as the need for new sports facilities. Once a list of ideas had been generated, and everyone in the group responded, the ideas were discussed and the five most promising were selected. Each group then reported its conclusion to the full assembly.

When several small groups present their conclusions, it is common for their reports to be collated and assigned to appropriate committees for further work. Although anecdotal reports (Moore, 1987; Thissen et al., 1980) suggest this procedure to be useful during planning and policy making, it has not been subjected to empirical evaluation.

Crawford slip method

There are times when ideas collected during the divergent thinking phase are not winnowed. For example, when developing a training manual or listing the full range of an organization's needs, the goal may be to collate as many ideas as possible (cf. Ballard and Trent, 1989). In this instance, the concern is to optimize divergent thinking, but convergent work is primarily a matter of categorization and organizing, rather than of evaluation and selecting.

The **Crawford slip method** has proven to be useful for such tasks. Crawford (1983) describes it this way: "Assemble the relevant people; define the target subjects; get everyone to write their ideas—one at a time, in a single sentence, on individual slips of paper; collect and classify all slips; edit the results into final form." Since the method is based entirely on written input, it can be used with groups of any size. Every person who has relevant information or experience should be included. The final collation of results can be performed separately by one or more editors.

Although the Crawford slip method has not been subjected to empirical scrutiny, Ballard and Trent (1989) cite apparently successful applications to the preparation of training manuals, design of curricula, diagnosis of an organization's needs, improvement of services, and planning a new product. In sport settings, these applications would seem to be particularly useful for enhancing facility operations, service delivery, or program design.

Dialectical decision making

Some decisions have major consequences for the organization. For example, the decision may result in substantial expense, or it may precipitate an irreversible choice among strategic alternatives. In such cases, the evaluation of ideas may be very important. In particular, it might be of interest to determine whether a decision is consistent. In other words, do different groups reach similar conclusions? If they do not, it can be helpful to probe the assumptions from which differences emerge. The best choice may be easier to identify after scrutinizing the assumptions on which different options are based (Byrnes, 1998).

Dialectical decision making (Mitroff and Emshoff, 1979) is a useful technique in such cases because it requires group members to engage in multiple phases of convergent thinking. This has the added advantage that it can foster the synthesis of several different options. Further, since the full group is divided into smaller subgroups, dialectical decision making can also reduce groupthink and group polarization (Macy and Neal, 1995; Schweiger et al., 1986).

The key to dialectical decision making is to develop two or more separate analyses of the decision problem. Each analysis is developed by a group working independently of other groups. At this phase, there are two possibilities: Each group can be instructed to develop its analysis in terms of what it deems the best possible alternatives. On the other hand, if it is important to examine fully a preexisting set of alternatives, each group could be assigned one alternative with the instruction to prepare an analysis that best supports it.

Once each group completes its analysis, group members are recombined to discuss the different analyses and to formulate a new analysis that builds on those of the small groups. At this phase, there are three possibilities: (1) The entire group can be convened to discuss the separate group analyses. (2) One new group can be constructed by assigning a member from each of the original groups. The new group consists of persons who did not work together during the preceding phase. (3) Several new groups can be constructed, each containing one member from each of the original groups.

If more than one new group is constructed, a further round of recombinations is possible. In this case, the process of analyzing, recombining, and reanalyzing can be continued for as many iterations as desired. Through successive recombinations and reanalyses, new insights may emerge, or an apparent consensus may develop.

Combining dialectical decision making with other techniques. Dialectical decision making focuses primarily on the analysis of alternatives. As such, it is fundamentally a tool for convergent thinking phases. In contrast, brainstorming, the nominal group technique, synectics, and the Crawford slip method focus primarily on the divergent thinking phase of group decision making. Thus each of these four methods (or a combination) could be used to generate the ideas that will subsequently be analyzed through dialectical decision making. Similarly, when ideawriting sessions have been done in a multigroup fashion, further analysis can be accomplished through group recombinations like those used in dialectical decision making. Again, key components of the various techniques can be adapted or combined as needed for a specific decision task.

Delphi

There are times when the persons required for a decision task cannot meet together. On other occasions, status differences among participating experts threaten the group's impartiality. In such instances, the **Delphi technique** (Delbecq et al., 1975) can be useful. It is an excellent tool for pooling expert judgment.

The first step of a Delphi process is to establish the **Delphi panel** of experts. Delphi panelists will work anonymously; they are not told who the other panel members are. All correspondence from them goes to a **facilitator** who is not a member of the panel. Panelists remain at their home sites and communicate by mail or electronic mail. Although any number of panelists can be included, execution becomes increasingly labor intensive as panel size grows.

Once the panel is selected, each panelist is sent the Delphi question. Relevant data may also be included. Imagine, for example, that we want to determine experts' best judgment about new directions for sport policy. We might send our panel data on recent trends in sport participation, attendance at sports events, and audience ratings for sports on television. The accompanying Delphi question might ask, "What are the keys to enhancing public interest in sport over the next decade?"

Each panelist prepares a written response. The responses are collated and sent to panelists along with any supporting material (articles, statistics, etc.) that one or more individuals want to share. (When necessary, the Delphi facilitator will remove names from material being shared to maintain panelist anonymity.) Each panelist then responds to the new material. The panelist can agree, rebut, clarify, expand, or synthesize. The process of responding, collating, and responding again continues through successive rounds (usually around five) until a group consensus or a clear majority and minority viewpoint have emerged.

Unlike the other methods discussed here, Delphi can take several weeks or months to complete. Even the process of obtaining a panel can prove time-consuming. Nevertheless, the technique continues to be widely used for planning and policy making (Linstone and Turoff, 1975; Tourism Forecasting Council, 1998).

CONCEPT CHECK

Group decision techniques can be divided into those useful in the divergent thinking stage and those useful in the convergent thinking stage. Brainstorming, the nominal group technique, synectics, and the Crawford slip method are used to avoid pitfalls during the divergent thinking phase of a group's work. On the other hand, dialectical decision making focuses primarily on the convergence of ideas. Ideawriting and the Delphi technique bring their methods to bear during divergent and convergent thinking phases. Components of several techniques can be combined as necessary to circumvent decision pitfalls.

FACILITATING GROUP DECISION MAKING AND PROBLEM SOLVING

Formal techniques for decision making do not relieve the manager from the task of facilitating the group's efforts. The adequacy of any decision depends, in part, on the adequacy of the processes by which the group reached its decision (Kleindorfer et al., 1993). Managing a group during decision making and problem solving is a key leadership skill. The requisite components are well studied and readily learned (Maier, 1963; Schwarz, 1994). Three pivotal skills are sequencing the process, assuring balanced participation, and maintaining a task-oriented climate.

Sequencing the process

Inadequate attention to the sequential elements of team building and problem deliberation is one of the most common causes of poor group performance. Although the necessary procedures and outcomes may seem self-evident to the manager, group members may not share the manager's expectations.

At the outset, the group's goals, purposes, and timetable must be clarified. Group members may arrive at a meeting with varied or fuzzy understandings of what it is the group is going to do. Communication is enhanced and misunderstandings are reduced if fundamental elements of the group's work have been agreed upon. For example, what is the problem to be solved? What choices are to be made? How much time is available for the group's efforts? How will the group's analyses and decisions be reported? To whom? Will implementation of the group's decision be delegated, or will it be the group's responsibility?

Once the group has agreed on its goals, purposes, and timetables, it must establish its methods for operation. The rules for group interaction must be specified, and a basic agenda outlined. Decision rules (e.g., voting, consensus) should be agreed on. If it is likely that the group will need to gather information during its deliberations, an appropriate procedure should be developed. If a formal decision technique (brainstorming, synectics, idea writing, etc.) is to be used, its methods and procedures should be described.

The group is now ready to begin its deliberations. Each of the decision techniques reviewed in this chapter is designed to prevent the group from plunging into choosing an option. When no formal technique is applied, the manager must make certain that the group spends sufficient time exploring members' thoughts about the problem. The group should first be directed to collect requisite information and to share ideas and opinions. Since it is useful to have a variety of proposals and viewpoints on the table, the group should be discouraged from evaluating each alternative as it is presented. Rather, the manager should encourage the group to elaborate and clarify each idea, and to find potential syntheses.

Figure 6–2 illustrates an ideal sequence of tasks when making a group decision. As the discussion progresses, more attention can be paid to evaluating and classifying the various proposals that have been formulated. At this stage, it may be useful to summarize the suggestions and concerns that have been forthcoming and to ask whether any additional matters require discussion. As the evaluation of ideas progresses, the manager can test group consensus by summarizing key points and asking whether these adequately reflect members' appraisal. The process is concluded when a consensus or a clear majority or minority viewpoint emerges.

Assuring balanced participation

The group's work can be compromised by social loafing or status influence. The group leader's task is to encourage the contribution and analysis of each member's best thinking. It is the leader's job to make certain that each member remains engaged and that each member's contribution receives adequate attention. To achieve those ends, it is useful to monitor who participates, how often, and with what impact. In this way, the leader seeks to identify persons whose ideas need to be queried or whose contributions require further examination. Four techniques are particularly useful for fostering balanced participation: *reinforcing, soliciting, prompting,* and *probing.*

The way in which points are received can affect members' subsequent willingness to contribute. Members are more willing to contribute when initial contributions have been welcomed. Body language (e.g., nodding, smiling) and verbal acknowledgment (e.g., "interesting point" or "that's something we should explore") encourage further participation. Writing the point on a blackboard or flip chart can also be reinforcing.

When members have not contributed for some time, the leader can reinvolve them by soliciting a contribution. The solicitations might be as simple as, "Fred, what do you think?" Or it might be useful

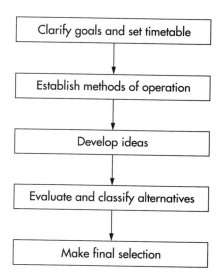

FIGURE 6–2   An ideal task sequence for group decision making.

to solicit a member's contribution in terms of the role he or she plays in the group. For example, the leader might ask, "Sally, how would that idea affect facility operations?"

If one or two members are dominating the discussion, the leader can prompt other views by saying something like, "So far we've spent a lot of time on Chris and Jim's suggestion, let's hear some other possibilities." If a member is preempting other discussion, the leader can point that fact out, "Bill, you've made your point, now we'd like to hear some other views."

Probing can be useful when the group has ignored an idea or has neglected to explore one. If the group seems to be ignoring a contribution, the leader can say something like, "Joe's suggestion seems useful; let's explore it a bit more." If the group has failed to explore a previous idea, the leader can ask, "Jane, can you say a little more about that point you made a few minutes ago?" Sometimes a contribution is ignored because members failed to fully understand it. If that seems to be the case, the leader can ask, "Lee, could you elaborate more on that point?"

Maintaining a task-oriented climate

If group members have a stake in the outcome of the group's deliberations, the discussion can become emotional. High emotions can distract the group from a focus on its task. In other instances, the group may fail to address relevant hot topics to avoid conflict. In so doing, crucial components of the decision may be neglected. Sometimes a lack of conflict is more detrimental to the group's function than the conflict would be (Tjosvold, 1993; Dooley and Fryxell, 1999). The confrontation of divergent views can clarify requisite needs for information and foster an appreciation of alternative viewpoints.

It is useful for the group leader to state at the outset that diverse views will be important for the group's work. Later, if emotions begin to run high, tension can sometimes be diffused by orienting group members to their common goal. The leader can reaffirm the value of fully exploring diverse views. It may even be appropriate to compliment the group on its frank and open discussions and to restate the group's common goal. If the emotional tone is still high, it may be useful to put the controversial issue aside temporarily and to refocus the group's attention on other aspects of the problem until emotions have cooled.

On some occasions, it may be important to face emotions directly. If a dispute between members is taken personally, the residual resentment can interfere with subsequent deliberations. In such instances, it may be necessary to put the decision task aside, openly discuss the hurt feelings, and reestablish consensus on group goals and processes.

Social norms in most management contexts disallow expressions of anger. This in turn can cause the group to avoid potentially controversial elements of a decision. When group deliberations seem to be skirting a delicate issue, an effective instruction might be, "It would seem useful to expand our discussion to include [the delicate issue]." By using leadership authority to steer the group onto a touchy subject, the leader reduces group members' sense of risk. For one thing, members need not fear recrimination for having raised the matter (since they did not). For another, controversial discussion was mandated by the group leader, who thus bears primary responsibility. Peer relations seem less threatened than if the issue had been forced by a group member.

CONCEPT CHECK

Managing group decision making and problem solving is a key leadership skill. A common source of poor group performance is inadequate sequencing of the decision process. Before beginning deliberations, the group should agree on its goals, purposes, timetables, and methods of operation. As the group works, the manager should ensure balanced participation by using such techniques as reinforcing, soliciting, prompting, and probing. Maintaining a task-oriented climate is vital, especially if the discussion has become emotional. The leader is responsible for seeing that controversial discussion and even conflict, when necessary, are not avoided.

SUPPORTING GROUP DECISION MAKING AND PROBLEM SOLVING

A variety of computer-based tools is available to aid group decision making and problem solving. These include *databases* to provide requisite information (Browne, 1993), procedures that break the task into *subproblems* (MacGregor and Lichtenstein, 1991), and *algorithms* (mathematical procedures) to help decision makers develop *quantitative models* of the *decision domain* (Watson and Buede, 1987). Current technologies allow **decision support systems** to be used by the group at the decision site and throughout the group's deliberations (Reagan-Cirincione, 1994; Nunamaker et al., 1991). In the optimal case, each group member has a terminal, and each member's input can be shared visually by projecting it onto a screen that is visible to the entire group. Sports Organizations are making increasing use of decision support technologies. Examples include databases of information about players' performances and contracts (Waggoner, 1989) and formal procedures for rating potential draft picks (Whittingham 1992, chapter 2).

Since it is expected that applications of decision support systems in sport settings will expand significantly in the next few years, it is helpful to consider some of the reasons that decision support is beneficial. A key value of decision support is that it can provide an empirical check on decision makers' judgments and assumptions. A substantial body of work shows that even experts make consistent (often predictable) errors (Byrnes, 1998). Poor judgments are often persistent because decision makers are typically overconfident about their judgments (Sniezek and Buckley, 1993).

The case of the "hot hand" in basketball provides an instructive illustration. After a player has executed a series of successful shots in close succession, coaches and administrators often believe that the player is on a hot streak. However, empirical studies of the phenomenon show it to be a statistical illusion (Gilovich et al., 1985). The probability of success in the player's next shot is in no way predicted by the streak of baskets preceding that shot. Nevertheless, the illusion of the hot hand has continued to condition marketplace estimates of a player's value (Camerer, 1989)—an example of decision error precipitated by fallacious judgment. Decision support systems can help reduce or eliminate biases like these by providing critical baseline data and necessary probability estimates (Kahneman and Tversky, 1982).

Another way that decision support systems can support the group's efforts is to help structure the task. Decision errors are diminished when decision makers are helped to elaborate their representation of the problem (Jungermann, 1980; Philips, 1983).

Facilitation of task sequencing can be particularly useful. Kleindorfer et al. (1993) describe the following five-step procedure: First, the system prompts the group to develop a single-sentence summary of its task. Second, the system displays and stores ideas as the group brainstorms. Third, the system streamlines the classification of the ideas. Fourth, the system provides algorithms to help the group rank or rate the ideas. Fifth, the system allows the group to assign tasks for implementing the decision.

A related form of structuring is to elicit from the group the attributes that members agree are important for judging the decision outcome. For example, in choosing a stadium site, city officials might be concerned about such factors as the impact on the local cost of land, local business, local residents, and local ecology, the adequacy of roads, and the accessibility by public transportation. Once the attributes relevant to decision makers are identified, the relative importance decision makers assign to each can be measured. For example, in the case of stadium siting, city officials might rate cost of land much more highly than they rate accessibility by public transportation. Thus cost of land would receive a proportionately higher weighting. After a weight is determined for each attribute, choices are assessed by identifying their attributes and applying the appropriate weights (Goodwin and Wright, 1998). These procedures have been shown to be effective (Reagan-Cirincione, 1994; Politser, 1991) and favorably received by users (John et al., 1983).

The limitations of short-term memory make it difficult for decision makers to absorb and use large quantities of new information (Sanford, 1985, chapter 5). One useful remedy is to simplify the decision problem by having a model or formula for rating alternatives. For example, eleven NFL teams use the BLESTO ratings of players to help them choose the players they will draft. The BLESTO ratings combine such elements as **player height, weight, strength, intelligence, injuries, 40-yard dash speed, position skills, lateral movement, aggression,** and **quickness** into an overall measure of player potential (Whittingham, 1992). Although team management does not rely solely on the BLESTO ratings, the ratings simplify each team's decision making by summarizing an otherwise unwieldy array of information. Research suggests that decisions based on models of this kind are, on average, higher-quality and less prone to error than are decisions based solely on impressions or qualitative judgments (Dawes, 1979).

CONCEPT CHECK

Computer-based group decision support systems provide decision makers with a check on judgments and assumptions. Group decision support systems can also help the group to structure its problem and sequence its deliberations. One particularly useful method of structuring the problem is to identify the relevant attributes of the decision and then rate their relative importance to the decision. Models that aggregate large quantities of information into overall ratings provide other useful tools for simplifying the group's decision task.

CRITICAL THINKING EXERCISES

1. You are an athletics director at a large university. In order to comply with Title IX requirements, you will have to drop at least one men's sport. In deciding which sport to drop, whom would you include in the decision process?
2. You are the marketing manager of a professional baseball team that has moved to a new city. In order to develop the marketing plan to promote your team, you have brought your staff together for a planning session. What decision technique or sequence of techniques would you use?

SUMMARY

1. In sport management, groups are involved in planning, generating ideas, problem solving, decision making, agenda setting, policy making, and governance.
2. When compared with individual problem solvers, groups can generate more ideas, locate more information, identify more perspectives, and formulate a decision that seems fairer.
3. When deciding whether to use a group for decision making, the manager should consider requisite decision quality, the amount of time available to make the decision, and whether implementation of the decision will require subordinates to have helped formulate the decision.
4. Persons who have requisite information or who must cooperate in decision implementation should be included on the decision team.
5. Groupthink and group polarization can be minimized by including outside experts, incorporating critical evaluators, or assigning someone the role of devil's advocate.
6. The group's efforts can be compromised by social loafing, status influence, limited creative flexibility, and plunging in.
7. Brainstorming is a useful technique for collecting a wide array of ideas. Brainstorming separates the phase of divergent thinking from the phase of convergent thinking. During the divergent thinking phase, members are encouraged to contribute as many ideas as they can.
8. The nominal group technique also collects a wide array of ideas by separating the phase of divergent thinking from the phase of convergent thinking. Group members are required to begin by silently writing their ideas. The ideas are then discussed and evaluated.
9. Synectics uses analogies to enhance the group's creativity.
10. Ideawriting requires group members to write their idea, to read each other's ideas, and to respond in writing. It can be used with small or large groups.
11. The Crawford slip method collects ideas by having participants write each idea on a single piece of paper. The ideas are then categorized and collated. The technique is particularly useful for developing training manuals, designing new services, or diagnosing an organization's needs.
12. Dialectical decision making breaks the group into two or more smaller groups. The analysis and decision of each smaller group is then used as input to formulate a final decision.
13. The Delphi technique obtains an estimate of expert consensus. Members of the Delphi panel work anonymously through several iterations of inquiry.
14. The various decision techniques can be modified or combined as the situation warrants.
15. The three pivotal skills for facilitating the group's work are sequencing the process, ensuring balanced participation, and maintaining a task-oriented climate.

16. Appropriate decision sequencing consists of the following: (a) establishing goals, purposes, and timetables; (b) presenting, elaborating, and clarifying ideas; and (c) classifying, summarizing, and evaluating.

17. Methods for ensuring balanced participation include reinforcing, soliciting, prompting, and probing.

18. To maintain a task-oriented climate, the group leader must see to it that the group does not skirt around important yet sensitive issues. When emotions run high, the leader must help the group to refocus on its common objectives.

19. Decision support systems can help the group by helping to sequence the task, by eliciting key decision attributes and values, by providing baseline data and probability estimations, and by formulating quantitative models for rating alternatives.

CASE STUDY

Court cases have always fascinated the public. The film Twelve Angry Men *takes one beyond the flash of the courtroom and is a classic example of the decision-making process.*

After viewing the film, consider the following:

1. What pitfalls were portrayed, and how did the group work together to circumvent them?

2. How might technical decision support have aided the group's work?

3. What facilitation techniques would have been useful had the jury foreman known how to use them? When?

4. What other techniques might have improved this group's process?

REVIEW QUESTIONS AND ISSUES

1. What are the relative pros and cons of group versus individual decision making and problem solving?

2. What criteria should be used to evaluate who should be included in the group?

3. List and describe six pitfalls to be wary of during group decision making and problem solving.

4. Explain the difference between divergent thinking and convergent thinking. Why is it useful for the former to precede the latter?

5. Briefly describe an appropriate task sequence for group decision making and problem solving.

6. Define the four techniques for ensuring balanced participation.

7. How should conflict be managed during group decision making and problem solving?

8. Give an example of a decision problem faced by sport managers that would benefit from technical decision support. What kinds of support would be most useful?

9. Write a stimulus question about a sport management problem. What kind of organization might seek to obtain an answer to such a question? If you were putting a group together to answer the question for such an organization, whom would you include? Why? What decision techniques would you apply? How? Why?

SOLUTIONS TO CRITICAL THINKING EXERCISES

1. There are two key objectives in this task. First, you want to make certain that you fully understand the pros and the cons of each possible choice. Second, you want to make certain that each group that will have to help to implement the fallout from this decision will be involved in helping to make the decision (so that they will feel more ownership of the decision). Thus, at a minimum, you would want to have your marketing director, sports information director, associate athletic directors, and compliance officer. You would also want to have athlete and coach representatives from each of the men's sports that is being considered for elimination. You would also want a representative from the alumni association, from the local community, and from relevant women's organizations.

2. The key techniques in this instance are those that foster divergent thinking. Therefore, brainstorming will probably be the key technique. It might be useful to use the nominal group technique as a means to minimize social loafing. If that were done, staff members would be asked to arrive at the meeting having done some initial work, or time would be allotted before the brainstorming begins for individuals to work independently. If the two

techniques were combined, the sequence would be: nominal group technique followed by brainstorming. If the manager was concerned about the possible limitations that could be imposed by groupthink, then dialectical decision making might be a reasonable alternative to nominal group technique and brainstorming.

REFERENCES

Ballard, J. A., and Trent, D. M. (1989). Idea generation and productivity: The promise of CSM. *Public Productivity Review, 12*, 373–86.

Bereiter, C., and Scardamalia, M. (1985). Cognitive coping strategies and the problem of inert knowledge. In S. S. Chipman, J. W. Segal, and R. Glazer (eds.), *Thinking and learning skills: Current research and open questions* (Vol. 2, pp. 65–80). Hillsdale, NJ: Lawrence Erlbaum Associates.

Browne, M. (1993). *Organizational decision making and information.* Norwood, NJ: Ablex.

Byrnes, J. P. (1998). *The nature and development of decision making.* Mahwah, NJ: Lawrence Erlbaum Associates.

Camerer, C. F. (1989). Does the basketball market believe in the "hot hand?" *American Economic Review, 79*, 1257–60.

Cannon-Bowers, J. A., Salas, E., and Converse, S. (1993). Shared mental models in expert team decision making. In N. J. Castellan, Jr. (ed.), *Individual and group decision making: Current issues* (pp. 221–46). Hillsdale, NJ: Lawrence Erlbaum Associates.

Carroll, J. S., Sterman, J., and Marcus, A. A. (1998). Playing the maintenance game: How mental models drive organizational decisions. In J. J. Halpern and R. N. Stern (eds.), *Debating rationality: Nonrational aspects of organizational decision making* (pp. 99–121). Ithaca, NY: Cornell University Press.

Catrambone, R., and Holyoak, K. J. (1987). Transfer of training as a function of procedural variety of training examples. In *Proceedings of the Ninth Annual Conference* (pp. 36–49). Hillsdale, NJ: Cognitive Science Society.

Chalip, L. (1995). Policy analysis in sport management. *Journal of Sport Management, 9*, 1–13.

Chalip, L. (1996). Critical policy analysis: The illustrative case of New Zealand sport policy development. *Journal of Sport Management, 10*, 310–24.

Choi, J. N., and Kim, M. U. (1999). The organizational application of groupthink and its limitations in organizations. *Journal of Applied Psychology, 84*, 297–306.

Collins, A., and Gentner, D. (1987). How people construct mental models. In D. Holland and B. N. Quinn (eds.), *Cultural models in language and thought* (pp. 243–65). New York: Cambridge University Press.

Crawford, C. C. (1983). How you can gather and organise ideas quickly. *Chemical Engineering,* July 15, 87–90.

Davis, J. H. (1992). Some compelling intuitions about group consensus decisions, theoretical and empirical research,

and interpersonal aggregation phenomena: Selected examples, 1950–1990. *Organizational Behavior and Human Decision Processes, 52*, 3–38.

Dawes, R. M. (1979). The robust beauty of improper linear models in decision making. *American Psychologist, 34*, 571–82.

Delbecq, A. L., Van de Ven, A. H., and Gustafson, D. H. (1975). *Group techniques for program planning: A guide to nominal group and Delphi processes.* Glenview, IL: Scott-Foresman.

Dooley, R. S., and Fryxell, G. E. (1999). Attaining decision quality and commitment from dissent: The moderating effects of loyalty and competence in strategic decision-making teams. *Academy of Management Journal, 42*, 389–402.

Fox, W. M. (1987). *Effective group problem solving.* San Francisco: Jossey-Bass.

Gick, M. L., and Holyoak, K. J. (1980). Analogical problem solving. *Cognitive Psychology, 12*, 306–55.

Gick, M. L., and Holyoak, K. J. (1983). Schema induction and analogical transfer. *Cognitive Psychology, 15*, 1–38.

Gilovich, T., Vallone, R., and Tversky, A. (1985). The hot hand in basketball: On the misperception of random sequences. *Cognitive Psychology, 17*, 295–314.

Goodwin, P., and Wright, G. (1998). *Decision analysis for management judgment.* 2d ed. Chichester, UK: John Wiley & Sons.

Gordon, W. J. J. (1961). *Synectics.* New York: Collier.

Hardin, R. (1982). *Collective action.* Baltimore: Johns Hopkins University Press.

Hollenbeck, J. R., Ilgen, D. R., LePine, J. A., and Hedlund, J. (1998). Extending the multilevel theory of team decision making: Effects of feedback and experience in hierarchical teams. *Academy of Management Journal, 41*, 269–82.

Hollander, E. P. (1964). *Leaders, groups and influence.* New York: Oxford University Press.

Holyoak, K. J., and Koh, K. (1987). Surface and structural similarity in analogical transfer. *Memory and Cognition, 15*, 332–40.

Hornsby, J. S., Smith, B. N., and Gupta, J. N. D. (1994). The impact of decision-making methodology on job evaluation outcomes: A look at three consensus approaches. *Group & Organization Management, 19*, 112–28.

Janis, I. L. (1982). *Groupthink.* 2d ed. Boston: Houghton Mifflin.

Janis, I. L., and Mann, L. (1977). *Decision making: A psychological analysis of conflict, choice, and commitment.* New York: Free Press.

John, R. S., von Winterfeldt, D., and Edwards, W. (1983). The quality and user acceptance of multiattribute utility analysis performed by computer and analyst. In P. Humphreys, O. Svenson, and A. Vari (eds.), *Analysing and aiding decision processes* (pp. 301–19). Amsterdam: North Holland.

Johnson-Laird, P. (1983). *Mental models.* Cambridge, MA: Harvard University Press.

Jungerman, H. (1980). Speculations about decision-theoretic aids for personal decision making. *Acta Psychologica, 45*, 7–34.

Kahneman, D., and Tversky, A. (1982). Intuitive prediction: Biases and corrective procedures. In D. Kahneman, P. Slovic, and A. Tversky (eds.), *Judgement under uncertainty: Heuristics and biases* (pp. 414–21). New York: Cambridge University Press.

Kerr, N. L., MacCoun, R. J., and Kramer, G. P. (1996). Bias in judgment: Comparing individuals and groups. *Psychological Review, 103,* 687–719.

Kleindorfer, P. R., Kunreuther, H. C., and Schoemaker, P. J. H. (1993). *Decision sciences: An integrative perspective.* New York: Cambridge University Press.

Koopman, P., and Pool, J. (1991). Organizational decision making: Models, contingencies, and strategies. In J. Rasmussen, B. Brehmner, and J. Leplat (eds.), *Distributed decision making: Cognitive models for cooperative work* (pp. 19–46). New York: Wiley.

Lamm, H. (1988). A review of our research on group polarization: Eleven experiments on the effects of group discussion on risk acceptance, probability estimation, and negotiation positions. *Psychological Reports, 62,* 807–13.

Lamm, H., and Myers, D. G. (1978). Group-induced polarization of attitudes and behaviour. In L. Berkowitz (ed.), *Advances in experimental social psychology* (vol. 11, pp. 145–95). San Diego: Academic Press.

Linstone, H. A., and Turoff, M. (eds.) (1975). *The Delphi method: Techniques and applications.* Reading, MA: Addison-Wesley.

Macy, G., and Neal, J. C. (1995). The impact of conflict-generating techniques on student reactions and decision quality. *Business Communication Quarterly, 58,* 39–45.

Madsen, D. B., and Finger, J. R. (1978). Comparison of written feedback procedure, group brainstorming, and individual brainstorming. *Journal of Applied Psychology, 63,* 120–23.

MacGregor, D. G., and Lichtenstein, S. (1991). Problem structuring aids for quantitative estimation. *Journal of Behavioral Decision Making, 4,* 101–16.

Maier, N. R. F. (1963). *Problem solving discussions and conferences: Leadership methods and skills.* New York: McGraw-Hill.

Mitroff, I. L., and Emshoff, J. R. (1979). On strategic assumption making: A dialectical approach to policy and planning. *Academy of Management Review, 4,* 1–12.

Moore, C. M. (1987). *Group techniques for idea building.* Newbury Park, CA: Sage.

Mulcahy, K. V. (1995). Rethinking groupthink: Walt Rostow and the national security advisory process in the Johnson administration. *Presidential Studies Quarterly, 25,* 237–50.

Neck, C. P., and Moorhead, G. (1995). Groupthink remodeled: The importance of leadership, time pressure, and methodical decision-making procedures. *Human Relations, 48,* 537–57.

Nijstad, B. A., Stroebe, W., and Lodewijkz, H. F. M. (1999). Persistence of brainstorming groups: How do people know when to stop? *Journal of Experimental Social Psychology, 35,* 165–66.

Nunamaker, J. F., Jr., Dennis, A. R., Valacich, J. S., and Vogel, D. R. (1991). Information technology for negotiating groups: Generating options for mutual gain. *Management Science, 37,* (10), 1325–46.

Osborn, A. (1948). *Your creative power.* New York: Charles Scribner's Sons.

Philips, L. D. (1983). A theoretical perspective on heuristics and biases in probabilistic thinking. In P. Humphreys, O. Svenson, and A. Vari (eds.), *Analysing and aiding decision processes* (pp. 525–43). Amsterdam: North Holland.

Politser, P. E. (1991). Do medical decision analyses' largest gains grow from the smallest trees. *Journal of Behavioral Decision Making, 4,* 121–38.

Putnam, L. L. (1986). Conflict in group decision-making. In R. Y. Hirokawa and M. S. Poole (eds.), *Communication and group decision-making* (pp. 175–96). Newbury Park, CA: Sage.

Reagan-Cirincione, P. (1994). Improving the accuracy of group judgment: A process intervention combining group facilitation, social judgment analysis, and information technology. *Organizational Behavior and Human Decision Processes, 58,* 246–70.

Reed, S. K., Dempster, A., and Ettinger, M. (1985). Usefulness of analogous solutions for solving algebra word problems. *Journal of Experimental Psychology: Learning, Memory and Cognition, 11,* 106–25.

Sanford, A. J. (1985). *Cognition and cognitive psychology.* New York: Basic Books.

Schafer, M., and Crichlow, S. (1996). Antecedents of groupthink: A quantitative study. *Journal of Conflict Resolution, 40,* 415–34.

Scheidel, T. M., and Crowell, L. (1979). *Discussing and deciding.* New York: Macmillan.

Schwarz, R. M. (1994). *The skilled facilitator: practical wisdom for developing effective groups.* San Francisco: Jossey-Bass.

Schweiger, D. M., Sandberg, W. R., and Ragan, J. W. (1986). Group approaches for improving strategic decision making: A comparative analysis of dialectical inquiry, devil's advocacy, and consensus. *Academy of Management Journal, 29,* 51–71.

Sniezek, J. A., and Buckley, T. (1993). Becoming more or less uncertain. In N. J. Castellan, Jr. (ed.), *Individual and group decision making: Current issues* (pp. 87–108). Hillsdale, NJ: Lawrence Erlbaum Associates.

Stein, M. I. (1975). *Stimulating creatively.* Vol. 2. New York: Academic Press.

Thissen, W. A. H., Sage, A. P., and Warfield, J. N. (1980). *A user's guide to public systems methodology.* Charlottesville, VA: School of Engineering and Applied Science.

Tjosvold, D. (1993). *Learning to manage conflict.* New York: Lexington Books.

Tourism Forecasting Council (1998). *The Olympic effect: A report on the potential tourism impacts of the Sydney 2000 Games.* Canberra, Australia: Tourism Forecasting Council.

Veno, A., and Veno, E. (1996). Managing public order at the Australian Motorcycle Grand Prix. In D. Thomas and A. Veno (eds.), *Community psychology and social change: Australian and New Zealand perspectives* (pp. 58–80). Palmerston North, New Zealand: Dunmore Press.

Vroom, V., and Yetton, P. (1973). *Leadership and decision making.* Pittsburgh: University of Pittsburgh Press.

Waggoner, G. (1989). It's a whole new ballgame! PCs and baseball. *PC Computing, 2* (6), 61–73.

Watson, S. R., and Buede, D. M. (1987). *Decision synthesis: The principles and practice of decision analysis.* New York: Cambridge University Press.

Whittingham, R. (1992). *The meat market: The inside story of the NFL draft.* New York: Macmillan.

WEBSITES

www.Olympic.org/IOC/e/facts/cities/candidate_city_intro_e.html
This site provides information about future host cities of the Olympic Games. It also provides detailed information about the processes and information required to bid to host an Olympic Games. It may be useful to consider the decisions that must be made in order to complete a bid. It may then be of interest to identify the stakeholders that would be implicated in each decision, and consider the decision techniques that might be applied to formulate each decision.

www.usbr.gov/Decision-Process/toolbox/pareitdo.htm
This site describes how to apply a decision process that uses polling and Pareto charts to reach a decision. It may be of some interest to consider the kinds of sport management problems to which this technique might be applied. It may also be useful to consider the pros and cons of this technique versus those discussed in this chapter.

CHAPTER 7

Human Resource Management in Sport

Frank Linnehan

In this chapter, you will become familiar with the following terms:

Strategic human resource management	Succession planning	External competitiveness
Human resource planning	Validity	Internal consistency
Core competencies	Content-related evidence	Broadbanding
Recruitment	Criterion-related evidence	Human resource development
Selection	Reliability	Training
Job posting system	Downsizing	Development
	Compensation	

Although what has been written about human resources' application to sport management is limited, the two disciplines have much in common. Human resource management (HRM) is the study of systems and activities in organizations that influence employee behavior. The human resources function in organizations can be thought of as a strategic, integrated collection of employee-centered activities and processes whose objective is to help the organization meet its short- and long-term goals. Typically, the human resource function includes such activities as staffing (recruiting and selecting personnel), rewards (i.e., compensation), and human resource development (HRD) (e.g., training and development, career development).

These activities are particularly relevant to sport and sport management. Administratively, coaches and their staffs are recruited and selected at every level, from high schools to the professional ranks. Not only must sport organizations be able to attract

quality candidates and select the right person for the job, but the owners of the teams must know how to adequately reward their staff as well. From a team perspective, recruiting, selection, and personnel development are critical to the success of amateur and professional franchises, as well as the athletic departments at colleges and universities. These activities are also essential to the performance of companies in the health and recreational industries who must staff and manage their facilities.

This chapter will first present a strategic view of human resources. It will then discuss recent developments and the applicability of HR activities to sport management in three areas: staffing, compensation, and human resource development.

STRATEGIC HUMAN RESOURCES

In the past, human resources was considered to be a loose collection of employee-related activities whose purpose was to maintain or enhance the satisfaction of the company's employees. Often, personnel departments were the repositories of soon-to-be retired managers who had lost their value to the organization. Fortunately, this perspective of HR is no longer relevant today and has been replaced with the concept of **strategic human resources management.** Strategic human resources management takes a long-term view of the organization and its HR practices, recognizes that external conditions, such as competition and the labor market, will affect the firm, and tries to integrate HR activities with the firm's overall business strategy (Anthony et al., 1998).

HR professionals and researchers have advanced the notion that human resources can and must add value to an organization by becoming a strategic partner to management (Barney and Wright, 1998). As strategic partners, HR managers are not only involved in the development and execution of a firm's strategic plan, but also create an HR strategy that will help the organization meet its goals. This strategy is often developed through the process of **human resource planning,** which is a formal or informal process that forecasts the human resource needs of an organization and develops strategies to meet these needs. One objective of the planning process is to identify gaps between the current capabilities of the company and those needed to achieve the firm's objectives (Lam & Schaubroeck, 1998). These gaps are then used in the planning process to develop action plans to meet the firm's goals. This process helps a firm to build a competitive advantage in the marketplace through its human resources.

Why has the perspective of HR changed? To a great degree, it has been in response to increased competition in the marketplace. Much like an owner of a local sporting-goods store who now must compete against a national chain, all organizations are being challenged to find ways to distinguish themselves from their competitors. In order to do this, firms rely on the use of their distinctive resources, which are called **core competencies.** These distinctive resources or core competencies can be thought of as what organizations learn over time (Prahalad and Hamel, 1998). Increasingly, progressive human resource practices are being viewed as a way to either create or sustain a firm's core competencies, and they may even be considered a

core competency of the firm itself (Cappelli & Crocker-Hefter, 1996).

In professional sports, for example, team performance is often crucial to the financial success of a franchise. Even the most loyal fans may lose interest in a team if it continues to post losing seasons. A subsequent decline in fan attendance will adversely impact the team's profitability. It could be argued that the truly successful franchises over the long term are those with the best front office or administrative staffs. These staffs are able to build unique, competitive advantages for the franchise through such HR-related practices as recruiting coaches and players, developing personnel, and structuring financial rewards that are competitive in the market, fiscally sound, and within league guidelines. These are the types of front office, human resource practices that can create a competitive advantage for successful sports franchises.

While recruiting and developing better players may improve a team's performance, can these and other HR practices actually help the performance of a business? The answer seems to be yes. In a study of over eight hundred firms, it was found that companies adopting high-performance HR practices had lower employee turnover, higher productivity, and higher profitability than companies that had not adopted these practices (Huselid, 1995). These HR practices included extensive employee training, the use of employee incentive plans, linking performance to future compensation, and the use of pre-employment tests in making hiring decisions. What this study did not show is which of these practices were most effective or if certain practices were more effective for some companies than others.

The idea that HR should be a strategic partner with business leads to the conclusion that the type of HR practices that will be most effective are those that are aligned with an organization's strategic plan. Conceptually, then, a close fit between a company's HR and business strategies should enhance a firm's overall performance. Evidence of this has been found and is the topic of the Focus on Research: Human Resource Strategy box.

From this strategic perspective of HR, we now turn our attention to a discussion of specific HR activities. We begin with the staffing process.

Focus on research: Human resource strategy

Aligning human resources and strategy among NCAA basketball teams

Using team records and surveys from 143 Division I men's basketball team coaches, Wright et al. (1995) explored the effects on team performance of aligning human resource practices with the preferred strategy of the coach. They identified the coaches' preferred and actual strategies and classified them as strategies built on (1) speed, (2) power, or (3) finesse.

The researchers found that coaches who preferred a strategy based on speed rated the importance of a recruit's athletic ability and speed-quickness higher than the coaches who preferred the power or finesse strategies. Thus, the coaches' preferred strategy influenced the type of player that was recruited. Second, teams actually using the coaches' preferred strategy had better performance (as measured by a higher power rating) than teams that used a strategy inconsistent with the preferred strategy of the coach.

STAFFING

Perhaps the most common activities associated with human resources are those that pertain to the recruitment and selection of employees. Very simply, **recruitment** is the process firms use to attract a sufficient number of qualified candidates to fill their job openings, and **selection** is the process used to decide which candidates to hire. Similar to business and educational organizations, assessing the talents and skills of prospective players is often the most critical component of a team's success. Unlike in many business organizations, however, the team's ability to make these judgments is subject to immediate scrutiny by the public. The media coverage now given to the draft of college athletes, coupled with the subsequent performance of the players, make this a highly conspicuous activity in most sport organizations.

Recruitment strategies are developed through a continuous assessment of a firm's strategic goals and the human resource needs to meet these goals. Both internal and external factors will influence a company's recruitment strategy. Externally, one such factor is the supply and demand for labor. Currently, the demand for people with information technology skills far exceeds the supply. This has led to a number of innovative recruitment strategies in the information technology industry, such as the use of smart agent software to actively search the World Wide Web for resumes of potential applicants (Greengard, 1998). These dynamics of the labor market, along with an increasingly competitive marketplace, have also caused many companies to look to nontraditional sources to fill their job openings. Today, more companies are making the decision not to recruit full-time workers and are using temporary employees to fill their needs. In fact, it is estimated that 20 percent of the new jobs that were created in the United States from 1991 to 1993 were filled by temporary workers (von Hippel et al., 1997).

When a company's recruitment strategy calls for hiring full-time workers, one of the first choices it must make is whether to look for applicants outside the firm or try to recruit from inside the company. This decision often depends on such factors as a company's level of commitment to the development of its employees, its business objectives, and the current capabilities of its work force. If an organization is committed to developing its employees, it will first look internally for job candidates before searching outside the firm. One way to do this is through a formal **job posting system** that communicates present job opportunities to employees. These openings are posted, often using a company's intranet, and employees who are interested may then apply and compete for the positions.

While job posting systems may be used to fill lower-level positions, internal candidates for senior-level positions are often identified through **succession planning.** Succession planning is the process of identifying and developing employees for senior and executive-level positions. Colgate-Palmolive, for example, has created an extensive executive development program for employees with high potential (Conner and Smith, 1998). The program identifies employees early in their careers who Colgate-Palmolive believes have the ability to manage at an executive level. For development purposes, these employees are given assignments that have significant levels of managerial responsibility early in their careers. Colgate-Palmolive believes these experiences will prepare them for their future roles as executive leaders.

While employees are often used to fill job openings, not all positions can be filled from a company's current work force. Accordingly, recruiting strategies will also identify external sources of job applicants as well. Traditionally, these sources have included advertisements in newspapers, on the radio, and in trade and professional publications; other external sources include employment agencies, executive search firms, colleges and universities, and, for many entry-level positions, school-to-work programs at the high school or junior college level.

Recently, the Internet has become a popular external recruitment source and promises to grow as more people gain access to the World Wide Web (Greengard, 1998). There are now more than 2,500 web sites listing job openings. These include all-purpose sites, such as E.Span (www.espan.com), The Monster Board (www.monster.com) and Career Mosaic (www.careermosaic.com), as well as specialized sites such as JOBTRAK (www.jobtrak.com), which is the largest online job listing site for college students (Greengard, 1998). In addition to these sources, many companies now advertise their openings on their own websites.

The effectiveness of a recruitment strategy in attracting qualified applicants depends not only upon applicant sources, but also on other factors such as the organization's reputation, jobs, and the recruiters themselves (Turban et al., 1998). Recruiters will often influence the applicants' perceptions of the job and the company. In turn, these perceptions will influence the attractiveness of the company to the applicant (Turban et al., 1998).

Thus, a company must look at its recruitment process as a marketing effort, paying particular attention to the quality of the messages it sends applicants, as well as how, and by whom, its messages are sent. These messages act as signals to prospective employees that either attract applicants to the firm or motivate them to search for other opportunities (Rynes et al., 1991). When applicants are attracted to the company, the firm is then faced with the challenge of selecting the right candidates for their jobs.

Employee selection is one of the most challenging tasks faced by any organization. Selection is a complex process of assessing fit between the applicant and the organization. At the most fundamental level, companies must assess how well the applicants' skills, knowledge, and ability fit the requirements of the position. Professional teams, for example, will rely on scouting reports of college players to assess a player's skills and ability. However, selection is also based on an assessment of person-organization fit on levels other than skills and ability (Kristof, 1996). In choosing employees, companies will try to assess the fit between organizational values and culture and the applicant's personal values and work attitudes. Thus, scouting reports of a player's ability are not the only information used in making selection decisions. Prior to drafting a college player or signing a free agent, coaches and team officials will often meet with the athlete to assess such personal characteristics as character and work ethic. In addition to assessing the fit based on these personal characteristics, fit is also evaluated on more tangible issues such as the financial incentives the organization can offer, compared with the applicant's requirements.

A wide variety of selection techniques can be used to determine this fit between the organization's needs and the applicant. Interviews, background and reference checks, ability tests, and personality assessments are among the most common. In choosing which techniques to use, organizations must insure that these techniques are both valid and reliable. The concepts of *validity* and *reliability* of selection techniques are critical in the hiring process.

The **validity** of a selection technique is concerned with two issues, (1) what the test or procedure (such as an employment interview) is measuring and (2) how well it measures it (Cascio, 1998). For these reasons, validity can be thought of as a measure of the accuracy of the assessment tool. Firms should try to collect different types of evidence for the validity of their selection techniques. Two of the most important are content-related and criterion-related. **Content-related evidence** is the extent to which a selection tool measures a candidate's performance on a representative sample of tasks, compared to all the tasks required by the job. For example, in softball, an outfielder's overall performance depends upon many factors, such as hitting for average, hitting for power, arm strength, speed, and the ability to catch a fly ball on the run. If a team uses a test that measures only the strength and accuracy of an outfielder's arm to make its selection decision, the validity of that test will be low, since it provides limited content-related evidence of what it is supposed to be measuring (i.e., the overall performance of the outfielder).

Criterion-related evidence is the strength of the relationship between what is used to predict performance (for example, a score on an ability test) and future performance. For example, suppose a selection committee that is interviewing candidates for the position of athletic director has decided it should assess each candidate's ability to work effectively with representatives from the media. The committee chooses to assess this ability by using a structured interview format. By structuring interviews (i.e., using the same questions for every candidate), the members of the committee will evaluate each candidate's ability based on the responses to their questions. A strong relationship between the committee's evaluation and the person's effectiveness in dealing with the media after being hired would be criterion-related evidence for the validity of using a structured interview format as a selection technique.

While it is important that all selection tools have evidence of validity, it is equally important that there is evidence they are reliable as well. *Reliability* is concerned with the consistency of what is being measured. Formally, **reliability** is the absence of unsystematic errors of measurement (Cascio, 1998). If certain skills are measured at different times or by different people, there generally will be some differences between them. In order for an assessment to be reliable, however, any differences in measurement should be due to chance and not to an error in the measurement technique. As an example, a person who wants to determine her speed in running the 100 meters decides to run this distance on two consecutive days. However, her times are different each day, which makes it difficult to assess her true speed. There may be many reasons for the differences in her times. She might have been more prepared the second day, the weather conditions may have been different, or perhaps she didn't have the same person timing her each day. All of these factors are potential sources of error in measuring her true speed and make this particular two-day test of speed unreliable. If a selection test is reliable,

it means that test scores (such as times in the 100-meter dash) should be consistent between evaluators and consistent over time. If they are not, a pre-employment test or selection tool is unreliable and should not be used by a company to make its employment decisions.

CONCEPT CHECK

Selection techniques must show evidence of validity and reliability. Validity is concerned with the accuracy of a pre-employment selection tool, while reliability is concerned with the consistency of the technique.

As we've seen, staffing strategies in organizations include decisions about employee selection and recruitment. However, staffing strategies also include a firm's decisions on the appropriate number of employees needed at any time. This assessment is done within the context of an organization's strategy, its competition and, perhaps most often, its profitability. Unfortunately, this assessment often leads firms to downsize their operations. **Downsizing** is a planned, systematic reduction in staff. Although earlier efforts at downsizing were simply intended to reduce the number of employees in an organization (and, along with that, its compensation and benefits expenses), many organizations now look to downsizing from a strategic perspective, to enable them to refocus on the areas of their competitive advantage (Bruton et al., 1996).

While these broad-based cuts in staff are endemic to many organizations today, other difficult staffing decisions must sometimes be made at the executive level. In professional sports, team owners and general managers are often faced with making the decision to change managers. The Focus on Research: Staffing box discusses the effects on a team's performance of managerial changes when they are made in the middle of a season.

Staffing processes, then, are one of the sets of HR activities that help a firm meet its strategic objectives. Another important set of these processes is related to the financial reward systems a firm develops. We now turn our attention to these reward systems.

Focus on research: Staffing

Manager/coach mid-season replacement and team performance

One of the most difficult decisions for the owner of a team is to replace a manager or coach. McTeer et al. (1995) studied the immediate and longer-term effects of a midseason manager/head coach change in four professional sports leagues: the NHL, the NBA, Major League Baseball, and the NFL. Across all four leagues, team performance improved for the remainder of the season. However, this improvement didn't last into the next season. In only one of the leagues (ice hockey) did team performance improve in the year following the change, compared to performance in the year prior to the change being made.

COMPENSATION

In 1975 Steven Kerr, a professor of management and a consultant with General Electric Company, criticized the compensation schemes of many organizations for rewarding the wrong types of behavior. One of the examples he used to illustrate this was the sports contract that includes incentives that are based exclusively on individual accomplishments for players who participate in team sports. Unfortunately, many of Kerr's criticisms about company compensation systems are as relevant today as they were in 1975.

The heart of most companies' reward systems is **compensation,** which is any type of financial or tangible return given to an employee as a result of employment (Milkovich and Newman, 1996). In addition to base salary, compensation also includes rewards that vary with performance, such as commissions, incentives, or bonuses, as well as the cost of company benefits offered to employees. The allocation of these rewards and the productivity of the employees in exchange for them is of critical importance to a firm's profitability.

Among other factors, compensation strategies usually take both the external competitiveness and the internal consistency or equity of pay into consideration (Milkovich and Newman, 1996). **External competitiveness** is determined by comparing a firm's compensation with that paid by other companies. To make this evaluation, a firm will review compensation data from companies across many different markets. This means obtaining salary information not only from organizations that are in direct competition with the firm, but from other sources as well. For example, it may also be important to review salary data from a broad occupational area, or from companies who are in different industries but who recruit applicants from the same geographical area. Today, the dramatic increase in international sources for recruitment has significantly expanded the geographical recruiting areas of most companies (Laabs, 1998).

After competitive data are gathered, a firm must decide its strategy, that is, if it wants to lead, lag, or match the current market rates. This decision will have an impact on other HR outcomes such as employee turnover, applicant pool size and characteristics, acceptance rates, selection costs, and the attitudes of its current employees (Klaas & McClendon, 1996). Similar to other business organizations, a professional sports team's compensation strategy will be at least partially dependent upon its revenues. Revenues for professional teams are generated from attendance, broadcast rights, and licensing fees. Thus, the size of a team's market can be a strong determinant of its compensation strategy. Teams in smaller markets are often unable to compete for talent in the free agent market. It is clear that teams in major markets, such as the New York Yankees in professional baseball, have chosen a compensation strategy that leads the market. Putting aside the owner's personal financial status, this strategy can be sustained over the long term only if the market continues to support it.

Besides external competitiveness, another area compensation strategies must address is the **internal consistency** of salaries. Internal consistency is measured by the equity of salaries paid across similarly valued jobs within a firm. To achieve internal consistency, a firm will first assess the value or worth of all its positions and create a pay structure that insures that salaries are similar for jobs with equal value to the company. Determining the relative worth or value of a position is often done through a formal job evaluation system. While there are a number of ways to do this, jobs are most commonly evaluated by systems that assign points to indicate the value of each position to a company.

Salary structures are created using the results of the company's job evaluation system. Job levels are determined by placing similarly valued jobs (i.e., jobs whose points fall within a specific range) into salary grades. The midpoint of the salary range for each grade is set to the market rate and a minimum and maximum is established for each range. Typically, the difference between the minimum and maximum for a range may be 10 to 25 percent for lower-level jobs, but as high as 120 percent for upper-level jobs (Milkovich and Newman, 1996). This range spread for each salary grade allows the firm some flexibility in its individual pay decisions.

By using competitive market data (to set the midpoints of each range) and assessing the value of jobs with a point system, salary structures based on these systems try to develop compensation structures that are both externally competitive and internally consistent. Although still very widely used, these types of pay structures with their narrowly defined, multiple pay grades are rapidly losing favor (Risher, 1997). Intense competitive pressures, along with the constant change required to meet these pressures, have created a need for greater flexibility to be competitive in the market. Today, there is less emphasis on the goal of internal consistency and much greater use of group and individual incentive plans to more closely tie pay to individual performance (Risher, 1997).

One way firms have tried to be competitive is to allow managers more discretion in rewarding high performers. To do this, many organizations are implementing a salary structure that is based on **broadbanding.** Broadbanding is the consolidation of hierarchical, narrow pay grades into a very limited number of bands with much broader pay ranges. Pay surveys in both the United States and Great Britain have found that 19 to 20 percent of firms are using broadbanding now, and 27 to 30 percent are considering its implementation (Wagner and Jones, 1994).

The wide range spreads characteristic of broadbanding allow companies to be more competitive in the market, as managers are no longer constrained by narrow salary ranges. Placing jobs in only a few salary bands also allows managers greater flexibility to differentiate pay between employees in the same job, based on their performance and individual contributions. Additionally, broadbanding can also encourage lateral, developmental transfers

across jobs that were previously in different salary grades (Brown, 1996). With the elimination of many management levels through downsizing and reengineering, the opportunity to move laterally within a company is particularly important.

> ## CONCEPT CHECK
>
> *Broadbanding creates a salary structure that replaces multiple salary grades with a limited number of pay grades. The use of broader salary ranges gives managers more discretion in salary decisions and allows salaries to be more competitive with the market.*

This emphasis on the external market and individual performance has also led to incentive pay becoming a larger component of an employee's total compensation. Although there are other factors that contribute to performance (Kohn, 1998), it has been argued that financial incentives are the single most influential factor (Jenkins et al., 1998). Typically, short-term financial incentive plans are based on goals established at the beginning of a plan year and tie the employee's pay to the achievement of these goals. Goals may be set at an individual, group, or team level, and even at the organizational level.

This emphasis on incentive-based pay, however, has contributed to considerable pay disparity between executive management levels and other employees. In its annual pay survey of chief executive officers of publicly held companies, the *Wall Street Journal* reported that L. Dennis Kozlowski, the CEO of Tyco International Ltd. was the highest paid chief executive officer in 1999 (*Wall Street Journal*, 1999). Mr. Kozlowski's total direct compensation was approximately $170 million, while the second highest executive, Mr. David S. Pottruck of Charles Schwab Corp. earned $127.9 million that year. For both CEO's, the largest component of their compensation was incentives based on the stock market performance of their corporations.

Pay disparity exists in many of today's sports teams as well. Free agents are given enormous salaries, often creating significant disparity between the lowest- and highest-paid players on a team. Although the effects of pay disparity have not been studied extensively in business, they have been explored in professional baseball and are presented in the Focus on Research: Compensation box.

Compensation systems, then, are important elements of a firm's human resource strategies.

Focus on research: Compensation

Performance effects of pay dispersion on individuals and teams

Using data collected from professional baseball, Bloom (1999) looked at the effects on individual and team performance of wide variations in pay across team members. The difference between the lowest-paid person and the highest is a measure of pay dispersion in an organization. For organizations with hierarchical or high pay dispersion, there is a concentration of pay at the top levels. Compressed or low dispersion occurs when pay is more equally distributed and there isn't a large disparity between the highest and lowest pay levels.

Bloom examined the effects of pay dispersion on the performance of 1,644 professional baseball players and twenty-nine teams during the years 1985 through 1993. He explored the effects of hierarchical pay dispersion on a player's offensive output and defensive performance, as well as on a team's winning percentage, fan attendance, and standing. He found that the greater the hierarchical pay dispersion, the lower the individual and team performance in every category except defensive performance. In explaining these results, he speculated that teams who actively participated in the free agent market and pay high salaries will increase pay dispersion, which may lower the performance of other players because of the feelings of inequity these high salaries create.

Ideally, these systems should promote and reinforce behavior that will lead to the accomplishment of an organization's objectives. Providing rewards for certain behavior on the job, however, will not be effective if employees don't possess the basic skills, knowledge, or ability to do their jobs. The third, and final, set of HR activities that will be discussed focuses on the development of a company's human resources.

HUMAN RESOURCE DEVELOPMENT

As organizations have been forced to change due to new technology, greater availability and access to information, and competitive global markets, scholars and organizational consultants are beginning to formulate different theories of the firm. One of these more recent theories views firms as learning organizations (Starkey, 1998) in which knowledge and the organization's ability to learn are seen as the firm's competitive advantages. While pure forms of learning organizations may not exist, these types of organizations share common characteristics, such as the belief that organizations and groups have the ability to learn, a commitment to continuous learning at every level, and the leadership and culture that support learning activities throughout the organization (Redding, 1997).

This view of the importance of knowledge and learning to a firm's success underscores the value of human resource development activities today. **Human resource development (HRD)** is the set of activities that promote learning and the acquisition of skills necessary to meet current and future job demands (Harris & DeSimone, 1994). HRD focuses on learning outcomes, specifically on the acquisition of knowledge, skills, and abilities (KSAs). It includes activities such as training and development as well as career development. While the definitions are often blurred, HRD professionals draw a distinction between training and development activities. **Training** is the process of trying to acquire KSAs for current or future jobs (i.e., the opportunity to learn), while **development** is the actual learning of KSAs (i.e., the results of learning) (Blanchard and Thacker, 1999).

Recognizing the importance of continuous learning, many companies have made substantial financial commitments to training their employees. In its 1999 state of the industry report, the American Society of Training and Development reported that annual training expenditures were $32.7 million in what it termed its leading-edge companies, with over 83% of all employees in these firms receiving some type of training over the course of the year (Bassi and Van Buren, 1999). As knowledge is becoming obsolete faster today than ever before, many companies have established corporate universities to insure that their employees have learning opportunities throughout their careers. There are now more than 1,600 of these universities in operation (Meister, 1998) which provide not only specific job skill training but also training in such areas as leadership, communication, and problem-solving skills.

Regardless of the type of training that is done, training departments are increasingly being held accountable to measure their results. Kirkpatrick (1994) has identified four levels on which training evaluations can be conducted: (1) the immediate reactions of the participants, (2) an assessment of the learning that occurs, (3) measuring changes in behavior on the job, and (4) determining the results of the training. At the most basic level, participants' reactions are typically assessed by a questionnaire given at the end of the training. To assess whether any learning has taken place, tests may be administered at the conclusion of the training, but these tests are not proof that the learning has been transferred to the job. The failure to transfer learning from the training environment to the job is a common problem of many corporate training programs (Rossett, 1997). The ultimate test of the training is not only its transfer to the work environment, but its result, that is, its impact on organizational performance. Unfortunately, despite the very limited correlation between trainees' reactions and the measurements on any of the other three levels (Alliger et al., 1997), many organizations continue to base their evaluation of training exclusively on the reactions of the participants alone.

Regardless of the extent to which they're used, formal training programs are not the only important HRD activities in organizations. HRD also includes activities focusing on career development. The traditional definition of a career was based on the premise of a long-term, relational contract between an employer and employee (Callanan and Greenhaus, 1999). This relationship was based on stability and mutual commitment, and career progress was defined as advancement through an organization's hierarchy. However, this type of psychological contract is no longer applicable, as such factors as shifts in employment opportunities, changing organizational structures and workforce characteristics have contributed to a dramatic shift

in what is considered a career today (Callanan and Greenhaus, 1999).

A career may be seen as a continual series of learning experiences over the course of one's life (Hall, 1996). Since these learning experiences will most likely not take place in a single organization, the responsibility for one's career has shifted away from the organization to the individual. Today, careers may more accurately be defined not by the progress one makes in a single organization, but by a feeling of psychological success, or the sense of accomplishment derived from achieving one's personal goals, whether these goals include professional achievement and/or personal happiness (Hall, 1996).

This need to achieve psychological success through one's career has a profound impact on the human resource practices of organizations that wish to motivate and retain their employees (Callanan and Greenhaus, 1999). Companies must strive to create environments in which continuous learning is encouraged and that offer the opportunity for self-assessment and evaluation. HR practices must help employees balance their work and family responsibilities and must be used to support the careers of their employees.

CONCEPT CHECK

The changing nature of the relationship between an employer and employee has had a significant impact on how careers are perceived. Although this new, shorter-term relationship has shifted the responsibility for career management to the individual, HRD activities in organizations are still used to facilitate personal growth, employee development, and career success.

Regardless of the experiences that will ultimately define your career in sport management, whether these include an administrator in a university athletic department, a coach, a player, or a manager in a sports-related industry, your success will depend upon getting others to enjoy their work, to be challenged, and to act in ways that support the organization's goals. The HR activities presented in this chapter can help you and your organization to accomplish these objectives.

CRITICAL THINKING EXERCISES

1. As the owner and general manager of a new professional sports franchise, one of your most important decisions is the selection and hiring of the team's first coach. What issues should you consider before beginning the recruitment and selection processes?

2. You are the store manager of a family-owned retail sporting goods outlet. Last year, your store had very high turnover of its sales staff. You believe the main reason for this is that the national sporting goods chain that opened a store near you can pay higher salaries to their employees. What actions could you take to reduce this turnover?

SUMMARY

This chapter has explored three specific areas of human resource activities in organizations: staffing, compensation, and human resource development. Strategic human resource management was presented as the mechanism that organizations use to integrate these activities so they support the strategic objectives of the firm. Besides defining and identifying recent trends in these fields, their relevance to sports and sports-related industries has also been discussed.

Thus, the chapter has offered the perspective that HR will contribute to an organization by integrating employee-related activities with the strategic objectives of a company. However, the HR function may contribute to an organization in other ways, focusing on more complex activities such as understanding human interaction to achieve fundamental changes in organizations, to insuring equitable treatment across all employee groups. These perspectives have been discussed by Frisby and Kikulis (1996) and are highly recommended for the interested reader.

CASE STUDY

Dr. Bill Watt was recently hired as the athletic director of a private university with a total student enrollment of 15,000. The athletic program has grown over the last five years and fields teams in men's and women's basketball and lacrosse, men's football and baseball, and women's softball and field hockey. The department currently employs thirty-six people, including administrative staff, faculty, coaches, and athletic trainers.

While he was being interviewed for the position, Dr. Watt learned that the men's and women's basketball teams are moving down from Division II to Division III next season. He also discovered that few of the employees in the department have been employed by the university for more than two years and that there are currently seven job openings that must be filled, one of which is the budget and finance manager of the department. The previous budget and finance manager was in the position only four months before leaving for another job.

The president of the university was very blunt with Bill during his job interview. She told him that morale in the athletic department was extremely low, and the previous AD was unsuccessful in his attempts to turn things around during his three-year tenure. She recommended that one of the first things Bill should do is to meet with the university's human resources director to discuss ways to address these issues. On this, his second day on the job, Dr. Watt is now preparing for this meeting.

REVIEW QUESTIONS AND ISSUES

1. The Human Resource function is a collection of integrated, employee-centered activities whose objective is to help the organization meet its short- and long-term goals. Strategic human resource management takes a long-term, externally focused view of these HR activities.

2. Employee recruitment strategies are influenced by factors external and internal to the company. Firms often recruit from their own employee base. A job posting system is used to fill lower-level jobs, while succession planning is used for upper-level positions.

3. All employee selection techniques must show evidence of both reliability and validity. Content-related evidence is an indication that the test measures all skills, knowledge, and ability required by the position, while criterion-related evidence is indicated by the relationship between test scores and job performance.

4. A compensation strategy is driven by the firm's desire for the external competitiveness of its salaries and the achievement of internal consistency between jobs within the company.

5. To compete in the marketplace, many firms have switched from a narrowly defined salary

grade system to broadbanding, which restricts the number of salary grades but uses wide salary ranges for each band. This structure offers greater discretionary judgment for managers.

6. Incentive plans are becoming more prevalent in compensation, but they may contribute to pay disparity in many organizations.
7. HRD activities promote learning and the acquisition of new skills. Training is the process of acquiring new KSAs, while development is the actual learning of these KSAs.
8. A career is no longer based on a long-term, relational contract between an employee and employer.
9. The new career concept of psychological success means that organizations must offer opportunities for continuous learning, self-assessment, and a balance between work and family.

SOLUTIONS TO CRITICAL THINKING EXERCISES

1. Before choosing any HR activity, it is important to have a clear understanding of the business strategy of the organization. Is your plan for the team to be competitive right away? Or are you more interested in developing younger players, which will take the team more time to be competitive in the league? You must also consider your financial resources. Finally, you must consider the responsibilities of the job itself. Will the head coach have control over all player decisions or will someone else in the franchise have this responsibility? The answers to these questions will help decide the type of coach you want (someone who has been successful in developing young players, for example), the recruitment sources you choose (for example, coaches with or without professional experience), and the personal characteristics of the candidate.
2. First, you must find out why your employees are leaving. People leave jobs for many reasons, not just for higher salaries. One of the best ways to find this out is to conduct exit interviews with the employees who are leaving and ask why they have decided to leave. It may also be a good idea to find out the salaries being offered by the national

chain. Think about the information you collect, why people work, and what they want from work. As a small store, what are your competitive advantages? Can you structure your jobs in such a way as to provide opportunities for your employees that the national chain is unable to do (flexible work hours, more responsibility in the store, or a chance to share in its profits)? Is it possible to create incentive plans for your employees that are based on individual or store performance?

REFERENCES

Alliger, G. W., Tannenbaum, S. I., Bennett, W., Traver, H., and Shotland, A. (1997). A meta-analysis of the relations among training criteria. *Personnel Psychology, 50,* 341–58.

Anthony, W. P., Perrewe, P. L., and Kacmar, K. M. (1998). *Human resource management: A strategic approach.* 3d ed. Orlando, FL: Harcourt Brace & Company.

Barney, J. B., and Wright, P. M. (1998). On becoming a strategic partner: The role of human resources in gaining competitive advantage. *Human Resource Management, 37* (1), 31–46.

Bassi, L. J., and Van Buren, M. E. (1999). The 1999 ASTD state of the industry report. *Training and Development, 53* (1), S3–S4.

Blanchard, P. N., and Thacker, J. W. (1999). *Effective training systems, strategies and practices.* Englewood Cliffs, NJ: Prentice-Hall.

Bloom, M. (1999). The performance effects of pay dispersion on individuals and organizations. *Academy of Management Journal, 42* (1), 25–40.

Brown, D. (1996). Broadbanding: A study of company practices in the United Kingdom. *Compensation and Benefits Review, 28* (6), 41–49.

Bruton, G. D., Keels, J. K., and Shook, C. L. (1996). Downsizing the firm: Answering strategic questions. *Academy of Management Executive, 10* (2), 38–45.

Callanan, G. A., and Greenhaus, J. H. (1999). Personal and career development. In A. I. Kraut and A. K. Korman (eds.), *Evolving practices in human resource management: Response to a changing world.* San Francisco: Jossey-Bass.

Cappelli, P., and Crocker-Hefter, A. (1996). Distinctive human resources are firms' core competencies. *Organizational Dynamics, 24,* 7–22.

Cascio, W. (1998). *Applied psychology in human resource management.* 5th ed. Upper Saddle River, NJ: Simon & Schuster.

Conner, J., and Smith, C. A. (1998). Developing the next generation of leaders: A new strategy for leadership development at Colgate-Palmolive. In Edward M. Mone and Manuel London (eds.), *HR to the rescue: Case studies of HR solutions to business challenges.* Houston, TX: Gulf Publishing Company.

Frisby, W., and Kikulis, L. M. (1996). Human resource management in sport. In B. L. Parkhouse (ed.), *The management of sport: Its foundation and application* (2d ed.). New York: McGraw-Hill.

Greengard, S. (1998). Putting online recruiting to work. *Workforce, 77,* 73–77.

Hall, D. (1996). Proteam careers of the 21st Century, *Academy of Management Executive, 10* (4), 8–16.

Harris, D. M., and DeSimone, R. L. (1994). *Human resource development.* Orlando, FL: Dryden Press.

Huselid, M. A. (1995). The impact of human resource management practices on turnover, productivity and corporate financial performance. *Academy of Management Journal, 38* (3), 635–72.

Jenkins, G. D., Gupta, N., Mitra, A., and Shaw, J. D. (1998). Are financial incentives related to performance? A meta-analytic review of empirical research. *Journal of Applied Psychology, 83,* 777–87.

Kerr, S. (1975). On the folly of rewarding A, while hoping for B. *Academy of Management Journal, 18,* 769–83.

Kirkpatrick, D. L. (1994). *Evaluating training programs.* San Francisco: Berrett-Koehler.

Klaas, B. S., and McClendon, J. A. (1996). To lead, lag, or match: Estimating the financial impact of pay level policies. *Personnel Psychology, 49,* 121–41.

Kohn, A. (1998). Challenging behaviorist dogma: Myths about money and motivation. *Compensation and Benefits Review,* March/April, 27, 33–37.

Kristof, A. (1996). Person-organization fit: An integrative review of its conceptualizations, measurement and implications. *Personnel Psychology, 49* (1), 1–48.

Laabs, J. (1998). Recruiting in the global village. *Workforce, 77,* 30–33.

Lam, S. S. K., and Schaubroeck, J. (1998). Integrating HR planning and organisational strategy. *Human Resource Management Journal, 8* (3), 5–19.

McTeer, W., White, P. G., and Persad, S. (1995). Manager/coach mid-season replacement and team performance in professional team sport. *Journal of Sports Behavior, 18* (1), 58–68.

Meister, J. (1998). Ten steps to creating a corporate university. *Training and Development, 52,* 38–43.

Milkovich, G. T., and Newman, J. M. (1996). *Compensation.* New York: McGraw-Hill.

Prahalad, C. K., and Hamel, G. (1998). The core competence of the corporation. In D. Ulrich (ed.), *Delivering results.* Boston: Harvard Business School Publishing.

Redding, J. (1997). Hardwiring the learning organization. *Training and Development, 51* (8), 61–66.

Risher, H. (1997). Emerging model for salary management. *Public Management, 79,* 10–14.

Rossett, A. (1997). That was a great class, but . . . *Training and Development, 51,* 18–24.

Rynes, S. L., Bretz, R. D., and Gerhart, B. (1991). The importance of recruitment in job choice: A different way of looking. *Personnel Psychology, 44,* 487–520.

Starkey, K. (1998). What can we learn from the learning organization? *Human Relations, 51* (4), 531–46.

Turban, D. B., Forret, M. L., and Hendrickson, C. L. (1998). Applicant attraction to firms: Influences of organization reputation, job and organizational attributes, and recruiter behaviors. *Journal of Vocational Behavior, 52,* 24–44.

von Hippel, C., Mangum, S. L., Greenberger, D. B., Heneman, R. L., and Skoglind, J. D. (1997). Temporary employment: Can organizations and employees both win? *Academy of Management Executive, 11* (1), 93–104.

Wagner, F. H., and Jones, M. B. (1994). Broadbanding in practice: Hard facts and real data. *Journal of Compensation and Benefits, 10,* 27–34.

Wall Street Journal, April 6, 2000. "Who made the biggest bucks."

Wright, P. M., Smart, D. L., and McMahan, G. C. (1995). Matches between human resources and strategy among NCAA basketball teams. *Academy of Management Journal, 38* (4), 1052–74.

WEBSITES

SHRM

www.shrm.org and http://www.shrm.org/hrlinks

This is the website of SHRM, the Society for Human Resource Management. This is an excellent site for those who are interested in learning more about current trends in Human Resources.

CHAPTER 8

Labor Relations in Professional Sports

Harmon Gallant

In this chapter, you will become familiar with the following terms:

Players' associations
Collective bargaining
  agreements
Standard player contract
Lockout
Sports agents
Salary cap
Revenue sharing
Competitive balance

Cartel
Free agency
National Labor Relations Act
  (NLRA)
Reserve system
Grievance procedures
Good faith collective bargaining
National Labor Relations Board
  (NLRB)

Commissioner
Negotiation impasse
Scope of collective bargaining
Agency shop
Arbitration
Final offer salary arbitration
Player strike
Collusion
Right of first refusal

Overview

To understand labor relations in professional team sports, it is necessary to examine the economic structure of the major sports leagues and the legal framework in which they operate. Labor relations between owners and players, and the labor laws which in large measure regulate their interactions, have become a central focus in the development of American professional sports. Today's professional sports leagues in baseball, football, basketball, and hockey are each evolving major industries. Other league sports, for example soccer, are not yet a significant factor, though they may become so in the future. Individual performer sports, including tennis, golf, and bowling, generate significant revenues but have organized in ways beyond the scope of this chapter. Similarly, college athletics generate sizeable revenue and fan interest, but this chapter will only consider the question of whether college athletes may be properly considered employees of their respective educational institutions and accordingly compensated. With respect to labor relations, the major development in the professional sports industries in the past quarter century has been the appearance of organized **players' associations.** These associations are now full-fledged labor unions, and they are recognized as an integral part of the bargaining process with ownership. The unions are well established, but the problems they are attempting to resolve are not easily defined or managed.

Labor law and labor relations are central to understanding the sports industries, but other elements also go into the mix. The sports industries are complex, despite a surface simplicity resulting from their product and the production process. It was not until the 1970s that the major sports had arm's-length bargaining and the **collective bargaining agreements** between players and owners that ensued. After more than two decades of litigation, player strikes, and contentious player-owner negotiations, many observers have hoped for a new era of cooperation. Such is not the case. Substantive progress has been made in resolving certain problems, but the true nature of labor-management issues in professional sports is just beginning to be understood and appreciated. By the 1990s, these issues reached crisis proportions in each of the major team sports, threatening the economic foundations on which the various leagues are based.

ECONOMIC BACKGROUND

The sports industries are different from other sectors of the American economy in several important respects. First, the basic product is the "on-field" game, and is therefore an experience for the consumer rather than a tangible product. It is a particular form of entertainment and is generally considered a segment of the entertainment industry. Second, each sport has individual characteristics that have led to differences in the creation and growth of the leagues in which business is conducted. For example, the various leagues have differences in the number of players per team, the size of the arena or stadium in which the games are played, and the number of games that constitute a championship season.

There are also the following elements to consider for each sport: the injury toll exacted on the players, how well the game is adapted to broadcasting (especially television), and whether or not the sport is able to attract national interest. As a result, the number of viable teams, and their total revenues, varies from league to league. Another factor, making its presence felt especially in the last decade, has been a substantial rise in the sale of licensed merchandise, such as trading cards and logo-imprinted apparel. Each of these factors must go into any analysis of the financial value of a professional sports franchise as a business concern (Berry and Wong, 1986).

Considered as an industry, sports is still in its developmental stage. The teams have grown from small businesses with entrepreneurial ownerships (individual or partnerships) into corporate undertakings. Despite media attention given to high player salaries, spiraling franchise sales prices, and

local and network television contracts, the overall dollar amount historically generated by the sports industries has been relatively small when compared with revenues of more established industries. This is because the product itself, the "game," has a rich history with traditions which are only now beginning to translate into revenues. As a result, a constant upward pressure can be seen on the financial side of sports. Precise figures have been generally unavailable because most professional clubs have been operated as partnerships or closely held corporations, with no obligation to reveal financial information to the public. By any reckoning, however, the professional sports leagues were a growth industry in the 1990s.

WHERE PROBLEMS OCCUR IN SPORTS LABOR RELATIONS

Each league's basic working agreements between players and owners include the collective bargaining agreement, the **standard player contract,** and league bylaws and rules. Team owners, general managers, and players, however, are not always familiar with their contents, and operating procedures often suffer as a result. Modern sports history contains many examples of owner-player conflicts resulting in litigation, when a careful consideration of the business relationship between owner and player might have avoided the need for court intervention. When agents and aggressive player unions are added to the equation, susceptibility to misunderstanding or simple miscalculation of interests during labor negotiations is greatly expanded. Some labor problems may be inherent in the basic structure of professional sports and prove less tractable. Within each sport, however, improvements in team and league administration should ameliorate many of the labor relations problems common in the professional sports environment (Staudohar, 1996).

CONCEPT CHECK

Because professional sports is not yet a mature industry, its principles of administration are still taking shape as the twentieth century draws to a close. Established industrial models are often inapplicable or improperly adapted to the operations of professional sports leagues.

COMPONENTS OF THE
LABOR-MANAGEMENT RELATIONSHIP
Management

The league itself, and its individual clubs, including all nonplayer employees, make up the management component of the labor-management relationship. Players, their agents, and the players' association represent labor's side.

This alignment of interests remains relatively constant, although conflicts often arise within the ranks on each side.

For example, occasionally individual club owners consider an action by the league contrary to their own interests. In the 1970s and early 1980s, Oakland Raiders owner Al Davis fought National Football League Commissioner Pete Rozelle and the other team owners over the right to relocate the franchise to Los Angeles. The right of an individual team owner to relocate a franchise over the objections of the league was an issue that affected the operation of the NFL far beyond this particular case. Since it affected the league's ability to govern its member clubs, the entire framework of labor relations within the league structure was also indirectly involved.

A similar case of conflict within management ranks occurred in baseball in 1992, when team owners decided to terminate the employment of Commissioner Fay Vincent and install Milwaukee Brewers owner Alan ("Bud") Selig as "acting Commissioner." Vincent was instrumental in ending the owners' 1990 **lockout** in spring training, and he was consequently perceived by the majority of owners as "pro labor" on the difficult labor relations issues then plaguing major league baseball. Public criticism of the Vincent firing extended to Congressional threats to repeal baseball's antitrust exemption unless a strong, independent commissioner was quickly appointed. The owners remained united in their determination to keep the commissioner's office out of their labor struggles. Their action, however, created a significant degree of player mistrust regarding their intentions in subsequent collective bargaining negotiations.

Labor

The labor component of our model includes players, their agents, and the certified labor unions that represent the players in collective bargaining negotiations with management. Elements on the labor side of the equation sometimes come into conflict with each other, just as they do on the management side. (See the case study on sports agents at the end of this chapter.)

Additional Factors

It is most common, however, for disputes to occur between elements on opposite sides of the labor-management equation. One source of conflict arises over the process by which **sports agents** negotiate contracts on behalf of individual players. Currently, league offices in football and basketball closely monitor individual player contracts, and nullify those deemed to violate the restrictions of current **salary cap** provisions. It is evident that in a number of areas, the interests of players, clubs, unions, and agents come into conflict, and not always from the expected direction.

A final concern involves the impact of external sources on the league's administration of operations, especially in labor relations. *Umpires* and *referees* are neither labor nor management elements according to our model, but they have become more active in union organization in recent years and they have a growing influence in their industries. *Television* and *radio broadcasts* have become absolutely vital to the revenue streams accruing to every professional sports team, and they have had a corresponding rise in influence over many administrative issues, including the way games are played and teams are operated. *Stadium* and *arena ownership* often involve municipalities, either in financing or operations or both, so that government becomes a crucial factor in a franchise's economic viability. Each of these external elements bears directly or indirectly on the relationship of labor and management in the classic model of the professional sports industries. One ignores a particular element at his peril (Berry, Gould, and Staudohar, 1986).

CONCEPT ✔ CHECK

A professional league, made up of a number of privately owned teams based in various cities, is the basic element in the economic analysis of professional sports. The infrastructure of a professional sports league can be described as follows: The league itself and its individual clubs make up the "management" side of the equation; the individual players, their agents and attorneys, and the players' association make up the "labor" side.

THE BASIC ELEMENTS OF MANAGEMENT AND LABOR

Leagues

Organized professional sports leagues in the United States began in 1876, when baseball's National League was formed. Several of its guiding principles have continued throughout the subsequent development of professional sports in this country. Individual clubs began by cooperating with each other regarding the market supply of producers and consumers. The producers were the players, who made the product by playing the games on the field, and the consumers were the fans, whose ticket purchases provided operating expenses and profits.

Each league allocates a territorial market to an individual member team, eliminating intraleague competition for the sports consumer within the territory. At the same time, the league expands to cover the major population centers throughout the country. In this way, a sports league becomes something of a *monopoly* and discourages the formation of rival leagues. The establishment of a viable team in a desirable market greatly decreases the chance a new league can be formed and succeed in that market. Nevertheless, the great expansion and shifts in American population centers in this century have given rise to a number of attempts to establish rival leagues. In basketball, football, and hockey, recent league mergers and expansions resulted from these attempts. In baseball, the American League in 1901 was the last successful attempt to challenge the monopoly enjoyed by an existing league.

To guarantee the league's overall health as an economic entity, each sport has a method of **revenue sharing.** Contracts with major commercial television networks are divided equally among the member teams in each league. With the great revenue increases in the past decade, the national television contracts have been the primary basis of team financial parity. Hockey has lagged behind the other three major team sports in the acquisition of network television contracts. Clubs contract individually for local broadcast revenue, and great discrepancies in these amounts (between so-called "big-market" and "small-market" teams) has been an issue of growing concern among team owners. Additionally, some leagues split gate receipts. The National Football League provides that 40 percent of regular-season and 50 percent of preseason gate revenues go to the visiting team. In baseball, the visiting team is given 20 percent, but in basketball and hockey there is no division of gate receipts to the visiting team.

A final allocation of league resources involves those necessary to make the product, which is the pool of player talent. A roughly equal division of these resources is necessary to ensure a competitive product from each team. It has been long established that a lack of **competitive balance** among the league's member teams will drive down fan interest and, ultimately, each team's revenues. For this reason, a number of devices have been created, over time, to control the distribution of player talent to each team. Not every device is used simultaneously by each league, but they have included initial player allocations to new teams, drafts of available professional and amateur players, restrictions on player movement to new clubs, and compensation to old clubs for lost players.

Any restriction on player movement to new clubs has had the perhaps unintended effect of suppressing player salaries within a given league. Before the advent of the free-agency era in 1976, only the existence of rival leagues, aggressively competing for player services, has effectively raised the level of player salaries within any professional sports league. Restrictions on mobility have been the primary concern of the players in modern labor negotiations. Players' unions consistently maintain that such restrictions illegally suppress player salaries by eliminating the market for their services (Staudohar, 1996).

> ### CONCEPT CHECK
>
> *Sports leagues have the appearance of joint ventures between club owners, but they have in fact operated as* **cartels.** *They have as a primary purpose to allocate and control the markets for production and distribution, and have therefore sought to eliminate, within the league, competition over producers (players) and consumers (fans). Any competition in modern sports leagues is avoided as much as possible, within the legal confines of contract, labor, and antitrust laws.*

Member clubs

Individual clubs within a professional sports league are nominally independent legal entities, free to make or lose money depending upon how they operate their businesses. Each team, however, is signatory to a league agreement, which governs the team's actions as a member of the cartel. In this regard, each team is an equal partner with every other team in the league, subject to league rules and severe disciplinary action for any breach. Therefore each member club must be considered as *both* a private business entity and a franchise, operated in accordance with league-wide concerns.

In other industries, it is possible for one firm to withdraw to another market. A sports team, however, must have an opposing team to play against to create the game, which is its final product. A professional sports team must stay within its league to stay in business, unless a rival league exists or can be formed. This is a powerful incentive for each member club to comply with its league's bylaws and rules to identify its individual interests with league-wide interests.

Each league has rules providing for disciplinary action, including expulsion, against members. The constitution and bylaws define the disciplinary powers of a commissioner; in the case of franchise cancellation or forfeiture, the matter is referred to the league's executive committee.

Sanctions have been imposed against league clubs or their owners in a number of situations. For example, league rules were violated by owners trying to improperly lure a player away from another club, so that "tampering" penalties were invoked, on separate occasions, against Atlanta Braves owner Ted Turner, and Oakland A's owner Charles Finley. In 1981, Milwaukee Brewers General Manager Harry Dalton violated a league "gag order" concerning ongoing collective bargaining negotiations, and sanctions were imposed. In 1994, NFL Commissioner Paul Tagliabue threatened to impose a $10,000 fine on any team owner who made public statements deemed unduly critical of the league's new collective bargaining agreement.

Traditionally, each club within a league endeavors to field the best team possible and thereby improve its economic performance. Some teams have sought to become more successful on the field through the acquisition of players in the free-agent player market, and this approach has driven up salaries in each sport. In baseball, the clubs unable or unwilling to compete for these players will, in theory, direct their resources to develop players for their farm systems and future player rosters.

As the player's right to declare himself a free agent has expanded, the pressures on each club to maintain performance levels by acquiring new players (usually other free-agent players) have also grown. But these pressures are balanced by certain economic realities. As a club approaches peak earnings, as determined by attendance and television revenues in its home market, there is a diminished incentive to spend money and improve the product. Spending more on player salaries would result in a reduction in short-term club profits, with no guarantee of improved on-field performance. Each league has a different proportion of owners who believe increased free-agent spending will translate into greater on-field success and consequently greater profitability. Each league has a different free-agent market as a result. What is common to each league at the present time is a belief by owners that an unrestrained free-agent market will destroy their league's viability in the long run (Berry and Wong, 1986).

Players

In each professional team sport, the players are the direct producers of the industry's product, the game; players *are* the product in the estimation of the public (the consumers). It is accurate to say the players are only a part of the game, but in many important respects, they are the most critical part.

With the advent of television, and the commercialization of the sports industries in the last quarter of the twentieth century, professional athletes have attained a cultural status at odds with their legal and economic status as mere employees. Many of the higher-paid stars are more aptly considered entrepreneurs or personal corporations. **Free agency** has given rise to a class of athletes properly considered independent contractors from a fan's viewpoint, and possibly in a strict legal sense as well.

From the players' perspective, since fans pay to see them perform, their compensation should be based on the revenues they generate. A player's career is also very short because of injury or the diminished performance of age, and this is another factor, in the players' view, entitling them to high salaries. Most players, therefore, are unified in their opposition to any club or league rules that suppress their salary levels. This is irrespective of any argument offered for their necessity, either the economic viability of certain teams or certain markets, fan loyalty, or competitive balance among clubs. As this chapter will explore more fully in considering the development of players' associations, these forces have had a powerful impact on the course of labor relations in modern professional sports (Berry, Gould, and Staudohar, 1986).

Agents and attorneys

With the advent of a free agency system in each of the major professional team sports, beginning with baseball in the mid-1970s, the marketing of players has been almost completely taken over by sports agents. Some agents are non-attorneys, but with the growing complexity and compensation of contracts, the players' need for the professional services of both attorneys and accountants has increased.

The influence of competent, ethical sports agents has been a positive one, resulting in higher salaries for their clients and the protection of the players' considerable financial resources. Problems and abuses in the player-agent relationship often result from a lack of professional requirements to enter the field. There currently exists a patchwork of individual state licensing provisions regulating sports agents, but in many contexts, agents can enter the contract negotiation process merely by declaring themselves as agents.

If an agent acts in an unethical manner, the result may be any of the following: misappropriation of client funds, recommendation of investments that violate federal securities laws, overcharging of fees for contract negotiation (usually by charging an up-front percentage of an amount the player may never realize), renegotiation of a player's contract without prior authority, or negotiations contrary to a verbal agreement with the client. Agent abuses can be as varied as the imagination of the agent. College athletics, especially football, have had numerous problems in recent years as a result of the involvement of agents. Funds have often been furnished by agents to college athletes during their eligibility to play, in contravention of NCAA rules. Agents have been known to sign college athletes to contracts of representation before the end of their senior-year playing season, also a violation of NCAA rules. Another common prohibited practice is for an agent to loan money to a promising, but still-eligible, college player in order to later represent him in professional contract negotiations. This is an incomplete list of the many devices which sports agents have used to circumvent established rules and ethical practice. The player-agent re-

lationship is an area where regulation by government licensing procedures, or self-governance by agents themselves, seems desirable. The role of the sports agent is substantial and can no longer be ignored by management. It affects the entire structure of professional team sports, and especially the structure of labor relations.

Players' associations

A note on player unions. Professional baseball players have sought to unionize at least five times. In 1885 they formed the National Brotherhood of Professional Ball Players, and through it they attempted to abolish the new reservation system. Three subsequent attempts to organize players failed, and only with the creation of the Major League Baseball Players Association in 1954, and union status in 1966, did players begin to bargain effectively with ownership. The significant development in this change was the passage of the **National Labor Relations Act** in 1935. This federal law created a public policy that granted unions the right to organize and bargain collectively, and it also required management to negotiate in good faith with a union representing a majority of employees. Before this enactment, player associations were merely voluntary associations, which players did not have to join and leagues did not have to recognize or deal with. True labor unions representing player interests then became part of the landscape in professional sports. The NBA Players Association was formed in 1954, the NFL Players Association was formed in 1956, and the NHL Players Association was formally recognized by the league in 1967.

The historical development of the major professional sports leagues has resulted in a two-tier system. Through the collective bargaining process, the players' associations have each established a minimum player salary in their respective leagues. Players have also collectively negotiated several other financial considerations, notably pension payments and rookie salary structures. Individual players, on their own behalf or through agents, negotiate their own contracts. Salary, contract length, guaranteed payments, and bonuses are currently the province of individual negotiations between player and club (Staudohar, 1996).

To fully understand the development of players' associations, and the collective agreements they have negotiated with ownership, we need to examine the reasons why professional athletes have considered it necessary to organize.

By 1966 it was evident that major league baseball's plan for player representation (in its decision-making executive council) did not adequately protect player interests. It was also clear that union membership had provided significant benefits for workers in diverse segments of American industry. Since player concerns over the **reserve system,** pensions, **grievance procedures,** and minimum salaries had gone unresolved for many years, the benefits of unionization became obvious. The prevailing attitude of players in all major sports was that ownership might not engage in **good faith collective bargaining** unless required to by law; it was, in fact, the establishment of player unions that created the mandate for collective bargaining. This process then transformed the employment relationship in professional team sports.

For many years, there was an active debate over whether player groups were really unions, capable of recognition under the NLRA. Even with official recognition, player unions have had a contentious relationship with management in the collective bargaining process. As a result, the recent history of each major professional sport has seen the players resort to three basic strategies to strengthen their position in the collective bargaining process: (1) antitrust litigation, (2) player strikes, and (3) arbitration of grievances. Antitrust litigation, which forms an essential part of the fabric of labor relations in sports, is considered elsewhere in the text (Jennings, 1990).

CONCEPT CHECK

In each of the four major professional sports, players' associations are now fully recognized as labor unions. As such, they are protected under the provisions of the National Labor Relations Act of 1935. Umpires and referees in these sports have, for the most part, organized in a similar manner.

A model of labor relations in the sports industry

Figure 8–1 shows the interaction of key elements in the sports industry's labor relations. This model has been developed over time to rationally resolve contending claims in the owner-player employment relationship. As in other industries, the principal issues in sports center on the distribution of money and power between players and owners. The government, through statutory enactments and court decisions, regulates the primary relationship, which is between management and labor. This relationship has been formalized under the NLRA-mandated system of union representation and collective bargaining and has in this way established the basic legal framework through which the sports industry is governed. The **National Labor Relations Board** and the federal courts have interpreted and applied laws pertaining to collective bargaining, the right to strike and antitrust policy in a variety of industries. Therefore each labor dispute in sports is affected by a large body of precedent.

1. *Management* operates through league offices, in conjunction with individual team ownerships. Questions of corporate planning and supervision are decided at this level. Leagues, operating through ownership committees, are responsible for the negotiation of collective bargaining agreements, national television contracts, setting procedures for player drafts, and rule-making to enforce various management prerogatives. Individual team owners have found it necessary to grant this authority to the league of which they are a part, but they retain power in several key areas. Team managements, we have seen, negotiate individual player contracts, but also establish rules for player movement between teams (subject to the collective bargaining agreement with the players' union), as well as hire their own front-office employees and coaches.

2. *Labor,* as a component of the industry model, is made up of the players and their unions. We have seen how players' associations evolved into unions; as such, their primary aim is to promote effective collective bargaining. The unions engage in five principal functions to further this objective: (1) organizing the membership to support union goals; (2) negotiating contract terms applicable to all players; (3) using pressure tactics, including strikes; (4) enforcing the terms of the collective bargaining agreement through grievance procedures under the NLRA; and (5) conducting meetings, voting on collective agreements and communicating with members, all of which provide internal union organization.

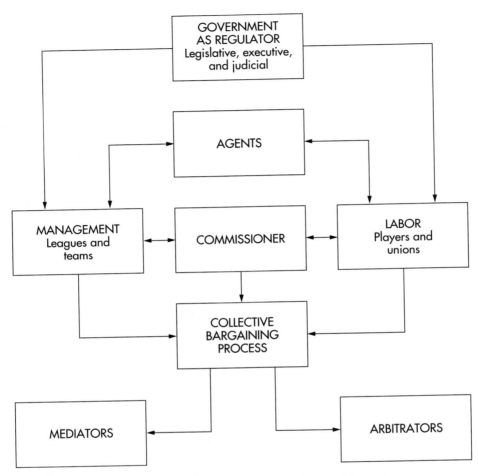

FIGURE 8–1   Interaction of elements in the sports industry's labor relations.
From Staudohar, P.D. (1996). Playing for dollars: labor relations and the sports business. Ithaca, New York, ILR Press.

3. The *commissioner's* role, at least in theory, serves both management and labor. The league commissioner is held forth as a spokesperson on league matters and a guardian of the public interest on questions of the "integrity of the game." In reality, league commissioners are selected and paid by, and serve at the discretion of, management. In 1992 the owners of major league baseball dismissed Commissioner Fay Vincent and installed one of their members (Milwaukee Brewers owner Bud Selig) as "acting Commissioner." It was not until 1998, however, that Selig was given permanent status. Selig is part of the owners' Executive Council, and collective bargaining on behalf of management is handled through the council's Player Relations Committee. Critics have suggested that Vincent's intercession to end the 1990 lockout during spring training was responsible for his ouster as commissioner, illustrating the tenuous nature of the commissioner's role once labor disputes in a particular sport become heated or reach a **negotiation impasse.** Current threats from Congress to repeal baseball's antitrust exemption often emphasize the absence of an impartial commissioner, and this again points to the intercon-

nected elements of the industrial model. The ultimate resolution of these issues is, at present, completely unsettled.

4. *Agents* are not a formal element of the industry model, since they are involved only in the negotiation of player contracts. Still, one must not underestimate their role in raising player salaries to unprecedented levels, and in marketing players for outside commercial activities. Management-player relations have become more adversarial in recent years as a direct outgrowth of agent participation.

5. *Mediators* and *arbitrators* are neutral parties who may become involved in the collective bargaining process through grievance procedures or impasses in negotiations. Paul Staudohar and other labor economists are of the opinion that the development of labor relations in sports will see mediation and arbitration replace litigation as the preferred method of dispute resolution, as it has in more mature industries (Staudohar, 1996).

CONCEPT CHECK

Players have gained greater economic power and freedom with respect to owners, largely through the efforts of player unions and sports agents. Management, labor, the commissioner, and agents all interact to create a model of labor relations built on collective bargaining procedures. Government regulations oversee the entire process.

Collective bargaining

Workers involved in interstate commerce, which includes athletes in professional team sports, are covered by the National Labor Relations Act of 1935, as amended. Section 7 of the NLRA provides for: (1) the right to self-organization, to form, join, or assist labor organizations; (2) the right to bargain collectively through representatives of their own choosing; and (3) the right to engage in "concerted activities" for employees' mutual aid or protection. This last element includes the right to strike and picket for legitimate ends. The law's provisions are administered by the National Labor Relations Board (NLRB) and enforced by the federal courts.

Unfair labor practices, by either management or labor, are prohibited by the NLRB. The Board also determines which issues are properly within the **scope of collective bargaining.** In professional sports, there are two areas that have been of special concern. One is the allegation that a team or employer has disciplined or discharged a player for participation in union activity. Another involves the allegation that an employer has refused to bargain in "good faith." In this context, the parties to negotiations are required to communicate through a series of back-and-forth proposals, while reasonably attempting to reach an agreement. In certain cases, good faith requires an employer to furnish basic financial information regarding its operation. Traditionally, owners of professional sports teams have been loathe to disclose this data to players' unions. To bolster their demand for a salary cap in major league baseball, the owners did submit financial information to the players union in 1994. Nevertheless, the interpretation and inferences to be drawn from the data are still very much at the center of the conflict.

Individual teams negotiate collectively as a league for the purpose of reaching a contract with that sport's players' union. All active league players are bound by the actions of the bargaining unit, and nearly all players are union members. Since the clubs join together to bargain with the union, the negotiated agreement applies uniformly to each team. It is important to remember that, although certain issues are deemed *mandatory subjects* of collective bargaining by the NLRB, the critical issue of individual player salaries has remained the province of individual club management. Salary caps have now been implemented pursuant to the collective agreements for basketball and football; as a result, individual salaries have come under the increasing scrutiny and intervention of league management. Like so many areas of sports labor relations, the league's power to restrict individual player contracts is an unresolved issue warranting future attention. The established industry model no longer considers individual player salaries to be solely a club prerogative. The NBA Players Association is also challenging basketball's college draft and salary cap in court.

Similar player-team-league conflicts can be expected to accompany the implementation of the salary cap scheme in football and basketball.

CONTENTS OF THE COLLECTIVE BARGAINING AGREEMENT

The following areas of concern are typical, but not exclusive, of the matters contained in collective agreements between the players' union and the league (Staudohar, 1996).

1. *Contract length.* It may provide for renegotiation of certain issues during its term, called a *reopener provision.* Most collective agreements in professional sports have been three to five years in length.
2. *Compensation,* including wages, pensions and fringe benefits. Unions in sports only negotiate minimum wage standards, as a rule.
3. *Utilization of labor,* such as work practices, overtime and health and safety concerns. It is here that rules on player *free agency* are made part of the collective agreement.
4. *Individual job rights,* including seniority and discipline. Violence, gambling, and drug abuse by players are regulated in these provisions and are currently matters of significant union and management concern.
5. *Rights of the parties in the bargaining process.* The players' union is usually accorded status as an **agency shop,** so that players electing not to join can be assessed a "service fee" by the union (usually the equivalent of dues).
6. *Methods of administration and enforcement.* Grievance procedures and **arbitration** are usually provided for in this section; if duly negotiated, a no-strike clause would pertain.

CONCEPT CHECK

The NLRA defines the scope of bargaining to include questions of wages (pay, benefits, and bonuses), hours, and working conditions. These areas are deemed "mandatory" subjects of collective bargaining, requiring good faith negotiating between employers and workers. The collective agreements in professional sports vary for each league.

BASEBALL AS A MODEL OF SPORTS LABOR RELATIONS

As America's oldest professional sport, baseball has provided a model of labor relations upon which the other major sports have been patterned. The modern players' union in baseball is the Major League Baseball Players Association (MLBPA). Formed in 1954, the union's early activities were primarily concerned with player pension and insurance issues. In 1966 Marvin Miller was hired as executive director of the MLBPA. Reflecting his background as a labor negotiator in the steel industry, Miller quickly transformed the MLBPA into an effective trade union. In 1968 he negotiated the first collective bargaining agreement between players and owners, resulting in higher minimum salaries, pension increases, and disability and health insurance benefits. To secure a good faith collective bargaining relationship between the parties, the agreement provided for a grievance procedure for the resolution of disputes.

Before 1968, players were permitted to file grievances, but their final disposition was reserved to the commissioner of baseball. The new agreement instituted a system of impartial grievance arbitration, with participants chosen by both sides. In this manner, baseball became the first professional team sport with genuine collective bargaining procedures (Staudohar, 1996).

BASEBALL'S LABOR RELATIONS IN THE COLLECTIVE BARGAINING ERA

The MLBPA's apparent goal during Miller's stewardship was the modification or outright elimination of baseball's *reserve system.* The reserve system was named after the provision in baseball's standard player contract known as the *reserve clause.* The reserve clause stated that if a player failed to sign a contract for the following season, his club could unilaterally renew the contract for one additional season under the identical salary and conditions. A second collective bargaining agreement was ratified in May 1970 for a period of three years. The players, however, went on strike for thirteen days at the start of the 1972 season. The issue was the amount owners would contribute toward player pensions. Since the strike forced the cancellation of eighty-six league games, payment for games missed as a result of the strike was another point of contention. A compromise was reached in the February 1973 collective bargaining agreement, with the owners giving in on pension demands and the players agreeing to forfeit salaries for games not played during the strike. The new agreement broke important new ground, since it provided for **final**

offer salary arbitration in cases where negotiations between owners and qualified individual players had reached an impasse. Under this new system, the club submitted the highest figure it was willing to pay, and the player submitted the lowest figure he was willing to accept, with an arbitrator choosing one figure or the other as a binding determination of the player's salary for the following season. The long-established practice of players negotiating salaries individually, with only minimum salary levels collectively bargained by the union, did not change.

Arbitration: The end of the reserve clause in baseball

It should be made clear that unilateral decisions by management on baseball's fundamental labor questions often result in harmful work stoppages. It was through the collective bargaining process that baseball's reservation system was finally toppled. In the 1973 agreement, the individual clubs and the players' union agreed to the use of a grievance-arbitration procedure, with a neutral third-party arbitrator presiding. The collective agreement addressed the reserve system issue in an ambiguous manner. The precise language, contained in Article XV, read as follows:

Except as adjusted or modified hereby, this Agreement does not deal with the reserve system. The Parties have differing views as to the legality and as to the merits of such system as presently constituted. This Agreement shall in no way prejudice the position or legal rights of the Parties or of any Player regarding the reserve system.

During the term of this Agreement neither of the Parties will resort to any form of concerted action with respect to the issue of the reserve system, and there shall be no obligation to negotiate with respect to the reserve system.

Despite language that appeared to remove the reserve system from inclusion in the collective bargaining agreement, the agreement also incorporated by reference the Uniform Player's Contract, which still contained the "reserve clause." This latent contradiction went unresolved until Jim "Catfish" Hunter brought a grievance against his Oakland A's club in 1974. Hunter claimed that the team's failure to purchase an annuity under the terms of his player contract was a breach allowing him to become a free agent, eligible to negotiate with any other club. The case went to arbitrator Peter Seitz, who ruled the A's owed Hunter the

amount of the annuity plus interest and that Hunter was a free agent. The courts upheld the arbitration ruling, and Hunter signed a five-year, $3.75 million contract with the New York Yankees. This was the highest salary in baseball history at the time, and it emboldened players to test the reserve clause under the grievance-arbitration procedure.

In 1975 Andy Messersmith of the Los Angeles Dodgers and Dave McNally of the Montreal Expos played without renewing the signed contracts under which they had played the previous season. At the end of the season, each declared himself a free agent eligible to negotiate and sign with any other team in baseball. The players argued, in effect, that the reserve clause in their 1974 contracts only bound them for one additional year, while the owners maintained the reserve clause was perpetual.

In October 1975 the MLBPA filed a grievance on behalf of Messersmith and McNally, asking an arbitrator to declare both players free agents. The owners, citing Article XV of the collective bargaining agreement, contended the grievance was not subject to arbitration, since issues relating to the reserve system were expressly excluded from the contract. The players union answered this argument by declaring that Article XV had been accepted only to pursue the Curt Flood antitrust litigation. The arbitrator, again Peter Seitz, ruled the issue was arbitrable for the reason offered by the union, then went on to side with the players on the question of the reserve clause's applicability for only one year after a signed contract expired (Jennings, 1990).

Seitz's final ruling declared that in the absence of an existing contractual relationship between team and player, the reserve clause had no effect. A signed contract allowed the team to exercise one option of the reserve clause per player for a period of one year. McNally and Messersmith were declared free agents who now could negotiate with any team in either league without restriction. The arbitration ruling was upheld on appeal in federal court, and the modern era of free agency in professional sports was born.

Baseball: Two decades of unrest

Once the existing reserve system had fallen, players and owners still had to negotiate a new reserve system that would fairly balance the needs of both parties. Nearly twenty years later, the issues remain unresolved. In 1976 the MLBPA under Marvin

Miller agreed to a new system in which players could become free agents after playing six major league seasons. This gave each major league team, in effect, a six-year guarantee on a player's services. After this period expired, if the team and player could not agree to a new contract, the player became a free agent.

In 1972 the players had struck briefly at the start of the season over a pension dispute, and eighty-six games were lost. (The championship race in the American League's Eastern Division was compromised as a result.) In 1976, spring training was shut down for seventeen days because of a collective bargaining dispute over the free agency question. The owners had announced they would not open spring training camps without a new collective bargaining agreement, but Commissioner Bowie Kuhn intervened to open the camps on March 17, and the season continued. A new four-year agreement was signed on July 12, 1976, adopting a six-year free agency provision with players eligible for salary arbitration after two years. A similar lockout occurred during 1990 spring training. Before 1994, however, the only major disruption to a championship baseball season was the 1981 players' strike.

Negotiations between owners and players in 1980 sought to reach a new collective bargaining agreement to take effect in 1981. In the 1976 agreement, the players still had the right to grievance and salary arbitration, but they had finally modified the onerous effects of the reserve clause. Beginning in 1976, players were permitted to become free agents under certain conditions and thereby sell their services to a new team for more money.

By 1980 owners were trying to regain control over player mobility and, consequently, control over player salaries. At issue was the question of whether teams losing players to the free agency market should be compensated by the teams that signed them. The owners' logic was that compensation would dampen the free-agent market and keep player salaries from explosively escalating (Dworkin, 1981).

Baseball's owners and players reached an impasse on the free agency compensation question in 1981. When the owners announced they would unilaterally impose a compensation plan in the absence of an agreement with the players, the union set a strike date of May 29. The union then filed an unfair labor practice charge with the NLRB, claiming the owners had refused to bargain in good faith when they denied the union's request for financial data. The union delayed the strike for two weeks while the NLRB sought an injunction in federal court. An injunction would have prevented the owners from implementing the compensation plan and would have delayed the strike for another year. The court refused to intervene, and the players went on strike on June 12, 1981.

Once collective bargaining negotiations reach an impasse and breakdown, the ultimate weapon of the union is the **player strike.** Each of the major sports has a multiple-employer bargaining structure, so when the players strike, every team is shut down. Corollary businesses, such as network and local television companies and stadium concession stands, are adversely affected. Hotels, restaurants, bars, and airlines also lose revenue when games are cancelled due to a work stoppage. Baseball has endured five such stoppages since 1972, but none as catastrophic as the 1994 strike.

Preparing for the 1981 strike, baseball's owners had purchased $50 million in strike insurance from Lloyd's of London, and they had also created a $15 million strike fund. Players lost salaries as the strike dragged on, but remained unified in their opposition to ownership's demand for a compensation provision. After 713 league games had been cancelled and fifty days had elapsed, the unpalatable prospect of wiping out the remainder of the season brought both sides to a compromise. Free agency rules were tightened, but no compensation was required for players moving to new teams. The players had preserved the right to move to other clubs, and the era of dramatic salary increases continued (Jennings, 1990).

Collusion

In 1985 the free-agent market collapsed when no contract offers for new free agents were forthcoming. The owners were eventually found by the courts to have engaged in **collusion,** agreeing among themselves not to bid for free agents and guaranteeing that no offers were made. The courts found that since an existing market had already been established, the owners had acted wrongfully. A $280 million damage award was split up among those players who had found no market for their services as free agents in the years 1985 to 1987.

The 1994 impasse

By 1993, with the expiration of the current collective bargaining agreement, player salaries under free agency had increased to the point where the average salary was $1.2 million per season. Owners claimed that the continuation of several franchises in the game's current economic condition required revenue sharing between so-called "large-market" and "small-market" teams. The owners tied the plan to the acceptance of a salary cap by the players' union in a new collective agreement. The owners maintained they had to control player salaries to ensure the survival of the game. The players refused to accept a cap system, and when the owners threatened to unilaterally impose a salary cap at the end of the 1994 season, negotiations for a new agreement reached another impasse. On August 12, 1994, the players went on strike rather than complete the season and allow the owners to impose the new system. On September 14, 1994, the owners canceled the remainder of the championship season, as well as all postseason playoffs and the World Series. Despite the owners' resolve to "explore all avenues to achieve a meaningful, structural reform of baseball's player compensation system," the collective bargaining mechanism had broken down, and the sport and business of major league baseball ground to a halt.

Months of unproductive negotiations ensued, and in late February 1995 labor negotiations between major league baseball's players and owners broke down. William J. Usery, Secretary of Labor under President Ford and a former director of the Federal Mediation and Conciliation Service, had been appointed in October 1994 by President Clinton to move the parties back to the bargaining table. The player strike had brought a premature end to the baseball season, and direct negotiations between the parties had ended in early September. By the following February, it was clear that Usery had failed to achieve his presidential mandate.

On December 22, 1994, the owners announced they would unilaterally implement a salary cap provision after declaring an impasse in collective bargaining negotiations. The players had long maintained such an action was in violation of federal labor law, and in late January the general counsel of the National Labor Relations Board advised club owners he was about to file a complaint with the NLRB. The purpose was to seek an injunction in Federal court, and force baseball to return to its *status quo ante* prior to the owners' December 22 action. Richard Ravitch, the head of the Player Relations Committee for the owners, left office on December 31, and a committee headed by Boston Red Sox owner John Harrington became directly involved in negotiations for the first time.

The owners took several contradictory steps in early February 1995. On February 3 they promised to restore the pre-salary cap system, but on February 5 they declared that individual clubs could no longer directly sign players to contracts; this function would become the exclusive province of the owners' Central Bargaining Committee. On February 9 the owners announced the end of salary arbitration procedures, long viewed by many of them as an inflationary device in the determination of a player's market value.

As matters deteriorated in early February, Usery emphatically denied he had made any final or formal recommendations to the President for ending the impasse. The two sides seemed more intransigent and irreconcilable than ever. The owners maintained that without a salary cap the economics of baseball were not viable, and the players' union steadfastly held that if a player and his club could not agree on what the player should be paid, the player should be free to seek employment with a new team.

On March 31, 1995, U.S. District Court Judge Sonia Sotomayor in New York granted the injunction sought by the NLRB, preventing the owners from implementing the salary cap system and its attendant provisions. The following week the Second Circuit Court of Appeals, acting through a three-judge panel, denied the owners' request for a stay of the injunction, and ultimately upheld the District Court's ruling. In response to this judicial action, the players' union announced it would voluntarily end its strike and return to the field to play the 1995 championship season.

After an abbreviated spring training, and the abrupt dismissal of replacement players prepared to proceed with a regular season schedule of games, major league players returned to begin a shortened 144-game schedule. There is still no assurance that a collective bargaining agreement can or will be reached in the foreseeable future, and it is not clear how long the sides will continue to function without one. Fans showed their displeasure with both sides by curtailing game attendance by about 20 percent.

TABLE 8-1   *The case for and against a baseball salary cap*

Year	Total revenue	Players' total payroll	Percent of total revenues
1985	$720,192,000	$322,557,000	45
1986	798,148,000	355,582,000	45
1987	914,109,000	391,369,000	43
1988	1,007,474,000	443,554,000	44
1989	1,214,833,000	503,373,000	41
1990	1,363,605,000	587,750,000	43
1991	1,539,217,000	736,591,000	48
1992	1,665,106,000	914,014,000	55
1993	1,879,737,000	997,548,000	53

Data from *USA Today*.
For the projected 1994 season, since cancelled, players' salaries were expected to be 58% of baseball's total projected revenues of approximately $1.7 billion.

Table 8-1 helps put the numbers and dollar amounts that led to the 1994–95 conflict into perspective. Figure 8-2 charts the increase in players' salaries since the beginning of free agency, and Table 8-1 tracks the change in baseball's total revenue with the percent of players' payroll.

With renewed popularity in 1998, baseball attendance drew closer to its average before the 1994–95 strike. By mid-1999, game crowds averaged 27,919, just under the 27,967 average a year earlier; attendance was up 10.5 percent from 1995 (25,260), but was off 11.7 percent from the pre-strike average (31,612). Saturday telecasts on Fox averaged a 17 percent increase over the prior year. "I believe baseball is more popular today than ever before," Commissioner Harry "Bud" Selig maintained. Small-market owners argue they cannot generate sufficient revenue to field competitive teams, even with the poorest clubs receiving $12 million to $13 million from revenue sharing in 1999. In response, Selig formed an economic study committee, which was scheduled to report in early 2000.

The labor agreement with players was to expire after the 2001 season. Between 1972 and 1999, baseball had nine work stoppages, and the salary cap issue was the most divisive. The 1995 collective bargaining agreement avoided a salary cap by implementing a "luxury tax" on teams with the highest salaries. Some owners still feel a salary cap and revenue sharing system are necessary for the league's economic survival, but the players' union is still strongly opposed to the plan. As of mid-1999 there were no proposals by either side to extend the collective bargaining agreement beyond its scheduled termination. Whether the dispute over the salary cap leads to yet another work stoppage is open to conjecture. Donald Fehr, MLBPA executive director, believes the owners and players have improved their relationship. Fehr and Selig were antagonists during the 1994–96 labor dispute, but communicate now in a positive manner. Tables 8-2 and 8-3 show the growth of top player salaries by the end of 1998.

Owners are concentrating on marketing efforts instead of potential labor issues with the players. Seattle opened a new stadium July 15, 1999, and new ballparks were to open in 2000 in Detroit, Houston, Milwaukee, and San Francisco. The Montreal Expos draw only 8,789 per game at Olympic Stadium, and questions also persist regarding ownership, location, and stadium financing for the Minnesota Twins and Oakland Athletics.

The umpires' lockout

In the midst of major league baseball's labor dispute between owners and players, problems arose with the umpires' union. The union had a four-year collective bargaining agreement which expired on December 31, 1994, and in the absence of a new agreement with the owners they were locked out of spring training camps as of January 1, 1995. Replacement umpires were then hired in contemplation of a 1995 major league season to be played by replacement baseball players.

At issue in the negotiations between the owners and the umpires was the existing salary structure for major league umpires, as well as corollary issues of severance and bonus pay. Richie Phillips, executive director of the Major League Umpires Association, asked for a 53 percent raise over the current compensation scale, which paid a $60,000 minimum annual salary for rookies up to a maximum $175,000 annual salary for veterans with twenty-five years of major league service. The umpires also demanded payment of 1994 postseason bonuses, which had been cancelled because there was no postseason in 1994, and an increase in severance payments

TABLE 8-2   *Highest baseball salaries*

NEW YORK (AP)—Baseball contracts with average annual values of $8 million or more. Figures were obtained by The Associated Press from player and management sources and include all guaranteed income but not income from potential incentive bonuses. There is no distinction for money deferred without interest:

Player, club	Years	Average salary
Mo Vaughn, Ana	1999–04	$13,333,333
Mike Piazza, NYM	1999–05	$13,000,000
Pedro Martinez, Bos	1998–03	$12,500,000
Bernie Williams, NYY	1999–05	$12,500,000
Greg Maddux, Atl	1998–02	$11,500,000
Barry Bonds, SF	1999–00	$11,450,000
Gary Sheffield, LA	1998–03	$11,416,667
Albert Belle, CWS	1997–01	$11,000,000
Sammy Sosa, Cubs	1998–01	$10,625,000
Mark McGwire, StL	1998–00	$9,500,000
Matt Williams, Ari	1999–03	$9,000,000
Raul Mondesi, LA	1998–01	$9,000,000
Ken Griffey Jr., Sea	1997–00	$8,500,000
Tom Glavine, Atl	1998–01	$8,500,000
Pat Hentgen, Tor	1999	$8,500,000
Ivan Rodriguez, Tex	1998–02	$8,400,000
Roger Clemens, Tor	1997–99	$8,250,000
Andres Galarraga, Atl	1998–00	$8,250,000
Darryl Kile, Col	1998–00	$8,000,000
Kenny Lofton, Cle	1998–00	$8,000,000
Al Leiter, NYM	1999–02	$8,000,000
David Cone, NYY	1999	$8,000,000
Todd Stottlemyre, Ari	1999–02	$8,000,000
Brian Jordan, Atl	1999–03	$8,000,000
Roberto Alomar, Cle	1999–02	$8,000,000

from $200,000 to $500,000. The union took the familiar tack of filing an unfair labor practices charge with the NLRB, alleging that American and National League owners had failed to bargain in good faith after the expiration of the old agreement.

The end of the players' strike, occasioned by an injunction prohibiting the owners' unilaterally imposed salary cap, led to a hastily restructured regular season. As regular-season games commenced they were staffed by replacement umpires. After several days, in which players expressed growing displeasure with the level of umpiring, the owners unceremoniously dismissed the replacements and reached an accord permitting the regular union umpires to return to work. The new four-year agreement provided for undisclosed wage-scale increases to be phased in over the course of the contract, and no maximum salary for umpires with more than twenty-five years of major league service.

The owners faced a labor confrontation with umpires after the 1999 season. Selig wanted to shift control of umpires from the leagues to the commissioner's office, and the three-way relationship between owners, players, and umpires had deteriorated significantly since MLB acted indecisively in the 1996 Roberto Alomar spitting incident. Public reprimand and fines for umpires is especially unpalatable to the umpires union and its director, Richie Phillips.

CONCEPT CHECK

The concept of a standardized pay schedule, determined by age, position, and seniority, is common in many industrial settings, but has been consistently excluded from labor relations in professional sports. Sports has a two-tier system, and individual player salaries are not subject to collective bargaining. Note, however, that team challenges to salary cap strictures are blurring the traditional division of areas affected by collective bargaining.

RECENT HISTORY: THE FREE-AGENT ERA IN THE OTHER PROFESSIONAL SPORTS
Football

Historically, each of the major professional sports has devised some form of reservation system to hinder a player's freedom to move from one team to another. Compensation systems and other league actions effectively destroyed the player's right to free agency, even with the one-year reservation system.

Beginning in 1947, football players had to sign a standard player contract, which bound them to

TABLE 8-3   *Salary progression chart*

NEW YORK (AP)—A look at how the top salary in baseball has escalated, based on average annual values of multiyear contracts. Figures were obtained by The Associated Press from player and management sources and include all guaranteed income at the time of signing, but not income from potential incentive bonuses. There is no distinction for money deferred without interest:

Date	Player	Club	Average salary
Nov. 25, 1998	Mo Vaughn	Anaheim	$13,333,333
Oct. 26, 1998	Mike Piazza	N. Y. Mets	$13,000,000
Dec. 12, 1997	Pedro Martinez	Boston	$12,500,000
Aug. 10, 1997	Greg Maddux	Atlanta	$11,500,000
Feb. 20, 1997	Barry Bonds	S. F. Giants	$11,450,000
Nov. 19, 1996	Albert Belle	Chi. White Sox	$11,000,000
Jan. 31, 1996	Ken Griffey Jr.	Seattle	$8,500,000
Dec. 8, 1992	Barry Bonds	S. F. Giants	$7,291,666
March 2, 1992	Ryne Sandberg	Chicago Cubs	$7,100,000
Dec. 2, 1991	Bobby Bonilla	N. Y. Mets	$5,800,000
Feb. 8, 1991	Roger Clemens	Boston	$5,380,250
June 27, 1990	Jose Canseco	Oakland	$4,700,000
April 9, 1990	Don Mattingly	N. Y. Yankees	$3,860,000
Jan. 22, 1990	Will Clark	San Francisco	$3,750,000
Jan. 17, 1990	Dave Stewart	Oakland	$3,550,000
Dec. 11, 1989	Mark Davis	Kansas City	$3,250,000
Dec. 1, 1989	Mark Langston	California	$3,250,000
Nov. 28, 1989	Rickey Henderson	Oakland	$3,000,000
Nov. 22, 1989	Kirby Puckett	Minnesota	$3,000,000
Nov. 17, 1989	Bret Saberhagen	Kansas City	$2,966,667
Feb. 16, 1989	Orel Hershiser	Los Angeles	$2,633,333
Feb. 15, 1989	Roger Clemens	Boston	$2,500,000

their teams for an additional season at not less than 90 percent of their previous season's salary. In the National Football League, the compensation system was known as the *Rozelle Rule* because Commissioner Pete Rozelle was charged with the task of awarding compensation to those clubs that had lost players to free agency. The practice did have the owners' desired effect of discouraging free agent signings and holding down player salaries. Player dissatisfaction with the NFL's system led to strikes and antitrust litigation, which in turn led to a liberalized free agency system in the 1993 collective bargaining agreement.

In 1974, professional football faced a situation very similar to the baseball impasse. The 1970 collective bargaining agreement had expired, and the Rozelle Rule governing the movement of players between teams was a sticking point. The rule allowed a player whose contract had expired to sign with a different club, but it also required the signing club to compensate the player's former club. If the two teams could not agree, it was left to the commissioner to award players, draft choices, or cash to the former team. The effect of the rule, which was part of league bylaws, was to destroy the free-agent market for players, since no team wanted to risk losing top players or draft choices at the sole discretion of Rozelle.

The NFL players went on strike during the summer of 1974 to break the deadlock, but after six weeks the strike failed, and the players returned. Scabs and rookies had crossed the picket lines to enter training camp, and the 1987 player strike was broken in similar fashion. Nevertheless, the union in each instance had one weapon left in its arsenal—antitrust litigation. This is the one avenue unavailable to baseball players. From 1976 until 1993, NFL players won a series of court victories against the owners, and accomplished what the player strikes never could. The court decisions set the stage for the current free agency system in football.

Professional football survived its free agency crisis largely because of the John Mackey case, filed in a Minnesota federal court in 1975. The trial judge held that the Rozelle Rule was an illegal conspiracy in restraint of trade. As such, it violated antitrust law and denied the players the right to contract freely for their services. It was, in effect, a group boycott or "refusal to deal" by the owners, something the law clearly prohibited. The federal appeals court upheld the ruling, but warned that a rule governing player movement could be exempt from antitrust law if it was the product of bona fide arm's-length negotiations during collective bargaining. But no such actions had occurred between the owners and the union to save the Rozelle Rule. The court stated:

It may be that some reasonable restrictions relating to player transfers are necessary to the successful operation of the NFL. . . . We encourage the parties to resolve this question through collective bargaining. The parties are far better situated to agreeably resolve what rules governing player transfers are best suited for their mutual interests out of court (*Mackey v National Football League,* 543 F.2d 606 [8th Cir., 1976]).

It took another generation of court action to get rid of the successor to the Rozelle Rule, "Plan B" free agency. Plan B also undermined the free-agent market and unfairly held down player salaries, but it was successfully challenged by a 1993 antitrust suit (*McNeil v NFL*). This forced the owners back into collective bargaining negotiations with the players' union.

The collective bargaining agreement between NFL owners and the NFLPA took effect in the 1993 season. It provides that players with five years'

experience can offer their services on the open market once their current contracts expire. A salary cap provision took effect in 1994, setting combined player salaries at 64 percent of designated gross revenues flowing into the league. The cap fell 1 percent per year until 1996, then remained stable at 62 percent. A complicated exemption system for free agents was also instituted, allowing each team to designate one "franchise" player, who then must be paid a "top five" equivalent salary for his position to be exempted.

Of all the major sports leagues we have examined, the National Football League appears to have the most stable labor-management relationship. Considering the league's bitter legal battles and work stoppages of the past, this is surprising. But it is a testament to the determination of NFLPA executive director Gene Upshaw and NFL Commissioner Paul Tagliabue. Both men recognized the necessity of improving their relationship, and so were able to forge a sense of cooperation and mutual interest rarely present in the collective bargaining taking place in the other professional sports. In February 1998 the league owners and players' union agreed to extend the current collective bargaining agreement through the end of the 2003 season. This guarantees football's place as the only major sport that did not cancel games during the 1990s due to labor discord.

From 1989 to 1999, total league revenues increased from $970 million to $3.5 billion. The valuation of franchises also escalated throughout the decade. Between 1960 and 1988, Jack Kent Cooke paid $15 million to acquire sole ownership of the Washington Redskins. In 1999, the team was sold by his estate for $800 million. The expansion Cleveland Browns franchise was purchased from the league in the summer of 1998 for $530 million. The Dallas Cowboys, to take another example, were purchased by Jerry Jones for $95 million in 1988; ten years later, Forbes magazine (December 14, 1998) estimated the team's value at $413 million.

The average NFL team's player payroll is about $47 million per year. Players have shared in the league's sustained prosperity during the past decade; salaries have continued to rise despite restraints on free agency such as a hard salary cap. The huge television contracts of 1994 and 1998, spurred by network rivalries and a determination first by Fox then by CBS to participate in the league's broadcast packages, have been fundamental to the league's success. The inclination of cities and states to fund new stadium construction has also played a part. But the other key element has been the lack of turmoil in the league's labor relations.

The working relationship of Upshaw and Tagliabue contrasts with the adversarial relationship between NBA commissioner David Stern and NBPA executive director Billy Hunter. The NFL principals meet regularly to discuss a wide range of issues, including all aspects of the governance of the game. By contrast, during the 1998 NBA lockout, Stern accused prominent player agents of sabotaging the negotiations, while Hunter accused Stern of trying to divide the union.

The National Football League is the new paradigm of positive labor relations in sport. (M. Freeman, "NFL Labor Peace Through 2003," the *New York Times,* Nov. 8, 1998). Franchise values steadily appreciate, fan interest is high, and perhaps most essential, there is a working partnership between the league's commissioner and the head of the players' union. Accordingly, for sports leagues to ensure satisfactory collective bargaining it may be necessary for the principal negotiators to develop respect, trust, and the conviction that each side's interests are inextricably connected to their counterpart's.

A significant court decision affecting the NFL's labor situation was rendered in *Brown v Pro Football, Inc.,* 116 S. Ct. 2116 (1996). In 1992, Antony Brown and the players' union brought an antitrust action against the Washington Redskins and the NFL. They claimed that the Redskins, under a plan devised by the league, set Brown's salary as a member of the team's six-player "development squad" at $1,000 per week; they further alleged that this was a wage-fixing restraint in violation of the federal antitrust laws. Although the union had sought to make these wages a matter of negotiation between the player and his team, there was no collective bargaining provision regarding the issue. After the union and league reached an impasse in collective bargaining negotiations, the league unilaterally imposed the salary scale.

The lower courts held that this action unfairly restricted a player's ability to freely market his services to the highest bidder, and was a price-fixing restraint subject to antitrust law. The United States Supreme Court let stand an appeals court decision reversing the ruling; this overturned the $30 million judgment awarded to the affected players by the trial court. The Supreme Court held that the nonstatutory labor exemption extended even to unilateral employer action taken after an impasse in the bargaining process was reached. This opinion ends any hope the players had that they could participate in collective bargaining and still seek protection from the antitrust laws. Only union decertification will overcome the nonstatutory labor exemption.

Basketball

In the National Basketball Association, players signing the uniform player contract were originally bound to one team throughout their careers. If the player refused to sign a tendered contract, the team could unilaterally renew his contract for the following season at the same salary rate he was then earning.

In March 1973, a three-year contract was signed between the NBA and the players' association (NBAPA), the league's first collective bargaining agreement. The NBAPA had filed an antitrust suit against the league in 1970, seeking to halt a merger between the league and the rival American Basketball Association. A month before the NBA's first labor agreement, the U.S. District Court ruled "the player draft, uniform player contract, and reserve clause were analogous to devices which were *per se* violations of the antitrust laws" (*Robertson v NBA,* 389 F.Supp. 867, 1975), and upheld an injunction against the merger. In February 1976 the case was settled out of court when the league agreed to drop the requirement of compensation for free agents, beginning in 1980. Additionally, 1976 would be the last year a standard player contract would contain an option clause. As a result, beginning in 1980, NBA players were allowed to become free agents, subject only to the **right of first refusal** by the team that the player sought to leave. This mechanism allowed the player's old team to resign him by matching any offer tendered to the player by a prospective new team.

In April 1983 the NBA brought professional sports into the salary-cap era.

The NBA lockout of 1998–99. Prior to the 1998–99 season, the National Basketball Association took great pride in the fact that no regular-season or play-off games had ever been lost to a work stoppage. The other major professional team sports, by contrast, suffered from serious labor discord throughout the 1980s and 1990s; often seasons were curtailed due to lockouts and strikes. In the case of Major League Baseball, the cancellation of the 1994 playoffs and World Series seriously undermined fan interest in the sport, creating a 20 percent decrease in attendance for the following two seasons.

In 1994, when the NBA began negotiations for a new collective bargaining agreement, the union leadership's primary goal was the elimination of three provisions from the expiring contract: the salary cap, the college draft, and the "right of first refusal," which allowed a team to retain a free agent player by matching an opposing club's salary offer. The owners refused to reach a new agreement without these elements, and the 1994–95 season was played pursuant to a no-strike, no-lockout moratorium. The union then filed an antitrust lawsuit, alleging that the three provisions created an unlawful restraint of competition, and constituted an unlawful price-fixing agreement among horizontal competitors, in violation of the Sherman Antitrust Act. The players also argued that by collectively imposing terms of employment after the prior agreement had expired, the owners were acting as an illegal cartel.

The players' claims were rejected in the federal district court, and the Second Circuit affirmed the ruling in *National Basketball Association v Williams*, 45 F. 3d 684 (2d Cir. 1995). The court held that the antitrust laws do not prohibit employers form bargaining jointly with a union, from implementing their proposals in the absence of a collective bargaining agreement, or from using economic force to obtain agreement to their proposals. In effect, the court declared that the multi-employer bargaining of the NBA was exempt from the antitrust laws under the "nonstatutory labor exemption" recognized by courts in prior cases.

This set the stage for some unusual developments at the bargaining table. In April 1995 Charles Grantham abruptly resigned as executive director of the players' union and was replaced by a former league deputy commissioner, Simon Gourdine. At Gourdine's insistence, a tentative agreement was reached between owners and the union. Several influential player agents objected to the proposed agreement because it greatly restricted the growth of the top player salaries. NBA ticket prices in 1995 were the highest of the four major team sports, the teams had the smallest rosters (twelve players per team), and consequently average salaries, based on computing a designated percentage of total league revenues, were the highest of all the major sports leagues.

On June 30, 1995, the owners declared a lockout, the first in league history, and froze all dealings with players. They also moved to restructure the proposed collective bargaining agreement to make it more acceptable to the dissident players and their agents. At the urging of several powerful agents, a number of players (including superstars Michael Jordan and Patrick Ewing) tried to have the union decertified; the goal was to nullify the proposed collective bargaining agreement. This strategy was also designed to destroy the owners' antitrust immunity under the "nonstatutory labor exemption." After decertification, the players could pursue a litigation strategy, attacking the salary cap, draft and right of first refusal on antitrust grounds. The NFLPA had succeeded with this strategy, though their antitrust litigation (*McNeil v NFL*) was settled with a new collective bargaining agreement, not a court judgment.

A decertification election was set for September 1995. A faction of players and agents was now in conflict with the players' union over who would control the direction of negotiations. The owners believed a union defeat over decertification would result in another round of antitrust litigation, so they sought to head off the decertification election. In early September, the players voted emphatically (63 percent) not to decertify, the lockout was lifted, and the 1995–96 season proceeded on schedule without the cancellation of any games. On September 15, 1995, the league and union reached a new agreement to run through the 2000–2001 season.

One result of the 1995 negotiation was that top player agents such as Richard Faulk, and the union's legal counsel, Jeffrey Kessler, became part of the collective bargaining process. The union was still in turmoil; Gourdine was replaced as executive director by Billy Hunter. Finally, the owners saw that a lockout could be an effective technique in conducting negotiations, and they would soon use it again as a preferred tactic in dealing with an uncooperative union.

The six-year agreement approved in 1995 contained a clause allowing the owners to reopen negotiations after three years, if the percentage of "basketball-related income" devoted to player salaries exceeded 51.8 percent. On March 23, 1998 the owners voted 27–2 to reopen negotiations at the conclusion of the season, claiming player salaries for the 1997–98 season would total 57 percent of the league's $1.7 billion total revenue. This percentage would later be disputed by the union, but it was the basis on which the owners invoked the "reopener" clause. The league, through Commissioner Stern, also claimed that nearly half of its twenty-nine franchises were losing money.

Over the next three months, the owners' and players' negotiating committees met a total of nine times. The owners had already signed a four-year, $2.64 billion television rights contract with the NBC and Turner networks, raising each team's *pro rata* share from $9 million to $22 million. But player salaries had increased by 50 percent over the previous five years, and the owners were determined to make changes to the salary cap provisions in the prior labor agreement. In 1994, the owners demanded the so-called "Larry Bird exemption," allowing teams to exceed the salary cap in order to match another team's offer to players who qualified for free agency; in 1998 they reversed their position and demanded the "Bird exemption" be abolished. In salary cap parlance, this would change a "soft cap" to a "hard cap." The players' union argued that the new television contract belied the owners' claims of economic hardship, and refused to grant the demand for a hard cap. On June 22, 1998, the final meeting between the sides ended after only thirty minutes, and a few days later the league announced a lockout beginning on July 1.

The NBA enjoyed tremendous popular growth throughout the 1980s and 1990s; though overall attendance was stable during 1997–98, some teams experienced 15 to 20 percent attendance declines and decreased sales of licensed apparel. Much of the league's success was due to the extraordinary popularity of Michael Jordan and the Chicago Bulls, who became a worldwide marketing phenomenon. But steadily increasing aberrant behavior by NBA players, including domestic violence, on-court violence, and weapons, traffic, drug, and alcohol charges, reflected negatively on the sport and disaffected many fans.

Still, the single most polarizing issue in the labor negotiations of 1998 was the explosive rise in player salaries. We have traced the growth of player salaries in professional team sports during the collective bargaining era, but basketball posed an especially dramatic case. In 1977, for example, Kareem Abdul-Jabbar's $625,000 annual salary with the Los Angeles Lakers was the league's highest. In 1987, Patrick Ewing of the Knicks topped the list with an annual salary of $2.75 million, and in 1997, due to the Bird exemption, Chicago's Jordan was the highest paid at $30 million per year.

Long-term contracts were part of the problem. In 1996, Shaquille O'Neal signed with the Los Angeles Lakers for seven years at $123 million. The following year the Minnesota Timberwolves signed 21-year-old Kevin Garnett for $126 million over seven years. Garnett had entered the NBA directly from high school and was still establishing himself as a player; his salary represented potential value rather than compensation for proven performance. By 1997, 15 percent of total salaries were going to the nine highest-paid players, while about 20 percent of the players made the league's minimum salary. As always, the issue boiled down to how to divide the revenues between the players and owners.

The five principal issues in the 1998 negotiations were: the salary cap, free agency, minimum salaries, the rookie pay scale, and discipline of "aberrant" player behavior.

Here is a summary of the provisions under discussion:

SALARY CAP Basketball's salary cap is highly complex. It was designed to limit team payrolls, while guaranteeing the players a percentage of overall league revenues. In its first year of operation, 1984–85, the cap was $3.6 million per team; in 1997–98 it was $26.9 million, and in 1998–99, $30 million per team. The NBA's salary cap is "soft," meaning it permits exceptions. For example, a team could replace an injured player for up to 50 percent of the injured player's salary, and not affect the cap. Clubs could also sign one free agent for $1 million every two years and not affect the cap. Most crucial was the "Bird exception," allowing teams to sign their own free agents regardless of cap restrictions. Players demanded the soft cap be retained, while owners insisted it be replaced by a hard cap, permitting no exceptions. As negotiations began, players demanded that 60 percent of total revenues be assigned to player salaries, while owners offered them 50 percent.

FREE AGENCY If teams had to count salaries paid to retain their own free agents against the salary cap, salaries would be significantly reduced. It is clear why players favored keeping the Bird exception and owners demanded its removal.

ROOKIE PAY SCALE Under the prior agreement, all first-round draft picks had to sign three-year, guaranteed contracts, after which they became free agents. The contracts could be extended after the first two years, and owners did not want to lose top draft picks to free agency. So the extensions offered to players like Garnett, if they showed great potential after two years, drove the market price of still-unproven players into the $20 million per season range.

MINIMUM SALARIES Under the old agreement, the league's minimum salary was $272,500. The union sought a pay scale that increased the minimum according to the player's seniority in the league.

PLAYER DISCIPLINE The NBA sought to add marijuana, opiates, alcohol, and performance-enhancing drugs to the list of substances covered by the league's drug control program; only heroin and cocaine had been covered since the program's inception in 1984. (A well-publicized 1997 *New York Times* survey claimed that 60 to 70 percent of the league's players smoked marijuana.) The league also wanted the authority to punish players for misdemeanor charges, attacking fans and team officials, and refusing to accept a trade to a new team.

The 1998 negotiating team for the owners was Commissioner David Stern, deputy commissioner Russell Granik, and legal counsel Jeffrey Mishkin. The players were represented by NBPA executive director Billy Hunter, union president Patrick Ewing, and legal counsel Jeffrey Kessler. After the lockout took effect, there was intense daily media scrutiny, and negotiations took place, in labor relations parlance, in a "fishbowl atmosphere." This is usually a highly undesirable negotiating situation, and Stern declared that any NBA owner speaking to the media directly would be subject to a $1 million fine.

Most negotiating was done through the media, anyway; while face-to-face bargaining was rare, it was usually hostile. The league's strategy was to secure itself economically and wait the players out. The league's television contracts were guaranteed in the event of a lockout, with repayment for lost games interest-free and not due for three years. The issue of whether players with guaranteed contracts would be paid during the lockout was referred to an arbitrator. The union argued that the owners could have put language into the guaranteed player contracts, declaring no payments would be made in the event of a work stoppage; this is a routine clause in baseball contracts. The union reasoned that the lack of such language in the contract justified payment during a league-imposed lockout. It is not customary in other industries for employees to be paid during a lockout resulting from collective bargaining. In this case, the arbitrator ruled that the owners were not responsible for paying the "guaranteed" contracts. (*In the Matter of National Basketball Players Association and National Basketball Association*, arbitration decision issued October 19, 1998). The media consensus was that this decision gave the owners significant leverage in the dispute.

On November 1, 1998, the regular season was scheduled to begin, but on that date the NBA lost its unblemished record regarding games lost to work stoppages. The two sides were close on a number of issues as the year ended, but the league announced that if no agreement was reached by January 7, 1999, the entire season would be cancelled. Stern directly mailed to each player a nine-page letter outlining the owners' most recent proposal; Hunter then sent each player a nineteen-page union response. Stern declared that his letter included the owners' final offer, and he asked that the rank-and-file union members be allowed to vote on it. The union leaders agreed, seeking to prevent the players' growing unhappiness over negotiating tactics. A vote was scheduled for January 5, 1999.

A media poll of player attitudes towards the owners' proposal indicated a probable 2–1 vote against ratification. With the season, and perhaps the viability of the league, depending upon the vote's outcome, Hunter and Stern met for a marathon bargaining session. They reached a compromise agreement, and within hours the union ratified 179–5, and the owners approved 29–0. The season, comprised of fifty regular-season games per team rather than the regular 82-game schedule, began on February 5, 1999.

THE TERMS OF THE AGREEMENT The owners dropped their demand for a hard salary cap, but obtained a cap on individual player salaries. This is a new concept in collective bargaining agreements in professional sports. Players with up to five years' service have a $9 million maximum annual salary, six to nine years' service an $11 million maximum, and ten or more years a $14 million maximum. Players who signed higher contracts before the new agreement do not have to negotiate new, lower salaries.

Salary cap exceptions remain: A team can sign two extra players each season, one at the average salary, the other at the median salary, even if it puts the team over the cap. For the first three years of the seven-year agreement, no team has a limit on total salary spending.

For the fourth through the sixth year, players are guaranteed 55 percent of league revenues. The extension of the agreement to a seventh year is at the owners' option; if exercised, the players are guaranteed 57 percent in the final year. Players' paychecks will be subject to a 10 percent escrow tax if salaries exceed 55 percent of income in the fourth, fifth, and sixth years. Raises are limited to 10 percent per year, unless a free agent player re-signs with his old team, in which case the raise is limited to 12 percent.

The contract length for rookies remains at three years, and the club has an option to renew in the fourth, with the right of first refusal in the fifth year. This means clubs can keep a draft choice for five years before he becomes an unrestricted free agent; under the old system, rookie players were bound for only three years before free agency. The minimum salary was raised to $287,500 for rookies; a sliding scale for veterans increased the minimum to $1 million for ten or more years service. Players will be tested once each season for drugs; marijuana and illegal steroids are now on the prohibited list. NBA players who test positive at training camp must undergo a mandatory counseling program. A second positive test brings a $15,000 fine, and any third or subsequent positive test results in a five-game suspension. All players will be tested when training camps open in October, and rookies will be tested four times per season on a random basis. The league is allowed to impose slightly higher fines and longer suspensions for player misconduct.

THE EFFECT OF THE NEW COLLECTIVE BARGAINING AGREEMENT After the NBA's shortened 1999 season was completed (fifty regular-season games per team and a normal playoff schedule), the union announced that the average NBA salary increased to $2.64 million from $2.37 million, and the median salary increased from $1.4 million to $1.68 million. In his annual state of the union address, Hunter reviewed the financial outcome and impact of the new collective bargaining agreement and claimed the following:

The players' share of basketball-related income increased from 57 percent in 1997–98 to 59 percent in 1999. Salaries increased 17 percent as a whole. The number of players earning $1 million or more increased from 61 percent to 71 percent. The number of players earning between $1 million and $4 million annually rose from 44 percent to 50 percent. Fifteen players signed contracts under the new "middle-class exception," which allows teams to exceed the salary cap to sign free agents. Aside from the ten players who signed the maximum six-year, $71 million extensions going into the final year of their rookie scale contracts, only two players, Rik Smits of Indiana and Jayson Williams of New Jersey, received the maximum allowable salary. Young star players who signed six-year extensions, such as Allen Iverson and Ray Allen, can earn upwards of $200 million over their careers if they maintain their level of excellence.

Another result of the lockout was that NBA owners acquired more control over player salaries than any other sport's owners. During the lockout, NBA teams lost about $1 billion in revenues and players about $500 million in salaries, but because the season and playoffs were salvaged, further losses were avoided. Paul Staudohar, a leading observer of labor relations in professional sports, believes the new collective bargaining agreement could reduce the influence of agents. The fixed salaries for long-term contract extensions eliminated agents from that aspect of negotiations. Since the objective of collective bargaining is to represent all players, it is desirable that the process restores this function to the union instead of individual player agents.

Salaries, though moderated, are likely to continue to rise. Staudohar suggests the following to improve the league's labor prognosis: avoid union decertification and antitrust litigation, maintain a stable union leadership, keep agents on the collective bargaining sideline, encourage players to improve on- and off-court behavior, and restore the lost notion of a cooperative partnership between owners and players (Staudohar, 1999).

Questions for further discussion

1. The National Labor Relations Act governs collective bargaining negotiations between employers and labor unions. Section 8(d) of the act requires the two sides to collectively bargain "in good faith with respect to wages, hours, and other conditions and terms of employment." Does this requirement mean the NBA owners were required to negotiate in good faith with the players over the disputed "Larry Bird exception"?

2. "Good faith bargaining" does not require either side to make concessions or agree to proposals against their will, only that each side communicate to the other through proposals and counter-proposals. The extreme tactics of strike and lockout are justified only after an *impasse* is reached, and an impasse can occur only when one side insists on the acceptance or removal of a provision and refuses to modify its position. Do you think there is sound logic behind the NLRA's scheme for (1) good faith bargaining and (2) reaching impasse before invoking certain tactics? Did the owners bargain in good faith over the Bird exception? Did the circumstances under which the owners declared the lockout meet the NLRA requirements? Should the union have litigated the issue of whether an official impasse had been reached by late June, 1998? Irrespective of the negative ruling, do you agree with the union's decision to arbitrate the "guaranteed contract" payment issue?

The WNBA collective bargaining agreement of 1999. In 1997, two new professional basketball leagues were created: the American Basketball League (ABL) and the Women's National Basketball Association (WNBA). Both were women's leagues seeking to capitalize on the growing interest in women's college basketball and the success of the U.S. women's basketball team at the 1996 Olympics in Atlanta. The WNBA was set up as a summer league, while the ABL played a fall/winter schedule in direct competition with men's college and professional basketball. From their inception, the two women's leagues competed for the best players, and for supremacy in an untested sports market.

Originally there were eight teams in the WNBA. Instead of individually owned franchises, each team was owned by the league itself. The WNBA was organized as a joint venture of the NBA team owners. An operating agreement was granted by the WNBA to local management groups designated to run the teams, in exchange for a share of the profits. This allowed the new league to benefit from the NBA's marketing capital and know-how, and proved decisive in the competition with the American Basketball League. In December 1998, after its second season, the ABL declared bankruptcy and ceased operating. About 90 ABL players were left to seek employment in the WNBA, the sole remaining American professional women's basketball league, or in the professional women's leagues in Europe.

The WNBA was created and operates on the "single entity" ownership model, that is, individual franchises are owned by the league. Players are not employees of the team they play for; rather, they are employed by the WNBA itself. This marks a critical difference from the men's professional leagues in the four major sports. The U.S. Supreme Court has ruled that a company and its subsidiaries are not treated as separate entities regarding antitrust law, and so can't violate the statute's prohibition of "conspiracy, contract or combination" in restraint of trade; see *Copperweld Corp. v Independent Tube Corp.*, 467 U.S. 752 (1984). This allows the WNBA to conduct its operations without fear of antitrust scrutiny.

After its second year, the players of the WNBA voted to affiliate with a certified players' union. The new union then designated the NBPA, and executive director Billy Hunter, as its authorized representative in collective bargaining negotiations with the league. The WNBA was represented in collective bargaining negotiations by President Val Ackerman. The key issue involved salaries: the league minimum was $15,000, with incremental raises dependent upon draft position and seniority, up to a maximum salary of $50,000. Bonuses could be earned for most valuable player awards and other incentives. The overall pay structure was much less than the standard of the defunct ABL, whose league average was about $80,000 for forty-four regular-season games. With a thirty-two-game schedule and twelve teams set to play in 1999, the WNBA was unwilling to significantly increase salaries, and WNBA players were still marginally "professional" (i.e., able to earn a living solely from their sport). Many WNBA players continued to play overseas to supplement their earnings.

Another issue was the number of former ABL players allowed to fill roster positions on WNBA teams in 1999. The players' union wanted to limit the number to twenty-four, or two per team, while the league argued that four to six ABL players should be allowed on each team's roster. The players' union also wanted expanded health coverage (including maternity leave), retirement benefits, the right to appeal disciplinary action against players, and a percentage of league revenue derived from licensed merchandise.

Talks between the players' union and the league management began in March 1999. The league was to hold a tryout camp in mid-April in Chicago, and the college and former-ABL player draft was scheduled for April 27, and the league's third season was to begin on June 10. By mid-April it appeared the WNBA might lose part or all of the season. On April 14, the two sides announced an agreement had been reached and the season would proceed as scheduled. The four-year collective bargaining agreement increased the minimum annual salary to $25,000 for rookies and $30,000 for veterans. By the fourth year those amounts would increase to $30,000 and $40,000, respectively. Additional increases could be negotiated by individual clubs and players based on merit.

The number of ABL players per team was set at three, except that the league's two new expansion teams, Orlando and Minnesota, would be allowed five. In 2000, all limits on ABL players would be removed, and four new teams would then enter the league through another expansion. The contract provided for renegotiation in its third year, and a no-strike, no-lockout moratorium in the final year. This encourages negotiations to proceed smoothly toward the next collective bargaining agreement.

On April 23, the WNBA players prepared to vote on the contract ratification, but the proposed agreement suddenly was repudiated by both sides. The union stated it believed ABL players would not be classified as rookies, but the league disagreed. Further disputes involved the number of league-mandated promotional appearances by players, and how many games must be played to guarantee a player's full salary. On April 29 the agreement was revived and quickly ratified by the players and the league. Compromises were reached on the remaining issues: the former ABL players would be treated as rookies only for 1999,

and each team was limited to three, as draftees or free agents (five for the expansion teams). After 1999 there would be no limits on former ABL players. One feature unchanged from the league's original standard player contract is that rookies are paid according to where they are selected in the draft.

The minimum pay scale remains as originally agreed. Each player will each get a 401(k) retirement plan with mandatory team contributions, graduate school tuition, a $100,000 life insurance plan, plus year-round health and dental benefits (including maternity leave). Salaries are guaranteed for players who appear in sixteen games. Finally, the union will receive $100,000 annually from WNBA licensing royalties.

The WNBA's first experience in collective bargaining succeeded because the NBA's nearly disastrous 1998–99 labor negotiation was still fresh in the minds of the parties. The principal actors were essentially the same, and the issues involved were very similar, albeit on a much smaller scale. If the WNBA continues to survive and prosper, the players' union will aggressively seek a bigger share of the economic benefits. As in each of the other major sports leagues, the central issues will be what is a fair division of revenue and power, and whether league management and the union can foster the idea of a cooperative enterprise between players and owners. These questions will require further consideration as the league matures.

Hockey

The National Hockey League also had a standard player contract that granted the team a right to own a player's services in perpetuity. In every sport the standard player contract is incorporated into the collective bargaining agreement. Hockey players relied on the collective bargaining process to eliminate the "perpetual" player reservation system. In 1975 the *Philadelphia World Hockey Club* case, 351 F.Supp.462, struck down the NHL's reserve system, and the owners subsequently recognized the players' right to become free agents after playing out an option season. Hockey retained the compensation award for teams losing free agents, a system referred to as equalization. An arbitrator awarded the compensation if the two clubs could not agree, although after 1982 no compensation was required for free agents aged 33 and over.

The National Hockey League's collective bargaining agreement expired on September 15, 1994. On October 1, in the absence of meaningful labor negotiations between the club owners and the players' union, the owners declared a lockout. Two months earlier, Commissioner Gary Bettman had announced major cutbacks in the package offered to the players by the owners. These included pension and medical benefit reductions, as well as reduced arbitration rights and roster sizes. The commissioner and owners were responding to what they perceived as a refusal to bargain by the players' association. The players, however, claimed that the owners' proposed wage structure was merely a disguised salary cap system, and they did not intend to proceed with negotiations until it was withdrawn.

One week before the lockout, Bettman announced that the 1994–1995 regular season would not begin without a new labor agreement, in order to protect the sport from a mid-season strike similar to the one which had recently damaged baseball. The players responded by promising not to strike during the season and playoffs if the owners would promise in return not to lock them out. The union's counterproposal to the owners featured a complex payroll tax, whereby club salaries beyond a determined amount would be taxed at a specified rate and the revenues derived from the tax would then be transferred to small-market, low-payroll clubs. The payroll tax was rejected by the owners on October 11, and the NHL season was formally postponed.

In mid-November 1994, as games were cancelled and lost revenues were mounting, a group of player agents entered the negotiations by advising league executives the payroll tax was unworkable. In its place, the owners substituted a revised free-agent provision that would allow less player movement between clubs. The owners also empowered the commissioner to cancel the remainder of the season if no agreement was reached by January 16, 1995; the theory was that a minimum fifty-game regular season was needed, and that playoffs had to be completed prior to July 1.

As the January 16 deadline approached, the owners resubmitted the payroll tax plan, and the union solidified in its opposition. On January 4, the union submitted its "final offer," with the payroll tax eliminated, and three days later the NHL Board of Governors responded with its own "final offer," dropping the payroll tax but raising to 32 the age for unrestricted free agency in the first half of the six-year agreement. The owners approved the amended proposal by a 19-7 vote, and on January 11, 1995, the players' union leadership, led by Robert Goodenow, accepted it pending ratification by the union membership. After a short training period, the league proceeded to play out a forty-eight-game regular season (pared down from its standard eighty-four-game length), and began the Stanley Cup playoffs just in time to conclude the season by the end of June.

At this writing, the NHL was still operating under the collective bargaining agreement that resulted from the 103-day lockout of late 1994 and early 1995. As in baseball and basketball, the central issue was whether the league would implement a salary cap. The agreement was for six years and was to expire on September 15, 2000. Both sides agreed to a four-year extension in 1999. To reach agreement, the players accepted the owners' proposal of a salary tax. As in the case of Major League Baseball, the owners' salary cap demand was withdrawn in lieu of the less-restrictive salary tax.

The hard salary cap places an absolute ceiling on each team's payroll and puts downward pressure on player salaries. The salary tax concept imposes a tax on each team whose payroll exceeds a specified amount. The revenues generated by the tax are then apportioned to the smaller-market teams, who by necessity have lower payrolls. In baseball and hockey labor negotiations, both sides agree that revenue sharing in some form is needed to ensure the economic survival of the small-market franchises; the issue is whether the salary cap accomplishes the desired result in the most efficient way.

In late 1994, the NHL's owners and players seemed to accept the need for a salary tax. Yet after the two sides traded widely differing salary tax proposals, the union declared that either a salary cap *or* a salary tax provision was unacceptable. The owners did not want to lose the entire season over this issue, as baseball had recently done to its severe detriment. The owners proposed a salary cap only for rookie draft picks, based on the player's draft round. The final agreement set a single cap, $850,000 per year, for all drafted players under age 25. The cap is "soft" because contracts can include performance bonuses (other than number of games played) that can exceed the stated cap limit.

The final agreement also placed restrictions on free agency, a compromise veteran players made to avoid a salary cap. The primary distinction is between "restricted" and "unrestricted" free agents. A player must be 32 years old before he can be designated an unrestricted free agent, which means his new team does not have to pay compensation to the team he is leaving. That age drops to 31 for the final three years of the agreement. (The prior agreement had set the age at 30.) There are actually four categories of unrestricted free agents under the new system, but in each case the players who qualify are not the top players in the league. Elite or average-skilled players are unlikely to meet the requirements of the various "unrestricted" groupings.

There are three categories of "restricted" free agents under the agreement, but compensation to the player's former team must be in the form of future draft picks. A predetermined schedule determines the number and draft rounds of the compensatory picks, and is based on the average annual salary of the restricted free agent's new contract. Under certain conditions, if the restricted free agent's old team wants to retain his services they must make a "qualifying offer," that is, a new contract proposal, to the player. The old team then acquires a right of first refusal and can re-sign the player by matching the offers of other teams. To complicate matters, certain restricted free agents (i.e., those lacking necessary playing experience) who receive a timely qualifying offer may negotiate only with their old teams.

Finally, the NHL has a system of salary arbitration wherein the owners and the union jointly appoint eight arbitrators from a national academy. Unlike baseball's system, in which the arbitrator must choose from one or the other salary proposals submitted by each side, the NHL's panel can set a fair salary regardless of the proposals submitted to them. Only restricted free agents are eligible for salary arbitration, and while the arbitrator sets the amount, the owner selects the contract's duration (one or two years). Salary arbitration is binding, *except* the owner can refuse to enter into any three contracts in a two-year period if the arbitration salary exceeds $550,000 (Staudohar, 1996).

The full intricacies of the NHL's collective bargaining agreement are beyond the scope of this chapter. When the current agreement expires, the issues of salary cap/salary tax, revenue sharing, and

free agency restrictions will return to the negotiating table. The NHL's prolonged work stoppage of 1994–95 destroyed a golden opportunity for hockey to fully capitalize on the labor woes of baseball and basketball, but it did impress both sides with the need to conclude negotiations before a season is completely lost by strike or lockout. If the owners and the players' union successfully navigate the next bargaining round, hockey will continue to grow.

League salaries

Table 8-4 charts the average salaries and total payrolls in the professional baseball league from 1998–99.

Salary changes

Tables 8-5a–c and 8-6 chart the average salaries in the professional baseball, basketball, hockey, and football leagues from 1984 to 1998.

Table 8-5b shows the terms and conditions of the salary cap in professional basketball.

ANTITRUST CONSIDERATIONS

Before the 1970s, players remained subject to the reservation systems imposed by each sport. This was not changed by early unionization attempts or the periodic appearance of rival leagues, which introduced competition for player services. As a result, players sought relief from the reserve clause through antitrust law prosecutions; their argument was that reservation was anticompetitive and a violation of the Sherman Act.

Baseball players were completely unsuccessful in this strategy. A 1922 U.S. Supreme Court decision by Justice Holmes held that baseball was a sport rather than a business, and as such was not covered by the antitrust laws. Subsequent legal challenges to the reserve clause by baseball players were denied, as the Supreme Court continued to uphold the earlier exemption and suggested Congress should be the one to abolish it.

The other major sports have been more successful in this tactic because the Supreme Court has refused to extend baseball's antitrust exemption to cover any other professional sport. The lack of an antitrust exemption has been the primary cause of eliminating player reservation systems in professional football, basketball, and hockey. The courts have taken the position that jointly bargained agreements, as contemplated by the National Labor

TABLE 8-4   *Major league baseball 1998–99 total payrolls and average salaries*

Team	1998 total payroll*	Average player salary*	1999 total payroll**	Average salary
Baltimore	69.0	2.56	78.9	2.9
New York (AL)	63.5	2.44	85.0	3.0
Cleveland	59.6	2.13	68.1	2.4
Atlanta	59.5	2.13	73.6	2.7
Texas	55.3	1.96	74.8	2.9
St. Louis	52.6	1.75	45.7	1.7
Seattle	52.0	1.68	49.9	1.9
Boston	51.6	1.78	59.6	2.2
New York (NL)	49.5	1.65	62.5	2.3
Chicago (NL)	49.4	1.83	60.2	2.1
Toronto	48.7	1.73	44.5	1.7
Los Angeles	48.0	1.65	79.3	2.8
Colorado	47.4	1.69	55.9	2.1
San Diego	45.4	1.74	47.8	1.7
Houston	40.6	1.45	51.6	2.0
San Francisco	40.6	1.56	44.9	1.8
Anaheim	38.7	1.29	51.8	1.6
Chicago (AL)	36.8	1.47	24.6	.9
Philadelphia	34.4	1.23	30.3	1.0
Florida	33.4	1.24	18.9	.7
Kansas City	33.0	1.18	23.7	.9
Milwaukee	32.4	1.12	41.4	1.5
Arizona	30.6	1.05	66.1	2.5
Minnesota	26.2	1.09	19.2	.7
Tampa Bay	25.3	.87	34.0	1.2
Detroit	22.7	.78	34.1	1.2
Cincinnati	22.0	.76	33.1	1.1
Oakland	20.1	.67	23.2	.9
Pittsburgh	13.4	.48	22.2	.7
Montreal	9.2	.35	16.2	.6

* All amounts in millions of dollars.
** 1999 salaries for rosters as of 15 July, 1999.

Relations Act, are the proper method of resolving labor questions in professional sports. How well the collective bargaining method actually works to resolve sports labor conflicts is still an issue, but the public policy of encouraging arm's-length bargaining between the parties remains.

COLLECTIVE BARGAINING AND ANTITRUST

The Sherman Act, an 1890 federal law prohibiting agreements that unfairly restrain trade, was clearly instrumental in helping players radically alter existing player reservation systems in football, basketball and hockey. The 1976 *Mackey* case in professional football is the leading precedent. The federal court (Eighth Circuit) ruled that a reservation system was not a per se violation of the Sherman Act, but the NFL's system was deemed improper because it was not a product of bona fide arm's-length bargaining between owners and players.

As stated, the National Labor Relations Act of 1935 granted workers the right to form and join

TABLE 8-5a   *Major league baseball average salaries 1984–87*

Year	Average salary	Percentage change
1984	$329,408	—
1985	371,157	12.7
1986	412,520	11.1
1987	412,454	(^{1})
1988	438,729	6.4
1989	497,254	13.3
1990	597,537	20.2
1991	851,492	42.5
1992	1,028,667	20.2
1993	1,116,353	8.5
1994^2	1,168,263	4.6
1995^2	1,110,766	−4.9
1996	1,119,981	.8
1997	1,380,000	23.2

[1]Less than 0.5 percent.
[2]Due to players strike in 1994–95, actual salary was less.
Source: Major League Baseball Players Association.

TABLE 8-5c   *Hockey average salaries, 1986–87 through 1996–97*

Season	Average salary	Percentage change
1986–87	$173,000	—
1987–88	184,000	6.4
1988–89	201,000	9.2
1989–90	232,000	15.4
1990–91	263,000	13.4
1991–92	369,000	40.3
1992–93	463,000	25.5
1993–94	558,000	20.5
1994–95	733,000	31.4
1995–96	892,000	21.7
1996–97	981,000	10.0

Source: 1986–87 through 1995–96, National Hockey League; 1996–97, National Hockey League Players Association.

TABLE 8-5b   *Basketball average salaries, percentage changes, salary caps, and ratios, 1984–85 through 1997–98*

Season	Average salary	Average salary percentage change	Salary cap (thousands)	Ratio of salary cap to average salary
1984–85	$340,000	—	$3,600	10.6:1
1985–86	395,000	16.2	4,233	10.7:1
1986–87	440,000	11.4	4,945	11.2:1
1987–88	510,000	15.9	6,164	12.1:1
1988–89	601,000	17.8	7,232	12.0:1
1989–90	748,000	24.5	9,802	13.1:1
1990–91	1,034,000	38.2	11,871	11.5:1
1991–92	1,202,000	16.2	12,500	10.4:1
1992–93	1,348,000	12.1	14,000	10.4:1
1993–94	1,568,000	15.6	15,175	9.7:1
1994–95	1,800,000	15.5	15,964	8.9:1
1995–96	2,027,261	12.8	23,000	11.3:1
1996–97	2,189,442	8.0	24,300	11.1:1
1997–98	2,418,982	15.5	25,000	—

Source: 1984–85 through 1994–95, National Basketball Association; 1995–96 through 1997–98, National Basketball Players Association.

TABLE 8-6   *Football actual expenditures,
1994–96[1]*

Team	Actual expenditures (millions)
Green Bay	$ 37.5
Tampa Bay	37.7
Cincinnati	38.5
Pittsburgh	39.0
Minnesota	39.1
Atlanta	39.5
Seattle	39.5
Houston[2]	40.0
San Diego	40.7
Philadelphia	40.8
Indianapolis	41.2
Chicago	41.3
Baltimore	41.3
Arizona	41.3
Washington	41.6
Detroit	41.6
St. Louis	42.1
Denver	42.1
Miami	42.2
Kansas City	42.9
San Francisco	43.2
New Orleans	44.7
New York Jets	44.7
Oakland	45.1
New York Giants	45.4
Buffalo	46.0
New England	46.3
Jacksonville	47.1
Carolina	47.4
Dallas	49.8

[1]The average salary cap for the three year period was
$37.5 million. The proration of signing bonuses over the
contract term raises compensation above the salary cap.
[2]In the 1997 season, Houston moved to Tennessee.
Source: National Football League Players Association.

unions, and to engage in collective bargaining with
employers. As player associations became certified
unions under the provisions of the statute, they acquired the power to use the collective bargaining
process in order to negotiate conditions of employment. Through this mechanism, and bolstered by
the court's willingness to apply antitrust law to the
league's operation, football, basketball, and hockey

players achieved a more equal position with the
owners. A new era of collective bargaining began in
this way.

Baseball owners continue to have the benefit of
an antitrust law exemption. There have been periodic Congressional hearings into the matter, and
revocation has been often threatened, but as of
June 2000 no action had been taken.

COLLEGE ATHLETICS

This final section addresses the question of whether
college athletes should be considered employees of
the universities they attend. If so, a model of labor
relations will need to be applied to college, as well
as to professional sports. Currently they are treated
as "student-athletes" with amateur status, and there
are strict rules promulgated and enforced by the
National Collegiate Athletic Association (NCAA)
governing the source and amount of permissible
income.

Since major college sports have become significant revenue producers in football and basketball, a
question of fairness is raised if the players are
prohibited from sharing in the profits they generate
for their schools. Additionally, if a scholarship
athlete is injured while performing, his or her right
to worker's compensation benefits will hinge on
whether he or she is considered an employee in the
estimation of the courts.

Some preliminary questions arise when courts
address these issues. Does the university have the
right to discipline or discharge the athlete? In
Coleman v Western Michigan Univ., 336N.W.2d224
(1983), the court defined employment by examining
the conditions under which college athletes perform. Before 1973, an athlete who did not withdraw
voluntarily from participation in sports, did not engage in serious misconduct, or did not fail to meet
minimum academic standards, could not have his
or her four-year scholarship withdrawn. After 1973
the NCAA gave coaches discretion over whether or
not to continue an athlete's scholarship from year to
year.

The second factor a court considers is whether or
not the university had the right to control or dictate
the activities of its student-athletes. Since coaches
can now make scholarship renewal decisions on the
basis of athletic performance, the athletes' activities
can jeopardize their scholarship status if at all contrary to the coach's desires.

A third factor is how dependent the athlete is on the benefits of his or her scholarship for the meeting of living expenses. In return for the athlete's services, the athletic scholarship generally provides for room, board, tuition, and books. The court in *Coleman* found this situation met the employment test; it should be noted that additional living expenses in the form of cash, transportation, and equipment have been the most-often violated rules as college players seek to increase the benefits paid them under their scholarships, and athletic programs and "boosters" are often willing to comply.

A related element is the intent that an employment contract exists between university and athlete. In the case of *Rensing v Indiana State Univ.*, 444 N.E.2d 1170 (1983), the Indiana Supreme Court ruled against the compensation claim of an injured football player, holding "there must be a mutual belief that an employer-employee relationship did exist." Since the NCAA rules expressly prohibited athletes from accepting pay for their services, the university could not have considered the athletic scholarship to be payment for services rendered.

In deciding the issue of university as employer, the final factor courts have considered in this context is whether the athlete's function was an "integral part" of the university's business. Obviously, the "business" of a university is education, and a student-athlete engages in sports. The proper test, it has been suggested, is whether the athlete's job is just as vital as that of nonacademic personnel, such as security and maintenance workers. It is certainly arguable that major college sports provide an essential public relations function for the school, keeping it in the public eye and encouraging continued identification of alumni with the institution.

Proposals to make student-athletes employees of their academic institutions have met varied responses from both the NCAA and legislative bodies. The current system is under intensive NCAA review, in an attempt to correct the most serious flaws, but a constant stream of violations and sanctions continue to result. For the foreseeable future, however, no fundamental change in the system should be expected.

In theory, the employment rights of college athletes could be created by a university initiative, but this has never been attempted. Similarly, college athletes could organize into a union and undertake collective bargaining but have not yet done so. For the present, court decisions considering these matters on a case-by-case basis are the only avenues open to college athletes. Legislation and NCAA regulations have been spotlighted by the media, but have offered no tangible results in this area.

CRITICAL THINKING EXERCISES

1. From the perspective of the commissioner of baseball, how crucial is the decision to take control over MLB umpires away from the American and National League presidents? Does your answer change if the transfer of authority causes the National League president to tender his resignation?

2. As head of an agency representing pro athletes, how much regulatory authority do you feel should be vested in the respective professional leagues' player associations? Should union employees participate in external investigations of sports agents, that is, by the government, the NCAA, or college athletic departments?

SUMMARY

1. Because players were historically denied the right to choose which team to play for, and to switch teams to raise their salary level, the owners were in a much more powerful position. They benefitted from the new revenues radio and television brought into the game, while players' salaries were suppressed far below the level a competitive labor market would have brought them.

2. In response to the reservation system, players in each sport formed players' associations, which evolved into labor unions. This in turn led to the system of collective bargaining between players and owners, which is where labor relations in each sport stand today.

3. The main focus of this chapter has been how employer-employee relationships have developed in America's four major professional team sports—baseball, football, basketball, and hockey.

4. The employer in each situation is the club, or team, and in each sport individual clubs have been organized into professional sports leagues. The employee is the professional athlete who performs on the playing field.

5. Occasionally, competing leagues have come into existence to challenge established operations, and they always have a significant impact on the employment relationships of their rivals.

6. At present, there is only one major league operating in each of the four major sports. While there is competition among the teams in a particular sport for free-agent players, championships and revenues, it is more accurate to view individual teams within a sport as joint venturers with a common interest in the competitive balance and financial soundness of the league as a whole.

7. Players have gained more power in recent years through the organization of player associations into effective labor unions. They have also realized substantial income escalation through the establishment of various free agency mechanisms in each sport, allowing them to change teams under certain conditions and thereby require employers to bid among themselves for player talent.

8. Free agency for players and the existence of rival leagues have been the two driving forces behind rising player salaries in the modern era of professional sports.

9. The labor crisis that each sport faces as the century draws to a close revolves around the question of the proper balance between the rights of team owners and professional athletes.

10. The current situation raises these key questions: What role, if any, should government play in regulating the employment relationship, particularly when labor negotiations between the parties reach an impasse? What rights should players and owners each have in the equation, and what is the public's interest (especially the fans') in the employment relationship?

11. These issues have moved to center stage in the last several years, as players and owners have become more adversarial and less trusting of each other's motives during collective bargaining negotiations.

12. The case of baseball illustrates how destructive the breakdown of labor relations can be. Each sport must answer the critical questions of the employment relationship for itself, but neglecting them jeopardizes their ability to put on the games, which constitute the economic product of professional sports.

13. College athletes have not been recognized as employees by their universities, nor have they organized into unions. Courts consider their status on a case-by-case basis.

CASE STUDIES

Player-Agent-Union Relations: A Case Study

We have examined how the creation and growth of viable players' unions led to free agency and, in turn, higher player salaries. Now we will look at union attempts to regulate the agents who represent player interests. Our case study involves a player agent and the NFL Players' Association.

  Regulatory Background. *After the* Powell *case, the NFLPA was recertified as the authorized union for collective bargaining. The union also restored a regulatory program for player agents, requiring them to be union-certified. This created a dual role for the union. In late 1996, the union sent all registered player agents a voluntary test on the terms of the new collective bargaining agreement; only one-third of the agents reportedly took the test, but most who did scored poorly.*

  Another concern is that agents are violating SEC rules by acting as financial advisors and giving their clients investment advice. The SEC has also investigated agent referrals; the NCAA restricts agent activities on college campuses, and some agents use financial planners to recruit new clients. An agent who signs a player referred by a planner gives them a "finder's fee" and also exclusive management of the player's finances. Failure to disclose the agent–financial planner relationship to the player in advance constitutes fraud.

  The NFLPA has instituted safeguards for its players in the past few years. In 1996 it reduced the maximum allowable percentage charged by agents for contract negotiation from 4 to 3 percent, the lowest in the major professional sports. In early 1997, the union instituted a stricter application process and mandatory testing of agents. But not all problems are caused by the agent's misbehavior. Some players have failed to pay earned commissions to their agents, and this results in arbitration. Players also have been known to quickly drop an agent when a lower fee is offered by a competing agent.

By 1998, 800 different agents represented the NFL's 1,200 active players. This is nearly twice the number of player agents in 1990. During this period, player salaries have nearly tripled, but the number of arbitration complaints between NFL players and their agents also rose significantly, a total of 88 cases between 1996 and 1998. This number far exceeds player vs. agent disputes in the other major sports leagues. Since 1996, according to the union's disciplinary summary statement, seven agents were found guilty of violating union rules, and two were suspended for a year and fined $5,000 for improperly providing money to college players. In conjunction with stricter union rules, several states have enacted laws making it illegal for agents to improperly contact college players. One of those states is Florida.

The "Tank" Black Case. William "Tank" Black is head of Professional Management, Inc. (PMI), one of the leading sports agencies representing professional football players. He offers players the following services: contract negotiations with team management, personal management services, marketing and public relations services, and post-career planning. PMI currently has forty players under contract and earns between $10 million and $15 million annually. In mid-April 1999, five of Black's clients were selected in the first round of the NFL draft.

In early May, the NFLPA announced that Black was under investigation since late January for possible violations of their sports agent regulations, though neither Black nor any of his clients were questioned until the week of the draft. The union announced Black was accused of having an employee try to bribe a Louisiana State University assistant football coach in order to sign tackle Anthony McFarland as a client. The University of Florida and Florida attorney general also announced investigations into Black's activities regarding four players at that school. NFLPA representative Trace Armstrong was reportedly present during the university police's questioning of the players. Black faces up to five years in prison and a $5,000 fine if he is found guilty of violating the state's agent law.

On May 19, 1999, the NFLPA issued a five-page complaint against Black detailing eight different types of alleged violations. Possible penalties extend from the agent's suspension and fine, to a lifetime ban on representing NFL players in contract negotiations. The NFLPA complaint alleged Black told an LSU assistant coach he had purchased a car for a University of Florida athlete still playing collegiate football, using the money of one of Black's professional clients. A Black employee allegedly offered the LSU coach $30,000 to persuade McFarland to sign with Black. McFarland subsequently signed with another agent.

The complaint further charged Black with selling his clients shares in BAOA, Inc., a publicly traded company, for $1 per share. The stock price was 5 cents per share when the complaint was issued. Another allegation was that Black provided cash to football players at Florida, LSU, and the University of South Carolina, through an employee, Alfred "Tweet" Twitty. Black was accused of arranging the purchase of a Mercedes-Benz automobile for Florida's Jevon Kearse on December 31, 1998 (two days before Kearse played his final college game in the Orange Bowl), as well as acquiring cars for three other Florida players who still had college eligibility. One player, Johnny Rutledge, said under oath that he accepted $500 payments from Black while still enrolled at Florida. Rutledge and former Florida players Kearse and Reggie McGrew made sworn statements admitting to receiving payments from Black. All four Florida players named in the complaint fired Black as their agent prior to the draft.

On June 22, 1999, Black filed a federal lawsuit in Washington, D.C., claiming the NFLPA's disciplinary proceedings violated his civil rights. The suit claimed that Black lost $10 million due to the termination of his representation of the four players, and that other potential clients were scared away. The suit asked that the court issue an injunction to suspend the NFLPA investigation and take over complete jurisdiction in the matter.

In early July 1999, Black's attorney filed a reply with the NFLPA, which included statements from the four former Florida players and affidavits from three other Black clients, all denying that payments had been made to entice them to sign with Black. A sworn affidavit from Twitty was also submitted, denying that he worked for Black or in any way induced players to sign with Black's agency. In addition to denying each of the eight allegations of wrongdoing in the NFLPA complaint, Black's response included bank records and sworn statements from car dealers that the car purchases in question were made on January 4 and 6, 1999, after the eligibility of the players involved had expired.

Black again claimed that the union and other agents had conspired to force him out of business. He stated that the sworn statements by players claiming he had provided them with cash were the result of undue pressure applied by the police during the Florida criminal investigations.

When Black's lawsuit against the union was filed, NFLPA general counsel Richard Berthelsen stated Black was being treated no differently than the fifteen other agents investigated by the union in the past two years. "We don't have time for witch hunts. They've apparently chosen to make the media the forum for the issue instead of our internal arbitration procedures."

Questions for Discussion

1. Should the union's investigation procedures for alleged agent misconduct also include due process guarantees for the accused? If so, how should they be worded?
2. How should the courts rule on sports agent Black's request for injunctive relief? Are the state and federal courts a better forum for the resolution of agent misconduct allegations and counterclaims, or should the matter remain within the union's internal arbitration procedures?
3. What is the proper role of the union concerning investigations conducted by state police agencies under a state sports agent law? Did the NFLPA overstep its bounds by being present during state police questioning of players?
4. Given the pressures put on top college players by sports agents, what is the proper regulatory function of the union regarding the player-agent relationship? What should be the NCAA's role in this process?

The Labor Dispute between the Umpires and MLB

One of the most unusual labor-management disputes in the history of professional team sports occurred during the summer of 1999. In mid-July the Major League Umpires Association, a certified labor union, voted to tender the resignations of 57 of the union's 68 members (11 did not participate), effective September 2, 1999.

Recall that the MLBPA players' union struck on August 12, 1994, and forced the cancellation of the playoffs and World Series at the end of that season. The umpires found themselves in a similar negotiating position with owners regarding their collective bargaining agreement, about to expire at the end of the 1999 calendar year. Instead of striking, however, the umpires adopted a mass-resignation strategy to force the owners to begin early negotiations on a new labor agreement. But the umpires were not unified behind their executive director, Richie Phillips, nor did they accurately gauge the response of their negotiating counterparts. It is customary for unions to begin collective bargaining a month or two prior to the expiration of an existing agreement. An added consideration for the umpires was the no-strike clause in the agreement then in effect.

At the time of the "resignation vote," Phillips announced the umpires' intention of forming a new corporation as soon as the resignations took effect, requiring the two major leagues to contract for umpiring services with the new entity. The union's goal was to win for the umpires the right to supervise themselves and make their own work schedules, including postseason assignments.

The union made an apparent miscalculation as to what response MLB would have to the resignation vote. Earlier in 1999, Commissioner Selig announced his office would assume responsibility for umpire supervision, a power previously residing in the two league presidents. (In September, National League president Leonard Coleman would resign in protest over this transfer of power over umpires.) But even in mid-July, Selig's newly appointed "executive vice president of baseball operations," Sandy Alderson, was acting on behalf of baseball's owners in the umpires dispute. Alderson announced the leagues would accept twenty-two of the resignations that had been submitted to his office, nine in the American League and thirteen in the National, and would hire twenty-five replacement umpires from the minor leagues to begin work in early September.

In March 1999, Phillips had been granted a new five-year contract by the umpires' union; after the events in July, it was clear that a faction of umpires, mostly in the American League, were opposed to his continued presence. Once management made clear its intention to accept resignations and hire replacements, twenty-seven umpires withdrew previously tendered resignations, or refused to submit letters in support of the union's plan. By early August, Alderson accepted the resignations of twenty-two union umpires and announced twenty-five new umpires would be hired from the minor leagues.

With the situation rapidly deteriorating and pro-Phillips umpires publicly exchanging recriminations with the dissident umpires, the union filed an unfair labor practice charge with the National Labor Relations Board. A complaint was also filed on July 26 in the federal court in Philadelphia, challenging MLB's attempt to replace the twenty-two umpires and seeking an injunction to prevent it. Phillips argued the resignation strategy was merely an attempt to circumvent the current labor agreement's prohibition against umpire strikes.

The 1995 agreement had been reached after a lockout that had caused the umpires to miss eighty-six games at the start of the season. Tensions between labor and management were heightened by a September 1996 incident in which Baltimore's Roberto Alomar spat on umpire John Hirschbeck, and received a penalty regarded as unduly lenient by the umpires. (Hirschbeck, ironically, later emerged as one of the leaders of the anti-Phillips faction.) Then on July 2, 1999, tension escalated when umpire Tom Hallion was suspended for three days by NL president Coleman as punishment for bumping a player during an on-field argument. The umpires were prepared to strike then, according to Phillips, but he was able to substitute the resignation tactic in order to comply with the no-strike provision.

The umpires' union voluntarily withdrew its federal lawsuit on August 10th, pursuing instead the NLRB complaint and submitting the matter to binding arbitration pursuant to the terms of the current bargaining agreement. The union's argument was that of the twenty-two resignations that MLB had accepted, the determining factor was apparently union support rather than seniority or performance rating. This, if proven, would support the union's contention that the action constituted an unfair labor practice, and should be enjoined.

By late August, the union discussed whether to call a strike before the resignations were to take effect in early September. Instead they chose to seek an injunction in federal court, to keep MLB from accepting their resignations and fielding the replacements who had been hired. The federal judge in Philadelphia, J. Curtis Joyner, declined to intervene on the umpire's behalf. On September 2, the twenty-two umpires were relieved of their positions, and the replacement umpires began working major

league games without incident. The displaced umpires accepted a settlement by which they would be paid the remaining portion of their 1999 salaries, along with health benefits and termination pay, in exchange for their voluntary waiver of any rights to continue working as umpires in 1999, including pursuit of the unfair labor charge with the NLRB. The terminated umpires are to share in a post-season bonus pool, but may not engage in any strike of work stoppage as per the collective bargaining agreement.

Still at issue is the right of MLB to fully terminate the twenty-two umpires, by which their careers as umpires would effectively end. The matter is now a grievance to be heard by the American Arbitration Association, but the process by which each side struck names from a list of potential arbitrators was delayed in mid-September.

Question for Discussion

1. What tactics, if any, should the umpires' union have adopted to force management to the bargaining table in July? Why didn't the union wait for the customary bargaining phase to begin one month prior to expiration?

2. What impact did the apparent lack of union solidarity have on the effectiveness of the "resignation strategy"?

3. If you were the commissioner, would you have taken the same action regarding the transfer of authority over umpires? What effect did the National League president's resignation have, if any?

4. What do you think MLB's negotiating posture will be when the collective bargaining agreement expires? What will the umpires' union do in the wake of the failed resignation strategy, and their acceptance of the "settlement agreement" in September?

5. How will the arbitrator rule on the union's claim that the resignations should be rescinded and the twenty-two terminated umpires be restored to their jobs?

REVIEW QUESTIONS AND ISSUES

1. What devices can be invoked by each side when an impasse is reached during the collective bargaining process?

2. Is it desirable that players continue to perform when negotiations break down, or is

their strike weapon the ultimate guarantee that a collective bargaining agreement will be reached?

3. Should government agencies intervene when collective bargaining negotiations reach an impasse? If so, at what level?

4. What is the proper role, if any, of a league commissioner in labor negotiations between players and owners?

5. Are player salaries too high or too low? What standard of comparison is appropriate?

6. Is a salary cap a viable method of controlling operating costs of professional sports teams? Is it the best method? Should teams be required to reveal their financial information, especially their profitability, to the players' union when a cap on salaries is sought? To the public?

7. If a percentage of ownership revenues is designated for player salaries under a cap system, which revenues should be included? What is a fair percentage?

8. Should the free market alone determine player salaries in professional sports? What about the fans' need to have players stay with one team for a certain period to encourage team loyalties and rooting interest?

9. Has the development of players' unions been a positive influence in the history of professional team sports? Can you think of a better system to protect the interests of the major factions, specifically the players, owners, and fans?

10. Is the two-tier system of contract negotiations desirable?

11. What labor issues do you think should be resolved through the collective bargaining process?

12. How can collective bargaining negotiations be encouraged when an impasse occurs between management and players?

13. Assume collective bargaining negotiations reach an impasse. When, if ever, should players call a strike? When, if ever, should owners field replacement players?

14. In the event of a players strike, is a player-owned league a rational economic decision? How would fans respond?

15. In the 1994 baseball strike, were the owners' actions designed to undermine, or "break," the players' union? How can this analysis be made?

GLOSSARY*

Arbitration The process of referring disputes between employers and employees (or between two rival unions) to the decision of impartial adjudicators. Although an arbitrator's decision is legally binding, arbitration differs from judicial processes in two important respects: (1) the disputants have voluntarily agreed to refer the matter to arbitration and have themselves selected the arbitrator, except in rare cases, such as during wartime, when the government may require and appoint arbitrators; (2) the arbitrator holds the hearings, and these are usually much less formal than court proceedings. Also, the arbitrator does not rely solely upon the presentations at these hearings, but if he deems it necessary he may make independent investigations. (See *compulsory arbitration*.)

Bargaining rights Refers to workers' rights to bargain collectively with their employers as established by law and judicial interpretations.

Cartel A group of businesses or nations that agree to influence prices by regulating the production and marketing of a product.

Certification of union An official action or order of the proper government agency (e.g., the National Labor Relations Board) specifying that a union is free from employer domination and includes a majority of the employees in its membership and hence must be recognized by the employer as the collective bargaining agent for all the employees in the collective bargaining unit.

Collective agreement A contract signed by an employer (or his representative) and a union specifying the terms and conditions of employment of those covered by the contract, the status or relation of the union to the employer, and the procedures to be used for settling disputes arising during the term of the contract.

Collective bargaining The process of employer-union negotiation for the purpose of reaching agreement as to the terms and conditions of employment for a specified period.

*From Peterson, Florence. (1945). *American Labor Unions*, U.S. Dept. of Labor, Bureau of Labor Statistics; Harper and bros., New York, p. 248 et. seq.

Compulsory arbitration The process of settlement of employer-labor disputes by a government agency (or other means provided by the government), which has the power to investigate and make an award that must be accepted by all parties concerned; not to be confused with voluntary agreements between employers and unions to have their disputes submitted for final determination by an impartial agency.

Conciliation An attempt to settle disputes between employers and workers. The term is used interchangeably with *mediation,* although technically mediation is a more passive act of intervention. In the narrow sense, a mediator is a go-between who offers no advice and who may conceivably be able to effect agreement between parties who refuse to face each other. A conciliator, on the other hand, gets the disputants together and takes an active part in the discussions by offering suggestions and advice. Acceptance of the conciliator's recommendations, however, is voluntary.

Labor relations A general term used in connection with any or all matters of mutual concern to employers and employees. Sometimes given a more limited meaning to indicate the kind of recognition in effect between an employer and union. (See *NLRA.*)

Lockout A temporary withholding or shutting down of work by an employer, in protest against employees' actions or to coerce them into accepting his terms.

Mediation An effort by an outside person to bring the employer and worker representatives into agreement. Mediation in its very essence implies voluntarism. Whether performed by a government or a private agency, the parties concerned voluntarily refer the dispute to the mediator with the understanding that her role is to assist them in reaching a settlement rather than make a settlement for them, as in the case of arbitration. (See *arbitration* and *conciliation.*)

Monopoly Control of the production and distribution of a product or service by one or more firms acting together. The effect is lack of competition, higher prices, and nonresponsiveness to consumer needs.

Monopsony Dominance of a market by one buyer or group of buyers acting together.

National Labor Relations Act (Wagner Act) A federal statute passed in 1935 that guarantees to employees in any industry or plant engaged in interstate commerce "the right to self-organization, to form, join, or assist labor organizations, to bargain collectively through representatives of their own choosing, and to engage in concerted activities, for the purpose of collective bargaining or other mutual aid or protection." It established the National Labor Relations Board, whose function is to eliminate on the part of the employer unfair labor practices that impede collective bargaining, to settle controversies with regard to representation of employees, and to certify which union, if any, shall represent the workers in an appropriate bargaining unit.

Strike A temporary stoppage of work by a group of employees in order to express a grievance or to enforce a demand concerning changes in working conditions. Government statistics exclude all strikes lasting less than one day or involving fewer than six workers and make no distinction between strikes and lockouts.

SOLUTIONS TO CRITICAL THINKING EXERCISES

1. MLB Commissioner Selig felt the transfer of control over umpires to his office from the respective leagues was a necessary element in consolidating management control over the game into a central office. His action led directly to the resignation of National League president Leonard Coleman, the highest-ranking black official in an American professional sports league; a variety of management issues were thereby raised.

2. The players' associations in each of the professional sports leagues have asserted their right to regulate agents who represent active league players. Requirements vary from league to league, and include devices such as posting bonds and passing written tests to substantiate a knowledge of the league's collective bargaining agreement. In the "Tank" Black case, it was argued that it was improper for the NFLPA to assist state authorities in an investigation, or even to be present during interrogations.

REFERENCES

Berry, R., and Wong, G. (1986). *Law and business of the sports industries.* Vol. I Professional Sports Leagues; Dover, Massachusetts: Auburn House.

Berry, R., Gould, W., and Staudohar, P. (1986). *Labor relations in professional sports.* Dover, Massachusetts: Auburn House.

Burk, R. (1994). *Never just a game: players, owners, and American baseball to 1920.* Chapel Hill, North Carolina: The University of North Carolina Press.

Cosell, H., and Whitfield, S. (1991). *What's wrong with sports?* New York: Pocket Books.

Dworkin, J. (1981). *Owners versus players: Baseball and collective bargaining.* Dover, Massachusetts: Auburn House.

Jennings, K. (1990). *Balls and strikes: The money game in professional baseball.* New York: Praeger.

Johnson, A., and Frey, J. (Eds.) (1985). *Government and sport: the public policy issues.* Totowa, New Jersey: Rowman and Allanheld.

Kochan, T., and Katz, H. (1988). *Collective bargaining and industrial relations.* 2nd ed. Homewood, Illinois: Irwin.

Lowenfish, L. (1990). *The imperfect diamond: A history of baseball's labor wars.* New York: Da Capo Press.

Miller, M. (1991). *A whole different ball game: The sport and business of baseball.* New York: Birch Lane Press.

Noll, R. (Ed.) (1974). *Government and the sports business.* Washington, D.C.: The Brookings Institution.

Quirk, J., and Fort, R. (1992). *Pay dirt: the business of professional team sports.* Princeton, New Jersey: Princeton University Press.

Sands, J., and Gammons, P. (1993). *Coming apart at the seams.* New York: Macmillan.

Scully, G. (1989). *The business of major league baseball.* Chicago: The University of Chicago Press.

Shropshire, K. (1995). *Agents of opportunity: sports agents and corruption in collegiate sports.* Philadelphia: University of Pennsylvania Press.

Sommers, P. (Ed.) (1992). *Diamonds are forever: the business of baseball.* Washington, D.C.: The Brookings Institution.

Staudohar, P. (1996). *Playing for dollars: Labor relations and the sports business.* Ithaca, NY: ILR Press.

Staudohar, P. (1999, April). Labor relations in basketball: The lockout of 1998–99. *Monthly Labor Review,* 3–9.

Staudohar, P. (1998, Spring). Salary caps in professional team sports. *Compensation and Working Conditions,* 3–11.

Staudohar, P. (1997, Fall). Baseball's changing salary structure. *Compensation and Working Conditions,* 2–9.

Zimbalist, A. (1998). Perspective: Team profits and labor peace. *The New York Times* (July 5), A13.

WEBSITES

The *New York Times*

www.nytimes.com

The sports section of this website provides an excellent source of news reporting on labor relations developments in each of the four major professional sports leagues. It also will provide links to timely Associated Press wire stories by Ronald Blum, the sports labor relations reporter.

The Sports Server

www.sportserver.com

This site is a service of the *Charlotte News & Observer* ("Nando"), and it allows the student to select each major sport. After choosing a sport, go to the desired sports league, or the link to NCAA college football or basketball. Once chosen, the link to "News and Features" will provide a daily list of wire service stories, archived for two weeks. Labor relations developments can be tracked this way, and the student can be sure to stay current.

PART III

Issues of Policy

CHAPTER 9

Ethics

Scott Branvold

In this chapter, you will become familiar with the following terms:

Absolutism	Moral norms	Deontology
Relativism	Moral principles	Theory of justice
Rationalization	Ethics	Principle of proportionality
Morality	Teleology	Ethical code
Values	Utilitarianism	

Overview

This chapter provides the foundation for a rational application of the principles of ethics to the ethical problems that confront the sport manager. Such principles, some would argue, are not being applied systematically or with any consistency in matters of moral uncertainty. Many would suggest that the present ethical environment is in an abysmal state in all facets of life. Members of society are regularly exposed to new accounts of unethical and illegal activities in many basic social institutions, including government, business, and even religion.

There are numerous examples of political corruption reaching even the highest levels of political power. The business world has also been confronted with ethical problems, some of monumental proportions. Insider trading scandals, frequent disregard for consumer safety and the environment, and outsourcing of work to third world countries

are but examples of the ethical quagmire with which business must be concerned. Although the "caveat emptor," or "let the buyer beware" ideology may not be as prevalent or acceptable as it once was, many consumers are still skeptical, and frequently uncovered scams and schemes have done little to ease the apprehension. White (1993) suggests that the very nature of capitalism presents a variety of ethical questions. Capitalism encourages the accumulation of wealth and maximizing self-interest but can lead to materialism, greed, and callous indifference toward others. Businesses in a free market may choose to meet consumer wants by providing products that are harmful or addictive (e.g., tobacco, alcohol, gambling). Competition in business can produce the same "win at all costs" attitude often seen on the playing field and may result in unethical actions and behaviors. There is a certain level of cynicism and mistrust in many of our fundamental social institutions that is not surprising given the amount and extent of the ethical misbehavior to which the public is regularly exposed.

A debt of gratitude is owed to Dr. R. Scott Kretchmar, whose insightful and substantive comments aided greatly in the preparation of this chapter.

The business of sport has not been immune to or isolated from the ethical problems so prevalent elsewhere. It is largely a romanticized ideal that sport is a haven for fair play, sportsmanship, and "a level playing field." That ideal has been tarnished with monotonous regularity both on and off the playing field. College athletic programs are being investigated for a variety of violations, and college athletes are involved in sports gambling scandals. There is a long list of famous athletes who are as well known for their actions and exploits off the field as they are for their performances on it. Even the heroics of Mark McGwire are tainted by his use of androstenedione, a legal supplement banned by many sport organizations. Olympic athletes are barred from competition for drug use, while International Olympic Committee officials are selling their votes to the highest bidder. Professional franchise owners are accused of extorting subsidies from communities by threatening to move to another city, and athletes are accused of greed and disloyalty for their "show me the money" attitude.

Whether the ethical climate in society and business today is significantly different from other eras or generations is probably subject to debate. In simpler times, conduct was influenced by a more unequivocal set of guidelines. This ethical **absolutism** maintains that there is an eternally true moral code that can be applied with strict impartiality. Increasingly, actions appear to be guided by a sense of **relativism,** a belief in which right and wrong are determined by the situation rather than a set of absolute rules. (Robin and Reidenbach, 1989). The consequences of this relativistic approach include confusion about standards and expectations of behavior and greater latitude within which to rationalize one's actions.

Rationalization of actions occurs in a variety of ways. Perhaps the chances of getting caught are slight, or the penalties are minimal. In some circumstances, behavior is justified by saying "Everyone else is doing it!" or "Who's going to be hurt?" Some may excuse their behavior as just being a one-time occurrence or a sign of the times. Actions may also be rationalized because the stakes are sufficiently high to be worth the risks. For example, the economic incentives of successful college football and basketball programs may be enough to produce recruiting improprieties. This contingent view of what is acceptable may actually create confusion about the nature of ethics. Individuals charged with ethical misconduct often defend their actions by saying "I have broken no laws." Rather than viewing the law as the floor for acceptable behavior, many view the law as the standard for ethical conduct. The result is an increasingly regulated society that relies on the law rather than on ethical standards to achieve fairness and justice. Kristol states, "It is a confession of moral bankruptcy to assert that what the law does not explicity prohibit is therefore morally permissible" (Solomon and Hanson, 1983). It seems that rules are now viewed as barriers to get around rather than guidelines by which to live. A monument to this perspective is the voluminous NCAA manual, which undergoes frequent revisions to close the loopholes that are continually sought in order to beat the system. If this represents the standard most people and organizations use to guide their actions, then an ethical crisis does indeed exist.

FUNDAMENTAL CONCEPTS

Developing a foundation for ethical analysis first requires an understanding of the fundamental concepts of *morality* and *ethics*. These terms are often used interchangeably, and although one must not get bogged down in semantics, a brief discussion of distinctions between the two terms is appropriate.

Morality has been defined as the special set of **values** that frame the absolute limitations on behavior. It may include such basic rules as "Don't steal" (**moral norms**), as well as a more general system of duties and obligations (**moral principles**) (Solomon and Hanson, 1983). Rokeach (1973) defines a value as an enduring belief that guides personal behavior and shapes personal goals. He characterizes two types of values; instrumental values (e.g., ambition, courage, honesty), which are viewed as the means to terminal values (e.g., freedom, happiness, security).

De George (1982) and Beauchamp and Bowie (1988) place emphasis on morality's concern with the "good and bad" or "right and wrong" character of actions within the context of social customs and mores of any particular culture. They also stress the idea that morality is based on impartial considerations and that individuals cannot legitimately create their own personal moral codes.

De George (1982) defines **ethics** as a systematic attempt to make sense of our moral experience to determine what rules should govern conduct. This definition suggests that ethics is the study of morality.

Beauchamp and Bowie (1988) and Velasquez (1988) seem to support this idea, while stressing that ethics involves the justification and application of moral standards and principles.

CONCEPT CHECK

Although the terms morality *and* ethics *are often used interchangeably, ethicists do note some semantic differences between them. Morality provides the set of values that limit behavior, whereas ethics involves the application of and justification for moral principles.*

PERSONAL MORAL DEVELOPMENT

Often morality is viewed as a matter of personal conscience, with everyone entitled to their own moral opinion. However, morality is much more objective than many perceive. Moral development involves the ability to distinguish right from wrong; this ability to make moral judgments and engage in moral behavior increases with maturity (Cavanaugh, 1984).

Lawrence Kohlberg (1976) has developed perhaps the most widely accepted model of individual moral development, which involves three developmental levels with each level subdivided into two stages.

Level I: Preconventional. At this level, a child can respond to rules and social expectations and can apply the labels "good," "bad," "right," and "wrong." These rules, however, are seen as externally imposed (such as by parents) and in terms of pleasant and painful consequences (for example, a spanking for wrongdoing or a piece of candy for desirable behavior). The child does not have the ability to identify with others, so the motivation for action is largely one of self-interest. Stages 1 and 2 within level I reflect largely instrumental orientations. The behavior is not motivated by a moral sensitivity but simply by the consequences of an action—at first avoiding punishment and later receiving rewards and praise.

Level II: Conventional. At this level the expectations of family and peer groups become primary behavioral influences. The individual exhibits loyalty to the group and its norms and begins to identify with the point of view of others. This level is characterized by conformity and a willingness to subordinate individual needs to those of the group. The first stage within this level (stage 3) focuses on a "good boy/nice girl" morality, in which good behavior involves conforming to the expectations of family and friends. Actions are guided by stereotypes of what is normal behavior and are frequently judged by intention. The next stage of this level (stage 4) is termed the *law and order* stage. Right and wrong extends to conforming with societal laws, and there is a recognition of socially prescribed duties, responsibilities, and obligations. De George (1982) contends that most adults live at this conformity stage of development and that many never go beyond it.

Level III: Postconventional or Principled. At level III, there is an attempt to find a self-chosen set of moral principles that can be justified to any rational individual. Proper laws and values are those to which any reasonable people would want to commit, regardless of social position or status. The first stage (stage 5) within this level has a social contract orientation. There is an awareness of conflicting personal views and a sense that the rules should be upheld impartially because they are the social contract. A primary concern in this stage is that laws and duties are based on their overall utility as guided by "the greatest good for the greatest number." Cavanaugh (1984) points out that this stage is the "official" level of moral development of the United States government and the Constitution. The final stage (stage 6) is based on the acceptance of universal ethical principles. At this stage, appropriate action is defined by the conscious choice of universal ethical principles that are comprehensive and consistent and deal with justice, equality, and human dignity. The motivation for adherence to these principles is a basic belief in their encompassing validity and a willingness to commit to them (Cavanaugh, 1984; Kohlberg, 1976; Velasquez, 1988).

CONCEPT CHECK

Kohlberg's model of moral development describes the progression of moral reasoning from the childlike motivations of avoiding a spanking to the mature moral reasoning of taking a principled stand based purely on the "rightness" of the principle. Kohlberg's level III has at its roots the most widely accepted normative ethical theories, which serve as the basis for ethical analysis.

THEORIES OF ETHICS

Normally, references to ethical theories or ethical decision rules take the form of simple ethical maxims, such as the following (Laczniak and Murphy, 1985):

1. *The golden rule:* Act toward others the way you would want them to act toward you.
2. *The utilitarian principle:* Act in a way that results in the greatest good for the greatest number.
3. *Kant's categorical imperative:* Act in such a way that the action taken under the circumstances could be a universal law or rule of behavior.
4. *The professional ethic:* Take only actions that would be viewed as proper by an impartial set of professional colleagues.
5. *The TV test:* Act in such a way that the actions could be defended comfortably in front of a national television audience.

While these maxims may serve as handy rules for ethical conduct, the purpose of this section is to provide a more comprehensive foundation for ethical analysis. Several authors have developed theories for the ethical analysis of actions and decisions. Most of these theories are either teleological, deontological, or some combination of the two.

Theories based on **teleology** (from the Greek meaning "end") assess the morality of actions on the basis of the consequences or results of those actions; the most widely studied of these theories is **utilitarianism.** Jeremy Bentham (1748–1832) and John Stuart Mill (1806–1873) were the most influential developers of utilitarianism, which is predicated on the idea of "creating the greatest good for the greatest number." Actions are evaluated by judging their consequences and weighing the good effects and bad effects. The attempt is to achieve an optimal balance of benefits versus harms on those affected by the action. Applying utilitarianism to decision making requires selecting the action that will produce the greatest net social benefit. The good of the group supersedes the good of the individual (Beauchamp and Bowie, 1988; De George, 1982; Robin and Reidenbach, 1989). The major criticisms of the utilitarian approach include (1) the difficulty in measuring utilitarian value, (2) the opportunity for unjust net consequences, and (3) the lack of concern for how results are produced (Beauchamp and Bowie, 1988).

The deontological, or formalistic, approach to ethical analysis was formulated primarily by Immanuel Kant (1734–1804), with more contemporary work done by William D. Ross and John Rawls. **Deontology** (derived from the Greek for *duty*) is based on the idea that what makes an action right is not the consequences but the fact that the action conforms to some absolute rules of moral behavior. Kant's categorical imperative statements serve as guidelines for what would be considered moral behavior. Moral action would (1) be universalizable (that is, it would make sense for everyone in a similar situation to take the same action), (2) demonstrate respect for the individual (that is, others are never treated simply as means), and (3) be acceptable to all rational beings (Tuleja, 1985). Kant's vision was one of universal and consistent application of the rules of morality. His critics maintain that the theory is too vague and imprecise. There are also claims that it does not help resolve the issue of balancing conflicting individual rights and has too little regard for consequences (Velasquez, 1988).

Ross put forth a theory that combined certain aspects of utilitarianism with Kantian theory. He postulated that action is bound by the duties of fidelity, gratitude, justice, beneficence, self-improvement, and noninjury. These are seen as universal moral obligations above and beyond the law, but there is a recognition that some exceptions may exist (Laczniak and Murphy, 1985).

John Rawls has also formulated an influential ethical approach called the **theory of justice.** The major premise behind his proposals is that rules and laws of society should be constructed as if we did not know what roles we were to play in that society (what Rawls terms the "veil of ignorance"). This creates an objectivity and fairness to the ethical principles that guide actions (Cavanaugh, 1984).

CONCEPT CHECK

The most widely accepted ethical theories are either teleological or deontological in nature. Utilitarianism is the most prominent teleological theory, and its focus is on consequences of actions and "creating the greatest good for the greatest number." Deontology has a more absolute orientation, suggesting that what makes an action right is not consequences but adherence to basic moral laws.

MODELS FOR ETHICAL ANALYSIS

The ethical theories in the previous section provide the foundation for numerous models that can aid in evaluating moral dilemmas. An approach suggested by Tuleja (1985) has a utilitarian orientation in which actions are evaluated on the basis of their effect on various constituent groups or stakeholders. For example, a college athletic administrator must weigh the interests of a number of constituencies, including school administration, athletes, coaches, alumni, fans, faculty, media, and community, when making decisions.

Many of the models use a combination of the basic theories to provide a multidimensional approach to dealing with ethical questions. Goodpaster (1984) summarized three avenues for ethical analysis, one based on utility (maximum benefits), one based on rights, and one based on duty or obligation. Garrett (1966) developed a theory specifically with the business manager in mind that combines concern for outcomes (utilitarianism) and process (deontology) and adds the dimension of motivation. These three components (means, ends, and intentions) are synthesized into what Garrett calls the **principle of proportionality,** which states that undesirable side effects of an action can be accepted if and only if there is some proportionate reason for doing so (Laczniak and Murphy, 1985). One might use the principle of proportionality to evaluate the process being used to provide more gender equity in interscholastic and intercollegiate sport. The means for this was federal legislation (Title IX). One consequence (end) of increasing opportunities for females has been, in many cases, lost opportunities for males. The ethical analysis would involve weighing the undesirable side effect of the process against the benefits achieved.

Cavanaugh (1984) has also suggested a tridimensional approach to ethical decision making that includes characteristics of both teleological and deontological theories. He uses utility, rights, and justice as the ethical evaluation criteria. If conflicts arise among the three criteria, further analysis must be done based on the relative importance of the criteria, the freedom with which the action is taken, and the nature of the undesirable effects. Figure 9–1 provides a flowchart of steps to guide this ethical evaluation process; it is rather simplistic

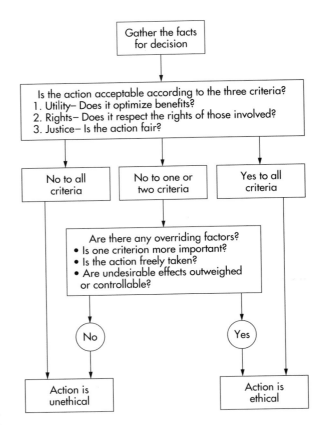

FIGURE 9–1 Flowchart for ethical decision making. From Cavanaugh, G. (1984). *American values* (2nd ed). Englewood Cliffs, New Jersey: Prentice-Hall.

but does provide a starting point that can be useful in ethical analysis.

CONCEPT CHECK

The models for ethical analysis are built on the foundations of basic ethical theories. They are not designed to provide indisputable answers to every ethical dilemma, but they can provide a systematic methodology for assessing ethical questions and clarifying the alternatives. Cavanaugh's model is but one of many approaches that may be useful in the quest for ethically sound decisions.

PERSONAL ETHICS AND ORGANIZATIONAL RESPONSIBILITY

The distinction between personal and professional ethics is a difficult matter to address. Ultimately, organizations are collections of individuals and decisions are made and carried out by individuals. This would seem to indicate that the ultimate responsibility for ethical behavior rests with the individual, thereby demonstrating the importance of personal ethics. If this is the case, however, how is it that people who consider themselves to be basically honest and compassionate can act so irresponsibly at times? It seems as if a different set of values is applied on the job than is applied outside the workplace. One author cites a former corporate vice-president who says, "What is right in the corporation is not what is right in a man's home or in his church. What is right in the corporation is what the guy above you wants from you" (Jackall, 1988).

Circumstances may arise in which professionally defensible behavior is not always congruent with the guiding principles of ordinary norms. Honesty is a basic virtue; yet, at the personal level the "little white lie" may be a justifiable action for some situations. Are the standards of honesty at the professional level any different?

Advertisers use the "white lie" in many cases; the term *puffery* has even been coined to describe the practice of stretching or bending the truth with inflated claims and exaggerations. Indeed, advertising is often considered one of the most ethically suspect aspects of business operations. Chonko (1995) notes that criticism of advertising practices often occurs when efforts to persuade result in inaccurate, manipulative, or deceptive messages. A recent advertisement for a Continental Basketball Association (CBA) franchise encouraged people to purchase tickets to see a team whose roster was purported to be filled with future National Basketball Association (NBA) stars. Anyone familiar with professional basketball recognizes the extravagance of such a claim, yet many would not question the ethics of such an advertisement. Professional football and hockey downplay the role of violence in their sports, yet continue to allow the use of some of the most violent action footage to promote their sports. In this case, behavior is inconsistent with principles and does not adhere to the ideal societal standards of virtue. The frequency of departure from these standards and, perhaps more importantly, the willingness to routinely accept such departures are basic ethical concerns.

Milton Friedman, a prominent American economist, maintains that businesses are amoral entities and the corporate executive's only responsibility is to maximize profit. Yet even this extreme proponent of free market capitalism recognizes that this must be accomplished within the framework of basic societal rules of law and custom. Work values may be developed through conscious organizational effort, or they may evolve without organizational attention. When results are the primary or perhaps only organizational value supported, the consequence may be an "anything goes" ethical climate. Kristol states, "Businessmen have come to think that the conduct of business is a purely "economic" activity to be judged only by economic criteria and that moral and religious traditions exist in a world apart, to be visited on Sunday perhaps" (Solomon and Hanson, 1983). There are likely to be situations in which unethical behavior will produce greater profits, especially in the short run (Robin and Reidenbach, 1989). In a social environment in which immediate gratification is an increasingly pervasive mindset, the temptation and pressure to cut corners naturally increase.

Organizations that ignore or even reward unethical behavior are likely to have personnel who behave unethically. Sims (1994), Cialdini (1996), and Frank (1996) are among the many authors who have addressed the costs to organizations that tolerate socially irresponsible actions and the benefits of operating ethically. All mention the internal problem of dealing with the cost of monitoring dishonest employees as well the external problem related to the organizational image and reputation. The cost of drug testing athletes and the International Olympic Committee's tarnished reputation over influence peddling are examples of the damage than can be caused by disreputable activity. Benefits such as enhanced customer loyalty, increased goodwill, and avoiding litigation provide valuable return for behaving ethically.

In sport, the scoreboard and the record book have become the final determinants of value and worth for many (Gibson, 1993). Stoll and Beller (1993) contend that this perspective has a tremendous influence on the moral reasoning of sport participants. Their studies indicate that a negative relationship exists between moral development and sport participation and that there is a decrease in moral reasoning the longer the athlete competes in organized sport. This view of sport success is also likely to influence the decisions of sport administrators as they attempt to attract the public's attention and support. Since box office success is usually linked to winning, sport managers are subject to some of the same pressures that athletes encounter.

The role models of an organization will set the tone for the behavior of the entire organization. The leadership will determine what the dominant perspective is toward ethical behavior. The demands, expectations, and traditions of an organization will be the behavioral guides. The organizational leaders must set clear, unambiguous expectations for the ethical conduct of their employees. When this is done, employees must then be given the authority to act and be held accountable for the ethical quality of their actions. It takes integrity and courage to act on one's values, especially when the stakes are high. An organization, through its leaders, must work diligently to create a climate in which ethical conduct is a matter of habit rather than one of expedience.

CONCEPT CHECK

The relationship between personal and professional ethics is difficult to determine with great precision. Individuals will bring a personal set of values to the job, but to what extent that set of values will influence job behavior depends on a number of factors, including the strength with which those values are held, the integrity and courage of the people holding those values, the ethical environment within the organization, and the role models and leaders that influence the work environment.

ETHICS AND THE PROFESSIONALIZATION OF SPORT MANAGEMENT

Professions carry with them prestige, status, respect, and autonomy and have traditionally been allowed more control to set their own standards and to be self-regulating and self-disciplining. As sport management strives to move toward a more professional status, autonomy does have particular

relevance with regard to ethics. Standards are frequently expressed in the form of an **ethical code,** often developed and enforced by a professional organization. Many businesses and professional business organizations have also developed ethical codes and creeds. The following boxes contain

---

American Advertising Federation's code of advertising ethics

1. Truth—advertising shall reveal the truth, and shall reveal significant facts, the omission of which would mislead the public.
2. Substantiation—advertising claims shall be substantiated by evidence in possession of the advertiser and the advertising agency prior to making such claims.
3. Comparisons—advertising shall refrain from making false, misleading, or unsubstantiated statements or claims about a competitor or his products or services.
4. Bait advertising—advertising shall not offer products or services for sale unless such offer constitutes a bona fide effort to sell the advertised products or services and is not a device to switch consumers to other goods or services, usually higher priced.
5. Guarantees and warranties—advertising of guarantees and warranties shall be explicit, with sufficient information to apprise consumers of their principal terms and limitations or, when space or time restrictions preclude such disclosures, the advertisement shall clearly reveal where the full text of the guarantee or warranty can be examined before purchase.
6. Price claims—advertising shall avoid price claims that are false or misleading, or savings claims which do not offer provable savings.
7. Testimonials—advertising containing testimonials shall be limited to those of competent witnesses who are reflecting a real and honest opinion or experience.
8. Taste and decency—advertising shall be free of statements, illustrations, or implications which are offensive to good taste or public decency.

Adapted from American Advertising Federation, 1101 Vermont Ave., NW, Suite 500, Washington, D.C. 20005.

World marketing contact group marketing creed

1. I hereby acknowledge my accountability to the organization for which I work, and to society as a whole, to improve marketing knowledge and practice and to adhere to the highest professional standards in my work and personal relationships.
2. My concept of marketing includes as its basic principle the sovereignty of all consumers in the marketplace and the necessity for mutual benefit to both buyer and seller in all transactions.
3. I shall personally maintain the highest standards of ethical and professional conduct in all business relationships with customers, suppliers, colleagues, competitors, governmental agencies, and the public.
4. I pledge to protect, support, and promote the principles of consumer choice, competition, and innovative enterprise, consistent with relevant legislative and public policy standards.
5. I shall not knowingly participate in actions, agreements, or marketing policies or practices which may be detrimental to customers, competitors, or established community social or economic policies or standards.
6. I shall strive to insure that products and services are distributed through such channels and by such methods as will tend to optimize the distributive process by offering maximum customer value and service at minimum cost while providing fair and equitable compensation for all parties.
7. I shall support efforts to increase productivity or reduce costs of production or marketing through standardization or other methods, provided these methods do not stifle innovation or creativity.
8. I believe prices should reflect true value in use of the product or service to the customer, including the pricing of goods and services transferred among operating organizations worldwide.
9. I acknowledge that providing the best economic and social product value consistent with cost also includes: A. recognizing the customer's right to expect safe products with clear instructions for their proper use and maintenance; B. providing easily accessible channels for customer complaints; C. investigating any customer dissatisfaction objectively and taking prompt and appropriate remedial action; D. recognizing and supporting proven public policy objectives such as conserving energy and protecting the environment.
10. I pledge my efforts to assure that all marketing research, advertising, sales promotion, and sales presentations of products, services, or concepts are done clearly, truthfully, and in good taste so as not to mislead or offend customers. I further pledge to insure that all these activities are conducted in accordance with the highest standards of each profession and generally accepted principles of fair competition.
11. I pledge to cooperate fully in furthering the efforts of all institutions, media, professional associations, and other organizations to publicize this creed as widely as possible throughout the world.

Draft approved by World Marketing Contact Group in Verona, Italy, September 1976.

---

examples of advertising ethics and marketing ethics codes. However, many researchers question the impact some of these codes have had, contending that they lack depth or are filled with platitudes that do little to guide behavior (Robin and Reidenbach, 1989). De George (1982) recommends that a code should (1) be regulative, not simply a statement of ideals, (2) protect public interests and not be self-serving, (3) be specific and relevant to the specialized concerns of the members, and (4) be enforceable and enforced.

The American Psychological Association's nine principles for ethical standards can serve as a guide to the development of an ethical code: (a) responsibility, (b) competence, (c) moral and legal standards, (d) public statements, (e) confidentiality,

(f) welfare of the consumer, (g) professional relationships, (h) utilization of assessment techniques, and (i) pursuit of research activities (American Psychological Association, 1977).

Developing a code of ethics for sport managers is a problematical undertaking. The breadth of the field makes it very difficult to create a code that has much specificity. In addition, no organization fully accommodates the tremendous variety of practitioners and academicians in the field.

Zeigler (1989) expressed a need for those involved in sport management to develop a sound approach to ethics as it relates to their duties and responsibilities and suggested that a comprehensive code of ethics needed to be developed. This served as the impetus for the North American Society for Sport Management (NASSM), which approved an ethical creed for sport managers in 1989. This creed is one of the few efforts made in the area of sport management to formally address the issue of professional ethics.

An increasing number of sport organizations are also addressing the issue of ethical conduct. Some examples include most of the major coaching associations in North America, the National Association of Academic Advisors for Athletics, the United States Olympic Committee, and the International Health, Racquet and Sportsclub Association. Perhaps a cooperative effort that includes various academic and professional associations in the field such as the National Association for Sport and Physical Education (NASPE), NASSM, and closely related occupational and professional groups can produce guidelines that might serve as the foundation for organizations to develop ethical codes tailored to their own operational needs.

CONCEPT CHECK

One of the characteristics of professionalization is the autonomy that provides opportunity for self-regulation. This often manifests itself in a formalized approach to ethical standards and conduct. Increasing attention is being paid to ethics in many business fields, as reflected by both ethics training and the development of formal codes of ethics. Various sport and recreation organizations have also made efforts to deal with pertinent ethical concerns in formal and proactive ways.

DEVELOPMENT OF ETHICAL SPORT MANAGERS

As the study of sport management becomes more formalized, one must examine the relationship of ethics and the future of sport management preparation and practice. With the number of academically prepared practitioners in sport management likely to increase substantially, the move toward a greater professional status will probably continue. This trend has implications for the preparation of graduate and undergraduate students in sport management programs. More material dealing with ethically sensitive issues and more sport ethics and philosophy courses are being developed and included in the curriculum. (The American Assembly of Collegiate Schools of Business [AACSB] accredited business schools are required to include instruction on ethics within their curricula [Laczniak and Murphy, 1985; Robin and Reidenbach, 1989].)

Petrick and Quinn (1997) identify several dimensions of management integrity that should be cultivated to produce ethical conduct. Ethical development can be viewed as a sequential process that begins with ethical awareness (perception of and sensitivity toward ethical situations). The next step can be termed assessment or reasoning to make ethical judgments. The third step progresses to ethical conduct or action. Without movement to this stage, ethics would have little practical impact. This involves the leap between talking about what is right and acting on it. Ultimately, the desire is to help prepare sport managers to exert ethical influence on those around them.

There are ethical issues in virtually every area of sport management coursework. Topics such as honesty in advertising, accuracy in advertising and sales, price gouging, collusion, ticket scalping, and product safety have clear ethical dimensions. Ambush marketing (the effort of a company to affiliate with an event without paying a sponsorship fee) is another subject that raises very interesting ethical questions. Gender and minority equity, athlete exploitation, performance supplements, social responsibility, conflicts of interest, and privacy rights are but a few of the other issues with complex ethical considerations within the sport industry.

Certainly there are many ethical issues and predicaments that surround the practice of sport management. One response to these ethical challenges is a more concerted attempt to provide ethical training to both prospective and practicing sport management professionals. Several studies indicate that ethics committees and employee ethics training programs are becoming more prevalent in mainstream business firms (Robin and Reidenbach, 1989; Sims, 1994). This is likely to occur in sport businesses as well, and two particular reasons stand out. With the attention that many sport enterprises receive, unethical actions result in negative publicity that can be very damaging to public support. A very different concern has to do with the increasingly international nature of the sporting business. The international community may have a very different perspective on what actions are ethical and unethical. Reconciling the different cultural mores will require a far more conscientious effort of ethical preparation.

CONCEPT CHECK

Attention to ethical considerations is increasingly a part of the training for sport managers. It is likely that more concerted efforts will be made to emphasize ethical training in both educational and job settings. The goal is to have sport managers exhibit ethical sensitivity, sound ethical judgment, and a willingness to act and lead in an ethical manner.

NASSM Creed

Professional members of the North American Society for Sport Management, living in a free, democratic society, have respect for the worth and dignity of all people in our society. As professionals we honor the preservation and protection of fundamental human rights. We are committed to a high level of professional practice and service, professional conduct that is based on the application of sound management theory developed through a scientific body of knowledge about sport and developmental physical activity's role in the lives of all people. Such professional service shall be made available to clients of all ages and conditions, whether such people are classified as accelerated, normal, or special insofar as their status or condition is concerned.

As NASSM members pursuing our professional service, we will make every effort to protect the welfare of those who seek our assistance. We will use our professional skills only for purposes which are consistent with the values, norms, and laws of our society. Although we, as professional practitioners, demand for ourselves maximum freedom of inquiry and communication consistent with societal values, we fully understand that such freedom requires us to be responsible, competent, and objective in the application of our skills. We should always show concern for the best interests of our clients, our colleagues, and the public at large.

There are many examples of ethical misconduct in all segments of society, and certainly sport is no exception. The focus of this chapter is to encourage an examination of the ethical dimensions of decision making and to provide a framework for a logical and reasoned approach for dealing with the moral and ethical choices that are certain to confront the sport management professional.

Professional behavior is grounded in personal values, but professional conduct does not always coincide with those personal values or the ideals of societal norms and virtues. To raise the level of professionalism in sport management, it is essential to take a proactive approach to ethical training. Ethical guidelines need to be carefully developed, and prospective sport managers should be schooled in the use of a systematic and analytical approach to the ethical dilemmas that they will undoubtedly encounter.

There is certainly a need for an increased awareness of and concern for the ethical issues of sport management; this is something that can be accomplished in a variety of ways. Incorporating ethical issues into existing academic coursework and developing courses in the ethics of sport are logical beginnings. The development of a code of ethics can begin to assist in providing a framework for ethical analysis. Beyond the classroom, practitioners must provide an environment in which a high standard of ethical conduct is the norm. Strong role models must be available and high expectations clearly outlined, and practitioners must be willing to accept that ethical behavior will not always bring the short-term, immediate benefits so demanded in this culture. The professionalization of sport management will ultimately be a cooperative venture between academics and practitioners in the field. How each partner in this endeavor deals with the issue(s) of ethics will be important in determining the status and prestige of sport management in both the academic and business communities.

CRITICAL THINKING EXERCISES

1. As the marketing director of the athletic department at a major university, you are responsible for generating revenue through the sale of promotional opportunities, including advertising at athletic venues and in the department's printed material. Often these opportunities are sold as part of a promotional package. Recently a large beer company approached you with a proposal for a wide-ranging promotional package at a premium rate. The issue of alcohol and campus life is a particularly sensitive one at your institution, which has a reputation as a party school, and recurring incidents of binge drinking have resulted in a substantial amount of negative publicity. What are the ethical considerations that should be addressed as you weigh this proposal?

2. The annual Regatta Festival is a week-long event with substantial media coverage in your community. Your chain of Sport-o-Rama sporting goods stores in the region sells many water-related recreational products. The Regatta sales staff has discussed with you the possibility of your company becoming an official sponsor of the event, but the price is quite steep in your judgment. You also feel you have little competition in the region and can capitalize on the event's presence without being an official sponsor. You plan a big store-wide sale on regatta week with a newspaper flyer. You are also considering the distribution of discount coupons at various sites along the race course. What ethical issues should be considered as you assess your marketing alternatives as they relate to this event?

SUMMARY

1. Numerous examples of ethical misconduct exist in many of the basic social institutions, and sport is certainly no exception.

2. The relativistic approach to ethics creates an ambiguous behavioral environment, and action is frequently guided by legal standards rather than ethical standards.

3. Ethics and morality are interrelated concepts that provide guidelines for acceptable conduct.

4. Moral development starts with a very self-centered motivation, progresses to conforming with social norms, and ideally reaches the stage in which there is a reasoned belief in and commitment to universal moral principles.

5. Teleology and deontology are the two primary categories of ethical theory.

6. Maxims such as the golden rule are used as "rules of thumb" for ethical conduct, but more extensive frameworks for ethical analysis have been developed.

7. Many useful models have been developed to systematize the task of ethical decision making. Several of these models incorporate characteristics of both deontology and teleology.

8. Personal ethics must serve as the foundation for professional ethics, but the ethical environment in the workplace will influence behavior.

9. Organizational and industry standards of conduct are often not congruent with personal standards, and the differences may be difficult to reconcile at times.

10. There are often long-term consequences to unethical behavior that can outweigh the short-term gains.

11. The development of a code of ethics is a step that can be taken to formalize ethical standards and expectations.

12. The North American Society for Sport Management (NASSM) has developed an ethical creed for sport managers.

13. Ethics training is becoming more prevalent in the academic and business settings.

14. Ethical development should progress from ethical sensitivity to ethical judgment to ethical conduct and leadership.

CASE STUDY

You are the athletic director at XYZ State University, a school of 15,000 students that is a member of NCAA Division I-AA. Your athletic program is comprised of sixteen sports, but financial constraints have limited your ability to do all you would like with the program. Football has never been a primary revenue source as it is with some major Division I institutions, and attendance has dwindled over the past few years. In fact, football currently produces a larger net loss than any other sport in the program. Nevertheless it holds a very strong traditional place on campus and in the community. The demands of gender equity have also forced resources to be reallocated and have strained the budget to the extent that either new revenue must be found to maintain the program or cuts will need to be made.

One option you are considering is dropping football. Such a proposal would create a furor on campus and in the community, but it has some merit financially and minimizes gender equity problems. Another option presented itself to you recently. The athletic director at MEGA University, a major Division I football power, called to see if you would consider playing them in football at their 90,000 seat stadium for a sizeable guarantee. XYZ and MEGA U. played each other on a regular basis several years ago, with MEGA U. routinely winning by six to eight touchdowns. There is virtually no prospect that the outcome would be much different now. The revenue produced from such a game would certainly ease some of your immediate financial problems, however.

Aside from the purely financial considerations of the scenario presented, there are some important ethical questions that must be addressed. As you weigh the options present, how would you respond to the ethical issues presented in this situation.

1. *Who are the various constituents who will be affected by your decision? How are they likely to react?*
2. *Is it appropriate to place the burden for the department's financial problems on the shoulders of an overmatched football team? What are the possible consequences?*
3. *How might either of these options be rationalized as the best decision?*
4. *What constitutes gender equity? Are there any ethical dimensions to dropping football as a method for achieving gender equity?*

ETHICAL SITUATIONS FOR DISCUSSION

The situations presented here are but a few examples of the ethical issues that can arise in sport. One or more of the following suggestions may help to make these situations more useful exercises: (1) Evaluate how each situation might be dealt with at stages four, five and six of Kohlberg's model of moral development. (2) Evaluate each situation from both teleological and deontological points of view. (3) Use one or more of the five maxims on p. 165 to assess the appropriate actions in each situation. (4) Apply Cavanaugh's model for ethical decision making (or some other model of ethical analysis) to the situations in order to arrive at an ethically reasoned response or decision.

1. What are the ethical considerations to be addressed in the decision to use drug testing as a screening tool for prospective employees? What about the use of lie detector tests? Would you submit to such testing? Why or why not? At what point do these tests become an invasion of privacy or a threat to basic constitutional rights?

2. Are the ethical considerations cited above the same for drug testing college and/or professional athletes? If athletes should be randomly tested, should all students? Professors? Administrators? Should drug testing be concerned only with performance-enhancing substances?

3. Bill Frieder accepted the coaching job at Arizona State just before his Michigan basketball team was to start play in the NCAA basketball tournament in 1989. At that point he was relieved of his duties at Michigan, and his assistant took over the team (which went on to win the NCAA title). Without being privy to all the details of the situation, it may be difficult to be overly critical of the parties involved, but the situation poses some interesting ethical questions. What are the ethical responsibilities of the coach to his team? To the University of Michigan? To Arizona State University? What ethical standards should Arizona State University be held to in this circumstance? Given that the letter of intent date for signing recruits is shortly after the completion of the NCAA tournament, what does Arizona State have to gain and lose by waiting

until after the tournament is completed before publicly consummating the deal?

4. It is relatively common practice now for professional baseball teams to offer to pay for the college education of high school draftees as an enticement to get them to sign a professional contract out of high school. Are there any ethical concerns surrounding this practice if baseball administrators are also aware that this is a benefit that players often will not ever use? Is this simply "good business?"

5. Al Davis, the owner of the Oakland Raiders, moved the team from Oakland to Los Angeles in the early 1980s, primarily because of the tremendous financial potential of a major market like Los Angeles. Oakland had supported the team well and the team had been very successful playing there, but from a business perspective Los Angeles was deemed to be a more profitable locale. After extensive litigation, the courts affirmed that Mr. Davis indeed had every right to move the franchise wherever he desired. Do professional franchise owners have any ethical obligations to the communities that support them? If so, what are they? Are they different from those of any other business operation?

6. The difference between serving the public well (social obligations) and serving as the social conscience is sometimes difficult to determine. Several examples involving health and fitness clubs may serve to amplify this issue. Should health clubs serve alcoholic beverages in their lounge areas? Should they have cigarette machines? Should they provide tanning beds for those who wish to use them? From a business standpoint, each of these may be a profitable service. From a health standpoint, there are various levels of concern about each of these services. What ethical consideration comes into play in making the decision about the provision of such services? By not providing such services, are you playing the role of social conscience and limiting people's freedom to make their own choices?

7. Organizational image is the primary concern of the public relations effort. In many sport organizations the media are important players in the manipulation of that image, and the ethics of this relationship may bear scrutiny on both sides. Is it appropriate to curry the attention of the media by providing free tickets, food, transportation, accommodations, and so on? Should these favors be provided only for favorable coverage? Should the media accept such favors? What are the risks to each party and to the general public with such an arrangement?

8. In many circumstances it may be the actions of others that pose a personal ethical quandary. In such situations the question of how you tolerate or deal with such behavior becomes the ethical dilemma. Do you report a fellow employee who is skimming small amounts of money from the cash register? Do you accept an outstanding prospective athlete's transcript that you know has been altered? Do you report a supervisor who is providing inside information to a favored supplier about competitors' bids on athletic equipment? Should such actions ever be ignored? What actions should be taken under these circumstances?

9. Employee and consumer safety are often cited as ethical problems that arise when organizations attempt to balance economic and safety concerns. For example, many considerations go into the decision on what type of playing surface to install. Are there ethical dimensions to this decision? Should artificial turf be used if the incidence of injury or the severity of injuries is higher than on natural surfaces? How much more dangerous would the surface have to be before the risks outweigh the benefits?

10. Personnel matters are often very subjective, and judgments are often influenced by personal philosophies and biases rather than clear-cut personnel policies. The Houston Oilers withheld a starting offensive lineman's pay for a game he missed to be with his wife during the birth of their child. How should such a situation be handled? Does the quality of the player or the importance of the game influence the decision you would make in such a circumstance?

REVIEW QUESTIONS AND ISSUES

1. Cite examples that depict the ethical climate that exists in society and in sport.
2. How are the concepts of ethics and morality related?

3. Discuss the contention that stage four of Kohlberg's model for moral development is the stage from which most adults tend to function ethically.
4. What are the primary characteristics of teleological and deontological theories of ethics?
5. What are the strengths and weaknesses of Cavanaugh's model for ethical decision making?
6. What is the relationship between personal and professional ethics?
7. Can ethics be taught in a college classroom, or is it too late to affect or influence the ethics of college students?
8. What is the responsibility of an organization's leadership with regard to the level of ethical conduct exhibited by its employees?
9. What can an organization do to encourage high standards of ethical conduct? How can ethical codes be utilized in this process?
10. Is all legal behavior ethical? Is all ethical behavior legal? Defend your position.
11. What are the strengths and weaknesses of the ethical creed approved by the North American Society for Sport Management (NASSM)?
12. What role does ethics play in the professionalization of sport management?
13. Discuss what barriers you see that impede the ability of the field of sport management to develop an encompassing ethical code.

SOLUTIONS TO CRITICAL THINKING EXERCISES

1. A utilitarian view would likely address the benefits versus the costs of accepting such a proposal. The financial benefits of accepting such a proposal are quite clear and could be justified or rationalized in a variety of ways. Additional revenue may provide more or higher-quality opportunities for athletic participation. This proposal may also reduce the time and effort required to produce necessary resources. There are social costs to accepting this proposal, including the promotion of a product that has some negative social consequences and in an environment in which many of those exposed to the promotional efforts cannot legally use the product. There are some mixed signals being sent when the institution tries discouraging underage and excessive drinking on campus while, at the same time, providing a forum for a company that encourages alcohol consumption. The inconsistency of such action poses an ethical quandary for the institution's decision makers.

2. Using Cavanaugh's model for ethical decision making, three questions need to be addressed. First, if the company decides to use the event without paying a sponsorship fee, are benefits to the parties involved optimized? The benefits to Sport-o-Rama are quite high, while the benefits to the Regatta Festival are nonexistent. In fact, the Regatta Festival is damaged by such an action because it may undermine the value of sponsorship. It is unlikely that the total benefits are optimized if Sport-o-Rama takes this approach. Second, do the actions of the parties respect the rights of the other? This is a more difficult issue to assess. The Regatta has a right to sell the benefits of affiliation and to protect itself from those who may try to benefit from the event without paying for the association. Sport-o-Rama also has certain rights to communicate freely with consumers as long as it does not cross legal lines associated with using protected names, trademarks, and logos. The balance of rights is a difficult issue in this circumstance. The third question is one of justice or fairness. Is it fair for Sport-o-Rama to benefit from this event without providing any compensation? Would Sport-o-Rama feel the same way if another company was using an event sponsored by Sport-o-Rama in a similar way? Is it fair for the Regatta Festival to demand compensation from anyone who associates with this community event in any way? The response to these three issues will provide the foundation for an ethical decision.

REFERENCES

American Psychological Association. (1977). *Ethical standards of psychologists.* Washington, DC: APA.

Beauchamp, T., and Bowie, N. (1988). *Ethical theory and business.* 3d ed. Englewood Cliffs, NJ: Prentice-Hall.

Cavanaugh, G. (1984). *American business values.* 2d ed. Englewood Cliffs, NJ: Prentice-Hall.

Chonko, L. (1995). *Ethical decision making in marketing.* Thousand Oaks, CA: Sage Publications.

Cialdini, R. (1996). Social influence and the triple tumor: Structure of organizational dishonesty. In D. Messick and A. TenBrunsel (eds.), *Codes of conduct: Behavioral research into business ethics* (chapter 2). New York: Russell Sage.

De George, R. (1982). *Business ethics.* New York: Macmillan.

Frank, R. (1996). Can socially responsible firms survive in a competitive environment? In D. Messick and A. TenBrunsel (eds.), *Codes of conduct: Behavioral research into business ethics* (chapter 4). New York: Russell Sage.

Garrett, T. (1966). *Business ethics.* Englewood Cliffs, NJ: Prentice-Hall.

Gibson, J. (1993). *Performance versus results: A critique of values in contemporary sport.* Albany, NY: State University of New York Press.

Goodpaster, K. (1984). *Ethics in management.* Boston: Harvard Business School.

Jackall, R. (1988). *Moral mazes: The world of corporate managers.* New York: Oxford University Press.

Kohlberg, L. (1976). *Moral development and behavior: Theory, research, and social issues.* New York: Holt, Rinehart, & Winston.

Laczniak, G., and Murphy, P. (1985). *Marketing ethics.* Lexington, MA: Heath.

Petrick, J., and Quinn, J. (1997). *Management ethics: Integrity at work.* Thousand Oaks, CA: Sage Publications.

Rokeach, M. (1973). *The nature of human values.* New York: The Free Press.

Robin, D., and Reidenbach, R. (1989). *Business ethics: Where profits meet values systems.* Englewood Cliffs, NJ: Prentice-Hall.

Sims, R. (1994). *Ethics and organizational decision making: A call for renewal.* Westport, CT: Quorum Books.

Solomon, R., and Hanson, K. (1983). *Above the bottom line.* New York: Harcourt Brace Jovanovich.

Stoll, S., and Beller, J. (1993, March). *The effect of a longitudinal teaching methodology and classroom environment on both cognitive and behavioral moral development.* Paper presented at American Alliance for Health, Physical Education, Recreation, and Dance. Washington, D.C.

Tuleja, T. (1985). *Beyond the bottom line.* New York: Facts on File Publications.

Velasquez, M. (1988). *Business ethics: Concepts and cases.* 2d ed. Englewood Cliffs, NJ: Prentice-Hall.

White, T. (1993). *Business ethics.* New York: Macmillan.

Zeigler, E. (1989). Proposed creed and code of professional ethics for the North American Society for Sport Management. *Journal of Sport Management, 3,* 2–4.

WEBSITES

www.Depaul.edu/ethics/

A very complete site providing a wide range of information about business ethics including an on-line journal, links to other sites, and a compilation of ethics resources on the web.

www.ethics.ubc.ca/

The Centre for Applied Ethics website with clear and useful applied ethics information, codes of ethics, and links to a variety of ethics-related sites.

CHAPTER 10

Tort Liability and Risk Management

Betty van der Smissen

In this chapter, you will become familiar with the following terms:

Tort	Immunity statutes	Waiver
Intentional tort	Gross negligence	Informed consent
Assault and battery	Good Samaritan laws	Secondary assumption of risk
Defamation	Independent contractor	Comparative fault
Invasion of privacy	Governmental immunity	Reckless disregard
Negligence	Indemnification	Negligent supervision
Proximate cause	Shared responsibility legislation	Sexual harassment
Duty	Reasonable and prudent	Deliberate indifference
Unreasonable risk	professional	Avoidance
Standard of care	Foreseeability	Transference
Imputed	Primary assumption of risk	Retention
Doctrine of respondeat superior	Inherent risks	Reduction

Overview

This chapter has two major parts. The first discusses basic legal concepts, primarily in the field of tort law. Who is liable in negligence actions is set forth in a section on the doctrine of respondeat superior. The standard of care required of sport managers is described, and then the defenses, which one may use when sued. There are brief sections on intentional torts, such as defamation and assault and battery (player toward player violence) and on products liability (equipment). The last section on legal concepts addresses some legal concerns related to employment torts, particularly physical violence and sexual child abuse by those who work with youth, and sexual harassment.

The second part applies the legal concepts in focusing on managing "risk exposures" to reduce loss, especially liabilities related to personal injuries of participants and spectators. The four phases in the development of a risk management plan are set forth, with emphasis on the analysis of risks and control approaches (phase 1) and operational procedures to ameliorate risk (phase 3).

Law is pervasive in all of sport management. In a study (Lea and Loughman, 1993) of NCAA schools, it was found that the areas of law for which athletic departments frequently sought advice were:

Area	Percent	Area	Percent
Employment/ personnel	67.29	Insurance	29.91
Execution of contracts	61.68	Television contracts	28.97
Licensing	46.73	Corporate sponsorship	28.97
Title IX	45.79	Merchandising	25.23
Contracts with vendors	45.79	Facility construction	23.36
Radio contracts	32.71	Booster fundraising	22.43
Patent or trademark	31.78	Breach of contract	20.56
Americans with Disabilities Act	29.91	Facility management	20.56

Most of these topics are addressed in various chapters of this book. Advice on aspects of tort liability, the focus of this chapter, was sought by the athletic departments regarding player injury (31.78%), coaches' liability (28.97%), medic's liability (24.30%), and players' liability (20.56%). However, when asked about legal actions brought against them in the past five years, they indicated that nearly one-third (31.43%) had negligence liability actions and just slightly less than one-fifth had NCAA compliance (19.05%) and general administration (17.14%) actions. On the other side, slightly less than one-third (29.27%) of the schools had brought (initiated) marketing actions and about one-fifth (20.73%) general administration actions against others. This chapter addresses selected basic legal concepts of tort liability and sets forth some risk management guidelines for policies and practices to reduce the risk exposure.

THE FIELD OF TORT LAW

Tort comes from the Latin *torquere,* meaning to twist, tortus. It is a private or civil wrong against a person, an injury to the person, to property, or to one's reputation. The wrongdoer is called a *tortfeasor.* There are two categories of torts, intentional torts and unintentional torts. An **intentional tort** requires an *intent* to harm. The most common intentional torts in sport and athletics include **assault and battery, defamation,** violence of one player against another player, hazing, and **invasion of privacy.** In contrast, an unintentional tort, or **negligence,** has no intent to injure, but injury does occur. Both require that the act done was the **proximate cause** of the injury, and that actual damage occurred.

Negligence

Negligence is an unintentional breach of **duty,** an act of omission or commission that exposes the person with whom one has a special relationship to an **unreasonable risk** of injury, causing damage. There are four elements of negligence, and all four must be proven (occur) for a person to be held liable.

1. *Duty. A special relationship* must exist between the injured person and the alleged "wrongdoer," wherein there is a *duty owed* to not expose to or to protect the injured person from unreasonable risk of injury. Usually the relationship is obvious—player and coach, instructor and student, leader and participant, spectator and event sponsor, supervisor and facility/equipment or area user. However, if one who holds a lifesaving certificate is sunning on the beach with a friend, and a swimmer is struggling in the water, there is *no* special relationship requiring the sunbather to rescue the swimmer. There may be a moral responsibility but not a legal duty. However, if the sunbather decides to attempt a rescue, a special relationship is established from this voluntary act, and a duty arises to perform the rescue without negligence. There also may be a special relationship wherein the duty to protect is nondelegable. Such has been held in respect to a school and an athlete (*Wagenblast v Odessa School District,* 1988).

2. *The Act.* Whether or not there is an unreasonable risk and a breach of duty is determined by whether *the act* to protect is in accord with the **standard of care** a professional should give to the person with whom there is the special relationship (see subsequent section on standard of care).

3. *Cause.* The failure to provide the appropriate standard of care is *the cause* of the injury.
4. *Damage. Actual damage* occurred.

CONCEPT CHECK

A tort is a wrong against a person, which injures the person, property, or reputation. The four elements of negligence (unintentional tort) are the duty, the act, proximate cause, and damage.

The doctrine of respondeat superior. In the field of torts, the action is brought by the person injured against the program sponsoring organization or provider of the service and those who represent the organization or provider. Who is liable? A corporate entity is liable for the negligence of its employees, interns, and volunteers; that is, the negligence that injures another is **imputed** to the corporate entity under the **doctrine of respondeat superior,** "let the superior respond." Some refer to this as *vicarious liability.* However, if the employee or volunteer in injuring another acted outside the scope of his or her authority or responsibility, committed an intentional tort (act to harm), or engaged in illegal activity, then the employer is not liable for such injury and does not have vicarious liability. But, the individual "stands alone" and is personally liable for any damages that may be awarded due to the injury.

Inasmuch as both the corporate entity and individuals are sued, it is important to know that in addition to the corporate entity being held liable, the employee or volunteer is individually liable for injury caused by his or her act. In regard to volunteers, about two-thirds of the states have **immunity statutes** for volunteers servicing nonprofit organizations, which encompass sport. Nevertheless, the laws in about one-half of these states are specific to sport volunteers. In 1997 the federal Volunteer Protection Act, covering both nonprofit and public entities, was passed. The federal and the various state laws are very similar. Although the volunteer is immune from liability for ordinary negligence, the corporate entity (nonprofit organization or public agency) remains liable. However, the volunteer retains personal liability for **gross negligence,** that is, acts which exhibit considerable lack of care, of an aggravated character, as distinguished from a mere failure to exercise due care (ordinary negligence), manifesting an indifference toward and disregard for the duty owed, but falling short of willful conduct to injure.

Do the **Good Samaritan laws** protect employees or volunteers? In all but a couple of states, such laws do not protect them because there is a duty owed to not expose participants to unreasonable risk. Good Samaritan laws generally apply only to citizens who see an injured person, recognize the need to render aid, and do so "out of the goodness of their heart" and not because they have a duty toward the person in need. They are immune from ordinary negligence but not gross negligence.

And what about game officials or individuals hired for a specific task, such as teaching swimming lessons or conducting an aerobic fitness class? It depends on whether their status is as an employee, for which the corporate entity is liable, or is as an **independent contractor,** which shields the corporate entity from liability (see shifting liability by contract under Transference).

Administrators or supervisors are *not* personally liable for the acts of employees under them. However, they may be liable for acts that enhance the likelihood of injury. For example, such acts may include hiring incompetent personnel (e.g., uncertified lifeguards), failure to have appropriate rules and regulations for the safety of participants, lack of a supervisory plan, and failure to act on maintenance hazards after notice. They also are liable for negligent hire and deliberate indifference (see later section).

Depending on the state, there may be **governmental immunity** for *public* agencies (e.g., schools, municipalities, state institutions) under tort claim statutes. Even in those states that provide for immunity from negligent acts related to the conduct of activity, there usually is liability for dangerous conditions of facilities and areas. However, many tort claims statutes do provide for either authorization of insurance coverage or **indemnification** of employees acting within the scope of their responsibility, that is, the reimbursement for any damages award levied against them.

In some states there is **"shared responsibility"** legislation. This is directed toward specific activities, for example, the Ski Responsibility Acts, which retain the liability of managers (corporate entity). Also used for injuries as a result of operations' negligence, such as ski lift malfunction, but places responsibility on skiers for skiing within their ability and knowing how to ski.

CONCEPT CHECK

Under the doctrine or respondeat superior, the negligence of the employee or volunteer is imputed to the corporate entity, making the corporate entity liable.

The standard of care. Often one hears about acting like "the reasonable and prudent person." What one must add to that phrase is "for the situation," and the situation in sport is that of a **reasonable and prudent professional.** When one accepts a responsibility, the expectation is that the task will be performed according to accepted standards or practices of the profession. The standard is not determined by the background of the person in charge, such as experience, skill, credentials held, maturity, or knowledge. There is not one standard for beginners and inexperienced persons and another for persons of some years of experience. The participant is owed a duty to be protected from unreasonable risk of harm regardless of who is in charge. The standard is situational and has three determinants. What are the desirable professional practices for (1) the nature of the activity, whether simple or complex; (2) the type of participants, whether exuberant youngsters, physically disabled, persons with mental deficiency (the person in charge must understand the clientele and know how to work with them); and (3) the environmental conditions—is it hot and humid, a Class V river; is there lightning, a muddy field, or slippery floors. The leader must be able to "read" the environment and know what to do to protect the participants.

The standard of care is determined by **foreseeability.** Under the circumstances that existed (the situation) could a reasonable and prudent professional have foreseen or expected or anticipated that the participants would be exposed to an unreasonable risk of injury? If so, then there is a responsibility to act to protect the participant. For example,

if there is lightning, a reasonable and prudent professional at a golf course or at a swimming pool would foresee potential injury to golfers or swimmers and ould act to get golfers off the course and swimmers out of the water. On the other hand, in one case, a group of youth were properly racing in the pool, and a 14-year-old dove into the pool, hitting and injuring one of the racers (*Benoit v Hartford Accident and Indemnity Co., 1964*). The injured swimmer sued, alleging improper supervision. "No," the court said, because the youth watching had always behaved and, thus, it was not foreseeable that this youth would dive into the racers. It must be emphasized, though, that the standard is foreseeability by a professional, not the ordinary person. It behooves every professional to keep up on the best, and latest, practices of the profession.

CONCEPT CHECK

The standard of care required is that of a reasonable and prudent professional. A professional must act to protect the participant or spectator if an unreasonable risk is foreseeable.

Defenses. If one is sued in tort, what are the defenses? Among the various defenses there are three basic types: immunity, contract, and common law. As indicated in the section on the doctrine of respondeat superior, some individuals and agencies or associations, by statute, may be immune from liability in certain situations and for certain types of acts. Or, as discussed in the later section on risk management, liability may be shifted to another corporate entity or individual by contract. In neither of these two defenses are the circumstances evaluated on their merits as to whether there was negligence.

The defense most commonly used relates to common law, specifically, the elements of negligence and assumption of risk. An effort is made by the defendants to prove that one or more of the elements was not present and, thus, there would be no liability. Because there seldom is an issue related to whether there was a duty owed or whether the act was the proximate cause of actual damage, most defenses focus on the second element of negligence, the act. In considering "the act," one must look not only at what the defendant(s) (providers of the activity or service) understood or did but also at what the plaintiff (injured) did.

First it should be asked whether an unreasonable risk could be foreseen in the situation by a reasonable and prudent professional, so as to give rise to a duty to perform an affirmative act to protect. If no, then that is a defense. If yes, then the critical question regarding the provider is, was the standard of care given the same as that which is desirable by the profession or standard-setting organization, or did it fall short? Expert witnesses will be brought in to the trial by the defendant to "prove" the care given was, indeed, appropriate, while the plaintiff will have expert witnesses to counter, and the jury will decide "the truth," that is, was the defendant negligent in how the situation was handled? Remember from previous discussion, there are three aspects of a situation that determine the standard of care required. The defendant also will include in its defense something about assumption of risk by the participant—the consent (primary assumption of risk) and the conduct (secondary assumption of risk or contributory fault) of the injured plaintiff.

CONCEPT CHECK

The three basic types of defenses are immunity, contract, and common law.

PRIMARY ASSUMPTION OF RISK (*Baker v Briarcliff School District*, 1994; *Bush v Parents Without Partners*, 1993; *Ferraro v Town of Huntington*, 1994; *Giovinazzo v Mohawk Valley Community College*, 1994; *Hammond v Board of Education*, 1994; *Laboy v Wallkill Central School District*, 1994; *Schiffman v Spring*, 1994; *Zalkin v American Learning Systems*, 1994.) **Primary assumption of risk,** as a defense, is based on *consent* of the injured party and is a bar to recovery. There are three essential components that go into this consent. First, the participation must be "free and voluntary"; the individual must not be coerced into participating. Second, the individual consents only to those risks that are inherent in the activity, that is, those that are integral to the activity and without which the activity would lose its character. For example, if a person were injured on the pool deck while doing "flip flops," such activity would not be considered inherent in swimming, but extraneous.

Also the participant does not assume any risks occasioned by the negligence of the provider, such as defective equipment or improper instruction. The third component for valid consent is knowledge of the activity, understanding in terms of one's own condition and skill and appreciation of potential injuries. If a participant is experienced and highly skilled, he or she should be fully cognizant of the risks when consenting to participate. On the other hand, if the participant is a beginner, then it is very important that the provider give appropriate instructions and supervision as the participant is learning. In the later '90s the consent concept has been extended to include "open and obvious" field conditions, played on voluntarily.

Primary assumption of risk can be either *implied*, knowing the risks encountered, one participates anyway, or *express*, usually a written or oral statement saying specifically that the **inherent risks** are assumed. In some literature and in a few jurisdictions, the term *express assumption of risk* may be used synonymously with waiver. However, as described in a subsequent section, a **waiver** is a contract to not hold the provider liable for ordinary negligence and really has nothing to do with inherent risks. The term **informed consent** also is often used synonymously with primary assumption of risk, for, indeed, the participant must be "informed" before consenting. But informed consent really came from the medical and research fields in that the client, or subject, is informed of the "treatment" to be done and what results can be expected.

SECONDARY ASSUMPTION OF RISK/CONTRIBUTORY FAULT (*Wattenberger v Cincinnati Reds, Inc.*, 1994; See also cases cited under Primary Assumption of Risk.) **Secondary assumption of risk** is really contributory negligence or fault, in that it is not an acceptance of the inherent risk of the activity but refers to the *conduct* of the participant, that is, it is the participant's behavior that contributes to one's own injury. Such behaviors could include, for example, failure to obey rules, to heed *warnings,* or to follow the sequence of instructions given by the leader. Previously, in the majority of states, any amount (even 1%) of contributory *negligence* or fault by the injured would bar recovery of any award by the injured. But at the turn of the decade only two states still adhere to this point of view, and most states have merged contributory fault into the concept of **comparative fault** (see next subsection). If the provider (defendant) expects to have available secondary assumption of risk or contributory fault as a defense, two practices are essential. First, the provider must set forth appropriate rules, give proper warnings, and instruct as to the desirable sequence. The participant must be informed orally or by written statement as to expected behaviors. Second, there must be a documentation system of just what was "informed" and the practices of the provider in the conduct of activities or services, as well as the behavior or conduct of participants.

CONCEPT CHECK

Primary assumption of risk is when the participant is aware of the inherent risks of the activity and consents to those risks in engaging in the activity. Secondary assumption of risk is when the participant engages in conduct that contributes to one's own injury.

CONCEPT OF COMPARATIVE FAULT Comparative fault is not really a defense but a method of computing a damages award—how much the plaintiff receives. The jury determines the percentage of contributing fault accorded to the plaintiff and the percentage of fault for all defendants aggregated; then the award is made in respect to the ratio of fault. There are two methods provided in the statutes.

About one-third of the states have what is called the "pure form"; that is, the plaintiff can receive whatever percentage the defendant is at fault. For example, if the plaintiff was 10% at fault and the defendant 90%, the plaintiff would receive 90% of the award. Or, if the plaintiff were 80% at fault, only 20% of the award would be received. The other method is the "50/50" approach. Some states say if the plaintiff's fault is "not greater than" the defendant's fault, then the plaintiff may receive the proportionate amount of the award, otherwise no award. Other states, however, will say the plaintiff's fault must be "not as great as" or "less than" the defendant's to receive any pro rata share (plaintiff does not receive an award if fault equal to that of defendants). But, whatever the statutory language, the basic interpretation is that when the plaintiff contributes more than 50% of the fault toward the injury, then there is no award. Thus, the defendant seeks to establish as much contributing fault on the part of the plaintiff as possible, making a documentation system essential. Figure 10–1 depicts comparative fault percentages and the amount of award.

CONCEPT CHECK

Comparative fault is a method of awarding damages in ratio to the fault of the defendants compared with contributing fault of the plaintiff.

CONSENT	CONDUCT	
Plaintiff's primary assumption of risk	Plaintiff's fault secondary assumption of risk	
		If plaintiff's fault greater than 50%, no award under 50/50 rule
No award	0% ———— 50%	
Defendant not negligent	0% ——————————————— 100%	
	under "pure" form, pro rata award for any percentage	
	100% ——————————— 0%	
	Defendant's negligence (fault)	

FIGURE 10–1   Comparative fault continuum.

WARNINGS AND PARTICIPATION FORMS The foregoing defenses are based on the participant having sufficient information to make an informed decision to agree to participate and assume the inherent risks (*consent*) or to engage in the activity in a certain manner, notwithstanding the circumstances (*conduct*). Integral to providing this information are warnings and participation forms.

The essence of warnings is communication to the participant as to how one engages in activity, what is required not to have unreasonable risk of injury, or the condition of the physical environment, including equipment, and the modifications desirable to help prevent injury. For effective communication there are four criteria for a warning: (1) obvious and direct, cannot be subtle; (2) specific to the risk, cannot be generalized but must indicate the risk; (3) comprehendible, in language understandable by the one being warned; and (4) location, at the point of hazard, or at the time when such warning is appropriate. Warnings can come in various forms of communication—oral instruction, video, pictures, posters, literature, signs,—and often it is desirable to use more than one form for emphasis and reinforcement. Warnings are essential in all aspects of programs and services, in skill instruction, use of fitness equipment, swimming on the beach, golfing in inclement weather, slippery dance floors, uneven surfaces or depressions on sport fields, bleacher seat protection, and use of eyeglass guards. Because warnings regarding how to participate to reduce the likelihood of injury are so pervasive, it is understandable that warnings have become one of the most important risk management tools. However, to utilize warnings to show contributing fault, the sport manager must keep complete records of the warnings and the behavior (conduct) of the participant related thereto, specifically when the participant ignores or violates the warning.

CONCEPT CHECK

Warnings are efforts to communicate to the participants how to conduct themselves to reduce their exposure to risk or possible injury.

Agreement to participate forms can be used both to provide information regarding the nature of the activity and appreciation of possible injury, which provides a base for primary assumption of risk defense, and to set forth expectations for the participant, an element in secondary assumption of risk. Although such forms are not a contract and should not be confused with waivers (exculpatory clauses), they do give some documentary evidence of an effort to inform and educate the participant. Even though participants may be minors, they should sign the form, since it is they who are to understand about the activity and the expectations, both as related to activity performance and general behaviors. It is desirable that both the parents and the leader go over the form with the minor.

Intentional torts

There are several intentional torts of which the sport manager should be aware, and procedures for addressing the potential risks should be incorporated into the risk management plan. Intentional torts often are categorized into (1) disturbance of intangible interests causing emotional and mental stress, such as defamation and invasion of privacy; (2) interference with property, such as trespassing, and (3) interference (physical) with person, such as assault and battery. Only a few of the selected torts that are most apropos to sport are discussed.

Disturbance of intangible interests. Athletes and coaches, particularly, are public figures and subject to invasion of their privacy and very critical comments, often emotionally distressing. However, for liability, such actions must be extreme, going beyond the boundaries of social decency.

Invasion of privacy, the intentional tort, should be distinguished from invasion of privacy, the human right. For the latter, which includes considerations related to drug testing, see chapter 12. One of the potential risks of invasion of privacy comes from the use of photos in promotion. Authorizations should be received from all persons whose pictures appear. Often a photo permission statement will be included in a form for athletic team participation, beginning with youngsters, and on registration or entry forms for tournaments and races.

Defamation is a tort with which all public figures have to deal, but the courts are quite "generous" to fans, commentators, and the public in general in what they can say without defaming [*Stepien v*

Franklin, 1988; *Stockard v Moss*, 1997; *Poncin v Arlt*, 1988; *Washington v Smith*, 1996]. To be held for defamation, a person must communicate, either by written (libel) or spoken (slander) word, to a third person with malice to injure one's reputation, and in fact does so. Truth is a complete defense; however, "fair comment" also is a defense. To be fair comment the statements must involve the activities of the sporting world or whatever professional endeavor in which the public figure is engaged. This must not be malice to injure.

CONCEPT CHECK

Defamation is a statement to a third person with intent to injure one's reputation. Truth is a defense.

Interference (physical) with person. There are several types of torts within physical interference with person, including player against player violence, assault and battery, corporal punishment and physical discipline, and child abuse. One also must recognize the involvement of sport in criminal actions, such as criminal assault and battery. Intoxication and hazing also are concerns.

PLAYER AGAINST PLAYER VIOLENCE One of the concerns in sport has been the aggressiveness in sport with one player injuring another player. There are several legal approaches focusing on intent and consent. Under the first approach, *negligence,* there is no intent to injure, and it is said that a player in engaging in the sport consents to the aggressive play (contact) as permitted by rules or *common usage.* In other words, the player assumes the risks inherent in the sport and aggression is considered in many sports as inherent. However, as to both intent and consent, it is a matter of when the aggressive act that caused injury took place, during the ongoing game play or "after the whistle blew" and play had stopped, with a player usually consenting to the first and not in the latter, which evidences intent to injure since it was after play had officially stopped. Usually the negligence suit is brought against the sponsor of the activity, rather than the individual player, for failure to protect the injured from this "unreasonable risk" encountered, namely, failure to control player behaviors. The second approach is *civil assault and battery,* an intentional tort. However, to prove intent against a player is very difficult when aggressive physical contact is often a part of the game. The defense usually is consent to such conduct by the injured player because it is common practice in play.

In an effort to place responsibility for injury, yet deal with the intent issue, the concept of **reckless disregard** has been developed; that is, the player who injures another player acting in disregard for the safety of that other player inferentially *intends* the injury. Situations on which court actions have been brought include a college ice hockey player "butt-ended" with an other player's stick, a pick-up basketball game, a softball player's injured ankle in a collision at second base, being struck by a baseball bat thrown by a fellow player during gym class, a collision in a polo match, and a racquetball player hit in the face by an opponent's racquet. However, in the mid-90s a modification was evidenced in several law cases in which negligence was construed very broadly and held to be an appropriate standard to govern recreational team contact sports, in that the negligence standard can subsume all factors of sport and can be flexible to permit vigorous competition. It was stated that if a participant creates an unreasonably great risk, then that person is negligent. There is a duty to protect a fellow player from such risk. Regardless of which liability concept is used, it is important that players recognize that they must assume some responsibility for their acts of undue aggression that injure another. As one case involving soccer put it, deliberate, combative, and reciprocal confrontation is intentional misconduct. (*Bentley v Cuyahoga Falls Bd. of Educ.*, 1998; *Crawn v Campo*, 1994; *Davis v Greer*, 1996.)

Criminal assault and battery is a fourth approach, but not only must malicious intent be shown but also the suit must be brought by the public prosecutor. One cannot consent to criminal acts. Few cases, therefore, are brought on criminal assault and battery. Some states (e.g., Iowa and Colorado) have enacted a statutory exception for assaults occurring in sport participation (the players).

HAZING Hazing, not only among college fraternities, but also within sport-related groups (teams, band), has become of such concern that approximately three-fourths of the states have passed laws making hazing a crime. A high school football player was injured on the team bus during a hazing incident; the coach failed to prevent the hazing. In a Texas situation, a student was killed from alcohol intoxication during initiation into the lacrosse club. The hazing violated both state law and university regulations. A third case involved hazing at a football camp run by the school board [*Reeves by Jones v Besonen*, 1991, *Haben v Anderson*, 1992, *Tryanowski v Lodi Board of Education*, 1994, *Caldwell v Griffin Spalding County Board of Education*, 1998].

CONCEPT CHECK

A player may be held liable for violence (injury) to another player, but more often, the provider of the activity is sued for negligence for failure to control the player's behavior.

Employment torts

The field of personnel law is extensive and specialized, and several other chapters address different aspects. However, in the 1990s another aspect has become important, employment or workplace torts. Both intentional torts and negligence are involved. The direct act (by the employee) that injured another person, usually a participant, was intentional, but the possible prevention of such act rests in negligence on the part of the corporate entity or employer (administrator, supervisor). The liability for these torts deviates from that usually considered under the doctrine of respondeat superior, which holds that usually a corporate entity is not liable for intentional torts of an employee, since such acts are considered outside the scope of authority and responsibility and not for the benefit of the employer (*Bratton v Calkins*, 1994). The liability is based on a prior act of an administrator or supervisor, who performed his or her responsibilities negligently, and, because of that negligence, the participant was exposed to an unreasonable risk with the potential of injury. And, this negligence is imputed to the employer, as well as retained by the individual. Because civil rights and performance appraisal are addressed in other chapters, only those workplace torts concerned with the employment process and sexual harassment are included in this chapter.

Employment process Four girls (students), including the 16-year-old manager of the girls'

basketball team, were allegedly sexually abused by the basketball coach (*Doe v Coffee County Board of Education*, 1992); action was brought against the school for an alleged sexual molestation of a 13-year-old student by the recreation supervisor (*Doe v Village of St. Joseph*, 1992); a supervisor of a city recreation center (and gymnasium) allegedly sexually molested several girls 6 to 7 years old and a boy 8 or 9 years old and shot one minor's parents (*Williams v Butler*, 1991). Actions in these three cases were brought on negligent hiring, a tort recognized at the turn of the '90's decade by a majority of the states, and by the mid-1990s, at least three-fourths of the states had enacted legislation regarding criminal background checks of persons applying for positions, especially for schools, day care centers, and private and public sport and recreation programs and services where children are involved. However, the federal law and many state laws have been amended to include the disabled and the elderly.

Negligent hiring refers to employing without an adequate background check a person, either paid on volunteer, who has a propensity to inflict harm on others, e.g., participants, especially physical and sexual child abuse, but also violence in general. Such person is considered unfit, in contrast to incompetent. The legal question rests on foreseeability. Did the employer do a "reasonable and adequate" background check so that there was no foreseeability of this type of act occurring, or if more had been done to check would such possible behavior have been foreseeable (Camacho, 1993). The standard for checking is very high for situations where the employee or volunteer has direct contact with children.

Although negligent hiring is the most frequent allegation and one that must be protected against, one also must be aware of negligent supervision, negligent training, negligent referral, and negligent retention actions. **Negligent supervision** involves an administrator or supervisor either failing to properly supervise the conduct of an employee or ignoring or being "deliberately indifferent" to an employee's on-the-job conduct, as was alleged in regard to a male elementary school teacher/coach's acts of molestation against three members of the boys' basketball team while engaged in fundraising activities for summer basketball camp (*D.T. by M.T. v Indp. School District*, 1990).

To not discharge when there are indicators of an employee being unfit as related to criminal or psychiatric attributes is negligent retention. Negligent retention was the allegation regarding a 55-year-old park employee who worked at the neighborhood playground in general maintenance but who also checked out basketballs, games, and ropes. When a 9-year-old child returned a jump rope to him at the maintenance shed, as she usually did, this time he closed and blocked the door and for more than 2 hours repeatedly raped, assaulted, and sexually abused the child and then threatened to kill her. When finally released, the child ran home to her mother, who took her to the hospital. Knowing of the employee's past criminal record, the city had not complied with its own procedures for placement of such persons, and thus this was considered a breach of duty to an invitee to a public park and negligent retention. Further, it was held that governmental immunity was inapplicable in this situation. $2.5 million dollars were awarded in damages (*Haddock v City of New York*, 1990). (See also *Cavarretta v Dept. of Children & Family Services*, 1996; *Rosa H. v San Elizario Indep. Sch. Dist.*, 1997; *Mueller v Community Consol. Sch. Dist.* 54, 1997).

CONCEPT CHECK

Negligent hiring refers to an employee or volunteer being unfit, having a propensity for violence and child abuse, rather than an employee or volunteer being incompetent.

Sexual harassment. There are two forms of sexual discrimination under Title VII of the Civil Rights Act of 1964. One is non–sexually motivated and the other form is sexually motivated, referred to as **sexual harassment.** The Equal Employment Opportunity Commission (EEOC) defines sexual harassment as unwelcome sexual advances, requests for sexual favors, and other verbal or physical conduct of a sexual nature, when

1. submission to such conduct is made either explicitly or implicitly a term or condition of an individual's employment;
2. submission to or rejection of such conduct by an individual is used as the basis for employment decisions affecting such individuals; or

3. such conduct has the purpose or effect of unreasonably interfering with an individual's work performance or creating an intimidating, hostile or offensive work environment.

The first two descriptions are known as *quid pro quo* sexual harassment, because a sexual favor is being asked for in return for a more favorable work assignment, salary, promotion, etc. There is no harassment unless the person requesting the favor holds "power" over the person from whom the favor is requested, that is, has the authority to affect the work position. The third aspect describes a hostile work environment: the employee is subjected to unwelcome sexual harassment that affects the individual's work performance. There is much litigation over hostile work environment and, as with negligent hiring, to do nothing as an administrator or supervisor brings liability to the individual and the entity where there might otherwise be none. For this reason it is essential that all entities establish a policy and procedures on hostile work environment (sexual harassment) that is included in any employee manual and employee training. It is imperative that the appropriate supervisor or administrator take action immediately on any complaint and that the procedures are followed. To do otherwise is called **deliberate indifference** which brings liability to the employee individually and to the corporate entity. (*Koop v Indep. Sch. Dist.*, 1993; *Faragher v City of Boca Raton*, 1998.)

RISK MANAGEMENT

What can be done about tort liabilities related to operations? It is imperative that each agency, organization, business enterprise, or other corporate entity have a risk management plan, up-to-date and implemented. There are many operational policies and practices that can ameliorate the risk exposures. There are two types of risks: the risk of financial loss and the risk of personal injury. Of course, in addition to personal injury causing pain and suffering to an individual, there is often the loss of capability to perform both work-related tasks and personal enjoyment tasks, all of which usually translate into "damages," or financial loss.

A risk management plan is more than safety checklists! It is the systematic analysis of one's operations for potential risks or risk exposures and then setting forth a plan to reduce such exposures. It is an integrating opportunity. Not only is it a diagnostic process of preventive actions that forestalls problems, but it also encourages professional practices and increases employee and volunteer pride, loyalty, productivity, and confidence, as well as promulgates good stewardship of human, financial, and physical resources.

A risk management plan has four phases in its preparation: (1) analyzing risks and determining approaches to control, (2) obtaining statements of policy related to the recommended policies from the policy-making entity, (3) setting forth the desirable operational practices identified and formatting it into a plan, and (4) implementing the plan.

Phase 1: Analysis and control approaches

There are three steps in phase 1: (1) identification of risks, (2) estimation of the frequency and severity of each risk, and (3) determining alternative approaches to controlling the risks. This analysis should include all legal aspects of one's corporate entity operations (a legal audit), but this chapter will consider primarily those aspects most related to torts. Initially, this phase should be done very extensively and then reviewed and updated annually as circumstances change, for example change in activities or services, financial circumstances, or personnel.

Assessment. The first two steps can be done together. One identifies all of the actual and potential risks in the operation of activities and services. This can be done more systematically if categorized. See the accompanying box as a start (see page 188).

Maintenance and program staff should be involved, as well as supervisors and administrators because they are the ones with direct contact with the clientele and have to keep up the facilities, areas, and equipment. Then, as one identifies the risks, the frequency of exposure and potential severity of injury should be assessed. Frequency and degrees of severity can be characterized with descriptive words. The accompanying box provides a guide for this (see page 188).

The risks, so characterized, can be placed on a matrix to facilitate determining the appropriate control approach, the third step (Figure 10–2).

Alternative control approaches. Now that the risks have been identified and frequency and severity determined, what can be done? There are

four basic approaches: **avoidance, transference, retention,** and **reduction.**

AVOIDANCE Avoidance is when one chooses not to offer or to discontinue an activity or service because of the perceived liability. The trampoline is a good example. Some schools, camps, voluntary and private for-profit agencies have chosen to discontinue use, while others will not authorize it. Avoidance is often used when someone does not want to offer an activity or service, "the liability risk is too great." This is an improper use of avoidance. It should be used when one cannot provide the appropriate leadership, facilities, and equipment, and thus the activity has an undesirable risk exposure. It is not the activity that is "hazardous" but the way in which it is conducted that may make it hazardous.

TRANSFERENCE Transference is to transfer or shift the liability to another. The most common is the purchase of insurance. A premium is paid, and the insurance company accepts responsibility for the potential financial risk that may be incurred. Insurance usually is carried on "risks" of high severity, but low frequency, such as participant's catastrophic injury or loss of a major facility by fire.

Another method to transfer risk is by contract (see chapter 11). There are several useful ways for the sport manager to use this approach of shifting liability. First, is independent contractor, that is, a person or company is contracted to provide a particular service and assumes the risks incurred in providing the service. Second, when one has a facility or equipment others would like to use, the lease or rental agreement should include a clause of indemnification and a clause contracting the user to assume the risks and also to provide indemnification to the leasor. Also, it is good to specify that the user is responsible for the proper conduct of any activities for which a facility is used, that the user of equipment knows how to use the equipment, and for both facilities and equipment the behavior of the participants. A third, and very effective, way for adults, is an exculpatory agreement, commonly referred to as a *waiver* or *release*. It is a contract between the provider and the participant not to hold the provider liable for injuries that may occur due to ordinary negligence. Most states hold waivers valid, if properly written. The criteria for a valid contract must be met (see chapter 12). Two key principles in writing or evaluating waivers are

---

Categories for risk assessment

1. Property exposures
   (Real and personal property, including areas and facilities, buildings, inventories, objects on loan, equipment leased and owned; office, athletic training equipment and supplies; program equipment, e.g., waterfront and water craft)

   - Fire damage
   - Damage caused by natural elements, e.g., hail, tornado, flood, lightning, wind, rain
   - Vandalism and malicious mischief
   - Theft and mysterious disappearance
   - Damage to property of others

2. Public liability (excluding negligence in program services)

   - Malpractice by personnel
   - Products liability, e.g., equipment, food
   - Contractual liability, including indemnity provisions, e.g., endorsements, "hold harmless" clauses
   - Natural hazards
   - Advertiser's liability
   - Intentional torts, e.g., libel and slander, false arrest or detention, assault and battery, invasion of privacy
   - Dram shop and host liquor
   - Discrimination or civil liberty violation

3. Public liability, negligence in program services
   List types of bodily injuries that might occur in conducted or supervised activities, programs or services provided, e.g., swimming, sports league, and on physical facilities and areas where the activities are not supervised, e.g., city park, reservoir lake, parking areas, playgrounds. Do this in some detail so that one assesses the likelihood and extent of risks one might incur. Then, group by type for an overall view of bodily injury risk potential. Some of the types of bodily injury that might be listed include the following:

   - Death
   - Quadriplegia or other paralysis
   - Brain damage
   - Loss of limbs
   - Loss of senses (vision, hearing)
   - Injury of internal organs
   - Strains, sprains, fractures of bones, ligaments, joints
   - Cuts, punctures, abrasions

---

(1) make clear that it covers all aspects of activity participation and injury from whatever cause, including negligence; and (2) the format should provide for conspicuousness of the exculpatory language in a print size that is easily readable.

RETENTION Retention is the acceptance of the risk within the budget or financial structure of the agency, organization, or business enterprise. This method is used primarily for risks of low severity but high frequency, and could include "losses" or risks such as for physical injuries by providing athletic training room or emergency treatment or for property damage from vandals or theft or for advertising liability.

REDUCTION The three following approaches all relate to potential financial risks, or "losses," and one may use all three for a specific risk, depending on the nature of the risk. The fourth approach, reduction, however, addresses the reduction of exposure through operational management. All risks

FREQUENCY OF OCCURRENCE

	High or often	Medium or infrequent	Low or seldom
High or vital	A Avoid or transfer	B Transfer	C Transfer
Medium or significant	D Transfer	E Transfer or retain	F Transfer or retain
Low or insignificant	G Retain	H Retain	I Retain

SEVERITY OF INJURY OR FINANCIAL IMPACT

FIGURE 10–2   The matrix of severity and frequency of potential losses and suggested control approach.

should be approached from *both* the financial and the operational management perspectives. Other generic risk managment plans in this chapter give some pointers on reducing liability exposure.

CONCEPT CHECK

Risk management is the assessment of exposure to loss and the attempt to reduce such exposures. Risk control approaches include avoidance, transference, retention, and reduction.

Phase 2: Statements of policy

As one reviews alternative approaches to managing risks, there will be certain areas in which the organization's governing body will need to set forth policies, on which then the operating procedures (phase 3) will be based. For example, What is the policy regarding medical insurance for injuries? Is the family's insurance to be used first? Will the organization cover "minor" expenses of treatment (e.g., ambulance, emergency room, emergency first aid, and athletic training room treatment)? Should only catastrophic insurance be carried by the agency, or should an athlete (or parents) be required to carry such? What is the policy relating to travel—no personal participant cars are to be used, no staff cars to be used, organization insurance to cover staff and volunteer cars, only school vehicles to be used, all transportation is hired as independent contractor? There will not be many, but there are some important policy decisions where there are alternative choices. Usually the sport administrator and/or risk manager will make recommendations for policy.

Frequency and severity descriptors

Severity degrees from a financial perspective

- Vital — Losses that would be catastrophic in nature; private enterprise would go bankrupt, tax-based agency would have to increase taxation or bond debt financing, or other special funding would have to be done for the corporation to survive
- Significant — Losses would require a cut-back in services or financial reallocations
- Insignificant — Dollar losses can be handled with operating revenues

Severity degrees as seriousness of an injury

- High — Fatal accident or injury resulting in quadriplegia or severe brain damage
- Medium — Disabling injury of a lesser severity but of a permanent nature or for an extended time
- Low — Temporary disability or of minor permanent disablement

Frequency of occurrence, likelihood of an injury or risk to occur, levels

- High or often — What is high or often will depend on the risk being evaluated; for some risks, often might be yearly, while for certain minor cuts and bruises it might be weekly; thus, in evaluating the frequency, the nature of the risk must be considered
- Medium or infrequent — Occurs occasionally and probably more often than you would like
- Low or seldom — Really a rare occurrence

Phase 3: Operational practices and procedures

In this phase, the operational practices and procedures are set forth for the reduction of risk exposure. These must be in detail and specific to all aspects of operations. Of course, each organization will offer its own activities and services and, thus, risk management details will vary from organization to organization. For this reason, a generic outline of tort liability–related aspects to be covered in the risk management plan is set forth. Many of the desirable practices will be discussed in other chapters, and there is considerable literature on operation details. Risk management is more than safety checklists. A risk management plan is an integrating opportunity, integrating many operational elements. Although an organization should have a complete legal audit, only operational elements relating to tort liability are included in the generic outline (see accompanying box).

Phase 4: Implementation of risk management plan

A risk management plan encompassing risk analysis, statements of policy, and operational procedures is of little value unless implemented.

Risk manager. Every organization should have a person designated as "the risk manager." This would be a specific position in larger organizations, or an assigned responsibility in smaller organizations. To say all personnel are responsible for risk management is not satisfactory, because everybody's business is nobody's business. There must be a specific person responsible for overseeing risk management. It is this person's responsibility to see that a risk management manual is prepared and regularly updated and that personnel are not only "in-serviced," relating to risk management practices and procedures, but also that these are carried out. This person also is

Aspects of operational practices: a generic outline for a risk management plan

I. General supervisory practices*

  A. Supervisory plan: a critical dimension

   - Should be written
   - Must be communicated to staff
   - In-service education program related to responsibilities
   - Assignment of personnel in accord with
     - Competence related to the activity or function
     - Suitability to handle clientele (participants)
   - Location and number of supervisors
     - Areas of responsibility
     - Pattern of circulation

  B. Management of behavior

   - Discipline policy and procedures
   - Distinguishing horseplay, rowdiness, assault and battery
   - Crowd control for large events (plan for control)
   - Drug abuse
   - Child abuse
   - Intoxication
   - Antisocial behaviors

  C. Rules and regulations

   - Establish minimum for safety of participants
   - Communicate to participants by various media
   - Enforce consistently and fairly

  D. Identify dangerous situations and conditions: procedures for remedying

   - Physical conditions which are hazardous—inspections (see III Environmental Conditions)
   - Activities being engaged in a dangerous manner (see II Conduct of Activities and Services)

  E. Security (protection against criminal acts)

   - Security plan should be in place for the premises generally, at spectator events
   - Safety of person and property—rape, kidnapping, robbery, shootings
     - Concept of foreseeability of felonies

  F. Care of the injured and emergency procedures

   1. The emergency procedure plan (in-service the procedures)
   - Rendering the first aid (in-service review of "life-saving" first aid only and those types of injuries most apt to happen)
   - Emergency procedures following aid
     - emergency equipment
     - hierarchy of care, e.g., trainers, physician
     - transportation arrangements
     - know where emergency treatment permissions for minors are
     - check vehicles, routes, insurance policies if using participant's   *(continued)*

*The focus of general supervision is supervision of participants and areas and facilities, not other staff. Supervision of staff is a different type of supervision.

Aspects of operational practices: a generic outline for a risk management plan **(continued)**

- Disposition and follow-up
- Media contact

2. Accident reporting

- Distinguish accident forms, treatment forms, statistical reporting forms, and insurance forms—know role of each
- Information necessary on an accident form to be useful if get in lawsuit
  - Identification of information
  - Location of accident (diagram)
  - Action of injured
  - Sequence of activity
  - Preventive measures by injured
  - Procedures followed in rendering aid
  - Disposition
- Inservice how to complete form properly
- Maintaining of records in documentation system
  - Who stores (maintains)
  - Length of time
  - (S/L + 2–3 years, after reaching age of majority)

G. Emergency plans, as appropriate

- Disasters (tornados, fire, flood)
- Runaway children
- External violence, riots, demonstrations

H. Crisis management plan

- Catastrophic injury
  - Shootings
  - Drownings
  - Quadriplegia

- Dealing with
  - Family
  - Co-participants
  - Media

I. Employment torts (selected aspects; most agencies have a separate personnel manual)

- Negligent hiring
- Sexual harassment—the hostile workplace
- Disciplinary and task performance appraisal

II. Conduct of activities and services

A. Adequacy of instruction and progress

- Skills with progression
  - Instruction for safety, courtesies of the game
  - Protective devices and equipment
  - Rules and regulations

(continued)

Aspects of operational practices: a generic outline for a risk management plan **(continued)**

   B. Use of warnings and participation forms (see Defenses on pp. 180 and 181)
   C. Maturity and condition of participants

- Age, developmental stage, size
- Physical, emotional, social maturity
- Skill and experience
- Mental and physical capability
- Temporary state of condition, physically and emotionally
- Any permanent disabilities that must be considered as related to the specific activity

   D. Transportation

- Type of vehicles (leased, chartered, school only)
- Maintenance of vehicles
- Drivers
- Riding to and from events
  - Supervision and permissions
- Routes
- Sharing expenses
- Insurance coverage

III. Environmental conditions (see also chapter 14, Managing the Facility)

   A. Equipment

- Appropriate equipment to the activity and participants and adequate protective devices and instructions on how to fit or use
  - Maintenance of equipment is absolutely essential
- Products liability
  - Distinguish inherent hazard in equipment or defect in materials or workmanship from negligence in professional's judgment in use or fit of equipment
  - Do you sell equipment? If so, you may be in the "chain of liability."
  - Standards or approved equipment (not always adequate for activity) a standard is only minimum (CPSC and ASTM standards)
  - Liability chain: manufacturer, retailer, concessionaire, you; number of states have laws limiting the length of time after manufacture and sometimes limits seller's liability
- Rentals
  - On rental agreement, have disclaimer regarding behavior of user and injury to third parties
  - Your responsibility is to have equipment in A-1 shape!
  - Do not assess ability of person renting equipment
  - Beware of donations of used equipment

   B. Layout of facility

- Layout and design, especially
  - Rest rooms/shower areas
  - Architectural barriers for the handicapped
  - Layout of activity areas for safety and monitoring
- Vehicular and pedestrian traffic pattern/flow for safety
  - Ease of supervision and control, e.g., entry control
  - Safety, e.g., hidden and/or dark areas

(continued)

Aspects of operational practices: a generic outline for a risk management plan (continued)

- Law enforcement of the premises

C. Maintenance of areas and facilities
Remember, premise-related injuries are the responsibility of both the owner of the premise and the activity sponsor.

- Inspection records/system (actual vs. constructive notice, liable for both)
  - Surfaces/floors
  - Field maintenance
  - Aquatic facilities
  - Hazardous materials
  - Showers and locker rooms
  - Debris, cleanliness, weeds
  - Contracting premise repairs
- Also, parking areas
  - Pedestrian ways and trails
  - Protective barriers (fences, gates, trails)
- Elements of maintenance inspection system
  - Ongoing, part of job description, done daily
  - Formal checklist; detailed, checked, dated, and signed
  - Critical parts inspection; needs a specialist to check condition
  - External, "a pair of eyes" not so familiar with the operation; may be paid consultant or exchange of services with another camp
- How much time do you get to repair? This depends on the following:
  - Density of use
  - Likelihood of an injury
  - Severity of injury if occurs

D. Health hazards (safe work environment)

- OSHA standards (and State OSHA)
  - Haz/Com and Exposure Control Plan (art materials, maintenance supplies)
  - Blood-borne pathogens (HIV/AIDS) standards
- Sanitation of food service areas, aquatic areas, bathhouse
- Care of poisons and inflammables
- Environmental audits (contaminants)
  In one case the users of the park (members of soccer club, children playing), township park employees, and neighbors sued, claiming exposure to toxins from forty years of dumping waste into a landfill, which became a park (*Redlands Soccer Club v U.S. Dept of Army,* 1992).

in charge of the information and documentation system, which is an integral part of all risk management. There also, must be monitoring of the plan. Neither the implementation of the plan nor its effectiveness assessment just happens. Responsibilities must be assigned and structure set in place to facilitate risk management.

Employee involvement. There should be active interaction between employees and administrators and supervisors. Many organizations establish a special risk management committee, often called the *safety committee,* but risk management is more than safety. This committee is vital not only to the implementation of the plan but also to its review and update.

Manual. Guidelines for operationalizing the procedures should be put together into a risk management manual to provide an authoritative guide and immediately available reference for all levels of employees, such as the top administrator or executive, athletic director and coach, the school principal and teacher, youth agency executive and physical director or field staff, program staff, and maintenance supervisor. Not all employees need a full copy of the manual, but it should be available, and pertinent aspects definitely should be given to the employees in accordance with their responsibilities.

Information/documentation system. There must be a system maintained specifically to have available data for risk management. It should include participant forms, health and accident forms, operations information, program data and documents, etc.

Public relations. There should be a public relations program directed toward the concerns of risk management. It is well known that an irritated, unsatisfied customer or participant is prone to bring legal action much quicker than a person toward whom care, concern, and taking care of "minor" expenses are exhibited.

Monitoring the plan. Risk management is an ongoing process; not only must it be integrated into the very fiber of an organization, but also its effectiveness and the cost efficiency of risk management practices must be systematically evaluated and adjustments made, as appropriate.

SUMMARY

1. Unintentional tort or negligence was discussed in relation to who is liable, the standard of care required, and the defenses that may be used when one is sued for negligence.
2. The concepts of primary and secondary assumption of risk and comparative fault were set forth in terms of both defenses and operational practices.
3. Intentional tort, particularly violence of players against players and defamation, was described.
4. Employment torts, especially negligent hiring and sexual harassment, was introduced as an important concept in youth sport.
5. The four phases of the process of risk management were discussed. They are as follows: (1) analysis, (2) statements of policy, (3) operational practices, and (4) implementation.
6. A generic outline of operational practices and procedures for management (reduction) of risk exposures, focusing on supervisory practices, the conduct of activities and services, and the environmental milieu was presented.
7. The implementation of a risk management plan through identifying a risk manager, involving employees, establishing an information/documentation system, and monitoring the efficiency and effectiveness of the plan was set forth.

CASE STUDY

Use this case study as a review of the concepts of negligence and issues in sport management liability. The scenario is adapted from the case cited. You should review the actual case, a catcher-base runner collision in an informal softball game [Crawn v Campo, 643 A.2d 600 (N.J. 1994)].

A group of individuals regularly participated in informal softball each week. The composition of the teams varied week to week, but with a core group and friends or bystanders filling in to make a complete team. There were no independent officials, although the game was played under the general rules of softball. The plaintiffs were generally agreed that there was a no-slide rule, since whenever a player did slide, the other team seemed to invoke the rule. However, there was some difference among the plaintiffs as to the scope. That is, was the rule a general no-sliding or one that merely prohibited runners from purposely running into infielders in order to break up a tag or double play. They did all agree that the purpose was to prevent injuries. On the other hand, the defendants insisted that no rule governed sliding at all.

On this day, a runner (defendant) was on first base. A ball was hit to the shortstop, who flipped it to the second baseman for a force-out. However, the runner slid into second base, taking the legs out from beneath the second baseman. After that play, the plaintiff witnesses stated that the other players reminded the defendant runner that sliding was prohibited; the runner acknowledged the rule and indicated his willingness to abide by it. Defendant

*runner, however, testified that his slide into second
base did not result in any warning about sliding.*

*With the runner now on second base (he was
safe!), the next batter hit a ball to right field. As the
outfielder relayed the ball to the first baseman, the
defendant runner rounded third and headed for home.
The plaintiff catcher testified that he was standing on
the first-base side of home plate, left foot touching the
right side of the plate, body turned toward first ready
to receive the relay throw from the first baseman. As
defendant runner approached the plate, he lowered his
body and barrelled into catcher's left side, reeling
catcher backwards, and with runner ending up on top
of catcher's lower leg. The catcher maintains that the
runner had plenty of room to run past him and touch
home plate, since catcher was on first base side. The
plaintiff catcher alleges that defendant runner
deliberately ran into him to dislodge the ball from his
glove to avoid the out. The defendant testified that
when he approached home plate, the catcher was
straddling the plate with a foot on either side, so the
only way to reach home plate and avoid a tag was to
slide. He slid feet first into the catcher's left leg,
resulting in a torn knee ligament, which required
surgery.*

REVIEW QUESTIONS AND ISSUES

1. Was the conduct of the defendant base runner negligence, reckless, or intentional? Under which conduct, if any, was defendant liable to plaintiff? What is the standard of care that should be adhered to in this type of informal softball game? Does it differ from a league competition game? If so, how? If this had been an "instructional" game, such as Little League or a physical education class, what difference, if any, would it make in bringing the lawsuit?

2. Should informal recreational activities, such as this softball game, serving a societal interest to many people, in the interests of public policy, be accorded partial immunity for simple negligent conduct and have liability only for the more egregious (notably bad) or willful and wanton behaviors? What about the immunity statutes for volunteer athletic coaches in some states? What type of liability protection do such statutes give?

3. Did the plaintiff catcher, in playing this informal softball game under usual rules of the game, assume inherent risks of the game of softball? What are the inherent risks? Was this action an inherent risk? If the catcher did assume the risk, should defendant be liable? Is this type of injury foreseeable in an informal game like this one? Foreseeable by whom? If so, or if not, what difference would it make in liability?

4. What effect does a rule, like a no-sliding rule, have on the liability of the players? If this had been a sponsored game, would it be any different if a rule were violated? If there indeed, was a warning to defendant when he slid into the second baseman, what difference, if any, would that make on his liability to the plaintiff?

5. What if this had been a league game under sponsorship and the adults playing had signed a "waiver"? Who would be liable and for what? What would the waiver have "waived"?

6. If protective equipment had been involved, such as catcher's equipment, either not having it on or not in good condition so that it did not adequately protect, what would the issues of liability be? [*Baker v Briarcliff School District,* 1994, a field hockey situation.]

7. If a muddy field had been involved and the base runner slipped and seriously injured himself, or slid into the catcher ostensibly unintentionally, or if the catcher in taking position slipped into the pathway of the runner, what would the issues of liability have been? [See *Schiffman v Spring,* 1994, a soccer situation.]

8. If you were the owner of the ball diamond being used, what risk management strategies might you use to reduce your risk exposures related to the environmental conditions of the field? First, identify what risk exposures you would have (include both financial strategies and reduction).

9. You are the sponsor of a softball league and in charge of the management of the teams, the concessions and spectators, the officials, et al. What risk exposures would you have in the

areas of supervision and conduct of activity? What risk reduction strategies (operational practices and procedures) would you use to reduce your risks?

REFERENCES

Baker v Briarcliff School District, 613 NYS 2d 660 (1994).

Benoit v Hartford Accident and Indemnity Co., 169 So. 2d 925 (1964).

Bentley v Cuyahoga Falls Bd. of Educ., 1998 WL 78679 (Ohio Ct. App.).

Bratton v Calkins, 870 P. 2d 981 (Wash. App. 1994).

Bush v Parents Without Partners, 21 Cal. Rptr. 178 (1993).

Caldwell v Griffin Spalding County Bd. of Educ., 503 S.E. 2d 43 (Ga. App. 1998).

Camacho, R. (1993). How to avoid negligent hiring litigation, 14 *Whittier Law Review* 787–807.

Cavarretta v Dept. of Children and Family Services, 660 N.E. 2d 250 (Ill. Dec. 1996).

Crawn v Campo, 608 A.2d 465 (N.J. Super. 1992), aff'd/rev'd in part, remanded 630 A.2d 368 (N.J. Super. 1993), leave to appeal granted 636 A.2d 516 (N.J. 1993), aff'd as modified 643 A.2d 600 (N.J. 1994).

Davis v Greer, 1996 WL 596 556 (Tex. 1996) denying application for writ of error sub. nom. *Greer v Davis,* 921 S.W. 2d 325 (Tex. Ct. App. 1996).

Doe v Coffee County Board of Education, 852 S.W.2d 899 (Tenn. App. 1992).

Doe v Village of St. Joseph, 415 S.E. 2d 56 (1992).

D. T. by M. T. v Indp. School District No. 16, 894 F.2d 1176 (10th Cir. 1990).

Faragher v City of Boca Raton, 118 S.Ct. 2275 (1998) rev'g 111 F. ed 1530 (11th Cir. 1997), reinstating 864 F. Supp. 1552 (S.D. Fla. 1994).

Ferraro v Town of Huntington, 609 NYS 2d 36 (1994).

Giovinazzo v Mohawk Valley Community College, 617 NYS 2d 90 (1994).

Haben v Anderson, 597 N.E. 2d 655 (Ill. App. Ct. 1992).

Haddock v City of New York, 554 NYS 2d 439 (1990).

Hammond v Board of Education, Carroll County, 639 A.2d 223 (1994).

Koop v Indep. Sch. Dist., 505 N.W. 2d 93 (Minn. Ct. App. 1993).

Laboy v Wallkill Central School District, 607 NYS 2d 746 (1994).

Lea, M., and Loughman, E. (1993). Crew, compliance, touchdowns & torts. The Entertainment and Sports Lawyer, Vol. II, No. 3, Fall, 1993, pp. 14–25. Schools in NCAA Divisions I–A, I–AA, I–AAA, and II were included in the study.

Mueller v Community Consol. Sch. Dist., 678 N.E. 2d 660 (Ill. Dec. 1997).

Poncin v Arlt, 428 N.W. 485 (Minn. App. (1988)).

Redlands Soccer Club v U.S. Dept of Army, 801 F. Supp. 1432 (M.D. Pa. 1992).

Reeves by Jones v Besonen, 754 F. Supp. 1135 (E.D. Mich. 1991).

Rosa H. v San Elizario Indep. Sch. Dist., 887 F. Supp. 140 (W.D. Tex. 1995), rev'd/remanded 106 F. 3d 648 (5th Cir. 1997).

Schiffman v Spring, 609 NYS 2d 482 (1994).

Stepien v Franklin, 528 N.E. 2d 1324 (1988).

Stockard v Moss, 580 A.2d 1011 (D.C. App. 1990), aff'd 706 A.2d 561 (D.C. 1997).

Tryanowski v Lodi Bd. of Educ., 643 A.2d 1057 (N.J. Super. 1994).

Wagenblast v Odessa School District, 758 P.2d 968 (1988); see also *Seal v Carlsbad Indp. School District.,* 860 P.2d 743 (N.M. 1993).

Washington v Smith, 893 F. Supp. 60 (D.D.C. 1995), aff'd 317 U.S. App. D.C. 79, 80 F. 3d 555 (1996).

Wattenberger v Cincinnati Reds, Inc., 33 Cal. Rptr 2d 732 (1994).

Williams v Butler, 577 So.2d 1113 (La. App. 1991).

Zalkin v American Learning Systems, 639 So.2d 1020 (Fla. App. 1994).

SUGGESTED READINGS

References on various topics have been cited throughout the chapter. It would be helpful if students looked up these cases and articles to obtain further insights.

The law is a dynamic field and ever relevant to what is happening in society; therefore, it is essential that sport managers endeavor to "keep up with the times." How? Rather than give some specific articles to read, resources are indicated.

Books

This chapter, including tables and figures, is based on Dr. van der Smissen's three-volume reference book:

(SSLASPA has an extensive resource list of books on both amateur and professional sports, including risk management.)

Daugherty, Neil, David Auxter, Alan Goldberger, and Gregg Heinzmann. (1993). *Sport, physical activity, and the law.* Champaign, IL: Human Kinetics Publishers.

van der Smissen, Betty. (2000). *Legal liability and risk management for public and private entities.* 2d ed. Cincinnati: Anderson Publishing Company.

Wong, Glenn M. (1994). *Essentials of amateur sports law.* Westport, Connecticut: Praeger 2nd edition.

Newsletters and magazines

Athletic Business each issue has a *Sports Law Report.*

From Gym to the Jury

> *The Center for Sports Law and Risk Management*
> 8080 North Central Expressway, Suite 400
> Dallas, TX 75206
> 12 pp. Newsletter, 6 issues per year

WEBSITES

The Sports Lawyers Association (focus on professional sports)
www.sportslaw.org/sla.html

For information on current issues the local papers will have articles, but of special value is *USA Today*
www.usatoday.com/sports/scores.htm

The New York Times
www.nytimes.com

CHAPTER 11

Contract Law and Sport Applications

Linda A. Sharp

In this chapter, you will become familiar with the following terms:

Offer	Specific performance	Restrictive covenant
Acceptance	Actual authority	Covenant not to compete
Consideration	Apparent authority	Rollover clause
Legality	Perquisites	Promissory estoppel
Capacity	Liquidated damages	Indemnification
Statute of Frauds	Termination for cause	Certificate of insurance
Monetary damages	Reassignment clause	Additional insured

Overview

The purpose of this chapter is not to provide one with the skills necessary to draft contracts nor to solve challenging issues of contract interpretation. However, after studying the material herein, the student should (1) appreciate the extent to which numerous issues in sport management are related to contract law, (2) become familiar with some basic tenets of contractual interpretation and contract law, (3) become conversant with various contractual transactions in sport settings (e.g., an employment contract with a coach, a game contract, a sales contract, an athletic grant-in-aid, a facility lease, a contract with a game official, or a contract with a team physician) and the important aspects of each transaction from an administrative perspective, (4) understand the role of legal counsel in helping one draft and interpret a contract and acquire a preventive mentality, and (5) realize that a document's strength is dependent upon each party's respective power in negotiating the transaction.

It would be ludicrous to suggest that anyone, absent legal training, should draft contracts for an organization. However, it is important to be informed about contract law, to be able to choose legal counsel wisely and be able to converse with him or her in a knowledgeable manner. Contracts simply represent a determination of how parties wish to structure a particular undertaking. Therefore, the more legal counsel knows about one's business and about the transaction in question, the better the document should be. Do not assume counsel knows what you want to accomplish; your role is to educate counsel about the transaction in the context of a particular sport setting.

As discussed earlier, risk management is a very important concept for your business. The principles of risk management extend well beyond the realm of personal injury, and one should adopt a preventive mentality in conjunction with all contractual dealings. Normally, for a transaction of any magnitude, extensive negotiation takes place. Therefore, you have the luxury of time to allow you and your legal counsel to structure a transaction so that it best protects your interests.

In conjunction with the preventive mentality, it is important to understand that attorneys draft a document envisioning the *worst-case scenario*. Any contract, drafted poorly or well, will work for the parties when their relationship is amicable because the parties do not question their obligations or look for ways to get out of the relationship.

However, with contracts, just as in life, parties may not maintain an amicable relationship throughout the entire term of the contract. It is when a relationship sours that the parties need the guidance of a contract. Therefore, even though it may seem perverse to envision the termination of a transaction when the parties are happily engaged in entering into a contract, it must be done to protect the client. If the relationship goes awry and the parties need to seek judicial relief, the contract must be explicit in its terms and provisions for termination.

There are, of course, drafting and negotiation advantages to being the party that drafts the document. However, there is a tenet of contractual interpretation that may come into play. Any ambiguity in a document will be resolved by a court against the party that drafted the document. In view of this interpretive canon, the drafting party must take extra precautions to draft a document that is clear and incapable of multiple interpretations.

FORM CONTRACTS

Every business has a number of repetitive transactions for which *form contracts* may be used. These documents are drafted by legal counsel to fulfill a particular need. Therefore, it is ill-advised to change such a document without the advice of counsel. Although the temptation may be great to alter a clause or strike a word or phrase, this tampering can cause unintended interpretive problems for a court.

In interpreting a contract, courts try to adhere to the parties' intentions as evidenced in the document. However, in doing so, the court is reading the document as an *integrated whole;* every part of the contract should be consistent with every other part. When people make piecemeal changes to a document, they may unwittingly alter other parts of the document

because they may not understand the way that various parts of the document fit together. Therefore tinkering with a form contract may result in a great deal of harm.

Alternative form contracts or clauses should be prepared by counsel so that these acceptable variations from the standard form may be used by administrators. Also, periodic review of form contracts is advisable to make sure that they are still in concert with the transaction. Businesses sometimes change the way that they do something but do not change the underlying contract. When this happens, numerous problems may result.

INTRODUCTORY CONTRACT PRINCIPLES

"A contract is a promise, or set of promises, for breach of which the law gives a remedy, or the performance of which the law in some way recognizes a duty" (Restatement, Second, Contracts, 1981, Sec. 1).

The major legal concepts involved in the formation of a contract are offer, acceptance, consideration, legality, and capacity.

1. An **offer** is a conditional promise made by the offeror to the offeree. An offer usually includes the following essential terms: (1) the parties involved, (2) the subject matter, (3) the time (and place) for the subject matter to be performed, and (4) the price to be paid.
2. An **acceptance** can be made only by the party to whom the offer was made.
3. **Consideration** involves an exchange of value wherein one party agrees through a bargaining process to give up or do something in return for another party's doing the same. Consideration is often viewed as the essential term needed in a contract to make it legally enforceable. Without consideration, there may be a promise to do an act, but it may not be legally enforceable as a contract.
4. **Legality** means that the underlying bargain of the contract must be legal for the contract to be considered valid by the courts. The courts will not enforce illegal contracts, such as gambling contracts, contracts with unlicensed professionals, contracts with loan sharks, and so forth.
5. **Capacity** is defined as the ability to understand the nature and effects of one's acts. In

regard to contracts, the general rule is that anyone who has reached the age of majority (18 in most states) has the capacity to enter into a contract.

STATUTE OF FRAUDS

In general, oral contracts are enforceable, assuming the parties have evidence to show on what terms they are in agreement. However, the **Statute of Frauds** provides that there are certain types of agreements that must be written to be enforceable. Among these agreements, which may be applicable to a sport setting, are (1) agreements for the sale of land or an interest in land, (2) agreements for the sale of goods in excess of $500, and (3) contracts not to be performed within one year from the date of the agreement (Calamari and Perillo, 1998). For two sport cases dealing with the third aspect, see *Cooper v Peterson*, 626 N.Y.S.2d 432 (Sup. Ct. 1995) and *McInerney v Charter Golf, Inc.*, 680 N.E.2d 1347 (Dec. 1997).

REMEDIES

The purpose of damages in contract law is "to place the aggrieved party in the same economic position he would have had if the contract had been performed" (Calamari and Perillo, 1998). Thus, the purpose is compensatory, not punitive, and punitive damages may not be recovered in a contract action, except in rare circumstances, such as fraud.

The court will not award damages based on mere speculation. Damages must be proven with reasonable certainty (Restatement, Second, Contracts, 1981, Sec. 352). Generally, damages may be recovered for those items that arise naturally from the breach as well as damages that are in the contemplation of the parties at the time the contract is entered into (Calamari and Perillo, 1998, Sec. 14.5).

The usual type of award in a contract action is **monetary damages.** For example, in a contract for the sale of goods, the usual measure of damages is an amount equal to the difference between the contract price and the market price. School A contracts with Store B to buy a certain brand and model of football at $50 per unit. Store B, however, breaches the contract and refuses to sell School A the footballs promised. School A, therefore, gets bids from other stores in the area for the same brand and model football. The best price that School A can get

is $60 per ball. Therefore, the damages incurred by School A are $10 times the number of balls to be purchased.

Another remedy, available only in cases where monetary damages will not adequately compensate the injured party, is **specific performance.** This remedy provides that the breaching party must perform the act as promised in the contract. The remedy is limited to cases in which a sales contract for a unique item is breached. For example, if you contract to purchase the original jersey worn by Babe Ruth on August 18, 1921, and the seller refuses to convey that item to you (breach), the appropriate remedy may be specific performance. Monetary damages cannot cure the breach because you cannot purchase that particular Ruth jersey anywhere else for any amount of money.

However, specific performance may *not* be used in a personal-service contract (e.g., an employment contract). For example, if Shaquille O'Neal decided to breach his employment contract with the Los Angeles Lakers, the Lakers could not compel him to perform as specified in his contract. This restriction on the availability of specific performance exists for two basic reasons: (1) to make someone do something against his or her will is not looked favorably upon by the law because it resembles involuntary servitude, and (2) there are severe enforcement problems in this type of situation. In regard to the latter point, one can see the inherent difficulty in ensuring that Shaq was playing to the best of his abilities if the court forced him to perform. How would a court enforce whether he got enough rebounds or blocked enough shots? Therefore in an employment situation, the court will not order a person to complete a personal-services contract for his or her current employer.

Another type of remedy is *rescission and restitution,* which is an action to cancel a contract and to restore the parties to the status occupied prior to the contract. This remedy may be available in cases involving fraud, duress, or mistake.

A final remedy is *restoration,* in which the court allows the parties to rewrite a contract to conform to their true intentions. This remedy is appropriate in cases of mutual mistake or where, through oversight, all of the contract terms were not specified.

Last, there is the principle of *mitigation,* wherein the nonbreaching party must make reasonable efforts to lessen the consequences of the breach. For example, in the sale of the footballs mentioned above, School A had an obligation to obtain the footballs for the lowest price available from the vendors to which School A had reasonable access. Therefore, if one store offered the footballs at $75 per ball and another store offered the same footballs at $60 per unit, School A, under the principle of mitigation, should accept the $60 bid so that the contract damages sustained are $10 per ball, not $25 per ball.

AUTHORITY TO CONTRACT

In order for business to be conducted, employees within an organization are given the ability to contract with outside parties in certain limited areas up to a specified monetary limit. This limit, conveyed to the employee, is known as the person's **actual authority.** What happens if the employee exceeds actual authority when contracting with a third party? Can your organization be held accountable for that particular transaction?

For example, assume that the business manager in an athletic department has actual authority to contract up to $5,000. However, the manager signed a contract with equipment Vendor X for $7,500. What argument will Vendor X use to enforce the contract against the university regardless of the fact that the business manager exceeded actual authority? Vendor X will use the principle of **apparent authority** to try to bind the organization. "Apparent authority arises when an organization acts in a way that manifests the agent's authority to a third party and the third party reasonably relies on the manifested authority of the agent" (Wiesner and Glaskowsky, 1995). Therefore, the vendor will argue that it had no actual knowledge of the real limit of authority possessed by the business manager; and absent that information, it was reasonable business practice to rely upon the business manager's ostensible authority to engage in a transaction of this nature. There are two key points to remember: (1) the vendor does *not* know the actual limit of authority, and (2) the transaction must be a reasonable exercise of authority in view of the transaction in question, based on trade custom and established business practices. Therefore, while it may be reasonable for a vendor to believe that a business manager may have actual authority of $7,500, it would be ludicrous to suggest that a business manager would be able to contract for the renovation of a facility worth $500,000. Because a vendor cannot use the concept of apparent authority to its advantage if it has actual knowledge of an employee's limit of authority, you may wish to construct documents so that it is clear to a third party (e.g., by a line for a countersignature) that any transaction in excess of X dollars may not be entered into by only one employee.

EMPLOYMENT CONTRACT

For the purposes of this discussion, you are the athletic director at Books and Balls University (BBU), a Division I institution that values both academic and athletic achievements. You are overjoyed that you have reached a preliminary understanding with I. M. A. Scholar, a highly regarded coach, to head your football program. University legal counsel will be meeting with you in approximately one hour to discuss the particulars of the Scholar contract. What are the major points that you will address?

Termination clauses

Although you are euphoric at the prospect of securing Scholar for BBU, your euphoria must give way to the harsh reality that coaching contracts are frequently breached. It is not uncommon for a university to terminate a coaching contract without cause before the term of the contract expires—a breach of contract by the university. Likewise, a coach may decide to leave a school for another coaching opportunity prior to the end of the contract term—a breach by the coach. Therefore you must give great attention to the termination clauses because they may have severe economic ramifications for the parties. Draft these clauses with the worst-case scenario in mind—that a party to the contract may wish to breach.

Breach by the university

The basic principle of contract law to keep in mind is that the breaching party is responsible for all damage that reasonably flows from the breach and for damage that is in the contemplation of the parties at the time the contract is made. Therefore it is beyond dispute that the coach would be entitled, upon breach by the university, to his salary and the normal benefits of university employment (e.g., health insurance and pension benefits). However, the matter of dispute often becomes the coach's entitlement upon breach to **perquisites** (i.e., those benefits that the coach received because he was in the position of head football coach). The seminal case for this issue is *Rodgers v Georgia Tech Athletic Association*, 303 S.E.2d 467 (Ga. Ct. App. 1983). In this case, Pepper Rodgers, the former football coach at Georgia Tech, was fired from his position with two years remaining on his contract. Although Georgia Tech, the breaching party, paid his salary for those two years, Rodgers sued for the value of the benefits and perquisites that were received from the Georgia Tech Athletic Association and from other sources by virtue of his coaching position. These perquisites included such items as (1) profits from radio and television shows, (2) profits from his summer football camp, (3) the use of an automobile and payment of auto expenses including gas, maintenance, repairs, and insurance, (4) memberships in a number of country and tennis clubs, and (5) housing in Atlanta for Rodgers and his family. These extensive perks, numbering twenty-nine items, greatly exceeded the value of Rodgers' salary.

The Georgia Court of Appeals found a legal basis on which Rodgers could recover in regard to some of the alleged perquisites because the rather nebulous language in the contract did not make it clear exactly what the defendant athletic association was responsible for in the event of breach. Further, using contract principles related to damages, the court decided that even though some of the perquisites were not provided by the Georgia Tech Athletic Association, some of the items could have been contemplated as a probable result of the breach and were, therefore, recoverable.

In view of this precedent, it is important that the university try to limit the items for which it could be responsible in the event BBU breaches its contract with Scholar. Therefore, the contract should state explicitly what items the university intends to provide as compensation. From BBU's viewpoint, it must be clear that the university provides no other compensation and is not responsible for any other compensation. The purpose of this clause is to limit the amount recoverable by Scholar should the university terminate Scholar's contract without cause.

Obviously, when Scholar and his attorney negotiate the contract with you and BBU's counsel, Scholar will take the position that the university should be responsible, upon breach by the university, for all perquisites, regardless of the source. BBU will take

the position that it is responsible only for the compensation it provides (i.e., salary and pension and health benefits). Usually, the parties will arrive at some mutually satisfactory amount that will be paid upon breach. This amount, which is known as **liquidated damages** or *buyout*, is compensation that is reasonably related to the amount of damages that will actually be sustained in the event of breach. The parties cannot quantify the exact amount of damages in advance; they can, however, stipulate a reasonable estimate of the probable loss (Restatement, Second, Contracts, 1981, Sec. 356(1)). This type of clause is recommended, but the parties should be sure to draft it as discussed above and not to draft it as a *penalty clause*. Penalty clauses are written into a contract in order to sanction the breaching party, and the monetary sanctions do not actually bear a relationship to the amount of damage to be incurred. Courts will not uphold penalty clauses.

Breach by the coach

It is not only the university that may breach an employment contract; coaches often breach their agreements. This possibility should be addressed in the employment contract. It is legally permissible to include a clause that provides that Scholar would be liable to the institution for liquidated damages (buyout) if Scholar breaches the agreement. For example, Vanderbilt University, in a recent case, was successful in having the liquidated damages clause held reasonable and enforceable against its former football coach. See *Vanderbilt Univ. v DiNardo*, 174 F.3d 751 (6th Cir. 1999).

Although the possibility exists to include such a contract clause, BBU may wish to consider the operational ramifications of doing so. If BBU gets the reputation of being inflexible in drafting such provisions, it may deter some coaches from taking a position with BBU. This is an issue in which the legal aspects need to be balanced against administrative realities. The legal provisions that may be used to protect BBU are only one facet to consider.

Termination by the university for cause, and coach's responsibilities

In the previous discussion, the breaching party could be held liable for damages. However, if the university terminates the contract for a justifiable reason—for cause—it is not in breach and does not owe damages to the coach. In fact, BBU's ability to

terminate for cause is based on the fact that Scholar would have failed in some way to meet his obligations under the contract and is in breach.

Therefore it is important to specify Scholar's responsibilities so that, if necessary, BBU may allege that Scholar failed to meet one or more of these responsibilities. There are numerous programmatic responsibilities Scholar must take on—including budgeting, scheduling, recruiting, evaluation of coaching staff, and public relations that should be addressed. Further, the contract should explicitly address Scholar's obligation to abide by all NCAA, conference, and university rules and regulations. BBU also should incorporate specific language that directs Scholar to make every effort to ensure that the academic requirements of all student-athletes are met.

In stating Scholar's responsibilities, BBU also may wish to consider the inclusion of a **reassignment clause** stating that, although the intent is to hire Scholar as football coach, BBU reserves the right at any time during the term of the contract to reassign Scholar to other duties, usually administrative, that are in line with Scholar's abilities. This clause is used by BBU to retain flexibility and to permit it to reassign Scholar without a claim by Scholar that he was hired *only* to coach football and that a reassignment would serve as a *constructive discharge* (i.e., a breach of the contract by the university). For example, a former university basketball coach unsuccessfully claimed that the university breached his employment contract when it offered him reassignment as the golf coach or rules compliance coordinator, since a statutory provision allowing reassignment was incorporated into the coach's contract. See *Monson v State of Oregon*, 901 P.2d 904 (Or. Ct. App. 1995).

Restrictive convenant

In addition to the buyout clause, there are two other methods that BBU may consider to induce Scholar to stay for the entire term of his contract. First, if BBU has the resources, it may be possible to offer Scholar an extra monetary incentive to honor the entire contract period. This bonus could be in the form of cash, a base salary increase, or the forgiveness of mortgage payments. For example, Barry Alvarez, the current football coach at the University of Wisconsin-Madison, will receive a bonus of $1 million if he continues to coach at that university

until the expiration of his fifteen-year contract (Greenberg and Gray, 1998).

A second mechanism for keeping a coach from breaching a contract is the **restrictive covenant** or **covenant not to compete.** This clause basically provides that if a coach breaches the employment contract, he or she is prevented from or limited in taking other employment opportunities that are in competition with the university position just vacated. These clauses are disfavored in law because they place restrictions upon the right to pursue one's livelihood, so they must be narrowly drafted in terms of time period, scope, and geographic area. The enforceability of these clauses varies widely and is controlled by state law (Restatement, Second, Contracts, 1981, Sec. 188).

Term of employment

The term of employment may be for a stated number of years, or a **rollover clause** may be used. Note that universities in some states are forbidden by law from entering into an agreement that exceeds one year.

BBU should negotiate for a term with a fixed number of years, perhaps with an option to renew, but BBU does not want a rollover clause in the contract. The rollover clause provides that a coach always has a commitment from the university for a specific number of years. At the end of each year, the contract's term is automatically renewed for another year unless one party notifies the other of the intention not to roll over. For example, if BBU entered into a three-year term with Scholar using the rollover clause, Scholar would continue to have a three-year term at the end of each year in which BBU let the term roll over.

Rollover clauses are often poorly drafted and result in an ambiguous understanding of what the term actually is. It also puts the university in the position of having to give years of notice of its intention to let the contract expire, which is poor personnel relations (Stoner and Nogay, 1989).

Disclosure of outside income

The NCAA requires that a coach obtain prior written approval from the university's chief executive officer to receive all athletically related income and benefits earned from outside sources (NCAA Bylaw 11.2.2). This mandate must be incorporated into the coaching contract. The income may include, but is not limited to, consultation fees from shoe or equipment manufacturers, fees from sports camps, housing benefits, complimentary ticket sales, or income from radio and television programs.

CONCEPT CHECK

The negotiation and drafting of a coaching contract should be approached in a comprehensive fashion. Parts of the contract fit together and cannot be altered without affecting other aspects of the agreement. Termination provisions must be drafted in conjunction with both the duties and responsibilities section and the compensation section of the employment contract. If the university breaches the agreement (terminates without cause), it wants to limit the amount of compensation it owes the coach to salary and health and pension benefits, whereas the coach wants to receive compensation for all the perquisites received by virtue of the coaching position. Usually a liquidated damages or buyout clause will be drafted to deal with this. A buyout clause also may be drafted to protect the university if the coach breaches. Further, the drafting of the document must take into consideration applicable state law, NCAA regulations, and university regulations and policies.

GAME CONTRACT

The athletic director at BBU is negotiating with Sports "R" Us University (SRUU) to play a nonconference football game at SRUU in the fall of 1996. Both BBU and SRUU are football powerhouses, and this game will certainly sell out SRUU's 90,000-seat stadium. What are the essential elements in the game contract that will be drafted for this contest?

Location, date, and time

Football schedules for Division I institutions are determined many years in advance, and it is imperative that no scheduling conflicts arise. Make sure that the date and time listed in the contract are in accord with the preliminary negotiations. If a neutral site is chosen for a particular contest, one team should be designated as the home team.

Game officials

Because this is a nonconference game, the contract should indicate how the officials will be chosen. There may be provision for a split crew or for a neutral crew of officials.

Guarantees

It is important that the remuneration that BBU will receive for participating in this game is set forth precisely. The remuneration (*guarantee*) may be a fixed amount or a percentage of the net revenue for the game. BBU may receive—in addition to the above or in lieu of all or a portion of the above—hotel, travel, and/or meal expenses. If BBU is to receive a percentage of the net game revenue, the term *net revenue* should be defined. Also, a date should be set on which BBU will receive its compensation. For example, if BBU plays SRUU in early September but the contract provides for payment at the end of the season, SRUU would have use of that money for several months. If the guarantee is a large sum of money, this could result in substantial gain for SRUU. Therefore, BBU wants the money as soon as possible after the contest. To avoid any disputes pertaining to the calculation of the guarantee, there should be a provision for auditing the pertinent documentation.

Complimentary tickets

The number of complimentary tickets allocated to each team must be negotiated, and issues pertaining to bench and sideline passes, and admission of the band and cheerleaders must be addressed.

Broadcast rights

Radio rights generally belong to the home team. Television rights also belong to the home team unless there are conference agreements that take precedence.

Termination provisions

Although it may be unethical to do so, the reality is that sometimes a party may breach its game contract, often because of the prospect of greater financial gain by playing another school. This eventuality must be considered and provided for by incorporating a liquidated-damages clause. Liquidated damages is a method that makes a reasonable estimate of the damages to be sustained in the event of breach. In this situation, if SRUU breached this contract and BBU had negotiated for a percentage of net revenue, the liquidated-damages provision would approximate this amount. Penalty clauses may not be used. For example, it would not be appropriate to provide that if SRUU breached the agreement it would pay BBU $1.5 million as a penalty for breaching the agreement. If, however, the damage to be sustained would actually approximate $1.5 million, that figure would be upheld as a reasonable estimate of the damage to be sustained. Also, schools may wish to consider a clause that allows for the cancellation of a contract for cause should one school be subject to NCAA penalties that may prevent the team from being seen on television. If the contest was scheduled to be televised, considerable income may be lost, and a school should have the option of cancelling a contract if a large amount of money from broadcast rights would be lost.

Because of the recent spate of teams leaving previous conference affiliations, many conferences have notice provisions to which their teams must adhere in order to leave a conference without breach.

> **CONCEPT CHECK** ✔
>
> *Game contracts must set forth the particulars of a transaction and make sure that all economic provisions are properly defined. Guarantees are an important consideration for revenue-producing contests. Termination clauses should be drafted with the concept of liquidated damages in mind.*

SALES CONTRACTS

The business manager for athletics at BBU is negotiating with a national hotel chain for the provision of pregame meals for its men's basketball team at various locations during the upcoming season. What are important aspects of contracts for the sale of goods or services? What points should the athletic manager be especially cognizant of for this type of transaction?

Use of the vendor's contract

In many situations, a sales transaction drafted by the vendor will be used. One must remember that the document was drafted by the vendor's legal counsel to protect that company's best interests. Therefore the athletic manager should be prepared to seek amendments to language that is unfavorable to BBU. The vendor might approach the document as if it were carved in stone and incapable of alteration. However, if the vendor wants to retain business, the document, even though it is a standard form, *can* be altered.

Quantity and quality of goods and services

A contract should clearly indicate the quantity of goods ordered and describe the goods and services with particularity. For a team meal contract, the athletic manager should be aware of the notification provisions regarding the number in the athletic-team party. There will be a clause providing that BBU must give certain notice to the hotel regarding the exact number of meals to be prepared. Failure to attend to such a provision may result in paying for more meals than are actually needed or not having enough meals ordered to satisfy the size of the party.

Price of goods and services

What is the price of the goods and services? When is payment due? Are there provisions for the establishment of credit? Is there a discount for early payment? In the team meal context, there is sure to be a provision in the hotel contract in which any increase in the meal's cost from the date the contract was signed to the date of actual service will be passed on to BBU. This type of clause is unacceptable; and if the athletic business manager has the necessary negotiating power, the contract should read that the price agreed to on the date of the contract is fixed, regardless of increases in food prices, cost of labor, etc. One way to structure this is to agree on a *cap on price increases*—an agreement to increases of X%, but anything beyond that will be assumed by the hotel. The use of a cap on price increases is important in any sales transaction in which the contract is signed well in advance of the actual date of performance.

Guarantees

Although the law implies warranties concerning goods, these apply only relative to the fitness of the items for their purposes. BBU, as the buyer, may not find the goods to be satisfactory, but this may not be a breach of warranty. BBU wants some *guarantee* that if the goods are unsatisfactory it will receive monetary compensation or alternative goods that are satisfactory. In the team meal contract in question, BBU should make sure the vendor does not have a clause allowing "reasonable substitutions" in the meal. The hotel's view of what is a reasonable substitution may be greatly at odds with a coach's or trainer's view of what is a reasonable substitution. In this situation, the business manager should negotiate for *no* substitutions by the hotel unless the substitutions have been approved by the team trainer or other appropriate team representative.

Cancellation provisions
The timing of cancellation should be set. In addition, the method by which a party may cancel should be delineated (e.g., notice by registered mail at least X days prior to the transaction). If no specific method of cancellation is set, it is important to cancel in such a way that documents the cancellation.

Options for renewal
Often a party may negotiate a favorable contract that may be renewed at the same favorable terms by giving notice to the other party in a time frame specified in the contract. A buyer should make sure there is a system to keep track of such dates so there is no chance of failure to renew a favorable contract.

> **CONCEPT CHECK**
>
> *Some important aspects of sales contracts are (1) quantity and quality of goods and services, (2) the price of goods and services and method of payment, (3) guarantees regarding the satisfaction of the buyer, (4) cancellation provisions, and (5) options for renewal. As a buyer, a cap for price increases should be set and "reasonable substitutions" should be defined and allowed only with the approval of the buyer.*

ATHLETIC GRANT-IN-AID

The athletic director at BBU will meet soon with Jerry Jock, a former football player whose grant-in-aid was not renewed for his senior year. Jerry had received an athletic scholarship for three years, but the football coach decided not to award Jerry a scholarship for his senior year on the basis that Jerry was not contributing enough to a winning effort. The notice of nonrenewal was given as required by NCAA regulations. Further, the form used by BBU to award athletic financial aid clearly states that

"the maximum length of any grant-in-aid to a student-athlete is for a period of one academic year." According to the contract language, no reason was needed by the coach to refuse to renew Jock's grant-in-aid. Is there any basis on which Jock and his lawyer can attempt to make a case that BBU should renew Jock's grant-in-aid? What if Jock was given verbal assurances by an assistant coach when he was recruited that he would be given aid for all his years at BBU, provided he retained academic eligibility? What if Jock relied on that assurance in choosing to attend BBU? Does it help Jock's case that BBU's practice is to grant automatic renewal of aid from year to year and that this was an expectation held by all BBU athletes?

Many courts have analyzed the athletic scholarship as a contract between the student-athlete and the university. The university extends an offer for a scholarship, which is accepted by the athlete who chooses to attend that school. The consideration by the university is the grant-in-aid, and the athlete's consideration is participation in the sport. The grant-in-aid document evidences this agreement, which is limited to a year's aid by the NCAA.

In the case of Jerry Jock, his attorney would not make an argument based on the language of the contract itself. Rather, the relief sought—renewal of the scholarship for his senior year—is predicated on an argument based on another doctrinal principle: **promissory estoppel,** the elements of which are (1) a *promise* is made that should reasonably be expected to induce reliance, (2) there is *reliance* upon the promise, and (3) *injustice* to the promisee results from the reliance. In an action based on promissory estoppel, detrimental reliance is being used as a substitute for the contractual element of consideration (Restatement, Second, Contracts, 1981, Sec. 90). Since this doctrine has both elements of contract law and tort law, it has sometimes been characterized as a "contort" (Cozzillio and Levinstein, 1997).

In this type of case, the courts are trying to remedy an injustice that resulted because one party relied on a promise made by another party. In this case, the assistant coach made a promise to Jock that he would have aid for his years at BBU. Jock relied upon this promise as evidenced by his choice to attend BBU. The injustice would be the economic loss Jock would suffer with the loss of his scholarship in his senior year. The court would also look at the relationship between the parties and find the reliance factor to be heightened because a representative of the football program of a powerful institution made this representation to a relatively naive 18- or 19-year-old person. This *disparity in bargaining power* would make a stronger case for Jock.

The representations made by coaches as to "full rides" for four years are in conflict with the written grant-in-aid, which is restricted to a one-year term. This may subject schools to possible liability based upon promissory estoppel in a case such as the one just described.

For example, it has been reported that the University of Arizona recently settled a claim by a former baseball player for $125,000. The player had claimed that he was cut from the team due to poor athletic performance despite the coach's promise of a "multi-year" scholarship which was contingent only on acceptable academic performance and lack of misconduct. (Perspective, 1999). This type of situation poses a difficult administrative response, because coaches may argue that if forced to divulge the reality of the one-year scholarship, they may be at a recruiting disadvantage with schools that offer the prospect a complete four- or five-year package. This issue has both legal and ethical ramifications.

CONCEPT CHECK

Although the grant-in-aid document states that the scholarship period is only one year, coaches often recruit athletes based on contrary representations. If the athlete relies upon such representations to his or her detriment, the remedy of promissory estoppel may apply.

FACILITY LEASE*

The general manager of the Grand Central Arena (GCA), a multipurpose facility that houses a variety of sporting events, concerts, and the circus—is in charge of preparing leases for upcoming events.

---

*There are documents of this nature that are titled *license* instead of *lease*. It is beyond the scope of this chapter to discuss the technicalities of this legal distinction, which has important ramifications. The traditional distinction, however, is "that a lease is a conveyance of exclusive possession of specific property, for a term less than that of the grantor, usually in consideration of the payment of rent, which vests an estate to the grantee. . . . A license, on the other hand, merely makes permissible acts on the land of another that would otherwise lack permission" (Friedman, 1997, Sec. 37.1).

Hoosier University (HU), a well-known basketball powerhouse, wants to lease the facility next year for a game with its rival University of Horseland (UH). What are some critical elements of this lease transaction that protect the interests of GCA, the lessor, in this transaction?

Rental

From the lessor's perspective, it is important to derive a profit on the transaction regardless of the economic success or failure of an event. Therefore a base rental amount normally is designated, with provision that the lessee will pay this amount *or* a percentage of the gross receipts derived from ticket sales, whichever is the greater amount. In this way the lessor is guaranteed a certain amount; but if the event proves profitable, lessor will derive benefit from that occurrence. The term *gross receipts* must be defined precisely to avoid disputes.

Restrictions on the use of facilities

It must be clear for what purpose the lessee is using the facility and should be restricted to that purpose only. In this case, the use would be restricted to a basketball game between HU and UH. Further, the lessee (HU) agrees to be bound by all applicable federal, state, county, or municipal ordinances and by the operating rules and regulations of the facility. Limitations on the use of advertising in the facility and restrictions on alterations of any part of the facility are set.

Concessions

Lessor may reserve and retain the rights and revenues relating to the facility's concessions. A comprehensive list of what this encompasses should be included. If GCA agrees to allow HU to sell concessions, a percentage of those receipts shall be taken by GCA. Any restrictions relating to the sale of alcoholic beverages must be noted.

Liability and insurance issues

The lessor wants to structure the lease so that any occurrence that transpires during the term of the lease will have monetary ramifications for the lessee and not for the lessor. For example, if this point was excluded in the lease, what would GCA's liability be if during the pregame warmup a GCA employee, in the scope of his or her duties, acted negligently, resulting in injury to a spectator? Under usual tort principles, GCA could be held liable under respondeat superior because its employee acted negligently while in the scope of employment. Obviously, this outcome is not favorable to GCA; and as lessor, GCA wants to incorporate language into the lease that may alter this outcome.

Therefore, GCA will put an **indemnification** provision into the lease that states that HU "will indemnify and hold harmless GCA against any and all claims for loss, injury, or damage to persons or property, including claims of employees of lessee or any contractor or subcontractor, arising out of the activities conducted by lessee, its agents, members, or guests." Basically, indemnification is a method to protect an entity from financial loss in the event of a judgment against it. The indemnification agreement comes into play after an award has been made. Lessee (HU) would reimburse GCA for the amount of recovery.

Note that this provision is written very broadly to protect the interests of GCA. It is written so that it includes any occurrence related to the use of the facility, even if a GCA employee is at fault. Even though it may seem suspect to have a provision whereby the lessee basically assumes the financial ramifications of something it may not have caused, this type of provision is an accepted part of commercial transactions, and will be enforced by the courts, assuming that it is drafted properly.

Of course, an agreement to reimburse a party after a judgment rendered against it is a useless provision if the indemnifying party has no assets. That is why the insurance provisions are critical. GCA will mandate that HU provide insurance as specified in the lease by GCA. As evidence of this, HU will provide GCA with a **certificate of insurance** from HU's insurance carrier that attests to the coverage mandated by GCA. Also, GCA wants to have direct access to the insurance proceeds should something occur. This can be accomplished by having HU name GCA as **additional insured.** Doing this means that for the purposes of insurance coverage which is applicable to this lease, if an occurrence arises for which insurance is applicable, GCA is named on the policy as an insured party as is HU.

Relationship of the parties

GCA does not want to be considered a partner or joint venturer with HU. This is essential because a partner is responsible for obligations incurred by any other partner. GCA wants it made clear that there is no partnership between the parties; rather, the only relationship that exists is one of lessor-lessee. A statement to the effect that HU's employees are not agents or employees of GCA should be included to avoid any implications of respondeat superior for the actions of these persons.

CONCEPT CHECK

The facility lease signifies that the lessor allows the lessee to use the facility for a particular time period, for a designated purpose, and for a specified amount of compensation. The rental amount is often a minimum fixed amount that may increase if the percentage of gross receipts reaches a certain level. The lessor wants to protect itself from any economic ramifications of possible occurrences resulting in liability or loss during the term of the lease. It does so by incorporating indemnification provisions and mandating that the lessee obtain a certificate of insurance and place the lessor as additional insured on the applicable policies.

CONTRACTS WITH GAME OFFICIALS
The courts generally have held that game officials are considered independent contractors and not employees of a school district or university. However, to protect the contracting organization from a worker's compensation claim, should the referee be injured during the event, the contract should clearly reinforce the referee's independent contractor status. This will also protect the organization against liability under respondeat superior should the referee act negligently.

CONTRACTS WITH TEAM PHYSICIANS
Usually a university does not wish to be considered the employer of a team physician. Therefore the document developed to reflect the agreement between the parties should state that the physician is rendering services as a consultant for which she or he will be paid a lump sum. It is important to reinforce the fact that the physician is an independent contractor and is not acting as the agent, employee, or servant of the university.

CRITICAL THINKING EXERCISES

1. As an athletic director, you want to insure that your business manager is not able to bind the athletic department (university) to a contract that exceeds his actual authority of $5,000. Explain the concept of apparent authority and what you can do to keep a third party from using this concept to your disadvantage.

2. Bearing in mind the doctrine of promissory estoppel, discuss what type of training you, as athletic director, might wish to provide to your coaches in regard to their recruiting techniques.

SUMMARY

1. Adopt a preventive mentality in your contractual dealings, and work with legal counsel to draft documents that best protect your interests.

2. To protect your interests, contracts should be drafted by envisioning the worst-case scenario.

3. Form contracts are helpful to use in repetitive business transactions and should not be altered without consulting legal counsel.

4. The major legal concepts involved in the formation of a contract are offer, acceptance, consideration, legality, and capacity.

5. The Statute of Frauds provides that certain transactions must be in written form to be enforced by a court. These transactions include (1) contracts for the sale of goods in excess of $500, (2) contracts for the sale of land or an interest in land, and (3) contracts that cannot be performed within one year from the date of the contract.

6. The usual type of award in a contract action is monetary damages that attempt to compensate the aggrieved party for the loss of his or her bargain.

7. Specific performance is available only in those cases in which monetary damages will not suffice (e.g., a sales contract for a unique item). Specific performance is not applicable to personal-service contracts.

8. A third party may be able to enforce a contract against an organization even if an employee exceeded his or her actual authority in doing so, if the third party can show that it was reasonable to believe in the employee's apparent authority to engage in that transaction.

9. Termination clauses are important aspects of employment contracts with coaches. If the university breaches the contract, it wants to limit the damages recoverable to the coach's salary and related health and pension benefits. The coach, however, wants compensation for all the perquisites that he or she lost upon contract termination.

10. Liquidated damages, or buyout, are agreed-upon compensation to be paid by a breaching party when a contract is terminated without cause. This cannot be a penalty but rather must be compensation reasonably related to the amount of damages to be sustained upon breach.

11. If a university wishes to terminate a coach's employment contract for cause, the responsibilities of the coach need to be specifically stated in the contract.

12. A restrictive covenant provides that if a coach breaches an employment contract, he or she is prevented from or limited in taking other employment opportunities that are in competition with the university position just vacated.

13. Game contracts need to set forth the particulars of the event. Guarantees are an important aspect and must be defined carefully. Termination provisions should incorporate liquidated-damages clauses.

14. Sales contracts must address (a) quantity and quality of goods and services, (b) the price of goods and services and method of payment, (c) guarantees regarding the satisfaction of the buyer, (d) cancellation provisions, and (e) options for renewal.

15. The university athletic grant-in-aid is limited to a one-year term by NCAA regulation. If coaches make representations to the contrary, upon which an athlete relies to his or her detriment, promissory estoppel may apply.

16. The facility lease signifies that the lessor allows the lessee to use the facility for a particular time period, designated purpose, and specified amount of money. The lessor wants to protect itself from the economic ramifications of any

possible occurrence resulting in liability or loss during the term of the lease. It does so by incorporating indemnification provisions and mandating that the lessee obtain a certificate of insurance and place lessor as additional insured on the applicable policies.

17. Contracts should be structured so that game officials and team physicians are considered independent contractors.

CASE STUDY

You are the legal counsel for J. J. Starbucks, men's basketball coach at Wheatland University (WU), a Division I university. Starbucks has come to you for advice regarding his employment contract with WU. Although the term of his contract does not expire for another two years, Starbucks is concerned that the university may try to terminate his contract before next season because the basketball team just finished with its worst record in twenty years. Several prominent boosters are putting pressure on WU's board of trustees to fire Starbucks immediately.

Apart from the poor performance of his team, Starbucks has been a model coach. He carefully abides by all NCAA, conference, and university rules and regulations. Starbucks closely monitors the academic performance of his team, and the graduation rate of his players exceeds the university's rate for nonathletes. In addition, he is active in the community and volunteers his time to a number of projects.

Starbucks has told you he has heard rumors that the university may try to reassign him to other duties—namely, as facility manager. He strongly opposes this reassignment, even if the university continues to honor his current contract.

Starbucks' base salary is $100,000 per year. He receives a number of perquisites, including payment for radio and television shows, profits from his summer basketball camp, and income from a shoe contract with a major manufacturer. The value of the perquisites equals $150,000 per year, bringing Starbucks' total annual income to $250,000.

You have reviewed Starbucks' employment contract and have established that there is no reassignment clause nor any buyout provisions in it. Further, the language in the contract is rather nebulous, making it unclear exactly what WU is legally responsible for in the event of their breach of the contract.

1. *What arguments will you raise on behalf of Starbucks if WU wants to reassign him to an administrative position?*
2. *How will you respond if WU alleges that it can terminate Starbucks for cause?*
3. *If WU terminates Starbucks' contract without cause, what damages should your client recover? Respond to WU's contention that WU is not responsible for the perquisites that Starbucks received as part of his compensation. Use the Rodgers case to strengthen your argument.*

REVIEW QUESTIONS AND ISSUES

1. How can you apply a preventive mentality to your contractual dealings? Explain the worst-case scenario in drafting contracts.
2. Explain the use of form contracts. Why is it ill-advised to make changes to such a document without the assistance of legal counsel?
3. Explain the concepts of offer, acceptance, consideration, legality, and capacity.
4. Explain the Statute of Frauds. Give two examples of how it could pertain to transactions in sport settings.
5. What are the types of remedies available in breach-of-contract actions? What is the purpose of monetary damages? When is specific performance applicable? Can it be used to compel someone to perform an employment contract? Why or why not?
6. Explain the principle of mitigation.
7. Contrast the concept of actual authority with apparent authority. Give an example of when a third party might argue that apparent authority could bind an organization to a contract.
8. What are some major points to address in an employment contract between a coach and a university? Discuss the role of the termination clause in the event the university breaches and the concepts of perquisites and liquidated damages/buyout. Contrast liquidated damages with a penalty clause.
9. If a coach breaches an employment contract with a university, is the principle of liquidated damages/buyout legally applicable? Aside from the legal issues, why might an

athletic director hesitate to incorporate such a provision into an employment contract?

10. For what purpose might a university put a reassignment clause in a coach's contract?

11. What two methods, besides the buyout clause, might a university incorporate into an employment contract to induce a coach not to breach his or her employment contract? What are the limitations of the restrictive covenant?

12. What is a rollover clause? What are its disadvantages for a university?

13. Explain the guarantee provisions in a game contract. What related provisions should be incorporated to protect an institution's interests if it will be the recipient of the guarantee?

14. What are the important elements in any sales contract? If you were dealing with a hotel contract to serve team meals, what additional provisions should you be cognizant of?

15. What are the elements of promissory estoppel? How could it apply in an athletic grant-in-aid scenario?

16. From a lessor's viewpoint, what are some critical provisions to incorporate in a lease? Explain the concept of indemnification and its relationship to requiring a certificate of insurance and being named as an additional insured on lessee's policy.

17. Why structure a relationship with game officials and team physicians so that they are considered independent contractors?

SOLUTIONS TO CRITICAL THINKING EXERCISES

1. Apparent authority arises when a third party has no knowledge of the actual authority possessed by the business manager and the third party reasonably relies upon the business manager's ostensible authority to engage in a transaction. To avoid apparent authority, you can convey actual notice of authority possessed to your vendors through policies and procedures. You can also use countersignatures on your documents so that it is clear to the third party that your employee does not have the authority to bind your organization in a transaction in excess of a certain dollar amount.

2. To avoid the prospect of reliance by athletes upon coaches' promises of four- or five-year "full rides," you can train coaches to recruit by promising only what is contained in the grant-in-aid document, i.e., that a scholarship period is yearly. Renewals of scholarships are to be made on a yearly basis and at the discretion of the coach. This information should be accurately conveyed by coaches as they recruit for their teams.

REFERENCES

American Law Institute. (1981). *Restatement (second) of the law of contracts*. St. Paul, MN: American Law Institute.

Calamari, J. D., and Perillo, J. M. (1998). *The law of contracts*. 4th ed. St. Paul, MN: West Publishing Co.

Cooper v Peterson, 626 N.Y.S.2d 432 (Sup. Ct. 1995).

Cozzillo, M. J., and Levinstein, M. S. (1997). *Sports law: Cases and materials*. Durham, NC: Carolina Academic Press.

Friedman, M. (1997). *Friedman on leases*. 4th ed. New York: PLI.

Greenberg, M. J. (1992). Representation of college coaches on contract negotiations. *Marquette Sports Law Journal* 3:101–9.

Greenberg, M. J., and Gray, J. T. (1998). *Sports law practice*. 2d ed. Vol. 1. Charlottesville, VA: Lexis Law Publishing.

McInerney v Charter Golf, Inc., 680 N.E.2d 1374 (Dec. 1997).

Monson v State of Oregon, 901 p.2d 904 (Or. Ct. App. 1995). *Perspective* (June, 1999), 5.

Rodgers v Georgia Tech Athletic Association, 303 S.E.2d 467 (Ga. Ct. App. 1983).

Stoner, E., and Nogay, A. (1989). The model university coaching contract (MCC): A better starting point for your next negotiation. *Journal of College and University Law*, 16, 43–92.

Vanderbilt Univ. v DiNardo, 174 F.3d 751 (6th Cir. 1999).

Wiesner, D. A., and Glaskowsky, N. A. (1995). *Managing the legal factor: Business law text and cases*. Cincinnati, OH: South-Western College Publishing.

WEBSITES

Sports Lawyers Association
www.sportslaw.org/sla.html
Students interested in professional sport legal issues related to contracts and collective bargaining can get information pertaining to this association, which has student membership and publishes a very informative newsletter.

For the Record Online
www.marquette.edu/law/sports/frontline.html
This site, sponsored by the National Sports Law Institute at Marquette University Law School, has a number of articles focussing on current issues in sports law and stories supplementing its newsletter, *For the Record*.

CHAPTER 12

Constitutional and Statutory Law

Annie Clement

In this chapter, you will become familiar with the following terms:

First Amendment
Freedom of religion
Freedom of speech
Freedom of the press
Invasion of privacy
Searches and seizures
Fourth Amendment
Drug testing
Fourteenth Amendment
Procedural due process
Affirmative action

Evaluation
Equal-protection clause
Title IX
Disparate impact
Civil Rights Restoration Act
  (1987)
Civil Rights Act (1991)
Equity in Athletics Disclosure
  Act
Sexual harassment
Sherman Act (1890)

Antitrust
Clayton Act (1914)
Norris-LaGuardia Act (1932)
National Labor Relations Act
Collective bargaining
Interstate commerce
Reserve clause
Rozelle Rule

Overview

The United States Constitution is the primary law of the nation. In addition, each state has its own constitution or primary law. Federal and state statutes, executive orders, and city ordinances are laws enacted by legislative bodies to ensure efficient management at all levels of government. Statutes often contain descriptions of administrative and enforcement authority. Federal government powers are limited to the U.S. Constitution; the remaining powers are within the individual states' jurisdictions. State courts are bound by the U.S. Constitution and respective state constitutions. Constitutional and statutory laws may be litigated in state and federal civil courts; statutory laws may be enforced by agencies designed to carry out the particular laws.

The First, Fourth, and Fourteenth Amendments to and Article 1 of the U.S. Constitution play an important role in the interaction between sport management professionals and their clients. Historically, the First and the Fourth Amendments applied only to actions of federal agencies; today, as a result of the incorporation of the Fourteenth Amendment in a cause of action, state agencies (such as recreation commissions and schools) are covered.

This chapter discusses the freedoms of religion, speech, and press of the First Amendment and the search and seizure, drug testing, and privacy elements of the Fourth Amendment. Fourteenth Amendment due process in the context of employment, equal protection, and relevant statutes will be discussed. Article 1 of the Constitution provides the foundation for antitrust and labor law analysis.

FIRST AMENDMENT

The **First Amendment** states, "Congress shall make no law respecting an establishment of religion, or prohibiting the free exercise thereof; or abridging the freedom of speech, or of the press; or the right of the people peaceably to assemble, and to petition the Government for a redress of grievances" (U.S. Constitution, First Amendment). First Amendment rights are the freedoms of religion, speech (including symbolic protest), and press. In making a decision about the freedoms of religion, speech, and press, the courts balance the needs of the public against the rights of the individual.

Freedom of religion

Under the First Amendment's **freedom of religion clause,** the government may not enact laws that aid a particular church or religion. Also, the First Amendment guarantees the right of religious belief and the freedom to practice that belief. The amendment separates church and state, and protects people in their religious beliefs. The establishment clause of the First Amendment allows, for example, free bus transportation and textbooks to parochial schools and prohibits salary supplements to non-public school teachers and tuition reimbursement to lower-income families.

Two First Amendment areas of litigation important to sport managers are prayer at public sport events and the leasing of public facilities to religious groups.

Prayer in public sport events. In *Lee v Weisman* (1992), the U.S. Supreme Court found that conducting a religious exercise at a high school graduation was in violation of the First Amendment to the U.S. Constitution. The court held that "the Constitution forbids the state to exact religious conformity from a student as the price of attending her own high school graduation."

In *Chaudhuri v State of Tennessee, Tennessee State University, et al.* (1997) the Sixth Circuit of the United States Court of Appeals ruled that nonsectarian prayer did not violate the establishment clause of the United States Constitution. A Hindu professor challenged the use of invocations and benedictions at events such as graduation. The court distinguished the *Lee v Weisman* case from *Chaudhuri,* stating that the plaintiff in *Chaudhuri* was older and that he was not coerced to participate.

Doe v Duncanville Independent School District (1993) considered the prayer issue in relation to athletic events. Jane Doe, as a member of Duncanville's Reed Junior High School basketball team, was subjected to prayer (usually the Lord's Prayer) in the locker room after each game, during practice, at pep rallies, and at the year-end award ceremony. Although Doe refused to participate in the prayers, she did not file a complaint until she felt she could no longer continue to function normally in the prayer-intense environment. Her motion to the court was for a temporary restraining order and a preliminary injunction to stop prayer in her school. Doe's motion was granted; the defendant school appealed. The U.S. Court of Appeals for the Fifth Circuit agreed with the lower court and with Jane Doe. However, the court of appeals did have one exception: to maintain the *Mergens* decision, which allowed student-initiated prayer (*Board of Education of Westside Community Schools v Mergens,* 1990). Thus, student-initiated prayer was allowed in the Duncanville Independent School District, while administrator-, coach-, or teacher-initiated prayer was prohibited.

The 1998 decision of *Chandler v James* found an Alabama statute unconstitutional and held that student-led prayer at athletic events, or in schools, was a violation of the First Amendment.

Leasing of public property to religious organizations. *Lamb's Chapel* (1993), a U.S. Supreme Court decision involving leasing or other use of a public facility, is considered under religious freedom and freedom of speech. The State of New York authorized local school boards to use school property, not in use for school purposes, for a number of purposes; religious purposes were not included. The church, through its minister, made two formal requests to use a school facility for the showing of a religious film series on family values and child rearing. The church's request was denied. The district court granted Lamb's Chapel summary judgment, holding that the denial of the church's access to the school premises to exhibit the film violated the church's freedom of speech. Although both of these cases involved public school properties, similar decisions could be expected in public recreation environments.

Freedom of speech

Freedom of speech is the freedom to speak, to remain silent, to discuss with others, and to advocate and communicate ideas. Ideas can be conveyed, but language that is obscene, libelous, or slanderous is not protected. Verbal or expressive speech in public is not to be suppressed unless it interferes with the normal mainstream of society or causes harm to others. The courts will examine the following points to determine whether speech should be protected:

1. What: subject of speech
2. To whom speech is directed
3. Where: location of the speech
4. How: manner of delivery

Speech may be symbolic protest or merely speaking out. For example, the wearing of black armbands—first by high school students protesting the United States' involvement in the Vietnam War (*Tinker v Des Moines School District,* 1969), and the system for selecting a homecoming queen (*Boyd v Board of Directors of McGehee School District,* 1985) have served as models of symbolic protest.

In *Tinker,* junior and senior high school students in Des Moines, Iowa, violated school policy by wearing black armbands to protest the U.S. government's military involvement in Vietnam. They were suspended from school and told they could return when the armbands were removed. The U.S. District Court "upheld the constitutionality of the school authorities' action on the grounds that it was reasonable in order to prevent disturbance of school discipline." The U.S. Court of Appeals for the Eighth Circuit, in reversing and remanding the lower court's decision, stated that the Constitution did not permit state officials to deny a form of expression that "neither interrupted school activities nor sought to intrude in the school affairs or the lives of others."

African American football players refused to play the homecoming game after discovering what they perceived to be an illegal process for selecting the homecoming queen (*Boyd v McGehee School District,* 1985). They were suspended. The court found that the football players had grounds for their belief that the contest had been manipulated.

Numerous other sport groups, including Olympic athletes, have used actions to symbolize their feelings. In general, the courts have permitted such gestures and have denied them only when the actions were thought to be disruptive of the peace of the setting or to threaten the safety of members of society.

Dambrot v Central Michigan University (1993) was a First Amendment challenge to Central Michigan University's "discriminatory harassment policy" and the university's decision not to renew the basketball coach's yearly contract. The issue was the coach's use of the word *nigger* in a locker room pep talk. The coach, Mr. Dambrot, was white; most of the players were African American. Plaintiff coach claimed the word was used in a "positive and reinforcing" manner. When the use of the word became known outside the locker room, the coach asked the athletic director to interview members of the team. The athletic director found that the African American players were not offended.

A player who had left the team complained of the incident to the university's Affirmative Action Office, which found that Mr. Dambrot had violated the university's discriminatory harassment policy and suspended him for five days. The coach, in an effort to provide his side of the incident, gave an interview to the student newspaper, which led to a student demonstration. The coach's contract was not renewed, with the basis for nonrenewal the university's perception that the events and campus disruption would render him unsuccessful as a coach. One week later, Mr. Dambrot brought suit against Central Michigan University (CMU) for violation of his due-process rights, violation of the Elliot-Larson Civil Rights Act, and for defamation, a violation of his First Amendment right to free speech. A number of the basketball players joined him in the suit.

Dambrot was successful in his challenge of the constitutionality of CMU's discriminatory harassment policy, and the court permanently enjoined the university from further enforcement of the policy. CMU was successful in its termination of the coach, and both parties agreed to dismiss, without prejudice, the defamation count. CMU's discriminatory harassment policy was found to be vague and a suppression of speech described as both illegal and remarkable. No direct relationship was found on most of the issues for the team members who had joined their coach in the suit.

Plaintiff Dambrot relied on a theory that when CMU's policy was found to be unconstitutional under the First Amendment's suppression of speech, his sanction and termination would be a violation of his First Amendment rights. The court's response was that even though CMU's policy was found unconstitutional, Dambrot's statements had not been analyzed under the freedom-of-speech analysis used by the court in public-employee termination. The public employee "is required to show (1) that his speech was on a matter of public concern, (2) that if it was, then it was entitled to protection (after a balancing test is applied), and (3) that any First Amendment violation was a substantial factor in termination" (*Connick v Myers*, 1983). The court found Dambrot's statements not a matter of public concern and therefore not protected by the First Amendment.

Freedom of speech permits speech that does not interfere with the normal functioning of society or cause harm to others. This analysis takes on specificity when the person speaking is a public employee speaking out while on the job.

Coaches claiming slander among other legal complaints in employment discrimination are Stockard (*Stockard v Moss*, 1997), Campanelli (*Campanelli v Bockrath*, 1997) and Washington (*Washington v Smith*, 1996).

Bessie A. Stockard became head basketball coach at the District of Columbia University in 1978; in 1981 her contract was not renewed. Members of the basketball team approached the athletic director to determine why their coach had been fired. The athletic director told the players that Stockard has misappropriated funds. When Stockard learned of the accusation she filed suit. "The complaint sought compensatory and punitive damages, alleging breach of contract, libel and slander, tortuous interference with contract, intentional infliction of emotional distress and sex discrimination" (564). All but the slander and breach of contract claims were dismissed; $18,000 was awarded for breach of contract and $300,000 for slander.

The court of appeals reversed the decision, stating that Stockard should have used the local appeal process before making court claims.

Campanelli, like Dambrot, used unacceptable words in attempting to motivate athletes. The University of California, Berkeley coach's speech was described as "profane and abusive . . . speech to his players was 'different' because of the 'personal nature' of his criticism" (1995, 1476). He was fired under the at-will clause in his employment contract, for verbally and psychologically abusing the athletes. Campanelli filed two claims, one in federal and one in state court under a number of legal theories, including defamation. The claims were consolidated. The Superior Court found that the "defendant's statements to the press were opinion, not fact, and that they were substantially true" (1997, 3). The First Appellate District Court affirmed the Superior Court's decision.

Marian Washington, an experienced and prominent head coach of the University of Kansas women's basketball team, sued Joseph C. Smith, president of the Women's Basketball News Service, for comments he made about her coaching ability. (*Washington v Smith*, 1996) The statement was, "the Jayhawks are loaded with talent. . . . But Coach Marian Washington usually finds a way to screw things up. This season will be no different" (556). Washington filed suit for defamation. The district court granted Smith summary judgment; his statements were not actionable. The United States Court of Appeals, District of Columbia, affirmed the trial court's decision.

Freedom of the press

Freedom of the press is freedom to write and draw, which is similar to freedom of speech. Absolute freedom of thought and belief are guaranteed. In *Marcum v Dahl* (1981), female basketball players at the University of Oklahoma filed a complaint after being notified that their scholarships for the coming year would not be renewed. The incident started when plaintiffs commented to the press that if the current coach was hired for the following year they would not play. Plaintiffs contended that the refusal of the defendants to renew their scholarships was motivated by the plaintiffs' statements to the press, that the comments to the press were constitutionally protected by the First Amendment, and that the failure to renew the scholarships was in derogation of their First Amendment Rights. The court concluded "that the plaintiffs' First Amendment rights were not violated by the defendants' refusal to renew the plaintiffs' athletic scholarships."

Freedoms of speech and press depend upon the circumstances under which they are used; certain language is not protected. Courts use a test that considers the clear and present danger of the speech or press and balances the interests to be protected.

Invasion of privacy

Invasion of privacy, closely related to the Fourth Amendment's search and seizure clause, is often found in drug testing and the reporting of a suspicion of drug use. This right has been challenged among amateur and professional athletes. The state's interest with reference to drug testing is the health of athletes, particularly that of minors, and the establishment and maintenance of the natural competitive qualities of the performers. The athletes' interest is privacy. Details of invasion of privacy will be discussed under the Fourth Amendment.

CONCEPT CHECK

The First Amendment to the U.S. Constitution provides for freedom of religion, speech, and press. Freedom of religion guarantees all persons the right of belief and the freedom to practice their beliefs. The First Amendment separates church and state and protects people in their religious beliefs. Two areas of First Amendment concern to sport managers are prayer in public sport events and the leasing of public property by religious organizations.

FOURTH AMENDMENT

"The right of the people to be secure in their persons, houses, papers, and effects, against unreasonable **searches and seizures,** shall not be violated, and no warrants shall issue, but upon probable cause, supported by oath or affirmation, and particularly describing the place to be searched, and the persons or things to be seized" (U.S. Constitution, **Fourth Amendment**). The system for analyzing facts under the Fourth Amendment is the same as that used in a First Amendment analysis: balancing the needs of the state against the needs of the individual.

Searches of lockers (*In the Interest of Isiah B.*, 1993) and testing for drugs at the high school (*Acton v Vernonia School District*, 1995, and *Todd v Rush County Schools*, 1998), college (*University of Colorado v Derdeyn*, 1993; *Hill v National Collegiate Athletic Association*, 1994) and professional (*Reynolds v The Athletic Congress of the U.S.A*, 1994, 1992) levels have been the primary subjects of litigation in sport management.

School locker searches

A Wisconsin case (*In the Interest of Isiah B.*, 1993), in which a random search of students' lockers was conducted following the school's identification of guns on school property, was found to be a violation of the students' Fourth Amendment rights. The state argued that each student had received a written policy establishing the school's right to ownership and control of the lockers.

This decision and the drug-testing decisions that follow place a responsibility on professionals to make and enforce policies and penalties and to make these policies and penalties known to students and their parents, when appropriate, and to participants, when necessary. Proof, by signature, of participants' knowledge of rules and penalties, is also recommended.

Drug testing

Leaders in athletics believe that **drug testing** is necessary for the safety and health of the athletes and to maintain fair competition.

"Analysis of drug testing programs in industry shows that when the test was a part of the pre-employment examination of all employees, the courts tended to uphold the test; but when the test was given to persons employed for many years, it was not upheld. In order for the test to be upheld among veteran employees, there has to be reason to believe that the employee is on drugs" (Clement, 1998).

The following examples are taken from intercollegiate, Olympic, and secondary athletics. Challenges are to league rules, university policies, and standards employed in the drug-testing industry. *University of Colorado v Derdeyn* (1991, 1993, 1994) involved the constitutionality of the drug-testing program for intercollegiate athletics at the University of Colorado-Boulder. The university's drug-testing policy was instituted to prepare athletes for the mandatory NCAA drug-testing policies to which the university had agreed. The tests "ranged from random testing of athletes' urine samples obtained under direct visual observation to a system that depended on "reasonable suspicion" based, in part, on random rapid-eye-movement examinations.

A bench trial determined that the program violated the students' Fourth Amendment rights and their rights under the Colorado Constitution. Also, the consent given by the students for the conduct of the tests was found to be coerced. This decision was affirmed by the Colorado Supreme Court. The court stressed that when student consent was not voluntary, it could not be used to validate an unconstitutional search. The University of Colorado's petition to the U.S. Supreme Court for a writ of certiorari was denied May 4, 1994, and their petition to the same court for rehearing was denied June 20, 1994.

In January 1994, the Supreme Court of California ruled in *Hill v National Collegiate Athletic Association* (*NCAA*) that the NCAA drug-testing program did not violate the plaintiff's California constitutional right to privacy. Individual student privacy was balanced against the NCAA's need to maintain an equitable form of competition and a safe playing environment. In contrast to the presentation by Colorado in the previous case, the NCAA presented a history of problems in athletics that suggested a need for supervision of drug use among participants.

Hill v NCAA was the result of a long struggle in which Hill and the parties to the case, prior to Hill, were successful in the trial court and the court of appeals. The trial and appeals courts examined the invasion-of-privacy issue with the NCAA, under an analysis used with federal agencies that required the NCAA to prove a compelling state interest and the absence of alternative methods for accomplishing its goal.

In the Supreme Court of California (1994), the NCAA was treated as a private actor and asked to adhere to a far lower standard of privacy that noted that private actors did not have the power of the government but had a right of association. The court stated that persons choosing to be elite athletes agree to a whole series of intrusions, including the reporting of medical information to trainers and coaches, dressing in same-sex locker rooms, and frequent physical examinations. Further, the court noted that the "NCAA's rules contain elements designed to accomplish the purpose, including (1) advance notice to athletes of testing procedures and written consent to testing,

(2) random selection of athletes actually engaged in competition, (3) monitored collection of a sample of a selected athlete's urine in order to avoid substitution or contamination, and (4) chain of custody, limited disclosure, and other procedures designed to safeguard the confidentiality of the testing process and its outcome."

Acton v Vernonia (1995, 1994 and 1992) and *Vernonia School District 47J v Acton* (1995) resulted in a United States Supreme Court decision that upheld the right of public schools to randomly test athletes for drugs. A policy was created for the random testing of athletes for drugs in response to the community's sense that drug use was expanding. Wayne Acton's parents refused to consent to the drug testing policy and brought a cause of action against the school system for violation of their son's Fourth and Fourteenth Amendment and Oregon Constitution rights.

The district court found for the school; the Ninth Circuit Court of Appeals reversed. The Supreme Court accepted the case on certiorari. The Supreme Court reversed the Ninth Circuit and found for the school, confirming the district court's decision. The reasoning of the Court was the same as the reasoning found in *Hill*.

Todd v Rush County Schools (1998) found the Seventh Circuit Court of Appeals upholding the school policy that required all students engaging in extracurricular activities to submit to random drug testing. At the same time the Supreme Court of Colorado ruled that a random drug test of members of a school marching band was unconstitutional. (*Trinidad School District No. 1 v Lopez*, 1998.)

The Court noted that, "although band members wear uniforms, they do not undergo the type of public undressing and communal showers required of student athletes. . . . The band director also testified that marching band members do not shower together after a performance" (1107). A comparison of these cases suggests that a person's previous history of privacy has become important to drug testing decisions.

Reynolds v International Amateur Athletic Federation (*IAAF*) (1991) was a case that challenged the management and accuracy of drug tests. Reynolds, a world-class runner, was randomly tested in August 1990 by the IAAF following a meet in Monte Carlo and found to have the anabolic steroid nandrolone in his system. He was suspended from competition for two years and was ineligible for the 1992 Olympics. Reynolds appealed his suspension, but he was unable to obtain the information he needed to prepare for the internal hearing scheduled for January 1991. As a result of his inability to prepare for the hearing, he filed a lawsuit enjoining The Athletic Congress (TAC) and the IAAF from conducting the hearing. Reynolds based his case on evidence that his positive test was an error and that a similar test, taken seven days later, showed no trace of the banned substance.

In March 1991, the court held that Reynolds failed to exhaust his administrative remedies and stayed the action. In June 1991, the Sixth Circuit Court of Appeals vacated the judgment and ordered the case dismissed. The decision resulted from Reynolds' refusal to use TAC's administrative procedures.

Reynolds then used the recommended administrative procedures by participating in an arbitration session governed by the Amateur Sports Act and the U.S. Olympic Committee's constitution. The arbitration decision exonerated Reynolds, finding strong evidence that the urine sample tested did not belong to Reynolds. IAAF refused to accept the arbitrator's decision or to lift Reynolds's two-year suspension because the arbitration had not been conducted under IAAF or international rules. Reynolds appealed the IAAF's refusal to accept the arbitrator's decision to TAC, a procedure required by IAAF rules. TAC made the same positive decision that the arbitrator had made, finding strong evidence that Reynolds's drug test results were in error. Again, IAAF refused to accept the decision and decided to conduct its own arbitration in London in May 1992. IAAF found the drug test to be valid and upheld the two-year suspension.

Reynolds then filed an action against IAAF in the Southern District of Ohio alleging breach of contract, breach of contractual due process, defamation, and tortious interference with business relations. He requested a temporary restraining order that would allow him to compete in the Olympics and money damages. IAAF refused to appear in the case, stating that the district court did not have jurisdiction over the IAAF. The district court issued a temporary restraining order that prevented the IAAF from interfering with Reynolds as he prepared to try out for the 1992 U.S. Olympic team.

In June 1992, the district court, following a hearing in which TAC now opposed Reynolds, issued a preliminary injunction permitting Reynolds to participate in the Olympic trials. Its findings were that the court had personal jurisdiction over the IAAF and that Reynolds would be likely to succeed in a court of law on the merits of his claim. Note that TAC, which had supported Reynolds in the earlier hearings, now opposed him.

On the afternoon of the above decision, TAC filed a motion asking for a "stay" of the court's decision. The stay was granted, and it stopped Reynolds from entering the Olympic trials. The next morning, Reynolds filed an emergency motion with the U.S. Supreme Court, Justice Stevens, asking that the district court "stay" be vacated (removed). Reynolds' request was granted; he could compete in the 1992 Olympic trials.

IAAF announced that athletes who competed with Reynolds at the U.S. Olympic trials would be barred from competing in the Barcelona Olympics. TAC filed an application to the Supreme Court to bar Reynolds from competing, but the court refused to hear the request. Reynolds was allowed to compete in the trials and made the team as an alternate for the 400-meter relay. IAAF refused to let Reynolds compete in the 1992 Olympics, and TAC removed him from the team roster.

In September 1992, Reynolds filed a supplemental complaint to the district court. IAAF did not respond; TAC did not appear in the proceedings. The district court awarded Reynolds $27,356,008, including treble punitive damages. In February 1993, Reynolds began garnishment proceedings against four corporations with connections to the IAAF to obtain his damage award and brought suit against the federation. This time, the Sixth Circuit Court of Appeals (Reynolds, 1994) decided that it did not have jurisdiction (authority) over the IAAF, an international agency. As a result of the court of appeals' decision, the judgment of the district court (for Reynolds, with money damage) was reversed and remanded to the district court, where, according to the ruling, the district court would probably also dismiss the case for lack of personal jurisdiction over IAAF.

Reynolds not only identifies problems associated with drug testing but the complexity of national and international court rules when a decision to suspend an athlete is challenged.

CONCEPT CHECK

The Fourth Amendment provides a right for persons to be secure against unreasonable searches. Locker searches and drug testing are Fourth Amendment areas of interest to sport managers. Lockers belong to the agency that owns the lockers and can be searched without probable cause. Persons using lockers should be made aware of their rights.

Drug testing is important to athletics to ensure the safety and health of athletes and to maintain equitable competition. Results of court decisions show that random drug testing has been prohibited in universities when permission for the tests was found to be coerced but accepted when the NCAA took the leadership in obtaining permission.

FOURTEENTH AMENDMENT

The **Fourteenth Amendment** states, in part, "No State shall make or enforce any law which shall abridge the privileges or immunities of citizens of the United States; nor shall any State deprive any person of life, liberty, or property, without due process of law; nor deny to any person within its jurisdiction the equal protection of the laws" (U.S. Constitution, Fourteenth Amendment). All state actions are covered under the Fourteenth Amendment to the Constitution; private actions are not covered. Private actions can become covered as a result of explicit statements in the many statutes used in conjunction with the U.S. Constitution. Analysis under these laws is the balancing of the interests of the state against the rights of the individual. Procedural due process and equal protection are the areas of greatest significance to the professional sport manager.

Procedural due process

Procedural due process is a system that enables members of society to be assured of fair treatment. It provides an opportunity for an individual to be heard, to defend personal actions, and to be assured of fair treatment before a right or privilege is taken away. Due process systems are used so often that professionals will need to tailor a system to meet their needs from time to time. Because many factors enter into the formulation of a due process system, consultants in law and the area to be covered should participate in the design of the system. The following are basic concepts to consider in creating a system:

1. Knowledge of charge and complaint
2. A right to a hearing in which one may choose to use an attorney or other counsel
3. Opportunity to respond to charges with adequate time to prepare the response
4. Opportunity to present witnesses and to question witnesses presented by others

Employers and administrators have a number of well-defined responsibilities to their employees. Procedural due process becomes a constitutional issue in the hiring process and the evaluation system.

Equitable hiring process. Hiring systems differ among businesses. For years, the most popular employer-employee relationship was known as "at will." The employer had a task to be done, sought out a person believed capable of carrying out the task, and offered the job and a wage, and both mutually agreed to the arrangement with a handshake. When the employer no longer wanted or needed the employee, the employee was asked to leave. If the employee no longer enjoyed the work environment or had a better offer, he/she was free to leave. "Two weeks' notice" has grown to be a popular termination period in this type of work relationship. Another characteristic of at-will employment is that the reason for termination is seldom public knowledge and often is unclear to one of the parties involved in the agreement. Many people continue to be employed in this manner today. In addition, most part-time employment is at will.

Labor unions have made drastic changes in the at-will employment pattern in the past fifty to seventy-five years. Labor unions are private associations formed to represent groups of workers with common needs and a common desire to obtain the best wages possible for the entire group. They also negotiate contracts with individual businesses.

Employment contracts are another form of employer-employee work relationship. They are written agreements that identify tasks to be accomplished, the period of employment, and salary. Such contracts are specific agreements between one employee and a particular business.

Contract, labor union, and at-will relationships are the employer-employee relationships most often used in business and industry in the United States.

Today's employment environment is subject to federal laws created in an effort to remedy discrimination based on race, color, sex, age, religion, national origin, and handicaps. The Equal Pay Act (1963) and a number of Executive Orders of the 1950s and 1960s paved the way for discrimination legislation in employment. Title VII of the Civil Rights Act (1964), the Age Discrimination in Employment Act (1967), the Rehabilitation Act (1973), and the Americans with Disabilities Act (1990) have fashioned the framework for most civil rights legislation. Title VII of the Civil Rights Act (1964) prohibits discrimination in the work environment due to race, color, sex, religion, or national origin. Affirmative action and equal-opportunity employment are the results of Title VII. The Age Discrimination in Employment Act established a protected group for persons forty to sixty-five years old; the rehabilitative acts accomplished the same goal for the handicapped. Although the acts mentioned here refer to government contractors only, the Supreme Court has extended the requirements concerning race discrimination to private employers.

The Equal Employment Opportunity Commission (EEOC) is the federal government agency responsible for administering most of the discrimination legislation and regulations. Under equal opportunity, when a job vacancy occurs, provision is made for all qualified individuals to be made aware of the existence of the vacancy, to submit papers for review, and to obtain the position if best qualified.

Affirmative action is a special program designed to remedy past discriminatory practices in hiring minority groups. It is used when discrimination has been found. The program provides an opportunity for the protected group to receive special attention in employment until such time as its number is proportional to the percentage of employees in the nonprotected group. For example, if 60 percent of the population available for a certain job is African American, an affirmative-action program will continue until a particular work force has a 60 percent African American membership. Affirmative-action programs are influenced by the availability of skill and talent and a past record of discrimination.

Employers may volunteer to an affirmative-action program or be required by the court or an administrative agency to establish one in response to a finding of discrimination.

Employment systems are designed to rapidly locate the best talent pool available for a particular job. Skilled talent is a high priority for any business, and most employers are equally interested in being equitable in their hiring practices. The decisions in *Griggs v Duke Power Company* (1971), *Equal Employment Opportunity Commission v Atlas Paper Box Company* (1989), and *Ward Cove Packing Company v Atonio* (1989) provide guidance to administrators in designing and implementing systems for hiring and evaluation.

Evaluation

Employees must receive a fair and equitable **evaluation** based on the elements in the job description and the day-to-day tasks of the job. *Griggs v Duke Power Company* (1971) is a court decision that has played a significant role in establishing the need for job requirements that are directly related to job performance for both hiring and evaluation. If certain specifications—such as a college degree or a specific in-service training—are given a high priority in evaluation, then evidence must exist to show that the requirement is essential to successful job performance.

The results of evaluations are to be discussed with and be made available to employees. Where serious deficits in work habits are identified, a due process system must exist to permit employees to present their side of the situation. Opportunity must also exist for rehabilitation of deficits and for the monitoring of the success or failure of the rehabilitation program.

Policies on termination must be established—if possible, in writing. A system of warnings preceding termination, including a rehabilitation program, should be in place. These policies must be related to job responsibilities and executed in such a way that the rights of the employee are paramount.

Evaluation of personnel should be directly related to the position description and the day-to-day responsibilities of the job. Even though a specific system of evaluation is employed by an industry, it is expected to evaluate performance in line with the elements identified in *Griggs v Duke Power Company* (1971), *Brunet v City of Columbus* (1986), *Ward Cove*

Packing Co. v Atonio (1989), and the procedural due process system of the Fourteenth Amendment to the U.S. Constitution. Under *Griggs, Brunet,* and *Ward Cove,* procedural due process is the basis for employee evaluation and initial employment in state and federal agencies. Only those skills and knowledge directly related to the job and the day-to-day tasks of the work environment may be included. (Private agencies may or may not adhere to this system.)

A fair evaluation system is based on the description of and tasks demanded by a job. It should include the opportunity for the employee and employer to assess the execution of those tasks. When disagreement about the successful execution of the tasks occurs, a process must be available to resolve the dispute.

A procedural due process system should be available for use at any time. Its availability is essential when an employee receives a negative evaluation or is to be suspended or terminated. The procedural due process system should be included in the employee handbook or in related documents. Procedural due process is an appeal process that contains but is not limited to the following steps:

1. Written notice of all charges against the employee, including dates, times, and details of the specific charges that, if proven, would justify a penalty.
2. Establishment of a time and date for a hearing. Adequate time should be provided to enable the employee to prepare for the hearing.
3. Representation, including legal representation, may or may not be permitted in the hearing. This decision is made at the time of the establishment of guidelines, not shortly before a specific hearing. Also, the decision to use legal counsel and the technique of cross examination is made at the time the system is created.
4. The hearing provides the opportunity for all sides to present their case. All versions of the problem are presented.
5. An impartial panel shall hear the presentation. The status and authority of the panel and its leader must be known to all parties.
6. Effort should be made, if possible, to negotiate a viable settlement.
7. A decision is made. The decision should be accompanied by a written report of the rationale for the decision.
8. The proceedings should be recorded and made available to the employee.
9. In most employment environments, it is assumed that the next level of appeal will be to a court of law. When the problem concerns discrimination, the appeal may be to an administrative agency.

Tarkanian v NCAA (1987), *NCAA v Tarkanian* (1988, 1993), and *University of Nevada v Tarkanian* (1994) involved a number of legal theories, including due process. The NCAA began investigating the University of Nevada-Las Vegas (UNLV) shortly after Jerry Tarkanian became head basketball coach in 1973. In 1976, after a 2½-year investigation, the NCAA Committee on Infractions confronted UNLV with a report of seventy-two violations that they alleged occurred between 1970 and 1976. Six additional violations were added at a later date. The Nevada State Attorney General's Office investigated the allegations by interviewing the persons accused. UNLV submitted responses—including a large number of affidavits, sworn statements, and documentary evidence—to support the denial of specific rule violations.

The NCAA held a hearing and found thirty-eight violations of NCAA rules, naming Tarkanian in ten of them. Further, they "directed UNLV to show cause why additional penalties should not be imposed against it if it did not suspend Tarkanian from involvement with the university's intercollegiate Athletic Program for two years" (*Tarkanian v NCAA,* 1987).

In September 1977, UNLV, after conducting a hearing on the matter, suspended Tarkanian. Tarkanian brought suit against UNLV and obtained an injunction, which is a court order that directs a party to stop doing or to do some specific act. In this case, the court directed UNLV to stop the suspension of Tarkanian, or to let him return to his coaching position. The court then reversed the injunction for Tarkanian's failure to be willing to include the NCAA in the law suit (*University of Nevada v Tarkanian,* 1979). In essence, the court said that Tarkanian had to sue the NCAA in addition to UNLV.

In July 1979, Tarkanian sued again, this time naming both UNLV and NCAA, and received another injunction stopping his suspension. Tarkanian argued that he was without a formal procedural due process, but NCAA rulings do not include procedural due process for persons accused of violations.

In August 1987, the Supreme Court of Nevada held that the NCAA, as an actor in a state agency, was required to use a procedural due process and that Tarkanian had a right to due process. The NCAA petitioned the U.S. Supreme Court (*NCAA v Tarkanian*, 1988). It reversed the Nevada court's decision, stating that NCAA actions were not state actions and therefore the NCAA did not have to provide Tarkanian with an opportunity for procedural due process. This decision held (contrary to an earlier decision regarding television contracts) that the NCAA was a private organization that UNLV had the freedom to join or not join. The U.S. Supreme Court remanded the case back to the Nevada Supreme Court, stating that UNLV was in charge of disciplining faculty members and that UNLV, as a state agency, was required to adhere to procedural due process.

Tarkanian then moved for an order imposing costs, including attorney fees, against UNLV. His motion was granted in June 1992, and UNLV appealed. Tarkanian was awarded attorney fees. He was not able to obtain a financial settlement from the NCAA, but he did receive a settlement from UNLV.

The results of the Tarkanian Supreme Court decision place the responsibility for evaluating, reprimanding, and terminating state employees in the hands of the state agency and prohibit state agencies from carrying out third-party orders. This case prohibited UNLV from carrying out the NCAA's request to suspend Jerry Tarkanian without a procedural due process opportunity.

Concept Check ✓

Successful employee-employer relationships are created in the employment process. To affect positive relationships, attention must be paid to the preparation of a comprehensive job description, obtaining qualified candidates, and careful screening, interviewing, and selection of candidates.

These successful relationships are maintained when the employer provides an equitable evaluation system. Should an employee not be making satisfactory progress on the job, a carefully constructed procedural due process system should be used, first to counsel the employee toward success and then, if that is not possible, to provide the employee with full legal rights in the termination process.

EQUAL PROTECTION

The Fourteenth Amendment's **equal-protection clause** states, "No State shall make or enforce any law which shall . . . deny to any person within its jurisdiction the equal protection of the laws." An equal-protection challenge must show that groups of people are being treated differently, without justification, than is the total population. A regulation that arbitrarily or unreasonably subjects an identified group of people to a regulation violates the *equal-protection* clause.

An equal-protection challenge in scholastic or collegiate sport might be a complaint by a group of people (women) that they are being treated different from others (men) in athletics and that no justification exists to warrant the difference in treatment. One woman or a group of women (class action) might retain an attorney and bring a legal action against a public school or a college for sex discrimination under the Fourteenth Amendment to the U.S. Constitution.

The first use of the Fourteenth Amendment in sport discrimination suits is believed to be Jerry Hunter's 1956 defense to a charge of the crime of participating in a wrestling competition (*State v Hunter*, 1956). The court denied her constitutional claim, stating "that there should be at least one island on the sea of life reserved for men that would be impregnable to the assault of women."

Among the cases that prompted the creation of Title IX of the Educational Amendments of 1972 and influenced their operating guidelines were *Brenden v Independent School District* (1973), *Hollander v Connecticut Interscholastic Athletic Association, Inc.* (1971), *Reed v Nebraska Athletic Association* (1972), *Haas v South Bend Community School Corporation* (1972), *Bucha v Illinois High School Association* (1972), and *Rittacco v Norwin School District* (1973).

Brenden, Hollander, Reed, and *Haas* were complaints in which high school women requested the opportunity to participate on men's teams when no team was available to women. In most cases, the high school league had established the rule; the school district was merely enforcing the rule. Hollander's challenge to run on the cross-country team was denied. Reed's request to play on the golf team was granted, as was Brenden's request to play tennis. Haas was granted an opportunity to play on all men's teams in which no team existed for women. Note should be made that the requests were granted in Nebraska, Minnesota, and Indiana and denied in Connecticut.

Two class action suits, denied by the courts, were *Bucha* (1972) and *Rittacco* (1973). Bucha challenged the events selected for women swimmers. At that time, females were not permitted to perform in long-distance events. Rittacco challenged a Pennsylvania law that prohibited mixed teams and competition. This was one time in which the courts ruled for separate-but-equal opportunities; separate-but-equal opportunities were always denied in litigation involving race.

Title IX of the Education Amendments (1972)

Title IX states that "No person in the United States shall, on the basis of sex, be excluded from participation in, be denied the benefit of, or be subject to discrimination under any education program or activity receiving Federal financial assistance" (Title IX of the Education Amendments of 1972). Title IX, a federal statute, extended the principles articulated under the Fourteenth Amendment to all schools, public and private, that rely upon federal and state funds. Title IX is enforced by the Department of Education, which can withhold federal funds for violation of the statute. *Cannon v University of Chicago* (1979) extended Title IX to private or individual causes of action; *North Haven v Bell* (1982) extended the law to employment.

Title IX was envisioned by its creators as a way of convincing young women to participate in mathematics and science programs and to aspire to careers similar to those selected by men. The originators of Title IX did not view it primarily as a means of creating equity in athletics. Shortly after Title IX was implemented, athletics, a visible component of most school programs, became a public focus.

Many of the complaints in the early days of Title IX were resolved within the school districts, by other agencies, or by the Office of Civil Rights. Among the few complaints that went to court were *Yellow Springs Exempted Village School District v Ohio High School Athletic Association* (1981), *Gomes v Rhode Island Interscholastic League* (1979), and *Petrie v Illinois High School Association* (1979).

In *Yellow Springs*, a school district, not a student, brought action against the state high school league that the rule on contact sports was unconstitutional and in violation of Title IX. Middle-school girls had tried out and made the men's basketball team. The school district was forced by the Ohio High School Athletic Association to eliminate the qualified girls or withdraw from the league. The U.S. District Court, Southern District of Ohio, ruled for the female student athletes; the court of appeals reversed. The court was asked to rule on Title IX in general but refused to do so.

In an effort to divert attention from athletics, three cases—two in athletics, *Othen v Ann Arbor School District* (1981, 1982) and *Bennett v West Texas State University* (1986), and one general university case, *Grove City v Bell* (1984)—successfully petitioned the courts to make Title IX "program specific." *Grove City* is the one that has been favored by the popular press. *Program-specific* meant that only those programs receiving direct federal funding were subject to Title IX. Sports, seldom financed from federal dollars, were freed from the Title IX jurisdiction. The *Othen, Bennett,* and *Grove City* rulings brought the Title IX investigative system of the Office of Education to a halt. Title IX was no longer important to athletics.

It should be noted that the Fourteenth Amendment to the U.S. Constitution and various state civil rights laws continue to be used effectively in the quest for equal opportunity for women in sport. The results of decisions using the U.S. Constitution and state laws has led to the new civil rights legislation.

Equity for women in athletics has been influenced by (1) the Fourteenth Amendment equal-protection clause, particularly disparate-impact theory referred to as "equity by enrollment," (2) Title IX, (3) decisions in *Haffer* (1987), *Ridgeway* (1988), *Blair* (1989), *Franklin* (1992), and *Roberts* (1993), and (4) the Civil Rights Acts (1988, 1991). These major elements in the quest for gender equity are presented, in chronological order, in the following pages.

DISPARATE IMPACT

The legal theory that has had the greatest impact on today's cases is **disparate impact,** a theory that evolved in employment discrimination litigation and that involves practices that appear to be neutral in their treatment of different groups but fall more harshly on one group than another (*Teamsters v United States,* 1977). *Hazelwood* (1977), provided a method of analysis for use in identifying patterns and practices of discrimination under disparate impact that includes history, statistics, procedures, and

TABLE 12-1   *Equity by enrollment*

	Enrollment	Participation (%)	Berths	Scholarships
Male	14,000	47	282	141
Female	16,000	53	318	159
Totals	30,000	100	600	300

specific instances. Disparate-impact theory in sport is "participation by enrollment."

To achieve equity in athletics under the theory of disparate impact, an institution of higher education or a secondary school must show that the percentage of females and males given the opportunity to play in sport is the same as the percentage of females and males attending the institution. An institution with a student body of 30,000—16,000 females and 14,000 males—with 600 berths in competitive athletics, 300 under scholarship, is summarized in table 12-1.

Under the disparate-impact theory, the quality of all opportunities must be equal. Budgets do not have to be equal, but resources must enable the field hockey team, for example, to reach the same level of competence as the opportunities provided for the football team. Assistant coaches, trainers, and others must be adequately prepared to enable males and females to achieve an equal level of recognition in their sports.

The equal-protection clause of the Fourteenth Amendment, Title IX of the Education Amendments (1972), and various state equal-rights statutes provide protection against and avenues of redress for discrimination, and they have been used most often in athletics. Generally, female high school athletes have employed the Fourteenth Amendment to gain entry to sports; college athletes have used Title IX for the same purpose. When available, both collegiate and scholastic female athletes have used state equal-rights statutes. (See Heckman [1992]; [1997] and Clement [1998] and Vargyas [1994] for detailed discussions of these cases.)

LEADING CASES

Ridgeway (1988), *Haffer* (1987), and *Blair* (1989) are cases that have charted the course in discrimination and that will assist the professional in analyzing programs for equity.

Ridgeway v Montana High School Association (1988), the most comprehensive decision in athletics at the secondary level, was a class action suit brought on behalf of all Montana high school girls against the High School Athletic Association alleging violation of Title IX, the Fourteenth Amendment to the U.S. Constitution, and the Montana Constitution. The plaintiffs claimed discrimination existed in the number of sports, the seasons of play, the length of seasons, practice and game schedules, and access to facilities, equipment, coaching, trainers, transportation, the school band, uniforms, publicity, and general support. The parties accepted an agreement that provided for equal opportunity and placed a court-appointed facilitator in charge.

Haffer v Temple University (1987) concerned Temple University women currently participating in athletics and those who had been deterred from participating because of sex discrimination. Their claims focused on three basic areas: the extent to which Temple University afforded women students fewer "opportunities to compete" in intercollegiate athletics, the alleged disparity in resources allocated to the men's and women's intercollegiate athletic programs, and the alleged disparity in the allocation of financial aid to male and female students. The complaint alleged discrimination in opportunities to compete, expenditures, recruiting, coaching, travel and per diem allowances, uniforms, equipment, supplies, training facilities and services, housing and dining facilities, academic tutoring, and publicity. These actions were in violation of the Fourteenth Amendment and the Pennsylvania Equal Rights Amendment. The court ruled for the plaintiff in all areas except meals, tutoring, facilities, and scheduling.

Blair v Washington State University (1989) was similar to the foregoing decisions, except that the trial court chose to exclude football in the equity calculation. The plaintiff appealed the football decision, and the Washington Supreme Court reversed the decision, requiring that football be included in all calculations for finance and participation. Although this decision is precedent only for the State of Washington, it serves as an example in other states.

Civil Rights Restoration Act (1987)

The **Civil Rights Restoration Act (1987)** restored Title IX to its original strength and removed the program-specific status. Title IX was once again applied to an entire institution and to all of the institution's programs.

Civil Rights Act (1991)

The **Civil Rights Act (1991)** strengthened disparate-impact theory by placing the burden of proof on those who practice discrimination, not on those who suffer discrimination. For example, when discrimination is alleged in a university athletic department, the athletic department and the university have the burden of proof: They must show evidence of equitable participation in intercollegiate athletics and in intramural and club sports and must demonstrate that no discrimination occurred or currently exists.

Further, the 1991 Civil Rights Act provided the victims of intentional discrimination with the right to recover damages, including compensatory and punitive damages. Punitive damages are based on reckless indifference. Incidentally, the U.S. Senate, in its deliberations, suggested that this legislation would be effective in encouraging voluntary settlements.

Although most schools and colleges openly admit inequities in their athletic programs, many claim that they do not intend to discriminate and that the courts will find it extremely difficult to prove they are intentionally discriminating. Given the fact that in January 1992 the U.S. Office of Education circulated a memo to college and university presidents warning them to be careful of sex discrimination laws when they make decisions about eliminating sport teams, it does not seem that it will be difficult to prove that a college president who ignores the memo has intentionally discriminated (Lederman, 1992).

Franklin v Gwinnett County Public Schools

Franklin, a sexual-harassment complaint, enables victims of discrimination to be compensated under Title IX. In February 1992, the U.S. Supreme Court granted money damages under Title IX (*Franklin v Gwinnett County Public Schools,* 1992). Judges White, Blackmun, Stevens, O'Connor, Kennedy, and Souter "held that a money damage remedy is available for an action brought to enforce Title IX." Prior to this case, civil rights complaints in athletics have requested that the number of sports or the opportunities for participation in sports be added and schools

be prohibited from dropping women's sports. Now plaintiffs may request monetary compensation for lost opportunities.

Equity in Athletics Disclosure Act

Within the 1994 reauthorization of the Elementary and Secondary Education Act is a provision requiring schools to publish male/female enrollment and athletic participation ratios. Schools are to list varsity team membership; operating and recruiting expenses; number, gender, and salary of coaches; student aid; and revenue generated by sports programs.

Fair Play Act

This legislation, introduced in 1997 and effective in 1998, requires that the information obtained in the **Equity in Athletics Disclosure Act** be published. It is to be available to the student consumer who wishes to make an informed decision in selecting a school. Currently it is published on the Internet. The impact on litigation that will result from the publishing of the information is unclear.

1990s cases

Among the institutions of higher education filing equity complaints in 1992 and 1993 were the University of New Mexico, Bowdoin College, Rutgers University, Auburn University, College of William and Mary, Indiana University of Pennsylvania, the University of Texas, five institutions in California, Colorado State University, Brown University, and Colgate University.

Since 1993, cases have been filed and in most situations settled in *Favia* (1993 [1], 1993 [2]), *Boucher* (1996), *Pederson* (1996), *Beasley* (1998, 1997), *Horner* (1994), and *Adams* (1996). All but *Horner* and *Adams* are at the collegiate level.

Many of the higher-education cases occur in response to budget cuts that affect both men's and women's sports. The courts are ruling that women's sports cannot be cut until equity by enrollment, or proportionality, is achieved.

Roberts v Colorado State Board of Agriculture (1993 [1], 1999 [2], 1993 [3]) saw current students and former members of the women's varsity fast-pitch softball team bring suit challenging the elimination of Colorado State University's softball and baseball teams in June 1992 in response to budget cuts. The district court and the U.S. Court of Appeals, Tenth Circuit, have required the university to hire a coach and put softball back into its program.

In *Cohen v Brown University* (1997, 1996, 1995, 1993, 1992), women gymnastics and volleyball team members brought a class action suit against Brown University, a private college, following the demotion of their teams from varsity to club status. The U.S. District Court for the District of Rhode Island issued a preliminary injunction restoring the teams to varsity status (1992). The U.S. Court of Appeals, First Circuit, affirmed. The district court, after a lengthy trial, found Brown University to be in violation of Title IX and ordered the institution to submit a plan of compliance in 120 days (1995). Brown University failed to meet the requirement. Brown University appealed. The United States Court of Appeals, on November 21, 1996, upheld the district court's ruling that Brown University had violated Title IX; Brown University's petition for writ of certiorari to the United States Supreme Court was denied (*Brown University, et al. v Cohen, et al.*, 1997).

Cook v Colgate University (1992, 1993) and *Bryant et al. v Colgate* (1996, 1997, 1998) saw former members of the women's ice hockey team bring suit to elevate their sport from club to varsity status. Colgate University was ordered by the district court and the court of appeals to make ice hockey a varsity sport, and the university appealed.

Favia (1993) was a class action suit by female athletes requesting that the field hockey and gymnastics teams at Indiana University of Pennsylvania be reinstated. Plaintiffs won; defendants asked that gymnastics be replaced with soccer. The district court said no; the court of appeals reversed and let soccer replace gymnastics. In a similar case, members of the lacrosse and softball teams brought an action against Syracuse University claiming that the university failed to accommodate the needs and interests of women. Their claims included insufficient athletic scholarships and other benefits for women. The 1996 decision granted class certification for "all present and future female students at Syracuse University who are interested in and able to play varsity lacrosse, but are not able to do so because it is not a varsity sport " (20, 21).

Pederson et al. v Louisiana State University et al. (1996), a case consolidated with a complaint by Pineda, claimed the unequal treatment of female varsity athletes. Intent has become important to contemporary cases because the courts have to find intent before they award punitive damages. In this case the court had trouble determining the women's status as varsity athletes. The court found the university in violation of Title IX; however, the court stated that the university did not intend to harm the women. The "Court holds that the violations are not intentional. Rather, they are a result of arrogant ignorance, confusion regarding the practical requirements of the law, and a remarkably outdated view of women and athletics which created the byproduct of resistance to change" (918).

Beasley, an injured female athlete, sued Alabama State University for discriminatory treatment of women in scholarships, medical treatment, training, facilities, coaching, and opportunities to participate in sports. Defendants were successful in obtaining summary judgment, although the facts of this case differ from the other cases we have observed.

Horner (1994) and *Adams* (1996) are cases involving high school students. Twelve female high school slow-pitch softball players succeeded in their cause of action under the equal protection clause against the Kentucky State Board of Education in their quest for equal sports for women and sanction for slow-pitch softball. Tiffany Adams's equal protection claim was for a chance to try out for the wrestling team. She was granted the injunction to try out for the team.

Coaches' salaries

At the same time, coaches began filing suits and receiving damage awards.

Sanya Tyler, women's basketball coach at Howard University, received a verdict of $1.1 million in her equal-pay claim (Wong and Barr, 1993). And Oklahoma State University's women's golf coach has sued under the Equal Pay Act.

As Marianne Stanley began to negotiate a new contract as head women's basketball coach at the University of Southern California (USC), she decided—based on her outstanding coaching record—to request a multiyear contract for a salary similar to that paid to the men's basketball coach. She also asked for increases in the salaries of her assistant coaches. USC refused her request and told her that they would find another coach because she was no longer under contract. She was forced to accept a salary in the range in which she had been paid previously or lose her job. Stanley brought suit against USC for $8 million, alleging sex discrimination and retaliation, wrongful discharge, breach of implied contract, and conspiracy (*Stanley v University of Southern California*, 1994). Although she lost an injunction that would have enabled her to retain her position, she continues in her action against the university.

Many women have filed claims for sex discrimination in coaching women's sports; few have been successful in the courts. Their successes do not mirror the highly successful court decisions that women sport participants have achieved in litigation.

Sexual Harassment

Sexual harassment, a violation of state and federal laws, is becoming one of the most highly discussed legal topics. Its origins in legal theory are found in Title VII of the Civil Rights Act of 1964, Title IX of the Education Amendments of 1972, and various state statutes. There are two types of sexual harassment; quid pro quo and hostile environment. *Quid pro quo* means that certain benefits are conditioned on a sexual relationship. For example, sex for grades. *Hostile environment* occurs when the workplace allows persons to use sexual innuendoes to intimidate and insult others. It is classified as unwelcome behavior.

Meritor Savings Bank v Vinson, was the first Superior Court decision in sexual harassment. The *Meritor* decision determined that quid pro quo harassment was a violation of Title VII of the Civil Rights Act of 1964. Meritor had accepted her supervisor's sexual advances in order to keep her job.

In 1992, the Supreme Court extended the *Meritor* decision to public schools (*Franklin v Gwinnett*). Franklin had a sexual relationship with a coach/teacher. When she tried to file a complaint about the incident with the school she was discouraged from pursuing it. Franklin used Title IX as her legal theory.

It was *Harris v Forklift Systems, Inc.* (1993) that defined hostile environment—a workplace permeated with discriminatory intimidation, ridicule, and insult. The United States Supreme Court, using Title VII, found for the plaintiff.

In 1997 the Supreme Court extended sexual harassment to all sexual relationships (*Oncale v*

Sundowner Offshore Services, Inc., 1998). Oncale, an oil rig worker, quit his job after being grabbed and threatened in a shower by two male co-workers, one a supervisor. The court held that Title VII protected persons from same-sex and opposite-sex sexual harassment.

Burlington Industries, Inc. v Ellerth (1998) and *Faragher v City of Boca Raton* (1998) were decisions for persons who were harassed but suffered no threat to their jobs. Ellerth quit her job with the company after being subjected to continuous sexual harassment. She refused all the advances, suffered no job discrimination, and failed to inform persons in authority in the company of the advances even though she knew that the company had a sexual harassment policy.

The Court held that "under Title VII, an employee who refuses the unwelcome and threatening sexual advances of a supervisor, yet suffers no adverse, tangible job consequences, may recover against the employer without showing the employer is negligent or otherwise at fault for the supervisor's actions, but the employer may interpose an affirmative defense" (2259).

Beth Ann Faragher, a lifeguard for the City of Boca Raton, brought an action against the city and her immediate supervisor on the city's beach for sexual harassment. "The supervisor had created a 'sexual hostile atmosphere' at work by repeatedly subjecting Faragher and other female lifeguards to 'uninvited and offensive touching' by making lewd remarks, and by speaking of women in offensive terms, and that this conduct constituted discrimination in the 'terms, conditions, and privileges' of her employment in violation of Title VII of the Civil Rights Act of 1964" (2277).

The district court found for Faragher, holding that employees of the city had knowledge of the harassment and had failed to report it to supervisors. The Eleventh Circuit Court of Appeals reversed. The Supreme Court of the United States reversed the decision of the Eleventh Circuit Court, finding for Faragher.

Alida Star Gebser, a high school student, had a sexual relationship with one of her teachers (*Gebser v Lago Vista Independent School District,* 1998). The couple was discovered having sex by the local authorities; the teacher was arrested. Gebser did not report the relationship to school authorities. Gebser brought a cause of action under Title IX against the school district. The district did not have or circulate a policy or grievance procedure for sexual harassment. The district court found for Gebser.

CONCEPT CHECK

Equal protection and Title IX are the leading legal theories of sex integration in athletics. They have been strengthened in recent years by the Civil Rights Acts of 1987 and 1991. The Civil Rights Act of 1987 restores Title IX to full strength, countering the Grove City ruling that Title IX was program-specific and no longer covered athletics. The Civil Rights Act of 1991 gave money damages, compensatory and punitive, in Title IX decisions.

Disparate impact is the legal theory functioning when an athletic department is examined for conformity with Title IX.

ARTICLE 1 OF THE U.S. CONSTITUTION

Article 1, Section 8, Number 3 states that Congress shall have the power "to regulate commerce with foreign nations, and among the several States, and with the Indian tribes"; Number 18 gives Congress the power "to make all laws which shall be necessary and proper for carrying into execution the foregoing powers, and all other powers vested by this Constitution in the Government of the United States, or in any department or officer thereof." This congressional authority has been further expanded by the Sherman Act (1890), the Clayton Act (1914), the Norris-LaGuardia Act (1932), and the National Labor Relations Act, a result of amendments to the Wagner Act (1935) and the Taft-Hartley Act (1948). Antitrust and labor relations theories in these laws influence the rights of players and team owners in professional sports.

Labor laws

Sherman Act (1890). The **Sherman Act (1890)** set the stage for the evolution of **antitrust** law. Its purpose was to promote competition in the business sector through regulations designed to control private economic power. Professional sport, a private business operated to make a profit, comes under the labor laws. Section 1 of the Sherman Act states, "every contract, combination in the form of trust or

otherwise, or conspiracy, in restraint of trade or commerce among the several States, or with foreign nations, is declared to be illegal. Every person who shall make any contract or engage in any combination or conspiracy hereby declared to be illegal shall be deemed guilty of a felony."

Section 2 states that "every person who shall monopolize, or attempt to monopolize, or combine or conspire with any other person or persons, to monopolize any part of the trade or commerce among the several States, or with foreign nations, shall be deemed guilty of a felony."

The Sherman Act regulates interstate commerce, including goods, land, and services. Price fixing, for example, is outlawed. Violations of the act are examined by the courts using a rule-of-reason test that balances the illegal practice against the anticompetitive effect. Procompetitive and anticompetitive goals are examined in an effort to find the least restrictive means to reach a legitimate procompetitive goal. For example, is the restraint of a professional player's movement from one team to another the least restrictive method of maintaining equity in competition? Is the restraint of a professional player to a one-year contract commitment to a particular team a viable method of maintaining equity in competition?

Clayton Act (1914). Sections 4 and 6 of the **Clayton Act (1914)** are significant to professional athletes as they negotiate individual contract components and collective-bargaining agreements. Section 4 states that "any person who shall be injured in his business or property by reason of anything forbidden in the antitrust laws may sue therefore in any district court of the United States in the district in which the defendant resides or is found or has an agent, without respect to the amount in controversy, and shall recover threefold the damages by him sustained, and the cost of the suit including a reasonable attorney's fee. The court may award under this section . . . simple interest in actual damages for the period beginning on the date of service of such person's pleading."

Section 6 states that "the labor of a human being is not a commodity or article of commerce. Nothing contained in the antitrust laws shall be construed to forbid the existence and operation of labor, agricultural or horticultural organizations, instituted for the purpose of mutual help, . . . or to forbid or restrain individual members of such organizations from lawfully carrying out the legitimate objects thereof; nor shall such organizations, or the members thereof, be held or construed to be illegal combinations or conspiracies in restraint of trade under the antitrust laws." The Clayton Act strengthens and defines the Sherman Act. The act gives direction to athletes seeking redress for violations of antitrust and labor laws. Unfortunately, baseball's exemption from antitrust laws, discussed later, has denied baseball professionals a means of redress.

Norris-LaGuardia Act (1932). The following is taken from the interpretation of Section 102, Public Policy of the United States in the Act: "Whereas under prevailing economic conditions developed with the aid of governmental authority for owners of property to organize in the corporate and other forms of ownership association, the individual unorganized worker is commonly helpless to exercise actual liberty of contract and to protect his freedom of labor, and thereby to obtain acceptable terms and conditions of employment, wherefore, though he should be free to decline to associate with his fellows, it is necessary that he have full freedom of association, self-organization, and designation of representatives of his own choosing, to negotiate the terms and conditions of his employment, and that he shall be free from the interference, restraint, or coercion of employers of labor, or their agents, in the designation of such representatives or in the self-organization or in other concerted activities for the purpose of collective bargaining or other mutual aid or protection; therefore, the following definitions of and limitations upon the jurisdiction and authority of the courts of the United States are enacted."

The **Norris-LaGuardia Act (1932)** defines, and in some authors' opinions, restricts the incidents in which federal courts can grant an injunction in labor disputes. In the 1945 *Bradley* case, the U.S. Supreme Court pointed out that corporations that engaged in price control of products, created monopolies, or violated other aspects of antitrust laws would lose their labor union antitrust exemption.

The Norris-LaGuardia Act (1932), and the sections of the Clayton Act that it reinforces, protects union activity from antitrust scrutiny. Union-management agreements that are a product of "good-faith" negotiations receive protection from antitrust law. The exemption or protection applies where restraint on trade primarily affects only the parties to the collective-bargaining agreement. This restraint is a mandatory subject of bargaining, and the exemption is a product of arm's-length negotiation. This reasoning is used in nearly all antitrust actions in professional sport.

National Labor Relations Act. Under 29 U.S.C. 157, the **National Labor Relations Act,** "Employees shall have the right to self-organization, to form, join, or assist labor organizations, to bargain collectively through representatives of their own choosing, and to engage in other concerted activities for the purpose of collective bargaining or other mutual aid or protection, and shall also have the right to refrain from any or all of such activities except to the extent that such right may be affected by an agreement requiring membership in a labor organization as a condition of employment."

It is an unfair labor practice for either an employer or a labor organization to restrain or coerce an employee in the exercise of his or her rights. It is also an unfair labor practice for a labor organization to refuse to bargain collectively with an employer that is the official representative of its employees. The National Labor Relations Board (NLRB) is authorized by the act to hear and render decisions on unfair labor practices. It also has the power to petition the U.S. district court for appropriate temporary relief or a restraining order. The National Labor Relations Act guides businesses and members of unions, including athletic-player unions, in negotiations and in implementing collective-bargaining agreements in sport.

Antitrust cases

Through the years, sport has presented some unique issues to the courts for antitrust examination. The sport industry differs from other businesses in many ways. A consumer who is unhappy with the goods or services of a typical business can seek out another source of supply, while in sport there is no real substitute for the college and professional sports market. Gary Roberts (1991) notes that a legal problem in antitrust claims in sport is defining "the relevant market that the plaintiff claims has been monopolized. The market definition must include both a product and a geographic dimension—for example, professional football entertainment in the United States."

Another unique characteristic of sport is that its product (or service) is the competition between teams. Equity (a level playing field!) must be maintained to enable live spectators and television audiences to observe close, exciting, and competitive encounters. League owners are forced to work together to secure the league while at the same time engaging in fierce competition with the other members of the league.

Only in sport does a player join a **collective bargaining** unit and then negotiate individually for additional resources. In business and industry, the employee is either a member of a union, accepting the results of a collective-bargaining agreement, or an independent worker, negotiating an individual employment contract. Athletes, upon employment, automatically become members of a players' union, which negotiates basic elements of the work, economic, and fringe package. All athletes accept the results of this agreement, and outstanding athletes then bargain, usually through their agents, for additional economic and work-related privileges.

Unique among sports are the three U.S. Supreme Court decisions that exempted baseball, prior to 1998, from all antitrust laws. In *Federal Baseball Club of Baltimore v National League of Baseball Clubs* (1922), the Supreme Court held that baseball was exempt from the Sherman Act because it did not meet the definition of **"interstate commerce."** Justice Holmes stated that professional baseball "business is giving exhibitions of baseball, which are purely state affairs."

The suit, for treble damages, had been brought by members of the Federal League against the National and American Leagues, challenging restraints on player movement in professional sports. The **reserve clause,** a part of all players' contracts, bound a player to a team until the team released him or contracted him to another team. Further, the reserve clause prohibited other teams from making offers to signed players. Once a player signed the initial contract, all control of his future was placed in the owner's hands. The system was justified to maintain competitive balance by preventing one team from hiring all the good players.

In 1953, the Supreme Court had a chance in *Toolson v New York Yankees* to reverse its earlier decision and deny baseball the antitrust exemption awarded in 1922. The issue was that the reserve clause was an alleged violation of the Sherman and Clayton Acts. The plaintiffs focused their complaint on television in an effort to demonstrate interstate commerce. The court reaffirmed *Federal Baseball*, saying that the business of baseball had operated successfully for thirty years and the antitrust exemption should stand. The two dissenting justices, Burton and Reed, argued that during those thirty years baseball had become big business, with significant impact on interstate commerce, and should be subject to the antitrust laws.

Flood v Kuhn (1972) involved the professional player Curt Flood, who was traded to another club without his knowledge. The Supreme Court, in maintaining baseball's antitrust exemption, noted that professional baseball's long-standing exemption from antitrust law was an established aberration not held by other sports but that it should be allowed to stand.

As a result of these decisions, state courts have issued similar holdings in response to antitrust claims in baseball.

Curt Flood Act of 1998

The Curt Flood Act of 1998 provides: "It is the purpose of this legislation to state that major league baseball players are covered under the antitrust laws (i.e., that major league baseball players will have the same rights under the antitrust laws as do other professional athletes, e.g., football and basketball players), along with a provision that makes it clear that the passage of this Act does not change the application of the antitrust laws in any other context or with respect to any other person or entity" (P. L. 105-297).

Players filing antitrust complaints. Although other sports profit from minor antitrust exemptions, baseball's exemption has not been extended to all sports. Television network pools, blackouts of non-local telecasts when the home team is playing at home, and blackouts of home team games when it is playing in home territory constitute antitrust exemptions. These exemptions exist in a number of sports, but football appears to profit most from them.

In 1974, football players decided to challenge the Rozelle Rule under antitrust law (*Mackey v National Football League*, 1992). The **Rozelle Rule** was a practice started in the 1960s that required a team signing a veteran free agent to compensate the team that lost the player. Compensation was usually a player or draft-choice trade. Although different from baseball's reserve clause, a system football players had previously worked under, the new Rozelle Rule was viewed as equally offensive. Even more difficult for football players to understand was the fact that football was subject to antitrust law, which should have given them greater freedom.

The district court found that the Rozelle Rule violated the Sherman Act. The Eighth Circuit Court of Appeals affirmed the district court. Following the *Mackey* decision, a right-of-first-refusal compensation was developed through the collective-bargaining system. Under this rule, owners were permitted to match outside players' offers and by so doing retain a player's service. The right of first refusal was not popular with players; they believed that it gave too much control to the owners. In light of the fact that the first-refusal system of compensation was negotiated by the players' union and that unions usually have limited antitrust exemptions, the players had a difficult challenge in their many trips to court to attempt to change the first-refusal system (*Powell v National Football League*, 1991). Finally, in *McNeil*, Judge David Doty played a major role in crafting contract provisions that have become the current standard. Teams now have exclusive rights over players for their first three years in the league; in years four and five, players remain under a limited right of first refusal; and at the end of year five, players become unrestricted free agents. Salary cap implementation is accompanied by free agency in the fourth year. A number of categories, such as "franchise player" and "designated transition player," have been established to accommodate the needs of outstanding talent. These arrangements are the subject of current debate in newspaper sports pages.

Owners filing antitrust complaints. Two cases, *Piazza v Major League Baseball* (1994) and *Sullivan v National Football League* (NFL) (1994), discuss professional team owner antitrust problems. *Piazza* was a suit filed by a partnership that attempted to buy the San Francisco Giants and move them to Tampa/St. Petersburg. The partnership was outbid by a purchaser who promised to keep the Giants in San Francisco but paid $15 million less than the amount offered by Piazza. Among the many legal theories in the complaint were antitrust issues. The court denied Major League's motion to dismiss based upon the antitrust exemption, holding that the exemption was limited only to the reserve clause and that the reserve clause was not an issue in this case.

In *Sullivan* (1994), the plaintiff, founder of the New England Patriots, received a jury award of $38 million, trebled to $114 million, from the National Football League for violating antitrust laws by restricting him from selling stock in the club to the public. The damage award was reduced to $17 million in December 1993. In September 1994, the First Circuit Court of Appeals set aside the entire award and ordered a new trial, which has not yet been conducted.

Antitrust in sport can best be described as a theory in process. Through the years, labor law has been applied by the courts differently, in various sports and in various owner-player situations.

CONCEPT CHECK

Article 1 of the Constitution and the Sherman, Clayton, Norris-LaGuardia, and National Labor Relations Acts establish the antitrust and labor relation theories and laws that influence the rights of players and team owners in professional sports. The Sherman and Clayton Acts promote competition and prohibit monopolies; the Norris-LaGuardia Act addresses the needs of the individual; and the National Labor Relations Act provides a road map for collective bargaining.

Professional athletes have used the courts to gain freedom from contract restraints imposed by team owners. While considerable progress has been made, the fight continues.

CRITICAL THINKING EXERCISES

1. Analyze the *Dambrot* and *Campanelli* cases according to the elements found in the First Amendment to the Constitution. Do you agree or disagree with the Court's decision? If you wish to obtain more information before making your decision, look up the case on Lexis/Nexis Universe.

2. Create a secondary or collegiate sports program that will meet the requirements for equity under the Fourteenth Amendment to the United States Constitution. Identify the school enrollment.

SUMMARY

1. The U.S. Constitution is the primary law of the country, and each state has a constitution or primary set of laws. In addition, federal and state statutes have been enacted by legislative bodies to ensure efficient management of the federal and state governments.
2. The First Amendment to the U.S. Constitution includes the rights of religion, speech, and press.
3. The Fourth Amendment to the U.S. Constitution involves privacy rights.
4. Under the First and Fourth Amendments, the courts balance the needs of the state against the needs of the individual.
5. Primary elements of the Fourteenth Amendment are due process and equal protection.
6. Procedural due process enables an individual to be heard, to defend his or her actions, and to be assured of fair treatment before a right or privilege is taken away.
7. Hiring-system agreements include at-will, labor unions, and employment contracts.
8. The primary federal laws affecting employment are the Equal Pay Act (1963), Title VII of the Civil Rights Act (1964), the Age Discrimination in Employment Act (1967), the Rehabilitation Act (1973), and the Americans with Disabilities Act.
9. Affirmative action is a program designed to remedy past discriminating practices in hiring minority groups.
10. An effective system for hiring personnel includes preparation, identification of job responsibilities and requirements, obtaining an applicant pool, screening applications, interviewing, selecting, and documenting the entire process.
11. Employee evaluations are tailored with due process in mind.
12. An equal-protection challenge must show that groups of people are being treated differently, without justification, than the general population.
13. Title IX states that "No person in the United States shall, on the basis of sex, be excluded from participation in, be denied the benefit of, or be subject to discrimination under any education program or activity receiving Federal financial assistance."
14. Disparate impact involves practices that appear neutral in their treatment of different groups but fall more harshly on one group than another.
15. The Civil Rights Act (1987) restored Title IX to its original strength. Title IX was eroded between 1972 and 1987 by a number of court cases that narrowed its scope.
16. The Civil Rights Act (1991) strengthened disparate-impact theory by placing the burden of proof on those who practice discrimination and provided for both punitive and compensatory-damage recovery.
17. Article 1 of the U.S. Constitution and the Sherman, Clayton, Norris-LaGuardia, and National Labor Relations Acts identify the rights of players and team owners in professional sports.
18. The Sherman and Clayton Acts promote competition and prohibit monopolies.
19. Violations of the Sherman Act are examined by the courts using a rule-of-reason test that balances the illegal practice against the anticompetitive effect.
20. The National Labor Relations Act serves as a guide for collective bargaining.
21. Sports differ from business and industry in market, product definition, and employment agreements.
22. Three U.S. Supreme Court decisions, *Federal Baseball, Toolson,* and *Flood,* have maintained baseball's antitrust exemption.
23. The Rozelle Rule was a practice that required a football team signing a veteran free agent to compensate the team that lost the player.
24. Under the right-of-first-refusal compensation, owners were permitted to match outside players' offers and by so doing retain a player's service.
25. Owner litigation is threatening baseball's antitrust exemption. Only time will tell whether

the exemption is the reserve clause or all of baseball.

CASE STUDY I

The equal-protection clause of the U.S. Constitution and Title IX assist the athletic administrator in determining equity in sport. A high school district has a student population that is 55 percent female and 45 percent male and a sports budget of $85,000 for boys and $65,000 for girls. One hundred and forty boys participate in sports, while female participation is 100.

Analyze equity in this setting using the equal-protection clause and Title IX.

CASE STUDY II

Professional baseball players are automatically members of a players' union and reap the benefits of union membership. In addition, many players employ an agent to negotiate additional wages and benefits. Owners have reserved various rights in arriving at player agreements. Among them are the reserve clause, trading players to other teams, and the Rozelle Rule.

How do athletes' agreements, including owners' rights, differ from employment agreements in business and industry?

REVIEW QUESTIONS AND ISSUES

1. Using the results of court decisions, explain the U.S. Constitution's First Amendment freedoms of religion, speech, and press.
2. Can a school locker be searched under the Fourth Amendment?
3. Explain the balancing system used by the courts in First and Fourth Amendment decisions.
4. Trace the court decisions in the *Reynolds* case in an effort to understand the rights of the Olympic Committee.
5. Explain procedural due process, identifying when and how it is used.
6. How do the results of the *Tarkanian* court decision fit into the due process system?
7. Explain the relationship between the Fourteenth Amendment's equal-protection clause and Title IX of the Education Amendments (1972) in athletics.
8. Explain disparate-impact theory.

9. Chart a local athletic department participation rate to see if it would meet the current court ratio of equity within 5 percent.
10. How do labor laws define antitrust relationships?
11. Explain the rule-of-reason test.
12. How does the National Labor Relations Act serve as a guide to collective bargaining?
13. Identify and explain the unique characteristics of sport as a business.
14. Contrast baseball's antitrust exemption with the treatment of other sports under antitrust law.
15. Explain the Rozelle Rule, which was challenged in the *Mackey* case.
16. Explain the results of the *McNeil* decision and its impact on collective bargaining.

SOLUTIONS TO CRITICAL THINKING EXERCISES

1. The First Amendment freedom of speech is the freedom to speak, to remain silent, to discuss with others, and to advocate and communicate ideas. Ideas can be conveyed, but language that is obscene, libelous, or slanderous is not protected. Dambrot used the "n" word as a means of motivating his basketball team during a locker room pep talk. The university fired Mr. Dambrot for violating a university discriminatory harassment policy. Dambrot sued, challenging the university's policy under the First Amendment and his firing under contract. The court found Dambrot's statements not a matter of public concern and therefore not protected by the First Amendment.

Was Dambrot's statement one of public concern? Was his statement obscene, libelous, or slanderous? When does a pep talk to motivate athletes become libelous? Campanelli also used unacceptable words in motivating athletes. His speech was found to be profane and abusive and very personal to the players. He was fired from his at-will employment contract. Campanelli filed claims in federal and state courts. He also lost his First Amendment claims. Again, the speech had little to do with the coach's constitutional rights or ability to express his views on broad global issues and contained obscene and libelous statements.

Students might consider what can and cannot be used in a public school setting in motivating students. Remember that no statement can be obscene, libelous, or slanderous.

Participation rate under equity

	Enrollment	Participation %	Berths	Scholarships
Males	6,400	40%	240	120
Females	9,600	60%	360	180
Total	16,000	100%	600	300

REFERENCES

Acton v Vernonia School District, 66 F. 3d 217 (1995) and 23 F. 3d 1514 (1994) and 796 F. Supp. 1354 (1992).

Adams v Baker, et al., 919 F. Supp. 1496 (1996).

Beasley v Alabama State University, et al., 3 F. Supp. 2d 1325 (M. D. Ala. 1998); 966 F. Supp. 1117 (1997).

Bennett v West Texas State University, 799 F. 2d 155 (5th Cir. Ct. 1986).

Blair v Washington State University, 740 P. 2d 1379 (Wash. 1989).

Board of Education of Westside Community Schools v Mergens, 496 U.S. 226, 110 S. Ct. 2356 (1990).

Boucher, et al. v Syracuse University, 95-CV-620, United States District Court of the Northern District of New York (1996).

Boyd v Board of Directors of McGehee School District No. 17, 612 F. Supp. 86 (1985).

Brenden v Independent School District, 342 F. Supp. 1224 (1972), affirmed 477 F. 2d 1292 (1973).

Brunet v City of Columbus, 642 F. Supp. 11214 (1986); appeal dismissed, 826 F. 2d 1062 (1987); cert. denied, 108 S. Ct. 1593 (1988).

Bryant, et al. v Colgate University, et al., 93-CV-1028 (1996 U.S. Dist. ct. for the N. Dist. of N.Y.) and No. 93-CV-1029 (FJS), 1997 U.S. Dist. LEXIS 21518 and 996 F. Supp. 170 (1998).

Bucha v Illinois High School Association, 351 F. Supp. 69 (1972).

Burlington Industries Inc. v Ellerth, 118 S. Ct. 2257 (1998).

Campanelli v Bockrath et al., No. C93-3038 FMS, 1997 U.S. Dist. Lexis 7981 and 44 cal. App. 4th 572 (1996) and 100 F. 3d 1476 (1996).

Cannon v University of Chicago, 441 U.S. 677 (1979).

Chandler v James, et al., 985 F. Supp. 1094 (ND Ala. 1998).

Chaudhuri v State of Tennessee, Tennessee State University, et al., 130 F. 3d 232 (1997).

Civil Rights Restoration Act (1987), Public Law 100–259, 102 (1987).

Civil Rights Act (1991), Public Law 102–166 (1991).

Clayton Act (1914), 15 USC 15, 4 and 6 (1914).

Clement, A. (1987). Legal theory and sex discrimination in sport. In Adrian M., ed., *Sports women.* Basel, Switzerland: Karger Press.

Clement, A. (1998). *Law in sport and physical activity.* Dubuque, IA: Brown & Benchmark.

Cohen, et al. v Brown University et al., 101 F. 3d 155 (1996); 879 F. Supp. 185 (1995); 991 F. 2d 888 (1993); 809 F. Supp. 978 (1992) and *Brown University, et al. v Cohen, et al.,* 117 S. Ct. 1469 (1997).

Connick v Myers, 461 U.S. 138, 103 S. Ct. 1684 (1983).

Cook v Colgate University, 992 F. 2d 17 (2d Cir. 1993); 802 F. Supp. 737 (NDNY 1992).

Curt Flood Act of 1998, P. L. 105–297, Sect. 2, 112 Stat. 2824.

Dambrot v Central Michigan University, 839 F. Supp. 477 (1993).

Doe v Duncanville Independent School District, 994 F. 2d 160 (1993).

Equal Employment Opportunity Commission v Atlas Paper Box Company, 868 F. 2d 1489 (1989).

Faragher v City of Boca Raton, 118 S. Ct. 2275 (1998).

Favia v Indiana University of Pennsylvania, 7 F. 3d 332 (3rd Cir. 1993), 812 F. Supp. 578 (1993).

Federal Baseball Club of Baltimore v National League of Baseball Clubs, 259 U.S. 200 (1922).

Flood v Kuhn, 407 U.S. 258 (1972).

Franklin v Gwinnet County Public Schools, 112 S. Ct. 1028; 117 L. Ed. 2d 208; 60 USLW 4267 (1992).

Gebser v Lago Vista Independent School District, 118 S. Ct. 1989 (1998).

Gomes v Rhode Island Interscholastic League, 441 U.S. 958; 99 S. Ct. 2401 (1979); 469 F. Supp. 659 (1979) vacated as moot, 604 F. 2d 733 (1979).

Griggs v Duke Power Company, 401 U.S. 424, 91 S. Ct. 849 (1971).

Grove City College v Bell, 465 U.S. 555, 79 L. Ed. 516, 104 S. Ct. 1211 (1984); 687 F. 2d 684 (3d Cir., 1982), pet for cert. Granted, 103 S. Ct. 1181 (1983).

Haas v South Bend Community School Corporation, 289 NE 2d 495 (1972).

Haffer v Temple University, 524 F. Supp. 531 (ED Pa. 1981), affirmed 688 F. 2d 14 (3d Cir. 1982) and 678 F. Supp. 517 (ED. Pa. 1987) and 115 FRD 506 (ED Pa. 1987).

Harris v Forklift Systems, 510 U.S. 17 (1993).

Hazelwood School District v United States, 97 S. Ct. 2736 (1977).

Heckman, D. (1992). Women and athletics: A twenty year retrospective on Title IX. *University of Miami Entertainment and Sport Law Review 9* (1):1–64.

Heckman, D. (1997). Scoreboard: A concise chronological twenty-five year history of Title IX involving interscholastic and intercollegiate athletics. *Seton Hall Journal of Sport Law 7* (2): 391.

Hill v National Collegiate Athletic Association, 865 P. 2d 633 (1994).

Hollander v Connecticut Interscholastic Athletic Association, Inc., Civil No. 12-49-27 (Super. Ct., New Haven, Conn., March 1971); appeal dismissed 295 A. 2d 671 (1972).

Horner v Kentucky High School Athletic Association, 43 F. 3d 265 (6th Cir., 1994).

In the interest of Isiah B., 176 Wis. 2d 639; 500 NW 2d 637 (1993).

Lamb's Chapel v Center Moriches Union Free School District, 113 S. Ct. 2141; 124 L. Ed. 2d 352 (1993).

Lederman, D. (1992). U.S. Draft memo on sex equity in college sports, *Chronicle of Higher Education 38* (22):1.

Lee v Weisman, 505 U.S. 577 (1992).

Mackey v National Football League, 790 F. Supp. 871 (1992).

Marcum v Dahl, 658 F. 731 (1981).

McNeil v National Football League, 790 F. Supp. 871 (1992).

Meritor Savings Bank v Vinson, 477 U.S. 57 (1986).

National Labor Relations Act, 29 USC § 157.

NCAA v Tarkanian, 102 L. Ed. 469 (1988); 795 F. Supp. 1476 (1992); 10 F. 3d 633 (1993).

Norris-LaGuardia Act (1932), 29 USC § 102 (1932).

North Haven v Bell, 102 S. Ct. 1912, 72 L. Ed. 299 (1982).

Oncale v Sundowner Offshore Services, Inc., 118 S. Ct. 998 (1998).

Othen v Ann Arbor School District, 507 F. Supp. 1376 (ED Mich. 1981); affirmed on grounds not involving Title IX, 699 F. 2d 309 (1982).

Pederson, et al. v Louisiana State University, 912 F. Supp. 892 (1996).

Petrie v Illinois High School Association, 75 Ill. App. 980, 394 NE 2d 855 (1979).

Piazza v Major League Baseball, Civil Action No. 92-7173 (ED Pa. 1994); 836 F. Supp. 269 (1993); 831 F. Supp. 420 (ED Pa. 1993).

Powell v National Football League, 764 F. Supp. 1351 (1991); 930 F. 2d 1293 (1989); 690 F. Supp. 812 (1988); 678 F. Supp. 777 (1988).

Reed v Nebraska Athletic Association, 341 F. Supp. 258 (D. Neb. 1972).

Reynolds v The Athletic Congress of the U.S.A. Inc., 23 F. 3d 1110 (1994); 841 F. Supp. 1444 (1992).

Ridgeway v Montana High School Association, 858 F. 2d 579 (9th Cir. 1988); 633 F. Supp. 1564 (1986); 638 F. Supp. 326 (1986).

Rittacco v Norwin School District, 361 F. Supp. 930 (1973).

Roberts, G. R. (1991). Professional sports and the antitrust laws. In Staudohar, P. D., and Mangan, J. A. eds. *The business of professional sport,* Chicago: University of Illinois Press.

Roberts v Colorado State Board of Agriculture, 998 F. 2d 824 (1993, [1]); 814 F. Supp. 1507 (D. Colo. 1993, [2]); and

Colorado Board of Agriculture v Roberts, 510 U.S. 1004; 114 S. Ct. 580 (1993, [3]).

Scholz v RDV Sports, Inc. (1998).

Sherman Act (1890), 15 USC 1 and 2 (1890).

Stanley v University of Southern California, 13 F. 3d 1313 (1994).

State v Hunter, 300 P. 2d 455, 208 Ore. 282 (1956).

Stockard v Moss, 706 A. 2d 561 (D.C. 1997).

Sullivan v National Football League, 34 F. 3d 1091 (1994); 839 F. Supp. 6 (1993); 785 F. Supp. 1076 (1992).

Tarkanian v NCAA, 741 P. 2d 1345 (1987); 810 P. 2d 343 (1989); 114 S. Ct. 1543 (1994); petition to U.S. Supreme Court for writ of certiorari denied.

Teamsters v United States, 431 U.S. 324 (1977).

Tinker v Des Moines School District, 393 U.S. 503 (1969).

Title IX of the Education Amendments (1972), 20 USC 1681 (1976).

Todd v Rush County Schools, 133 F. 3d 984 (1998).

Toolson v New York Yankees, 346 U.S. 356 (1953).

Trinidad School District No. 1 v Lopez, 963 P. 2d 1095 (1998).

University of Colorado v Derdeyn, 863 P. 2d 929 (Colo. 1993); 832 P. 2d 1031 (1991); 114 S. Ct. 1646 (1994); petition for writ of certiorari denied; 62 USLW 3843 (June 20, 1994); petition to U.S. Supreme Court for rehearing denied.

University of Nevada v Tarkanian, Supreme Court of Nevada, No. 23494 (July 7, 1994); 594 P. 2d 1159 (1979).

Vargyas, E. J. (1994). *Breaking down barriers: A legal guide to Title IX.* Washington, D.C.: National Women's Law Center.

Vernonia School District 47J v Acton, 515 U.S. 646; 115 S. Ct. 2386 (1995).

Ward Cove Packing Co. v Atonio, 104 L. Ed. 2d 733 (1989).

Washington v Smith, et al., 80 F. 3d 555 (1996) and 893 F. Supp. 60 (1995).

Wong, G. M., and Barr, C. A. (1993). Equal paybacks. *Athletic Business* (September).

Yellow Springs Exempted Village School District v Ohio High School Athletic Association, 647 F. 2d 651 (1981).

WEBSITE

www.cnn

Examines recent court decisions of interest to the public.

www.lexis.com

Contains most state and federal cases at the appeals level or higher. Also contains law reviews and other legal periodicals.

CHAPTER 13

Sport Governance

Matthew J. Robinson
Mireia Lizandra
Sue Vail

In this chapter, you will become familiar with the following terms:

Interscholastic competition
State athletic associations
National Federation of State
  High School Associations
Executive director
Board of directors
Interscholastic athletic
  conferences
National Collegiate Athletic
  Association
Inter-university governance
  structure
NCAA Division I
NCAA Division II
NCAA Division III
Dominant provision
Division-dominant
  provision
Common provision
Federated provision
Executive Committee
NCAA National Office

Intercollegiate athletic
  conference
Student-athlete advisory
  committee
Athletic board
Player-controlled league
Owner-controlled league
Commissioner
International marketplace
Olympic movement
Olympic Games
Olympism
Olympic Charter
International Olympic
  Committee (IOC)
International federations (IFs)
National Olympic committees
  (NOCs)
Organizing committees of the
  Olympic Games (OCOGs)
the Session
the Executive Board

the President
Association of National Olympic
  Committees (ANOC)
United States Olympic
  Committee (USOC)
Amateur Sports Act of 1978
National governing bodies
  (NGBs)
National federations (NFs)
National sport organization
Bill C-131
Coaching Association of Canada
National Coaching Certification
  Program
Fitness and Amateur Sport
Sport Canada
Canadian Olympic Association
  (COA)
Calgary Olympic Development
  Association
Provincial sport organization
  (PSO)

Overview

As the new millennium begins, it can be expected that sport as an institution will continue its growth in scope, recognition, and importance in the global community. As this growth continues, governance takes on an increased importance at all levels of sport. In the United States, the National Collegiate Athletic Association has restructured its governance structure to provide more autonomy to the membership divisions. In professional sport, although the owners still have the most say in governance, players have gained more power in the governance of their respective sports through collective bargaining. Internationally, the increased recognition and national emphasis given to international competition and the financial benefits associated with hosting the Olympics has led to increased scrutiny of the role of the International Olympic Committee. This is also true with the various international sport federations. These governance structures are instrumental in creating the rules and policies that promote fairness and safety in competition. They enforce those rules to enhance the credibility of sport at all levels.

The following chapter will examine the governance of sport in five different environments: the interscholastic, intercollegiate, and professional levels in the United States, the international governance structures and sport governance in Canada.

INTERSCHOLASTIC ATHLETICS GOVERNANCE

Sport and athletic competition in American high schools has a long and distinguished history. The inclusion of physical activities in the academic curriculum can be traced to the Turner Societies in Germany during the nineteenth century and to English private schools that promoted individual physical activities as well as cooperation through the physical with rugby football (Baker, 1988). In America, where the public school system made obtaining an education possible for all citizens, school sports were touted as potentially powerful tools for formulating the kinds of attitudes and behaviors associated with effective citizenship. Ath-letic participation provided the practical lessons in cooperation and social discipline required for those living in an industrial society (O'Hanlon, 1995).

Interscholastic competition is athletic competition that features athletes from different high schools competing against each other. The earliest form of interscholastic competition at the turn of the twentieth century was student initiated. A 1907 study of high school athletic programs revealed that the students ran one out of six programs. This changed dramatically as faculty and administration expressed concerns over commercialism, poor sportsmanship, and cheating (O'Hanlon, 1995). The faculty took the position that varsity sports could promote sound values if they were properly regulated. This position has been the rationale for the creation of sport leagues and **state athletic associations.** State high school athletic associations strive to regulate and standardize competition between schools through the enforcement of eligibility rules and other rules governing competition between schools. This movement was successful, for by 1924 all but three states had established a state athletic association (O'Hanlon, 1995). The faculty had wrested the control of athletics away from the student and placed it in the hands of educators.

As society saw the varied benefits of varsity athletic competition, the emphasis on interscholastic competition grew, as did the number of sports offered. Early interscholastic competition included football, basketball, and baseball for males, but through the twentieth century, varsity athletic programs included other sports as well as opportunities for females to compete. By the later part of the twentieth century, high school sport programs were the single most significant dimension in the entire sport enterprise (VanderZwag, 1998). Over 17,000 high schools are members of the **National Federation of State High School Associations,** and over six million male and female athletes compete in interscholastic competition (www.nfhs.org). This number does not include the millions who participate in high school *intramural programs* or sport instruction offered through physical education classes. Intramural programs are athletic programs housed within academic institutions and promote competition among the students from a particular academic institution.

The governance of interscholastic athletic competition involves four dimensions: the individual school district where the school is located, the athletic conference in which a school's athletic program competes, the state athletic association that governs sport in a particular state, and the National Federation of State High School Associations (NFHS), which oversees high school athletics in the country (figure 13–1).

The NFHS is the national service and administrative organization for high school athletics located in Kansas City, Missouri. The NFHS's role is to provide leadership and national coordination for interscholastic athletic competition in the United States by publishing playing rules for sixteen boys' and girls' sports and providing educational services and programs for the members of fifty-one state associations whose members make up the NFHS. The organization has a board of directors consisting of representatives from eight geographic districts as well as individuals who hold several at-large positions. The board of directors oversees the activities of the organization and establishes its policies and procedures. The NFHS does not possess any enforcement powers, and the rules it establishes are not mandatory or enforceable.

The state associations govern athletics in each state. These state associations have the power to establish rules and in most cases possess enforcement powers. The extent of these powers varies from state to state. The majority of the state associations exist for the purpose of providing uniform standards for athletic competition within the state; offering state championships; ensuring that athletic competition is fair, safe, and sportsmanlike; and providing an environment that emphasizes the overall development of the participants.

A state association will have an **executive director** and a staff that run the day-to-day operations. The executive director is a hired employee who oversees the direction of the state association and is responsible for implementing the association's policies and procedures. Although the executive director implements, the rules that govern athletic competition come from the members. Most states act as representative democracies where authority lies within the member institutions. A state association will have a **board of directors**. A board of directors is a governance body consisting of representatives from various districts within the state and that is empowered to make policy decisions on behalf of the members. These individuals represent the interests of their respective districts. At the district level, there is a district committee with representatives from each of the conferences or leagues that compete within the district. There will also be various district committees that will ensure the operation of the state association.

Membership in **interscholastic athletic conferences** is usually based on geographic location. In some instances, school size and whether a school is private or public are considered in conference formation. At the conference or league level, there is a board or committee that consists of representatives from each member institution. The representatives who serve in the governance structure are usually the principals or athletic directors from the member institutions. The representatives at the various levels elect them. Therefore each member institution has a say in creating the legislation it will have to follow.

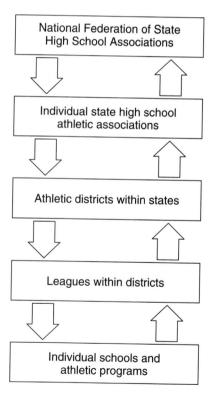

FIGURE 13–1 Governance structure for interscholastic athletics in the United States of America.

Even with a comprehensive governance structure in place, the actual administration of high school athletics is primarily conducted on the local level. Most policy and procedural decisions are made at the school district or school level (Covell, 1998). The local schools must be cognizant of and operate within the rules established by the state association. A *school board* or *board of education* is an elected body made up of individuals living within the boundaries of a school district who have the authority to establish the policies and procedures and allocate resources for all school district programs, including athletics. The school board approves budgets, determines the feasibility and allocation of resources for the building of athletic facilities, votes on the hiring and firing of athletic department personnel, and votes to establish policies for the school district's athletic programs.

Within each individual school district, the athletic director has the responsibility of implementing those policies established by the school board for the athletic programs within the district. These programs usually include interscholastic athletic teams on the high school or secondary level as well as the middle school level. The most extensive athletic programs exist at the high school level, with the middle school programs serving as feeder programs for the high school programs.

In larger school districts where there may be more than one high school, there will be a district-wide athletic director as well as an athletic director at each individual high school. The district athletic director oversees the athletic program for the entire district, while the school athletic director oversees the athletic program at his or her high school. The district-wide athletic director will be supervised either by the superintendent of the school district or an assistant superintendent for extracurricular programs. In the case of the high school athletic director, he or she is supervised by the high school principal.

Concept Check

The governance of interscholastic athletic competition involves cooperative efforts among the individual schools, athletic conferences, state athletic associations, and the National Federation of State High School Associations. Each level has its own governance structure and plays an integral role in the overall governance of interscholastic competition in the United States.

INTERCOLLEGIATE ATHLETICS

Intercollegiate athletics have played an integral and visible role in sport and society during the twentieth century. The **National Collegiate Athletic Association** is the largest and most influential governing body in intercollegiate athletics. The NCAA had operating revenue of over $275 million for the 1997–98 year, and $213 million of that revenue came from the broadcast rights to the NCAA Men's Division I Basketball championships as well as several other championships (National Collegiate Athletic Association, 1998c). The NCAA offers championships in sixteen male sports, fourteen female sports and three coed sports, and over 35,000 male and female student athletes had the opportunity to compete in those championships (National Collegiate Athletic Association, 1998a).

The first documented intercollegiate athletics event was a crew race pitting Harvard against Yale in 1852 (Sack and Staurowsky, 1998). Harvard was the victor, and a rematch occurred in 1855. Athletic competition between institutions of higher learning expanded to include baseball in 1859, and in 1869 Princeton and Rutgers competed in the first intercollegiate football game (Davenport, 1985).

In its earliest stages, students administered intercollegiate athletics, but athletics eventually became integral to the institutions. Important athletic contests generated large gate receipts, and success, especially in football, brought prestige to a college. This arrangement was satisfactory with administrators until the athletic operations became so large that the students could no longer control them (Nelson, 1982). The hiring of professional athletes to play was a common practice, athletes moved from school to school at will, enticements were offered to gifted athletes, and athletes only attended classes during their respective seasons.

Faculties at institutions expressed concern over the student-run programs and took action to address the problems. In the early 1880s Princeton's faculty took action with the creation of the first athletic committee, which was formed to settle questions related to the athletic program (Smith, 1995). By the end of the nineteenth century, most institutions had created some type of faculty body that oversaw athletics, but the rules established by the individual institutions often led to either competitive advantages or disadvantages for individual institutions. These conflicts led to discussions of an **inter-university governance structure** to develop consistent rules that all institutions would follow.

Early attempts at inter-institutional governance were not successful. Resolutions passed by a conference of faculty members from East Coast institutions in 1882 were not accepted by other institutions due to a lack of consensus on the various individual resolutions (Smith, 1995). In 1898 faculty, alumni, and student representatives from seven of the eight current Ivy League institutions (Yale was missing) met at Brown University to address the reform of intercollegiate athletics (Sack and Staurowsky, 1998). Issues addressed at the Brown conference included athlete eligibility, pay for play, and the faculty role in the governance structure. This meeting did not present any enforceable rules for the governance of intercollegiate athletics, but it did offer a model for the governance of athletics within the university environment. Institutions, conferences, and national governing bodies adopted many of the recommendations later.

The first athletic conference, the Intercollegiate Conference of Faculty Representatives, was established in 1895. Better known as the Western Conference or Big Ten Conference, it provided a blueprint for the control and administration of athletics by faculty representatives from the member institutions. Many of the rules the Big Ten established in regard to eligibility and payment of players were later adopted by the national regulatory body, the National Collegiate Athletic Association, which came into existence at the turn of the century.

The impetus behind the creation of a national regulatory body was an alarming number of deaths in college football in 1905. President Theodore Roosevelt intervened from the White House and called for changes that would debrutalize the game (Lewis, 1969; Michner, 1976; Savage, 1929). Roosevelt's decree led to the formation of the Intercollegiate Athletic Association of the United States in 1906. The purpose of the organization was stated in its chief objective: "The regulation and supervision of college athletics throughout the United States, in order that athletic activities in the colleges and universities may be maintained on an ethical plane in keeping with the dignity and high purpose of education" (Lewis, 1969, p. 721).

The organization, which started with thirty-nine members, took on its current name in 1910. In the NCAA's early stages, it was primarily a regulatory body, and its annual convention served as a forum for the open discussion of problems in intercollegiate athletics. The organization's power grew because of the increased belief in faculty control of athletics. The NCAA promoted the formation of conferences in the model of the Big Ten, and in turn these conferences encouraged its member institutions to follow the NCAA's lead (Davenport, 1985).

The scope of the NCAA's responsibilities grew as more institutions and conferences became members. Stern (1979) noted that from its origins in 1906 to 1948, the NCAA increased its influence by mandating rules of play, offering educational material and meetings, offering administrative recommendations for athletic programs, instituting championship play in 1921, awarding financial incentives, and encouraging United States Olympic team participation.

In 1948 the NCAA membership established the *Sanity code* with the intention of developing guidelines for recruiting and financial aid and enforcing those guidelines. The Sanity Code was ineffective as abuses in the aforementioned areas increased in number and seriousness. Ultimately it was abandoned by the membership (Tow, 1982). The ineffectiveness of the Sanity Code led to binding legislation in 1952 that delegated enforcement powers to the policy-making body of the NCAA, the NCAA Council. The NCAA also hired its first full-time executive director, Walter Byers. The NCAA had become a regulatory body with the power to investigate abuses of and enforce the NCAA rules and punish offenders (Byers, 1995; Stern, 1979; Tow, 1982).

The NCAA is the definitive governance organization in intercollegiate athletics. It is a voluntary organization of over 1,200 institutions, conferences, and organizations devoted to the sound administration of intercollegiate athletics (National Collegiate Athletic Association, 1998b). The member institutions of the NCAA are diverse, with different educational missions, enrollments, and athletic philosophies. To address the diverse interests of its members, in 1974 the NCAA adopted Article 11 of the NCAA constitution. Article 11 established criteria and philosophies for the three NCAA Divisions.

NCAA Division I institutions strive for regional and national excellence, recognize the dual objective of serving both the university and general public, and strive to finance their athletic programs through funds generated by the athletic enterprise. It also should be noted that those institutions that are classified as Division I must offer a minimum number of scholarships (National Collegiate Athletic Association, 1998b). **NCAA Division II** institutions offer financial incentives, but on a more modest scale, place an emphasis on scheduling fellow Division II institutions within a geographic region and accept the dual objective of their athletic programs serving the general public and campus (National Collegiate Athletic Association, 1998b). **NCAA Division III** institutions, on the other hand, strive to place the emphasis on the student-athlete instead of the spectator, award no financial aid, give primary emphasis to in-season competition and treating athletic paticipants no differently than the other members of the student body (National Collegiate Athletic Association, 1998b).

The NCAA constitution has 33 *articles* that serve as its basis for governance. The NCAA's *constitution* consists of six articles that address the purposes of the association, its structure, its membership, its legislative process, and role of institutional control. The organization also has fourteen articles that serve as its *operating bylaws*. These bylaws address ethical conduct, conduct and employment of athletics personnel, amateurism, recruiting, eligibility, financial aid, awards and benefits for student-athletes, playing and practice season, championship and post-season football, enforcement, division membership, committees, football television plans and regulations, and athletics certification.

These bylaws are the product of the legislation adopted by the membership. There are four types of legislative provisions or bylaws. A **dominant provision** is a rule that applies to all members of the association. A **division-dominant provision** is specific to a division and must receive a two-thirds majority vote by the membership to pass. A **common provision** is one that applies to more than one of the three divisions of the association. A **federated provision** is a rule that is adopted by one of the divisions and only needs a simple majority of the membership present to pass (National Collegiate Athletic Association, 1997). The division-dominant and federated rules are each division's interpretation of articles based on each division's philosophy. A classic example is that Division I is allowed to award financial aid based on athletic ability, while Division III is not. Also, Division I recruiting rules are much more stringent than the recruiting rules in place for Division III.

Finally, the NCAA has four *administrative articles* that set forth the policies for the implementation of general legislative action, the NCAA championships, the enforcement program, and athletics certification program. All of this information is made available to the membership in the form of the NCAA manual. This publication is found in every NCAA member institution's athletics department. Athletic directors, compliance coordinators, and coaches use the manual to ensure that they are operating within the framework of the NCAA by-laws and to understand the operations of the NCAA as a governing body.

In the past, the NCAA was structured so that each institution had one vote, so that a Division III institution had the same power as a Division I institution when voting on legislation that affected the NCAA. In 1996, the NCAA was *restructured* to give more autonomy to the three divisions. In the restructured NCAA, there is an **Executive Committee** that has representation from all three divisions, but with the majority of the board coming from Division I institutions (figure 13–2). Division I has a board of directors consisting of institutional chief executive officers, while Divisions II and III have Presidents Councils consisting of institutional CEOs. Below this level, each division has a Management Council consisting of athletics administrators and faculty athletics representatives, and in the case of Division III, institutional CEOs also.

Divisions II and III still meet at an annual convention, and the members vote on legislation that will affect the respective divisions. Division I's structure is based on conference representation. Legislation is approved by a fifteen-member board of directors who represent the various Division I conferences, rather than by a vote of the 305 Division I members at an annual convention. At all three levels there is a committee structure that assists in the governance of each division. The committees consist of presidents, athletics directors, faculty athletic representatives, coaches, and student athletes.

There are ten convention committees that perform duties associated with running the annual convention and other special meetings of the respective divisions. There are thirty standing general committees that are appointed by the NCAA Council or the Executive Committee to perform those duties necessary to the operation of the NCAA. There are also rules committees without

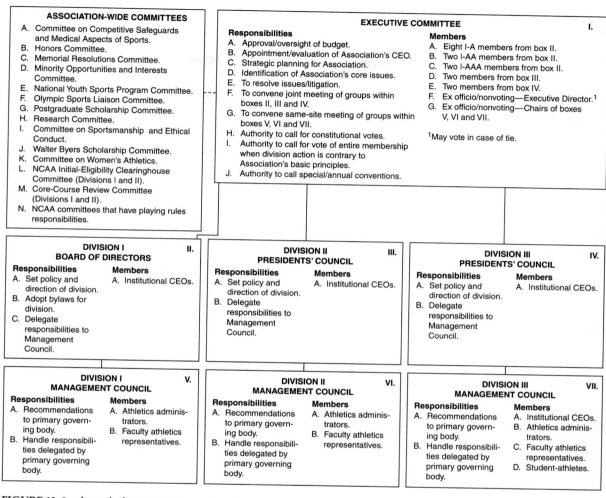

FIGURE 13–2 Association governance structure.
© National College Athletics Association.

championship administration responsibilities, sports committees with playing rules and championship administration responsibilities, and sports committees with only championship administration responsibilities. These committees are responsible for formulating the rules of play for the respective sports and hosting the championships in each sport. Finally, there are special committees established by the association to address specific issues or concerns.

The **NCAA National Office** is not involved in the legislative process but rather works for the membership. The office does so by providing services,

hosting championships, conducting educational workshops, educating the membership on rules, and investigating rules violations. The NCAA national office receives the most recognition in the area of investigating violations. In this capacity the members of the NCAA staff are investigating institutions and their staffs for violating rules that the members created. The national office is headed by an executive director and is divided into the following departments: Championships, Education Services, Enforcement and Eligibility Appeals, Finance and Business Services, Membership Services, and Public Affairs.

There are 112 conferences represented in the NCAA (National Collegiate Athletic Association, 1998c). In most cases, an **intercollegiate athletic conference** consists of institutions with the same institutional and academic missions and level of commitment to athletics, and is located in the same geographic region. In recent years at the major college level, institutions have either joined conferences or switched conferences, and geography has not been as major a factor as in the past. Air travel has made it possible for institutions to belong to conferences outside a geographic region. This is best demonstrated by Penn State University becoming a member of the Midwest-dominated Big Ten Conference and Notre Dame, a Midwestern university, joining the Big East Conference. Barr (1998) cited four reasons for a school to change conference affiliation or to join one: (1) exposure from television contracts with existing conferences, (2) potential revenues from television and corporate sponsorship through conference revenue-sharing; (3) difficulty for independent schools in scheduling games and generating revenue; and (4) the ability of a conference to hold a conference championship game in football which has the potential of generating millions of dollars for the members of a conference with twelve members.

Institutions belonging to the conference must adhere to the rules established by the conference. At times the rules that the conference establishes may be more stringent than those established by the NCAA, but they cannot be less stringent. The conferences have executive directors and conference offices that handle the day-to-day operations of the conference and are responsible for organizing the conference championships for its members as well as enforcing conference rules and offering interpretations of both conference and, when necessary, NCAA rules. The members of the conference establish the rules for the conference members. The governance structure of each conference differs in that in some conferences, the control rests in the hands of the presidents of the institutions, while in others it may rest in the hands of the athletic directors.

The NCAA states that the control and responsibility for the conduct of intercollegiate athletics should be placed in the hands of the individual institutions. The chief executive officer of each institution is responsible for how an institution conducts its intercollegiate athletic program (National Collegiate Athletic Association, 1997). Each institution must appoint a *faculty athletics representative*. The duties of the faculty athletics representatives are defined by each institution. They must be persons who hold faculty rank at the institution. An institution must also establish a **student-athlete advisory committee** consisting of current student-athletes so that they have a voice in how athletics are conducted on a particular campus. Some institutions choose to establish an **athletic board** consisting of athletic administrators, institutional administrators, alumni, faculty, and student-athletes to establish policies for the athletic programs.

CONCEPT CHECK

The NCAA is a membership-driven organization. The members of the association created the legislation that is enforced by the NCAA executive director and national office. The NCAA addresses the diversity of its membership by offering three divisions from which an institution may choose. Each division has established its own governance structure through the restructuring of the NCAA in 1996, but still all three division are involved in the overall governance of the NCAA.

PROFESSIONAL SPORT

Professional sport has been a part of the sport landscape in America since the early part of the nineteenth century. *Professional sport* constitutes participants being financially compensated for their talents and services. There are four major sport leagues in the United States: football, basketball, baseball, and hockey. There are professional tours in men's and women's golf, tennis, ice skating, beach volleyball, bowling, and skiing. Several auto-racing circuits exist, and professional boxing and horseracing have been fixtures on the American sport scene since the 1700s. Professional sport leagues also exist in indoor and outdoor soccer, women's basketball, lacrosse, and roller hockey. Minor leagues in baseball, basketball, hockey, and soccer exist for the purpose of player development for major sport leagues.

The four major team sport leagues are the most recognizable and profitable entities in professional sport. The National Football League has thirty-one teams and will be adding a thirty-second in 2002.

The average current value of an NFL franchise is $277 million (Ozanian, 1998). The National Basketball Association also has thirty teams, and its broadcast contract with the National Broadcast Company and Turner Broadcasting is worth $300 million a year (Ozanian, 1998). The National Hockey League has twenty-six teams, and the average team will generate over $25 million through attendance (Ozanian, 1998). Major league baseball, the oldest professional team sport league, has thirty teams divided into two leagues (Ozanian, 1998). The 1998 World Champion New York Yankees drew over two million fans and paid over $69 million on player salaries (Ozanian, 1998).

The first all-professional sport team in America was the Cincinnati Red Stockings baseball team formed in 1869. The team's manager, Harry Wright, raided other clubs for their best players and paid them to play. The ten-man team had a payroll of $9,300 (Baker, 1988). In 1871 the National Association of Professional Baseball Players was formed. It was a ten-team **player-controlled league** where the players organized the teams, determined player salaries, and developed the schedule. The league existed for five turbulent years, during which twenty-five different clubs came and went, gambling ran rampant, players changed teams on a regular basis and teams would not appear for scheduled games in order to save travel money (Baker, 1988; Helyar, 1994).

In 1876 William Hulbert initiated the creation of the eight-team National League to replace the troubled player-controlled league. The National League set a precedent for all professional sport leagues that would follow in other sports because it was an **owner-controlled league** and the players would be employees. Many of the governing practices set forth by the National League are still in effect in all professional sport leagues today. The constitution of the National League provided for a central office and a five-man board of directors selected by the owners, with one serving as the president of the league. There was no player representation within the governance structure. The league constructed a seventy-game schedule, and teams could be expelled for not finishing a season. It also hired umpires who worked for the league and not for the teams in individual cities, forbade gambling within ballparks, and did not allow Sunday play to improve the credibility of the league (Baker, 1988).

Two key elements of the governance of early professional baseball were the *salary cap* and the *reserve clause*. The owners viewed these as means to ensuring the financial viability of the league and its member teams. The salary cap instituted in 1889 placed a limit of $2,500 on a player's salary (Helyar, 1994). The reserve clause restricted the movement of players. The rule stated that once a player signed a contract with a club, he was the club's property unless he was traded to another team or released. These two measures ensured that the owners would keep the salary costs down and would therefore leave more profit for the owner. The National League thrived under the owner-controlled format, but the players did not have much say in the governance of the game and little control over their careers (Miller, 1991).

The National League was the lone professional team sport league at the turn of the twentieth century. Eventually a minor league circuit named the Western League moved East, renamed itself the American League and did battle with the National League for players and spectators (Helyar, 1994). The American League did not have a salary cap and did not recognize the National League's reserve clause, and it began to offer the National League's best players higher salaries. The two leagues sued for peace in 1903 and combined to create the major leagues. Each league would recognize the reserve clause, and a National Commission was established with the president of each league and members agreed upon by both. The body oversaw professional baseball for seventeen years.

In the wake of the Black Sox Scandal of 1919, the National Commission was viewed as ineffective in governing baseball. It was decided that only an outsider of impeccable integrity could do the job of restoring baseball's good name after the gambling scandal at the 1919 World Series (Heylar, 1994). Judge Kennesaw Mountain Landis accepted the position as the **commissioner** of baseball on the condition that he had absolute authority to act in the best interests of baseball. Landis held the position of commissioner of baseball for twenty-four years. There have been eight commissioners who have since followed Landis.

Professional football, hockey, and basketball followed baseball's path as professional sport leagues. Professional football's origins were in small industrial towns in the Midwest. The National Football

League was formed in 1920 when men from town teams in Ohio met in Canton, Ohio to discuss cooperation in scheduling, player salaries, and to agree on not stealing one another's players (Fox, 1994). Eventually there were fourteen charter teams from Ohio, Indiana, Illinois, and western New York. The league's first president was football legend Jim Thorpe, and he was followed by Joe Carr a year later. Carr would serve as president of the NFL until his death in 1939.

Carr took a league of small-town teams and led its transformation into a thriving big-city league. Under Carr's leadership, teams were prohibited from paying college players to turn professional, by not allowing a player to join the league until his class graduated. Carr was also responsible for introducing the player draft to professional sport (King, 1996). He also introduced a standard player contract to ensure continuity on teams and established Sunday as game day.

Early professional basketball consisted of teams *barnstorming* across the country with no set season or schedule. A stable national league for pro basketball started in 1946. Two years later it would take on the name of the National Basketball Association. The league's first commissioner also served as commissioner of the American Hockey League. The early owners of professional basketball teams were also the owners of arenas as well as the hockey teams that played in the arenas. This was the case for many years in Boston and New York (Gorman and Calhoun, 1994). These owners viewed basketball as a way to increase the usage of the arenas. Professional hockey was primarily played in Canada; in fact, a team from the United States was not able to compete for the Stanley Cup until 1916 (Gorman and Calhoun, 1994). The league only had six teams until it expanded to twelve teams in the 1960s.

Each of these sports followed the owner-controlled governance structure created by baseball. The governance structures for the four major sport leagues are very similar. Each league has a commissioner, a board of governance or committee structure consisting of the owners and front office personnel of the franchises, and a league office. The owners hire the commissioner of each league. The owners also decide and pay the commissioner's compensation and determine the commissioner's duties and responsibilities (Miller, 1991). The owners also have the power to remove the commissioner. A commissioner will serve a term, and at the end of the term the owners will vote whether or not to renew the term. The commissioner has the responsibility of protecting the best interests of the sport, but it can be argued that since the owners pay the commissioner's salary, he/she represents the owner's interests. This was demonstrated by the role that David Stern, the NBA's commissioner, played in representing the owners against the players in negotiations related to the owners' lockout of the players during the 1998–99 NBA season.

Professional sport commissioners have had a significant impact on the growth of the respective sport leagues. Pete Rozelle, the commissioner of the National Football League from 1960 to 1989, helped shape the modern professional sport landscape. Rozelle saw the benefits of televised sport and was instrumental in the United States Congress passage of the *Broadcast Act of 1960*. This law enabled the NFL to negotiate a television contract with a network. Rozelle recognized that the success of professional football was tied to the success of the league. Revenue from network television contracts would be divided equally among all of the teams in the league and thus ensure the viability of all of the franchises. He was instrumental in the merger of the AFL and NFL and proposed the idea that the AFL and NFL championship game be known as the Super Bowl. He initiated NFL Properties, which sells NFL licensed products and generates millions of dollars for NFL teams each year. He also participated in negotiations for television contracts that provided large financial rewards for the NFL teams. The other sport leagues followed the NFL's lead set by Rozelle.

Stern is credited with saving the NBA as it struggled with low attendance, low television ratings, high salaries, and a poor public image in the early 1980s. Stern became commissioner in 1984 and was able to negotiate with the player's association a salary cap to limit a player's salary. But the salaries would be tied to the success of the league. The players would receive 53 percent of the projected gross revenue of the league each year (Gorman and Calhoun, 1994; Halberstam, 1999). Stern also was successful in using the league's marquee players Magic Johnson, Larry Bird, Julius Erving, and Michael Jordan to market the NBA in the United States as well as globally.

Even though the commissioner is the most visible individual in the governance structure of professional sport, the owners do have the final say on the governance of their respective leagues. Through a committee structure, the owners propose rules and rule changes, vote on expansion and franchise relocations, negotiate the league's network broadcast contracts, and represent management in contract negotiations with the players' unions.

It has been through the players' unions that players have had a voice in the governance of their respective sports. Through *collective bargaining agreements* players have a say in areas such as compensation in terms of minimum salary, fringe benefits, and pension; rules for the use of labor, such as games per week, and starting times related to travel; terms of free agency; individual job rights; methods of enforcing the collective bargaining agreement; discipline; injury protection; economic issues such as meal money and travel expenses; and rules for agent certification (Greenberg, 1992). Collective bargaining led to the end of the reserve clause in baseball in 1975. This led to free agency in baseball and set a precedent for free agency in other sports (Miller, 1991). For more on collective bargaining in sport refer to chapter 8, "Labor Relations in Professional Sports."

The commissioner and the league office are responsible for running the day-to-day operations of the league. The league office handles the scheduling of contests, oversees the umpires and referees, administers special events like All-Star games and championships, fines and suspends players for breaking league rules, conducts public relations, advertising, and marketing for the league as a whole, and implements licensing agreements.

CONCEPT CHECK

The governance structure for the four major sport leagues are similar in that each professional league has a commissioner, a board of governance or committee structure, and a league office. The owners still have ultimate say in the policies that are developed, but the commissioner, an employee of the owners, is very influential. The players have gained more influence in the governance of professional sport through the rise of players' associations and collective bargaining.

INTERNATIONAL ATHLETICS GOVERNANCE

As the world moves into the twenty-first century and moves toward a global economy, sport, like other businesses, is playing a major role in the **international marketplace.** Television has been a vehicle to this global expansion. It has created a global viewership. Along with sport merchandise consumption and a wider sport fan attendance, major sport leagues and sporting events have reached millions of people in hundreds of countries. Sporting events have crossed domestic boundaries: the Opening Day game of the 1999 Major League Baseball season was played in Monterrey, Mexico between the San Diego Padres and the Colorado Rockies in front of 26,000 fans and televised to almost 200 countries (Wissot, 1999). The Nagano Winter Olympic Games were televised approximately in 160 countries, and the total global television coverage increased 55 percent (International Olympic Committee, 1998). Super Bowl XXXIV will be telecast in more than 185 nations.

In addition, the advent of cyberspace has influenced all aspects of the global economy, including sport. Every day, millions of people around the world access a vast wealth of sports information by simply logging onto their computers. ESPN.com was accessed by 3,856,000 people in February 1999. CBS SportsLine.com had 2,810,000 visitors the same month (Liberman, 1999).

To this end, it is obvious that the scope of knowledge for the future sport manager goes beyond the domestic domain. Understanding sport at the international level will help you to become a better sport manager no matter what field you pursue in sport management. This chapter will address the governance and management of sport at the international level. We will focus on the **Olympic movement** since the **Olympic Games,** as the single largest international sporting event, is the pinnacle of event management (Thoma and Chalip, 1996).

OLYMPIC MOVEMENT AND OLYMPISM

Before explaining the governance and management of Olympic sport, we need to become familiar with two concepts: *Olympic movement* and *Olympism.* Historically, Pierre de Coubertin is considered the founder of Modern **Olympism.** The **Olympic Charter** (International Olympic Committee, 1997) states:

Olympism is a philosophy of life, exalting and combining in a balanced whole the qualities of body, will and mind. Blending sport with culture and education, Olympism seeks to create a way of life based on the joy found in effort, the educational value of good example and respect for universal fundamental ethical principles. (International Olympic Committee, 1997, p. 8)

Under Coubertin's initiative the International Athletic Congress of Paris was held in June 1894. During the Congress the **International Olympic Committee** was constituted on June 23, 1894.

The *Olympic Charter* continues, stating:

The Olympic movement led by the International Olympic Committee, stems from Modern Olympism.

The goal of the Olympic movement is to contribute to building a peaceful and better world by educating youth through sport practiced without discrimination of any kind and in the Olympic spirit, which requires mutual understanding with a spirit of friendship, solidarity and fair play (International Olympic Committee, 1997, pp. 8–9).

The Olympic movement includes the International Olympic Committee, the **international federations** (IFs), the **national Olympic committees** (NOCs), the **organizing committees of the Olympic Games** (OCOGs), the national associations, clubs, and the persons belonging to them, particularly the athletes. It also includes other organizations and institutions as recognized by the International Olympic Committee (International Olympic Committee, 1997).

THE INTERNATIONAL OLYMPIC COMMITTEE

The International Olympic Committee (IOC) is a nongovernmental, nonprofit organization with headquarters in Lausanne, Switzerland. It is considered the supreme authority of the Olympic movement.

The Olympic Charter is the codification of the fundamental principles, rules, and bylaws adopted by the International Olympic Committee. It governs the organization and operation of the Olympic movement and stipulates the conditions for the celebration of the Olympic Games.

The International Olympic Committee owns exclusive rights to:

- The Olympic symbol—represented by five interlocked rings. It represents the union of the five continents and the meeting of athletes from all over the world at the Olympic Games. The Olympic symbol can be used alone, in one or in several colors (blue, yellow, black, green, and red).
- The Olympic flag—It has white background and the Olympic symbol in its five colors is located in the center.
- The Olympic motto—"Citius, Altius, Fortius" or "Swifter, Higher, Stronger"
- The Olympic anthem
- The Olympic Games—The Olympic Games consist of the Games of the Olympiad and the Olympic Winter Games. The term *Olympiad* is frequently misused. It does not refer to the Games themselves but rather to the four-year period following the Games. The Games of the Olympiad are held during the first year of the Olympiad, which they celebrate. Beginning in 1994, the year of the XVII Winter Games, the Olympic Winter Games are held during the second calendar year following that during which an Olympiad begins (International Olympic Committee, 1997).

These Olympic marks become very important because they are the trading tools of the International Olympic Committee (Thoma and Chalip, 1996).

The International Olympic Committee is governed by its members. The International Olympic Committee chooses and elects its members from people the IOC considers qualified. Some of the requirements to become an IOC member are: (1) they must be nationals of a country in which they have their domicile or their main center of interests and in which there is a national Olympic committee recognized by the International Olympic Committee; (2) they must also speak at least one of the languages used at International Olympic Committee Sessions.

Some of the rules that apply to the IOC members are:

- IOC members are representatives of the International Olympic Committee in their countries and not delegates of their countries within the International Olympic Committee. For example, an IOC member from Mexico represents the International Olympic Committee in Mexico and not Mexico in the International Olympic Committee.
- There cannot be more than one IOC member elected in a country. However, in those countries in which either the Games of the Olympiad or the Olympic Winter Games have been held, the IOC may elect a second member. For example, since the United States has held more than two Games of the Olympiad, the IOC has appointed two IOC members from the USA, Anita DeFrantz and Jim Easton.

When the International Olympic Committee was founded, there were fourteen members. Currently there are 105 IOC members and twenty-three honorary members. They retire at the end of the calendar year when they turn 80 years, unless they were elected before 1966, in which case they are members for life. The retiring age and the way the members are elected are likely to change after recommendations from the IOC 2000 Reform Commission later in 1999.

IOC governance

The IOC is governed by three bodies:

- The Session
- The Executive Board
- The President

The general assembly of the members of the International Olympic Committee is called a *Session*. The **Session** is the supreme body of the IOC. It is held at least once a year. The president can request an extraordinary session. The main function of the Session is to adopt, modify, and interpret the Olympic Charter. Its decisions are final. The Session may delegate powers to the Executive Board. The official languages of the session are French, English, German, Arabic, Spanish, and Russian.

The **Executive Board** consists of the IOC president, four vice-presidents, and six additional members. All the members of the Executive Board are elected by the Session, by secret ballot, by a majority of voters cast. The Executive Board is responsible for managing IOC finances, preparing the annual report, submitting the names of persons it recommends for IOC membership, establishing the agenda for IOC Sessions, etc. The vice-presidents and the additional six members are elected for a period of six years.

A **president** heads the International Olympic Committee. The IOC president is elected by secret ballot from among its members, for a period of eight years. The president may be re-elected for successive four-year terms. He supervises all the activities of the International Olympic Committee.

The president nominates special commissions or working groups to study certain specific subjects and formulate recommendations to the Executive Board. These commissions have a significant role, and they can propose recommendations to the International Olympic Committee. The members appointed in these commissions are a mix of IOC members, IFs and NOCs representatives, consultants, and technicians in specific areas. Examples of these special commissions are the Finance Commission, Medical Commission, and Press Commission, and the two latest commissions are the IOC 2000 Reform Commission and IOC Ethics Commission.

CONCEPT CHECK

The Olympic Movement is comprised of the International Olympic Committee, the International Federations, the National Olympic Committees, the Organizing Committees of the Olympic Games, the national associations, clubs, and the persons belonging to them, particularly the athletes. The International Olympic Committee (IOC) is the supreme authority of the Olympic Movement. It is governed by three bodies: the Session, the Executive Board, and the president.

The National Olympic committees

The national Olympic committees are the organizations responsible for the development and protection of the Olympic movement in their respective countries. The Olympic Charter (International Olympic Committee, 1997) specifies in Rule 31 the NOC requirements:

- Propagate the fundamental principles of Olympism at national level within the framework of sports activity and otherwise contribute, among other things, to the diffusion of Olympism in the teaching programs of physical education and sport in schools and university establishments.
- Ensure the observance of the Olympic Charter in their countries.
- Encourage the development of high performance sport as well as sport for all.
- Help in the training of sports administrators by organizing courses and ensure that such courses contribute to the propagation of the fundamental principles of Olympism.
- Commit themselves to taking action against any form of discrimination and violence in sport.

The national Olympic committees are responsible for the representation of their respective countries at the Olympic Games and at the regional, continental, or world competitions patronized by the IOC. They also have the authority to designate a city as a candidate to host the Olympic Games.

The NOCs are grouped into regional organizations. These are as follows:

- Association of National Olympic Committees of Africa (ANOCA) based in Cameroon. ANOCA organizes the African Games. There have been seven editions of the African Games.
- Olympic Council of Asia (OCA) based in Kuwait. OCA organizes the Asian Games every four years.
- The European Olympic Committees (EOC) based in Italy.
- Oceania National Olympic Committees (ONOC) based in the Fiji Islands.
- Pan American Sports Organization, which encompasses the National Olympic Committees of North, South, and Central America (PASO) based in Mexico. PASO organizes the Pan American Games. The games have taken place every four years since 1951. (Association of National Olympic Committees, 1998).

The common objective of these regional associations is to uphold the Olympic Charter and promote sport in their regions. The umbrella organization for all the National Olympic Committees is the **Association of National Olympic Committees (ANOC).**

CONCEPT CHECK

The national Olympic committees are the organizations responsible for the development and protection of the Olympic movement in their respective countries. They are responsible for the representation of their respective countries at the Olympic Games and at the regional, continental, or world competitions patronized by the IOC. They also have the authority to designate a city as a candidate to host the Olympic Games.

The United States Olympic Committee

The **United States Olympic Committee (USOC)** is the organization that provides leadership and guidance for the Olympic movement in the United States and around the world (United States Olympic Committee, 1997). The **Amateur Sports Act of 1978** appointed the USOC as the coordinating body for all Olympic-related athletic activity in the United States. It designated the USOC as the sole authority for supervision and development of sports contested in the Olympics and Pan American Games. The USOC was also given the responsibility of promoting and supporting physical fitness and public participation in athletic activities by encouraging developmental programs in its member organizations. The USOC member organizations include Olympic and Pan American sport organizations (the national governing bodies), affiliated sport organizations, community-based and education-based multisport organizations, athletes' representatives, armed forces, Disabled in Sports, state fundraising organizations, associate members, and representatives of the public sector.

The Amateur Sports Act granted the USOC exclusive rights to the symbol of the International Olympic Committee, the USOC emblem, and the words "Olympic," "Olympiad," and "Citius, Altius, Fortius" in the United States.

The Amateur Sports Act also included provisions for recognizing **national governing bodies (NGBs)** for the sports on the Olympic (winter and summer) and Pan American Games programs. It gave the USOC the general authority, on a continuing basis, to review matters related to the recognition of NGBs in the act.

The federal government has no direct authority over the USOC. In turn, the USOC obtains almost no funding from federal sources. The majority of USOC revenue is derived from private fundraising, licensing, and sponsorship agreements. Sports outside the Olympic movement and Pan American Games (including professional teams and leagues) are subject to neither the USOC nor federal oversight.

The USOC also supports the bid of U.S. cities to host the winter or summer Olympic Games or Pan American Games. After reviewing the bids, the USOC may endorse one city per event as the U.S. bid city. The USOC has developed an internal bid process to choose a U.S. bid city for the 2007 Pan American Games. The same process has been put in place for a U.S. bid city for the 2012 Olympic Games. Currently eight cities are bidding to become the American candidate city for the 2012 Olympic Games (United States Olympic Committee, 1999).

USOC's organizational structure

The organizational structure of the USOC includes volunteer leadership consisting of the officers, an executive committee, a board of directors, standing and special committees, and an executive director and paid staff. There is also an Athletes' Advisory Council to serve as a source of opinion and advice to the board and all other USOC committees.

- The officers of the USOC consist of a president, three vice presidents, a secretary, and a treasurer.
- The executive committee has the responsibility for supervising the conduct of the business affairs of the USOC according to the policy guidelines prescribed by the board of directors.
- The board of directors establishes the policies to be followed in carrying out the purposes and objectives of the USOC. It meets twice a year, unless otherwise decided by the members. It has the authority to amend the USOC constitution and bylaws, admit new members or terminate the membership of current members, and to receive and review reports of the executive committee, executive director, and all committees or other persons, concerning USOC activities.
- The standing and special committees are part of the USOC structure for the purpose of making recommendations to and reporting to the board of directors and executive committee and carrying out other functions assigned to them.
- The Athletes' Advisory Council helps to improve communications between the USOC and currently active athletes and to serve as a source of opinion and advice to the board of directors.

CONCEPT CHECK

The United States Olympic Committee is the organization that provides leadership and guidance for the Olympic movement in the United States. It is the sole authority for supervision and development of sports contested in the Olympics and Pan American Games. The organizational structure of the USOC includes volunteer leadership consisting of the officers, an executive committee, a board of directors, standing and special committees, and an executive director and paid staff. There is also an Athletes' Advisory Council.

International Federations

The international federations are international nongovernmental organizations recognized by the International Olympic Committee to administer one or more sports at world level and to encompass organizations administering such sports at national levels (International Olympic Committee, 1997). In the United States, the **national federations (NFs)** are known as national governing bodies (NGBs). For example, for the sport of baseball, the International Baseball Association (IBA) is the international federation and USA Baseball is the national governing body for baseball in the United States. For another example, the Fédération Internationale de Basketball (FIBA) is the international federation for basketball. USA Basketball is the national governing body for basketball in the United States, and the Federación Española de Baloncesto is the national federation for basketball in Spain.

The role of the international federations is to establish and enforce the rules for their respective sports and to ensure the development of their sports throughout the world.

We can categorize the international federations as follows:

- Recognized international federations whose sports appear on the Olympic program have the status of International Olympic Federations. There are two categories: the International Olympic Summer Federations (see table 13-1) and the International Olympic Winter Federations (see table 13-2). As such, they participate in annual meetings of the IOC Executive Board.
- Recognized international federations whose sports are not part of the Olympic program (see table 13-3).

In order to discuss common problems and decide on their event calendars, the summer Olympic Federations, the winter Olympic Federations, and the recognized federations have formed associations:

- The Association of Summer Olympic International Federations (ASOIF)
- The Assembly of International Winter Sports Federations (AIWF)
- The Assembly of IOC Recognized International Sports Federations (ARISF)

TABLE 13-1   *International Olympic summer federations*

International Amateur Athletic Federation (IAAF)
International Rowing Federation (FISA)
International Badminton Federation (IBF)
International Baseball Association (IBA)
International Basketball Federation (FIBA)
International Amateur Boxing Federation (AIBA)
International Canoe Federation (FIC)
International Cycling Union (UCI)
International Equestrian Federation (FEI)
Fédération Internationale d'Escrime (FIE)
Fédération Internationale de Football Association (FIFA)
International Gymnastics Federation (FIG)
International Weightlifting Federation (IWF)
International Handball Federation (IHF)
International Hockey Federation (FIH)
International Judo Federation (IJF)
International Federation of Associated Wrestling Styles (FILA)
Fédération Internationale de Natation Amateur (FINA)
Union Internationale de Pentathlon Moderne et Biathlon (UIPMB)
International Softball Federation (ISF)
The World Taekwondo Federation (WTF)
International Tennis Federation (ITF)
The International Table Tennis Federation (ITTF)
Union Internationale de Tir (UIT)
International Archery Federation (FITA)
International Triathlon Union (ITU)
International Sailing Federation (ISAF)
International Volleyball Federation (FIVB)

TABLE 13-2   *International Olympic winter federations*

Union International de Pentathlon Moderne et Biathlon (UIPMB)
International Bobsleigh and Tobogganing Federation (UIPMB)
World Curling Federation (WCF)
International Ice Hockey Federation (IIHF)
International Luge Federation (FIL)
International Skating Union (ISU)
International Ski Federation (ISU)

TABLE 13-3   *Recognized international federations*

International Federation of Sports Acrobatics (IFSA)
Fédération Aéronautique Internationale (FAI)
The International Mountaineering and Climbing Federation (UIAA)
World Confederation of Billiards Sports (WCBS)
Confédération Mondiale Sports Boules (CMSB)
International Dance Sport Federation (IDSF)
World Amateur Golf Council (WAGC)
World Karate Federation (FMK)
International Korfball Federation (IKF)
International Federation of Netball Associations (IFNA)
International Orienteering Federation (IOF)
International Roller Skating Federation (FIRS)
International Federation of Basque Pelota (FIPV)
Federation of International Polo (FIP)
Fédération Internationale des Quilleurs (FIQ)
International Racquetball Federation (IRF)
International Rugby Football Board (IRFB)
International Life Saving Federation (ILS)
International Water Ski Federation (IWSF)
World Squash Federation (WSF)
World Underwater Federation (CMAS)
International Surfing Association (ISA)
International Trampoline Federation (FIT)

- The General Association of International Federations (AGFIS/GAISF), which also includes other sports federations.

All of the sports included on the Olympic program have an international federation. After each Olympic Games, the International Olympic Committee reviews the program and determines whether new sports and/or new events can be added. At this time, international federations that are recognized by the International Olympic Committee but are not included on the Olympic program can petition to be included. We need to take a step back and realize that an international federation needs to request its recognition to the International Olympic Committee. The IOC will grant two years of provisional recognition and after these two years, the IOC grants final recognition in writing.

So, when an international federation petitions to be included in the Olympic program, it has to comply with some requisites. In order for a sport to be included on the summer Olympic program it must be practiced by men in at least seventy-five countries on four continents and women in at least forty countries on three continents.

To be included on the winter Olympic program, it must be practiced in at least twenty-five countries on three continents. The sport is admitted to the program of the Olympic Games at least seven years before the Olympic Games. A *discipline* (a branch of an Olympic sport comprising one or several events) must have a recognized international standing to be included in the program of the Olympic Games. The standards of admission for disciplines are the same as those for sports. An example of a discipline would be beach volleyball. An *event* (a competition in an Olympic sport or in one of its disciplines and resulting in a ranking) must have a recognized international standing both numerically and geographically and must have been included at least twice in world or continental championships. Only events practiced by men in at least fifty countries and on three continents may be included in the program of the Olympic Games.

No international federation is obligated to keep the sport it governs on the Olympic program. Each IF establishes its own eligibility rules for its sport. An international federation can have a set of eligibility rules for the Olympic Games, which must be approved by the International Olympic Committee, and another set of rules for all other international competitions (for example, world championships).

CONCEPT CHECK ✔

The international federations are international nongovernmental organizations recognized by the International Olympic Committee for administering one or more sports at world level and encompassing organizations administering such sports at national levels.

Organizing Committees of the Olympic Games

The bid process to host the Olympic Games is lengthy and highly scrutinized. When a city is chosen to host the Olympic Games, an organizing committee of the Olympic Games (OCOG) has to be formed. The International Olympic Committee entrusts the organization of the Olympic Games to the national Olympic committee of the country of the host city as well as to the host city itself. In the case of the 2004 Olympic Games, the International Olympic Committee has entrusted the Hellenic Olympic Committee and the city of Athens with organizing the 2004 Games of the Olympiad. For this purpose, an organizing committee of the Olympic Games has been formed, *Athens 2004*.

From the time of its constitution to the end of its liquidation, the organizing committee must comply with the Olympic Charter, the contract entered into between the IOC, the national Olympic committee, and the host city, and the instructions of the IOC Executive Board. For an organizing committee of the Olympic Games there are many areas to address, including operations, accommodations, accreditation, logistics, host broadcasting, television rights, medical, Olympic Village, security, technology, tickets, transportation, and sport competitions (Thoma & Chalip, 1996).

THE CANADIAN AMATEUR SPORT SYSTEM

Around the rinks and the playing fields, the pools, the ski hills and trails in Canada, emulating their heroes, are thousands of young Canadians of all backgrounds, learning together. Cheering them on, coaching them, and enduring the endless rounds of car pools and early morning ice times are the parents who through their countless hours of "parent duty" experience the positives of sport as well. Sharing a cup of coffee at five a.m. in a cold rink can be an incredible stimulus to conversation and the beginning of a better understanding among Canadians. It's cold out there at five a.m. whether you are French, English, male or female.

For the Love of Sport (1992)

INTRODUCTION

Although we are neighbors, and Canada and the United States influence each other in many areas, the way in which our respective amateur sport systems have developed over the past thirty years is distinctly different. This section has three purposes:

- To help you to understand the evolution of the Canadian amateur sport system;
- To help you to understand the current structure and governance of the Canadian amateur sport system; and

- To help you to understand what changes are needed in the Canadian system for the next decade.

Sport management as a profession and a discipline was first recognized in the early 1970s when the federal government, under then–Prime Minister Pierre Trudeau, responded to a task force report on sport, which moved the management of sport from the proverbial kitchen table to the boardroom. **National sport organizations (NSOs)** were formally recognized by the federal government and received funds to support athletes and organizational development. At the same time, universities began to offer programs to train physical educators, and the research and practice of sport-related subjects, including sport administration/management, was recognized as a discipline.

Since the birth of the formalized sport system in Canada, federal, provincial, and municipal governments have played a major funding and policy role. To this day, the system is largely dependent upon public funds to provide athletes, coaches, and recreational participants with ongoing programs and services. Throughout the 1990s, all levels of government implemented major cutbacks in their sport budgets, and this had a crippling effect on many aspects of the system.

In essence, the high level of government involvement in sport over the years has been a two-edged sword. On one hand, the foundation for the Canadian sport system would not have developed as rapidly or as uniformly without government support. On the other hand, a financial overreliance on government leadership and funding has evolved, leaving sport vulnerable to political whimsy and the financial constraints and priorities of the government in power.

As we pass the turn of the century, the Canadian sport system is in jeopardy. The cutbacks in government funding reflect not only Canada's attempt to reduce its deficit but also indicate the government is questioning the contributions of the sport system. From a high-performance perspective, Canada has not produced the number of medals that many politicians feel is critical for continued support. From a health perspective, sport is not yet seen as an essential contributor to a healthy lifestyle, although more cause-effect research supports this position as each year passes. Generally speaking, sport in Canada is not viewed as an integral part of the culture, as it is in many European countries.

Concept Check

The high level of government involvement in the development and maintenance of the Canadian sport system has been a two-edged sword. On one hand the system could not have developed so rapidly or uniformly; on the other hand, an overreliance on government leadership and funding has evolved.

The evolution of the amateur sport system in Canada

In 1959 the Duke of Edinburgh, Prince Philip, made a speech to the Canadian Medical Association decrying the state of fitness of Canadians and challenging the medical profession to take steps to rectify this deficiency (Macintosh and Bedecki, 1987). At the same time, Canada's weak performance at the Olympics and other international games did not go unnoticed by members of Parliament.

As a result, in September 1961 **Bill C-131,** an Act to Encourge Fitness and Amateur Sport, was passed in the House of Commons with unanimous consent. The purpose of the act was to provide access to sport and fitness for all Canadians. The act had a 5 million budget attached to it, which allowed for the establishment of the base of the Canadian sport system as it exists today. A sport presence was also established within the federal government bureaucracy, Fitness and Amateur Sport, a branch of the Department of Health and Welfare. This government branch was to assist in shaping the development of the amateur sport system in Canada.

It took the better part of ten years to plan for the implementation of the Canadian sport system, and then around 1970 the system started to take shape. It was in 1971 that Hockey Canada (now the Canadian Hockey Association, after a merger with the Canadian Amateur Hockey Association in the mid-1990s) was formed to address Canada's poor showings at international competitions. Particip-ACTION came into being with a mandate to make Canadians more aware of the importance of physical activity, and ultimately to become more physically active. The **Coaching Association of Canada** was birthed and from that the **National Coaching Certification Program** was developed and implemented. University programs were established to do research and to educate students about the value of sport and physical activity. Finally, a National Sport and Recreation Center was created in Ottawa to house the offices of all of the newly formed national sport organizations (e.g., Basketball Canada, Canadian Figure Skating Association). Provinces followed suit with the creation of provincial sport centers to house the offices of provincial sport organizations.

Over the next few years, a number of federal-provincial cost-sharing agreements were set up for sport program development across the country. Problems arose when Quebec refused to participate, and many of the smaller provinces were unable to find their share of the cost-sharing agreements. These agreements were discontinued in the late sixties and deemed unsuccessful in encouraging mass participation sport. At that point the ten provinces independently developed their sport systems based upon the resources and priorities of each. Interestingly enough, in spite of the independent development, each provincial sport system parallels the national system in large measure.

A number of other policy papers and reports were developed by the federal government through the 1970s and 1980s that tried to further define the roles of governments and to develop the sport delivery system. In 1976 the **Fitness and Amateur Sport** branch of the Department of Health and Welfare received its own minister of state, the Honourable Iona Campagnolo. This was viewed by the sport community as a stronger commitment by the federal government to supporting the growth of fitness and amateur sport in Canada. Unfortunately, it turned out to be just a "stopover" for junior ministers to gain some experience before receiving more prestigious posts. Between 1976 and 1984, the branch had eight different ministers, each with different priorities and different policy thrusts that were imposed on the sport community. These were challenging times.

In spite of many policy changes, federal and provincial monies allocated to the sport system continued to grow through the 1980s, allowing the sport bureaucracy to flourish and expand. Canada

was the envy of most other governments in the Western industrialized nations who were striving for international supremacy (Macintosh and Bedecki, 1987, p. 180). Over that time period the federal government funded between sixty and seventy national sport organizations and supported everything from the rental of office space and staff salaries to athlete assistance stipends and travel expenses (figure 13–3).

In the mid-1980s, then–Minister Otto Jelinek, a former world-class figure skater, challenged the national sport organizations to obtain 50 percent of their funding from private sources and established a Sport Marketing Council to encourage all NSOs to become more financially self-reliant. Unfortunately, the amateur sport bureaucracy had become very dependent on public funding over the previous twenty years, and many of the NSOs felt that the federal government would and should continue to support amateur sport at the same level. Because

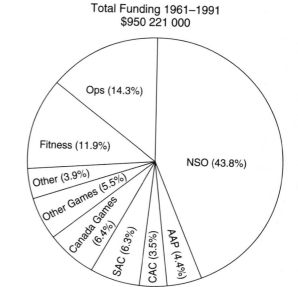

AAP - Athlete Assistance Program, which began as the Grants-in-Aid to Student-athletes Program
CAC - Coaching Association of Canada
SAC - Canadian Sport and Fitness Administration Centre, originally the National Sport and Recreation Centre (NSRC)

FIGURE 13–3   Distribution of funds among core FAS programs.

the government had always provided for sport, most were not motivated to search out other sources of funding beyond membership fees and government grants. However, much to the disbelief of many sport leaders, government funding for sport in the 1990s reached an all-time low.

It has only been in recent years that many sport leaders are beginning to understand that the government's priorities are not necessarily those of sport and that the monies received by sport must be used to address the government's priorities, which are generally less to do with athlete and infrastructure development and more to do with national identity and international prestige.

Structure and roles within the current Canadian sport system

The Canadian sport system was built by government in the image of government and is in every way a bureaucracy, with all of the strengths and limitations of that type of an organizational structure.

In the late 1980s and early 1990s, many members of the sport community felt that too great a portion of the federal monies were being used to support the development of the infrastructure and not enough funds were reaching the athletes and being used for athlete development. In 1992, Fitness and Amateur Sport released a task force report entitled *Sport: The Way Ahead*. This report was prepared in response to several broader policies documented in the *Report of the Commission of Inquiry into the Use of Drugs and Other Banned Practices Intended to Increase Athletic Performance* (Dubin report), which was released in 1990. Specifically, the task force was asked to examine the purpose and place of sport in society, the underlying values and ethics that should shape its conduct, the roles and responsibilities of the Canadian NSOs, and the federal government's future role in sport policy and programs (Minister of State, Fitness and Amateur Sport, 1992, p. 8). Among the many recommendations in this report was an emphasis on the need to design and implement new community-centered models for the development of sport, to be created in partnership with provincial governments and other stakeholders (Minister of State, Fitness and Amateur Sport, 1992) (figure 13–4).

The emphasis on the development of community -centered sport remains a central theme in the Canadian sport community; however, there has been little success in re-creating the system in the way that

the task force report was suggesting. Large gaps still exist between what is happening at the community level and provincial and national sport programming. Part of this issue relates to the complex sport bureaucracy that has evolved in Canada. Each NSO has its own delivery system for its programs and services, and it is rare for sports to work together to address the common sport needs of participants and athletes in a province or a community. Combine this with what is often a competitive attitude by the sport leaders within one sport organization where the provincial sport members refuse to cooperate or share information with their national counterparts. The same problem often applies to the relationship between Provincial Sport Organizations (PSOs) and their respective community clubs. Unfortunately, the situation has worsened in recent years, as public funding for sport has been reduced and competition for new resources has become more intense.

The harsh reality of reduced funds to amateur sport appeared in the mid 1990s as the federal government began to act on redefining and streamlining its role in funding amateur sport. Drastic cuts were made across the board, crippling many sport organizations. The number of NSOs receiving federal support was cut in half. When federal and provincial governments decided that it was time to reduce the deficit, sport was seen as a "frill" that could be done without.

CONCEPT CHECK

In the 1990s when the federal and provincial governments made drastic cutbacks to sport funding, national and provincial sport leaders began to realize that government's priorities were not the same as sport's priorities.

The current role of Canadian governments in sport. The federal government, now through **Sport Canada,** a branch within the Department of Canadian Heritage, continues to fund amateur sport at the national level through national sport, multisport, and multiservice organizations. The annual support varies from year to year. Generally, the more successful its athletes are internationally, the greater the funding support to a national sport organization.

The federal government supports sport to the extent that sport allows it to meet such objectives as

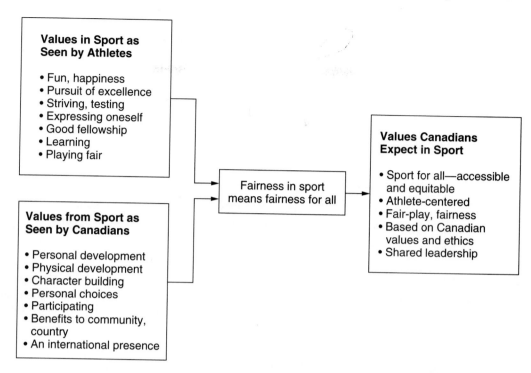

FIGURE 13-4   The values of sport to Canadians.

assisting Canada in having a strong international presence or contributing to the country's sense of heritage. These funds are used to provide athlete assistance (e.g., living expense money while the athlete is training), administrative assistance for the national office (e.g., staff salaries, board of directors meetings), coaches' training and travel, and monies in support of travel to or the hosting of major national or international games. Each sport organization must submit complete documentation and meet stringent funding guidelines to receive financial support from the federal government (figure 13–5).

A very similar process takes place at the provincial level with provincial governments. Each of the ten provinces has different priorities for funding provincial sport organizations and provides differing amounts of grant monies on an annual basis. In Ontario, for example, the provincial government recognizes and values sport's contributions to profiling Ontario nationally and internationally.

Currently, given the government's desire to reduce health care costs, it recognizes physical activity as a vehicle to a healthier lifestyle for Ontarians and is supporting sport to play a bigger role in health promotion.

Municipal governments provide funding to support community sport across towns and cities in Canada, primarily through their respective departments of parks and recreation or departments of community services. Municipal governments, up until the last five years, delivered many sport programs directly to community members. Recently, more and more are working in partnership with community sport organizations which then deliver such activities as tennis lessons, figure skating lessons, or swimming lessons.

The role of the Canadian Olympic Association (COA).

The **Canadian Olympic Association** is dedicated to developing and advancing sport and the Olympic Movement

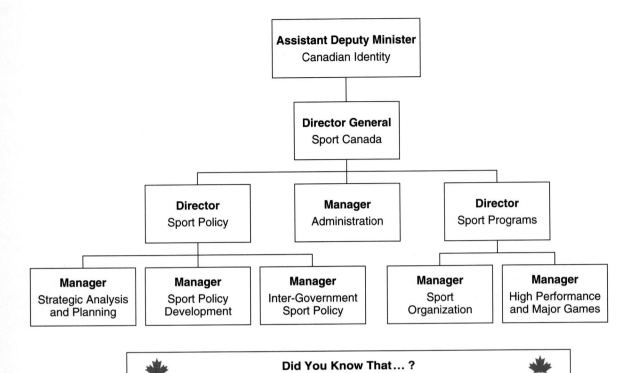

FIGURE 13–5   Sport Canada's organizational structure.

for all Canadians from coast-to-coast-to-coast (*COA Annual Report,* 1997, p. 2).

This is the mission statement of the COA. It is a not-for-profit, nongovernmental organization, the second largest contributor of financial assistance to Canadian athletes, coaches, and sport organizations (next to the federal government). The COA is governed by a volunteer board of directors and has thirty-five employees located in regional offices across Canada. In 1997, the COA generated over $7 million, primarily from marketing initiatives in sponsorship, licensing, and special events, and spent over $11 million on athletes, national sport organizations, and sporting events (*COA Annual Report,* 1997, p. 8). It also is responsible for the Canadian Olympic Foundation, which manages several segregated funds in excess of $100 million.

The role of the Calgary Olympic Development Association (CODA).

Committing to the legacy of the 1988 Calgary Olympic Games to the complete development of Canadian Olympic Winter sport athletes. (*CODA Annual Report,* 1998, inside cover)

As indicated in its mission statement, the **Calgary Olympic Development Association's** primary responsibility is to winter sport athletes and organizations. In 1998, CODA's revenues exceeded $200 million (*CODA Annual Report,* 1998). The CODA board of directors has grown the 1988 Olympic Games legacy from $80 million to $200 million in a decade and will contribute to the support of winter sport athletes and facilities even more substantially for the coming decade. The organization is now in discussions with the COA to look at more ways to collaborate to better serve Canadian athletes.

The role of the Coaching Association of Canada (CAC). Established in 1971, the CAC has the mission to "enhance the experience of all Canadian athletes through quality coaching" (CAC website). This mission is achieved by: establishing education, training, and ethical standards for coaching in Canada; improving the development and delivery of the 3M National Coaching Certification Program; creating a national, self-regulated, professional association that advocates on behalf of the coaching profession and establishes, promotes, and enforces the professional standards set by its members; and encouraging the marketplace to support more paid coaching positions.

The 3M National Coaching Certification Program, one of the major programs of the CAC, provides information and training to promote coaching excellence and establishes minimum behavioral standards for active coaches. The program is designed to increase knowledge about general theory, provide technical information, and transfer knowledge to practice through experiential learning. Levels 1 through 3 of the NCCP teach fundamentals for coaches at the community, regional, and provincial sport levels. Levels 4 and 5 are aimed at coaches developing athletes for national and international competition.

Through the 3M National Coaching Certification Program, coaches have been certified in every province and territory. Between 1994 and 1996 over 150,000 coaches were certified in Canada, and almost 20,000 theory and technical courses were offered (The Contribution of Coaching in Canada, 1998, p. 22).

The roles of national and provincial sport organizations. There are approximately sixty national sport organizations (NSOs) in Canada, each serving a different sport (e.g., Basketball Canada, Tennis Canada). Each of these not-for-profit organizations has a twofold mandate to provide Canadians with opportunities to participate (participation development) and to support the development of high-performance athletes (high-performance development). High performance means that the athlete is skilled enough to be able to compete at a national or an international level. Almost all of these organizations received financial support from

the federal government in the 1970s and 1980s, but less than half are now eligible. Generally, if the NSOs can produce athletes who bring home medals from international competitions, they are supported by government funding.

Each NSO is governed by a volunteer board of directors, generally comprised of people who represent each province or region across the country, and often the board will have representation from members of the business community who are well connected and can assist with revenue generation. The role of these governing boards is to make policy decisions that will provide a framework for those within the organization to work toward common goals. In reality, what often happens is that boards become tangled up in the technical aspects of the sport (e.g., who should be on the national team) and lose sight of their respective mandates as "trustees of the game." The memberships of NSOs are generally comprised of each province, and each pays a membership fee based on population size. Some NSO memberships are based on "regional" boundaries rather than provincial boundaries, and still others have individual or club-based memberships at the national level.

NSOs have differing staff complements. Generally, all have an executive director, general manager, or chief executive officer who reports directly to the board and who is responsible for carrying out the policy decisions of the board through his or her staff. Other staff positions in a national office could include national coaches, technical directors, and program coordinators (e.g., coaching, competitions). Staff sizes range from less than five to greater than fifty for organizations such as the Canadian Figure Skating Association and Tennis Canada.

CONCEPT CHECK

It is the role of each national sport organization to address both the development of high-performance athletes and to increase participation. Often the organization's role in high performance takes precedence, sometimes at the expense of growing the sport and making it accessible for all Canadians.

Each NSO in Canada is governed by an international sport federation, which establishes the rules of the sport and, among other things, determines

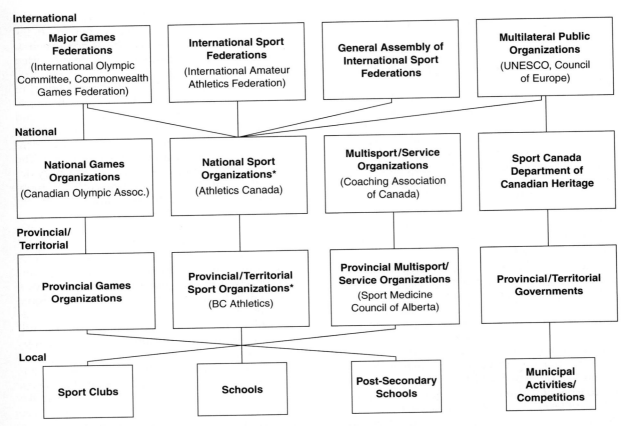

International

| Major Games Federations (International Olympic Committee, Commonwealth Games Federation) | International Sport Federations (International Amateur Athletics Federation) | General Assembly of International Sport Federations | Multilateral Public Organizations (UNESCO, Council of Europe) |

National

| National Games Organizations (Canadian Olympic Assoc.) | National Sport Organizations* (Athletics Canada) | Multisport/Service Organizations (Coaching Association of Canada) | Sport Canada Department of Canadian Heritage |

Provincial/ Territorial

| Provincial Games Organizations | Provincial/Territorial Sport Organizations* (BC Athletics) | Provincial Multisport/ Service Organizations (Sport Medicine Council of Alberta) | Provincial/Territorial Governments |

Local

| Sport Clubs | Schools | Post-Secondary Schools | Municipal Activities/ Competitions |

*Also includes associations for athletes with disabilities (e.g., Canadian Blind Sport Association)

FIGURE 13–6 The Canadian sport community infrastructure. Organizations in parentheses are cited as examples.

where its respective international competitions will be held. There are also a number of other national sport organizations with which each NSO needs to communicate (figure 13–6).

Each NSO has a provincial counterpart, and some have associations in the North West Territories and the Yukon. It is the mandate of each **provincial sport organization (PSO)** to provide participation opportunities and athlete development opportunities for the people in its province. Just as the national mandate of the NSO is often skewed more toward high-performance development (sometimes at the expense of participation development), so are the activities of the PSOs (e.g., Ontario Tennis Association, Athletics Ontario). A strong focus on participation or grassroots development is a difficult, time-consuming,

and resource-consuming commitment, and the results are not immediate, which discourages many PSO boards from fully realizing their mandates in this area.

The memberships of PSOs are most often comprised of community sport clubs, be they private or public. Each club pays a fee to access the programs and services of the PSO, and this fee is usually based on the number of members in that club. Ironically, in some provinces, the relationship between the PSO and its member clubs is competitive rather than collaborative. This is an issue that can have many negative ramifications for that sport.

Community sport organizations. There are hundreds of thousands of community sport clubs across Canada, and they comprise the heart of the amateur sport system. Without community sport, there would be no sport. It is here that children are exposed to the sport experience for the first time, and the extent to which that experience is positive and will have an impact on that child for the rest of his or her life. Community sport organizations are generally volunteer-driven, usually by a small group of dedicated people or sometimes by one community champion. Interestingly enough, although there are often several sport clubs or minor sport organizations in one small town, seldom do they join forces to advocate or to generate revenue. Further, seldom is there collaboration with the parks and recreation department or recreation director in that town, both of whom are providing sport programs and services. School sport is the other major sport delivery partner at the community level, and too often schools have parallel sport systems that do not communicate with sport clubs or parks and recreation. The impact that this is having on the system is huge. Many precious resources and programs are being duplicated.

Sport participation in Canada

In 1992, Statistics Canada found that 9,600,000 Canadians aged fifteen and older participate regularly in sports, while 4,400,000 of these participate through sports clubs or organizations. The Canadian sport system supports 3,000,000 registered athletes of national and provincial sport organizations, 850 carded high-performance athletes, 400,000 coaches, and 1,000,000 volunteers (strengthening the Canadian sport system, 1998, p. 23).

It was also found that men were more likely to report regular participation in a sport. One-third more men than women participated regularly. Twice as many men participated through clubs, leagues, recreation programs, and provincial sport organizations (strengthening the Canadian sport system, 1998).

Forty percent of people participating regularly in sport are between the ages of 15 and 34, while 34 percent are between the ages of 35 and 54 and 26 percent are in their retirement or preretirement years.

The ten most popular sport activities for men are: hockey, golf, baseball, alpine skiing, tennis, volleyball, cross country skiing, soccer, and softball. The ten most popular women's sports are: swimming, alpine skiing, cross country skiing, volleyball, golf, bowling, baseball, tennis, basketball, and badminton.

Hockey, baseball, soccer, and swimming are the most popular activities among young boys. For younger girls, swimming was the most popular activity, followed by baseball, soccer, gymnastics, and alpine skiing.

Many factors influence sport participation. Research on Canadian children has found that the following factors have a positive influence on children's participation: fun, learning and skill improvement, being with friends, success and winning, and physical fitness and health. Children drop out of sport due to competitive stress, parental pressure, lack of fun, lack of playing time, limited opportunities for improvement, and/or dislike of the coach (The contribution of coaching in Canada, 1998, p. 24).

A time for change in the Canadian sport system: Beyond 2000

The Canadian sport system has made a number of significant strides over the past thirty years. Its stability over that period of time, due to a steady flow of government dollars, made it the envy of most other countries. The achievements of organizations like the Canadian Figure Skating Association and the internationally acclaimed National Coaching Certification Program attest to the success of the system. More recently, the use of a partnered approach to implement a multisport high-performance system and an influx of new monies from the federal government to support disabled sport are evidence of continued commitment and forward thinking.

However, there are many issues plaguing the Canadian sport system. From a high-performance perspective, Canadian athletes and teams have not been dominating the national and international scene, even in hockey, which has always been used as a barometer of success. The sport community has not been able to replace these funds through other sources, and consequently it has had less money to support athlete development as well as grassroots development.

The sport delivery system overall is still structured in a very redundant and isolated fashion. Each NSO and PSO as well as many community sport clubs are trying to operate exclusively rather than collaborating with other sport organizations or community groups to reduce costs and improve service.

Many sport organizations are still overly dependent on government support and look to government officials to provide leadership and policy direction, still not understanding that sport's priorities are not necessarily the government's priorities. The following chart indicates some of the paradigm shifts that need to take place if the Canadian sport system is to continue to grow and prosper.

Paradigm shifts needed in the Canadian amateur sport system

Element	From	To
Structure	centralized	decentralized
Funding	single funding source (public)	diversified funding sources (public and private)
Leadership	government-directed	sport-directed
Policy-Making	government-centered	sport-centered
Delivery System	vertical and duplicative	partnered and cost-efficient

---

So what can be done to improve the Canadian sport system?

John Bales, president of the Coaching Association of Canada, identified three issues that need to be addressed:

- The current partnership between sport and government is vague and confusing.
- The current organization of sport is ineffective.
- There is a void in national leadership for sport (Strengthening the Canadian sport system, 1998, pp. 4–5).

Canada's high-performance athletes and their coaches have pointed to facility access as a primary need. Sport Canada and such organizations as the Canadian Olympic Association, the Coaching Association of Canada, the Calgary Olympic Development Association, and the provincial governments, have joined forces to create six multisport training centers across Canada. The creation of these centers is one of the most promising consequences of the growing acceptance by Canada's sport leadership that the key to survival is partnership.

The centers are meant to provide athletes with all of the services that they may need, to support athletes in the regions where they live, and to create an environment that attracts the best coaches and experts. Although the centers network is now operational, Bayles notes that the need for new facilities has not been addressed as the budgets for the centers just cover annual operational costs, not facility development. He recommends that the federal government commit $50 million per year for a five-year period to sport facility construction and upgrading (Strengthening, 1998, p. 7).

Sport Canada, the federal agency responsible for providing funds to NSOs, now restricts its funding to thirty-eight organizations (down from sixty-three organizations in the late 1980s), leaving almost half of Canada's national sport organizations in financial limbo with no link to the national system. Sport Canada's budget of approximately 60 million is a minor investment in a system that addresses so many of the government's priority issues. Bayles recommended that Sport Canada's budget be increased by $40 million to $100 million annually.

CONCEPT CHECK

The amateur sport delivery system in Canada is in need of a major overhaul. NSOs and PSOs, as well as many community sport clubs, deliver their sport programs to the same target populations and often end up competing with each other rather than looking at ways to work collaboratively toward common goals, saving time and money.

The Canadian sport system needs to become self-led. The current leadership has become too dependent on government to define its future. While this was a necessary and desirable relationship in the early years of the development of the Canadian system, it is time for the children to leave the home of the parents and start fending for themselves. This is not to say that governments should not continue as funding partners for NSOs and PSOs, but the sport system needs to establish its own leadership structure, make policy decisions, and decide what the best use of its collective resources is. To this end, Bayles recommended that a Canadian Sport Confederation be established that would take over the consultative and programming function of

Sport Canada and assume responsibility for the delivery of technical sport programs, including national sport centers, coaching, sports information, sport science and medicine, and athlete assistance services (Strengthening, 1998, p. 9). He also advocates for the creation of multisport clubs at the community level, to provide more services to more people at less cost.

So far, Bayles's recommendations have yet to be implemented. The health of the Canadian amateur sport system will depend upon the willingness of sport organizations and their potential partners to let go of the past and grab hold of the future, collectively growing sport for athletes and participants alike.

CRITICAL THINKING EXERCISES

1. What are the major similarities and differences between the governance of interscholastic athletics and intercollegiate athletics?
2. If Paris and Lyon, two French cities, are interested in bidding to host the 2008 Olympic Games, what national Olympic committee will be responsible for appointing one of the two as the bid city?
3. How many IOC members could Japan have at most?
4. Should government subsidize not-for-profit sport organizations? Many people think that government should continue to fund, others disagree, feeling the public dollars would best be spent in other areas. What do you think and why?
5. How does the Canadian sport system need to change to reduce the duplication of resources and to better serve both athletes and recreational participants?

SUMMARY

1. The public school system in the United States made obtaining an education possible for all citizens, and school sports were viewed as a powerful tool for formulating the kinds of attitudes and behaviors associated with effective citizenship.
2. State high school athletic associations strive to regulate and standardize competition between schools through the enforcement of eligibility rules and other rules governing competition between schools.
3. High school sport programs are the largest dimension in the entire sport enterprise, with over 17,000 high schools being members of the National Federation of State High School Associations and over six million male and female athletes competing in interscholastic competition.
4. The governance of interscholastic athletic competition involves individual schools, athletic conference, state athletic associations, and the National Federation of State High School Associations cooperating to ensure effective governance of interscholastic competition.
5. The majority of the state associations exist for the purpose of providing uniform standards for athletic competition within their states; offering state championships; ensuring that athletic competition is fair, safe; and sportsmanlike; and providing an environment that emphasizes the overall development of the participants.
6. Even with a comprehensive governance structure in place, the administration of high school athletics is primarily conducted on the local level. The local schools must recognize and operate within the rules established by the state association.
7. A school board is a body made up of individuals living within the boundaries of a school district that has the authority to approve budgets, determines the feasibility and allocation of resources for the building of athletic facilities, votes on the hiring and firing of athletic department personnel, and votes to establish policies for the school district's athletic programs.
8. In its earliest stages, students administered intercollegiate athletics, and this arrangement was satisfactory with administrators until the athletic operations on campuses became so large that the students could no longer control them. Faculties expressed concern and took action with the creation of the faculty athletic committees that oversaw athletics at institutions.
9. Early attempts at inter-institutional governance were not successful, but ultimately a national inter-institutional body was created in the form of the NCAA. The

NCAA increased its influence by mandating rules of play, offering educational material and meetings, offering administrative recommendations for athletic programs, instituting championship play in 1921, awarding financial incentives, and encouraging United States Olympic team participation.

10. The NCAA became a regulatory body with the power to investigate abuses of and enforce the NCAA rules and punish offenders in 1952.

11. The member institutions of the NCAA are diverse, with different educational missions, enrollments, and athletic philosophies. To address the diverse interests, the NCAA created three divisions, each with its own philosophy, criteria for membership, and governance structure.

12. The NCAA constitution has thirty-three articles that serve as its basis for governance.

13. Fourteen of the articles serve as the organization's operating bylaws. A bylaw can either be a dominant, a division-dominant, a common, or a federated provision.

14. In 1996, the NCAA was restructured to give more autonomy to the three divisions.

15. In all three NCAA divisions, there is a committee structure that assists in the governance of the division. The committees consist of presidents, athletic directors, faculty athletic representatives, coaches, and student athletes.

16. The NCAA national office is not involved in the creation of legislation, but rather serves the members of the organization. The national office is headed by an executive director and is divided into the following departments: Championships, Education Services, Enforcement and Eligibility Appeals, Finance and Business Services, Membership Services, and Public Affairs.

17. An intercollegiate athletic conference usually consists of institutions with the same institutional and academic missions and the same level of commitment to athletics that are located in the same geographic region.

18. Institutions belonging to a conference must adhere to the rules established by the conference. The rules that the conference establishes may be more stringent than those established by the NCAA, but they cannot be less stringent.

19. Due to financial considerations, it has been commonplace for institutions to change conferences or to decide to join one. It has also been commonplace for institutions to overlook the geographic considerations when joining a conference.

20. The NCAA placed the responsibility for the conduct of the athletic program in the hands of the president of each institution. Governance on campus must include a faculty athletics representative and a student athlete advisory board. An institution may choose to create an athletic board to be involved in governance.

21. The National League established a precedent for all professional sport leagues because it was an owner-controlled league and the players were employees.

22. Two key elements of the governance of early professional baseball were the salary cap and the reserve clause. The owners viewed these as means to ensuring the financial viability of the league and its member teams.

23. The governance structures for the four major professional sport leagues are very similar. Each league has a commissioner, a board of governance or committee structure consisting of the owners and front office personnel of the franchises, and a league office.

24. The commissioner and the league office are responsible for running the day-to-day operations of the league. The commissioner, who is an employee of the owners, and the league office handle the scheduling of contests, oversee the umpires and referees, administer special events like All-Star games and championships, fine and suspend players for breaking league rules, conduct public relations, advertising and marketing for the league as a whole, implement licensing agreements.

25. Through a committee structure, the owners propose rules and rule changes, vote on expansion and franchise relocation, negotiate the league's network broadcast contracts, and represent management in contract negotiations with the players' unions.

26. This chapter addressed the Olympic movement as a model of international sport management. Sport is a global business. In becoming a better sport manager, one must not limit one's knowledge to the domestic

arena. Because we are involved in a global economy, it is important for the sport manager of the future to understand the globalization of sport. The Olympic movement is probably the best example of this globalization. Specifically, the focus has been on the Olympic movement because the Olympic Games are often used as a model for international sporting events. It is important to understand the structure of the Olympic movement, including the International Olympic Committee, the national Olympic committees, the international federations, the national governing bodies or national federations, and the organizing committees of the Olympic Games. Specifically, we have described the United States Olympic Committee for its role in the Olympic movement and its reputation as the most developed NOC in the world.

27. The Canadian sport system was created by the federal government in the early 1960s.
28. After 1970 a number of national sport and multisport organizations came into being, including the Coaching Association of Canada, Hockey Canada, and ParticipACTION.
29. Although government funding of sport increased steadily through the seventies and eighties, drastic cuts took place in the 1990s when the government was questioning the significance of sport's contributions to its objectives and in light of the focus on reducing the deficit.
30. National sport organizations are not-for-profit agencies governed by volunteer boards of directors that use government funds and other revenue sources to serve their members.
31. The sport system in Canada is based on a bureaucratic structure that is duplicative and competitive, often not providing the best service to athletes or participants.
32. Changes need to be made in the Canadian system to reduce this duplication and help NSOs to better serve their mandates in high-performance athlete development and participation development.

CASE STUDY I

East State University, an NCAA Division I institution, has been a member of the Large Eastern Athletic Conference since its inception in 1950. East State, which annually fields an outstanding football team, also fields twenty-one intercollegiate athletic teams and has a reputation of being an outstanding academic institution. ESU annually wins the LEAC football championship, because the fellow LEAC institutions field weak football teams. Only four times in the past ten years has a LEAC institution besides ESU gone to a bowl game. The LEAC is better known for the academic reputation of its members than their athletic reputation. ESU has been successful in several other male and female sports, but is not known for competitive men's or women's basketball programs.

The Middle West Athletic Conference is interested in having ESU join its conference so it can have two six-team divisions and have a conference championship football game. The MWAC is perennially the strongest football and basketball conference in the country, often sending four or five teams to bowl games as well as six or seven teams to both the NCAA men's and women's basketball tournaments. If ESU joined the MWAC, the closest conference school would be 400 miles away and the farthest 1,000 miles. The MWAC consists of large universities with strong commitments to athletics, but with less than reputable academic traditions.

As a member of the ESU athletic board, you have a vote on whether ESU joins the MWCA or not. How would you vote? Please weigh the pros and cons of the decision and offer the rationale for why you would vote the way you would.

CASE STUDY II

The board members of the Fédération Internationale des Quilleurs (International Bowling Federation) have decided in their last meeting to pursue the inclusion of bowling in the Olympic program. They understand that such effort will take some years. You, as the executive director of the Fédération Internationale des Quilleurs, have been asked to put together a long-term plan with the objective to have bowling be included in the Olympic program. What steps will you need to follow in order to have bowling be included in the Olympic program? What are the International Olympic Committee requirements for a sport to be included in the Olympic program? When will you present the request to the International Olympic Committee? What would be the first Games in which bowling could be included as an Olympic sport?

CASE STUDY III

To lead the growth of tennis and foster the pursuit of excellence for all players.

This is the mission statement of Tennis Canada. As the chief executive officer of this national sport organization, you have been concerned about participation in the sport. Club membership numbers have stayed much the same over the past several years, and although clubs are serving their members well, it is important for Tennis Canada to play a role in growing the game.

You commissioned a study to find out how many people were playing tennis in Canada and where they were playing. Upon completion of this market research, it became clear that a significant number of people were playing tennis but that most of them were being introduced to the sport on public courts provided by parks and recreation departments, outside of the tennis club "family." In fact, about two-thirds of the adults and half of the children who had played tennis at least once in the past year had played in the summer on public courts. You know that the tennis club system has little communication with the municipal parks and recreation system, and that in some communities, due to funding cuts, parks and recreation departments are not maintaining some public tennis courts or continuing their tennis programming. Also, some municipalities do not offer tennis because they do not have qualified instructors in the community.

Given this information, and your knowledge of the sport system in Canada, what actions might you take to ensure that Tennis Canada fulfills its role in stimulating participation and growing the game?

REVIEW QUESTIONS AND ISSUES

1. For what reasons do state interscholastic athletic associations exist?
2. What is the role of a school board in the governance of interscholastic competition?
3. How did the NCAA increase its influence over the governance of intercollegiate athletics between 1906 and 1948, and what steps were taken to make the NCAA a regulatory body in 1952?
4. Compare and contrast the philosophies of NCAA Divisions I, II, and III.
5. Define a dominant provision, a division-dominant provision, a common provision, and a federated provision.
6. With the restructuring that occurred in the NCAA in 1996, discuss the differences in the governance structures among the three NCAA divisions.
7. What are the criteria for intercollegiate athletic conference membership, and what have been the potential rationales for institutions joining or switching conference affiliation in the 1990s?
8. Define the role of the NCAA membership and the national office in the governance of intercollegiate athletics.
9. What are the components of governance within an NCAA institution?
10. What impact did Pete Rozelle as NFL commissioner have on the modern professional sport landscape?
11. For what innovation is David Stern, commissioner of the NBA, responsible? How did it help save the NBA from financial difficulties?
12. What issues does a collective bargaining agreement address?
13. Define the Olympic movement.
14. Discuss the relationship among the International Olympic Committee, international federations, national Olympic committees, and organizing committees of the Olympic Games.
15. Name your national Olympic committee and define its organizational structure.
16. Name the two international sport competitions for which the United States Olympic Committee is responsible according to the 1978 Amateur Sport Act.
17. Not all the international federations are part of the Olympic program. Do you see it as an advantage or a disadvantage to be part of the Olympic program?
18. Why did the Canadian federal government decide to use public funds to support sport?
19. What year was Bill C-131 enacted to encourage both fitness and amateur sport development?
20. When did the Canadian government decide to reduce funding to sport organizations and why?
21. In addition to the federal government, what other organizations play a role in funding athlete development?

22. For what program is the Coaching Association of Canada known internationally? What does this program provide?
23. How does a national sport organization link with its community clubs to deliver its programs?
24. What types of paradigm shifts need to be made in the Canadian sport system and why?
25. What is the mandate of the proposed "Canadian Sport Confederation"?

SOLUTIONS TO CRITICAL THINKING EXERCISES

1. Similarities: Both governance structures are set up to be representative democracies. The members have a voice in the rules that are created, adopted, and enforced by governing bodies.

   Differences: At the intercollegiate level, a great deal of governance power is at the national level with the NCAA. The bylaws created by the NCAA membership are practiced and enforced by a national governing body. In the case of interscholastic governance, the national governing body is not a legislative body. The state athletic associations have a greater influence over the governance of athletics in individual states.

2. Since Paris and Lyon are both in France, the French Olympic Committee, *Comité National Olympique et Sportif Français,* will have the authority to designate the city as a candidate to host the 2008 Olympic Games.

3. The IOC can elect a maximum of one member in a country. However, in those countries in which either the Games of the Olympiad or the Olympic Winter Games have been held, the IOC may elect a second member. Since Japan has been the host of the Games of the 1964 Olympiad, the 1972 Winter Games in Sapporo, and the 1998 Winter Games in Nagano, it can have two IOC members.

4. Government departments and agencies fund organizations that provide services and do things that the government wants done. Often, these are services that the government feels are important but which it cannot deliver, so it delegates the job to voluntary organizations. The not-for-profit sport organization receives public funds with strict funding guidelines attached. This often puts the sport organization at the mercy of changes in government policies and programs, leaving it in a very precarious financial position.

   The government may even try to interfere in the sport organization's management on the grounds that the money comes from the public purse and the government therefore has a duty to be involved in the organization's day-to-day administration. Sport leaders ought not to accept such interference. For while it is natural that they should be accountable to their members, they should not be accountable to the state, which is not a member.

   On the other hand, sport is an important part of the cultural fabric of our society and pivotal in maintaining our national identity. It is government's responsibility to support those organizations that contribute to these areas. Government funding provides the seed, the starting point, from which sport organizations can reach out and gain wider individual and business support.

   Governments should be involved in supporting the sport system in Canada. However, sport organizations have been overly dependent on government funding for too long. Sport leaders need to diversify their sources of income and their services and find ways to increase their self-financing in order to be less dependent on government funding and less vulnerable to the changing political winds.

5. The structure of the sport system in Canada is very bureaucratic, and as such it is subject to many layers of administration and duplication. Each national sport organization has its own delivery system for its programs and services, and more often than not, all are trying to reach the same target markets at the same time. From a high-performance perspective, each NSO has independently trained its own national-level athletes. From a participation development perspective, a single high school or elementary school might have at least a dozen sport organizations that want to reach children with their programs. It is difficult for a school principal or physical education teacher to respond to all of these requests or

to make decisions about what is best to offer the child. Sometimes the education leader will just reject all requests because it is too time-consuming to sort out the advantages and disadvantages of each proposal.

It is a similar situation between the sport system and the municipal recreation system in Canada. Both offer sport programs, but often there is very little communication between sport leaders and recreation leaders, so often both end up offering the same services in a community when resources and energies could be combined.

REFERENCES

Association of National Olympic Committees. (1998). *Year-book 1998.*

Baker, W. J. (1988). *Sports in the western world.* Rev. ed. Urbana, IL: University of Illinois Press.

Barr, C. A. (1998). Collegiate sport. In *Principles and practices of sport management.* Gaithersburg, MD: Aspen Publishing.

Byers, W. (1995). *Unsportsmanlike conduct: Exploiting college athletes.* Ann Arbor, MI: The University of Michigan Press.

Calgary Olympic Development Association. (1998). *Annual Report.* Calgary, Alberta: CODA.

Canadian Olympic Association. (1997). *Annual Report.* Toronto, Ontario: COA.

The contribution of coaching in Canada. (1998). *Coaches Report, 5* (2), 18–24.

Covell, D. (1998). High school and youth sports. In *Principles and practices of sport management.* Gaithersburg, MD: Aspen Publishing.

Davenport, J. (1985). From crew to commercialism—the paradox of sport in higher education. In D. Chu, J. Seagrave, and B. Becker (eds.), *Sport in higher education* (pp. 5–14). Champaign, IL: Human Kinetics.

Fox, S. (1994). *Big leagues: Professional baseball, football, and basketball in national memory.* New York: William Morrow.

Gorman, J., and Calhoun, K. (1994). *The name of the game.* New York: Ernst and Young.

Greenberg, M. J. (1992). *Sport law practice.* Charlotteville, VA: Michie.

Halberstam, D. (1999). *Playing for keeps: Michael Jordan and the world he made.* New York: Random House.

Helyar, J. (1994). *The lords of the realm: The real history of baseball.* New York: Villiard.

International Olympic Committee. (1997). *The Olympic Charter.* Lausanne, Switzerland: IOC.

International Olympic Committee. (1998). 1998 Broadcast analysis report: Preliminary results. *Olympic Marketing Matters,* (13), (Summer 1998), 6.

King, P. (1996). *Football: A history of the professional game.* New York: Sports Illustrated.

Lewis, G. (1969). Teddy Roosevelt's role in the 1905 football controversy. *Research Quarterly, 40,* 717–24.

Liberman, N. (1999). TV partners provide juice to websites. *Street & Smith's SportBusiness Journal, 2,* (3), 21.

Macintosh, D., and Bedecki, T. (1987). *Sport and politics in Canada.* Kingston, Ontario: McGill-Queens University Press.

Macintosh, D., and Whitson, D. (1990). *The game planners.* Kingston, Ontario: McGill-Queens University Press.

Michner, J. (1976). *Sports in America.* Greenwich, CT: Fawcett Crest Books.

Miller, M. (1991). *A whole different ballgame.* New York: Fireside.

Minister of State, Fitness and Amateur Sport. (1992). *Sport the way ahead.* Ottawa, Ministry of Supply and Services, Canada.

National Collegiate Athletic Association. (1997). *1998–99 NCAA Division III Manual.* Shawnee Mission, KS: NCAA.

National Collegiate Athletic Association. (1998a). *1997–98 NCAA Annual Reports.* Shawnee Mission, KS: NCAA.

National Collegiate Athletic Association. (1998b). *1997–98 NCAA Manual.* Shawnee Mission, KS: NCAA.

National Collegiate Athletic Association. (1998c). *1998 NCAA Financial Report.* Shawnee Mission, KS: NCAA.

Nelson, D. (1982). Administrators' views of athletic governance. In J. Frey (ed.), *The governance of intercollegiate athletics* (pp. 49–57). West Point, NY: Leisure Press.

O'Hanlon, T. P. (1995). School sports as social training: The case of athletics and the crisis of World War I. In D. K. Wiggins (ed.), *Sport in America: From wicked amusement to national obsession* (pp. 189–206). Champaign, IL: Human Kinetics.

Ozanian, M. K. (1998). Selective accounting. *Forbes* (December 14, 1998), *124* (1).

Sack, A. L., and Staurowsky, E. J. (1998). *College athletes for hire: The evolution and legacy of the NCAA's amateur myth.* Westport, CT: Praeger.

Savage, H. J. (1929). *American college athletics.* New York: The Carnegie Foundation for the Advancement of Teaching.

Smith, R. A. (1995). Preludes to the NCAA: Early failures of faculty intercollegiate athletic control. In D. K. Wiggins (ed.), *Sport in America: From wicked amusement to national obsession* (pp. 151–62). Champaign, IL: Human Kinetics.

Sport Canada. (1996). *Status of the High Performance Athlete Survey.* Ekos Research Associates Inc.

Sport Ontario. (1992). *For the love of sport.* Toronto, Ontario: Ministry of Tourism and Recreation.

Stern, R. (1979). The development of an intercollegiate central network: The case of intercollegiate athletics. *Administrative Science Quarterly, 24,* 242–66.

Strengthening the Canadian sport system. (1998). *Coaches Report, 5* (2), 4–11.

Sutton, W., and Gladden, J. (1998). Professional sport. In J. B. Parks, B. R. K. Zanger, and J. Quarterman (eds.), *Contemporary sport management* (243–62). Champaign, IL: Human Kinetics.

Thoma, J., and Chalip, L. (1996). Sport governance in the global community. Morgantown, WV: Fitness Information Technology.

Tow, T. C. (1982). The governance role of the NCAA. In J. Frey (ed.), *The governance of intercollegiate athletics* (pp. 108–16). West Point, NY: Leisure Press.

United States Olympic Committee. (1997). *97/98 Fact Book.* Colorado Springs, CO: USOC.

United States Olympic Committee. (1999). *Olympic Beat 14* (4), (May 1999).

VanderZwag, H. J. (1998). *Policy development in sport management.* 2d ed. Westport, CT: Praeger.

Wissot, Michael. (1999). Swinging for foreign fences is new "international pastime." *Street & Smith's SportBusiness Journal, 2,* (2), 40.

WEBSITES

The National Collegiate Athletic Association
www.ncaa.org
This site is where the nation's colleges and universities speak and act on athletic matters at the national level.

International Olympic Committee
www.olympic.org
Students planning to pursue a career in the international sport marketplace can use the information available in this website to become more knowledgeable about the governance of international sport.

United States Olympic Committee
www.olympic-usa.org
Students planning to pursue a career in the Olympics can look at this website and find out more about the United States Olympic Committee, considered the most developed NOC in the world.

Sport Canada, Department of Canadian Heritage
www.pch.gc.ca/sportcanada/
This site describes Sport Canada's mandate, structure, programs, and policies. It also overviews the sport system in Canada, major games and sporting events, and selected "sport facts." For information on specific Canadian sport organizations there is a link with the majority of sport and multisport organizations in the country.

Coaching Association of Canada
www.coach.ca
This site describes the mission and major programs of the CAC, including the 3M National Coaching Certification Program and other related programs. There is a link to the Canadian Professional Coaches Association, as well as information about "coaching tips," conferences, and seminars.

PART IV

Facilities

CHAPTER 14

Managing the Facility

Aaron Mulrooney and Peter Farmer

In this chapter, you will become familiar with the following terms:

In-house
Request for proposals (RFP)
Mission statement
Booking
Tentative-hold reservations
Contracted reservation
Boilerplate contract
Promoter
Earned media
Respondeat superior
Event coordinator

Housekeeping
Setup and breakdown
Walk-up sales
Will-call location
Performance scale
Point of sale
Private seat license (PSL)
Stocking
Convenience foods
Vendors
Hawkers

Bootleggers
Budget cycle
Generally accepted accounting
   practices (GAAP)
Event settlement
House expenses
Internal auditing process
External audit
Standard operating procedures
   (SOPs)

Overview

Professional management can influence the supply of sports events and well-organized services, and provide the patron with an enjoyable time. Management philosophy will determine the number and type of staff, as well as the extent of services provided in-house as opposed to those that are contracted out. The quality of management for major sport facilities can determine the ability of the facility to attract and retain tenants. Income and profitability for the facility owner, staffing requirements, building condition, and service levels (fan comfort) also are affected by management. This chapter will investigate the various types of facility management and the major components of the management team.

TYPES OF MANAGEMENT

There are a number of management alternatives: those operated by their owners, by the primary or anchor tenants, by not-for-profit entities, or by private management companies.

Owner

This management organization may be public or private (Laventhol and Horwath, 1989). If owned or operated by a government agency, operational efficiency is constrained or reduced by the regulations and procedures that are often associated with governmental bureaucracy. Such items as purchasing procedures; contract approval processes (often by the legislative body); hiring, promotion, and dismissal of personnel; and other government policies (including just plain politics, such as patronage) are just a few of the operational performance areas of the building that are affected by bureaucracy. To alleviate this situation, many publicly owned facilities have moved toward independent authorities, such as not-for-profit operations and private management companies (Laventhol and Horwath, 1989).

The main problems facing privately owned and managed facilities are enormous costs and human resources. Because of these burdens, many privately owned facilities have opted to move toward not-for-profit operations and private management companies.

Not-for-profit operations

These entities generally involve a commission or a board of directors, appointed by a governmental body to act as an agent of the local government (Laventhol and Horwath, 1989). This board is exempted from numerous government regulations and procedures in order to run an efficient facility. Over time, however, the quality of the board may deteriorate as political patronage and reputation become standard operating procedure.

Private management: The future alternative

Although sport facilities have traditionally been owned and governed by public authorities, the situation appears to be changing. Sport facilities were originally designed as a community economic-impact entity, but many facilities have become a drain on community resources. In difficult economic times, this burden on the taxpayer can be significant.

If a facility has significant problems or is unable to realize its managers' expectations, alternative management organizations, other than an **in-house** group, should be considered. One of these alternatives is private management. This type of management enables the governmental or institutional entity to maintain control over the facility, but with the opportunity to:

- Reduce or eliminate an operating deficit
- Offer patrons improved service
- Increase the quantity and quality of the events booked
- Become part of a larger facility network, which would facilitate greater opportunities
- Provide greater operational flexibility concerning policies and overall operational structure

These advantages have enabled this facility management alternative to experience dramatic growth over the past decade. It is interesting to note that a number of different types of management groups—ranging from hotels, to food service groups, to specialty facility management groups have entered this competitive arena. Each of these management groups evaluates a facility's needs based on its current financial picture, staffing requirements, marketing needs, event scheduling, and the political situation.

PRIVATE-MANAGEMENT SELECTION PROCESS

After resolving any obvious internal problems and disagreements, the facility's governing body will initiate the private-management selection process. The first step is the issuance of a **request for proposals (RFP)** (IAAM, 1990). This formal process begins with the issuance of statements outlining what is expected from a contracted management organization. Materials should be attached to provide the responding management organization with an overall picture of the facility's present situation. Such items as long- and short-term plans and projections, actual and projected budget and income, annual and usage reports, and existing contracts should be included.

The second step is dispatching the RFP document to all major management groups, as well as prominently displaying it in all appropriate trade and professional publications. The RFP bid response period varies from thirty to ninety days, depending upon conditions. The RFP also should indicate whether the bid will be a public process, open to the press, and whether bid proposals will be available to competitors (IAAM, 1990).

Third, all interested participants/bidders will be provided with a facility tour and an in-depth examination of the RFP. Addenda will be prepared as a result of the meeting between bidders and the facility's governing body.

Fourth, all proposals that are received before the deadline are reviewed by a designated body and finalists are determined. All bidders will be notified as to their success or failure in the bidding process. The finalists are provided with an opportunity to give a personal presentation to the review body. At this stage, the bidders have the right to know about their competition and the stage of the decision process. It is important that flexibility be part of the process, because bidders sometimes need to change their proposals as new information becomes available.

Fifth, following the personal presentations, one bidder should be selected to proceed into the negotiation stage, which involves representatives from both groups as well as legal assistance. Negotiations are initiated through a written document based on the RFP and the proposal. An agreement is apparent when there is resolution of the differences between these two documents.

The final (approval) stage comes at the end of the negotiation phase, when the final authority (e.g., the commission or state legislature) approves the contract (IAAM, 1990).

CONCEPT CHECK

Although many facilities are managed by their owners or by not-for-profit governmental agencies, the current trend is toward contracting with private management companies. These companies should be required to submit competitive bids through the request-for-proposals (RFP) process.

OPERATIONS

Operations are the most complex and comprehensive function in all of sport facility management. Facility operations managers have a wide variety of departmental responsibilities, including event coordinating, engineering, security, maintenance, and housekeeping. They must possess an adequate knowledge of budgeting, cost control, methodology, and negotiation skills to effectively complete their job responsibilities.

Operations of a sport facility vary significantly from the operations management of most businesses, although the underlying principles are similar. Operations management in a major sport facility focuses on how services are produced, rather than the production of those services, which is the traditional definition of operations management.

Management teams

A sport facility is operated by a management team. This team, depending upon the facility's size and function, is headed by an individual titled general manager, CEO, or executive director. Other members of this team oversee marketing, public relations, advertising, and operations. This section focuses on management functions, especially those associated with the general manager's office. These functions include philosophy, mission, policies and procedures, organizational elements, booking and scheduling, contracts, the management manual, and evaluation procedures.

Policies

A policy is a definitive course of action selected from various alternatives, in light of given conditions, to guide and determine present and future decisions. Policies are developed from the **mission statement,** which should be the basis for establishing all aspects of the operational procedures (Thompson and Strickland, 1990). A policy is the reason—the why—behind management's decision to function in a particular manner.

Procedures

Procedures are the "how" of accomplishing policies. They are the established, traditional way of doing something, and they include a series of steps to be followed by facility staff members to accomplish their assigned duties. From the outset, the manager will encounter numerous problems, from change orders to equipment purchases to overseeing the entire project to ensure that the final product is what was intended. Prior to the facility's opening, the building manager should establish a philosophy and tone, as well as appropriate building policies and operational procedures. These general policies and procedures should then be effectively communicated to staff, tenants, and the general public in a manner that clearly reflects the parameters under which the facility is to be used.

Philosophy

The philosophy of the facility manager should provide a basis for establishing guidelines and a proper orientation to operations. This philosophy may be based on the attitude that the facility should either serve the community without concern for profit and proper management control or exhibit fiscal responsibility through the control of appropriations and revenues, with the goal of breaking even or earning profit. A combination of the two approaches might be preferable to the either/or philosophy, but local circumstances might dictate the final choice.

Mission statement and goals and objectives

The operation of all facilities is guided by a mission statement or an operational direction. While many facility organizations, especially those tied to government agencies or large corporations, have formal mission statements, others operate with general and wide-ranging guidelines. It is these mission guidelines that provide the parameters for developing an organization's budget.

Goals and objectives that support and justify the facility's mission, or statement of purpose, need to be developed. They should be developed by competent management and compiled from input from all operational personnel (Hitt, 1985).

Goals are the achievable statements of purpose, or expectations, provided by management personnel. If fulfilled, they justify the fiscal resources requested in the budget document. Generally, sport facility goals are not as formalized as in other industries (e.g., increase sales by 18 percent and open new markets in the South).

Objectives are the supporting qualifications of the specified goals, not the goals themselves. All objectives should be measurable, quantifiable, and subjective. Most facilities, depending on their size, are departmentalized, but management should involve all personnel, regardless of their duties. This participative-management approach (a bottom-up rather than top-down approach) is vital if all personnel are expected to support the mission, goals, and objectives of the facility.

CONCEPT CHECK

To be successful as an entertainment complex, a sport facility must define its mission, philosophy, procedures, and policies, as well as establish specific goals and objectives.

ORGANIZATIONAL AREAS

Within a facility, there are important operational areas that need to be considered in order for the facility to operate smoothly and effectively, including:

- Booking and scheduling
- Marketing, public relations, and advertising
- Security
- Safety and medical services
- Housekeeping and maintenance
- Box office
- Concessions and novelties
- Traffic and parking
- Financial management
- Risk management

BOOKING AND SCHEDULING

Event booking and scheduling is one of the most important areas of concern in maintaining a facility. A facility without events has little or no purpose. Events are the primary source of revenue and the lifeblood of any facility. In addition, booking and scheduling and public relations are the departments most responsible for molding the facility's image by direct association with the sponsor and by their ability to coordinate the facility's schedule.

To comprehend the different approaches to scheduling, a facility's mandate must be understood. Facilities differ not only in their public/private management approach but also in their mission. A public facility is obligated to provide for the scheduling of community events, whereas a private facility, depending upon its formation agreement, may limit charitable and nonprofit activities.

A privately operated facility has the ability to promote its own events, although many do not because of legal ramifications. A privately managed facility can actively court business and aggressively seek to attract events by bidding or presenting comprehensive proposals to promoters.

Whatever the facility's purpose and mission in attracting and promoting events, the general approach to booking is reserving a specific space, within a specific facility, for a specific date, at a specific time, for an agreed-upon amount of money. **Booking** is the act of engaging and contracting an event or attraction.

Attracting an event

The first step in securing an event is the development of a positive public image. One key to developing a positive image is the production of a facility brochure, detailing the specifications of the building, staff, types of events, and event suitability. A well-planned and -produced informational brochure should be directed to all individuals who might be interested in securing the facility for a planned event. Events that are successful should be featured prominently in future facility publications, which should be revised annually.

Other elements in attracting events are maintaining visibility with local and national promoters, visiting appropriate trade fairs and conventions, and networking with other facilities. Success in booking an event is much more likely to result not from walk-in trade but from whom you know.

Scheduling

Scheduling is the reservation process and coordination of all events to fit the facility's available time. This reservation process involves scheduling a series of like events (e.g., football games or symphony concerts) and providing the best possible event mix to fit the facility's usage. Event dates must be properly spaced (not overlap). Individuals responsible for scheduling must have an in-depth knowledge of operational functions and be able to secure the appropriate number of events for the facility while not overtaxing the staff, overworking the building, overspending the budget, or saturating the marketplace.

For the scheduling process to maintain its cohesiveness, it is imperative that the record of scheduled events be solely under the control of a single individual who writes and erases information from the scheduling book. Changes in arrangements and notification of event alterations are this designated individual's unique responsibility.

Reservation process

There are two categories of reservations for space in a public facility, tentative and confirmed.

Tentative-hold reservations are made when an organization requests a specific date and time on the facility calendar but no actual contract has been prepared. If another organization desires the same date and time and can provide the necessary earnest money, the facility scheduler will contact the original tentatively scheduled organization and inquire about its intention to book the facility. It is not uncommon to have a succession of first, second, and third tentative holds on a given date or set of dates because they are often requested a year or more in advance.

After notification, confirmation will be requested and a contract readied. Customarily, the facility notifies the scheduled organization of its placement and any resultant changes in the schedule.

A confirmed reservation, or **contracted reservation,** refers to an organization that has placed a deposit for the agreed-upon date and time and contract negotiations have commenced. A facility should establish guidelines concerning the length of time a tentative hold may remain on record. At the same time, the facility should be as flexible as possible about the confirmation period. Different types of events require different confirmation and condition deadlines, depending on circumstances and the promoter's reputation. Any facility that hopes to maintain its integrity must adopt a reservation system that is fair and reasonable.

Contracting

After an organization confirms a tentative hold, the next step is to negotiate the contract. A contract consists of an offer, an acceptance, and a consideration. The concluded agreement creates obligations for all parties involved. After negotiations are finished, there are five requirements to complete a contract:

1. Consideration: legal value (money) and mutual obligation of both parties
2. A valid offer and a valid acceptance
3. The substance of the contract must be legal
4. A specific duration (time) for the contract
5. A written and/or verbal contract

It is necessary that qualified individuals design, prepare, and understand the contents of the contract, which should consist of mutually agreed-upon terms. This will ensure that the facility is not bound to terms in an agreement that it cannot meet.

Most facilities do not retain a full-time attorney to create a contract for each new facility event. Instead, a boilerplate contract containing a standard form is used. The **boilerplate contract** is similar to an apartment lease, with language in a standard form and with appropriate "fill-in-the-blanks" to address specifically agreed-upon terms.

Boilerplate contracts provide consistency and generally reflect a situation favorable to all parties. Variations in language concerning events provide a more streamlined contractual device. Addenda may be used to create a more customized form, enable modification or elimination of contract clauses, or clarify changes that have been agreed upon by both parties.

Contracts should be kept as simple as possible to avoid confusion and to expedite the contractual process. Large facilities that host a variety of events use three basic boilerplate contract forms, each addressing different event types:

- Ticketed events, open to the public, require language addressing ticket sales, gate proceeds, ushers, and ticket takers. Addenda usually refer to elements concerned with insurance, special financial arrangements, and promotions. Public events require more precise contractual procedures because the facility attempts to preserve the security of patrons and maintain building control.

- A nonticketed or closed event, such as a convention or trade show, deals with display booths and banquets but not invitations or ticketing. Contracts for these events are less complex because the event is not open to the public, thus reducing liabilities.

- A small event held in a facility's meeting room, such as a prom or a seminar, eliminates the need for the manpower of a large event that uses the arena. The contract in this case is simple and straightforward.

In contract negotiations, the main objective is to maintain control and direction for the facility. The facility maintains control over the building during an event by providing security, ushers, ticket takers, first aid, and special insurance arrangements. Such control reduces the facility's liabilities.

CONCEPT CHECK

The booking and scheduling process is an important aspect of achieving success in a facility. Events must be properly scheduled and contracted so that all parties know their rights and responsibilities. Formal policies and procedures will make this phase of facility management operate more smoothly.

MARKETING AND PROMOTIONAL-STRATEGY DEVELOPMENT

During the negotiation stage, the **promoter(s)** and facility marketing organization should be in contact to determine the type and extent of facility involvement with the proposed event. The level of facility involvement will hinge on the event type and the promoter's approach to marketing its event.

In some cases, the client(s) will undertake the entire marketing operation, from contact with the local media (radio, television, and newspapers) to promotions being run in the facility on the day of the event. This type of control will depend upon the experience and expertise of the promoters in the development of their events. Client-controlled promotion will limit the cost of the event to the facility but also lower the amount of revenue due to the facility at the time of settlement.

In most cases, promoters will not have developed ties with the local community and media. If this is true, they will often want the event's entire marketing campaign to be organized by the facility marketing organization. This marketing responsibility requires the development of a marketing plan.

Initial marketing efforts

After the establishment of the initial marketing assumptions (based on research) and the marketing plan and budget, the real work begins. The first phase, depending upon the event and the results of market research initiatives, begins with the establishment of contact with the local media. This initial contact includes discussion of the purchase of media time or space, and sets up some form of trade/promotion with these media. It is imperative that this media advertising be targeted at the appropriate audience (O'Shaughnessy, 1988).

At the same time, the group sales department attempts to contact corporations and service groups in an attempt to book groups for the upcoming event. Such promotional activities as press conferences and star athletes visiting key "publics", commonly known as **earned media,** should be planned and carried out. According to Will Peneguy of the New Orleans Super Dome, these public-awareness activities should be scheduled in close proximity to the actual event, while the initial media contact could be as much as a year in advance.

CONCEPT CHECK

Awareness and information are the keys to a successful marketing campaign. Once these are achieved, the job of attracting people to a facility becomes easier.

SECURITY

Security functions usually fall under the jurisdiction of the operations department in most facilities. In large facilities a full-time, in-house security staff is employed. This compounds the responsibilities of the operations manager, because in-house security officers are employees of the facility and it assumes liability for any negligent actions on their part under the legal doctrine of **respondeat superior.**

Therefore it is vitally important that proper rules and procedures be established, written, and made accessible to all members of the security department (Jewel, 1992). These rules and procedures should provide security personnel with a clearly delineated picture of restrictions and limitations, and what specific behaviors are expected of the staff within the scope of their employment. This area is a constant source of legal headaches for a facility.

It is vital that all employees, from administration to ticket-takers, understand facility policies and required responses. Any problem that arises must be resolved quickly, with limited public knowledge of the incident. A facility that has stringent policies and procedures that are developed for the protection of patrons will help reduce liability.

Alcohol

The majority of patron problems involve the excessive consumption of alcohol. However, most of today's facilities have minimized this problem by adopting strict policy guidelines pertaining to alcohol distribution during events. The essence of this policy is that there are specified times within a game, concert, or other event when alcohol will not be available for sale. To ensure that this policy is adhered to strictly, beverage sellers should be educated to recognize signs of unacceptable intoxication or purchases attempted by underage patrons. Even with strict policies concerning alcohol consumption, problems are inevitable.

SAFETY AND MEDICAL SERVICES

An emergency is any incident or situation that has resulted in, or could cause, the injury of employees, patrons, or visitors. Examples of potential emergency situations are bad weather, fire, bomb threat, medical emergency, airplane crash, utility loss, and hazardous material. These situations can occur in a facility at any time, but how prepared are facilities to handle them when the situation arises?

Authority

It is important that a definitive chain of command be established to maximize coordination and direction in emergency situations and to quickly deal with such emergencies. During any event in a public facility, a staff member should be empowered with the authority to take charge and make decisions when a problem arises. This staff member is usually the **event coordinator** or the operations manager, whose responsibility is to ensure that every facet of the event goes according to schedule and that problems are resolved in a professional and timely manner.

Emergency response training

Response to an emergency situation by the facility staff must be prompt and professional. The difference between a well-trained response and an erratic, poorly trained response could be the difference between life and death. An emergency response plan should be devised for all perceivable emergency situations. It is vital to thoroughly train all personnel who will most likely be involved in these response procedures.

Emergency response procedures

Each facility is unique—different from all other facilities—so, it is necessary for each facility to develop its own emergency response procedures. A detailed plan covers facility staffing, physical attributes, event type and classification, and type and numbers of appropriate emergency medical personnel per event. Constant communication with emergency medical staff, strategically positioned with the necessary response equipment and supplies, is required for immediate and appropriate reaction.

Emergency procedures are vital in large-scale situations, such as a bomb threat, a fire, or a mechanical failure (figure 14–1 provides a bomb threat procedure). In each instance, a specific procedure should be followed to ensure maximum safety. An evacuation plan must be understood and implemented correctly by the entire facility staff. Safe evacuation of patrons, in a professional and orderly manner, will minimize panic and resultant injuries. In most large facilities, ramps and other nonmechanical exit devices are employed in emergency situations; elevators or escalators should not be used under any circumstances. When an unusual situation develops, where no specific plan has been established, management must select the most appropriate and efficient response choice.

Date _____

Time _____

Keep caller talking. Give excuses (can't hear, bad connection, etc.)

Caller's message (exact) _____

_____

_____

Where is the bomb? _____

What time will it go off? _____

What does it look like? _____

What kind of bomb is it? _____

Why are you doing this? _____

Who are you? _____

Details of caller

Man/ Woman/ Child   Old/ Young

Voice: loud – soft – raspy – high pitch – pleasant – deep – intoxicated

Manner: calm – angry – rational – irrational – coherent – incoherent – emotional –
          righteous – laughing

Speech: fast – slow – distinct – distorted – stutter – nasal – slurred – lisp

Background noises: Factory – trains – planes – bedlam – animals – music – quiet –
          office machines – voices – street – party – kids

Language: excellent – good – fair – poor – foul

Accent: local – foreign – race

DO NOT DISCUSS THE CALL WITH ANYONE ELSE!

FIGURE 14–1   Bomb threat procedure.

CONCEPT CHECK ✓

Establishing security and emergency procedures is of the utmost importance when managing a facility. Improper security procedures can result in the injury of patrons and lawsuits against the facility. Providing emergency services also has legal ramifications, but the facility is ethically bound to provide a safe and enjoyable environment.

HOUSEKEEPING AND MAINTENANCE

Housekeeping and maintenance are functions designed to keep a facility clean and prepared for patrons. The task of cleaning a facility is one that cannot be underestimated.

Housekeeping in a facility is not like cleaning a house, because the areas to be cleaned and maintained are vast and varying: bleacher seats, portable seats, large restrooms, loges, carpets, tile and concrete floors, and numerous stairwells, elevators, and upholstered seats, to name just a few.

Maintenance and housekeeping duties consist of many different functions and responsibilities. Maintenance components include structural maintenance, equipment maintenance, **setup** and **breakdown** of events, and custodial functions (Jewel, 1992). Maintenance management also requires awareness of and adherence to federal and state regulations, as well as the ability to implement preventive maintenance and safety plans within the facility. Housekeeping is the physical cleaning and arrangement of the facility and its furnishings. (Figure 14–2 can be used as a guide for a maintenance schedule.)

Once the general mission statement has been developed, a plan for housekeeping and maintenance should be established. Management should consider the facility type, location, relationship to

---

Concourse Restroom Maintenance

Condition of restrooms at the start of shift

MEN EAST _____	WOMEN EAST _____
MEN NORTH _____	WOMEN NORTH (2) _____
MEN WEST _____	WOMEN WEST _____
MEN S.E. _____	WOMEN S.E. (2) _____
MEN S.W. _____	WOMEN S.W. _____

Record of maintenance during shift

Restrooms	Time (maintained and/ or checked)					
MEN EAST						
WOMEN EAST						
MEN NORTH						
WOMEN NORTH (2)						
MEN WEST						
WOMEN WEST						
MEN S.E.						
WOMEN S.E. (2)						
MEN S.W.						
WOMEN S.W.						

Maintenance needed or repairs to be made: _____

_____

Attendants on duty: _____ Date: _____

FIGURE 14–2 A sample maintenance schedule.

other facilities in the community, traffic access, usage level, types of groups using the facility, available labor, sources of revenues, and financial bottom-line responsiveness. This plan should establish guidelines concerning purpose, operation, storage, staffing, inventory, repair, and safety:

- Purpose: A facility should provide clean, well-organized, and safe spaces and equipment for events, lessees, and audiences.
- Operation: To operate effectively, a facility should have space and equipment set according to event requirements before the lessee's move-in time. It should operate the event efficiently by answering all late requests in a timely manner and maintaining an acceptable level of cleanliness in all areas during the event. Every attempt should be made to prevent safety violations. At the close of any event, all equipment should be secured, all refuse should be disposed of, spaces and equipment should be cleaned and returned to their original status, and all deficiencies should be reported and corrected in a timely manner.
- Storage: The storage of equipment should allow for quick identification and inventory; maximum space utilization; convenience to using area; protection against tearing, bending, scarring, water or dust accumulation, broken parts, and/or damage of any other kind; proper spacing; and safe handling.
- Operations staff: The operations staff should be organized into two or three departments, such as housekeeping/arrangements, engineering, or technical. These areas may be further subdivided. The housekeeping/arrangements section could be subdivided into such groups as (1) setup crew(s), providing for setup and striking events, and (2) deep-cleaning crew, which would be scheduled to complete major cleaning tasks, such as carpet shampooing, tile stripping and waxing, and glass washing.
- Housekeeping/arrangements: All setup crews should be comprised of a foreman, one or more leadmen, and part-time workers as required. These crews will operate eight hours

per shift, three shifts per day, seven days per week.

CONCEPT CHECK

A clean and well-maintained environment does much to improve the mood of the patrons. Housekeeping and maintenance should have high priority when managing a facility.

BOX OFFICE

The box office is probably one of the most important areas in sport facilities today. The box office, although not a complicated operation, is the public's initial contact with the facility and the entity that financially drives the operation, collecting the majority of revenue for all events.

Too often the box office area is the least-thought-about area in facility planning. It is assumed that people will tolerate confusion and discomfort to buy a ticket for a desirable event. This may be true, but to make patrons feel good about spending their money, the box office should be organized and easily accessible to the customer.

The size of the box office area should accommodate the sale and distribution of tickets. An adequate number of windows should be available to handle an unexpected number of **walk-up sales.** Sales windows should be located on all sides of the facility rather than just at the main entrance (Jewel, 1992).

To adequately serve the public, each sales window should be capable of selling the entire price range of tickets and generate sales of 400 to 700 tickets during the night. This figure will vary depending on the type of ticket-selling machines that are being used and the speed of the machines' operators. Therefore it is safe to assume that if you have an 18,000-seat facility it should have eighteen to twenty-four windows available for ticket sales. Although this is an optimum number of windows, most sport facilities will not have enough space for this many windows. The previously mentioned ratio of windows to projected sales is a useful rule of thumb, and with good record keeping and the use of historical data, one can gauge the number of ticket windows needed for a particular event. Nothing will turn a patron off faster than having to wait in line for a ticket and miss part of an event because of poor planning by the facility.

The main entrance to the facility should contain about 40 percent of the ticket-selling windows, with the other 60 percent distributed among the other entry areas of the arena. Box office lobbies should be of sufficient size to allow patrons to line up in front of the windows. (Remember, few people stand in line alone; the entire family or groups of friends stand in line together.)

Under normal circumstances, a covered area thirty to fifty feet deep should be provided in front of the selling windows. If possible, some ticket windows should be located on the outside of the building. This will allow for ticket sales in several locations and prevent lines from backing up against the turnstiles, which are generally adjacent to the ticket-selling windows. An outside ticket-selling window is also a good idea for the sale of tickets for future events, which would permit the sales without the need to open the building.

All box office windows should be located outside the turnstiles in an area that is easily accessible to the public. Specific windows should be designated for will-call and reservations, preferably in a separate area away from the main entrance. These windows tend to cater to the repeat business patron, and a separate window and entrance seem to promote future sales.

Box office personnel

Depending upon the size and mission of a facility, personnel number and designation vary considerably. As an important operational part of a facility, the box office requires a minimum number of full-time staff. Normally, the box office manager and two or three assistants are the only full-time staff members, with the remaining employees hired as part-time personnel.

The box office manager has the sole responsibility for the box office operation and supervision of all personnel. This individual is responsible for ordering, selling, and distributing event tickets, as well as for the final box office statement. Policy development, personnel selection and placement, safety, and discipline of box office personnel are additional responsibilities. The box office manager and his/her assistants work closely with promoters and all facility operations personnel.

Box office policies

Box office policies are relatively uncomplicated, with the ultimate goal to provide an efficient and secure service-oriented operation. Employees should be instructed in appropriate dress and attitude. Areas of policy should include

- Courtesy toward patrons
- Familiarity with event seating
- Efficient ticket processing

Working conditions

The box office generally operates from 8:30 A.M. to 4:30 P.M. on nonevent days and until intermission on event days, depending on ticket demand.

Public relations

All personnel should be instructed about the appropriate techniques for meeting and greeting the ticket-purchasing public and about proper dress and etiquette.

Equipment operations

Equipment operations include ticket counters (tickets divided into numerical sequence, by price breaks, or by rows and sections according to the seating plan); cash drawers for cash placement and stub count at the end of the day; computer terminals and printers for printing computerized tickets; cash registers; and telephones and answering machines to provide messages and record ticket orders.

Sales policies

When tickets are sold, all transactions involving the sale are final for the specific event. When an event has concluded, it is vital that all ticket sales, after accounting for unsold and complimentary tickets, equal the revenue generated. In other words, capacity minus total tickets sold equals unsold tickets plus appropriate evidence for all transactions.

Refunds and exchanges

The general rule is that *no* refunds or exchanges should take place. All sales are final. This rule results from the fact that the facility and its personnel are agents for the promoter and do not make the rules. Any refund or exchange policy must be approved in writing by the facility contractor or promoter.

Telephone orders

Procuring tickets by telephone is usually acceptable as long as certain restrictions are in place:

- A ticket for a seat should be held for only three days.

CHAPTER 14   *Managing the Facility*   **283**

- Telephone ticket orders should be accepted only if the promoter and facility management agree that this would be an appropriate sales method to be employed for a specific event. Telephone sales should be event-specific.
- All telephone orders should be recorded as cash transactions.

Mail orders

For convenience, patrons should be permitted to order tickets through the mail. This not only creates another avenue to sell tickets for that specific event, but permits the facility to provide information concerning future events when the tickets are returned to the patron.

Will call

Every facility should establish a **will-call location.** It is imperative that when a patron arrives for ticket pick-up, proper identification is produced before the tickets are provided to the patron.

Lost tickets

Refunds and exchanges are subject to the agreement of the promoter. However, in the case of a ticket lost prior to the event, the ticket manager should have the discretion to issue a duplicate ticket and void the original ticket. If the ticket manager decides that the patron should purchase a new ticket, then the original ticket can be returned to the box office for a full refund prior to the performance. This lost-ticket policy affects the facility's image, and every effort to resolve the situation should be encouraged without exceeding the limitations of prescribed authority.

Ticket purchases

The numbers of tickets purchased by a patron is up to the discretion of the box office manager and subject to the agreement of the promoter. There is usually no set limit to the number of tickets purchased.

Scalping

Scalping can be a serious problem, and although the facility and box office can do little to combat scalping, there are usually local laws that address the problem. In fact, most authorities arrest and fine scalpers.

Ticketing variables

There are a number of elements concerned with ticket sales and operations, such as the following:

- Capacity: The box office should strive to maximize revenue by selling every seat in the facility. It should be remembered that the configuration and capacity of each event is different, depending on the event type and requirements.
- Seating: There are two types of seating arrangement in a facility, regardless of configuration: (1) reserved, where a specific seat is designated for each patron. This type of seating arrangement is prevalent at events such as athletic contests and concerts. This arrangement provides the patron with "first come, best seat" when buying tickets. (2) General admission is a seating arrangement used primarily at lower quality, egalitarian productions. This arrangement implies that all patrons purchasing tickets will receive the same quality seating opportunity as those who purchase tickets in advance. Although both methods appear to have inherent inequities, a compromise arrangement is to provide tiered seating prices (e.g., ground floor: $30; 2d floor: $15; etc.), which all professional sport facilities use.
- Ticket type: The ticket is a contract (agreement) between the management/promoter and the purchaser of the seat. The box office manager should deal only with a reputable, bonded ticket company when ordering ticket stock. All tickets should be ordered well in advance of an event, to minimize the chance of error. This policy should be in place regardless of the ticket type (i.e., ticket roll or computerized tickets). Computerized tickets, although much more expensive than the traditional ticket stock, have certain advantages, such as event information printed on them: name of sponsoring organization, ticket price, program name, performance date and time, facility name, and seat location. Also, appropriate advertising can be included on ticket stock.

Ticket sales strategy

Although ticket sales strategy and policy will be codirected by the marketing department, it falls under the purview of the box office. Elements of this strategy are

- Pricing: The box office, the marketing department, and the promoter jointly develop a ticket sales strategy. A decision needs to be made regarding whether tickets will be sold on a house scale (i.e., pricing established by the box office) or by a **performance scale** (i.e., pricing established by the event promoter).
- Incentives: There are many traditional types of sales incentives that have been used, including discounted tickets or tickets that make use of unusual seating areas (e.g., standing room) or special circumstances. These are determined by the promoter and/or the box office. Group sales are made to groups for a price reduction, which is beneficial when an event has a lower ticket demand or corporate involvement is required. Season tickets predominate at athletic or theatrical events presented on a seasonal basis.

Daily reporting

A daily transaction or report form—which provides the facility with a record of daily transactions that have occurred—should be completed for all ticket sales, mail orders, and anything else deemed important by management.

Event summary

Although the event summary is prepared by the business office, the box office must initiate the process by providing event information at the conclusion of each event. The information should cover ticket prices; ticket categories, including complimentary or other special ticket classifications; and the number of tickets sold and unsold.

Computer ticket management

As facilities investigate various options to minimize personnel costs, eliminate cumbersome operational procedures, and become "auditor-friendly," a computerized ticket system is an ideal solution. This computer-operated system is dependent on software options. It provides the box office with patron information at the **point of sale,** organized either alphabetically, by postal code, or by subscriber number; a computerized mailing list, updated daily, which can be used for notification of upcoming events or to solicit patron response for a specified performance; and the ability to monitor ticket sales versus marketing efforts. If money is spent on advertising or direct-mail solicitations, these promotional efforts need to be compared to ticket sales.

Private seat licenses (PSLs)

Although some of these alternate revenue sources have been mentioned previously, **private seat licenses (PSLs)** are becoming important in ensuring profitability or that the "bottom line" is achieved. A PSL, in its truest form, is a one-time fee that gives an individual the right to will or pass on the tickets and the right to buy tickets for as long as the purchaser and the designee desire. Some facilities, however, have PSLs that have a limited duration. For example, Texas Tech University PSLs allow for a seat to be purchased for a period of ten years. The price of PSLs varies from $500 to $10,000, depending upon seat location and venue. For example, the Pittsburgh Steelers PSLs cost between $250 and $2,500, the Carolina Panthers up to $5,400, St. Louis and Nashville up to $4,500, and Cincinnati and Cleveland up to $1,500. The monies generated from PSLs, in most cases, go directly to the teams and do not have to be split with other teams or the leagues.

CONCEPT CHECK

The box office of a facility has enormous responsibilities. It must make sure that patrons can purchase tickets and enter the facility in a timely fashion. And because large quantities of cash are handled by the box office, reliable staffing is a must. Finally, the staff must be courteous, because the box office is the first contact the patron will have with the facility's personnel.

CONCESSIONS AND NOVELTIES

A facility's food service is the business operation that prepares, delivers, and sells food and beverages to customers. There are three forms of food service operations: concessions, catering, and novelties (which includes programs). In this presentation, catering will be included in the area of concessions.

Concessions

Concessions play a vital role in the success of a facility. A well-operated concessions department is often a major determining factor in the financial success of any sport facility. It is an accepted fact that food and drink go hand in hand with sports and recreation.

For example, during 1989–1990, the Superdome in New Orleans reported that concessions revenue amounted to $7.5 million, or 60 percent of its operating revenue. At a smaller sport facility, Fogelman Basketball Arena at Tulane University, a 72 percent net profit was reported on concessions operations in the facility in 1990.

In order for a concessions operation in a facility to survive, much more than serving good food at a reasonable price is required. It demands that management has a knowledge of marketing, financial management, business planning, purchasing, inventory management, business law, insurance, advertising, and personnel.

Stocking

Stocking is an important component of the concessions operation. The manager must initially decide which products to purchase based upon quality, price, service, and customer acceptance. The staff of a facility often taste-tests items to determine the best products. Today, the most popular foods appear to be hot dogs, nachos, popcorn, peanuts, soft drinks, and beer.

When deciding on the quality of products, one should scrutinize past records carefully. Nonperishable items (e.g., cups, napkins, and other paper goods) should be purchased in large quantities for the whole season. Perishable or time-sensitive items (e.g., hot dogs and buns) must be ordered fresh for every event. In large facilities, restocking takes about one week, while in smaller facilities it takes approximately five hours. Some interesting facts about concessions are:

- Beer and alcohol account for a high percentage of concession profits.
- Popcorn is probably the largest revenue producer in terms of margin. The cost of a box of popcorn is about five cents, while patrons pay $2.00 to $2.50 a serving.
- Concessions sales are constant one hour before a game; and 80 percent of sales take place at halftime, while only about 20 percent of sales take place after halftime.

Convenience foods

All the foods in concession stands are called convenience foods. There are three types of **convenience foods** that facilities stock: frozen, powdered, and dehydrated. Frozen foods include a large selection of fruit juices and meat, in a variety of sizes from individual servings to amounts sufficient for volume feeding. Dehydrated and powdered foods are appropriate for facilities because they can be stored for long periods of time without spoilage and are often packaged in bulk. They require only water or a short period of cooking for reconstitution. Some of the dehydrated and powdered foods on the market today are seasonings, soups of many varieties, milk, pastry mixes, sauces, gravies, and beverages.

The wide variety of convenience foods available enables concession stands to present a varied menu to the public and permits employees with limited knowledge and little training to prepare appetizing "fail-proof" dishes. Convenience foods enable operators to save money, time, and labor, especially in the areas of cleaning, trimming, packaging, storing, cooking, and serving.

The development of convenience foods and disposable packaging, containers, and utensils has enabled food service operations to become efficient and practical. Disposable products in common use are semirigid foil pans, plastic pouches, foil and plastic packets, foam containers, cardboard containers, and other disposable items, such as plates, cups, eating utensils, doilies, aprons, and uniforms. Boil-in-a-pouch and chemically generated foods have been developed to reduce both cooking time and cost.

Other developments involve foil and plastic packets that encase individual servings of condiments (e.g., tomato sauces, mayonnaise, salt, pepper, etc.) and foam or cardboard containers preshaped for specific carryout items. These disposable products enable minimally trained labor, with minimal equipment, to serve a variety of well-prepared convenience foods and other products that are easy to stock and dispense. These products also reduce sanitation problems.

The concessions operation should not only stock good food but also have adequate storage space and an appropriate location(s) for the spectators.

In large facilities, service elevators are located near the various storage areas and near all seats. There should be enough concession stands to serve the total number of seats, and any patron should be able to reach the nearest food stand in about forty to sixty seconds.

Concessions advertising

Concessions operations should be bright, colorful, well lit and decorated with attractive pictures of the food and beverages being served. Menu boards should be installed to clearly indicate products and prices. Signage should be in neon that is not the same color as the building. At large facilities, pictures of food should be displayed on the menu board. Pictures of brand name products, easily recognized by customers, eliminate questions about the quality of the merchandise. Further, to keep lines moving, most menus should list all prices in increments of 25 cents. Simple combinations should be listed on the menu in large, readable print to provide direction for the customer and to eliminate complex orders that can result in lost sales or patrons missing a portion of the event while waiting in line for food.

Concessions should be well organized, with clear indications of where patrons should line up for service. Equipment, food, and cash registers should be conveniently located so that customers can be quickly served by a single person in each selling section. It is important that employees be trained to manage large crowds and keep lines moving. At the same time, they should be encouraged to increase sales through suggestive selling techniques. They should attempt to convince the customer that all items are reasonably priced and that buying a larger size actually results in saving money.

Alcoholic beverages

In a facility operation, alcoholic beverages are the most profitable segment of the concessions operation. In fact, alcohol and beer manufacturers sponsor facilities and events to promote their products. There is a downside to this situation, of course, especially when there is community opposition to the sale of alcohol in the facility, particularly to the underaged and individuals who may drive an automobile after the event has concluded.

Another element that needs to be considered is the liability that the facility can incur if an accident occurs involving a patron who indulged in alcohol while attending a facility event. There have been lawsuits won by patrons where the facility, event, and concessionaire all have been held liable for fights or injuries due to the consumption of alcohol.

Concession maintenance

Employees should keep themselves well groomed and their workplace clean because customers may have a negative reaction to employees or concession stands that appear to be unclean. Large facilities usually employ a supervisor for every concession stand, and no employee is allowed to leave until the stands are spotless. At some large facilities (e.g., the Superdome, with 10,000 to 12,000 employees working concessions annually), most of the employees belong to nonprofit groups, such as softball leagues, Girl Scouts, Boy Scouts, or church groups, who volunteer their labor, with each group receiving a percentage of sales. To ensure cleanliness and compliance with health guidelines, floor drains and adequate ventilation and exhaust systems must be installed in stand and kitchen areas.

At the end of an event, employees must cope with a significant volume of refuse from disposable products. This debris should be removed through incineration, which requires a minimal amount of space because the paper items and some plastics are reduced to ash. A second method is to use a shredding machine that converts plastics and paper into a pulp by removing excess water and shredding the fiber. A third method, compression, packs refuse under pressure to reduce its size for ease of removal.

Hawkers/vendors

Another highly profitable aspect of the concessions operation is **vendors,** or **hawkers,** who take food or beverages to the patrons in their seats. Hawkers generate substantial sales because many patrons want food and beverage service but do not want to miss any of the event.

Trends

Recent trends in concessions operations now provide name-brand products (e.g., Popeye's Chicken and Domino's Pizza), for which the facility receives a percentage of sales. In the near future, many of the items served at concession stands will be more healthful foods, such as soup and salads. There will probably also be specialty operations, such as a sweet shop with a large assortment of candies or a hot dog shop with several combinations (e.g., cheese dog, chili dog, onion dog, or turkey dog). In the beverage area, there is often a demand during rush periods at sporting events for fast bar service. To satisfy this demand, computers have been used to control the mixing and pouring of any one of 1000 beverages in four seconds, with the liquor content in each being uniform.

Another recent innovation is to place frozen foods in an oven drawer and set a timer. After the correct time has elapsed, the oven automatically turns off and the door opens. The advantages of this innovative cooking equipment are that it saves time and requires much less space than conventional equipment.

Along with the recent trends of serving brand-name products, more healthful foods, specialty shops, and new equipment for bartending and cooking, new packaging has been developed. For example, the package of the future may be a rigid aluminum foil dish and cover with a pull tab, containing a hamburger, french fries, condiments, and wipe-and-dry towels. Pulling the tab before opening the cover will break a heat capsule that after thirty seconds will bring the contents to eating temperature. The ultimate development would be self-destruction of the container when its cover is replaced.

Food safety and sanitation practices

To control food contamination and the spread of disease, every employee must have knowledge of basic food safety and sanitation practices. Food services attract all types of bacteria, insects, and animal pests because they provide them with the three basic ingredients necessary to sustain life: food, water, and warmth.

To eliminate contamination, food service management needs to inspect delivery vehicles to ensure that they are properly refrigerated and sanitary. All products should be accredited and inspected by the appropriate government agencies. Upon delivery, crates or boxes should never be stored outside when unloading because insects can infest them and be introduced into the concessions operation. In addition, all spills should be cleaned up as soon as they occur, and food should be refrigerated until needed and cooked as soon as possible.

Another important way to inhibit food contamination is personal hygiene. Every employee must be aware that hands are a primary source of contamination. Every time employees scratch their heads or

sneeze, they are exposing their hands to bacteria that will spread to anything they touch. All employees should practice basic hygiene. For example, they should have short or controlled hair, clean hands and short nails, a daily shower or bath, clean clothes, and no unnecessary jewelry; be clean shaven; and not smoke in the proximity of the food and beverages. In addition, ill employees should not attend work, because they can expose the food preparation and service areas to bacterial contamination.

In most communities, there are regulations that affect food service operations. In fact, most employees are mandated to pass some form of medical examination (e.g., tuberculosis test) and complete a written examination concerning the handling of food.

Novelties

The success of novelty sales depends upon applying the appropriate formula to each situation. The following are four different novelty formulas that have been traditionally used:

- Flat fee: This negotiated fee is paid directly to the facility, usually for a nonticketed event (e.g., meetings, school graduations, or religious services). This fee should be collected in advance or be part of the deposit.
- Percentage of vendor sales: This is a common fee arrangement wherein the vendor pays the facility a percentage of the sales, ranging from 5 to 20 percent, depending upon the parties involved, facility, and event.
- Percentage of facility sales: In this arrangement, the facility, which is responsible for inventory and all sales, receives a percentage of total sales. This is a profitable method for the facility operation and is preferred because the facility knows the amount of inventory on hand and controls its flow. At the close of an event, with the final inventory completed, the vendor will receive a percentage of sales, ranging between 55 and 75 percent. The facility will then pay the sellers out of the facility's percentage of sales, which could range from 5 to 20 percent.
- Fee per person: This method is profitable for the facility and the easiest to handle by all parties. The vendor agrees to pay the facility a set amount per person in attendance,

including complimentary tickets. The fee will vary from event to event, depending upon the attraction and vendor items and may range from 1 cent to 25 cents per person. This fee should be collected in advance or by the first intermission, based on anticipated attendance or house capacity.

Sales personnel

Training can make a difference in the simple areas, such as appearance, uniforms, and the attitude of the vendors. However, training how to sell is extremely important if the operation is to generate profit. Another factor is the employment of experienced novelty-sales personnel. Although anyone can sell T-shirts or novelties, it takes a special ability, developed by experience, to generate the type of sales desired in a novelty operation.

Shoplifting is not limited to retail outlets. Novelty personnel should be trained to control their stock so that the only items that leave the stands are those that are sold. This is extremely important at such events as concerts, where a large number of people will want to purchase T-shirts and other items.

Splits and deals

If an event threatens to bypass the market and facility because of a better novelty deal in another facility, reworking the deal and split should be considered. There is no accepted standard formula to follow, because competition between facilities will dictate the requirements and generate the business.

Bootlegging

It is common practice for most major events, where novelties are sold, to obtain a federal injunction regarding copyright law infringement. This provides police with the authority to confiscate unauthorized merchandise and/or arrest its vendors. Local ordinances that govern the sale of items on the street can be most beneficial in eliminating **bootleggers.**

CONCEPT CHECK

Most patrons know that they will be paying more for food and other items within a facility. It is important that the sales staff and the products be of the highest quality. Patrons are becoming more and more demanding of concessions, and the facility must rise to meet these expectations.

TRAFFIC AND PARKING

Traffic flow is an extremely important part of a patron's visit to a major facility. There are two main components of traffic flow: the flow on the public streets to the facility and the flow within the parking lot if there is on-site parking. Figure 14–3 is a sample organizational roster that can be used to ensure that personnel are properly assigned to assist the flow of traffic in a facility's parking lot.

Although public streets are controlled by either the local police or the state highway patrol, the facility should make every effort to coordinate traffic flow in its lots with that of the public streets. One of the most common complaints at events that draw very large audiences is the time it takes to get into and leave the facility's parking lots. A trend in some of the newer facilities being built in urban areas is to take advantage of public transportation (trains and buses).

There are three common revenue-generating methods appropriate for a facility: a direct collection on a per-car basis; a dollar charge per ticket issued; and a flat rate for specific events. Additional sources of parking revenue can be generated from selling preferred, personalized parking spaces; per-event, all-event, season, or annual parking passes; valet parking for VIP parking at a standard fee per automobile; and marketing parking lots for new or antique cars, motor homes, ski or boat shows, carnivals, food festivals, grand prix races, driver safety school, and swap meets.

FINANCIAL MANAGEMENT

Every sport facility operation should have a business operations unit. In small facility operations, much of this function is delegated to one individual and the remainder, especially the tedious, time-consuming tasks, is contracted to an outside organization.

General accounting and finance concepts, for the most part, will be left to other courses that deal in depth with these functions. Discussion in this chapter will focus on the essential elements of the facility business operation: type and process, white papers, event settlement, auditing, payroll, risk management, and bad debts.

Budget

Although a sports facility operates on a day-to-day basis, the most important element of business operations is the development of the budget document. A budget is simply an estimate of receipts and

Parking Personnel Posting Sheet

Event: _____   Date: _____

Supervisors: _____   Supervisors: _____

_____   _____

Cashiers:

West: (1) _____
         (2) _____ _____
         (3) _____ Leader
Center: (4) _____
         (5) _____ _____
         (6) _____ Leader
East#1   (7) _____
         (8) _____ _____
East#2   (9) _____ Leader
         (10) _____
         (11) _____ _____
North   (12) _____ Leader
         (13) _____
         (14) _____ _____
         (15) _____ Leader

Time out:

East#1 :(1)_____(2)_____(3)_____
East#2 :(1)_____(2)_____(3)_____
West : (1)_____(2)_____(3)_____
North: (1)_____(2)_____(3)_____
Center :(1)_____(2)_____(3)_____

Misc Info: _____
_____
_____

Attendants:

East#1: (1) _____ (5) _____
         (2) _____ (6) _____
         (3) _____ (7) _____
         (4) _____ (8) _____
East#2: (1) _____ (5) _____
         (2) _____ (6) _____
         (3) _____ (7) _____
         (4) _____ (8) _____
West: (1) _____ (5) _____
         (2) _____ (6) _____
         (3) _____ (7) _____
         (4) _____ (8) _____
North: (1) _____ (5) _____
         (2) _____ (6) _____
         (3) _____ (7) _____
         (4) _____ (8) _____
Center   (1) _____ (5) _____
Lot: (2) _____ (6) _____
         (3) _____ (7) _____
North   (4) _____ (8) _____
Reserve: (1) _____ (2) _____

Loge: (1) _____ (2) _____
Point: (1) _____ (2) _____

FIGURE 14–3   Parking personnel posting sheet.

payments for a period of time, usually one or two years. It is also important as a predictive tool, for it can anticipate the flow of revenues and expenditures and be used as a tool of control. A budget is a guide to the financial expectations of a facility and an expression of management's plans (Garrison, 1982).

Political: Government budget process

Most sport facilities today are involved in one way or another with government. It is critical for a general manager to have some knowledge of the political process and methodology pertaining to the public budgeting process.

Most state and local governments operate on periods longer than one year—in many cases, a biennium (two years). Therefore, budget requests for public sport facilities may have to be submitted 1½ years prior to actual budget appropriation. By necessity, this projected budget is limited in scope and detail and is often inaccurate. Often, expenses are inflated and income deflated because of the numerous hearings, volatile economies, and the political nature of the budget process. Even though the final approved budget may seem to be "carved in stone," if the desired bottom line is not reached, political advocates can lobby for an adjustment to the budget.

Operational budget process

The submission of a budget request to a government agency does not hinder internal budget operations. Operational budget submissions are usually prepared up to sixty days before actual implementation. This time limitation provides limited flexibility when compared to the governmental product.

Budget cycle

There are four phases in the **budget cycle:** preparation, presentation and adoption, execution and postexecution, and audit.

The preparation of the budget begins with the establishment of the facility's mission, goals, and objectives. The overall objective of the entire process of preparing the budget is to end up with a budget that is coordinated into a well-balanced program. The program impact is the heart of any budget justification enabling the facility to achieve the stated mission if provided the requested resources (IAAM, 1990).

The next step is the actual preparation of financial data, which requires a review of past budget items. After review, the new financial data and their justifications are submitted as a draft that, hopefully, is acceptable to management. These materials provide information concerning the levels of personnel services, wages, benefits, materials, supplies, utilities, and services for the facility operation.

The presentation of a draft or revised budget document is a political process, particularly in large facilities. Initially, the budget document is circulated among proactive supporters for their input and approval. This document should be clear and precise and include any supporting documentation (e.g., letters, charts, comparison statistics, etc.) that may provide the reader with insight and understanding. After the supporters review the document and suggest changes, the revised document is circulated to the entire audience. At this time, the budget preparers must be ready to defend the document in an open forum. As soon as the document is approved and adopted by the assemblage, it is ready for interpretation and execution.

Once the budget is adopted, senior management (especially the general manager) is charged with its dissemination among the various facility departments. All budgeted groups, such as operations or engineering and maintenance, are obligated to maintain control over spending, using techniques such as monthly statements to maintain control of expenditures. Monthly meetings are recommended to ascertain whether budget goals and objectives are on target or need adjustment. It is important to remember that while certain budget limits are carved in stone, the budget document is flexible enough for some accommodation. Any substantial shift in facility goals and objectives will require a budget review and revision. The budget document and resulting implementation then must be altered accordingly. However, the prime directive, regardless of potential alterations, is to achieve the mission, goals, and objectives established at the outset of the process.

Simply put, this procedure evaluates whether or not all the budget assumptions were achieved and the mission fulfilled. In any budgeting situation, it is critical that fiscal budget limitations be adhered to. Overspending in any budget situation, private or public, is unacceptable. The evaluation process determines the level of success and is employed in the development of the next budget document.

Facility accounting

Accounting within a sport facility is similar to that of any other business operation. The only exception is that the operations involved with government demands are simpler and need not be responsive to stockholders, unlike a private facility operation. However, accounting procedures generally involve three fundamental accounting disclosures:

1. Managerial (internal) accounting is based on projections resulting from income and financial data. This information will be used to guide management's decision-making efforts.
2. Financial (external) account reports primarily involve an income statement, a balance sheet, and a cash flow statement. These reports are subject to auditing and must conform to the **generally accepted accounting procedures (GAAP)** that are used by accountants in preparing such reports (Walgenbach, Dittrich, and Hansen, 1980). External reports are not tax reports.

3. Tax accounting reports that are compiled in accordance with the guidelines of the taxation authority (e.g., the Internal Revenue Service).

All external communications are subject to an annual audit by an independent auditing firm, to report the financial status of the organization. It is important that these audits be objective and unbiased because the confidence of the public, as well as the stockholders or bondholders, is important to the future financial health of the facility management organization.

Event settlement

The **event settlement** process uses procedures normally involved in cost accounting or managerial accounting. This procedure is used to compute the operational costs of producing an event. Evaluation of this data guides management decisions, which in turn affect future events.

There are two costing systems employed in this event settlement procedure. The first is process costing, which is primarily used in industry and costs the entire operational process. The second is job order costing, where costs or expenses, such as labor and overhead, are identified by the job. The job order costing method is better suited to the special-order production needs of a sport facility (Davidson et al., 1988).

Sport facilities should analyze cost data both before and after an event settlement because they will (1) provide an operational measure in terms of dollars generated, (2) assist management in economic and negotiating decisions, (3) justify the need for greater funding, resources, and reimbursement, and (4) provide accountability. If an item is overlooked in the development of a settlement estimate at the end of an event, the facility or management group will have to suffer the loss, because recuperation will be impossible.

Any services associated with the production of an event are channeled into the costing of that event. These sources, known as **house expenses,** include such things as a plumber retained to unstop toilets and prevent a potential flood; stagehands and light operators; a specific facility setup configuration, such as a basketball floor; and the security guard assigned to the box office to protect the facility's deposits against theft. These services cannot be charged to the event promoter because they are the responsibility of the facility and are not recoverable cost items.

A cost accounting system enables the facility business office to itemize detailed contractual elements of the event/promotion and those that define the responsibilities of the facility's management (Garrison, 1982). Expenses must be collated and recorded; otherwise, facility management will absorb these expenses rather than pass them on to the promoter. The event settlement process, especially at a concert, usually begins about midway through the performance and may conclude before the end of the show. The only real concern after settlement is completed is that the show does not run over the projected time allotment; in that case, additional costs accrue to the facility management.

If the event settlement process has not been completed before the event has ended and the promoter has left, the likelihood of recapturing one's investment is probably "slim to none." Groups that have a good reputation and have been dealt with successfully over the years build up a level of trust and are considered stable operations. Their events are usually resolved within ten days of the event closure. With all other events, a facility would normally require a hefty deposit. In fact, it would be expected that in the majority of cases the rent would be paid thirty days in advance, rather than after the event.

Policies covering event settlement procedures are event-specific and part of the facility management philosophy. The bottom line is that every penny the facility spends for an event that is caused by the event must be accounted for and, hopefully, fully recovered by the facility.

Auditing

Regardless of business classification or location, safeguarding management's operating and financial controls are the objective of the audit process. There are two segments of the auditing process: the internal audit and external audit (Walgenbach, Dittrich, and Hansen, 1980).

Internal audit. The internal audit is a management tool that ensures that the company's assets are used properly and safeguarded at all levels. It is vital that all employees adhere to company policy and follow established procedures. There are two crucial elements within this **internal auditing process:** asset security and personnel compliance. Asset security involves the internal accounting control procedures. Substantial losses sometimes occur due to the theft of products or funds or the misuse of funds or equipment. It is important to realize that every employee is a *potential* thief. Personnel compliance attempts to provide personnel with operational guidelines to protect both the employee and the organization from potential future litigation. Appropriate supervision of employees should include random visitations to a facility—at night, on the weekend, or at unusual times. Management should attempt to vary its visits and not be predictable.

It is prudent to establish a paper trail, which is a collection of documents that can be used in an audit to substantiate any transactions involving the exchange of goods. Cash register tapes, purchase orders, requisitions, checks, contracts, ticket sale reports, and concession reports are often part of this paper trail. This information should be retained in the event of litigation arising out of employee dishonesty.

External audit. An **external audit** examines the organizational accounting records and financial statements to make certain that they are appropriately prepared and not misleading. The external auditor, usually a certified public accountant (CPA), tests and checks the accounting system underlying the financial statements, using the accepted American Institute of Certified Public Accountants (AICPA) auditing standards. This external audit is known as the *attest function,* which provides independent assurance as to whether appropriate procedures have been used.

Problem resolution

The internal auditing process should be an ongoing practice by management throughout the year, while the required external audit can be quarterly, although it is usually annual. Both of these audit processes are necessary to maintain the financial health and credibility of an organization. If an individual or group that is trusted and holds security clearance is involved in a facility problem, the penalty should be quick and should fit the crime. It is important that an example be set for all personnel. Management must have extremely tight control, because its credibility is on the line. If there is any infraction or other problem, swift action must be initiated to resolve the situation, keeping in mind any potential fallout.

Payroll

Payroll in a facility denotes, as in any other business, the compensation paid to employees on a regular basis. In a sport facility operation, the majority of employees are seasonal and part-time (employed no more than thirty-seven hours per week). These employees are usually paid on a weekly basis at an hourly rate. Full-time employees (employed at least forty hours a week) are paid biweekly or monthly. Overtime pay begins when an employee works more than forty hours a week. The rate of pay for this overtime is 1½ times the regular rate. Unionized employees are sometimes reimbursed at higher rates. Full-time employment is classified as either staff or management. The staff (line) classification usually includes hourly employees, while management is paid a salary, regardless of the time spent on the job.

The employee remuneration package consists of both wages/salary and deductions. Examples of some of these deductions are Social Security, federal income taxes withheld, state and local income taxes, state disability insurance, unemployment compensation, and any voluntary employee deductions. The employee's net (take-home) pay is calculated by taking the employee's gross pay (wages earned) and subtracting all the appropriate taxes and other deductions. At the end of the financial year, every employee, regardless of employment status, will receive a W-4 form prepared by the accounting division of the operation.

Payroll represents the largest portion of the total cost of any operation. All records pertaining to payroll must be maintained by the employer to prepare annual tax calculations and support the audit process. To satisfy government, union, and employee expectations, it is important to use a payroll method that is facility-specific and that satisfies all the conditions established. Instead of using a manual payroll operation, a facility can use one of several computer software applications available for calculating payrolls. These can be customized for a facility's special needs.

CONCEPT CHECK

Financial management is an extremely important aspect of facility management. Budget payroll and event settlement are probably the main features of financial management. To successfully manage this area, the facility manager must know something about accounting terminology and procedures.

RISK MANAGEMENT

Risk is defined as a hazard or the possibility of danger or harm. Risk management focuses on limiting exposure to harm in the facility (Berlonghi, 1990). The most common danger that a sport facility manager tries to minimize is injuries to patrons at the facility, which create the potential for lawsuits. These lawsuits can cause substantial monetary losses to the sport facility. The obvious goal of minimizing injuries and avoiding lawsuits and monetary losses may sound easy, but in fact it is a very complicated and difficult task to do correctly.

In order to be efficient at this task, the risk manager should identify the possible risks, assess their likelihood, calculate how to respond to the risks, and create standards and procedures (a strategic plan) for decreasing the risks.

Identification stage

In the risk identification stage, the facility manager must discover the various risks that may cause losses during any given event. There are primary and secondary factors that must be addressed in order to reduce the likelihood of losses to the sport facility. Primary factors are the base of operations at every sport facility, and each sport facility manager must consider them when trying to reduce risk. These factors are within almost complete control of the sport facility manager. It should be noted that while a well-trained staff is the risk manager's best tool for identifying risks, staff members can also be risks themselves.

Risk assessment

The assessment of risks should be systematic, using amount and frequency of loss as the two criteria. A matrix can be created that allows a consistent approach to the assessing process. Figure 14–4 gives the sport facility manager nine categories in which to classify any identified risk.

Risk treatment

The next stage, risk treatment, can also be accomplished with the use of a matrix. As you can see from figure 14–5, the matrix is now filled with various treatments for risks based on the three frequencies of occurrence and the three amounts of loss.

Avoidance

Clearly, one should avoid risks that cause a great amount of loss or occur often. For example, a sport facility should never hold an event that has caused

	High Frequency	Moderate Frequency	Low Frequency
High Loss			
Moderate Loss			
Low Loss			

FIGURE 14–4   Risk assessment matrix.

	High Frequency	Moderate Frequency	Low Frequency
High Loss	Avoid	Shift	Shift
Moderate Loss	Shift	Shift or keep & decrease	Shift or keep & decrease
Low Loss	Keep & decrease	Keep & decrease	Keep & decrease

FIGURE 14–5   Risk treatment matrix.

great damage to sport facilities elsewhere or that has equipment that is inherently dangerous, such as diving boards in swimming pools. Holding an event that has caused extensive property damage at other facilities and/or led to lawsuits would not be prudent. This type of event should be avoided altogether. The sport facility manager is an effective risk manager if he or she does not allow such an event to take place in the interest of eliminating all potential losses that might occur.

Transferring risks

This treatment of identified and assessed risks focuses on the sport facility manager's knowledge that certain losses will occur but it is difficult to determine the approximate losses involved and the frequency of occurrence. The matrix has identified these risks more or less as middle-of-the-road risks.

Looking at the matrix, however, does reveal that some very high losses are included. We do not wish to avoid these risks, because the frequency of their occurrence is moderate or below. Also, the risks that occur very frequently are moderate and therefore should not be avoided.

Keeping and decreasing risks

The final option for treating risks is to keep the risk and attempt to decrease the amount of loss the risk can cause. We can see in the matrix that risks that are to be kept and decreased are those that have low or very low potential for loss. A sport facility can accept these risks because there is very little chance of suffering substantial losses. Of course, this assumes that once the sport facility manager decides to keep the risk, proper precautions are taken to decrease the occurrence of and the monetary loss associated with the risk. This is accomplished by developing standard operating procedures, which is the final step in the risk management process.

Standard operating procedures

Under **standard operating procedures (SOPs),** the sport facility manager develops a strategic plan that will provide the most efficient and effective way to decrease the occurrence of risks. The strategic plan is basically a step-by-step set of instructions that give detailed directions for the appropriate courses of action, given the event and the risks associated with it. SOPs should be developed for both risks that are transferred and risks that are kept and decreased. (See figure 14–6 for an illustration of the risk management process.)

CONCEPT CHECK

It is extremely important to realize that risk management is a dynamic process that must continually be analyzed and modified. By following the risk management process, the facility manager can make the facility safer for patrons while reducing potential liability situations.

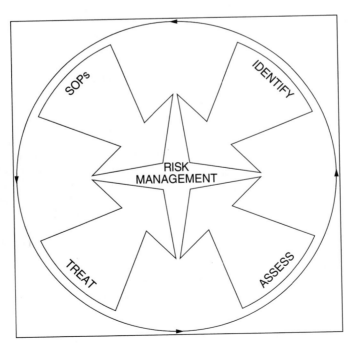

FIGURE 14–6 The risk management process.

CRITICAL THINKING EXERCISES

1. As a facility manager, what are the steps you would follow in a risk audit, and what are some things you would be looking for?
2. As a facility manager, how would you market a new facility? How does this differ from marketing events?

SUMMARY

1. The trend in facility management is toward private management companies rather than in-house operations. Private management companies are solicited through the request-for-proposals (RFP) process.
2. In order to effectively manage a facility, a mission statement—along with policies, procedures, goals, and objectives—must be established.
3. Booking and scheduling deals with obtaining events and contracting with the promoters of the events. It is important to have a good fit between the facility and the event in order for operations to be effective.
4. Marketing and promotions attempt to publicize events and attract patrons to them. Exposure is the key element in the success of the marketing campaign.
5. Proper security and emergency procedures must be developed in order to minimize lawsuits and provide a safe environment for patrons to enjoy the events.
6. The box office is in charge of ticket sales and admissions. It is an extremely important aspect of the facility because it handles a great deal of money and it is the first part of the facility that patrons deal with.
7. Concessions and novelties have become an increasingly important aspect of facility management. Expectations of patrons have increased to the point where concessions need to provide a higher level of food products and other items to meet these expectations.
8. Financial management deals with budgeting, event settlement, and auditing. These aspects of facility management require knowledge of the practices and principles of accounting and finance. Because many crucial decisions are based upon budget, event settlement, and auditing documents, it is extremely important that all of them be professionally prepared.
9. Risk management's purpose is to provide a structure to alleviate liability problems that could lead to significant financial losses. Also, the process of developing standard operating procedures for a facility provides a safe environment for the patrons.

CASE STUDY I

You have just been hired as the facility manager for the Coliseum. The president of the Coliseum wants you to create an operations manual that will help the building run more efficiently while making your job easier to perform. The following is a list of priorities given to you by the president of the Coliseum:

1. *Operations management: Describe and diagram the optimal organizational structure. This structure should include position descriptions and projected salaries.*
2. *Risk management: Describe the overall function of risk management within your arena. Give five potential risk management scenarios and explain in detail their resolution using risk management principles.*
3. *Marketing: Develop a marketing plan for your facility, including projected costs and benefits and two advertising campaigns for your facility.*
4. *Event management: Describe this process in your facility, including a chain of command for personnel (parking, security, ticket takers, ushers, etc.). Choose a special event that could be held at your facility, and describe what special-event management needs this event might create.*
5. *Concessions/food service: Describe the function of concessions in your facility. Give reasons why you would or would not own the concessions, have an agreement to get a percentage of concessions, or simply lease the space for concessions.*

CASE STUDY II

Assume that you are the facility manager at the Coliseum. Develop a standard operating procedure (SOP) for spills (something you forgot to do in your operations manual.) In this procedure, you need to describe what role, if any, the various departments would play in reporting, monitoring, and/or cleaning up spills.

After you have written your SOP, discuss the following problem. (Assume that the SOP has been put into effect and that it is reasonable in terms of implementation.)

A spill has just taken place, and the following events occur: (1) Three ticket takers see the spill and do nothing, (2) two security guards see the spill, but they are called to a fight and do not report the spill until fifteen minutes after they spotted it, (3) an usher immediately reports the spill but does not keep patrons from walking in the area, (4) the cleaning crew cleans the spill forty minutes after it was notified of it (forty-five minutes after it occurred), and (5) a patron slipped and fell because of the spill, broke an ankle, and is suing the Coliseum for $45,000.

REVIEW QUESTIONS AND ISSUES

1. Describe the advantages of contracting with private management companies.
2. What is RFP? Describe this selection process.
3. Define booking and scheduling.
4. Describe the reservation process. Comment on the statement that this process is not fair.
5. How does the mission of the facility influence its reservations and priorities?
6. How would you resolve a problem of two sport promoters desiring the same date and time?
7. Identify the four components of operations management.
8. List the operations manager's responsibilities.
9. When coordinating an event, what are the elements considered important from an operational perspective?
10. List the important elements concerned with the development of an emergency manual.
11. What measures need to be taken to ensure prompt and professional emergency response training for facility staff?
12. Define the terms *housekeeping, maintenance, engineering,* and *structural and equipment maintenance.*
13. List the elements of a maintenance and housekeeping plan.
14. Explain the following terms: *in-house food service management, concessions, stocking, convenience foods,* and *hawkers.*
15. Under what circumstances would you let an in-house food service management operation contract?
16. Explain the following terms: *novelties, bootlegging,* and *merchandising deals* with sport teams and athletes.
17. Why is the box office an important segment of the facility operation?
18. Identify the important components of box office operations.
19. What is a budget?
20. How does the political/government budget process differ from the private/operational budget?
21. Identify and comment on the phases of the budget cycle.
22. Describe the various budget types that can be involved in a facility budget.
23. Identify and describe the phases of a white paper. How does this apply to a sport facility?
24. Describe how event settlement works in a sport facility.
25. List internal auditing procedures that could be used in the various segments of the facility operation.
26. Why is it important to develop collections procedures?
27. Identify traditional revenue sources and operational segments in a facility.
28. List additional revenue sources.
29. Identify the essential elements of the risk management process, and describe the function of each.

SOLUTIONS TO CRITICAL THINKING EXERCISES

1. Identify, assess, treat, and develop standard operating procedures. Torn carpet, protruding objects, wet spots, lighting, access points, proper food preparation, etc.
2. Marketing a new facility is a fairly simple task. Marketers usually focus on the new amenities and try to build an exciting image to entice the patrons to come and see the new facility. The target market in event marketing is usually much narrower than when marketing a facility. So, in promoting an event, a marketer can use much more specific enticements to draw patrons to the facility.

REFERENCES

Berlonghi, A. (1990). *The special event risk management manual.* Dana Point, CA: Self-published.

Davidson, S., Maher, M., Stickney, C., and Weil, R. (1988). *Managerial accounting: An introduction to concepts, methods and uses,* Chicago: Dryden Press.

Garrison, R. (1982). *Managerial accounting.* Plano, TX: Business Publications.

Hitt, W. (1985). *Management in action.* Columbus, OH: Battelle Press.

International Association of Auditorium Managers. (1990). Unpublished proceedings, Ogelbay, Virginia, School for Public Assembly Facility Management.

Jewel, D. (1992). *Public assembly facilities.* Malabar, FL: Krieger Publishing.

Laventhol and Horwath. (1989). *Convention centers, stadiums, and arenas.* Washington, D.C.: Urban Land Institutes.

O'Shaughnessy, J. (1988). *Competitive marketing: A strategic approach.* Boston: Unwin Hyman.

Thompson, A., and Strickland, A. (1990). *Strategic management, concepts and cases,* Homewood, IL: BPI Irwin.

Walgenbach, P., Dittrich, N., and Hansen, E. (1980). *Principles of accounting.* New York: Harcourt Brace Jovanovich.

WEBSITES

FacilitiesNet

www.facilitiesnet.com/

This site for facility professionals includes industry news; an online bookstore; bulletin boards; *Building Operating Management, Maintenance Solutions, Energy Decisions,* and *Education* magazines; and information on products and equipment.

International Facility Management Association (IFMA)

www.ifma.org

Site includes publications, job opportunities, on-line library, product information, publishing opportunities in the *Facility Management Journal,* training seminars, and World Workplace conference. IFMA focuses on management and administration needs of facility managers.

PART V

Marketing

CHAPTER 15

Sport Marketing: Strategies and Tactics

Dianna P. Gray

In this chapter, you will become familiar with the following terms:

Sport marketing
Product extensions
Strategic planning
Demographics
Lifestyle
Product usage
Target market
Market segmentation
Market
Niche

Product
Services
Product benefits
Core product
Brand
Price
Bartering
Positioning
Promotion
Advertising

e-commerce
Sales promotion
Personal selling
Telemarketing
Public relations
Place
Distribution
Marketing plan

Overview

A thorough understanding of sport marketing theory and its application is a requirement for success in the sports industry. Sport has become one of the most conspicuous and omnipresent institutions in our society. The sports industry is the eleventh largest of all industry groups in the United States with a market value of $152 billion in 1995 (Meek, 1998). Whether employed in upper-level management, or in an entry-level position, the sport professional realizes that marketing is integral to the successful operation of the organization. The purpose of this chapter is to present concepts about sport marketing and to discuss the application of these concepts. This will be achieved by defining sport marketing and illustrat-

ing sports' unique characteristics; explaining the marketing management process; identifying and analyzing consumers; introducing the concept of marketing communication and the marketing mix; and developing a strategic marketing plan. The student who understands the strategic marketing management process will more fully understand the role of the marketing in the sport organization.

WHAT IS SPORT MARKETING?

A definition of *sport marketing* must be preceded by a definition and examination of marketing. Perreault and McCarthy (1999) define marketing as the performance of activities that direct the flow of goods and services from producer to user to satisfy the customer and accomplish the organization's objectives. Kotler (1997) defines marketing as the human activity directed at satisfying needs and wants through exchange processes. The American Marketing Association defines marketing as the "process of planning and executing the conception, pricing, promotion, and distribution of ideas, goods and services to create exchanges that satisfy individual and organization objectives" ("AMA Board," 1985). An emphasis on satisfying consumers' wants and needs is everywhere in today's marketplace; successful organizations are those that realize their objectives by satisfying customers' needs. Marketing is as much a way of conducting business as it is a theoretical concept.

The term *sport marketing* is said to have been coined by *Advertising Age* in 1978 to describe the activities of consumer and industrial product and service marketers who were increasingly using sport as a promotional vehicle. This is commonly referred to as marketing *through* sport; that is, *using sport* as a promotional vehicle or sponsorship platform for companies that market consumer and, to a lesser extent, industrial products. What is absent from this description is the marketing *of* sport. This aspect of sport marketing involves the specific application of marketing principles and processes to market goods and services directly to sports participants and spectators, or end users.

Many authors have developed definitions for the concept and practice of sport marketing (see for example, Brooks, 1994; Milne and McDonald, 1999; Mullin, Hardy, and Sutton, 1993; Shank, 1999; Stotlar, 1993), all of which encompass the essential elements of marketing. For our purposes, **sport marketing** will be defined as the anticipation, management, and satisfaction of sport consumers' wants and needs through the application of marketing principles and practice. Sport marketing begins and ends with the customer—whether an individual or organization—in mind.

A commonly asked question is whether sport as a product differs significantly from other goods and services. Virtually all sport marketers maintain that sport has certain characteristics in its core, extensions, and presentation that make the sport product unique, requiring an approach that may, at times, vary from the approaches of "mainstream" business marketing. What follows is a brief examination of sport's unique qualities that will alter traditional marketing approaches and dictate the "locus of control" of the sport marketer.

Intangibility and subjectivity

Simply put, the consumer takes nothing away from attending a sport event but impressions and memories. The wide variety of possible impressions and interpretations of the event pose a challenge for the sport marketer, namely to achieve a probability of consumer satisfaction. For example, consider a group of five people attending a major league baseball game. One member of the group might remember that parking was difficult and expensive; another might have been disappointed with the outcome of the game; a third may have been impressed by the quality of the pitching matchups; the fourth member of the group may have been disappointed in the lack of scoring; and the fifth person may remember enjoying the event because of the social interaction with the other members of the group. Each member of the group had an opinion that, although not necessarily related to the core product, or game itself, will influence future purchasing decisions about that product. In describing baseball, Veeck illustrates the intangibility of the sport product by stating, "The customer comes out to the park with nothing except the illusion that he is going to have a good time. He leaves with nothing except a memory" (Veeck and Linn, 1965).

Inconsistency/unpredictability

One of the great attractions of sport, for both participants and spectators alike, is the belief that on any given day, any team or individual, regardless of past performance, can win. This attitude would certainly describe die-hard Cubs fans! Many factors can affect the outcome of a game or contest. Such factors include injuries to players, player trades, momentum, motivation, and environmental conditions such as weather and time of year. These factors and the "lack of a game script" interact to guarantee that each game, event, or contest will be unique and the outcome will be "guaranteed."

Product perishability

The sport product can be sold no later than the day of the event. In reality, it should be sold well before the date to help ensure franchise stability, consumer interest, and product credibility. There is virtually no consumer market for yesterday's boxing match or basketball game. In professional sport, as well as basketball and football at "major" schools, tickets should be presold to guarantee stable revenue and to generate profits. If tickets are not presold, revenue will depend on performance, and if performance is poor or not up to expectations, revenue will suffer.

Emotional attachment and identification

Many studies have been conducted to measure the attitudes and behavior patterns of Americans regarding sport participation and attendance, as well as the effect of sport on the lives of Americans. The Miller Lite study of 1993, and the ongoing ESPN/Chilton Sports Poll reveal, among other findings, the tremendous effect sport has on the daily lives of Americans, not only in terms of sport participation, but also in attendance and media consumption of sport. A 1991 public opinion poll from a national sample revealed that 73 percent of the respondents were either "very interested" or "fairly interested" in watching sports, either in person or on TV (Lieberman, 1991). These studies also surveyed the *attitudes* of Americans toward sport, the results of which indicate that approximately 95 percent of American society is affected by sport (reading, discussing, listening, watching, or participating) each day.

Evidence of the prevalence of sport can also be seen by examining the growth of the sports industry. In 1987 sport was a $47.2 billion-a-year enterprise (Sandomir, 1988); by 1989 that figure had risen to $63 billion (Comte and Stogel, 1990). The most recent research on the economic impact of sport identifies it as a $152 billion-a-year industry, making it the eleventh largest industry in the U.S. (Meek, 1998). Sport is not simply another big business; it is one of the fastest-growing industries in the U.S., and it is intertwined with practically every aspect of the economy, from advertising and apparel, to computer technology and virtual reality games, to travel and tourism.

The development of properties divisions and merchandising departments in all professional and major college athletic programs has contributed to this sport frenzy by giving interested fans an opportunity to buy a variety of licensed apparel, uniform replicas or related team items. The increasing sales of caps, T-shirts, sweatshirts, jackets and other clothing emblazoned with Olympic marks, NFL individual

TABLE 15-1 *Super Bowl merchandise sales figures*

Super Bowl	Teams	Merchandise sales
Super Bowl XXIX	49ers–Chargers	$80 million
Super Bowl XXX	Cowboys–Steelers	$100 million
Super Bowl XXXI	Packers–Patriots	$130 million
Super Bowl XXXII	Broncos–Packers	$100 million
Super Bowl XXXIII	Broncos–Falcons	$90 million

Source: NFL Properties Inc.

and Super Bowl teams, and college and professional basketball teams, is just one indicator of the growing popularity of licensed merchandise. For example, even though Super Bowl merchandise sales vary widely, depending on the teams playing in the final game, apparel manufacturers have witnessed record sales figures in the past five years. Table 15-1 identifies recent Super Bowl merchandise sales.

Focus and "locus of control"

In mainstream business marketing, marketers play a critical role in determining the composition of their organizations' marketing mix, (how the four Ps will be blended and used) and product positioning. However, in sport marketing the marketer's input is inappropriate and thus is not actively sought. Players are acquired, traded, platooned, and used with no input from the marketer, whose responsibility is to market the game to a variety of market segments. Although the trade or acquisition of a particular player may help or hurt attendance, these decisions are not the purview of the sport marketer. The scheduling of the opposition is another factor that is outside the scope of the sport marketer's responsibility, yet it has a significant effect on attendance in team sports (Rudman and Sutton, 1989).

For example, in college football, league games are scheduled by the league office; only the scheduling of nonconference games is controlled by the home school. In 1999, eight schools in the sixteen-member Western Athletic Conference (WAC) left to form the new Mountain West Conference (MWC). One of the main reasons given for forming the new conference was that the traditional "rivalry" games, so important to the development of a strong athletic tradition, had been diminished when the WAC conference expanded to sixteen teams in 1995. The MWC reunites seven of the original WAC teams plus UNLV, and traditional rivalries are back in place (Patrick, 1999). Similarly, in participant sports, crucial factors such as weather, this week's gasoline costs, or the presence of road construction are outside the locus of control of sport marketers but have significant effects on demand at golf, tennis, and ski facilities. Thus the focus of the marketer is largely on the **product extensions** that are within (the locus of) his or her control. Table 15-2 summarizes the unique characteristics of sport, examining the market as well as the four Ps of the marketing mix.

CONCEPT CHECK

Sport marketing has unique characteristics and considerations not found in most areas of product marketing. Intangibility, subjectivity, inconsistency, unpredictability, perishability, emotional attachment and identification, social facilitation, public consumption, and focus and locus of control are factors that interact to form a series of challenges for the sport marketer.

TABLE 15-2 *Unique sport characteristics*

Market	Sport organizations compete and cooperate simultaneously
	Sport consumers consider themselves experts
	Wide fluctuation in consumer demand (seasonal, weekly, and daily demand differences)
Product	Intangible
	Subjective
	Produced and consumed on same site
	Inconsistent
	Perishable/no shelf life (must presell)
	Publicly consumed; affected by social facilitation
	Sport marketer has no control over core product
Price	Difficult to price using conventional methods
	Small percentage of total money spent by consumer goes to sport organization
	More money obtained from product extensions, TV, etc. (indirect revenues)
	Only recently required to operate as a for-profit organization
Promotion	Tremendous media exposure
	Businesses want association with sport
Place/distribution	Produced and consumed in same place
	Atmosphere contributes to enjoyment
	Sport marketer should focus efforts here
	TV and media; tickets

STRATEGIC MARKET MANAGEMENT

Strategic market management is a system designed to help management make better marketing decisions. A strategic decision is the creation, change, or retention of a strategy (Aaker, 1998). Philip Kotler (1997) defines the strategic market planning process as the managerial process of developing and maintaining a strategic fit between the organization's goals and resources and its changing market opportunities. The tangible result of this planning process is a marketing plan. Later in the chapter, the development of a marketing plan will be covered in detail.

Strategic planning

An essential component of the **strategic planning** process is conducting an environmental analysis (Aaker, 1998; Kotler, 1997). An environmental analysis is an assessment of the "climate," including internal and external factors that may or may not affect marketing efforts. For example, in intercollegiate athletics the environment would include the university itself, the athletic department, the local community, alumni, state government, media, boosters and corporate sponsors, and in this particular case, the federal government. How can the federal government affect the operations of an intercollegiate athletic program? It can enact legislation altering the tax-exempt status of gifts to the college athletic program, particularly contributions made to ensure "priority seating," a product requiring a donation for the "right to purchase" tickets. Such legislation could devastate athletic departments throughout the country and would affect not only the importance of marketing efforts, but also the scope and direction of those efforts.

It is important that the marketer conduct an environmental analysis of the historical market, as well as the present market climate and future market assumptions. In considering a city as a possible expansion site for a professional sports team, the league office would wish to understand the sports attendance history of that city, as well as sports and entertainment competition for the entertainment dollars of that city's populace. For example, if the city of Pittsburgh were being considered for a possible NBA expansion franchise, an environmental analysis would provide the following information:

Past professional basketball franchises
Pittsburgh Rens (ABL)
Pittsburgh Pipers (ABA)
Pittsburgh Condors (ABA)

It would also reveal that the Philadelphia 76ers played a limited schedule in Pittsburgh in the late 1960s.

Current sports competition
Pittsburgh Steelers (NFL)—some seasonal overlap
Pittsburgh Pirates (MLB)—some seasonal overlap
Pittsburgh Penguins (NHL)—direct competition
Pittsburgh Bulls (lacrosse)—some seasonal overlap, and also tenant
University of Pittsburgh—Division I college basketball
Duquesne University—Division I college basketball
Robert Morris University—Division I college basketball

In addition to these competitors, there are college basketball programs at the Division III, NAIA, and junior college levels. Also, as in all areas of the country, there are high school sport programs in basketball, hockey, and wrestling.

This type of research in the planning process provides a realistic assessment of the market and should also reveal past practices that were successful and those that failed. This process is one part of the situational analysis, which assesses strengths, weaknesses, opportunities, and threats (the SWOT analysis).

The sport marketer uses strategic market management to identify potential customers and then classify market segments. Once the segments are identified, the sport marketer then targets the appropriate market segment(s) and develops the core marketing strategy. This includes the selection of target market(s), the choice of a competitive position, and the development of an effective marketing mix to reach and serve the chosen consumers (Kotler, 1997).

The strategic market planning process justifies resource allocation, personnel decisions, media use, and ultimately organizational direction by defining organizational objectives. The strategic market planning process then enables the marketer to consider strategies that may be used in the organizational marketing efforts to achieve those objectives. Such strategies may be related to price, promotions, distribution, packaging, and positioning.

Consumer behavior

As stated earlier, the focus of marketing begins and ends with the customer/consumer. Kotler (1997) states that a customer orientation, backed by an integrated marketing approach aimed at satisfying customers, is the key to achieving the organization's goals. Knowledge of the consumer is so important for effective marketing that a variety of disciplines have studied it.

Marketing starts with an analysis of the consumer. Think of consumers as people who are trying to solve a problem. The consumers' problem could be described as the perceived difference between the *way things are* and the *way they wished them to be*. Thus, in an effort to satisfy needs, wants, and desires, consumers purchase goods and services. In other words, consumers purchase goods as one way of solving the problem of the *current situation* versus the *desired situation*. A young man feels he doesn't have a sufficiently masculine physique, so he joins a health and fitness club and begins a weight-lifting regime. An elderly woman concerned about decreased mobility and her resulting loss of independence enrolls in an aqua-robics class. The recent MBA graduate who wishes to impress colleagues and friends purchases a season ticket for the Los Angeles Lakers, an NBA franchise. As you can readily see, consumers must deal with a number of "problems" in their daily lives. A better understanding of why consumers behave as they do provides sport marketers with the information needed to effectively develop programs that solve consumers' problems, and to then communicate that to respective target audiences.

When one considers the diversity of sport and recreation participants, spectators, and the various sport and entertainment options available today, it is not difficult to hypothesize that each consumer may be seeking different attributes, and realizing different benefits and satisfaction from the same sport or activity. Whereas one fan enjoys the tension of a no-hitter, another is bored by the subsequent lack of offensive production.

The sport marketer seeks to maximize consumer satisfaction so that the spectator or participant will demonstrate repeat behavior. There are various ways to try to increase consumer satisfaction (i.e., increase the benefits and/or reduce the costs). However, knowledge of what motivates or deters the consumer from attending an event or participating in an activity is required before such attempts are made. On the surface, it may seem obvious why people watch or participate in sports. Nevertheless, the reasons for choosing one form of sport entertainment, or one activity over another, are not self-evident. It should be apparent then, that the study of why and how consumers decide to attend sports events, or engage in a particular sport activity, is an important yet complex facet of sport marketing.

What then, are the factors that motivate the consumption of various sport and leisure products and services? What are the factors that prevent or deter consumption of, or participation in sport?

There are at least three factors researchers have identified that appear to influence consumers' behavior about participation in, and consumption of, sports. Environmental, social, and cultural variables, collectively referred to as *sociocultural factors*, are known to influence behavior (Engel, Blackwell, and Miniard, 1995). The people with whom one associates, family, friends, and colleagues, have a potential influence on sport, entertainment, and activity decisions. One reason sport marketers collect demographic data on consumer markets is to develop marketing strategies based on the effects of sociocultural factors; people from the same environment tend to have similar interests and act similarly (Cialdini, 1993; Engel, Blackwell, and Miniard, 1995; Brooks, 1994).

Another important area that experts agree has some influence is one's personal or psychological state. Here is where sport marketers, in their effort to provide for consumers' wants, seek to better understand what is going on in the mind of the consumer. This factor includes one's attitudes, beliefs, and motivation. Attitudes and beliefs play a role in the consumers' psychological state because attitudes are a learned behavior and an expression of one's values and opinions. People have attitudes toward all objects, which may be positive, negative, or neutral. For our purposes, an attitude is an *index* of the degree to which a person likes or dislikes a sport or activity. How a customer feels about a particular sport or activity is based on information from previous experiences and is stored in the mind as an attitude (Engel, Blackwell, and Miniard, 1995). In an effort to build favorable attitudes toward a sport or activity *before* the customer even decides to try the sport, sport marketers emphasize the sport's various characteristics and benefits through promotional messages. This tactic is also used *after* customers attend a sports event or engage in an activity, in another effort to reinforce any positive attitudes held by the consumer.

Another aspect of one's personal/psychological state is motivation. While motivation is a complex area that is difficult if not impossible for the sport marketer to quantify, it is an important aspect of understanding consumer behavior. Motivation can be defined as a theoretical construct involving an internal need state that gives impetus to behavior, and a directional component that gives general direction to a variety of responses serving the same general function for the organism (Engel, Blackwell, and Miniard, 1995). Keep in mind that motivation is a theoretical construct that cannot be observed directly; only behavior can be observed. It is only after observing behavior that sport marketers can infer motives, and then design appropriate marketing communications and promotions. Mullin, Hardy, and Sutton (1993) have identified achievement, affiliation, health and fitness, and fun and entertainment as the four most frequently occurring motives in the literature on motivation and sport consumption. Determining customers' wants and needs is a basic axiom of marketing. However, accomplishing this is not as easy as it might appear.

Identifying and targeting sport consumers

To be successful in the highly competitive sport and entertainment business, the sport marketer must know something about the people who will be the

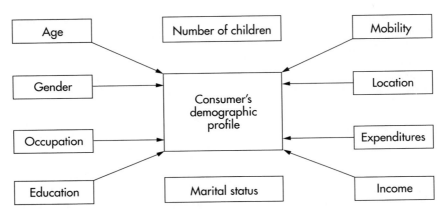

FIGURE 15–1   Factors that determine a demographic profile.

ultimate consumers. This learning process consists of examining the characteristics and needs of the target market, including the consumer's lifestyle and purchase decisions, so that product, distribution (place), promotion, and pricing decisions are made accordingly. By knowing as much as possible about the consumer, the sport marketer can satisfy the target markets, keep consumer dissatisfaction to a minimum, and remain competitive by maintaining or increasing market share.

Before beginning to plan ways of marketing a sport product or service, the sport marketer should answer some general questions about the consumer. First, who is the consumer of the product or service? Here the marketer is trying to obtain information about the *final consumer,* the person who actually decides to purchase the produce or service. Where does the consumer live? How does the consumer learn about the available sport and entertainment opportunities? To what forms of media is the consumer exposed? How far in advance of the event does the consumer decide to attend or participate? When does the consumer purchase the ticket to the event? What does the consumer do before the game (pre-event) and after the game (post-event)?

After getting general information about the sport consumer, the marketer seeks answers to more specific questions. At this stage, the marketer begins to compose a profile of the sport consumer by examining demographic and lifestyle information. Consumer **demographics** are the statistical descriptions of the attributes or characteristics of the population. By looking at demographic information, both indi-vidual characteristics and overall descriptions, the sport marketer can begin to develop consumer profiles that may pinpoint both attractive and declining market opportunities. Figure 15–1 illustrates some of the common factors that are used to determine a demographic profile.

One of the best ways to obtain demographic information is to conduct primary research, usually by means of a survey. This is not always feasible because of financial or time limits; however, there are several secondary sources of information. These sources give the sport marketer not only information about the general population, but also specific information about sport consumers. The federal government collects a wealth of data on its citizens. U.S. government sources include the *U.S. Census, American Statistics Index,* and *ASI Abstracts.* Population statistics from other sources such as chambers of commerce, convention and visitors bureaus (CVBs), public utility companies, and marketing firms can supplement the census data. Published sport-specific demographic data can be obtained from individual sport franchises, the national offices of the major sport leagues, sport marketing firms, institutions and private corporations that have commissioned studies, or university libraries.

The Simmons Market Research Bureau, Inc. and other marketing research companies annually conduct personal interviews with subjects on many consumer issues, including sport participation and live and televised sport viewing. Most university libraries have the results of these studies, a volume of which is usually devoted entirely to sport and leisure.

TABLE 15-3   *Secondary information sources: Print*

Print sources	Description
American Sports Analysis	Includes participation data for sports and other physical activity
Sporting Goods Industry Financial Performance	Published by the Sporting Goods Manufacturers Association (SGMA)
National Sporting Goods Association	Consumer demographics for sport-related products
Mediamark Research	Participation, sports attendance, spectating, and media habits reported
The Lifestyle Market Analyst	Demographic and lifestyle information on sport spectators and participants
The Almanac of Consumer Markets	Demographics, lifestyles, and segmentation techniques
Statistical Abstract of the United States	Summary statistics on social, political, and economic organizations in U.S. Breakdown of dollars spent on sporting events, goods, etc.
The Sports/Fitness/Leisure Markets	Fairchild publication; participation, spectating, and purchasing information
Study of Media and Markets; Kids Study	Participation, sports attendance, spectating, and media habits reported. Kids study (respondents aged 6–14); published by Simmons Market Research Bureau.

There are also a variety of serial publications and electronic databases (CD-ROMs) that offer the marketer demographic information. *American Demographics* is a monthly magazine that specializes in demographic data. Other secondary sources of demographic information include the Women's Sport Foundation, *The Sports Business Daily, Athletic Business, Club Business* (publication of the International Health and Racket Sports Association), *USA Today,* and local newspapers. Tables 15-3, 15-4, and 15-5 list additional print and electronic sources.

Zeroing in on your customer base

Although the information gathered from secondary sources can help the sport marketer to identify potential consumers, it is at best general information. Specific information about current consumers should be collected directly if possible. The tools available for this purpose—the survey, the exit poll, and the focus group—have proven to be effective. However, for the sport marketer the most feasible way of gathering information on current consumers is to conduct an in-arena or club members survey.

The following box identifies three common bases of segmentation and lists typical variables that may be used to generate questions for a survey

TABLE 15-4   *Secondary information sources: Periodicals*

Periodical sources	Description
Team Marketing Report	Monthly sport marketing and sponsorship newsletter
American Demographics	Demographic trends
Sporting Goods Dealer	Focus on sports equipment
Amusement Business	Stadium/arena statistics; entertainment marketing
Brandweek	Licensed merchandise figures for sport teams
SportBusiness Journal	Weekly sports business magazine; excellent coverage of sport business

of fans or patrons. Figure 15–2 is an example of such a survey.

Although demographics are valuable in giving the marketer an understanding of large-scale similarities and trends about the consumer and the market

TABLE 15-5   *Secondary information sources: Electronic*

Electronic/CD-ROM sources	Description
Nexis/Lexis (CD-ROM online)	Includes full text of newspaper, magazines, wire services, and broadcast transcripts. Relevant libraries and files: MARKET and TRENDS; MARKET and MKTRPT; SPORT; MARKET; and RPOLL (Roper Poll).
ABI/Inform Full Text Online	Full text of articles from over 1,000 academic, management, marketing, and business journals.
The Electric Library *http://www.elibrary.com*	Web-based free database; can search for articles using keywords; e-mail updates provided.

Bases of segmentation

Segments can be based on personal and geographic demographics and lifestyles.

Personal demographic segmentation measurements

Gender: Male or female
Age: Child, teenager, adult, senior
Education: High school, college, beyond college
Income: Low, middle, or high
Marital status: Single, married, divorced, or widowed

Geographic/demographic segmentation measurements

Population: Location, size, and density
Climate: Warm and Cold
Media present: Local, regional, and/or national
Commerce: Tourist, local worker, resident

Lifestyle segmentation

This segment includes, among other measurements, **product usage,** a key dimension for sport marketers. Other examples of lifestyle measurements include the following:

Social class: Lower-lower to upper-upper
Family life cycle: Bachelor to solitary survivor
Brand loyalty: None, some, complete
Beliefs and involvements: Causes people are concerned about
Attitudes: Neutral, positive, negative
Leisure interests: How people spend their nonwork hours

TABLE 15-6   *Typical psychographic variables*

Activities	Interests	Opinions
Work	Family	Themselves
Hobbies	Home	Social issues
Social events	Job	Politics
Vacation	Community	Business
Entertainment	Recreation	Economics
Club membership	Fashion	Education
Community	Food	Products
Shopping	Media	Future
Sports	Achievements	Culture

From Plumber, J. (1974), "The concept and application of lifestyle segmentation," *Journal of Marketing 38* (1): 33–37.

segments, the data do not reflect the cultural or social factors that influence consumers. The sport marketer also needs to identify consumer's concerns. What are the customer's preferences in music, entertainment, and television? What are the consumer's political, religious, or environmental concerns? One solution to this dilemma is to understand the market segment's values, attitudes, and lifestyles. Consumers' activities, interests, and opinions (AIOs) can be inventoried by asking respondents various questions about their work, sport activities, family, social life, education, and political preferences. Such analysis is important to sport marketers, because it presents a fuller picture of the consumer and helps sport marketers refine their demographic screening. Table 15-6 lists some of the variables explored in the activities, interests, and opinion categories.

INDIANA WOMEN'S BASKETBALL
Fan Survey

We'd like your help. In a continuing effort to better serve you and provide you with the best in college sports entertainment, we'd like your opinion. Please take a few minutes to complete and return this survey.

1. How many IU women's basketball games did you attend <u>last</u> season?

    ☐none   ☐one   ☐two   ☐three   ☐four
    ☐ five   ☐six   ☐seven   ☐ eight or more

2. Counting this game how many IU women's basketball games have you attended <u>this</u> season?_____

3. How many years (including this year) have you been attending Hoosier women's basketball games?

    ☐one   ☐two   ☐3 to 5   ☐6 to 10   ☐11 or more

4. Which time do you prefer regarding attending IU women's basketball games?

    ☐Friday night
    ☐Sunday afternoon
    ☐No preference
    ☐Not a factor in my decision to attend

5. How did you find out about <u>today's/tonight's</u> game? (check all that apply)

    ☐Team schedule card or poster
    ☐IU Credit Union
    ☐Newspaper
    ☐Radio
    ☐Television
    ☐Word of mouth

FIGURE 15–2   The first page of a questionnaire used by Indiana University to gather information about its fans.

Lifestyle marketing

Lifestyle marketing provides a platform for the delivery of products and services. Used strategically, it can cut through the clutter of the marketplace and communicate your message directly to your target audience. By knowing the consumer's **lifestyle,** the marketer can develop a relationship with the consumer and create the best match between the consumer and the sport product or service. Lifestyle segmentation includes, among other factors, **product usage**, an important dimension for sport marketers. Product usage is traditionally divided into light, medium, and heavy users. As shown in table 15-7, Mullin (1983) identifies four

TABLE 15-7 *Consumption rate groupings*

Usage segment	Identification pattern
Heavy user	Season ticket holders Club members and/or contract-time holders
Medium user	Miniseason plan users Heavy single-game/event ticket purchasers
Light user	Infrequent single-game/event ticket purchasers
Defector*	Individuals who have used the sport product in the last twelve months but who have not made a repeat purchase since that time
Media consumer	Individuals who do not go to the stadium or coliseum but rather "follow" the team or sport via the media
Unaware consumer	Individuals who are unaware of the sport product and its benefits
Uninterested consumer	Individuals who are aware of the sport product but choose not to try it

From Mullin, B. (1983). *Sport marketing, promotion and public relations*, Amherst, Massachusetts, National Sport Management.
*Levin defines *defectors* as people who have attended an organization's event at least once but have not returned within the last twelve months. In many cases, disenchanted heavy users become defectors; in other cases, defectors are individuals who did not gain sufficient satisfaction on the initial purchase or trial.

more sport-specific categories. Figure 15–3 shows a profile of Indiana Pacers games attendees by certain categories.

College, professional, and private sport and leisure organizations pay most attention to the heavy user, that is, the season ticket holder or the club participant who has a yearly rather than a three-month membership. The percentage of consumers who are heavy users varies from sport to sport, franchise to franchise, and club to club. Some baseball organizations rely heavily on the light user, the person who purchases a ticket one hour before the game. Other baseball organizations rely more on season ticket sales. Some football organizations sell out stadia every week and have long waiting lists of loyal fans who want to purchase season tickets, whereas others have difficulty selling out one game. In a similar fashion, fitness and health clubs put a great deal of effort into the renewal of annual memberships, usually at the end of the "indoor" season, since the late spring and summer months are low-usage months, even among heavy users, at most clubs.

Sport marketers should realize the importance of classifying consumer markets by product usage rate. The differing needs of light, medium, and heavy consumers must be satisfied as much as possible. Furthermore, the marketer should consider the light consumer's needs as much as the heavy user's, since today's light consumer could be tomorrow's medium or heavy consumer. An overdependence on the heavy or medium consumer at the expense of the light user could be shortsighted. For example, in the mid-1980s, the men's basketball program of Cleveland State University enjoyed great success. The team played in a small gymnasium to capacity crowds. Students, faculty, and the community alike had to stand in line for the opportunity to purchase single tickets the day of the game. Had they wanted, the Cleveland State Athletic Department could have presold the entire season. However, the administration did not want to alienate the light and medium users, knowing that in the next five years a new and much larger home arena would be built. If these consumers had been denied the opportunity to watch the team play occasionally, they might have lost interest in the team in the future. Knowing that selling out the new arena would be more difficult and the future financial success would depend on some of the light and medium consumers becoming season ticket

The Pacers **SCORE BIG POINTS**
with educated, executive sports fans.

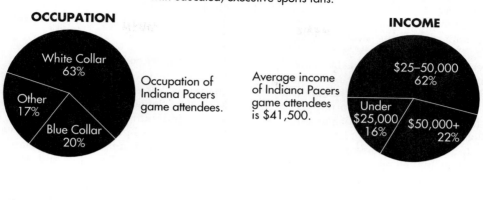

OCCUPATION

White Collar 63%

Other 17%

Blue Collar 20%

Occupation of Indiana Pacers game attendees.

INCOME

$25–50,000 62%

Under $25,000 16%

$50,000+ 22%

Average income of Indiana Pacers game attendees is $41,500.

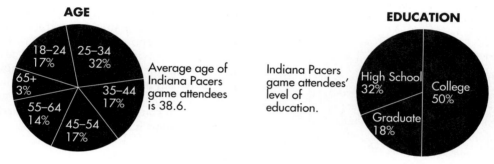

AGE

18–24 17%

25–34 32%

65+ 3%

35–44 17%

55–64 14%

45–54 17%

Average age of Indiana Pacers game attendees is 38.6.

EDUCATION

High School 32%

College 50%

Graduate 18%

Indiana Pacers game attendees' level of education.

FAMILY

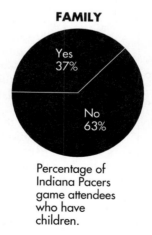

Yes 37%

No 63%

Percentage of Indiana Pacers game attendees who have children.

FIGURE 15–3   Demographics of all game attendees.

holders (heavy users), the marketing staff maintained opportunities for all three consumer levels. Near-sellout crowds when the new, larger arena opened verified this strategy.

Another example of this strategy is currently practiced by the Colorado Rockies, the MLB team headquartered in Denver. The Rockies typically sell out the majority of the stadium well before opening day. However, there is a section of the ballpark—the Rockpile—where the $4 tickets do not go on sale until four hours before the start of the game, thus allowing Rockies' fans who don't have season tickets a chance to attend a few home games. With more and more MLB teams selling out the entire stadium in the preseason, teams that provide an opportunity to purchase tickets for the occasional fan are assuring themselves of future customers as well as providing the team with tremendous public goodwill.

CONCEPT CHECK

Strategic market management is a systematic process by which managers evaluate the sport organization's strengths and weaknesses, measure the competition and external environment, and then develop a marketing strategy that matches the team's goals with the opportunities in the marketplace. Steps in this process include the selection of target market(s), the choice of competitive position, and the development of an effective marketing mix to satisfy sport consumers. Developing a profile of current consumers, including demographic and lifestyle information, is an important component of the strategic plan.

TARGET MARKETS: SEGMENTATION AND EVALUATION

Once a clear picture of just who the customers are has been determined, the sport marketer is ready to segment and select the **target market(s)** to which an appeal will be made. Theodore Levitt, in his classic book *Marketing Imagination* (1986), said that if marketers were not thinking about market segmentation, then they were not thinking. **Market segmentation** is the process of dividing the overall market into groups with relatively similar product needs so that a specific marketing approach can be developed to match those needs. The strategy of target

marketing is based on the concept that it is more profitable to zero in on a specific and often narrow market segment using a focused approach than it is to use the shotgun approach of trying to appeal to every consumer.

What are markets?

We have already used the word *market* often in this chapter. What exactly do we mean by the term? Marketers define a **market** as an aggregate people who, as individuals or as organizations, have needs for products in a product class and have the ability, willingness, and authority to purchase these products (Kotler, 1997; Perreault and McCarthy, 1999; Pride and Ferrell, 1997). You will often hear people refer to a market as the total population of people in a particular geographic area. However, this definition is more specific as it includes people seeking *specific products* in a specific product category. For example, weekend athletes are part of the market for athletic footwear and apparel and also part of the markets for sports equipment, training aids, nutritional supplements, instructional guides, magazines, video games, and other sport-related products. As you can see, many different markets exist within the sport industry.

Target market selection

Market targeting consists of the decision processes and activities conducted to find a market to serve. Market research should identify unsatisfied or partially satisfied needs. However, since there are an almost infinite number of differences in the population, and because not all needs are universal, it is highly unlikely that a marketer will be able to satisfy all needs. Once the market segments are identified, the marketer can then plan the strategy to reach the selected targeted segment or segments and initiate the exchange process.

There are three proven methods of defining and satisfying a target market: (1) mass marketing (undifferentiated), (2) marketing segmentation (concentrated), and (3) multiple segmentation (differentiated).

In mass marketing, a single, undifferentiated marketing strategy is used to appeal to a broad range of consumers. In market segmentation, the marketing plan is designed to appeal to one well-defined market segment or group of consumers. In multiple segmentation, a marketing plan

TABLE 15-8   *Methods for developing a target market*

Marketing approach	Mass marketing	Market segmentation	Multiple segmentation
Target market	Broad range of consumers	One well-defined consumer group	Two or more well-defined consumer groups
Product	Limited number of products under one brand for many types of consumers	One brand tailored to one consumer group	Distinct brand for each consumer group
Price	One "popular" price range	One price range tailored to the consumer group	Distinct price range for each consumer group
Distribution	All possible outlets	All suitable outlets	All suitable outlets—differs by segment
Promotion	Mass media	All suitable media	All suitable media—differs by segment
Strategy emphasis	Appeal to many types of consumers through a uniform, broad-based marketing program	Appeal to one specific consumer group through a highly specialized, but uniform, marketing program	Appeal to two or more distinct market segments through different marketing plans catering to each segment

From Evans, J. and Berman, B. (1994). *Principles of marketing,* New York, Macmillan.

is designed to appeal to two or more market segments, with specialized approaches developed for each well-defined consumer group. Table 15-8 compares the three methods for defining a target market.

Mass marketing. In the past, millions of dollars were spent marketing a product to some "typical" or "average" consumer. However, no company or organization can survive in today's competitive marketplace by selling to a mythical average customer. The mass-marketing or undifferentiated approach does not recognize different lifestyles or market segments; the focus of this marketing strategy is on the common needs of consumers, rather than on their differences. Within a mass-marketing approach, different consumer groups are not identified or sought.

Although a mass-marketing approach is not the sport marketer's principal method of reaching consumers, it does have a place in the marketing of the sport product. The Indianapolis Ice of the International Hockey League uses mass mailings as a low-cost way of getting ticket and game information to Indianapolis-area residents. The Ice, working with local banks and the Marsh store chains, uses statement stuffers* and schedule cards as its primary mass-marketing approach. Any entity that mails retail bills or statements, such as banks, utility companies, and department stores, or stores who will allow the display of pocket schedules can be approached for this cooperative venture.

Market segmentation. Nearly all businesses and organizations serve a multitude of market segments, and future market share will be won by the sport organizations that do a better job of identifying and

---

*Statement stuffers are coupons or advertisements that are sent to consumers with a bill or invoice. The company sending the bill absorbs the mailing costs, which usually does not entail cost beyond what was already involved in mailing the bill or invoice. The sport organization assumes the cost of developing and printing the coupon or advertisement. In addition to the obvious publicity for the sport organization, the company sending the bill or invoice engages in positive public relations, as well as association with a sport franchise.

targeting different market segments. A market segmentation or concentrated approach identifies and approaches a specific consumer market through one ideal marketing mix that caters to the specific needs of the chosen segment. Market segmentation is an efficient way to achieve a strong following in a particular market segment.

One caution should be noted. After identifying two or more potential market segments, the segment with the greatest opportunity should be selected as the target market, not necessarily the segment with the most consumers. The largest segment may not provide the greatest opportunity because of heavy competition or high consumer satisfaction with a competitor. Finding a **niche**[†] is a key to successful market segmentation.

Multiple segmentation. A multiple-segmentation approach combines the best aspects of the mass-marketing and segmented-marketing approaches. It is similar to the segmented-marketing approach except that the sport organization markets to two or more distinct segments of the market with a specialized plan for each segment. Sometimes a sport organization will market to consumers through a mass-marketing strategy to reach a very broad audience and also use a segmented approach geared to specific segments. The more unique segments there are, the better a multiple-segmentation approach will be.

For example, the Youngstown Pride, formerly of the World Basketball League, used an approach segmented by age groups. Youngsters between the ages of six and fifteen were targeted and invited to join the Pizza Hut Fan Club, a benefit of which was a free season ticket. Students (aged sixteen to twenty-two) were another segment and were targeted for a student season ticket, available for $75, which was $125 less than the regular season ticket price. Finally, consumers aged twenty-four and above were targeted with an offer of the regular season ticket, costing $200, because a reduced price was not necessary to attract these people to games. Brochures describing the appropriate offer were sent to these segments, followed by individual telephone calls.

Steps in planning a segmentation strategy

There are six steps in developing a segmentation strategy (figure 15–4). First, the sport marketer should determine the characteristics of consumers and their need for the product or service. In this step, demographic, psychographic, and lifestyle information are collected. Second, the consumers' similarities and differences are analyzed, and third, a consumer market profile is developed. These profiles help to define the market segments by

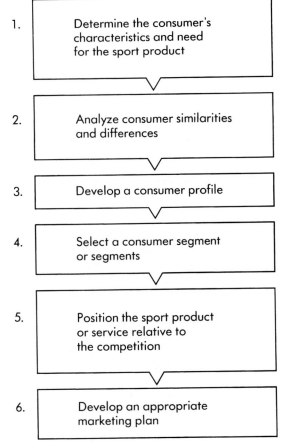

1. Determine the consumer's characteristics and need for the sport product

2. Analyze consumer similarities and differences

3. Develop a consumer profile

4. Select a consumer segment or segments

5. Position the sport product or service relative to the competition

6. Develop an appropriate marketing plan

FIGURE 15–4   Six steps in planning a segmentation strategy.

[†]Sport marketers try to find a unique position in the marketplace by distinguishing their sport product from competing products. This unique position is called a niche.

combining consumers with similar characteristics and wants into distinct groups.

At this point, as a fourth step, the sport marketer must make some decisions. The segment(s) that offer the greatest opportunity must be selected. The marketer decides how many market segments to pursue. The sport organization's financial and human resources must be evaluated and compared with the cost of developing this segment. The timing of the marketing efforts must be decided. Fifth, once a market segment has been selected, the organization must look at its competitors and, considering this competition, select a niche. The sixth and last step is to develop a marketing mix for each target market.

CONCEPT CHECK

For the best results, the sport marketer should develop a campaign that is highly focused and directed to a specific group of people. This practice is called target marketing. The three methods of reaching the target market(s) are mass marketing, market segmentation, and multiple segmentation. The sport marketer must identify and target different market segments to succeed in today's competitive marketplace.

FACTORS INVOLVED IN THE MARKETING OF SPORT: PLANNING THE MARKETING MIX

As has previously been defined, marketing is a complex process, and its success (to culminate in an exchange) requires the formulation of a methodology to attract and reach the potential consumer. That formula is composed of the traditional elements of the marketing mix—product, price, promotion, and place (distribution)—*plus* some other distinct, yet interdependent facets that vary with the nature of the product or service and also with the target market. An examination of these facets—positioning and packaging—will help you to understand the complexities of planning the *marketing mix.*

THE SPORT PRODUCT
Product versus service

A **product** is any item that can be offered for sale or barter to satisfy the needs of customers. In the broadest sense, the sport product is something designed to satisfy the needs and provide benefits to the sports participant or spectator. **Services**, which are also marketed by sport and fitness organizations, are activities or benefits that are offered for sale or barter to consumers. You will recall from the beginning of the chapter that there are many unique characteristics associated with the sport product. Attending a sports event is different from purchasing a piece of sports equipment, yet both can be classified as sport products. We can explain this by introducing the product-service continuum, with the products that are tangible, physical goods on one end and intangible, nonphysical services on the other. Figure 15–5 shows this continuum and presents some examples that help to differentiate between sports goods and services. **Product benefits** are the aspects of the product that satisfy the consumers' needs. A product is a bundle of tangible attributes and intangible benefits that buyers perceive they will obtain if they enter a transaction. The bundle includes everything, favorable and unfavorable, that a buyer receives in the exchange. Lazer and Culley (1983) identify a product as containing three dimensions: *attributes, benefits,* and a *support system* (figure 15–6). *Attributes* are associated with

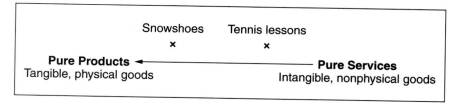

FIGURE 15–5   **The product-service continuum** reveals that sport products can fall anywhere along the line between pure product and pure service.

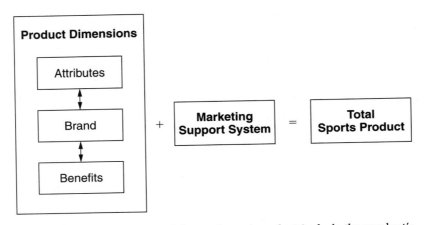

FIGURE 15–6   **Dimensions of the total sport product** include the product's attributes, brand and benefits, as well as the marketing support system.

TABLE 15-9   *Dimensions and elements of the total sports product*

Attributes	Benefits	Marketing support system
Team (*Denver Broncos*)	Thrill of winning	Ticket services
Seat location between the 40-yard lines	Expected enjoyment	"Customer satisfaction guarantee"
Athletes	Uncertain outcome	Media advertisements
Presence of superstars (*John Elway, Terrell Davis*)	Social interaction	Team website
Coach (*Mike Shanahan*)	Identification with the team	
Quality of the opponent	Fun and enjoyment	
The contest (*league play, Super Bowl*)		
Presence of promotional event or giveaway		

---

the **core product** itself and include such elements as ingredients, quality, style, design, color, and packaging. Attributes are the tangible product features and are observable, concrete, measurable, and intrinsic to the core product. A **brand** is a name, symbol, or character—separate or in combination—that designates a particular product and helps consumers to differentiate one product from another. A brand name is defined as the aspect of a brand that can be spoken, such as adidas, Denver Broncos, or the Ohio State University Buckeyes. The brand mark or mark (also called the logo) is the aspect of the brand that is symbolic or visual. One of the most discernible brands in the world is the Nike swoosh. *Product benefits* are defined as what the consumer

perceives as meeting his or her needs, such as comfort, increased self-esteem based on status, warmth, safety, pleasure, etc. Don't confuse features and benefits; features are elements of the product that deliver a benefit. The fourth element, called the *marketing support system,* includes any (if any) and all services provided in addition to the core product. Table 15-9 lists some of the various elements of the total sports product.

Attributes can change because of injuries, trades, weather, and so on. Benefits can change because of the result of the contest, other activities that occur with large crowds at sporting events, traffic congestion, parking, and crowd behavior. This is both a blessing and a curse for the sport marketer. The very characteristics of sport that endear it to the public—including player personalities, pomp and pageantry, ritual, uncertain outcome, emotion, public consumption, and opportunity for socializing—also make it difficult to market.

Marketing support systems are relatively recent refinements in the sport product. Certain teams have fan satisfaction guarantee programs (Cleveland Indians); most now have family seating sections and sections where no alcohol is sold or consumed, and most also have sales departments specializing in types of tickets sales (such as group, season, or corporate).

A product is generally seen as having a growth curve or life cycle (Figure 15–7). A product life cycle is the story of the product's sales. The four stages of the growth curve, introduction, growth, maturity, and decline, are accompanied by the formulation and implementation of strategies and procedures designed to ensure profitability and growth and minimize profit loss and product decline.

An excellent example of a sport-related product growth curve is the case of the Air Jordan basketball shoe. During its introductory stage, the Air Jordan basketball shoe was accompanied by an expensive advertising campaign and aided by an NBA ruling that the shoes, initially available in only black with red and white trim, solid red, or white with black and red trim, could not be worn in official NBA games. Jordan's on-court performance also aided the product's introduction and helped the product gain momentum through the growth stage. The growth stage was characterized by heavy demand and increased production and distribution outlets. As the sales of the shoe skyrocketed, market imitators began producing shoes of similar style, color, and quality, as well as shoes of lesser quality and similar appearance. During the maturity stage, the price of the shoe declined to meet market challenges, as well as to counteract declining growth.

As sales began to decline, Nike launched a new market offensive by introducing basic white and team color Air Jordan shoes, thus opening a new market by offering a product that high school and collegiate teams could wear, because the colors no longer were limited. Later strategies included the use of exotic leather, further technological modifications, the introduction of a clothing line, and the offering of the product for youth, toddlers, and babies. Moreover, although Michael Jordan has retired from the NBA, his signature shoes continue to be a desirable product.

CONCEPT CHECK

The sport product is difficult for the sport marketer to control, since it is intangible, unpredictable, perishable, and consumed as a social event. For these reasons, the product benefits and product extensions must be marketed. All products have a life cycle, which includes the introduction, growth, maturity, and decline stages.

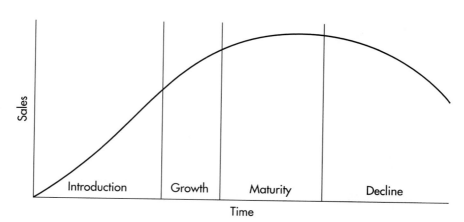

FIGURE 15–7 Product growth curve.

PRICE
What is price?
Let's start the discussion of this element of the marketing mix with an example: The money you pay for a ticket to a sporting event, concert, or movie is its price. The amount you pay for a tennis clinic in Hilton Head with Dennis Vandermeer, a new pair of Nike running shoes, or a pair of inline skates is also an example of price. **Price** is an expression of the *value* of a sports product or event. What you are willing to pay for any of the items just mentioned—the price—is a function of how much you value the product or service.

Price is very visible and intricately related to the other major elements of the marketing mix—product, promotion, and place (distribution). In addition, because of discounts, rebates, coupons, and promotional incentives, it is considered controllable and flexible. Price involves the determination of goods and services and the calculation of value of the exchange that can be used by all parties involved in the transaction (Kotler, 1997). In mainstream marketing, price tends to be an important strategic consideration and, in some cases, the most important component of the marketing mix. Sport, and in particular spectator sport, does not give price the same strategic importance as does mainstream business. In a study of 3,009 fan responses in two selected National Basketball Association cities, Rudman and Sutton (1989) found that the cost of tickets ranked fourth in importance in one city and fifth in another city, behind such considerations as opponent, team record, presence of superstars, and effect of the game on league standings.

We know that consumers equate price with value. A product that is deeply discounted or even free may be perceived as having little or no value. Bill Veeck would never give away tickets, no matter how poorly his team was performing. According to Veeck, "Tickets are the one thing I have to sell. To give them away is to cheapen the product I am selling" (Veeck and Linn, 1965). Similarly, when new sports leagues launch franchises in cities with existing professional sports teams, the new product usually is priced nearly the same as the existing product. To offer the new sports ticket at a lower price would tell the public that, in some way or another, the new product must be inferior to the existing product.

Pricing strategies
Early in the planning process, the sport marketer will have to choose a pricing strategy. Price is most commonly considered as an amount of money; however, it can be more broadly defined as anything of value that is exchanged. **Bartering,** also known as trading-out, is a common practice in sport marketing and consists of an exchange that does not involve money. Tickets, program ads, scoreboard space, and arena signage are valuable commodities to some companies. Sport organizations should use these commodities to trade for goods and services that are needed to execute the campaign.

The Ohio State University's director of marketing and sponsorships, David Brown, uses this strategy to trade women's volleyball and basketball tickets for radio advertising. The university gives 1,000 tickets to selected local radio stations in exchange for advertising equal to the face value of the tickets. For example, if the face value of the ticket were $5, the amount of advertising traded would be $5,000. The radio station gives tickets away in pairs over the air, resulting in a minimum of 500 "mentions." An additional feature of this trade-out agreement is that three additional "mentions" per giveaway are required, resulting in 15,000 advertising slots over the course of the season.

The University of Kansas tried to stimulate attendance at its football games by offering season tickets at two prices. Seats between the 10-yard lines were the higher priced at $90 each. The 7,000 seats located outside the 10-yard lines were priced at $65. This area would be called "Hawk's Nest," and since this area was sparsely populated in the past, all revenue would be "new" revenue. According to Doug Vance of the University of Kansas athletic department, "the reduced rate is intended to make it more affordable for fans to become season ticket buyers" ("Jayhawks," 1989).

The key to successful pricing strategies is to react to market demand and the elasticity or inelasticity (how price changes affect or do not affect the consumer and hence demand for the product) of consumer demand. In other words, does a price increase or decrease affect demand? In most cases, pricing strategies do not stand alone at all times. Promotional strategies and product positioning may alter perceived value and in some cases, actual price (for a time). Such strategies combined with pricing usually temporarily increase consumer demand for the product.

> ### CONCEPT CHECK
>
> *Price is a very visible element of the marketing mix and, although most often thought of as a dollar amount, can include anything of value that is exchanged. Exchanging tickets for services, especially advertising, is a form of bartering or trading-out, and is a common practice in sport marketing.*

Positioning

Before we go further and discuss promotion and advertising, it is important to understand the concept of **positioning**. One of the classics in the marketing literature is the book *Positioning: The Battle for Your Mind* (1986) by Ries and Trout. According to Ries and Trout, positioning "starts with a product, a piece of merchandise, a service, an institution, a company, or even a person. However, positioning is not what you do to a product. Positioning is what you do to the mind of the prospect. That is, you position the product in the mind of the prospect."

With so many sport products and services available today, each accompanied by countless advertisements, consumers have become immune to the plethora of traditional marketing communications.

Product: Tennis shoes

TARGET MARKET: Upper-middle class occasional athletes.
COMPETITION: Nike, Reebok, Converse, Prince, Diadora, Fila, New Balance.
PRODUCT'S BENEFITS: Wearer will look and feel better in the classic K-Swiss design; K-Swiss tennis shoes wear longer.
HOW DIFFERENTIATED FROM COMPETITION: K-Swiss uses a 25-year old, classic, primarily-white design; focus is on performance, not frills and gimmicks. The competition uses celebrity endorsers, bright colors, new-age designs with air-cushioned soles, and other innovations.

They do this in self-defense; there just isn't enough room in their heads to store every piece of information about every product. The result is that consumers either put products into neat little categories, or they ignore them.

The concept underlying positioning is relatively simple: find a hole (or niche) and fill it. People generally pick one or two product attributes to associate with a product, then file the information. When they need said attributes, the product associated with them comes to mind.

7-Up found a niche in the soft drink industry and outpositioned Coke. Even though Coke's marketing budget was many times larger, 7-Up was able to turn Coke's bigness (and their caramel coloring) against them. How? By positioning themselves as the Un-Cola. 7-Up represented an alternative beverage choice for those consumers who wanted a non-cola soft drink.

Positioning can use factors such as price, age, distribution, use, benefits, size, time, and technology to communicate its message (Ries and Trout, 1986). A classic example of the use of a positioning strategy in sport involved the Stowe, Vermont, ski resort area. A column in *Harper's Bazaar* by travel writer Abby Rand listed what she perceived to be the top ski resorts in the world. Stowe was one of the top ten. The complete list was Stowe; Aspen, Colorado; Courcheval, France; Jackson Hole, Wyoming; Kitzbuhel, Austria; Portillo, Chile; St. Christopher, Austria; St. Moritz, Switzerland; Sun Valley, Idaho; and Vail, Colorado. Seizing the opportunity to position itself as simultaneously elite and accessible, Stowe developed advertisements that showed the shoulder patches of the "top 10" ski resorts, with the caption, "Of the world's top ten ski resorts, only one is in the East. You don't have to go to the Alps or the Andes or even the Rockies to experience the ski vacation of a lifetime. You need only head for the Ski Capital of the East: Stowe, Vermont" (Ries and Trout, 1986). By mentioning the top ten ski resorts in the world, the advertisement created a list of elites in the consumer's mind, forming the basis for comparison of all resorts not on the list. Professional sports have been positioned as having the most talented athletes in the world, and this positioning has been the downfall of new sport leagues as they have tried to compete with the established leagues.

Another popular form of positioning used in spectator sports is to position a sporting event as more than the activity itself. This is done primarily through such promotions as "fireworks night," appearances by the Famous Chicken (formerly known as the San Diego Chicken), and so on. The positioning is that you are receiving something more for your money, a bonus. Family nights involve both promotion and pricing strategies that help position the sporting event as a "family affair," something wholesome and traditional that gives the family an opportunity to share an event. As mentioned previously, time of day is a positioning factor, and time of day has been used effectively to market a sport event as a "businessperson's special." A businessperson's special is a game (usually baseball) scheduled for early to midafternoon on a weekday. It is positioned as a way for a businessperson to entertain clients, reward employees, and so on. Taking the businessperson positioning a step further, professional basketball and hockey teams have created a ticket package aimed at the businessperson who may work late, have clients to entertain, and so on. The businessperson's special pack usually contains all weeknight games and is positioned as being tax deductible (as an entertainment expense) and an effective way to impress clients and sponsors. The package may also be developed to combine private club accommodations (if available), giving the businessperson additional reason to purchase the product.

Yet another interesting sport marketing example of positioning is seen in the competition for teams and vacationers between Florida's Grapefruit League and Arizona's Cactus League. (Note: The Grapefruit League and Cactus League are nicknames for the exhibition leagues composed of Major League Baseball teams using Florida and Arizona, respectively, for spring training.) The Cactus League has tried to position itself as the leader in certain factors that are weaknesses of the Grapefruit League. For example, the Cactus League emphasizes as its strengths dry heat for player conditioning, the number of playing dates available without inclement weather, the short travel distance between cities, and the proximity to the hometown. This positioning capitalizes on the Grapefruit League's weaknesses of high humidity, frequent rain, and longer travel distances between locations (Governor's Special Task Force on Cactus League Baseball, 1988). The key to this positioning is that very

little can be done to reposition the Florida league regarding the first two factors, which are natural conditions. Thus the Cactus League enjoys a natural geographic advantage and can concentrate other positioning efforts on facilities, community and corporate support, governmental involvement, and even attracting Japanese professional baseball teams.

Marketing research, and in particular consumer feedback and reactions, is the key to successful positioning. Marketing research is the key because your marketing solution is not inside the product or even inside your own mind, but inside the mind of the prospective consumer (Ries and Trout, 1986). The box shows how K-Swiss, a small athletic footwear company, positioned its shoe against Nike, Reebok, and other footwear manufacturers.

PROMOTION

Promotion, another of the "*Ps*" in the marketing mix, is a process in which various techniques are used to communicate with consumers. Sport promotions are most successful when the message the marketer wants to convey is directed toward one or more target markets.

The communication process

The communication process in sport marketing is no different from that used by marketers of other products. Knowledge of the communication process is useful in understanding how a message travels from its origin, the sport marketer, to its intended receiver, the fan or consumers. Figure 15–8 shows a communication model and its implications for sport marketers.

Let's examine more closely how the communication process works in sport marketing:

1. The *source* of the message is the sport marketer of the sport organization. Keeping the sport organization's philosophy and mission in mind, the sport marketer must decide what message will be sent about the product or service (team, club, event, lesson) and to whom (target market) the message will be directed. The communication process begins with the source or sender of the message.

2. The sport marketer *encodes* the message by choosing the words, sounds, symbols, or pictures to be used to communicate the intended message. In fact, the encoding is almost

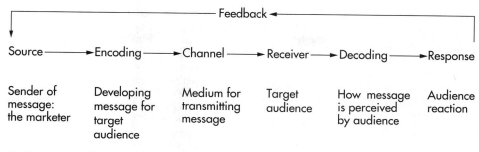

FIGURE 15–8   The communications model.

always done by an advertising agency hired by the sport organization.

3. The *channel* is the vehicle the agency uses to get the message to the receiver. This could take any number of forms, from a sponsor's sign to an ad placed in the newspaper or a commercial on radio, television, or the Internet.
4. The *receiver* is the target market that the sport marketer wants to receive the message.
5. The way the message is understood by the receiver or target market is the *decoding* aspect of the communication process.
6. The *response* is how the target market reacts to the message. Are consumers motivated to purchase the product or service, or do they merely acknowledge hearing or seeing the message?
7. *Feedback* or evaluation is a measure of the success in getting the intended message to the target market. Marketing research, ticket sales, and attendance indicators give the sport marketer feedback on how well the message was communicated.

At any or all points of the communication mechanism there is a possibility that noise* will distort the message. It is important, therefore, to learn how clearly the intended message is being received.

Promotional mix elements

The communications model (see figure 15–8) can be useful in planning marketing communications via the promotional mix, which includes advertising, personal selling, publicity, sales promotions, and sponsorship. Before implementing any promotion,

however, the sport marketer should map out the goals of the campaign. A key to the effective use of promotional strategies and activities is determining what you wish to accomplish and designing a specific promotional activity to reach this outcome. The following steps can serve as a general outline for planning a promotion:

1. *Define your target market.*
2. *Set measurable objectives.* What action do you want the target market(s) to take? What is your goal for this promotion?
3. *Determine the strategy.* How will you motivate the target market(s) to take the desired action?
4. *Research various promotional ideas.* Talk to other sport marketers, at both the professional and institutional (high schools and colleges) levels for ideas. Visit health and fitness clubs in your locale. Other sources for ideas include the library (for books that catalog promotions), marketing organizations, and local businesses.
5. *Select the promotional approach.* Choose one that is the most likely to be successful with your target market(s).
6. *Develop a theme for the promotion.* Devise a short, catchy slogan to attract the attention of the target market.
7. *Create support material.* This material should be in the form of advertising, sales promotions, and publicity.

Using spectator sport as an example and having a goal of increasing attendance, the marketer would need to know who attends and who does not attend, what promotional efforts have been used in the past, and how successful they were. Similarly,

---

*Noise is any interference that distorts the message or prevents the receiver from receiving or understanding the message.

the marketer needs to identify variables that attract fans or affect a fan's decision to attend or not attend a game. Marcum and Greenstein (1985), in a season-long analysis of selected professional baseball teams, identified day of the week, opponent, and type of promotion as factors affecting attendance. Hansen and Gauthier (1989), through a small cross-section of marketing personnel from a variety of professional sports, found that team quality, price, entertainment, competition, and convenience were factors affecting attendance. Table 15-10 ranks eleven attendance factors identified by Rudman and Sutton in a study of 3,009 fans that attended professional (NBA) basketball games in two selected cities.

Keep in mind that the promotional mix used for one product, event, or service may not be appropriate for another. Sometimes the emphasis will be on personal selling, and at other times, advertising will be the primary need.

Advertising. Because of the tremendous role of media in sport, **advertising** is probably the most crucial element of the promotional mix. Advertising, that is, presenting a paid message about the sport organization's product or service, is possibly the most readily identifiable form of communication in this country. Billions of dollars are spent annually on advertising, involving the following traditional and sport-specific media:

Newspapers
Magazines
Television
Radio
Athlete endorsements
Internet
Direct mail
Posters
Outdoor advertising
Painted transit advertisements
Ticket backs
Scoreboards
In-arena signage
Outfield fences
Pocket schedule cards
Game programs

One of the most popular forms of advertising used in sport marketing is endorsement. Endorsements feature a well-known or noteworthy athlete who endorses the benefits of a particular product or service. Miller Brewing Company used former athletes to endorse the qualities of its Miller Lite beer, namely taste and low calories. Nike has used a number of athletes to introduce and endorse its products, including Michael Jordan, Andre Agassi,

TABLE 15-10   *NBA attendance factors*

Factor	Cleveland		Indiana	
	Average score	Rank	Rank	Average score
Opponent	3.28	1	1	3.51
Superstar	3.10	2	2	3.45
Standings	3.08	3	5	2.54
Record	2.99	4	6	2.46
Price/cost	2.73	5	4	2.63
Game day	2.56	6	3	2.75
Weather	2.50	7	7	2.28
Arena access	2.30	8	9	2.09
Game time	2.27	9	8	2.24
Television	2.26	10	10	1.96
Event/promotion	1.83	11	11	1.82

Survey results are composed of the responses of 3009 people. Means reflect Likert scale, ranging from 1 (never) to 5 (always).

Mia Hamm, and Sheryl Swoopes. Endorsement contracts sometimes contain performance and morality clauses to protect the sponsor from damages resulting from association with a "tainted" athlete. Such contracts may require drug testing, may restrict the athlete's lifestyle, and may require that the athlete use the product.

Selecting the advertising medium is the first step. The key element in selecting the medium to carry the advertising message is determining which medium will best reach the target market. All of the media—newspapers, radio and television stations, magazines, and now the Internet—have conducted their own studies to describe the audiences they reach. The sport marketer should match the demographics and lifestyles of the sport audience with those of the advertising medium.

Another factor to be considered in selecting the medium is the cost of each. It is much more expensive to advertise on a national network affiliate than on a local cable network. Advertising via television may be the best way to reach the target market, but a limited budget may mean that other outlets, such as radio or outdoor advertising, have to be used. The sport marketer should also consider other creative advertising outlets, such as shopping cart placards, grocery bags, bus posters, banners on street light poles, or electronic messages such as marquees, in an attempt to convey a message to prospective consumers.

It is necessary to create an advertising plan to ensure continuity in the marketing communications effort. The following steps can serve as a guide for developing such a plan:

1. *Set objectives for advertising.* What does one want to accomplish? To create an awareness of a product or service? To rouse the consumer to action, that is, to purchase a ticket? To maintain current consumer's support? To improve an existing image? Reinforce a brand?
2. *Develop an advertising budget.* Research the costs of advertising in each of the media.
3. *Create an advertising theme.* Develop a catchy slogan relating to the team, event, or club.
4. *Select the media schedule.* When will each advertisement be run? Will the advertising be spread over the entire season or focus on the preseason?
5. *Create the advertisement.* This can be done in-house or by a local advertising agency.

6. *Evaluate the differences of the marketing message.* Use marketing research to evaluate the effectiveness of the advertising strategy. Precampaign and postcampaign testing, recall tests, and postcampaign purchase monitoring are common techniques used to measure advertising effectiveness.

The Internet. One of the fastest-growing and influential advertising media of recent years is the Internet. The advent of the Internet is unparalleled in the history of communications and advertising. The Internet surpassed fifty million users in just four years; it took radio thirty-eight years and television thirteen years to reach the fifty million–user milestone! Media watchers projected that there would be more than 150 million Internet users by the year 2000, matching—for the first time—the total number of cable television viewers ("The FANSonly," 1999).

The figures associated with the selling of goods and services using the Internet, called **e-commerce,** have been nothing short of remarkable. The Internet generated gross sales totaling $304 billion in 1998, and expected gross sales for 1999 have been set at $500 billion, with a projected figure of $950 billion by 2002 (Yow, 1999). In terms of Internet advertising, over $906 million was spent in 1997 and $1.8 billion spent in 1998. To put these figures in perspective, the advertising sales figure for television during its third year of existence was $834 million ("The FANSonly," 1999).

The Internet has already become a valuable source for sports-related information, and it is rapidly becoming a popular medium for sport marketers who wish to use its features to promote products, services, and events. As a communications and selling vehicle, it has immense and dynamic potential for sport marketing. Possibly the most attractive reason to market online is the demographic similarity of sports fans and Internet users. The typical Internet user can be described as entertainment-minded, college-educated males between the ages of eighteen and thirty-four (Gladden, 1996)—a very close match to the demographic profile of traditional sports fans. Other reasons for using the Internet as a communications and promotions medium is its flexibility and interactive nature, its ability to reach a focused target market, and its relative cost effectiveness (cost per thousand hits). However, as with other promotional tools, the risk of clutter and incorrect targeting of market segments can compromise the Internet's effectiveness. And it goes without saying that technology problems can undo an otherwise outstanding Internet promotion.

The Universities of Maryland (UMTERPS.com), Ohio State (OhioStateBuckeyes.com), UCLA (UCLABRUINS.com), Notre Dame (UND.com), Utah (UTAHUTES.com), California (CalBears.com) and dozens more are among the schools, conferences (e.g., Atlantic Coast Conference—THEACC.com; Mountain West Conference MOUNTAINWESTCONF.com), and events (e.g., Women's Final Four—WFINAL4.com; Wooden Classic—WOODENCLASSIC.com; Orange Bowl—ORANGEBOWL.org) that have aggressively developed a web presence. Many colleges and universities have partnered with the FANSonly network (www.fansonly.com), an Atlanta-based company that creates and manages a network of athletic websites, to develop interactive sites and Internet promotions. The school's websites allow them to conduct promotions, post news and information, provide webcasts of special events such as press conferences (during which the event can be watched in real time as well as be archived on the Internet site for later viewing), market and sell products and special events, and numerous other functions ("The FANSonly," 1999; Yow, 1999). Internet promotions can and should be supplemented with print, media (TV, radio, newspaper, and outdoor) and game-day promotions.

Sales promotion. Another aspect of the promotional mix, a **sales promotion** is any activity that cannot be called advertising, personal selling, or publicity. Sales promotions are various short-term activities that are designed to stimulate the purchase of a sports product or service. Sales promotions include many strategies, with those shown in table 15-11 being the most common.

Using a theme as part of a promotional strategy can be very effective. The theme should enable the intended audience to form a mental image, impression, or association with the product. Such was the case with the very successful promotion of the Oakland Athletics, titled "Year of the Uniform." This promotion was targeted at youth fourteen years of age and under and was designed to "guarantee" that the youth attended multiple games, because an individual needed to attend at least six games to receive the entire clothing set, and an additional two games for gifts such as balls and mugs. Attendance at "Year of the Uniform" games, which were strategically scheduled against quality opponents to maximize attendance and related nongate revenues, was 40 to 60 percent higher than on other days.

Personal selling. **Personal selling** is another form of promotion that can be very successful if the marketer capitalizes on its unique strengths and uses it in the right situations. Personal selling is direct interpersonal communication to inform and persuade. The advantage of personal selling in persuading and informing is that it enables the salesperson to interact with the prospect by explaining, questioning, and refuting objections. A common form of sport-related personal selling takes place in the health and fitness club industry. The personal selling usually takes place after the prospect samples the product through a free visit. At the conclusion of the visit the prospect is briefed about the benefits of membership and may or may not be offered a financial incentive to joint the club immediately. If the prospect has objections or reservations, the salesman has a list of responses to refute the objection and break down resistance. Although the methodology of personal selling does not include coercion, in some cases it is used in the hope of closing a sale.

Personal selling can take place face to face or through **telemarketing,** a form of personal selling using the telephone to inform and persuade and to offer the consumer an opportunity to purchase goods or services. Telemarketing has been a very effective sales tool for spectator sports. Telemarketing companies that specialize in the management of telemarketing campaigns and that train salespeople often contract to sell season tickets, group tickets, game plans, or selected individual tickets for professional teams, as well as for colleges and universities that face difficult marketing tasks or limited resources. The team or organization usually contracts to pay the telemarketing company's expenses and a percentage of income generated. The contract may or may not include a minimum payment regardless of the success.

Publicity and public relations. Publicity differs from advertising in that is *nonpaid,* nonpersonal communication about a product or organization. Usually the sponsor is not identified, and the message reaches the public because of its newsworthiness. Nonprofit agencies involved in recreation, such as the YMCA, YWCA, or YMHA, or national governing bodies (NGBs), such as those for USA

TABLE 15-11   *Sales promotion tools*

Tools	Examples
Coupons Redeemable certificates that offer a reduced price or voucher for an additional item with purchase.	Certificates found in the newspaper, direct mail coupon packets, or inserted in the product's package; some coupons can now also be found online and printed for future use.
Caveat: Overuse can undermine the perceived value of the product.	• The Colorado Rapids (MLS) target families by offering a 4 for 4 coupon in the Denver papers, selling four game tickets, hot dogs, soft drinks, and chips for $40.
Premiums, gifts, and giveaways Various promotional items given away to fans by a sponsor or the team; items usually exhibit both the team's and sponsor's marks/logo.	Caps, balls and pucks, water bottles, sports cards, schedule magnets, pennants, posters, umbrellas, tote bags, mugs, uniform shirts, etc.
Caveat: Although premiums and giveaways may increase attendance, careful planning is needed to make certain that you have enough items to distribute and/or that the promotional item cannot be used in a manner that might injure patrons or athletes (for example, baseball or hockey puck nights).	• *Sports Illustrated* and *ESPN* (the magazine) give away various promotional items when they receive a paid subscription (windbreaker or sweatshirt, watch, video, championship albums, etc.). • Sears, an NCAA Corporate Partner, gave away seat cushions to all ticket holders at the Women's Final Four.
Sampling A smaller portion or sample of the product is given to customers; a product is displayed/exhibited for the purpose of introducing fans to it.	Lip balm, sunscreen, nutrition bars, sports beverages, Band-Aids, analgesic creams, etc. • Exhibitions are a common way of introducing prospective fans to a new or unfamiliar sport.
Point-of-purchase displays (POPs) Eye-catching cardboard cutouts, banners or retail displays that call attention to the product and/or communicate special offers or price reductions to consumers.	Brochures, special packaging, eye-catching product arrangements, bottle tags, etc. • Anheuser-Busch develops unique POP displays for its Bud Light Super Bowl promotion.
Contests Contests and sweepstakes are used to create interest or awareness of a product. Contests pit contestants against each other; sweepstakes promotions are games of chance (no skill is necessary to play).	• United Airlines is sponsoring a sweepstakes to win two tickets to the 2000 U.S. Open tennis tournament; interested contestants may enter online or by mail. • The NFL sponsors the punt, pass and kick competition. (The NHL has a similar contest modeled after the PPK, the dribble, pass, and shoot competition.)

Swimming or gymnastics, usually depend on publicity as a primary tool to communicate with the public. A great deal of publicity comes through news releases. A news release tells about an event or activity that is newsworthy and that merits publicity through the appropriate media. A news release should tell the who, what, where, when, why, and how in a concise and timely format and should be electronically sent to the appropriate media personnel by the agency or organization. Most nonprofit agencies and organizations depend on publicity as the prime way of generating awareness of their missions and programs. To assist local YMCAs, the National YMCA office issues press kits for specific programs. For example, a press kit for youth soccer may provide a release containing information about soccer participation in the United States, and quotes from physicians or soccer players about the benefits of play and competition. Often the local program director merely inserts the information about registration, place, and time for the local program.

A unique form of publicity in professional sport involves the United Way and the National Football League. Television messages, paid for by the National Football League, promote and publicize various United Way agencies and services within the home cities of each National Football League franchise. These publicity spots are unique in that they also serve as advertisements for the National Football League by promoting the activities of its players and the charitable activities and functions of the league.

Public relations is a sport organization's overall effort to create a positive image for itself with its target public(s) and the community in which it operates. Public relations is the overall plan for conveying this positive message, but publicity is the tool that communicates the message.

CONCEPT CHECK

Promotion is the process of communicating with the consumer about the sport product. The sport marketer must be aware that interference or noise in the communication process may prevent the consumer from receiving or understanding the intended message. This knowledge is useful in planning and implementing the promotional mix. Elements of the promotional mix are advertising, sales promotions, publicity/public relations, and personal selling. The marketer develops promotional strategies to get the consumer's attention, arouse interest in the product, create a desire, and ultimately, motivate the consumer to purchase.

PLACE

Place in the marketing mix is the geographic location of the product, such as the stadium, arena, or club, and the target market, as well as the point of origin for distribution of the product or service. **Distribution** is the transfer or products, goods, and services from the producer to the consumer. Products move from producer to consumer through channels of distribution—any series of firms or people who participate in the flow of the product or service to the consumer (Perreault and McCarthy, 1999). The length of distribution channels varies; it may be direct or may require wholesalers, retailers, and assorted "middlemen." Probably the most unique aspect of this distribution process in the case of spectator sports is that the product does not move from the production site to a consumer outlet. The production and consumption occur at the same site—the stadium or arena. Thus, the consumption site in sport is perceived to be more critical than the distribution channels of traditional marketing. This same perception accounts for the emphasis on color and product extensions such as juice bars, lounges, and child care facilities in the construction of new comprehensive health and fitness clubs. Several factors associated with the location may affect the success of the enterprise. Among these factors are accessibility, attractiveness, and the actual location.

Accessibility has been described as a variable that affects fan attendance at professional sport (Marcum and Greenstein, 1985). Accessibility, or the relationship between the location of the product presentation and the location of the target market or consumer, is an important aspect of sport marketing. Accessibility is a convenience factor, and the consumer's perception of this convenience may significantly affect the success of the enterprise. Access factors such as highways, public transportation, transportation costs, route (direct or indirect) and length of time required all could significantly affect consumer traffic and success in reaching the target market.

Another function of the place concept is attractiveness. Is the place (area, facility, and so on) attractive (both inside and outside)? How does the attractiveness element function in attracting potential consumers? Do all of the qualities of the "place" combine to form a pleasing attraction, or do some elements conflict with other aspects, weakening the total attractiveness? For example, consider 3-COM Park (Candlestick Park), home to the San Francisco 49ers. A location at the mouth of the bay sounds very attractive, but when the location brings fog, wind and cold, the picturesque location is overcome by combined meteorological effects that make the place unattractive (Nelson, 1989). The construction of a new facility, especially a unique facility, as is the Toronto Sky Dome, can serve as an attraction and can become a marketing tool in itself. After the opening of the Sky Dome in June 1989, the Blue Jays enjoyed fifteen consecutive sellouts, and fifteen of the final twenty-two games were also listed as sellouts (Waddell, 1989).

Although the technological innovations of the Sky Dome (with its retractable roof) are greatly appreciated and ensure fan comfort, the new trend in facility design, especially in baseball, is to take the nostalgia and intimacy of the old ball parks' architecture but outfit them with all the modern amenities. New stadia are built with cup holders at every seat (some seats even sport an attached LED screen for ordering food and drinks, or for playing video games), game rooms, specialty restaurants, hot tubs, and more. Thus, the stadium becomes a permanent marketing tool that helps bring people into the ballpark. The success and attractiveness of Camden Yards (home of the Baltimore Orioles), Jacobs Field (home of the Cleveland Indians), Coors Field (home of the Colorado Rockies), and Bank One Ballpark (home of the Arizona Diamondbacks) support this type of facility design and construction.

The issue of location is also complicated by the location's appropriateness for the activity. The prestige of the facility or the public's opinion of the facility also affects its success. At the Air Force Academy in Colorado Springs, arguably home to some of the finest athletic facilities in the country, soccer and lacrosse are played at the varsity soccer field, a facility that seats 3,500. Although the matches in these sports rarely attract more than a few hundred spectators, the prestige of playing in a stadium helps recruit athletes and also implies that the sport is more important than it would be if it were played on a field in another part of the campus.

Establishing the distribution network

Another form of distribution is the sport media. Given the effect of the media on sport and the fact that most sport products cannot be physically delivered to the consumer, sport marketers use the media to develop their market. Marketing one's event through a wide broadcast and cable network not only generates widespread interest in and awareness of the product, but it can also have a direct effect on sales by creating media consumers. Media also

provides a lucrative revenue stream for sport franchises, particularly at the professional level. There is a considerable reliance on media revenues in major league football, baseball, and basketball. In fact, only the National Hockey League (NHL) relies more on gate receipts than media revenues. In all likelihood, media revenues will continue to increase if the recent NFL media contract of $17.6 billion is any indication.

Another way of distributing the product to consumers is via the telephone. The University of Kentucky uses a 900 number and an extensive radio network to get information about the Wildcats basketball team to its alumni and fans. Interested parties throughout the United States can call a 900 number for information about upcoming games, comments from the coaching staff, game statistics, and player profiles. In addition to the 900 system, any restaurant or similar establishment that has closed-circuit radio can arrange to broadcast Kentucky games live. Wildcat fans around the country can listen to Kentucky basketball games that they otherwise could not enjoy.

Ticket distribution

Even with a growing dependence on media revenues, the physical distribution of game or event tickets is an important part of the place aspect of the marketing mix. The goal of the ticket distribution system is to encourage consumer purchases by making the system as convenient and accessible as possible. Moreover, the ticket distribution system also serves to market and advertise the game. Strategies used by sport organizations include the following.

All sport organizations should have a comprehensive in-house ticket office that sells individual game and season tickets. The ticket office would also be involved in working with selling group tickets and the corporate sales program. Maintaining customer-oriented in-house ticket operations is a necessary tactic. This includes expanding the hours of operation so that consumers can come to the ticket office before or after work as well as during the lunch hour. The ticket office should be open late at least one evening a week. Telephone numbers, including toll-free numbers, should be available for the convenience of consumers who wish to charge their tickets to credit cards. Tickets should also be available for pickup by consumers just before the game at the will-call window.

Assuming there is availability, tickets can be also be sold online. Customized web ticket areas can be developed on the team's website, including off-line ordering forms and offering full online transactions.

Tickets can also be franchised to be sold by a third-party company such as Ticketmaster. The advantage of such a contract for the sport marketer is the connection with a well-established, highly visible network of ticket outlets. A consumer can go to any of these ticket outlets, and thanks to the computerized ticket system, buy the desired seat from the pool of available seats for a particular event. After the consumer selects the seat, the computer prints the event ticket. This a particular event. After the consumer selects the seat, the computer prints the event ticket. This system enables the consumer to choose a seat from all the unsold seats rather than having to select from a limited allotment of tickets. However, a disadvantage of this system is the sport marketer's loss of control over the operation and loss of ability to monitor consumer satisfaction. Franchised ticket outlets sell tickets for many organizations and do not promote any game or event. They also charge consumers a service fee, often as much as $5 per ticket sold.

Establishing a variety of authorized ticket outlets in the community is another popular strategy. This system is especially effective in areas where there are no third-party ticket outlets. The Houston Astros have a creative approach to ticket distribution with their Astros' van. The Astros' director of season ticket services says that no sell more tickets one must "go to the people rather than expecting them to come to you." In an agreement with a local automobile dealer and cellular telephone company, the Astros are given the use of a van, which transports ticket office personnel into the community to sell tickets to upcoming games.

The front office has set an ambitious schedule in which the van goes out every day during the season. On weekdays, the van travels to stores of the Astros' supermarket sponsor, and on weekends it tours shopping malls and major department stores. The van's schedule is announced at all home games, over the radio, and in the local print and electronic media. When the team is playing on the road, Orbit, the Astros' mascot, travels with the van.

So popular is this system that people wait at the announced sites, camera in hand, to take pictures of the mascot and to purchase tickets for games. This distribution system and promotion have realized positive results for the Houston team and have brought increased ticket sales, both in impulse buys and in renewals.

CONCEPT CHECK

The place element of the marketing mix is both the physical sport facility and the physical distribution of the product by means of tickets. The transfer of the product to the consumer is made through channels, that is, ticket outlets. Other ways of distributing the sport product include telemarketing, such as through toll-free numbers, and through the media.

Packaging

Packaging, or product presentation, is also a key factor in successful sport marketing. The importance of packaging in traditional marketing is underscored by the following quote, "Packaging as a medium of persuasion is an island of neglect" (Heller, 1989). In other words, too much is assumed about the consumer's point-of-purchase decision. The package should function as an advertisement and should make its promise loud and clear. Obviously, this philosophy has a great deal of merit for traditional products, but what does it mean for the sport product? Is there an effective packaging methodology for the sport product? With sporting goods and related sports products, the package can explain benefits, such as Nike's "air system" or Asics "gel system." Packaging also can explain the benefits of a "larger sweet spot" on a tennis racket or the strength and control of graphite skis. Is there a similar package concept for spectator sport?

The factors that make packaging spectator sport different are the same factors that make spectator sport different from more traditional products. That is, the intangibility of the spectator sport product requires the packaging to be composed mainly of expectations. Second, the packaging, because of the nature of the spectator sport product, is not used at the point of purchase, but must be informational and used before the actual event. Brochures, pamphlets, and "imagery-related" advertising are the essential packaging forms used for spectator sports. Highlight films, depicting the high points of the past season, are also integral to the packaging function in that they illustrate the "ingredients" in the product.

Some packaging techniques used in professional sports are selling groups of tickets for games held on weekends; "Super Saturday," a variation of the weekend package containing only Saturdays; or mini-vans, a group of games from the entire season combining strong and weak attractions. Other offers include promotional events, weekend and weekday games, limited game packages such as the Six Pack or Baker's Dozen, whereby the fan or the organization selects specific games. The benefits are the low initial cost of a limited number of games, the fact that seats are guaranteed, and usually a "free" or bonus game, that is, thirteen games for the price of twelve.

Another form of ticket packaging is the flex book, a series of coupons that may be redeemed at the box office for games of the customer's choice. The flex book is attractive because it enables the consumer to choose any games with no date restriction, and it usually offers the benefit of one "free" or bonus game. The limitation of the flex book from the consumer's perspective is that the seats are limited by availability, and consumers are cautioned to redeem their coupons as soon as possible to guarantee a seat for the games of their choice. In most cases, flex coupons are not redeemable at the gate on game day, forcing some planning by the consumer. On the other hand, the consumer may use all coupons for one game or may choose attend a variety of games, which gives the consumer a degree of discretion. The flex book is usually used in cases where demand is less than supply. When demand exceeds supply, packaging is limited and often is confined to season tickets and "mini" season tickets.

Another packaging technique is to combine the primary product with product extensions. An excellent example was devised by the Peoria Chiefs, a baseball club of the Class A Midwest League. The Chiefs designed packages for groups that included game tickets and concession or souvenir items for a discounted price. For example, an $8.50 group ticket (available to groups of twenty or more) included a general-admission ticket, popcorn or peanuts, a 22-ounce soda in a souvenir plastic cup, and a team yearbook (purchased separately the items would cost $10.50). According to the Chiefs' director of group sales, "The packages have been effective in luring groups to the park for the first time because it makes it

FIGURE 15–9 Product extensions—such as mascots, contests, halftime shows, and special events—add to the "sport package" by providing entertainment in addition to the core, or the game itself.

easy for people who haven't been here before" ("New Packages," 1989). Figure 15–9 illustrates how product extensions, such as a team mascot, add to the "sport package" by providing entertainment at the game.

CONCEPT CHECK

The four Ps (product, promotion, price, and place, plus positioning and packaging) are a formula that helps the producer to reach the potential consumer. These facets may be manipulated, emphasized, combined, and integrated to help achieve the correct formula.

MARKETING PLAN

The tangible result of the strategic planning process and the development of the marketing mix (four Ps) is the **marketing plan,** a document that becomes the framework for the marketing efforts of the sport organization. The sport marketer's research becomes

> *Your marketing plan should provide answers to the following questions:*
>
> 1. What is your product and how does it benefit your customers?
> 2. Who, exactly, are your customers?
> 3. What business are you in and what is your position relative to your competitors?
> 4. What barriers exist to keep competitors from taking your customers?
> 5. Who is/are your target market(s)?
> 6. How will you communicate with your customers? What is your positioning and advertising strategy? Do you have a creative theme?
> 7. What are the various promotional techniques and media channels you will use to reach your audience?
> 8. How much will it cost to market your product or service?
> 9. In what month will you implement the various promotional techniques and media messages?

most effective when it is incorporated into a systematic and formal marketing plan. The marketing plan enables a sport organization to establish strategies, objectives, and priorities, develop schedules and budgets, identify tactics, and initiate checkpoints to measure performance. Developing a marketing plan also helps the sport organization to recognize potential problems, opportunities, and threats that may emerge in the future. This section introduces the components of a marketing plan and outlines its most important elements. See the accompanying box for a list of important questions that should be considered in putting together a marketing plan.

Marketing plans generally fall into two primary categories: (1) new product plans and (2) annual plans. The *new product plan* is developed for a product, service, or brand that is new to the market. You can be certain that Nike, Wilson, Callaway, etc. develop complete new product marketing plans before committing resources to manufacture and distribution. Although the new product marketing plan may be sketchy in some areas, it is necessary to try to think through all contingencies before

embarking on a fully developed campaign. The new product marketing plan will have more unknowns than the annual marketing plan. The time frame for new product plans is from the introduction of the product through to its establishment in the marketplace (or the growth stage of the product life cycle).

The *annual marketing plan* is for products, events, services, programs, and brands that are already established. It is wise to formally review the organization's marketing agenda at least once a year—hence the term annual marketing plan. Keep in mind that the marketing plan is a road map for *future* marketing activities (both the new product and annual plans). Therefore, even with the annual plan there will be some unknowns.

Every marketing plan should be organized so that all important information is included. There are a variety of marketing plan outlines that will allow you to accomplish this. The outline that follows represents the typical plan. What is most important, however, is that your marketing ideas are presented in a logical and organized manner.

MARKETING PLAN OUTLINE

EXECUTIVE SUMMARY (The executive summary is an aspect of the final report and is written last, even though it appears at the beginning of the plan)

1. Introduce the problem.
2. Summarize the program/department's goals; describe the product or service being marketed; explain its differential advantage; sales; etc.
3. The executive summary presents an overview of the entire marketing plan.

I. Introduction
   A. Identify the organization's **mission statement.** The mission clarifies the basic values underlying management's marketing goals, decisions, and practices; it is, essentially, the organization's *reason for being.* Analyze relevant past and current marketing data; the development of a marketing plan begins with a clear understanding of "where we are."
      1. What does the organization produce and market?
      2. What are the customers' demands?
      3. How does the organization market its products/services to meet its customers' demands?

B. Background: Include history of the organization, previous target markets, and the organization's philosophy (written or unwritten), which may have an impact on their marketing approach.
   1. Who are the organization's primary stakeholders (customers, employees, owners)?
   2. Who is the ultimate customer (end user)?

II. Situational or Swot Analysis
A. Internal organizational (company) analysis: Identify **strengths and weaknesses** of the organization (program/team/department). If available, include in your report a copy of the organizational chart. Use the following categories to assist you in completing your STRENGTHS & WEAKNESSES analysis:
   1. Product: Describe your products.
   2. Management: Rate the management team at the organization in terms of ability, attitude, experience, and quantity.
   3. Employees: Evaluate the organization's employees in terms of the ability and number of adequately trained people (are there sufficient numbers of trained employees based on the organization's mission statement?).
   4. Budget and Finances: Even though capital budgets are not within the control of the sport marketer, it is important to know what the organization's capital resources are, as well as its budgeting procedures. Describe the financial issues that face the organization that allow or prevent it from having a competitive advantage. Review how resources are allocated. Does each manager know how much of the budget's resources he/she can use? What are the procedures for obtaining more budget dollars?
   5. Information: Review the organization's accounting system, inventory, customer sales, marketing, and employee records. Are they accurate and reliable? easily accessed? Does the organization have access to the information it needs?
   6. Customers: What do your customers want that you do not currently provide? What trade-offs are your customers willing to make (in terms of price, quality, convenience, reliability, etc.)? Do you have loyal customers?
B. External environmental analysis: Identify **opportunities and threats.** Review the economic indicators that are relevant to your product or service. Governmental agencies, trade association, library sources, and business publications are excellent sources of data concerning the economic conditions relative to sport. Use the following categories to assist you in completing your OPPORTUNITIES & THREATS analysis:
   1. Demographics: Who are the people who currently consume this product or service?
   2. Economic Climate: What are the economic factors and/or trends that affect the sport industry and in particular, this organization?
   3. Demand Trends: What is happening in your organization's industry? Is it growing, declining, or stable? Where are the company's products in terms of the product life cycle?
   4. Technological Trends: What impact does technology have on this organization? Does it affect the organization's product or service offerings?
   5. Government and Public Policy Trends: What local, state, federal, and/or international policies and regulations currently (or will in the near future) affect the organization?
   6. Macro-Environment Trends: Consider the political and sociocultural systems and their potential impact on the organization. What changes in social trends—population growth, aging patterns (baby boomers, etc.), public opinion of sport, ethical concerns, legal issues, etc.—affect the organization?
C. Competitive analysis: Knowledge of competitors and their affiliated brands is critical in designing effective marketing strategies. It is important to understand what the competition is doing even if you believe they are wrong. What are the competitors doing differently from this organization, that is, how are customers being satisfied by the competition?

1. The bulk of information about your competitors can be found by reviewing the following sources:
   a. Newspaper articles
   b. Annual reports (easily found online or in company CD-ROM)
   c. Company or department literature
   d. Trade journal articles
   e. Individuals
   f. The competitors
2. Describe your main competitors, their products, plans, resources, and strategies.
3. Evaluate the **strengths and weaknesses** of the competition's marketing strategy.

III. Customer analysis and target market-identification
   A. Customer Analysis
      1. List customers you serve
      2. Include customer demographics
      3. If available, include lifestyle information in this section.
         a. Examples include purchase frequency, brand or team loyalty, where tickets purchased or where service is enjoyed, activities, interests, opinions, etc.
   B. Target Market(s)
      1. Identify and select market segments that represent the most likely customers for your product or service.
      2. Describe your target market segment in detail, segmenting it however appropriate (e.g., demographics, psychograhics, geography, product usage, lifestyle, etc.)

IV. *Marketing* goals and objectives: Marketing objectives should be established to help the sport organization to achieve its goals. These predict market share, sales volume, and position in relation to price and quality. State them precisely.
   A. Summarize the organization's/sport franchise's goals.
   B. Summarize the marketing goals. Include short-term and long-term goals.
   C. State specific project goals and objectives. Objectives must be stated in such a way that results can be *measured*. Marketing objectives generally are stated in term of achieving X percent market share for a particular product or service, achieving X percent market penetration within certain market segments, and achieving X percent sales growth for all or selected product lines or tickets.
   D. Product portfolio and positioning. Examine the mix of product or service lines offered by the organization and identify how each is positioned.

V. Marketing strategy: How do you plan to achieve your objectives? In this section describe what is to be done to achieve the marketing goals and objectives identified in section IV. Your strategy may be trying to differentiate your product from the competition, or segmenting the marketing differently, or positioning (or repositioning) the product relative to competitors, etc. This section explains what you are planning to do strategically, given the current position of your product in the product life cycle. Be sure to consider how your main competitor(s) will likely respond to your marketing strategy (if applicable) and what you will do to counter this (avoid threats and exploit opportunities).

VI. Marketing tactics: How will you implement the marketing strategy(ies) identified above? Tactics explain *how* to carry out strategy. List every action required to implement each of the strategies identified.
   A. Tactics in this section are built around the following elements of the *marketing mix*: product or service; position; price; and distribution (place).
   B. Use the following to assist you in developing your marketing strategies:
      1. Describe the *product*. How will you *position* or *reposition* your event or product? Which of the three basic product tactics—introduction, change, or withdrawal—will you use to support your strategy and achieve your marketing goals?
      2. *Prices* must be established for each product line or service. Pricing objectives must match objectives for product lines. Describe the *pricing objective* for each product line or service. Identify which

pricing tactics—penetration pricing, meet-the-competition, skim pricing, promotional, etc.—you will use.

3. Describe the *distribution* for each product line or service. The use of new channels of distribution often offers opportunities to gain a competitive edge (differential advantage). Examples of distribution channels include direct mail, door-to-door sales, electronic shopping, site flexibility etc.

4. *Promotion* (include *advertising, publicity,* and *sales*). Before developing your budget, it is imperative that you determine what is desired of your promotions and advertising. Keep in mind that in every sport organization there are limited resources. Therefore, resources should be employed where they will have the greatest "bang for the buck."

   - Creative component: This is an essential core of your approach; what sets you apart; develop a *slogan* or *theme* for your campaign.
   - Promotion tactics: necessary to increase attendance, ticket or merchandise sales, create greater market share, or accomplish marketing objectives. Examples include sampling, give-aways, couponing, public relations, premiums, point-of-purchase displays, contests and sweepstakes, and specialty advertising. Sales promotions are especially useful for introducing new products or responding to extreme competition. Match your promotion tactics to your objectives and strategies for each event, product line, or service.
   - Identify the type (media, print, radio, television, specialty, direct mail, point of purchase, or other), the approximate cost, frequency, and size of the advertisement.

VII. Implementation and control
   A. Action Plan: Present a calendar or chart showing what promotions, ads, etc., will be used, and the month the activity is due to be completed.

   B. Budget: The proposed budget should reflect the projected costs associated with the marketing plan.
   C. Evaluation: How are you going to measure whether your goals and objectives are met?

VIII. Summary: State the differential advantage that your plan offers over the competition. Summarize the advantages, costs, profits, etc.

IX. Appendices: Include all information you deem relevant.

Sources of information that are helpful for this project include the following:
Predicasts Forecasts; US Industrial Outlook; Infotrac Business File; Survey of Buying Power; American Sports Analysis; Pedicasts Basebook; Study of Media and Markets; Valueline; Standard and Poor's Stock Reports; Moody's manuals; *SEC File; Market Share Reporter; Lifestyle Market Analyst;* 1995 United States Census; *Thomas Reporter; Rand McNally Commercial Atlas and Market Guide; SRDS Sports Advantage* or other Standard Rate and Data Service sources; journal articles; newspaper articles; and government publications.

CRITICAL THINKING EXERCISES

1. If you were the marketing manager for an NBA team, say the Denver Nuggets, how would you customize the elements of the marketing mix to try to increase attendance? How would you adjust the elements of the marketing mix if you worked for the Chicago Bulls or another NBA team?

2. As the associate athletic director of marketing for an NCAA Division I or II school, how would you price tickets for sports *other* than football? What factors would you consider when making your ticket pricing decisions?

SUMMARY

1. Sport marketing has its roots in traditional marketing but is also distinct in a variety of ways.

2. Sports are consumed for a variety of reasons, some of which may have little or no relation to the intent of the producer of the product. The sport marketer must be aware of these motivations for consumption of the product.

3. The marketing of the sport product should be strategically and systematically planned. The

strategic plan gives a framework to the entire marketing process.

4. Because of the unpredictability of the sport product, the sport marketer must market both the core product and the product extensions.

5. The focus of sport marketing is on identifying and selecting the target market(s) and then developing a marketing mix that will appeal to the selected target(s). To learn the needs of sport consumers, the marketer must conduct demographic and lifestyle analyses.

6. Sport marketing concepts act as a formula (the four Ps plus) and function in an interrelated manner to produce the effect that the marketer planned to achieve. Each of these factors can be manipulated to reach a target market, create awareness, provide information, or force a reaction.

7. Product usage information is crucial to sport marketing. Because product usage varies by strata, the marketer must develop strategies that address the needs of light, medium, and heavy users. Overemphasizing strategies targeted to the heavy users, particularly if it means neglecting light and medium users, could cost the sport organization in the future.

8. Positioning a product is necessary today because of the overwhelming volume of advertising. The concept of positioning is to differentiate, or position in the mind of the consumer, your product from your competitors' products. Positioning is the same as niche marketing.

9. The sport marketer must select a pricing strategy early in the marketing planning process. Price is the most visible and flexible component of the marketing mix, and it contributes to the consumer's perception of the value of the sport product.

10. Knowledge of the communication process is essential for the sport marketer and can be useful in planning the promotional mix. The promotional mix includes advertising, sales promotions, publicity, and personal selling. Before launching any promotion, the sport marketer should set the goals of the promotional campaign.

11. Advertising, because of its vast reach and high cost, and sales promotions, because of their flexibility, are important aspects of the promotional mix.

12. The marketing plan is a written document, resulting from the strategic planning process that guides the sport marketer throughout the season.

CASE STUDY

Nike: Going Global

Nike founder Philip Knight created what is now known as the Nike empire in 1962, when he started the company Blue Ribbon Sports. Nike, which in 1999 will likely generate revenues of more than $4 billion from U.S. footwear sales alone, currently holds the majority of the athletic shoe market with a 30 percent share. Knight's passion and drive for excellence influence the company's corporate culture and have been passed on to Nike's employees. The athletic footwear and apparel company's success is largely due to its ability to adapt its structure, management, and marketing processes to meet the demands of its competitive environment, both domestically and abroad. Nike has dominated the athletic footwear market for over two decades.

Recently, however, Nike has faced a slowdown in demand for its products abroad. The company remains the market leader in the U.S. but international sales are off, and domestic sales of basketball shoes have been slumping. Nike faces tremendous challenges in its global marketing efforts, particularly in China, where it began selling shoes and apparel in 1984. Although China's population of 1.2 billion represents a potentially lucrative market, U.S. marketers must surmount a number of obstacles, including an underdeveloped transportation system, uncooperative customs agents, thievery, government bias, and cultural differences in order to achieve any success. In spite of these obstacles, marketing research indicated that 15 percent of the Chinese population could afford to purchase Nike products. Nike chose to target highly populated cities first because it could more efficiently reach potential consumers through advertising and sponsorship of athletic teams.

Reebok is also interested in selling its footwear and apparel in China, and the competition between these two U.S. athletic footwear heavyweights is escalating. Moreover, both Nike and Reebok face stiff competition from China- and Hong-Kong-based athletic footwear companies, who price their products significantly lower than either Nike or Reebok. For the average Chinese citizen, a pair of Nike shoes would cost a few months' salary. However, with an improving

economy, more people should be able to afford Nike's products, and consequently, purchase them.
Questions to guide your analysis of Nike:

1. *Why is athletic footwear the ideal product for global marketing?*
2. *How should Nike position itself in the China market?*
3. *What other global opportunities exist for Nike now? Five years from now?*
4. *What threats do competing companies pose for Nike in China? In other global markets?*
5. *What advantages does Nike have in its competition with Reebok and other athletic footwear companies for leadership in the China market?*
6. *Are there any significant factors within the environment that could affect Nike's market position in the U.S.? Five years from now?*

REVIEW QUESTIONS AND ISSUES

1. What are the unique characteristics of sport, and how do these differences affect the marketing of sport?
2. Using the Target Group Index or Mediamark marketing reports (or similar marketing research database), identify the demographic and, if available, lifestyle profile of a sport's participant and spectating audience (e.g., NBA, NFL, World Cup Soccer, etc.).
3. What does the term *market segmentation* mean? What are the types of segmentation that are commonly used, and how does segmentation help the sport marketer to identify the target market?
4. Define the term *target market*. Discuss the steps in identifying a target market when marketing "official clothing" of a professional sports team (you might select one of the popular teams from the list in the chapter). How might this target differ from that of a target market for "official clothing" of a college or university?
5. What does the term *product* mean? Describe the attributes and benefits of a sport product or service.

6. What are the differences between core product and product extensions? Which of these concepts is more important to the sport marketer? Why?
7. What does the term *positioning* mean? How would you attempt to position a 3-on-3 basketball tournament (to be held for the first time on your campus) to students? To alumni? To the community?
8. What techniques and strategies would you use to promote your 3-on-3 campus basketball tournament? Justify your choices.

SOLUTIONS TO CRITICAL THINKING EXERCISES

1. The sport marketer cannot change the product; therefore, the price and promotion elements of the marketing mix would be the first choice for manipulation. Price could be changed to temporarily increase demand for tickets by developing a sales promotion, such as a four-for-four coupon. Other, non–price-related promotions could also be developed to increase interest in the games, such as a frequent fan series of promotions that encourage repeat attendance. Be careful, however, not to rely too heavily on sales promotions to increase demand.
2. The first step would be to determine the school's philosophy regarding charging for nonrevenue sports. Some schools do not charge for any sports except football, men's and women's basketball, and volleyball or hockey. However, if you do charge for nonrevenue sports events, a value must be placed on the worth of the event. Be careful not to charge too little for the event as it could result in a low perceived quality by potential fans. Another option for nonrevenue sports would be to develop a ticket package that would allow fans to choose various events.

REFERENCES

Aaker, D. (1998). *Strategy market management.* 5th ed. New York. Wiley.

Barnathan, J., Harbrecht, and Palmer (1994, December 12). "A tidal wave of Chinese goods." *Business Week*, 56.

"AMA board approves new definition." (1985, March 1). *Marketing News*, 1.

Brooks, C. (1994). *Sports marketing: Competitive business strategies for sports.* Englewood Cliffs, NJ: Prentice-Hall.

Sources: Barnathan, Harbrecht, and Palmer (1994, December 12). "A tidal wave of Chinese goods." *Business Week*, 56; Falson & Qiu (1996, March 3), "Jordan! Slam dunk! Pee-ow liang!" *New York Times*, section 4, p. 2; http:www.NikeBiz.com

Cialdini, R. (1993). *Influence: Science and practice.* 3d ed. New York: HarperCollins.

Comte, E., and Stogel, C. (1990, January 1). "Sports A $63.1 billion industry." *The Sporting News,* 60–61.

Engel, J., Blackwell, R., and Miniard, P. (1995). *Consumer behavior.* 8th ed. Fort Worth: Dryden Press.

Evans, J., and Berman, R., (1994). *Marketing.* 6th ed. New York, Macmillan.

Falson and Qiu (1996, March 3), "Jordan! Slam dunk! Peeowliang!" *New York Times,* section 4, p. 2; www.NikeBiz.com

FANSonly. (1999, March). *The FANSonly network: Your ticket to college sports!* Atlanta, GA: Author.

Gladden, J. (1996). "Sports market bytes: The ever expanding impact of technology on sport marketing, part I." *Sport Marketing Quarterly, 5* (3), 13–14.

Governor's Special Task Force on Cactus League Baseball. (1988). Office of the Governor, State of Arizona, Dwight Patterson, Chairman.

Hansen, H., and Gauthier, R., (1989). "Factors affecting attendance at professional sport events." *Journal of Sport Management, 3* (1), 15–32.

Heller, R. (1989). *The supermarketers.* New York: E. P. Dutton.

Jayhawks hope pricing change will attract fans. (1989, September). *Team Marketing Report,* 8.

Kotler, P. (1997). *Marketing management: Analysis, implementation, planning and control.* 9th ed. Upper Saddle River, NJ: Prentice-Hall.

Lazer, W., and Culley, J. (1983). *Marketing management.* Boston: Houghton Mifflin.

Levitt, T. (1986). *Marketing imagination.* New York: The Free Press.

Lieberman, S. (1991, September/October). "The popular cultures: Sports in America—a look at the avid sports fan." *Review of Public Opinion and Polling, 2* (6), 28–29.

Marcum, J., and Greenstein, T. (1985). "Factors affecting attendance at major league baseball, Part II. A within-season analysis." *Sociology of Sport Journal, 2,* 314–22.

Mason, J., and Paul, J. (1988). *Modern sports administration.* Englewood Cliffs, NJ: Prentice-Hall.

Meek, A. (1998). "An estimate of the size and supported economics of the sports industry in the United States." *Sport Marketing Quarterly, 6* (4), 15–21.

Milne, G., and McDonald, M. (1999). *Sport marketing: Managing the exchange process.* Sudbury, MA: Jones and Bartlett.

Mullin, B. (1983). *Sport marketing, promotion and public relations.* Amherst, MA: National Sport Management.

Mullin, B., Hardy, S., and Sutton, W. (1993). *Sport marketing.* Champaign, IL: Human Kinetics.

Nelson, K. (1989). San Francisco. *Sport Magazine, 80,* 10.

New packages boost Chiefs' group sales. (1989, August). *Team Marketing Report,* 4.

Patrick, D. (1999, August 27). "Mountain West reinstates traditional rivalries from WAC." *USA Today,* p. 3F.

Perreault, W., and McCarthy, E. J. (1999). *Basic marketing: A global-managerial approach.* 13th ed. New York: McGraw-Hill.

Plumber, J. (1974). "The concept and application of lifestyle segmentation." *Journal of Marketing, 38* (1), 33–37.

Pride, W., and Ferrell, O. (1997). *Marketing concepts and strategies.* 10th ed. New York: Houghton Mifflin.

Ries, A., and Trout, J. (1986). *Positioning: The battle for your mind.* New York: McGraw-Hill.

Rudman, W., and Sutton, W. (1989, September). The selling of the NBA: Market characteristics and sport consumption. Presentation at the National Basketball Association's Annual Meeting, Palm Springs, California.

Sandomir, R. (1988, November 14). The $50 billion sport industry. *Sports Inc.,* 14–23.

Shank, M. (1999). *Sports marketing: A strategic perspective.* Upper Saddle River, NJ: Prentice-Hall.

Stotlar, D. (1993). *Successful sport marketing.* Dubuque, IA: Brown & Benchmark.

Veeck, W., and Linn, E. (1965). *The hustler's handbook.* New York: The Putnam Publishing Group.

Waddell, R. (1989). "Attendance ups & downs for major league baseball teams." *Amusement Business, 101* (34), 18 and 31.

Yow, D. (1999, March). "New directions on the 'net." *Athletic Management,* 14–17.

WEBSITES

Professional sports

Official sites for major leagues; each team has a link on the league page so that each team can be reached.

www.nba.com
www.wnba.com
www.nfl.com
www.majorleaguebaseball.com
www.nhl.com
www.mls.com
www.NASCAR.com

Olympics

Information on the Olympics and Paralympics

www.olympics.nbc.com
www.olympics.nbc.com/usoc/paralympics

Sports Information

Sites that report on both the spectator and business aspects of sports.

www.ESPN.com
www.CBSSportsline.com
www.CNNSI.com
www.FANSonly.com
www.SportingNews.com
www.FoxSports.com

Sporting Goods Industry

SGMA's and National Sporting Goods Association sites

www.sportlink.com
www.ngsa.com

Sport Marketing

General sports marketing information

www.teammarketing.com
www.bizsport.com

CHAPTER 16

Sponsorship

Dave Stotlar

In this chapter, you will become familiar with the following terms:

Sponsorship
Exchange theory
Philanthropy
Advertising
Return on investment
Market research
Media exposure

Leveraging
Target markets
Demographics
Sampling
Merchandising
Sponsorship agreement
Legal counsel

Pricing
Cost-plus method
Competitive-market strategy
Relative-value method
Valuation
Ambush marketing
Vertical integration

Overview

On a worldwide basis, sport organizations and corporations have entered into partnerships wherein each agrees to assist the other in forwarding their own objectives. One such partnership is sport **sponsorship.** For sports organizations, it's an effort to obtain funds from sponsors to operate their sports events and programs. For corporations, it's a chance to get their products in the minds of consumers. This relationship originated decades ago, but it has increased in popularity and sophistication over the last fifteen years (Wilkinson, 1986; Ensor, 1987; Asimakopoulos, 1993; Graham, 1993; Irwin, 1993). It has been estimated that more than 4,800 U.S. companies involved in sports marketing and sponsorship spent $7.6 billion, up 15 percent over 1998. Contributing to this total were sixty-one companies that spent over $10 million each on sponsorship programs (1999 Sponsors' spending, 1998). Worldwide spending was $19.2 billion for 1999 with a growth rate of 11 percent.

PHILOSOPHICAL BASIS FOR SPONSORSHIP
Initially, sports professionals must develop an understanding of sponsorship from a philosophical view. Sport sponsorships are based on the **exchange theory:** "If you give me something, I'll give you something." Therefore the definition of a sport sponsorship is a situation wherein a sport organization grants the right of association to another company or organization. As we will see, the right of association can take many forms.

A determination must be made early in discussions between the parties involved regarding whether the exchange can be equal—*can* be equal as opposed to *will* be equal. Some sponsorship arrangements cannot provide equal value to both parties—for instance, the junior high school sports program that is asking for money to print its sports program. Any corporation that provides these funds is actually doing it for **philanthropy** rather than for financial reasons. However, a company that pays a fee to put its corporate logo on the side of a race car in the Indianapolis 500 may be able to generate an advertising value that substantially exceeds the amount paid. Irwin (1993) noted that "in years past, corporations provided financial assistance to sporting events and athletic programs for philanthropic purposes, [but] today's corporate interests are strictly promotionally motivated."

CONCEPT CHECK

Those who desire to obtain a sport sponsorship must make an initial determination with respect to their ability to deliver commensurate economic value in the exchange. If this criterion cannot be met, a philanthropic approach is mandated.

A key step in making a sponsorship proposal that appeals to a sponsor is to provide a comparison of the requested amount to competitive **advertising** costs and value. Each potential sponsor is engaged in other marketing activities, each of which has a price and a value. You must study and prepare data that show the benefit of sport sponsorship in terms that the corporation can evaluate. Remember, the person who agrees to give you the sponsorship must be able to defend her or his decision to the corporate management or stockholders.

A key component in the sponsorship process is the measurement of **return on investment** (ROI). Is there an equivalent increase in sales attributable to the sponsorship? Conventional data on the advertising and promotions conducted by corporations show that only about 16 percent of the promotions produced sales that were greater than the costs of the promotion (Abraham and Lodish, 1990). These authors also believe that if a promotion is not effective in increasing sales within a six-month period, it will never produce sales. With this in mind, it becomes essential for those entering a sport sponsorship to accurately and quickly measure the impact and success of the partnership. Recent data on VISA International's Olympic sponsorship produced data that measured a 3 percent increase in customer preference from before the Olympic games to after their completion. Although that may not seem like a large increase, 3 percent of a multibillion dollar industry is a considerable amount of money.

Sport managers must be fully cognizant of the data with which to demonstrate the accomplishment of specified corporate objectives. This should be provided by the sport organization or event owner, but it is occasionally collected by the sponsor. Motorola conducted its own market research to investigate the effectiveness of its motorcycle team sponsorship in Europe and found that it received a 6-to-1 return (IEG, 1993b).

CONCEPT CHECK

Sport organizations that use sponsorship as a marketing tool must be prepared to evaluate sponsorship in the same manner as other marketing efforts.

According to research data, "sponsorship may send a more convincing message than traditional advertising" (Performance Research, 1991). The study found that 70 percent of golf enthusiasts could recall the sponsors of events, whereas only 40 percent could remember the television commercials aired during the events. However, one should not underestimate the power of broadcasting commercial advertising during sports programs. Only about 8 percent of television viewers can recall commercials aired during nonsports programs.

During the 1990s, Princeton Video Images introduced a new advertising concept for sport events: virtual signage. Their technology "allows a broadcaster to electronically insert an image—generally an advertisement—onto any one-color surface, including a playing field or boundary" (Bernstein, 1998b, p. 24). The National Basketball Association has not allowed virtual signage, but Major League Baseball and the National Hockey League have used the technology on several national telecasts. The X Games and various professional tennis tournaments employed this technology extensively during the late 1990s. Considerable controversy exists concerning control of the images that are presented during the event. Facility owners protested these applications because they had often promised stadium advertisers that their signs would be seen by television audiences during events telecast from the facility.

The San Diego Padres encountered a problem when their TV broadcaster sold virtual signage during telecasts of home contests. The following year, the Padres specified in their broadcast contract that the team, not the broadcaster, would have the rights to any virtual signage inserted into Padres games (Bernstein, 1998b).

One can also have professional **market research** firms collect data for you. One such company is Performance Research, which conducts research in the area of sponsor exposure for companies involved in the trade. It conducts field-based research in such areas as aided and unaided recall, advertising awareness, responses to promotions, product usage, and brand loyalty.

During the Olympic games, Performance Research studied the recognition by consumers of Olympic sponsors (1992, 1994a, 1994b). Before the games, they found, 34 percent of consumers were still unaware that 1994 was an Olympics year and 43 percent could not name any Olympic sponsors. Of those who could name a sponsor, Coke was the leader, with an awareness of 22 percent. Studies conducted during the Olympics showed that 50 percent to 75 percent of those surveyed recognized Coke (Performance Research, 1994b; Stotlar, 1993).

Sports organizations have a variety of objectives, but two of the most prominent are finance and media exposure. Interestingly, these are the same objectives that sponsoring corporations seek.

CONCEPT CHECK

Establishing a base for a sponsorship relationship is paramount to its success. The sport organization and the sponsor must work together in all facets of the relationship. According to Wilkinson (1988), "in an ideal relationship between the organization and the sponsor, each helps the other meet its objectives."

Because sponsorship is "playing a more central role in corporate thinking, it becomes more important to understand consumer reaction to sponsorship efforts and to research the influence of sponsorship on attitudes" (Sandler and Shani, 1993). In general, only a few people feel that sport sponsorship is a "bad thing" (IEG, 1993c). At the same time, however, some consumers think that sports are becoming too commercialized.

Market research has found that the Olympic rings are the most recognized logo in the world, with 89.8 percent of the population able to correctly recognize the rings. Therefore, sponsors may desire to associate with the Olympic rings to enhance their recognition value. In addition, sponsors of the Olympics could benefit from the estimated worldwide TV audience of four billion viewers (TOP IV Programme, 1997).

Probably the most revealing data indicated that 69 percent of consumers felt that "the fact that a company is an official sponsor has no impact on my purchase habits" (Sandler and Shani, 1993). Although the research data are mixed in their summary of consumer reaction to sponsorship, you could argue that if the companies didn't think that it was a good investment, the billions of dollars now committed to sport sponsorship would disappear.

According to Irwin (1993), "without the support of corporations, the world of sport, as we know it, would collapse." This may seem dramatic, but the world of sport has become increasingly dependent on corporate sponsorships for operating revenues. For example, 40 percent of the U.S. Olympic Committee's 1996–2000 budget came from sponsorship and licensing revenue. Similarly, between 50 and 60 percent of the budgets for the Sydney and Salt Lake Olympic Games were based on sponsorship dollars (*Olympic Fact Book,* 1998). In addition, almost all of the top NCAA universities have corporate sponsorship programs in place (Irwin, 1993). Thus the relationship between sport organizations and sponsors must include advantages to all parties involved.

RESEARCHING SPONSORSHIP PROSPECTS

Many sports marketers fail to adequately prepare themselves to enter the sponsorship business. The key to success is the ability to research prospective companies. Probably the best place to start is to obtain a thorough understanding of the corporate sponsorship environment. The International Events Group (IEG) in Chicago has organized a corporation around the sponsorship industry, and its publication, *IEG Sponsorship Report,* is an important tool in researching prospective sponsors. Their research from World Cup '98 indicated that while 39 percent of the respondents said sponsorship made no difference in their intent to purchase or company loyalty, 50 percent said that they were more likely to switch brands because of a company's sponsorship of the event (*IEG Sponsorship Training Supplement*, 1999). In 1999, the International Events Group reported that the most active categories of sponsorship were media companies, packaged goods businesses, telecommunication firms, and banks and financial services corporations.

Sponsorship proposals are considerably more effective if they tie sponsorship elements specifically to objectives of the sponsoring corporation (Irwin, 1993). One of the more effective steps in investigating corporations' objectives and goals is gaining access to their corporate literature, such as the annual report. This document will tell you a lot about the inner workings of a company. There are, however, many things that a company doesn't want its shareholders to know that you need to know. From this perspective, you can read clippings from area papers or talk to people who do business with the company. Just knowing who holds what office is not enough; you have to know who the power brokers are in the organization.

One good example is the Coca-Cola Company. The best point of access for a sponsorship with Coke is the local bottler. More than 90 percent of the proposals funded by Coke come through to corporate headquarters with support from the local bottling company. The corporate belief is that if the local bottlers are in favor of an event and believe that it will have a positive impact on sales, then it's worth doing. However, the local distributor for other corporations may not have the money, the interest, or the authority to enter into this type of arrangement.

Additional research must be done on a corporation's prior sponsorship experiences. If it has had good experiences, your chances will be better; if it has had one or more bad experiences, you will have a difficult time demonstrating that your results will differ.

EXAMINING SPONSORSHIP OBJECTIVES

Irwin (1993) identified **media exposure** as one of the three most highly rated factors by sponsors in judging sponsorship proposals. *Telling* sponsors that they will get media attention is valuable, but *measuring* it provides data for legitimizing the corporation's involvement in sports marketing. Sponsors are increasingly demanding more sophisticated measurement of value. These measures typically parallel measures used to evaluate all corporate

marketing elements. Spoelstra remarked: "prove it to the decision-makers' boss" (Spoelstra, 1997, p. 172). In short, it helps them to help you. In a service-related business, it's your responsibility to provide them with these data.

Another consideration is **leveraging** media coverage through sponsorship. You are going to be spending money on advertising anyway, so why not seek a media sponsor and arrange for a four-to-one arrangement (for $4 worth of media space or air time, you give them $1 credit toward sponsorship). For instance, Digital Computer was approached by a minor league baseball team as sponsor. Digital Computer's goal was to produce a 5-1 return on their sponsorship investment. To assist digital in meeting their objectives, the team assembled all available sponsorship and media inventory including, field signage, program ads, and TV tags to parallel Digital's objectives. In the end, Digital provided $500,000 in sponsorship (50 percent product, 50 percent cash) and received an ROI of 9-1. This will give you more advertising for your dollar, your sponsors more media benefit, and the media source special-event associations (Spoelstra, 1997).

Irrespective of the validity of calculating the value of camera/action shots on an equal basis with actual ads, it gives the sponsors (or marketing managers) data with which to defend their decisions to use sport as a marketing vehicle. One company, Joyce Julius and Associates, provides support data to help event owners justify return on investment to sponsors. They calculate the total time that a sponsor's logo appears on the televised coverage of major events. Based on the cost of airing a thirty-second commercial during the event, they can determine the value of the sponsor's exposure. For example, data from the 1998 NASCAR Brickyard event indicated that each primary sponsor's logo was on screen for an average of 9 minutes and 14 seconds. The cost to advertise on ABC's broadcast of the event was $157,500 for a thirty-second advertisement (King, 1998).

The ability of sponsors to receive positive visibility and increase sales with favorable publicity has been shown to be an attractive mechanism for sponsors. Yet many sport organizations have experienced high levels of conflict between event management decisions and sponsors' satisfaction. During the 1996 Atlanta Olympic Games, conflict occurred in many of the cities where the Olympic Torch Relay was run. The relay was sponsored by Coca-Cola, yet managed by the Olympic Organizing Committee. The sponsors wanted the relay to always pass the local Coke distributor, whereas the planning committee often had other routes planned. Be careful not to jeopardize the integrity of your event for the desires of sponsors.

Before undertaking a sponsorship, most corporations develop a set of criteria for evaluating possible opportunities. This process has been discussed extensively (*IEG's Complete Guide to Sponsorship,* 1995; Irwin and Asimakopoulos, 1992; Irwin, 1993). To follow are typical factors to be considered beyond the media aspects previously discussed.

Target markets

There has to be a careful match between the **demographics** of the sponsor's consumers and the audience/participants of the sports event. In discussing their sponsorship of a golf tournament, one Acura (automobile) executive said the golfing market was its most desirable demographic target. Irwin (1993) stressed the importance of this when he said, "the audience profile, which is rapidly becoming the most important element of a sponsorship proposal, needs to go beyond simply reporting attendance figures and must comprehensively describe who attends the events." The sport organization has several avenues through which this information can be provided. The organization can collect its own data, or it can use secondary data collected by a commercial firm.

At the University of Northern Colorado, turnstile operators use Universal Product Code (UPC) scanners to record students' ID cards when they enter the stadium. With this information, the university can identify exactly who came to the game. Although only 50 percent of colleges collect this type of information, it is essential for sponsors. Consumer research firms such as Simmons Market Research Bureau also collect similar data on a nationwide basis. Their data can be used to relate to sponsors the "typical audience" for specific sports events. Their study of media and markets also provides data on television viewership of sports events. These will provide a rough idea of the audience profile for sports events.

The geographical reach of the sponsorship is also important. While once relegated to the southeastern part of the U.S., stock car racing now has a national

reach and has recently conducted races in Japan. Research commissioned by NASCAR indicated that its fans had the following characteristics: 78 percent male, 73 percent married, an average of 42 years old, 81 percent home owners, with 3.4 cars per household, and 87 percent earning $35,000 to $50,000 per year (Performance Research, 1994c). These data are imperative when attempting to select sponsors who have these people as their primary consumers. You simply cannot make a good match without good data.

Product sampling opportunities

"Qualitative research shows that **sampling** is the single best way to convert people" (*IEG's Complete Guide to Sponsorship,* 1995). To calculate the benefit for the sponsor, one can compare the cost of the sampling to the anticipated return. Sampling can convert about 10 percent of product users to the company's product. Assume that the typical consumer purchases $20 of the company's product per year, with a profit of $15. If the company spent $100,000 ($50,000 each for the sponsorship and for the cost of labor and products) for the sampling, there would need to be almost 7,000 conversions, which could only be realized if the event drew a crowd of about 70,000. Events can be both cheaper and more effective than other avenues of sampling. For example, many road races assemble "goodie bags" for participants, with product samples supplied by sponsors. For many years, U.S. Swimming also used this technique to provide a sponsor's sunscreen products for its members. In another example, Kodak uses its Olympic sponsorship to get 175,000 rolls of film into the hands of thousands of professional photographers who spend considerably more (or more often recommend corporate film purchases) than normal consumers (*Olympic Marketing Fact File,* 1998).

It is your responsibility to control sampling. Sponsors generally do not want consumers to take multiple samples, which would detract from product sales. Depending on the type of product, the timing of distribution is critical. You would certainly want to hand out the above-mentioned sunscreen to people on their way into the event on a sunny day. However, you may not want to provide cookie samples to incoming consumers because it could hurt your concession sales. For large or perishable products, it may also be wise to distribute them as people exit the venue. If you do any postevent research, it is also a good idea to ask about the samples provided.

OTHER CONSIDERATIONS
Client entertainment

People will pay incredibly large sums of money for the opportunity to play in a "pro-am" golf event with a top golfer. Although the power to invite business associates to a skybox still carries substantial weight in some sponsorship decisions, these affinity factors are declining. VIP parking and seating, hospitality suites (or tents), and specially designed event apparel are other perquisites that accompany sport sponsorships. In some corporations, sport sponsorships are considered "an ego buy used by CEOs to impress their partners" (McManus, 1989).

Some research has indicated that these elements are not primary factors in the decision to sponsor an event. Kuzma, Shanklin, and McCally (1993) found that client entertainment ranked significantly lower than other marketing elements. However, it should be noted that the events included in the study were amateur sports. Research regarding this factor for professional or world-class events (e.g., America's Cup, Olympics) may yield different results.

The management of an event is also a consideration for sponsors. In 1999, the scandal surrounding the award of the 2002 Olympic Winter Games to Salt Lake City caused great concern among sponsors. Several sponsors withdrew and the USOC executive responsible for overseeing sponsor recruitment and service, John Krimsky, resigned. The past history of the organizing committee and the professional reputation of the staff are critically important because the image of the corporate sponsor is being placed in the hands of the sport organization.

The image of the products and services offered must also result in a good match. Because sport is associated with a healthy lifestyle, many sponsors may seek to relate their products to that image.

Merchandising

Merchandising is an area in sport that experienced incredible growth during the 1980s and early 1990s. The merchandising and licensing business has, according to industry data annual sales that exceed $110 billion per year (Goldfisher, 1998). However, sales of sport-related merchandise diminished in the late 1990s because of changes in fashion trends. According to industry data, worldwide licensed apparel sales were $10 billion for 1998 (Rofe, 1999). U.S. professional sport leagues have traditionally been the industry leaders. The National Football League accumulated $3 billion in 1998 from licensed product sales, while the National Basketball Association realized $2.3 billion in sales. Major League Baseball was third in revenues at $1.85 billion, with the National Hockey League earning a little bit over $1 billion. The Women's National Basketball Association tripled merchandising earnings from 1997 to the 1998 season (Rofe, 1999; Bhonslay, 1999a). The profits generated from licensing are not limited to professional teams competing in league play. NASCAR was able to generate $600 million in licensed product sales (Bhonslay, 1999b).

Sponsorship options

Brooks (1994) suggests that sponsorship provides a variety of "athletic platforms" that can serve as the basis for sponsorship: individual athletes, facilities, or an event. Each of these must be selected in reference to corporate goals and objectives. A single platform will be a good fit for all companies. Individual athletes can give a corporation a personal touch.

Michael Jordan was the all-time leader in endorsements. His service as a spokesperson for Nike was arguably the most successful endorsement arrangement ever to occur in sport. However, few of the current athletes have experienced the marketing success of Jordan. As a result, many of the major corporations began to curtail their endorsement programs in the late 1990s. At one point, Reebok had over 130 NBA players under contract; they decreased their stable of NBA endorsees to less than ten during the 1999 season. Similar strategies were employed by Nike and Fila (Bernstein, 1998).

Tiger Woods, arguably the heir apparent to Jordan, signed a contract with Nike immediately following his final amateur match. The five-year, $40 million contract was one of the highest in the history of sport. Other sponsors to sign Woods included Titleist with an estimated $20 million for five years, $2 million from Rolex and $3 million per year from American Express. Electronic Arts secured Tiger to endorse a video game after his victory at the 1997 Master's. In total, Woods' 1998 endorsement earnings amounted to about $28 million per year (Lombardo, 1998).

Women have not been as successful in securing levels of individual endorsements equal to men.

The leading female endorsers were Monica Seles ($6 million), Steffi Graf ($5 million), Martina Hingis ($3 million), and Kristi Yamaguchi ($3 million). Seles's deals included Nike, Planet Hollywood, Yonex, and Sportline USA (Top 25, 1998). However, several marketing executives saw women's sport as a growth area for endorsements.

Each component in the platform that is made available for sponsors has its strengths and weaknesses. The task for sport managers is to find an appropriate fit between the company and the sport organization.

Sponsorship models

Conceptual models for managing sport sponsorships have been derived from field-based applications. The model presented (Irwin and Asimakopoulos, 1992; figure 16–1) has been derived from existing sponsorship proposals and agreements. By examining this model, administrators can gain the skills necessary to effectively work with sponsorship partners. Specific examples and procedures are presented for you to use as models in building sponsorships for your sport organization.

One aspect of sport sponsorships that has been difficult to foresee for many managers is that corporations often would rather deal with large projects than be burdened by a multitude of small ones. One of Volvo's specific recommendations for sport sponsorship is that high-cost deals are more profitable and less work than numerous small ventures (Volvo and Sport Sponsorship, 1990). Therefore, it is important to offer the company several options in its sponsorship agreement, ranging from exclusive ownership of all events and opportunities to smaller and less expensive options, such as in-kind donations or program advertising.

The framework for this, like any business relationship, is established through the **sponsorship agreement.**

SPONSORSHIP AGREEMENT

The laws pertaining to sports sponsorship are not well defined. The contracts between the sponsor and the event/property holder should be carefully constructed. Remember, consult your **legal counsel** so that all matters are included in the contract in clear language with mutual understanding. The most critical points to be addressed in the contract

include the following (IEG's *Complete Guide to Sponsorship*, 1995).

Terms like *title sponsor* and *official supplier* have no standard meaning in the industry. Therefore, you must clarify the rights the sponsor is getting and the rights the promoter is retaining. You also need to preserve the value of the sponsor's exclusivity. Avoiding competitors is only part of the problem. Developing an appropriate sponsor mix is also a consideration. You should carefully match each sponsor with other sponsors, products, and corporate image. For instance, based on the 1994 Olympic Winter Games, the U.S. Figure Skating Association may not want to offer the category "official legal counsel." Pizza Hut may not want an "official antacid" for an event if it

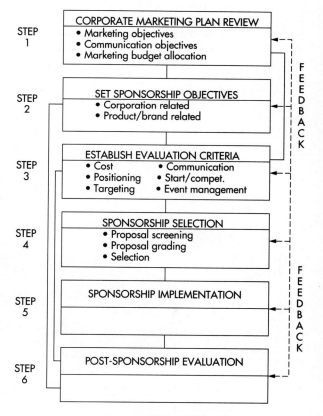

FIGURE 16–1   Six-step approach to sponsorship management.

(From Irwin, R. L. and Asimakopoulos, M. (1992). An approach to the evaluation and selection of sport sponsorship proposals, *Sport Marketing Quarterly*, pp. 43–51, December.)

were a title sponsor. McDonald's would not want to have Pepsi as the official soft drink because of its ties with Coca-Cola. If a soft drink company is secured, be sure to give attention to the contracts at the venue and any conflicts that might arise.

Each partner should strive to protect each other's trademarks and logos. Cooperation is always intended, but abuse can occur if the issue is not addressed. Typically, any use of an event logo or corporate trademark requires the owners' approval unless it is specially covered in the contract. Both parties need to be protected from liability through insurance. A sponsor does not want to be sued by an injured spectator or participant. Most events arrange for special coverage for all parties involved in an event. You might even have "insurance coverage" as a sponsorable category.

The agreement must include details on the use of the sponsors and event logos, including facilities and uniforms. Most sport organizations—including the IOC, USOC, NCAA, NFL, MLB, and NBA—have rules regarding the size of corporate logos that can be displayed on team uniforms. The primary catalyst in the logo issue was ski racers who, at the end of a race, immediately raised their skis in the air, with the logo facing toward the TV camera. Olympic gold medalist (1994) Diann Roffe-Steinrotter not only sported her Rossignol skis but lifted her Carrera goggles to reveal her Vail 99 headband promoting Vail as host of the 1999 World Cup ski finals (Carrier, 1994).

NASCAR strikes deals with sponsors and requires all drivers to place NASCAR's sponsors' logos on its cars for each race. Specific rules exist for the placement of the logos on the race cars (figure 16–2). The winning drivers of NASCAR races engage in a furious practice in victory lane: They constantly change hats sporting various sponsor logos. Not only does this give each sponsor its moment in the sun (and camera lens), but it's in the contract. Even the sequence is prescribed.

The NCAA published guidelines for all corporations involved in sponsoring its championships. In this document, the NCAA maintains absolute control over the sponsors' signs, advertisements, and even their specific wording. The NCAA document requires that "all advertising copy and promotional activities by NCAA national corporate partners utilizing the NCAA's name or registered marks must have prior approval of the NCAA" (National Collegiate Athletic Association, 1991).

One also needs to protect an event from being stolen. Many contracts contain a clause that prohib-

FIGURE 16–2 The ultimate fleet vehicle.
(From American Demogaphics, 14 (11), November 1992, a publication of Dow Jones & Co., Inc. Artwork courtesy of Gossage-McFarland Sports Marketing, Harrisburg, North Carolina.)

its the sponsor from staging a similar event for a specified number of years. However, problems can arise because of the difficulty of protecting the idea of an event or sponsorship. A situation such as this occurred with a national biathlon competition in the early 1990s. An agency representing the biathlon competition had proposed sponsorship to Adolph Coors Brewing Company. The event was conducted in 1988 and 1989 as the Coors Light Silver Bullet Biathlon Series, but when it came time for renewal in 1990, Coors delivered a form letter that stated "While COORS will evaluate your proposal for possible use in the future, it cannot make any commitments until the programs have been reviewed. . . . Please be advised that COORS may be developing similar or related projects, independent of any promotional ideas or proposals . . . submitted" (International Events Group, 1990). A few weeks after the event, the organizer received notice that Coors would not be renewing its contract and had, in fact, hired one of the agency's subcontractors to stage future events for Coors (International Events Group, 1990).

Protection against unfulfilled promises should also be addressed in the contract. If an event promises to deliver a designated number of spectators or TV audience share, it should be written into the contract and possibly backed financially through a letter of credit (Reed, 1990). The penalties (or bonuses) should be preset in writing so that all parties clearly understand the stipulations.

The types of event signage that will be available and the number, location, and responsibility for making and hanging them are all important matters to be covered in a contract. The actual production, installation labor, and postevent procedures are also essential points. Most sponsors do not want to risk their corporate image with the presentation of their logos on banners and signs (IEG's *Complete Guide to Sponsorship*, 1995). Therefore, most sponsors will oversee the production of an event's signage. However, organizers should be careful and supervise the installation. In one situation, at the (now defunct) Denver Grand Prix, Marlboro put up more than its allotted signs and erected them in places that had not been agreed to by event organizers. Only on the morning of the race did the organizers notice the problem, and it was too late to correct the situation. It's debatable whether it was an error or a strategic move by Marlboro to gain more exposure.

Most agreements control a sponsor's signs, advertisements, and even their specific wording. The difference between using the terms "official sponsor" and "official supplier" may mean thousands of dollars from a company, and one would not want to allow a minor sponsor to detract from the value sold to a major contributor.

Sometimes the selection and control of signage precludes existing signage in a local facility or secured by participating teams. Is your agreement enforceable regardless of the venue's or the team's previous sponsorship commitments? In constructing the sponsorship contract, remember the recent advent of virtual signage technology. You must make sure to include clauses that prohibit the modification of existing stadium advertising in the broadcast image. Without proper attention to these details, controversies are sure to surface. One Major Soccer League executive said that "the stadium takes a position that they have some proprietary interest in [virtual signage], our position is that they don't" (Bernstein, 1998, p. 24).

An organization's mailing lists and the use of individual athletes are often key factors in sponsorship. Many sponsors would like to use both for their benefit. You have probably kept records from advance ticket orders, season ticket holders, or association members. Corporations can use these to strengthen ties to consumers. Direct-mail campaigns are more effective if they come through an organization with which the consumer already has an association. Some sponsors like to use participants in their promotions. Be careful if you promise to provide them because they may not allow you to make agreements for their appearance with sponsors. If you have a participation contract with the athletes, this stipulation should be part of the contract. All participant agreements should also contain a clause that allows for photographs to be taken at the event that may contain an athlete's likeness and provide a release for that photograph's use by the event and sponsors.

There is a concern about the length of sponsorship agreements. There has been a steady increase in contract coverage over the past few years. Data have shown that long-term agreements (a minimum of three years) provide better results for both partners. Industry data indicated that the average length of a sponsorship agreement was five years (*IEG's Complete Guide to Sponsorship*, 1995). Therefore, the right of first refusal is always an element of interest. Sponsors generally like to have the right to future options for an event. They have placed their reputation on the line with you and should be accorded this consideration. Remember, this is a partnership that can benefit all of the participants.

Corporations occasionally enlist an agency to assist them with securing sport sponsorships. According to the industry leader, International Events Group (IEG, 1999), only 8 percent of sponsorship proposals resulted from contact through a sponsor's PR/ad agency. Fifty-seven percent of the successful sponsorship proposals came through a "cold call" (the property approaches the sponsor without previous contact).

Interestingly, 15 percent of agreements resulted from sponsors contacting a property directly. In 8 percent of the cases, the sponsorship came about through contact with a member of the sponsoring company's board. Seven percent of the time, the property used an outside agency to secure a sponsor (IEG, 1999).

There has been considerable confusion over the most successful approach strategy for sponsorship acquisition (IEG, 1999). The decision about entry channels, whom to contact at a particular company, varies considerably from one corporation to the next. All sponsors handle proposals differently. Some give a local distributor the authority to make decisions related to sponsorship, while others centralize sponsorship decisions at the corporate headquarters. You must evaluate point of access carefully for each of your potential sponsors.

According to Gearson (1994), if you want to use an agency to secure a sponsorship for your company, there are several factors to consider. Although many agencies create advertising campaigns and sponsorship proposals, some have little or no knowledge of the corporation's marketing plan. Sponsorship activities must be directly tied to the company's marketing plan, with significant measurement of resulting sales and revenue. Only as a partnership, where the company and the agency work together, can the end product be successful.

PRICING SPONSORSHIPS

The prices for sport sponsorship can range from a few hundred dollars to the $55 million each Olympic sponsor pays for World-Wide Partner status. Brooks (1994) details three different approaches to sponsorship **pricing**. The **cost-plus method** involves calculating the actual expenses incurred in providing the sponsorship package with an inclusion for profit for the organization. Expenses include all items included in the package, such as tickets, parking, dinners, souvenirs, and signage. A reasonable profit margin can be added, and the package ensures that the sponsorship will generate a profit.

The second method described by Brooks is the **competitive-market strategy.** The competitive market has changed since the 1990's. Early in the development of sport sponsorships, leverage was on the side of the event holder. Major events like the Indianapolis 500 would have many companies that wanted to sign sponsorship deals, and sometimes a bidding war erupted between potential sponsors. However, as more sport organizations and events entered the field, leverage shifted to the companies, which could then choose their options from a broad field of opportunities. As with any product pricing strategy, one must be competitive with alternative sponsorship options. The problem is trying to discover their price. With retail products, you can go to a store, pick up a company's product, and see how much is being asked. In the sponsorship business, it is difficult to know the pricing structure of competitors' packages.

Probably the most widely used method of sponsorship pricing is the **relative-value method.** Brooks (1994) reported that this strategy is based on the market value of each sponsorship component. For example, program ads could be compared to ads in the newspaper, scoreboard signage to billboards, and public-address announcements to radio advertising. The issue here is whether the comparison is legitimate. Is the same impact achieved? Is one message more powerful than another? The International Events Group (1992) reported that media impressions from event coverage are considerably less effective than a direct advertising message. If the event places the sponsor's logo in its media purchases, the value is about 10 percent of the media cost; however, if the event is given real advertising spots and space from a media sponsor, the value would be equal to the full rate offered to other advertisers.

Valuation is the most critical aspect of pricing. What is the *real* value of anything? You can offer a rental car company seats in the VIP section for the event as part of its package, but how much are those tickets worth: $50, $100, or what? Those seats will not be sold, anyway. They will all be distributed to sponsors, so just print $100 on the ticket (the ink doesn't cost anything!). It's perfectly legitimate because the rental car company is going to calculate its provision of cars at $75 per day, even though it could never get that on the open market. One should also accept in *trade-out* only those items that one would have had to purchase. During the 1990 Goodwill Games, a wine company donated thousands of bottles of wine as part of its sponsorship agreement. The organizers couldn't sell it, and there were only so many parties where it could be given away. The arrangement did not reduce costs for the organizers and did not yield the positive results anticipated by the sponsor.

The type of value exchanged is an important element in price negotiations. Industry data indicate that 47 percent of the sponsorships are cash payments from the sponsor to the event owner (sport organization). Twenty-eight percent of the deals are in-kind (product donations), with another 25 percent of the arrangements combining the two forms of exchange (International Events Groups, 1993a). In all of these negotiations, one shouldn't forget to include the associated labor costs for producing the sponsor's services.

IMPLEMENTATION

The execution of each detail prescribed in the sponsorship agreement is the implementation goal. Most sports administrators have developed highly successful planning and implementation strategies. Some of those used in the business world are also beneficial. Systems such as the Harvard project review, critical-path method (CPM), and project evaluation and review technique (PERT) provide a viable framework for sponsorship management.

The task of implementation does not fall only on the shoulders of the sport organization. A sponsor must clearly understand that purchasing a sponsorship is only part of its commitment. It must leverage its association across all of its marketing elements. A generally accepted ratio suggests that a sponsor must spend at least as much money promoting its association with the event (or sportsperson) as it paid for the rights. One expert said, "for every $600,000 you spend to sponsor an event, be prepared to spend another $600,000 aggressively

supporting and promoting that sponsorship through consumer tie-ins, advertising, and public relations" (Brewer, 1992).

CONTROVERSIES

In a 1998 settlement with major tobacco companies, forty-six states signed an agreement that restricted all tobacco sponsorship of sporting events by 2001. The accord specified that any sponsorship agreement in place prior to August 2, 1998, could be retained, but not renewed. The interpretation of the settlement "allows tobacco companies to tie into one series, event or team sanctioned by a single organization ("Landmark settlement," 1998, 1). Thus, sponsorship of NASCAR's Winston Cup series could continue, but other sporting events with tobacco sponsors would probably be adversely effected. In the coming years, more thorough guidelines are likely to evolve.

Another controversial issue in the sponsorship setting is **ambush marketing.** Ambush marketing has been defined as "a promotional strategy whereby a non-sponsor attempts to capitalize on the popularity/prestige of property by giving the false impression that it is a sponsor. [This tactic is] often employed by the competitors of a property's official sponsors" (IEG's *Complete Guide to Sponsorship*, 1995, 42). Several prominent examples of ambush marketing have developed within the sport industry.

During the 1994 Soccer World Cup, Nike cleverly distributed free hats during one of the final matches with Brazil. The hats were adorned with the Nike "swoosh" and the word "Brazil" in gold colors on a green background (Brazil's colors). Inside the stadium, Nike was assured a major "on-camera" presence even though Adidas was the official sponsor of the event.

To reduce ambush marketing during the 1996 Olympics, the Atlanta Organizing Committee, together with the IOC, established a fund to publicize the names of ambush marketers in national newspapers. The advertising copy stated that "Deceptive advertising is not an Olympic sport," and "Every time a company runs an ad like this, our Olympic team loses" (Myerson, 1996, D1). This tactic had the desired effect, as very few cases of ambush (or parasite marketing as the IOC calls it), occurred. In addition, the IOC reported that the Nagano Winter Olympics were relatively free from ambush marketing activities ("Ambush marketing," 1998).

A considerable debate has also developed over the supplements to coaches' salaries paid by many shoe companies. Do conflicts of interest occur? Does payment to a college or a coach mean that the college is endorsing one shoe over another? If it is a publicly funded institution, does the shoe contract have to go out for bids?

In 1997, Division I NCAA head coaches reportedly earned an average of $208,000 in outside income. Major controversies have developed concerning whether an individual coach should profit from an endorsement or whether the endorsement revenues should go to the institution. Steve Spurrier was the coach with the highest endorsement income at over $1.8 million (Pearson and Dodd, 1997). However, UCLA signed a school-wide sponsorship agreement with adidas in 1997 with a "six-year deal valued at over $18 million in cash, product and other in-kind contributions" (Mullen, 1998, 10).

It could be argued that college and university athletic programs can use the money garnered from sponsorships, but the situation is not void of potential problems. In 1996, the University of Wisconsin entered into a contract with Reebok ($7.6 million) that provided shoes, uniforms, and equipment for twenty-two sports and $2.1 million in cash for scholarships and student awards. Track coaches, upset about the selection of Reebok over a competitor's brand, made a series of unfavorable comments about Reebok. At this point, the media learned that the contract contained a clause that required the University to "take all reasonable steps necessary to address any remark made by any university employee . . . that disparages Reebok [or the] university's association with Reebok" (Naughton, 1996, p. 42). An enormous turmoil erupted when members of the Board of Regents and the faculty protested the clause as a violation of First Amendment rights to freedom of speech. In an effort to end the controversy, Reebok agreed to eliminate the clause from the contract (Naughton, 1996).

CONCEPT CHECK

Sport marketers should be aware that not all members of the community will embrace their involvement with all corporate sponsors. Many will see the association as counterproductive to the interests of sport.

TRENDS

In Stotlar's 1999 research, sport executives and sponsors were surveyed about the future direction of the industry. The study asked respondents to indicate where sponsorship dollars would be directed over the next three years. Participants on the team/property side provided the following data:

- 18.3 percent believed that local levels of competition would attract more dollars.
- 24.2 percent felt that the regional competitions would be more successful.
- 57.6 percent reported that national-level sport competition would receive the majority of sponsorship dollars over the next three years.

Sponsors responded in very similar ways:

- 13 percent believed that local competitions would attract more dollars.
- 21.7 percent felt that the regional level would be more successful.
- 56.5 percent reported that national-level sport competition would receive the majority of sponsorship dollars over the next three years.

In addition, 8.6 percent of the corporate sponsors thought that international sponsorships would begin to attract dollars away from the North American market for multinational corporations (Stotlar, 1999, 89).

Another significant trend is the advancement of "grassroots" (community-based) sponsorship. Greenwald and Fernandez-Balboa's 1998 research reported significant increases in the implementation of this strategy. They found that the factors similar to those cited for national-level sport sponsorship selection were identified for companies engaged in sponsoring grassroots sport. Most notably they discovered that increasing corporate exposure and consumer awareness were highly rated corporate objectives. Another advantage of grassroots sport sponsorship was that these situations provided an increased potential for product sampling and prototype testing. The authors noted that in grassroots sport sponsorship "corporations are increasingly pumping money into grassroots sports organizations, and in turn, grassroots sports organizations are better able to provide corporations with substantial returns on their investments (Greenwald and Fernandez-Balboa, 1998, p. 42). In the future, more companies will realize that speaking to consumers in a local environment is more persuasive than through nationwide involvement.

Vertical integration was another emerging trend uncovered by Greenwald and Fernandez-Balboa (1998) and the principal topic of Stotlar's address to the 1999 NASSM conference. This traditional business strategy is based on corporate control of all aspects of a business from manufacturing and production to distribution and final linkage with consumers at retail. Thus, ownership of a sporting event by a sponsor can yield total control and generate maximum exposure. In many cases, it has become less expensive to own the sport event/team than to sponsor it.

The primary U.S. example of this trend in sport is the case of Anaheim Sports (originally founded as Disney Sport). In this situation, Anaheim Sports owns the Anaheim Angels (MLB) and the Mighty Ducks of Anaheim (NHL). Through this ownership, they also control all broadcast rights and have significant influence in other media through corporate ownership of ABC-TV, ESPN, and ESPN2. In addition to owning the teams and the broadcast rights, they have controlling interest in Edison International Field (Angels venue) and own The Arrowhead Pond (Mighty Ducks venue) (*1998 Annual Report,* 1999).

Internationally, Rupert Murdoch (head of Australia-based News Corp.) typifies the trend. In 1998 he purchased the Los Angeles Dodgers and Dodger Stadium for $311 million and secured all television rights for their games for his FOX Network (Wertheim, 1998). In Europe, he made a $1 billion dollar bid (although ultimately voided by the Mergers Commission) through his media company BSkyB for England's Manchester United soccer club. In 1999, he was able to secure German TV rights for the Champions League (soccer) and acquired partial ownership of two Italian soccer teams. Murdoch's empire reaches around the globe including his Seven Network in Australia, which holds domestic Olympic television rights through 2008. In short, Murdoch's cable and media systems "reach two-thirds of the world's households that have a television set" (Wertheim, 1998, 40). Through these examples we can see that vertical integration will be the wave of the future.

LITTLE THINGS MEAN A LOT

Attention to little details can have a major effect on one's success. In this section, a few experiences, both positive and negative, are offered for review. During one event, where one of the major sponsors was a brewing company, a reception for sponsors was scheduled in a hotel executive suite. The person who planned the reception thought all of the details for the reception had been covered. The invitations had been sent out, the room decorations were assembled, name tags had been made, and the bar and bartender had been arranged with the hotel. However, when the bar was set up by the hotel, the sponsoring brewing company's beer was not available; only their competitor's product had been stocked by the hotel. Although the sponsor understood the problem, event organizers were monumentally embarrassed.

When the managers of a series of surfing events were searching for sponsors, they kept their staff busy switching the Coke and Pepsi in the corporate board room's refrigerator during negotiations between their two most promising sponsor candidates. Although it may seem trivial, one doesn't want to be pushing hard to secure Coca-Cola as a million-dollar partner and pull a Pepsi out of the refrigerator!

In another case, the event organizers were working hard to get all of their sponsorable categories filled. They were extremely happy when they secured Budget as their car rental company. The problem was that General Motors had been the primary title sponsor for several months. As they soon found out, Budget's rental fleet consisted primarily of Fords.

Often the presentation of ideas is just as important as the concept itself. For the Goodwill Games, organizers used computer-generated graphics to show the actual stadiums with sponsor signs in place. Although one may not be able to commission state-of-the-art computer graphics, sample program ads, banners, and gift items adorned with the sponsor candidate's logo can certainly be provided. This will not only show the sponsor what its money will buy, but show that you care about how the corporation is represented.

CRITICAL THINKING EXERCISES

1. As the coach of a college basketball team, you encounter a situation where your institution has signed an all-school agreement with Nike

to supply shoes and uniforms for the team. Your star player tries to wear the Nikes, but complains that her feet hurt. The player insists on wearing Reeboks. How would you resolve this issue?

2. As the event manager of a rodeo in Colorado, you have secured Coors Brewing Company as title sponsor of your event. Everything seems to be going well—the banners are up, the beer for the concession stand has been ordered, and the local Coors distributor will be on hand to award trophies to the winners. However, opening day of the rodeo at your final staff meeting, you learn that your volunteer who coordinates event entertainment arranged for the Budweiser Clydesdales to perform between shows. The Coors people are furious. How would you handle the problem?

SUMMARY

1. With industry leaders projecting a future growth rate in sports sponsorships of 15 percent per year, it is apparent that sport sponsorships will continue into the next century "1999 sponsors spending," 1998. It is essential for the sport manager to fully comprehend this marketing element.

2. The relationship between a sport organization and event owners involved with sponsorship must include advantages to both parties. A well-developed sponsorship can provide market value and increased profits for corporations, scarce operating revenues for sport organizations and events, and a full spectrum of sports events for participants and spectators.

3. Through a properly structured sponsorship agreement, one can ensure that benefits for both the sport organization and the sponsor(s) are achieved.

4. With models derived from existing sponsorship proposals and agreements, one can develop the skills necessary to succeed in the exciting world of sport sponsorships.

CASE STUDY

As the organizer of an event, you entered into a television agreement with a national cable network to televise the finals of your national swimming championship to ensure that your sponsors would have a platform for their message. In the agreement, you guaranteed the television appearance of Olympic 100 m freestyle gold medalist Chris Nathan. In your negotiations with Chris, you agreed to pay an appearance fee and all expenses to the meet, and Chris signed the contract. However, when the event began, it was clear that Chris was out of shape and was not swimming well. Chris did not qualify for the finals in the 100 m freestyle or any other event. On the morning of the finals, a network executive came to you with questions about your contract guaranteeing the television appearance of Chris. The network is demanding that unless Chris appears in a race, no broadcast rights fees will be paid and the event will not be aired. The major sponsors begin calling because they have heard that the event may be canceled from television. In the sponsorship contract, you guaranteed that the event would be televised nationally and that the sponsors' venue signs would have on-camera air time. How would you work to resolve this situation?

REVIEW QUESTIONS AND ISSUES

1. What are the essential elements for a well-written sponsorship contract?

2. What issues would need to be addressed if you were offered a considerable amount of sponsorship money by a local brewing company for your college?

3. Discuss the pros and cons of selecting an individual athlete as a representative for a company's products. In a group, select a product and athlete spokesperson.

SOLUTIONS TO CRITICAL THINKING EXERCISES

1. While there is no right or wrong answer, the students should cover several points. First they should consider reviewing the contract to determine if any provisions exist for solving the problem. In many of the contracts there is a provision that stipulates that the company will send a representative to customize shoes for any player who experiences difficulties with fit or comfort. Another solution could be to allow the player to wear the Reeboks, but cover or black out the logo. If the coaches think that the problem is not really an issue and choose to allow the player to wear the Reeboks without modification, the institution may risk losing the contract.

2. Perhaps the best solution would be to cancel the Budweiser performance. If they have already arrived and incurred travel expenses, your event should reimburse them and write it off as a loss. Another approach would be to visit with the Coors representatives and request suggestions from them to resolve the problem. One idea would be to make an announcement that the title sponsor, Coors has graciously allowed their primary competitor, Budweiser, to perform for the enjoyment of the audience. Ultimately, as the event manager, you have the authority to decide what occurs in the arena.

REFERENCES

1998 Annual Report. (1999). Burbank, CA: Walt Disney Company.

1999 sponsors spending: 7.6 billion. (1998, Dec. 21). *IEG Sponsorship Report, 1,* 4–5.

Abraham, M. M., and Lodish, L. M. (1990). Getting the most out of advertising and promotion, *Harvard Business Review,* (May–June), 50–60.

Ambush marketing: Under control in Nagano. (1998, Summer). *Olympic Marketing Matters,* 9.

Asimakopoulos, M. K. (1993). Sport marketing and sponsoring: The experience of Greece. *Sport Marketing Quarterly* (September), 2 (3), 44–48.

Bernstein, A. (1998a, June 22–28). High Tech a [virtual] sign of the times. *SportBusiness Journal, 24,* 36.

Bernstein, A. (1998b, June 22–28). High tech a [virtual] sign of the times. *SportBusiness Journal, 24,* 36.

Bernstein, A. (1998c, November 23–29). Reebok's future not in the stars. *SportBusiness Journal,* 7.

Bhonslay, M. (1999a, February 8–14). Women's goods don't score with fans. *SportBusiness Journal,* 28.

Bhonslay, M. (1999b, February 8–14). You did a great job for us—you're fired. *SportBusiness Journal,* 24.

Brewer, G. (1992). New spins on sports. *Incentive* (December), 42.

Brooks, C. M. (1994). *Sports marketing,* Englewood Cliffs, NJ: Prentice-Hall.

Carrier, J. (1994). Sponsors dig Olympic gold. *Denver Post* (March 18), 1A, 20A.

Ensor, R. J. (1987). The corporate view of sports sponsorships, *Athletic Business* (September), 40–43.

Gearson, R. F. (1994). What to expect from your ad agency. *Fitness Management* (January), 22–23.

Goldfisher, A. (1998, August 10–16). Cyberselling delivers global marketplace. *SportBusiness Journal,* 25.

Graham, P. J. (1993). Obstacles and opportunities for the marketing and sponsoring of sport in Russia. *Sport Marketing Quarterly,* 2 (2), 9–11.

Greenwald, L., and Fernandez-Balboa, J. M. (1998). Trends in the sport marketing industry and in the demographics of the United States: Their effect on the strategic role of grassroots sport sponsorship in corporate America. *Sport Marketing Quarterly,* 7 (4), 35–48.

IEG's Complete Guide to Sponsorship (1995). Chicago: International Events Group.

IEG Sponsorship Training Supplement: National Association of Sports Commissions. (1999, April 15). Chicago: International Events Group.

International Events Group. (1990). Coors proposal format. *Special Events Report* (June 25), 5.

International Events Group. (1992). Survey reveals what sponsors want. *Sponsorship Report* (September 7), 6–7.

International Events Group. (1993c). 1994 sponsorship spending will exceed $4 billion. *Sponsorship Report* (December 20), 1–2.

International Events Group. (1993a). 1994 quantifying sponsorship. *Sponsorship Report* (November 15), 4–6.

International Events Group. (1993b). Sponsorship report, assertions. *Sponsorship Report* (February 14), 45.

International Events Group. (1994). Crediting sponsors, *Sponsorship Report* (March 14), 4–5.

International Olympic Committee. (1993). Ambush marketing, Lausanne, Switzerland, International Olympic Committee.

Irwin, R. L. (1993). In search of sponsors, *Athletic management* (May), 11–16.

Irwin, R. L., and Asimakopoulos, M. (1992). An approach to the evaluation and selection of sport sponsorship proposals, *Sport Marketing Quarterly* (December), 43–51.

Irwin, R. L., and Stotlar, D. K. (1993). Operational protocol analysis of sport and collegiate licensing programs, *Sport Marketing Quarterly,* 2 (5), 7–16.

King, B. (1998, August 24–30). Virtual ads at the Brickyard worth virtually $300,000, says analyst. *SportBusiness Journal,* 8.

Kuzma, J. R., Shanklin, W. L., and McCally, J. F. (1993). Number one principle for sporting events seeking corporate sponsors: Meet benefactor's objectives. *Sport Marketing Quarterly* (September), 2 (3), 27–32.

Landmark settlement restricts tobacco marketers to one brand deal per year. (1998, November 23). *IEG Sponsorship Report,* 1–2.

Lombardo, J. (1998, May 4–10). 'Team Tiger' takes Woods to the top. *SportBusiness Journal,* 22–23.

McManus, J. (1989, February 13). Embarassment of riches. Sports, Inc. p. 52.

Mullen, L. (1998, August 31–September 6). Adidas ties up UCLA deal, said to be worth $18 million. *SportBusiness Journal,* 10.

Myerson, A. R. (1996, May 31). Olympic sponsors battling to defend turf. *New York Times,* D1, D17.

National Collegiate Athletic Association. (1991). *Guidelines for corporate participation in NCAA championships,* Document 7368, Mission, Kansas, July.

Naughton, J. (1996, July 5). U. of Wisconsin and Reebok remove controversial provision from $7.9 million contract. *Chronicle of Higher Education*, 42.

Olympic Fact Book. (1998). Colorado Springs: United States Olympic Committee.

Olympic Marketing Fact File. (1998). Lusanne: International Olympic Committee.

Pearson, B., and Dodd, M. (1997, November 21). Success pays off for college football coaches. *USA Today*, 4C.

Performance Research. (1991, May 14). *Economic slump*. Newport, RI: Performance Research.

Performance Research. (1992, Feb. 28). *Olympic marketing study: Can't beat the feeling*. Newport, RI: Performance Research.

Performance Research. (1994a, Feb. 8). *Olympic sponsorship study: What Olympics?* Newport, RI: Performance Research.

Performance Research. (1994b, Mar. 4). *Olympic sponsorship study: And you thought Nancy and Tonya were bad*. Newport, RI: Performance Research.

Performance Research. (1994c, Jan. 31). *Will the real NASCAR please stand up?* Newport, RI: Performance Research.

Reed, M. H. (1990). Legal aspects of promoting and sponsoring events. *Special Events Report* (March 26), 4–5.

Rofe, J. (1999, February 8–14). Winning record makes a sales slump. *SportBusiness Journal*, 23.

Sandler, D. M., and Shani, D. (1993). Sponsorship and the Olympic games: The consumer perspective. *Sport Marketing Quarterly* (September), 2 (3), 38–43.

Spoelstra, J. (1997). *Ice to the Eskimos*. New York: Harper Business.

Sponsors Report. (1991). CART/PPG Indy car world series, Ann Arbor, Joyce Julius and Associates, 9–14.

Stotlar, D. K. (1993). Successful sport marketing plans, Madison, Wisconsin. Brown and Benchmark.

Stotlar, D. K. (1999). Sponsorship in North America: A survey of sport executives. *International Journal of Sports Marketing and Sponsorship*, 1 (1), 87–100.

Stotlar, D. K. (1999). Vertical integration in sport. (Zeigler Lecture). Vancouver: North American Society for Sport Management Annual Conference.

TOP IV Programme. (1997, Summer). *Olympic Marketing Matters*, 8.

Top 25 female athlete endorsements. (1998, May 11–17). *SportBusiness Journal*, 25.

Volvo and Sport Sponsorship (1990, January, 29). Special Events Reports, pp. 4–5.

Wertheim, J. (1998 September 21). The Sky's the limit. *Sports Illustrated*, 40–42.

Wilkinson, D. G. (1986). *Sport marketing institute*. Willowdale, Ontario: Sport Marketing Institute.

Wilkinson, D. G. (1988). *Event management and marketing institute*. Willowdale, Ontario: Sport Marketing Institute.

WEBSITES

www.sponsorship.com

The International Events Group provides the most accurate and timely information on the sponsorship industry from sports and entertainment to events and fairs. This site offers information, news, and current events. It also has a job bank where candidates and properties can exchange employment-related information.

www.olympic.org

This is the website for the International Olympic Committee. It has news and information on Olympic-related matters in French and English. It also contains profiles on IOC sponsors and links visitors to websites for upcoming Olympic Games.

CHAPTER 17

Sport Licensing

Dick Irwin

In this chapter, you will become familiar with the following terms:

License	Trademark	Joint-use agreement
Licensor	License agreement	Promotional Licenses
Licensee	Exclusive agreement	
Royalty	Nonexclusive agreement	

Overview

Trademark licensing, a topic too frequently omitted from sport management and marketing texts, has become a primary responsibility of both amateur and professional sport administrators. The earliest form of sport-related licensing may have been when Roman athletes were paid for the use of their images on products sold at the Circus Maximus. Today, sport organizations and personalities grant, or **license,** second parties the right to produce merchandise bearing associated designs or individual likenesses.

The National Football League (NFL), under the direction of commissioner Pete Rozelle, was the first American sport organization to formally establish a licensing program in 1963, under the direction of NFL Properties (Rosenblatt, 1988). Following the NFL's pioneering efforts, the remaining major professional sport leagues, many national sport governing bodies, and major sporting events, from the Olympics to college bowl games, have become **licensors** of their associated logos, symbols, or designs. Furthermore, over 100 colleges and univer-

sities have followed suit and established licensing programs, frequently designating the department of intercollegiate athletics as the financial beneficiary as well as the home of program operations (Irwin and Stotlar, 1993). Much like their Roman-era predecessors, today's sport personalities have also granted manufacturers the right to use their likenesses on various products. Therefore it is imperative that today's sport managers be well versed in the field of licensing.

According to the Sporting Goods Manufacturers Association (SGMA), the sales of sports-licensed merchandise exceeded $10 billion in 1998 (figure 17–1). A number of factors have contributed to the fluctuation realized by each professional sport league. The National Football League has sustained steady growth due to increased popularity, the emergence of new stars, and the resurgence of teams such as the Denver Broncos and Atlanta Falcons. Meanwhile, the sales of merchandise bearing logos of National Basketball Association, Major League Baseball, and National Hockey

Sport-Licensed Products (U.S. retail sales in $billions)

Major Sports Leagues & Colleges/Universities

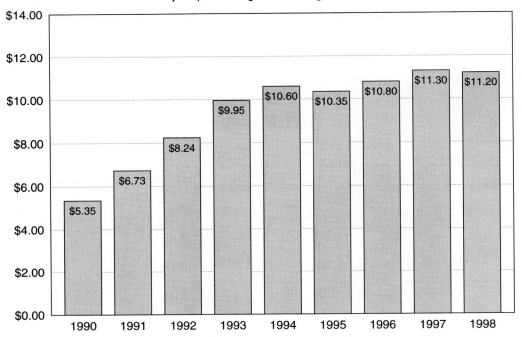

Source: SGMA estimate

FIGURE 17–1   Domestic sales of sport-licensed merchandise.

Association franchises were each significantly hindered by fan disenchantment with labor woes during the past few years as well as competition from other sport licensors.

Generating revenue from licensed merchandise is not limited to the four major professional leagues. Sport properties of all shapes and sizes have gotten into the licensing foray, including the 1996 Olympics, which generated $1 billion in sales ("A White Paper," 1999); World Cup '98, which realized $1.5 billion in sales worldwide (Meenaghan & O'Sullivan, 1999); NASCAR, where licensed product sales have been projected to total approximately $1 billion annually (Schaaf, 1995); the World Wrestling Federation, with sales in excess of $500 million (Ameson, 1999); collegiate athletic programs, which generated approximately $2.5 billion in annual sales (Loftus, 1999), and, even the minor leagues, where baseball alone generates over $32 million in licensed product sales ("A White Paper," 1999).

Battle, Bailey, and Siegal (1990) cited the following four factors as the primary contributors to the phenomenal growth in sales of college-licensed products that are applicable to the surge in sport licensed products:

1. The increasing popularity of American sports and resulting media coverage
2. Significant developments in imprinting technology
3. The maturation of licensing as an industry
4. The financial challenges facing sport managers

The prolific demand for these products has provided sport organizations and product manufacturers and retailers with a healthy revenue source. Manufacturers, or **licensees,** and retailers realize their profits from basic supply-and-demand principles, and licensing has provided an effective tool in expanding the marketplace for sport-logoed products. No longer must adoring fans attend an event or visit the campus bookstore to purchase merchandise bearing the logo of their favorite team. Now these items may be obtained at the local mall or ordered through the mail. This has led to the creation of "officially licensed outlets" that have tallied more than $600 million annually. In fact, the NBA offers retailers a "shop within a shop" concept that uses appealing design elements, branded fixtures, and interactive attractions as well as providing the outlet with access to exclusive proprietary products from the NBA Store. The NFL has opened several Play Football Endzone shops across the United States ("A White Paper," 1999).

The sport licensor derives its earnings in the form of a **royalty** fee, generally 6 to 10 percent of the manufacturer's wholesale price and typically passed on to the consumer through an increase in product price. The fee appears quite modest considering that the unlabeled product has little or no market value until the sport logo is affixed. Even so, major professional-sport franchises and a number of major colleges typically realize annual royalties in excess of $1 million. Professional athletes have also been able to generate significant supplemental income from licensing their personal name, likeness, and/or voice. Players generally receive 8.5 to 9 percent of the item's wholesale price, with contracts typically negotiated and payment secured by the player's union ("Old players," 1999).

A properly administered licensing program provides more than just financial dividends. The benefits of licensing, enjoyed by the licensor as well as the licensee, should include protection against unauthorized, counterfeit, or improper logo usage; promotion through the increase in popularity of both the sport property and the manufacturer; and, ultimately, the ability to profit from merchandise sales.

Protection and control of logo usage has been identified as the fundamental benefit of establishing a licensing program (Sykes, 1985). As the demand for logoed products has expanded, so have the abuses of logo usage. In addition to using the logo—a legally protectable property of the sport organization—without authorization, merchandise of poor quality bearing inappropriate statements or

images began to appear in the marketplace. Therefore it became necessary for the logo "owners" to regulate who was producing merchandise bearing the logo and how it was being displayed.

The logos used by professional sport franchises, college athletic programs, or sporting events are recognized as trademarks of those respective organizations. A **trademark** is defined as "any word, name, symbol, or device or combination thereof adopted and used by a manufacturer or merchant to identify and distinguish his goods" (15 U.S.C. 1127).

The classification of team logos as trademarks permits sport organizations, including university athletic programs, to capitalize on powerful trademark law aimed at restraining unauthorized production and distribution of merchandise bearing these marks. As the industry of trademark licensing has realized its greatest degree of growth, the laws that govern such activity have experienced considerable modification, providing the licensor with powerful ammunition in the fight against commercial counterfeiters. Therefore the sport licensing program administrator should become familiar with the laws that govern this activity in order to exploit them to their full potential.

Although not required for legal protection, consideration should be given to the actual registration of logos as trademarks. Federal trademark law, derived from the Lanham Act, renders the highest degree of legal protection and provides for both civil and criminal penalties to be levied against unauthorized product vendors (Bikoff, 1990).

CONCEPT CHECK

The logos used by professional sport franchises, college athletic programs, or sporting events are recognized as trademarks of those organizations, thereby qualifying for federal trademark law protection against unauthorized users.

A survey of licensing program administrators from the NBA, NFL, NHL, Major League Baseball, NCAA, and the U.S. Olympic Committee revealed that a majority of marks claimed by each program has been registered with the federal trademark commission (Irwin, Stotlar, and Mulrooney, 1993). In fact, several respondents indicated that hundreds

FIGURE 17–2 Trademarks of **A,** Georgetown University, **B,** University of Michigan, and **C,** University of Kentucky.

of logos had been federally registered as trademarks. Federal registration is denoted by the placement of a ® adjacent to the logo (figure 17–2). This level of protection does not come without a cost. The fee for federal trademark registration of a logo is several hundred dollars per mark per product category (Shinner, 1989).

Registration has not been mandatory to secure federal protection of organizational trademarks. Unregistered trademarks have been protected under unfair-competition principles (Ala, 1989). Reliance on unfair-competition principles, or common trademark law, has inherent disadvantages and will require the licensor to demonstrate that the manufacturer's use of the mark was likely to create confusion in the mind of the consuming public about the authenticity of the goods (Wong, 1986). In an effort to demonstrate such consumer confusion about the authenticity of unauthorized logo usage, the NFL successfully used consumer surveys as evidence in a case involving unregistered trademarks (*N.F.L. v Wichita Falls,* 1982). Frequently, licensors will request that a trademark symbol (™) be placed adjacent to unregistered logos as a means of demonstrating a claim of ownership.

In some instances, state registration, which is a more expedient and less expensive process, may be warranted when use of the organizational logos is limited to intrastate commerce. Such is the case with most school-oriented, regional sporting events and minor league programs. However, other than demonstrating that the logo in question has actually been registered, state registration offers no greater protection than common trademark law (Shinner, 1989). It is strongly recommended that the licensing program administrator consult with a legal specialist before making decisions about the registration of organizational logos, or for advice and support throughout the cycle of a licensing program, including the preparation, negotiation, execution, and adherence of the license agreement (Baghdikian, 1996). This is most relevant for sport licensing programs seeking international registration of associated marks, because trademark law varies from country to country as demonstrated in Shilbury, Quick, and Westerbeek's (1998) discussion of Australian trademark legislation.

The sport licensing program administrator must determine which logos are going to be licensed. An inventory of all names, symbols, designs, slogans, and images should be conducted in an effort to determine which items will be made available for commercial usage. Popular slogans such as the Minnesota Vikings' "Purple Pride" as well as the Atlanta Falcons' "Dirty Bird" had significant market demand and subsequent commercial value.

Attention should be directed toward all facility and venue names as well. For example, Pinehurst Golf Resort, host of the 1999 U.S. Open, is a registered trademark of Pinehurst, Inc., which requested that local businesses as well as the city discontinue their use of the word due to trademark infringement. Pinehurst, Inc. contends that the name and mark usage is limited to the golf course and resort. Businesses that previously included the term Pinehurst in their company name have responded by changing names in lieu of facing costly litigation (Welch, 1999).

The licensing administrator should also consider capitalizing on a provision within the Trademark Revision Act (1988) that has enabled licensors to claim or register a mark prior to its actual use (Ala, 1989). This is of particular interest when creating a team slogan or planning a season's advertising campaign. Early registration should guard against "accidental" reproduction, which can lead to cluttering or devaluing the organization's message. In turn, the organization has the opportunity to

maximize speculative commercial value of the proposed slogan. The Australian Olympic Committee's (AOC's) efforts to protect the marks planned for use in the 2000 Olympic Games date back to 1987, prior to the actual awarding of the Games. The AOC sought protection against unauthorized use of the Olympic symbol as well as other nominated Olympic designs (Shilbury, Quick, and Westerbeek, 1998).

Under the 1988 Trademark Revision Act, new franchises have capitalized on market demand for logoed merchandise well in advance of the team playing a game. This has allowed a majority of the expansion franchises, capitalizing on market enthusiasm and the team logos' novelty, to lead the way in merchandise sales. Teams such as the Colorado Rockies, Carolina Panthers, and the Anaheim Mighty Ducks all led their respective leagues in sales during their first year of operation. In fact, the Mighty Ducks sold over $300,000 worth of licensed merchandise at their first home game, while within a week of the Panthers being awarded an NFL expansion franchise at least one million licensed items were sold locally (Schaaf, 1995). Such may also be the case for the new franchises in Cleveland (NFL), Columbus (NHL), and Atlanta (NHL).

However, should the mark (registered or unregistered) not be used for an extended period of time (approximately ten years) or should the prior registration lapse, the potential exists for the mark to pass into the public domain, which has occurred for a majority of the marks associated with the Negro Baseball League. Only the Kansas City Monarchs and the Indianapolis Clowns have retained trademark protection of marks registered years ago as a result of continued use.

In an effort to fully employ the legal rights provided by trademark law, the licensing administrator must design and enforce written operational policies and procedures. In order to standardize program operations, a policy manual containing all operational policies and procedures should be drafted and stored in a readily accessible location, with additional copies available upon request. Informational brochures that reflect the licensing-program operational protocol should be prepared for circulation to prospective licensees and other interested parties. Suggested licensing-program operational protocols, derived from an analysis of licensing procedures for the NBA, NFL, NHL, NCAA, U.S. Olympic Committee, Major League Baseball, and 100 colleges will be addressed in the following sections.

LICENSEE RECRUITMENT

As advocated by Baghdikian (1996), the active recruitment of licensees is essential for any licensing program to flourish. The most common recruitment tactics employed by sport licensors have been personal contact, direct mail, and trade show networking (Irwin and Stotlar, 1993). Prospective licensees should be provided with operational policy material and details of licensor support programs aimed at generating awareness at the retailer and consumer level as well as protecting against unlicensed counterfeit competitors.

LICENSE APPLICATION PROCESS

However, sport licensors should practice diligence when granting licenses. Potential licensed product manufacturers should be able to demonstrate an ability to meet and maintain quality control standards, possess financial stability, and offer an aggressive, well-planned promotional strategy (Baghdikian, 1996). Therefore, prospective licensees should be required to complete a formal application. Approval criteria, such as royalty production standards, should be established for the review process prior to the issuance of any license.

PRODUCT REVIEW PROCEDURES

As a quality control measure, a thorough review should be conducted of each product under consideration for license, including the packaging, wrapping, and advertising literature, as well as an inspection of the production facilities. Lack of proper product screening may result in product liability litigation being brought against the licensor because consumers perceive a licensed product to be of higher quality (Kennedy and Geist, 1990). Therefore, it is imperative that a detailed evaluation be completed of all prospective licensees and their products.

LICENSE EXECUTION

When a licensee has met the established standards, a **license agreement,** or contract, should be executed. The antecedent to effective program enforcement has been the licensing agreement, because this covenant sets the legal parameters for the licensor-licensee relationship.

Types of agreements

Several types of licenses exist: exclusive, nonexclusive, joint-use, and promotional. An **exclusive agreement,** typically issued on a per-product-category or geographical basis, is more prevalent among professional-sport licensing programs, as demonstrated by the NBA's "less is more" philosophy (Nichols, 1994a). License exclusivity enables the licensor to limit the number of licensees producing goods in a particular product category or geographical region, thereby facilitating stronger "partnerships" with the licensor. Limiting the number of licensees allows for easier detection of unlicensed, counterfeit merchandise and expedites communication between the licensor and licensee. The licensee benefits from the "exclusive" classification as well as the limited competition. A number of the dominant licensed merchandise manufacturers have indicated a preference for more exclusivity among sport licensing programs (Klemm, 1991).

On the other hand, the execution of a **nonexclusive agreement** fosters competition among licenses within the same product category and allows "cottage" vendors to participate in the licensing industry. Unfortunately, claims have been made that the use of nonexclusive license agreements is leading to an oversaturation of the licensed product marketplace, adversely affecting the overall quality of goods (Klemm, 1991).

Two or more licensors may wish to execute a **joint-use license** agreement allowing their respective logos to appear together on merchandise. Cartoon characters and opposing teams make ideal joint licensors—for example, the NHL's incorporation of the Muppet characters within all twenty-six team logos on children's merchandise (Nichols, 1994b) and the NCAA's incorporation of participating team logos on national championship merchandise. Typically, the royalties generated from joint-use agreements are split evenly between the licensors.

Promotional licenses simply allow a licensee to use licensed marks in a short-term promotional campaign, such as a premium product giveaway by a local fast-food restaurant. Typically, the licensee is interested in capitalizing on the goodwill of the li-

FIGURE 17–3 A, Official licensed product logo for the NHL. **B,** National Football League shield. **C,** Major League Baseball logo. **D,** Licensed product logo for the NBA.
A, copyright, the National Hockey League. Artwork provided by and used with permission from NHL Enterprises Inc., New York. **B,** registered trademark of the NFL. Artwork provided by and used with permission from NFL Properties, New York. **C,** the Major League Baseball trademarks depicted herein were reproduced with permission from Major League Baseball Properties, Inc., New York. **D,** Used with permission of the National Basketball Association. Copyright 1995 NBA Properties, Inc., New York, 10022.

censor, while both parties benefit from the awareness generated.

Generally, all licenses, with the exception of the promotional license, are executed on an annual or biannual basis. Any breach of the agreement should result in automatic revocation, and renewal should be based on the licensee's sales activity and adherence to predetermined quality standards.

CONCEPT CHECK

Sport organizations and personalities license, or grant, second parties the right to produce merchandise bearing associated designs or individual likenesses.

COUNTERFEIT DETECTION AND REDUCTION

It is incumbent upon all licensing administrators to establish counterfeit detection and reduction procedures. The implementation of a systematic market surveillance program requiring staff members to regularly "police" or "shop" the local marketplace, including game day vendors, is vital to the overall success of licensing program operations. Unfortunately, a survey of collegiate licensing program administrators revealed that less than two-thirds had implemented such a program (Irwin and Stotlar,

1993). Therefore licensees, who have essentially paid for protection against unfair competition, should query the support provided by the licensor for the removal of counterfeit goods from the marketplace and only license with those actively protecting against pirating activities.

When "shopping," each staff member should be equipped with an up-to-date list of authorized licensees and copies of the licensing program policy manual. As a means of facilitating the recognition of licensed products by program "police agents," as well as the consuming public, each of the major sport programs has employed some type of identification label (figure 17–3). Professional-sport licensing programs employ the services of the Coalition to Advance the Protection of Sports Logos (CAPS) to assist with the counterfeit detection and reduction process (Bullington, 1994). Some of the organizations, such as the NBA, have their own internal intellectual property enforcement operations. According to Van Meter (1995), sport and collegiate licensing programs have joined forces in market surveillance and enforcement efforts. Such efforts have helped to limit the availability of counterfeit merchandise and have demonstrated a commitment to operating quality licensing programs.

Upon detection of counterfeit merchandise, staff members have the legal right to confiscate all products bearing organizational logos and should issue the vendor ***and*** the manufacturer a cease-and-desist notice. When faced with the difficulty of obtaining the names of counterfeit vendors and the fact that they will likely disappear after being served with papers, numerous college licensing programs have obtained "John Doe" temporary restraining and seizure orders against game day vendors who sell unlicensed logoed merchandise (Battle, Bailey, and Siegal, 1990). Counterfeit detection should be followed by personal contact, preferably from the licensing program's legal specialist, reminding the offending party of the licensor's rights and its intent to enforce these rights. If necessary, additional recourse may include litigation.

Each of the respective major professional leagues has at one time initiated litigation against manufacturers and/or vendors of unlicensed merchandise (Irwin and Stotlar, 1993). However, limited proceedings are available because most cases have been settled out of court. Although it has been reported that the NFL annually investigates more than 300 cases involving trademark infringement or unauthorized logo usage (Jones, 1984), the successful litigious record of licensors appears to have persuaded the pirates to cease production and/or distribution after receiving notification. A list of suggested case readings involving sport licensors has been provided at the conclusion of this chapter.

CONCEPT CHECK

*Upon detection of counterfeit merchandise, staff members have the legal right to confiscate all products bearing organizational logos and should issue the vendor **and** the manufacturer a cease-and-desist notice.*

ROYALTY AUDITS

As a means of verifying the accuracy of royalty reports—which accompany royalty payments and are typically provided by the licensee on a quarterly basis—the licensor may randomly conduct audits of licensees. These audits often reveal underpayments, commonly as a result of honest accounting errors. The licensor may choose to have these audits performed by a designated representative of the organization or use the services of an auditing specialist.

ROYALTY EXEMPTIONS

At the discretion of the licensor, exemptions from royalty payments may be granted. An exemption may be granted at either the producer or consumer level. Although sport organizations commonly employ a compulsory, nonexempt policy, college licensing programs generally exempt university departments (consumer level) from paying a royalty on items purchased from licensed suppliers that are only for internal consumption and are not available for resale, such as office supplies (e.g., letterhead stationery) and athletic equipment (Irwin and Stotlar, 1993). From a record-keeping perspective, the compulsory, nonexempt policy would appear to be more advantageous to both the licensor and licensee. Otherwise, it is the licensee who is held responsible and to whom purchasers are not required to pay a royalty.

LICENSING PROGRAM PUBLIC RELATIONS

According to Baghdikian (1996) the smooth running of the licensing program depends upon adequate liaison between the licensor (sport organization) and the licensee. Licensors should consider facilitating networking opportunities among current licensees and the retail community. This may be accomplished by distributing to retailers a licensed-product catalog, such as *Manny's Baseball Land*, the official catalog of Major League Baseball. It contains a list of all licensees and their representatives. Networking can also be done through mini-trade shows that allow licensees to display and take orders for the current year's licensed product line. Most important, it is recommended that licensors try to recognize manufacturers and retailers of licensed products with certificates of appreciation or point-of-purchase displays acknowledging the valuable relationship between the parties. Major League Baseball Properties has made a strong commitment to visit and service retailers of MLB-licensed products (Klemm, 1994).

CONCEPT CHECK

It is recommended that licensors try to recognize manufacturers and retailers of licensed products with certificates of appreciation or point-of-purchase displays acknowledging the valuable relationship between the parties.

LICENSING PROGRAM PRODUCT PROMOTIONS

It would behoove the sport licensing program administrator to employ an integrated promotional mix in an effort to enhance general awareness of licensed products to the consuming public. The most popular promotional media employed among sport licensing programs are direct mail, broadcast media, and trade publications (Irwin and Stotlar, 1993). Major League Baseball Properties plans to send its catalog to over four million households showcasing traditional products as well as hard-to-find collector items and autographed products, while the NHL.com Virtual Product Showroom provides visitors an opportunity to view official NHL merchandise ("A White Paper," 1999). In some cases, the licensor has contained costs by mandating in the license agreement that licensees must produce advertising materials that display the licensor's products (Irwin and Stotlar, 1993). A co-op advertising approach between licensor and retailer is employed by the professional sport licensing programs (Klemm, 1994).

CONCEPT CHECK

The sport licensor derives its earnings in the form of a royalty fee, normally 6 to 10 percent of the manufacturer's wholesale price, which has enabled major professional sport franchises and a number of major colleges to generate in excess of $1 million annually.

PROGRAM ADMINISTRATIVE ASSISTANCE

Although professional-sport licensing programs are administered exclusively with internal resources, administrative support can be obtained from a number of professional licensing agencies. Most college licensing programs have chosen to secure this type of administrative support and contracted with a licensing agency. A licensing agency, which typically represents several licensors as well as a bank of licensees, can provide services for legal consultation and representation, auditing, and promotions. Battle, Bailey, and Siegal (1990) have identified the following advantages of contracting with a licensing agency:

1. The size and diversification of staff and services
2. The strength provided by the number of licensors and licensees
3. Operational consistency and continuity
4. Leveragability of new programs
5. Licensor's ability to retain program control
6. The compensation system, typically a percentage of royalties generated

It would appear that the greatest strength of a licensing agency is its sensitivity to the practices of the industry. However, it should be noted that operational consistency has not yet been achieved among college programs contracting with a licensing agency (Irwin and Stotlar, 1993). Therefore if program administrative assistance is sought, a thorough investigation of the licensing agency is highly recommended. Licensing program administrators should query the staff's background, seeking assistance from agencies employing individuals who have gained experience working as licensors and licensees; request a list of current *and* former clients; request a copy of the agency's protection enforcement procedures; and request the submission of a promotional plan specific to the licensor's program.

It is difficult to imagine that the demand for sport-logoed products will continue to grow at the pace experienced over the past decade. However, sport-licensing administrators have already begun to develop programs that will maintain, if not stimulate, the sales volume of licensed products into the twenty-first century. The following sections highlight emerging trends within the field of trademark licensing.

DEVELOPING NEW PRODUCTS AND PENETRATING NEW MARKETS

In order to increase interest in and the popularity of hockey among new markets of fans, specifically those in warmer climates, the NHL is actively supporting the games of roller hockey and street hockey (Nichols, 1994b). Participants in these activities will of course need a jersey, a helmet, knee and elbow pads—and why not buy equipment emblazoned with an NHL logo? Therefore, in the spring of 1995, National Hockey League Enterprises launched a street hockey apparel line (Nichols, 1994b).

In an effort to overcome lackluster sales in the trading card industry, Major League Baseball has struck it rich in key product categories such as youth apparel and video games (King, 1999). As a way to further cultivate the youth market, Major League Baseball has teamed up with Hasbro and Mattel. While Hasbro produced action figures of several players Mattel introduced "Major League Baseball Barbie" ("A White Paper," 1999). Additionally, selected Major League Baseball players' voices and likenesses will be featured in a children's animated series developed by Hearst Entertainment and Mark Platt Productions ('Toon In, 1999). The WNBA also has taken a vested interest in appealing to the youth market and has launched an extensive line of children's apparel ("A White Paper," 1999). In an effort to lure interest among females, the NFL has collaborated with several licensees to design apparel of interest to women, while the NHL seeks to appeal to the high-end patron with its new stylish leather jacket from J.H. Designs ("A White Paper," 1999). Lastly, NASCAR's licensing program has provided the sport an opportunity to penetrate new, non-race markets (Hagstrom, 1998).

Similarly, teams have sought to increase sales through new logo designs and uniform modifications. In fact, this has become so popular that most of the major leagues have placed restrictions on the frequency of uniform changes. Other "new" products have been created via novelty items such as when the NFL celebrated its seventy-fifth anniversary and teams wore classic uniforms, with authentic replicas available at retail. The league netted approximately $40 million from the "Throwback" campaign (Shaaf, 1995).

Staying abreast of consumer trends is essential for the continued growth of licensed products.

INTERNATIONAL DISTRIBUTION

As the popularity of American sports has increased internationally, so have the sales of American sport-logoed products. Administrators of American sport and collegiate licensing programs are now taking a vested interest in the international marketplace, initiating efforts to ensure product distribution globally. Awarding franchises internationally, such as the NBA's newest additions of Toronto and Vancouver, virtually assures a stronger international following and subsequent merchandising opportunities. The recent influx of international players has sparked demand in foreign markets. With European-born players now accounting for almost one-quarter of the NHL's players, the NHL has aggressively sought opportunities to distribute merchandise globally. Unquestionably, events such as the Olympic Games and World Cup also see demand on an international scale. When considering international business, it is imperative that the licensing administrator explore the trademark laws in the anticipated countries of distribution and investigate the feasibility of consulting with a licensing agency familiar with international issues (see Shilbury, Quick, and Westerbeek, 1998).

LICENSEE EXCLUSIVITY

Following the NBA's less-is-more philosophy, other sport licensors are downsizing the number of their licensees (Nichols, 1994b). This has been advocated for collegiate licensing in an effort to facilitate industry standardization (Irwin, Stotlar, and Mulrooney, 1993), because several licensees have expressed a desire to terminate collegiate licensing activities (Klemm, 1991).

INTERNALIZATION OF PROGRAM OPERATIONS

Although at one time a majority of the sport and 87 percent of the collegiate licensing programs were assisted by licensing agencies, none of the sport programs and only 60 percent of the college programs remain (Irwin and Stotlar, 1993). It is projected that this internalization of licensing programs will continue as more administrators of sport and collegiate licensing programs become familiar with the operational complexities.

CRITICAL THINKING EXERCISES

1. What are the benefits of registering a team's logo as a trademark at the federal or state level?
2. How is revenue generated from a licensing program?
3. What is the difference between licensing and merchandising?

SUMMARY

1. The benefits of licensing include protection, promotion, and profit.
2. Several types of licenses can be granted: exclusive, nonexclusive, joint-use, and promotional.
3. A systematic market surveillance program requiring staff members to regularly "police"

the local marketplace, including game day vendors, is vital to the overall success of a licensing program.

4. The sport licensing program administrator should employ an integrated promotional mix in an effort to promote the availability of products to prospective licensees, retailers, and the general public.

CASE STUDY

As the athletic marketing director at Midwestern University, an NCAA Division II institution of approximately 6,000 students based in St. Louis, you have been assigned the responsibility of increasing the volume of licensed products in the retail outlets within the local marketplace (only one off-campus bookstore currently carries MU-logoed merchandise). No previous efforts have been made to secure additional shelf space, so you have no existing plan or model to follow. The campus bookstore obviously sells a variety of logoed items, but the general consensus is that they are not very appealing. Describe how you would approach this issue and the tactics you would implement to stimulate demand among licensees, retailers, and consumers.

REVIEW QUESTIONS AND ISSUES

1. What are the fundamental benefits of establishing a trademark licensing program?
2. Explain the differences between federal, state, and common trademark law.
3. Explain the inherent advantages and disadvantages of contracting with a licensing agency.
4. What effect does licensing have on the marketplace?
5. What emerging trends do you see that will have an impact on the sales of sport-licensed products?

SOLUTIONS TO CRITICAL THINKING EXERCISES

1. While protection exists for unregistered marks, the highest degree of protection in secured through trademark registration.
2. Typically, licensing program revenue is generated through a royalty fee. This is approximately 6 to 10 percent of wholesale costs, that is, the price charged by the licensee when selling the product(s) to a retailer.

3. Generally speaking, merchandising involves handling the sales of logoed products (including inventorying and supplying), whereas licensing allows the licensor to grant all responsibilities (production, distribution, and sales) to any number of external parties.

REFERENCES

A White Paper: Sports Licensed Products (1999). Sporting Goods Manufacturers Association. North Palm Beach, FL.

Ala, J. V. (1989). The new trademark law. *Case and Comment, 94,* (5), 3–7.

Ameson, E. (1999, June). Wrestling over sponsorships. *USA Today,* 12C.

Baghdikian, E. (1996). Building the sport organization's merchandise licensing program: The appropriateness, significance, and considerations. *Sport Marketing Quarterly, 5,* (1).

Battle, W. R., Bailey, B. B., and Siegal, B. B. (1990). *Collegiate trademark licensing.*

Bikoff, J. L. (1990). *The impact of product liability law on collegiate licensing programs.* Paper presented at the ACLA Fourth Annual Meeting, Santa Cruz, California.

Bullington, T. (1994). Counterfeiting: Screen printers pay high price for breaking licensing regulations. *Imprintables Today* (February 14), 30–32.

Hagstrom, R. G. (1998). *The NASCAR way.* New York: Wiley.

Irwin, R. L., and Stotlar, D. K. (1993). Operational protocol analysis of sport and collegiate licensing programs. *Sport Marketing Quarterly, 2,* (10), 7–16.

Irwin, R. L., Stotlar, D. K., and Mulrooney, A. L. (1993). A critical analysis of collegiate licensing policies and procedures. *The Journal of College and University Law, 20,* (2), 97–109.

Jones, C. B. (1984). Champions of confusion in trademark law: Champion Products v University of Pittsburgh. *Journal of Law and Commerce, 4,* 493–516.

Kennedy, E., and Geist, R. (1990). *ACLA Licensee Handbook.* Lansing, MI: Association of Collegiate Licensing Administrators.

King, B. (1999). MLB's lesson: Only time heals wounds. *Street & Smith's SportBusiness Journal, 1,* (39), 10.

Klemm, A. (1991). Maturation or saturation; has collegiate licensing gone overboard? *Team Licensing Business 3,* (5), 16–17.

Klemm, A. (1994). Young superstars twinkle in the 125th year of our national pastime. *Team Licensing Business 6,* (6), 36–39.

Loftus, M. (1999). Swoosh under siege. *U.S. News & World Report, 126,* (14), 40.

Meenaghan, T., and O'Sullivan, P. (1999). Player-sports meets marketing. *European Journal of Marketing, 33,* (3/4), 241–49.

National Football League Properties, Inc. v Wichita Falls Sportswear, Inc. 532 Supp 651 (1982).

Nichols, M. A. (1994a). NBA Properties: Building on the strength of the brand. *Team Licensing Business, 6,* (6), 26–29.

Nichols, M. A. (1994b). NHL Enterprises: The next frontier. *Team Licensing Business, 6,* (6), 31–35.

Old players seek fair share. (1999, June 8). Associated Press.

Rosenblatt, R. (1988). The profit motive. *Sports, Inc,* (December 5), 18–21.

Schaaf, P. (1995). *Sports marketing: It's not just a game any more.* Amherst, NY: Prometheus.

Shilbury, D., Quick, S., and Westerbeek, H. (1998). *Strategic sport marketing.* Sydney: Allen & Unwin.

Shinner, M. (1989). Establishing a collegiate trademark licensing program: To what extent does an institution have an exclusive right to its name? *Journal of College and University Law, 15,* (4), 405–429.

Sykes, W. D. (1985). The three ps of licensing. *The Canadian Bookseller* (March), 8–11.

'Toon In. (1999, June 8). *USA Today,* C1.

Van Meter, D. (1995). Sale of licensed products and services. In *Financing Sport* by Howard, D. R. and Crompton, J. L. Morgantown, WV: Fitness Information Technology.

Welch, W. M. (1999, June 11). Golf mecca tries to control name. *USA Today,* 3C.

Wong, G. M. (1986). Recent trademark law cases involving professional and intercollegiate sports. *Detroit College of Law Review,* 87–119.

WEBSITES

www.store.nba.com/

For students interested in viewing how a professional league promotes the availability of its licensed merchandise.

www.sportlink.com/research/index.html

This site provides an abundance of industry intelligence of interest to students studying sport licensing and promotions.

PART VI

Economics and Finance

CHAPTER 18

Economics and Sport

Michael A. Leeds

In this chapter, you will become familiar with the following terms:

Opportunity costs	Normal goods	Comparative advantage
Profits	Inferior goods	Absolute advantage
Marginal utility	Complements	Monopoly
Marginal cost	Substitutes	Monopsony
Marginal revenue	Supply	Negative externality
Sunk costs	Equilibrium	Positive externality
Demand	Excess supply	Multiplier effect
Substitution effect	Excess demand	
Purchasing power effect	Price ceiling	

WHAT IS ECONOMICS?

Economics is unlike any other discipline one encounters in college. It is not a set of facts to memorize or dates to remember. Instead, it is a way to interpret everyday events. It is little wonder that one finds economics departments in both colleges of liberal arts and colleges of business, since economics applies equally well to discussions of Microsoft's marketing policy and the status of women in developing countries. One economist has even used economic theory to divine the true meaning of *The Wizard of Oz*.[1]

The word *economics* comes from the Greek word *oikonomikos*, which literally means "household management." While it seems a long way from running a household to running a multinational corporation, economists point out that successful management of both boils down to putting the resources at hand to their best possible use. Economists have also estab-

lished basic principles of behavior that characterize how people decide what to do. These principles apply whether one is a stockbroker on Wall Street, an auto mechanic in Havana, or a Bedouin in Yemen. All that differs is the setting within which one applies these principles. This chapter will introduce several basic principles of economic behavior and show how they apply to the world of sports.[2] While each economist may come up with his or her own set of basic rules, some variation of the following will be at the core of anyone's list of economic principles:

- All our actions involve costs and benefits.
- Decisions are typically made on the margin.
- Freely functioning markets are typically the best way to allocate resources.

---

[1]Rockoff, 1990.

[2]For one example of a more complete list, see O'Sullivan and Sheffrin, 1998.

- People should specialize and trade with one another according to their comparative advantage.
- Under some circumstances markets fail, and government can increase social well-being.

The remainder of this chapter will explain each of these principles and show how each applies to the realm of sports.

COSTS AND THE NEED TO CHOOSE

Economists believe that individuals and groups base their decisions on comparisons of the costs and benefits of their actions. These costs often take the form of an explicit price tag. For example, if you spend $100 on tickets to a Philadelphia Flyers hockey game on Saturday night, then you have $100 less to spend on tickets to a Philadelphia Eagles football game on Sunday afternoon.

One need not spend money to suffer a cost. For example, if one friend offers to take you to an Eagles game while another offers to take you to a Flyers game that same night, you spend no money. However, since you cannot be in both places at once, you still endure a cost. Here the cost is the happiness you would have experienced if you had gone to the game you chose to miss. Economists call these missed chances **opportunity costs.** Opportunity costs can occur because of explicit expenditures (spending your money on the Flyers instead of the Eagles) or because of implicit expenditures (spending your *time* with the Flyers instead of the Eagles).

Opportunity costs also play a role in the decisions made by producers. In fact, they account for the difference between how economists and accountants view **profits.** To an accountant, profits are the difference between the revenues a firm takes in and the expenditures it must make in order to produce. Economists consider this picture incomplete, because it does not take into account the profits the firm could have made had it decided to produce something else. A firm could thus make sizable *accounting profits* but—because it could have made even higher profits doing something else—endure an *economic loss* (negative *economic profits*) at the same time.

The main advantage to using accounting profits as a measuring stick is the fact that one can readily observe them. One cannot really compute economic profits, because they involve opportunity costs and hence rely on a counterfactual question: how well

could the firm have done if it had produced something else? One can, however, infer the existence of economic profits or losses by looking at the behavior of firms. If the firms in an industry are making an economic profit, then the accounting profits in that industry exceed the opportunity costs, which are the profits that could be made elsewhere. Other firms, upon seeing the economic profits, have an incentive to enter the industry. If the firms in the industry are making an economic loss, then the accounting profits do not exceed the opportunity costs, and the firms in the industry have an incentive to leave. One can thus tell if firms in an industry are making economic profits by observing whether firms are entering or exiting the industry.

An example of how opportunity costs affect producers can be found in the move of the Brooklyn Dodgers to Los Angeles in 1958.[3] From 1903 to 1953, the so-called Golden Era of Baseball, no major league baseball teams entered, left, or changed cities. In the early-to-mid–1950s, several teams changed cities: the Braves moved from Boston to Milwaukee, the Athletics from Philadelphia of Kansas City, and the Browns from St. Louis to Baltimore, where they were rechristened the Orioles. All these teams, however, were losing money in cities that had other, more profitable teams (the Boston Red Sox, Philadelphia Phillies, and St. Louis Cardinals). The Dodgers' departure from Brooklyn was another matter entirely. When they moved, the Dodgers were the most profitable team in baseball.

At first glance, it seems incongruous that such a prosperous team should seek to leave while other, less profitable teams—like the Washington Senators, whom the city of Los Angeles initially sought to attract[4]—stayed put. The key to the move can be found in the notion of opportunity cost. While the Dodgers made considerable profits in Brooklyn, their owner, Walter O'Malley, recognized that having the Southern California market all to himself would bring untold riches. Thus, despite making considerable accounting profits in Brooklyn, the Dodgers were operating at an economic loss.

OPERATING ON THE MARGIN

In this era of multi-million-dollar contracts, team owners routinely complain that the high salaries they pay to their players force them to raise ticket

---

[3]The New York Giants also left for the West Coast after the 1957 season, but they were clearly following the Dodgers' lead.
[4]Sullivan, 1987, p. 42.

prices. Such reasoning sounds plausible. After all, if a firm's costs go up, it seems perfectly reasonable for the firm to try to recoup the cost, and the only way to do so is to pass the higher costs along to customers in the form of higher prices. However, applying such reasoning to free agents and ticket prices ignores one of the basic rules of economic behavior: people consider the *marginal* impact of their actions.

To see what marginal thinking is and to appreciate its importance, suppose that you are the lucky student who purchased the millionth copy of this textbook. As a prize, the publisher offers you a choice: it will send you either a one-carat diamond or a glass of water.[5] The choice seems absurdly easy; presumably everyone would take the diamond. Choosing the diamond, however, raises a serious problem. A diamond, after all, is a luxury item that has little practical use for most of us, while we all need water to survive. It seems absurd that someone would choose a glittery trinket over something that would keep her alive, yet that is what we would all do.

The key to the paradox lies in the need to distinguish between the total happiness, total utility, that we gain from a good with the *marginal* happiness—or **marginal utility**—that it brings. The total value of water to us dwarfs the total value of diamonds, but none of us considered total values when choosing the diamonds. We were concerned only with how much extra happiness or utility we would get from *one more* glass of water or *one more* diamond. The fact that water is readily available reduces the happiness one gains from one more glass of it—its marginal utility—almost to zero. Unless you are dripping in diamonds, the marginal utility of one more diamond will be very high, despite the fact that you realize that water is, on the whole, more important. (See figure 18–1.) Similarly, people and firms worry about how much more they have to spend to get a little more of what they want—its **marginal cost**—and do not worry how much they have already spent.

This simple insight has enormous implications. It tells us that we can predict human behavior by looking only at the benefits and costs of doing a little more. The benefits and costs of what came

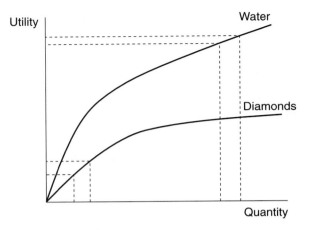

FIGURE 18–1 The total utility of water is much higher than the total utility of diamonds, but an extra diamond adds more utility than an extra glass of water.

before do not matter. Firms and people become as happy as they possibly can when they equate the marginal benefits with the marginal costs of their actions. Think of a firm's profits as a large pile of money. Additional revenues take the form of more dollar bills on top of the pile, while additional costs mean that the firm takes some bills off the top. The firm's profits rise with an additional sale, as long as it can put more bills on top of the pile than it removes. Profits fall when an additional sale removes more bills from the top than it adds. The firm will thus expand its sales as long as it can add to the height of the pile. The height of the pile will be maximized when the amount it adds and the amount it removes are equal, that is, when **marginal revenue** equals marginal cost. (See figure 18–2.)

Now suppose that a fire breaks out and burns away half the pile. Economic theory tells us that since the fire does not affect anything the firm will do in the future—it simply burned away profits from previous actions—the firm should not do anything differently. Setting marginal revenue equal to marginal cost still maximizes the height of the pile; the pile just is not as high as it once was. In effect, the economic principle of thinking marginally teaches us that we should ignore past costs—what economists call **sunk costs**—and let "bygones be bygones."

---

[5] This is one example of the classic "diamond-water paradox."

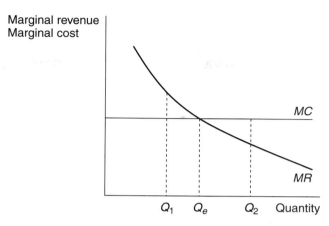

FIGURE 18–2   At Q_1 the firm can add more to revenue than to costs by producing more. At Q_e it can produce more revenue by producing less.

Consider now the impact of signing a free agent to a huge contract, such as the Dodgers' signing of Kevin Brown for $105 million. The contract adds greatly to the Dodgers' total costs. However, it has no impact on the Dodgers' marginal costs. To see why, one must first recognize that the Dodgers are not selling Kevin Brown. Rather, they are selling *tickets* that enable people to watch Kevin Brown (and others) play. Kevin Brown will cost the Dodgers $105 million whether they sell three million or three hundred tickets. Since they must pay him his salary no matter what, his salary represents a sunk cost and is irrelevant to any decision about tickets or ticket prices.

Still, teams do raise their ticket prices when they sign expensive free agents. They do so, however, not because they must but because they can. Signing a new star player excites the team's fans and makes them more eager to see the team play. This, in turn, makes them willing to pay a higher price to see the team play.

SUPPLY AND DEMAND

When people ask economists why it costs hundreds of dollars for a family of four to see a basketball game or why a highly educated social worker earns a small fraction of the salary of a minimally educated linebacker, the response invariably contains the phrase "supply and demand."

Understanding the forces of supply and demand will reveal the solution to several puzzles. Specifically, it will show

- why championship teams frequently raise ticket prices the next season.
- why it is so hard to get a ticket to a Duke University basketball game.
- why salaries in the NBA are so much higher than in the WNBA.

The **demand** for tickets to a Duke basketball game at the Cameron Arena (or for any good or service) is the relationship between the price of those tickets and the number of tickets that consumers are willing *and able* to buy. As seen in figure 18–3, this relationship is invariably negative: as the price of tickets falls, the number of tickets that consumers are willing and able to buy rises. The *demand curve*, which illustrates the relationship between the price of tickets and the number of tickets that consumers buy, slopes down.

The relationship is negative for two reasons. First, if the price of tickets to Duke games falls, consumers buy more tickets and fewer other goods (such as tickets to UNC games, textbooks, or pizzas). We call this displacement of other goods the **substitution effect,** because consumers substitute tickets to a Duke basketball game for other items they could buy.

The lower price of tickets also allows consumers to buy more tickets and *more* of other items as well.

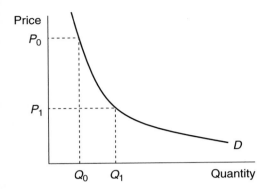

FIGURE 18–3   The number of tickets Duke fans are willing and able to buy rises from Q_0 to Q_1 as the price of tickets falls from P_0 to P_1.

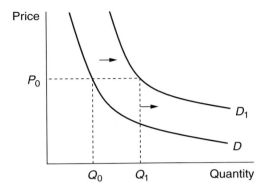

FIGURE 18–4   The increased demand for Duke basketball makes fans willing to buy more tickets at any given price.

Because consumers' money goes farther than it did, we call this impact the **purchasing power** (or *income*) **effect.** Increases in purchasing power will normally lead consumers to buy more of an item, so we call such goods **normal goods.** Sometimes, however, consumers will buy less of an item as their purchasing power rises. We call such items **inferior goods.** While many low-quality items (such as generic napkins, or poor cuts of meat) are inferior goods, the term need not imply that a good is bad. For example, as one's income rises to extremely high levels, one may buy fewer diamonds and more rubies. All "inferiority" means in this context is that one buys less of something as one's purchasing power rises. A good can be inferior for a given person at a given income level yet be normal for a different person with the same income or the same person with a different income level.

The willingness or ability of consumers to buy tickets to Duke games—and hence the position of the demand curve—may rise or fall for a number of reasons. For example, as the desire to consume a particular item increases, consumers become willing to spend more for that item. As teams become more successful, their fan base expands beyond a set of hard-core fans. The added interest of fans causes the demand for tickets to increase, pushing the demand curve out to the right (see figure 18–4).

As long as tickets to Duke games are normal goods, changes in income increase the number of

people willing and able to buy them. As a result, the demand for tickets should be higher among relatively wealthier groups[6] (again, see figure 18–4). This also means that the demand for tickets should be *pro-cyclical*, rising in good economic times and falling in bad times.

A decline in the price of another good will cause the demand for Duke tickets to rise or fall, depending upon whether the other good is a **complement** or a **substitute** for tickets. For example, a decline in the price of tickets for a Duke women's game will cause some fans to switch from going to men's games to going to Duke women's games. Tickets to women's games are substitutes for tickets to men's games. On the other hand, a decline in the price of Duke paraphernalia or parking fees around Cameron Arena will cause attendance at men's games to rise, since many fans also spend money on parking, t-shirts, or pom-poms (complementary items) as part of a trip to a game (see figure 18–3).

The **supply** of a good is also a relationship between price and quantity. This example relates the price of tickets to the number of tickets that Duke is willing and able to provide. Duke can increase the number of tickets it sells either by increasing the number of tickets it sells per game or by increasing the number of home games that it plays. As the

---

[6]This helps to explain why most sports—even those for which a majority of the participants are black—have primarily white fans.

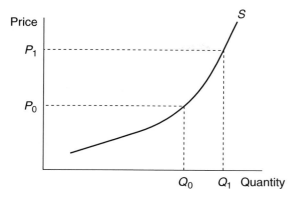

FIGURE 18–5   As the price of tickets rises from P_0 to P_1 the number of tickets Duke is willing and able to sell rises from Q_0 to Q_1.

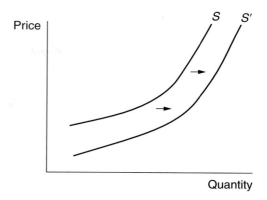

FIGURE 18–7A   Technological advances push out the supply curve.

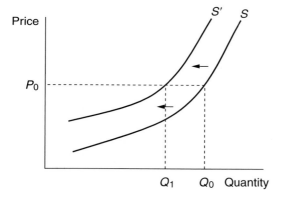

FIGURE 18–6   The higher costs of inputs makes Duke willing to supply fewer tickets at any given price.

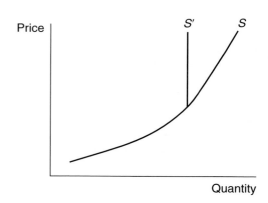

FIGURE 18–7B   A limit on the number of games shifts back a portion of the supply curve.

price of tickets rises, the marginal benefit of admitting another person to a game rises, and Duke has an incentive to sell additional tickets. The supply relationship is thus positive, and the *supply curve* slopes up, as seen in figure 18–5.

The position of supply curves also depends upon a variety of factors. If the cost of *inputs* to staging a ball game rises, then at any price the marginal cost of admitting another fan rises. This reduces the incentive for Duke to provide seats, and the supply curve shifts to the left (see figure 18–6).

Similarly, technological or institutional changes may affect the position of the supply curve. Changes in travel technology have enabled teams to get to and from away games more quickly and easily, allowing them to schedule more games, pushing the supply curve to the right (see figure 18–7a). The limits placed by the NCAA on the number of games that basketball teams may play shifts a portion of the supply curve back (see figure 18–7b).

Finally, the rewards to alternative activities may affect how much of a product a firm will want to provide for any given reward. If the price Duke could charge for admission to a women's basketball game rose high enough, it may inspire Duke to schedule more women's games and to decrease the number of men's games it stages, shifting the supply curve to the left (see figure 18–7b).

Taken alone, supply and demand simply express a series of "if/then" statements: if the price of a ticket to a Duke basketball game is P_0, then fans want to buy Q_0^d, tickets, while the university wants to sell Q_0^s. Neither one says how many tickets fans buy, how many tickets Duke sells, or what the price of a ticket is. To determine what actually happens, economists combine the concepts of supply and demand by literally combining the supply and demand curves into a single picture. Figure 18–8 shows that the two curves cross at the point labeled *e*. Economists call *e* the **equilibrium** point, because at that point the actions of consumers and producers are in balance. In this case the balance is between the quantity of tickets that Duke fans are willing and able to buy at the price P^e and the quantity that Duke is willing and able to sell at P^e. As a result, neither fans nor the university have any desire to alter either the price that is charged (the equilibrium price) or the quantity that is bought and sold (the equilibrium quantity).

The meaning of equilibrium becomes clearer when one sees what happens at prices other than the equilibrium price. If producers charge a price

above the equilibrium price (P^h in figure 18–9a), **excess supply** (also known as a *surplus*) results, because customers are willing and able to buy only Q^d while producers are willing and able to sell Q^s. Frustrated because they cannot sell all that they are willing and able to sell at the price P^h, producers will lower the price they charge in order to attract more customers. As the price of Duke tickets falls, more fans are willing and able to buy the tickets. A lower price of tickets, however, reduces the incentive Duke has to stage games for its fans, decreasing

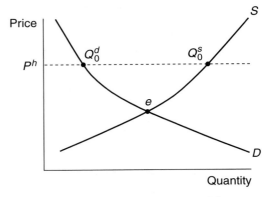

FIGURE 18–9A   Excess supply ($Q_0^s - Q_0^d$) occurs when price is below equilibrium.

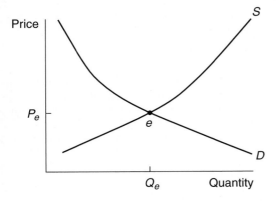

FIGURE 18–8   The equilibrium price and quantity occurs where supply and demand meet.

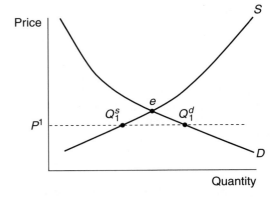

FIGURE 18–9B   Excess demand ($Q_1^d - Q_1^s$) occurs when price is below equilibrium.

the supply of tickets to Duke games. The larger quantity demanded and the smaller quantity supplied reduce the excess demand until the price reaches P^e, and the excess supply vanishes.

If producers charge a price below equilibrium (P^1 in figure 18–9b), **excess demand** (or a shortage) results, because producers are not willing and able to sell as much as consumers are willing and able to buy. In this example, frustrated Duke fans bid the price of tickets up, causing some fans to stop trying to buy tickets and increasing the incentive for Duke to increase the number of seats it can provide. Again, the price moves in the direction of P^e until the excess demand vanishes.

When demand or supply curves move, the equilibrium price and quantity also change. For example, if Duke were to win the NCAA championship this year, the demand for tickets next year would increase, because people would be more willing to buy tickets at any given price to see a champion play (figure 18–10). As a result, the equilibrium price and quantity of tickets to Duke games rise to P_1^e and Q_1^e. Similarly, if rising fuel prices sufficiently increase the cost of travel to Durham, NC, and thus increase the cost of staging a game, the supply curve would shift back, and the equilibrium price would rise to P_2^e while the equilibrium quantity would fall to Q_2^e.

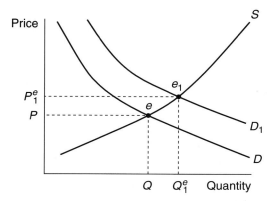

FIGURE 18–10 When demand rises the equilibrium changes from e to e_1 and equilibrium price and quantity rise.

Sometimes governments or other authorities decide that the market does not distribute goods or services appropriately. They feel the need to protect low-income residents from the high cost of housing by imposing rent controls. They try to protect the incomes of family farmers with price supports designed to keep the prices they receive high. In the sports world, governments try to protect fans from high admission prices with anti-scalping laws, while schools charge ticket prices to students that are well below the equilibrium price of tickets. Unfortunately, such policies often have unanticipated and undesirable consequences.

Universities often allow their students to purchase tickets at far below the equilibrium price. Their rationale is the desire to be "fair" to students who cannot afford to pay the equilibrium price. It is not clear, however, that a lower price is fair to the students, either. At an artificially low price, excess demand results, since students will be willing and able to buy more tickets than the university makes available (as was true for P^1 in figure 18–9b).

With price no longer determining who buys a ticket and who does not, Duke must come up with a new method of allocating tickets. The "method"—such as it is—can be found in the crowds of students that camp out for days as they wait for season tickets to go on sale. The students who show up first—and who wait the longest—are the ones who can buy the tickets. Such an allocation "mechanism" fails to lower the price of tickets. It simply replaces the explicit cost of a market price with the opportunity cost of the students' time. A first-come, first-served policy may be more "fair" to students who cannot afford to spend much money on basketball tickets, but it is less "fair" to students who cannot afford to spend much time waiting. Students with demanding classes or jobs will not be able to afford the "cheap" tickets.

The fact that a first-come, first-served policy tends to exclude students who prefer to spend their time doing other things may explain why schools adopt it as an allocation mechanism. Schools may reason that losing money on tickets sold to students who are willing to skip class or miss work to wait for a ticket actually increases their revenue overall. This policy is likely to attract students who are more rabid fans than would a price-based allocation mechanism.[7] The presence of rabid fans is likely to improve the performance of the home team. A more successful team will generate more publicity for the school and will increase the demand for tickets among nonstudents, allowing the school to charge an even higher ticket price to its alumni and outside supporters.

Some schools try to be even more "fair" by distributing the discounted student tickets according to a random lottery. Economists, however, would question whether such a system is fair at all. Under such a system a student who is only mildly interested in basketball (perhaps willing to pay only P^1 in figure 18–9b) may win the lottery, while a student who desperately wants to see Duke play (and is willing to pay P^h in figure 18–9a) loses out. Such a system may still work if the students could re-sell their tickets to those who place a higher value on their tickets.[8] Unfortunately, anti-scalping laws—again erected in the name of "fairness"—prevent such transactions from taking place. Anti-scalping laws prohibit the sale of tickets at prices above the official price listed on the ticket.

Economists call an official price that is set below the equilibrium price a **price ceiling.** Just as a ceiling prevents a helium-filled balloon from rising any farther, a price ceiling prevents the price from rising to its equilibrium level. Two problems result from a price ceiling. First, because the price is held below equilibrium, excess demand results (as in figure 18–9b), and some consumers who are willing and able to buy the tickets will be unable to do so. Second, if the excess demand for tickets is met randomly, some people who place a high value on the tickets will not receive them, while others who place a relatively low value on the tickets do. For example, a consumer who is willing and able to pay P^h may not win the lottery, while one who is willing and able to pay P^1 is. In the absence of anti-scalping laws the person who has the ticket can sell it to the person who wants it at an intermediate price, say P^e.

This secondary transaction benefits everyone. The buyer pays only P^e for a ticket she values at P^h, while the seller receives P^e for a ticket he values at only P^1. Anti-scalping laws prevent such transactions from taking place, however, as the official price of the ticket is set at P^1.

CONCEPT CHECK

Markets are in equilibrium at the price at which consumers are willing and able to buy the same amount that producers are willing and able to sell. At equilibrium there is no excess demand or excess supply. This occurs where the supply curve and the demand curve intersect. Price ceilings keep the price from rising to the equilibrium level. Excess demand results, frustrating consumers, and misallocating resources. Price floors keep the price from falling to equilibrium, frustrating producers, and again misallocating resources.

COMPARATIVE ADVANTAGE AND THE GAINS FROM SPECIALIZATION

While supply and demand tell us a great deal about what people do, they do not tell us everything. We know, for example, that no individual, household, or nation is completely self-sufficient. We all produce only a small amount of what we need in the course of a day. Think of the breakfast you had this morning or of the clothes you are wearing. Imagine how much time and effort it would have taken to provide all of that from scratch. Relying on others to produce most of the goods and services has vastly increased our standard of living. The same principle has been played out on an international scale by trade between nations that specialize in producing relatively few of their needs. Economists are almost universal in their advocacy of "free trade" among nations.[9]

The principle that people become better off by specializing in relatively few activities can also be found in the sports world. While it was once normal for football players to play both offense and de-

---

[7]Duke fans, the "Cameron Crazies," are renowned for rowdiness unexpected at an expensive, private university.
[8]College athletes' re-selling tickets at highly inflated prices has landed more than one college program in hot water with the NCAA.

[9]Frey et al., 1984.

fense, such players are now rare, and they typically play only one position full-time. The last player in the NFL to play both offense and defense full-time was "Concrete Charlie" Bednarik of the Philadelphia Eagles in 1962. At the college level, players routinely played both offense and defense until the mid-1960s.

The idea that we gain from specialization seems simple enough, but the principle behind it—the theory of **comparative advantage**—has been called "perhaps the most complex and counterintuitive principle of economics."[10] The basic message of comparative advantage is that specialization makes one better off only if one specializes in the correct activity. Initially, one might believe that people should specialize in what they are best at. This idea underlies the thinking of many politicians who oppose free trade. They fear that without protective legislation we shall soon not be able to produce anything, because developing countries will produce everything much more cheaply. This fear is unfounded. Even if a country produces everything more efficiently than we can—that is, if it enjoys an **absolute advantage** in producing the goods—it will still pay for that country to import some goods from us. That is, the other nation may be able to produce some goods slightly better than we can, but it can produce other goods much better than we can. The other nation will be best off if it specializes in the areas where its absolute advantage is greatest, where it enjoys a comparative advantage.

One can find a perfect illustration of the principle of comparative advantage in the career of Babe Ruth with the Boston Red Sox and New York Yankees. From 1915 through 1917, Babe Ruth was one of the best pitchers in baseball. During that period he won sixty-five games for the Red Sox and lost only thirty-three with an earned run average of only 2.02. As late as 1919 he started seventeen games for the Red Sox (and completed twelve) and had an earned run average of 2.97. After that year, however, Ruth was sent to the Yankees, for whom he pitched in only five games in fifteen years.[11] Instead, Ruth played right field, while the Yankees used pitchers who were clearly his inferiors.

Ordinarily, one would question the sanity of a manager who starts a lesser player in place of a star. In this case, the management of the Yankees recognized that Ruth enjoyed an absolute advantage over the Yankee pitching staff, since he would have done a better job than most of his team's pitchers. Using pitchers other than Babe Ruth probably cost the Yankees an extra run or two every fourth game because the other pitchers were not as good. However, the Yankees also recognized that they would score several additional runs every game if Ruth could concentrate on his hitting. The fact that Babe Ruth was an excellent pitcher but became a towering figure as an everyday player meant that he had an absolute advantage at both positions but had a comparative advantage as an everyday player. Because he specialized at what he was relatively best at, Babe Ruth—and the teams that he played for—are now acknowledged as among the best that ever played the game.[12]

CONCEPT CHECK

People should not try to be self-sufficient. They are better off when they specialize in one activity and buy what they lack from others. They should specialize in the activity at which they have a comparative advantage. One has a comparative advantage in the activity in which one is relatively best. One can be better than others at many different activities, but one has a comparative advantage only in that activity at which one's superiority is greatest.

WHEN MARKETS FAIL

Markets generally do a good job of allocating resources to their most desired use. Government intervention intended to improve the market outcome—such as the price ceilings previously discussed—actually produce a worse outcome. Under certain conditions, however, markets fail to perform properly. When markets fail, government intervention can lead to a socially preferred outcome. Three common sources of market failure, *monopoly* power,

---

[10]Buchholz, 1989, pp. 64–65.
[11]Data were taken from "Babe Ruth's Lifetime Stats" online at http://www.baberuth.com/stats.html.

[12]For a more complete treatment see Scahill, 1990.

monopsony power, and *externalities,* play a major role in the sports marketplace. In learning about each source of failure you will also learn

- The monopoly power of the NFL in negotiating media contracts played a major role in an $18 billion television deal.
- The monopsony power that leagues used to exert allowed them to keep the salaries they paid well below what the players were worth. The loss of this power led to an explosion of salaries.
- The positive externalities that cities see in having a professional franchise have led them to provide massive subsidies to millionaire owners.

A firm has **monopoly** power when it dominates a market enough to be able to set the price it wants for a product. When a firm operates in a *competitive* market, it has so many rivals selling the same product that it would lose all its business if it tried to charge more than the prevailing market price. A souvenir vendor selling a Cleveland Indians pennant for $6 will quickly go out of business if he is surrounded by vendors who are selling the same pennant for $5. Firms with monopoly power—a "monopolist" holds the greatest such power by being the only firm in the marketplace—can set the price that they deem best. Monopoly markets are thus marked by higher prices and—since demand curves slope down—lower output than competitive markets.

Firms that compete with each other in a market sometimes try to join together and exercise monopoly power that no one of them could exercise alone. They *collude* with one another by setting a common price and coordinating their sales policies. The U.S. government effectively outlawed most monopolies and collusive organizations, known as *trusts,* with the 1890 Sherman Act. The act and most of the legislation based on it covers two basic types of activities. It prohibits "every contract, combination, . . . or conspiracy in restraint of trade or commerce." It also makes it illegal for firms to "monopolize or attempt to monopolize, or combine, or conspire . . . to monopolize" trade or commerce.[13]

The government can deal with a monopoly by breaking it up into many smaller, competing firms, as the government sought to do with Bell Telephone in the 1980s. When the government feels that many small firms will operate far less efficiently than one large firm, it may allow the monopoly to remain intact but closely *regulate* its actions.

Professional sports and amateur sports have enjoyed a number of exemptions from our nation's antitrust laws. Baseball enjoys the most extensive exemption of any sport thanks to a 1922 Supreme Court decision that declared that baseball "was not within the scope of federal antitrust laws."[14] None of the other major sports, and no other industry, shares this blanket exemption from antitrust laws. The courts quickly recognized the illogic of baseball's exemption. Though they steadfastly refused to reverse their ruling on baseball, they did hand down repeated decisions that denied similar exemptions to other sports.

The other major sports have exemptions that are limited to specific activities, such as merchandise marketing and media contracts. Even these *limited exemptions* from the antitrust laws have played a major role in the development of several sports. The lifeblood of the National Football League, for example, is its national television contracts with CBS, Fox, and several cable channels.[15] In 1960, the NFL remained a distant second to baseball in popularity. Its games were typically played in baseball stadia and were televised (if at all) under low-paying, locally negotiated agreements.[16] All this began to change when Pete Rozelle was named commissioner of the NFL in 1960. Rozelle immediately sought to replace the collection of local TV markets with a single, centrally negotiated contract. Such a single, network-wide contract meant that stations that wanted to televise a football game had to deal with a single provider, giving the NFL monopoly power over the supply of games to television. The prospect of

---

[13]Quoted in Roberts, 1991, p. 135.

[14]Decision of Chief Justice Oliver Wendell Holmes quoted in Zimbalist, 1992.
[15]Sheehan (1996) claims that if it were not for its lucrative national TV deals, the NFL would be no more profitable than the NHL.
[16]The reliance of football on baseball can even be found in the names of the older teams. The Detroit Lions, Chicago Bears, and New York Giants played off the popularity of the Detroit Tigers, Chicago Cubs, and New York Giants.

monopoly power meant that Rozelle first had to obtain exemption from the antitrust laws. In 1961 Congress did extend a limited exemption to the sports not covered by baseball's exemption, allowing them to negotiate contracts as leagues rather than on a team-by-team basis (Leifer, 1995).

The monopoly power conveyed by the limited exemption gave football the power to restrict the number of games carried on television and to increase the broadcast fees it could charge many times over. Prior to being granted exemption from antitrust legislation, the New York Giants made $200,000 per year from their television contract, while the Green Bay Packers made only $30,000 (Leifer, 1995, p. 130). A recent contract that the NFL signed with ABC, CBS, and ESPN will pay the NFL $18 billion over eight years. When that sum is split evenly among the thirty teams, that works out to approximately $75 million per team per year. Inflation and the growing popularity of football (due in no small part to television) do not come close to explaining such astonishing growth in revenue.

The fact that the revenue goes to the league, not individual teams, and is then split evenly also helps to explain how the NFL can field competitive teams in cities as different as New York and Green Bay. Because the NFL gets so much of its revenue from a common source, the distribution of revenue is the most equal of all the major sports. As a result, football does not have a gulf between teams from "large markets" and teams from "small markets."

While monopolies typically operate in the market for goods and services, one generally finds **monopsonies** in the market for inputs like labor. For much of their history, the major sports teams held extensive monopsony power. Teams were able to limit their players' ability to sell their services to the highest bidder. One powerful tool at their disposal was the reserve clause, which effectively bound a player to his team for as long as the team wanted him.[17] With players unable to seek higher pay elsewhere, owners used this monopsony power

to depress wages well below those that would prevail in an open market.

While the reserve clause no longer exists in any major sport, teams still seek to limit player mobility and salaries. Hockey retains the greatest restrictions on mobility, as relatively few players become unrestricted free agents. Baseball has the fewest restrictions, though it has recently introduced a "luxury tax." The luxury tax forces teams that spend more than a specified amount to pay an additional sum into a central pool. This pool is then divided among teams with smaller revenues.

Football and basketball lie between hockey and baseball: Players have relatively easy access to free agency, but *salary caps* impose direct limits on the amounts teams can pay. Salary caps specify that players get a given share of the league's revenues.[18] This share of overall revenues is then split evenly among the teams. Thus, if a league with thirty teams has agreed to pay its players 60 percent of its $1 billion revenue, then each team has a "cap" of $20 million. To allow some room for negotiation, the cap is actually a band of possible amounts centering around the official cap. Teams have become so expert at exploiting loopholes in the salary cap regulations, however, that very few teams actually pay less than the amount specified by the salary cap. During the 1997–1998 season, Michael Jordan alone made more than the official salary cap of the Chicago Bulls. The NBA owners locked out players in 1998 in a successful effort to strengthen the team salary cap by placing limits on how much individual players can earn.

A third cause of market failure is the fact that an individual's or firm's decisions may affect innocent bystanders who have no say in that decision. Economists call such spillover effects *externalities*. An externality that has a deleterious impact on bystanders is called a **negative externality.** The best-known example of a negative externality is pollution. Pollution is a by-product of the production process that affects the health and well-being of individuals who have no say in what the firm does. Because the firm has no reason to account for the costs it imposes on innocent bystanders (it may not even be aware that it is imposing such costs), it does

---

[17]Professional soccer also placed restrictions on player movement through the use of "transfer fees." These fees force teams to provide monetary compensation to teams whose players they have signed.

[18]The definition of "revenue" has been the source of contentious bargaining between the leagues and the players' unions.

not build these costs into its production decisions, and therefore it overproduces. For example, a chemical factory may have production costs of $15 per gallon for the chemicals that it produces, while the pollution it discards into a nearby stream imposes costs of $10 per gallon on a nearby community. If the firm can charge $20 per gallon, it sees that its marginal benefits ($20) outweigh its marginal costs ($15) and will try to expand. The marginal cost to society as a whole, however, includes the pollution ($15 + $10 = $25). This means that society would be better off if the firm produced less.

The conflict between the private decision and the public desire lies at the heart of the market failure from externalities. Governments try to eliminate the conflict by getting the firm to "internalize" the externality. In this example that means getting the firm to account for the damage its pollution causes when it makes its production decision. This often takes the form of fines, taxes, or fees for "pollution permits."[19]

Not all externalities cause harm. A firm's production may convey unintended benefits on the surrounding community, creating a **positive externality.** A firm that creates a positive externality does not take account of the full benefits that it provides to society and produces too little as a result.

Governments try to encourage firms that provide positive externalities to produce more. This sometimes takes the form of patents or copyright laws that give the creator monopoly power over her crea-tion. In other cases, the government provides direct subsidies, such as the grants it provides to individuals and companies that perform basic research.

In recent decades, state and local governments have become increasingly involved in subsidizing sports teams. For example, in 1950 only one major league baseball team (the Cleveland Indians) played in a publicly built stadium. By 1985, seventeen teams were playing in publicly built stadia. In football, the Los Angeles Rams, Los Angeles Raiders, Cleveland Browns, and Houston Oilers all moved to smaller markets (St. Louis, Oakland, Baltimore, and Nashville) to occupy publicly funded stadia. Cities justify such subsidies for team

owners who can often be found on *Forbes* magazine's list of America's 400 wealthiest individuals by citing the positive externalities associated with a professional franchise.

Proponents of subsidies claim that the expenditures by fans who attend a sporting event create a ripple effect, not unlike the ripples one sees after throwing a pebble into a still pond. The initial impact is the spending by fans at the stadium and at area hotels and restaurants. The expenditure adds to the incomes of people associated with the team and with the city's hospitality industry in general. These people then spend some of their extra income on a variety of goods and services, adding to the incomes of yet another group of people, starting another round of expenditure. The initial expenditure thus generates additional income for a wide variety of people who have nothing at all to do with the team or stadium, so the initial expenditure might be multiplied many times over. Cities see this indirect **multiplier effect** as a way to stimulate economic growth and to generate tax dollars.

The debate over sports subsidies hinges on the size of the direct impact of the stadium and of the multiplier effect of the initial impact.[20] Most economists agree that the direct impact of a stadium is far smaller than one might believe. A stadium induces growth in a city's economy only if it generates new expenditure within the city's bounds. If a sports franchise draws fans away from some other form of entertainment—if, for example, fans stop going to a local college basketball game in order to attend a professional game—the franchise is rearranging existing expenditure, not generating new expenditure.

Multiplier effects can be similarly overstated. The size of a multiplier depends upon how much induced expenditure remains within the city. Smaller cities are especially likely to see "leakages" into surrounding communities, as people spend money in nearby towns. Regardless of the size of the city, most of the income accrues to a relatively small number of people earning unusually high incomes. These people generally live outside the team's "home" city and spend their time and money elsewhere. They are also likely to spend less of their additional income than are people of more modest means. Smaller induced

---

[19]One can buy such permits on the Chicago Mercantile Exchange.

[20]Noll and Zimbalist (1997) has an excellent discussion of the problems involved in measuring the benefits a franchise brings to a city.

expenditure further reduces the overall multiplier effect.

As a result of the confusion over direct impacts and multiplier effects, estimates of the value of franchises to cities vary widely. In one particularly egregious example, two studies of the impact that the loss of the Colts had on Baltimore's economy varied by a factor of one hundred fifty.[21]

CONCEPT CHECK

Externalities are side effects of a firm's production decision that affect innocent bystanders who have nothing to do with the firm's actions. Positive externalities confer benefits on innocent bystanders and negative externalities impose costs. Firms that impose negative externalities overproduce, since they do not absorb the full costs of their actions. Firms that confer positive externalities underproduce, since consumers do not pay for all the benefits they receive.

CRITICAL THINKING EXERCISES

1. You are a city official in Oakhurst, NJ. A minor league baseball team approaches you and offers to locate in Oakhurst if you will subsidize a new ballpark. What factors should you consider before responding?
2. You are the owner of a franchise that has just been fined $10 million for violation of antitrust laws. What should you do to ticket prices as a result?

SUMMARY

1. Economics explains why people behave the way they do. It states that people follow certain rules of behavior regardless of the social and institutional setting.
2. All our actions involve costs and benefits. Many costs do not involve explicit expenditures. Opportunity costs are the value of actions we could have undertaken but chose not to. Opportunity costs distinguish

an economist's view of profits from an accountant's view of profits. Opportunity costs explain why a highly profitable team like the Brooklyn Dodgers would choose to move to Los Angeles.
3. Decisions are typically made on the margin. People choose how much of a good to consume by weighing the marginal benefits and marginal costs. Firms base their production decisions on marginal revenues and marginal costs. Sunk costs, expenditures that have already been made, have no role in our decisions.
4. Freely functioning markets are typically the best way to allocate resources. The forces of supply and demand naturally push the market toward equilibrium with no central authority.
5. Demand curves show the quantity of an item that consumers are willing and able to buy at a given set of prices. Supply curves show the quantity of an item that producers are willing and able to sell at a given set of prices. The equilibrium price and quantity can be found at the intersection of the supply and demand curves.
6. Price ceilings impose artificial upper bounds to the price. Keeping the price below the equilibrium creates shortages and may prevent the people who most value the item from being able to obtain it. Anti-scalping laws often exacerbate the problem.
7. People should specialize and trade with one another according to their comparative advantage. The best pitcher on the great Yankee teams of the 1920s hardly ever pitched for them. Babe Ruth had an *absolute* advantage as a pitcher, since he was better than the other pitchers on his team. The other pitchers, however, had a *comparative* advantage over Ruth as pitchers because the cost to them of concentrating on their pitching was far less. They did not have Ruth's potential as an everyday player.
8. Under some circumstances, markets fail, and government can increase social well-being. Monopoly, monopsony, and externalities are three forms of "market failure."
9. Monopoly, a market in which there is only one firm, occurs when there is only one seller in a market. Sports leagues exert monopoly

---

[21]One cited a cost of $200,000 per year, while another said the cost would be $30 million per year (see Quirk and Fort (1992), p. 173).

power by colluding, agreeing on common pricing and output strategies. Monopoly power gives league members the power to charge higher prices than if they competed with one another. All the major sports leagues exert monopoly power over national TV contracts. The monopoly power of the NFL helps to explain its recent $18 billion agreement.

10. Sports teams used to be able to hold salaries below the equilibrium level by exerting monopsony power over their players. Monopsony exists when there is only one buyer in a market. Leagues owed their monopsony power to the reserve clause, which prevented players from selling their services on an open market.

11. Externalities consist of "innocent bystander effects," in which people who are not involved in the market decisions of producers and consumers are affected by those decisions. A negative impact results in a negative externality, and a positive impact results in a positive externality. Professional franchises often use positive externalities to justify the subsidies they demand from cities. They claim that the dollars spent on sporting events have multiplier effects on the local economy.

CASE STUDY

Free agency caused salaries in major league baseball to explode. In the first decade of free agency, the average salary rose approximately 700 percent, from about $51,500 in 1976 to over $370,000 in 1985. Owners grew increasingly alarmed as salaries rose to unprecedented levels. In an effort to control salaries, owners replaced Commissioner Bowie Kuhn with Peter Ueberroth, the man responsible for staging the highly profitable 1984 Olympic Games in Los Angeles.

Almost immediately, Ueberroth set out to discourage the owners from spending so freely for free agents. He delivered blistering lectures to them denouncing their free-spending ways and urged them to let each other know which free agents they wished to retain. His arguments had an immediate impact on the owners. Between the 1985 and 1986 seasons, roughly two-thirds of all free agents re-signed with their original teams without a single offer from another team. Salaries rose an anemic 5 percent. Between 1986 and 1987, average salaries actually fell

by 2 percent. Andre Dawson, one of the few stars to sign with a new team, did so only by presenting a signed contract to the Chicago Cubs and telling them to fill in whatever salary they wanted to pay.

The Major League Baseball Players' Association (MLBPA) immediately began to suspect that the owners were conspiring with one another. It responded by filing two separate grievances with independent arbitrators, charging that the owners were colluding with one another in violation of the terms of the collective bargaining agreement. Both arbitrators ruled in favor of the MLBPA. As a result, the owners were forced to stop their collusive behavior and to pay $280 million in damages.

REVIEW QUESTIONS AND ISSUES

1. Teams that win championships often raise their prices the following season. Use supply and demand to explain why.

2. A student on a full athletic scholarship at Temple University claims that her education costs her nothing. Explain the error of her reasoning.

3. Why did the Philadelphia Flyers raise ticket prices when they first signed Eric Lindros?

4. Neighborhoods with sports facilities often complain about traffic tie-ups, loud noises late at night, and increased crime rates. Explain how this shows that sports franchises can produce negative externalities as well as positive externalities.

5. Why did Deion Sanders give up a lucrative career as an outfielder to play football full-time?

6. Professional sports teams have "territorial rights" that prevent other teams in their league from moving close by. Explain how this gives teams monopoly power.

SOLUTIONS TO CRITICAL THINKING EXERCISES

1. You will want to weigh the costs and the benefits of the franchise. The largest benefit will be the increased spending that occurs in town. You must be careful to count only additional spending in town. You do not want to count expenditures that people make when going to a baseball game that they would have made on some other activity in town (e.g., going to the local cinema). You will want to apply the appropriate multiplier to the

added expenditure to account for the ripple effects of the added expenditure. Since Oakhurst is a small town and much of the economic impact is likely to spill over, the multiplier effect is likely to be small. You may want to account for intangible benefits like increased visibility and civic pride, although these are hard to quantify. Against these benefits you will want to measure the costs that a stadium will impose on Oakhurst. You will want to count explicit costs, like expenditures or subsidies, as well as implicit costs, like tax breaks or the value of land donated for the stadium.

2. The fine is a sunk cost. You will have to pay $10 million regardless of how many games you play or tickets you sell. If you want to maximize your profits, you should operate where marginal revenue equals marginal cost. The fine does not affect the profit-maximizing decision. It just means that the profits you make will be lower than before.

REFERENCES

Buchholz, T. (1989). *New ideas from dead economists.* New York: New American Library.

Frey, B., Pommerehne, W., Schneider, F., and Gilbert, G. (1984, December). Consensus and dissension among economists: An empirical inquiry. *American Economic Review* 74 (5), 986–94.

Leifer, E. (1995). *Making the majors: The transformation of team sports in America.* Cambridge, MA: Harvard University Press.

Noll, R., and Zimbalist, A. (1997). The economic impact of sports teams and facilities. In *Sports, jobs, and taxes: The economic impact of sports teams and stadiums,* ed. R. Noll and A. Zimbalist. Washington, DC: Brookings Institution Press.

O'Sullivan, A., and Sheffrin, S. (1998). *Microeconomics: Principles and tools.* Upper Saddle River, NJ: Prentice-Hall.

Quirk, J., and Fort, R. (1992). *Paydirt: The business of professional team sports.* Princeton, NJ: Princeton University Press.

Roberts, G. (1991). Professional sports and the anti-trust laws. In *The business of professional sports,* ed. P. Staudohar and J. Mangan. Urbana, IL: University of Illinois Press.

Rockoff, H. (1990, August). The Wizard of Oz as a monetary allegory. *Journal of Political Economy, 98* (4), 739–60.

Scahill, E. (1990, Fall). Did Babe Ruth have a comparative advantage as a pitcher? *Journal of Economic Education.* pp. 402–10.

Sheehan, R. (1996). *Keeping score: The economics of big time sports.* South Bend, IN: Diamond Communications.

Sullivan, N. (1987). *The Dodgers move west.* New York: Oxford University Press.

Zimbalist, A. (1992). *Baseball and Billions,* New York, Basic Books.

WEBSITES

"Sherman Takes the Field" at *http://userwww.service.emory.edu/~tyavero/antitrust/*

Examines the legal ramifications of the monopoly and monopsony power exercised by sports leagues. It also provides links to related sites.

"New Park Financing" at *http://www.wcco.com/sports/stadiums.html*

Examines several recent stadium deals, paying particular attention to the contributions made by states and municipalities. The link to *http://www.ballparks.com* lets you read about current and old stadia and arenas.

CHAPTER 19

Accounting and Budgeting

Elizabeth Barber

In this chapter, you will become familiar with the following terms:

Accounting
Balance sheet
Assets
Current assets
Long-term investments
Depreciation
Liabilities
Current liabilities
Long-term liabilities
Equity
Income statement
Gross sales

Net sales
Cost of goods sold
Gross profit
Gross margin
Operating expenses
Net income
Net profit
Net loss
Percentage column
Cash flow analysis
Journals
Budget

Object classification budget
Line item budget
Increment-decrement budget
Program budget
Performance budget
Planning programming budget
 system (PPBS)
Zero-based budgeting
Capital budget
Enterprise fund system
Fund accounting

Overview

The management of the annual budget or financial accounting statements will be the responsibility of all managers in the field of sport. The depth and breadth of their knowledge, of course, will be situation-specific, but all managers must be able to read and interpret financial statements and prepare and control an annual budget. The intention of this chapter is not to make the reader an accountant, but rather to help the future sport manager become accounting- and finance-literate. Most business operations will always retain the

services of a professional accountant, in addition to the on-site manager, but this is no reason for the sport manager not to be familiar with financial management.

Whether the enterprise is public (owned by the municipality or other government), nonprofit (college, university, YMCA, youth sport club, and the like), or private (in legal terms, the three forms of business ownership are sole proprietorship, partnership, or corporation, with examples being professional sport teams, health clubs, and retail stores), financial knowledge is imperative to the success of business operations. Managers who don't use proactive methods of financial control will soon find themselves unemployed.

Note: Otho G. Bendit, formerly of the University of Notre Dame, and Linda S. Koehler, University of the Pacific, contributed to this chapter.

The purpose of this chapter is to give the sport management student a finance and accounting overview. Issues dealing with profit or loss are among the most critical management functions for even the seasoned manager, so the importance of this chapter cannot be understated.

This chapter will cover two major topics. The first part of the chapter will discuss principles of accounting; financial statements, including balance sheet, income statement, and cash flow analysis. The second part of the chapter will discuss principles of accounting, along with different types of budgeting, for nonprofit organizations, municipalities, and government-owned operations.

DEFINITION AND ROLE OF ACCOUNTING

Accounting can be defined as the collection of financial data about an organization (Bendit and Koehler, 1991). The process includes gathering, recording, classifying, summarizing, and interpreting data. Accounting examines an enterprise's profit or loss, determines how it occurred, and determines assets and liabilities, all in relationship to the form of business ownership. These entities can be related to one another to provide information about the financial status of the business. This information helps the sport manager in the planning process and in making crucial financial decisions.

Cash versus accrual accounting

A manager who uses *cash-accounting* methods records revenues and expenses *only* when cash is actually received. For example, charge sales are not reported until the charge is paid or when the charge account has a zero balance. The same is true of charged purchases. When a business receives merchandise and the bill is not payable for thirty days, then the reporting of the expense only occurs when the bill is paid.

Accrual-accounting methods record revenues and expenditures as they occur—that is, a charged sale or a charged purchase is recorded on the same day it takes place under the accrual method.

Professionally speaking, the accrual method is the most often used because it is believed to show the most accurate picture of the revenue and expenditures of the business.

FINANCIAL STATEMENTS

A manager's primary task in financial management involves ensuring a profit for the enterprise, having current information on the financial condition of the business, and knowing the cash flow of the operation to prevent shortages. With this in mind, the following financial statements become the working tools of the sport manager. Financial statements are generally calculated annually, quarterly, and monthly in order to describe the financial condition of the organization (Crossley and Jamieson, 1997). These financial statements are normally used by private (for-profit) business enterprises, but in some cases of public/nonprofit ownership, a manager could be expected to use them. This is especially true of the balance sheet.

Balance sheet

The **balance sheet** is considered one of the most important financial statements. The four main uses of the balance sheet are that it (1) shows changes in the business over a period of time, (2) shows growth or decline in various phases of the business, (3) shows the business's ability to pay debts, and (4) through ratios, shows financial position.

Assets. The balance sheet is exactly what the name implies. It shows a balance in a business's assets as compared to the liabilities and owner's equity. On the left side of the balance sheet, one will find a listing of the assets (see table 19-1). **Assets** are considered to be what a business owns. The listing of assets is considered individual accounts. For example, the value that coincides with the asset called inventory would be backed up with an inventory account record. Assets can be divided into (1) current assets, (2) long-term investments, and (3) fixed assets.

Current assets are considered cash on hand and any asset that can be converted to cash within twelve months from the date on the balance sheet. Examples of current assets include accounts receivable (charges owed by customers), inventory (wholesale cost), temporary investments (e.g., interest-bearing bank accounts), certificates of deposits (CDs), stock in another business that will be converted within one year, and prepaid expenses (e.g., rent, insurance).

Long-term investments are any investments made by the business that have a maturity date beyond one year. One example would be a CD purchased with a five-year payoff date. *Fixed assets* are the items a business owns that cannot be sold without changing the business operations. Examples of fixed assets are real estate (land and buildings), furniture, equipment, and automobiles.

TABLE 19-1   *Balance sheet: ABC Sporting Goods yearly report*

Assets		Liabilities	
Current assets		**Current liabilities**	
Cash	$20,000	Accounts payable	$ 7,200
Accounts receivable	8,000	Short-term loans	0
Inventory	50,000	Interest payable	6,000
Short-term investments	5,000	Current portion of	
Prepaid expenses	3,720	long-term loan	12,000
Total current assets	86,720	**Taxes payable**	
Long-term investment	0		
		Accrued payroll	2,300
Fixed assets		Total current	
Land	0	Long-term liabilities	27,500
Building: $48,000 cost		Long-term liabilities	
accumulated (50 yr.)		Loans payable	72,000
depreciation of		Total liabilities	$99,500
$1920, book value	46,080		
Fixtures: $35,000 cost	28,000	**Equity**	
accumulated (10 yr.)			
depreciation of $7,000,		Montague's investment	20,000
book value		Hicklin's investment	20,000
Furniture: $10,000 costs	8,000	Plus net income	81,000
accumulated (10 yr.)		Less total partner	
depreciation of $2,000,		withdrawal	41,000
book value		Total partner equity	$80,000
Automobiles: $15,000 cost	10,700	Total liabilities and equity	$179,500
accumulated (7 yr.)			
depreciation of $4,300,			
book value			
Total fixed assets	85,100		
Total assets	$179,500		

Depreciation is a legal term used by businesses to lower the value of an asset as it gets older. After an asset is purchased and begins to be used in daily operations, the value of that item diminishes. The straight-line method of depreciation estimates the "life" of an asset, the amount of time one would expect this asset to last. For example, what is the life expectancy of a car? If it's estimated to be seven years and the original cost of the car was $14,000, then every year $2,000 would be deducted from the book value of the car listed on the balance sheet. This is not to say that in seven years the car does not have any *market value*, but rather, for the purpose of calculating the assets of this business, the car has been totally depreciated for income tax purposes because depreciation is tax-deductible (table 19-1).

The total amount of assets will be found at the bottom of the asset side of the balance sheet. It is computed by adding together the total current assets, long-term assets, and fixed assets.

Liabilities. **Liabilities** are considered a business's debt, how much money the business owes to other parties. Liabilities are found in the right-hand column of the balance sheet and are divided into current liabilities and long-term liabilities.

Similar to current assets, **current liabilities** are those debts that must be repaid within one year. Examples of current liability accounts include accounts payable (goods and services purchased on credit, usually payable within thirty days), short-term notes (amount of principal owed to a lender, totally payable within one year), the current portion of long-term notes (current principal amount due), interest payable (interest due on either short-term or long-term notes), taxes payable (only applicable to a corporation that owes corporate taxes), and accrued payroll (salaries or wages due).

Long-term liabilities include all the loans a business may have that are not currently payable. These are usually larger loans that were acquired to purchase large items (fixed assets), such as real estate, automobiles, and fixtures needed to open a business for operations.

All the current liabilities and long-term liabilities are added together to come up with the total for liabilities owed.

Equity. Owner's **equity** is the amount of money invested by owners. In a sole proprietorship, the business begins with the amount of money the owner invested from personal funds. In a partnership, it is the amount of money each partner invested individually. Earned income is added to the owner's investment. Subtracted from this amount are any withdrawals made by the owner. This amount would now be considered the total owner's equity. Equity is found underneath liabilities on the balance sheet (see the following box). This should be defined individually for each owner.

Equity equation

Owner's investment
+ Income earned
− Withdrawals made
Owner's equity

In a corporation, the equity would include all the stockholders' purchased shares of stock.

Once the total liabilities and the total equity are calculated, these two figures are added together. The combined values should equal (be balanced with) the total assets found in the column on the left in Table 19-1.

Income statement

Another extremely important financial document is the income statement. The income statement and the balance sheet are often used by bankers or interested investors when it comes to making decisions about lending to or investing in a business. The importance of these two documents cannot be overstated.

The purpose of the **income statement** is to analyze the success of a business. The profit (or loss) of a business is found in the income statement. This allows a manager to compare the cost of running a business with the sales generated. The purchases and distributions made to the owners rely on the income statement. An income statement is read from the top down. The top line is the gross proceeds, with the bottom line reflecting the net income (see table 19-2). The exact items found on the income statement will depend on the nature of business. The following information discusses typical items listed on many businesses' income statements.

Sales. *Sales* figures always appear first on an income statement. **Gross sales** are the total amount of revenue (excluding sales tax) that is generated. Revenue that is obtained through ticket sales, merchandise purchased, food service, memberships, etc., is considered gross sales. If a business has a return policy—where money is given back to dissatisfied customers—this amount should be subtracted from the gross sales figure. Other values that should be subtracted are called *allowances* (e.g., discounted sale price, cost of stolen or shoplifted merchandise, losses incurred from damages, and prompt-payment discounts). The resultant figure is called **net sales.**

The **cost of goods sold** (sales) must be calculated (see the equation in the following box). The beginning inventory's value is based on the wholesale

---

Cost of goods sold

Beginning inventory
+ Purchases
Total goods
− Ending inventory
Total cost of goods sold

TABLE 19-2   *Income statement: ABC Sporting Goods, yearly report*

	Amount ($)	% of net sales
Revenue		
Gross sales	273,200	101
Less sales returns and allowances	3,200	1
Net sales	270,000	100
Cost of sales		
Beginning inventory	50,000	18.5
Plus purchases	135,000	50
Total goods available	185,000	69
Less ending inventory	50,000	18.5
Total cost of goods sold	135,000	50
Gross profit	135,000	50
Operating Expenses		
Salaries and wages	22,000	8
Commissions	2,300	1
Advertising	1,500	0.5
Insurance	2,500	1
Depreciation	9,300	3
Interest	6,000	2
Office supplies	800	0.02
Utilities	2,200	1
Miscellaneous	7,400	2.7
Total operating expenses	54,000	20
Total operating income	81,000	30
Pretax income	81,000	30
Tax on income (corporation only)	0	
Net income (net profit)	81,000	30

cost of the merchandise. The value should be calculated on the first date of the income statement, usually the beginning of the year. The addition of the purchased inventory should include all purchases throughout the entire period (usually one year). From the total amount of merchandise, the ending inventory is subtracted. Ending inventory is the cost of the "remaining in inventory" on the last day of the year.

When the cost of goods sold is subtracted from net sales, the resulting value is called the **gross profit** or **gross margin.**

Operating expenses. **Operating expenses** include all other expenses a business accrues during day-to-day operations. Examples of operating expenses include salaries, insurance, rent or loan payments, advertising, and utilities. The income statement is used by most business owners to complete income tax forms. For that purpose, you will find such deductions as depreciation, even though it is not considered actual cash paid out by the business. Depreciation is used to replace fixed assets that have been used during normal business operations; in other words, it is considered the cost of doing business (Ellis and Norton, 1998).

Earnings before taxes and taxes due. A business owned as a sole proprietorship or a partnership is not responsible for paying federal income taxes. The owners of the business are required to declare the percentage of the business profit that is attributable to their specific percentage of ownership on their individual income tax. Only the corporation is required to pay corporate income tax on the business's profits. State or local municipalities may have separate laws that govern a specific location. The business owner should be aware of this; but if this isn't the case, this section of the income statement can be omitted.

Net income or net profit. **Net income** or **net profit** is the amount of money remaining after all expenses (liabilities) have been paid. This amount can be used for retained earnings for the business, divided among partners, or used to pay dividends to stockholders in the corporation. If the business accrues a **net loss** over the year, the amount of the loss will be shown in parentheses—e.g., (4800) represents a $4,800 loss.

Percentage column. The **percentage column** is a very useful management tool. It can show a manager what percentage of the net sales is being spent in specific areas of the business. If a particular percentage appears to be too high (higher than last year's income statement or higher than the standards set in this type of business operation), the manager will know that the expense should be lowered. For example, if the cost of goods sold in a retail operation is 75 percent of the net sales, most managers would consider this percentage too high. To remedy this situation, one could either raise the retail price so that net sales would increase or search for other wholesale vendors that would sell merchandise to the business at a lower cost, which would decrease the cost of goods sold.

Cash flow analysis

Cash flow financial statements serve a third purpose for the sport manager. The information found in the cash flow document is a detailed accounting of receipts (revenue) and disbursements (expenses). Cash flow does *not* tell the manager the business's financial condition (balance sheet), nor does it show the profit or loss (income statement) of the business. It only shows the manager "cash in" and "cash out." Cash flow is normally documented monthly. This gives the manager the ability to analyze the financial situation over a period of time. Also, after several years of business operations, the manager is able to see patterns of cash flow that might indicate the need for a short-term loan or, just the opposite, periods of time when cash is abundant and should be invested for maximum profit opportunities. Table 19-3 shows an example of a **cash flow analysis.**

Journals

Journals (sometimes referred to as *ledgers*) are the financial documents that the sport manager uses for recording all financial transactions during day-to-day operations. Most businesses use two basic record books: sales journals and disbursement journals (Pickle and Abrahamson, 1986).

Sales journals. Sales journals record cash sales and receipts of daily income. The journal headings are based on the exact specifications for the business. For example, a stadium operation might define its journal headings as ticket sales, concession sales, group sales, and Skybox sales. See table 19-4 for an example of a sales journal from a golf club.

A more detailed look at the sales receipts is warranted if the manager wants more specific information. In the case of the golf course's greens fees and pro shop sales, it might be appropriate to divide sales into cash and charge categories. Or membership dues could be divided into new memberships and renewals. The options are virtually unlimited, the point being that every business should design its sales journal in the manner deemed appropriate.

The sales journal can also be used to verify the amount of cash that is deposited in the bank daily. By adding the columns, it is easy for a manager to

TABLE 19-3 *Cash flow analysis: ABC Sporting Goods, 1st quarter 20XX*

	January	February	March
Sales			
Inventory			
Clothing	2,300	2,700	3,400
Equipment	10,540	1,500	9,900
Layaway paid	1,320	1,000	4,000
Total sales	14,160	5,200	17,300
Less cost of			
sales	7,300	7,000	7,200
Gross margin	6,860	(1,800)	10,100
Less expenses			
Salaries	1,200	1,200	1,200
Commission	800	300	0
Advertising	100	300	100
Insurance	0	1,250	0
Loan payment	700	700	700
Office supplies	150	70	50
Utilities	250	250	200
Miscellaneous	300	200	540
Total	3,500	4,270	2,250
Cash Flow			
A − B = C	3,360	(6,070)	8,850
Surplus (or deficit)			
Cash balance			
Cash at start	0	3,360	290
Cash flow	3,360	(6,070)	8,850
Bank loan (L)		3,000L	3,000R
or rent (R)			

see if discrepancies exist. The totals are also used for the income statement and cash flow analysis. All the financial statements should be used to cross-check one another.

Disbursement journal. The *disbursement journal* is similar to the sales journal in its format. The column headers are changed to reflect expenditures specifically defined by the individual business. Examples of disbursement category headings are payroll, all

TABLE 19-4 *Sales journal*

Date	Account or description	Greens fees ($)	Pro shop ($)	Food and beverages ($)	Lessons or tournaments ($)	Member fees ($)
June 1	Daily sales	366	127.43	100.20	55	1,500
June 2	Daily sales	824	447.60	275.75	110	9,000
June 3	Daily sales	455	235.75	155.45	0	500
June 4	Daily sales	875	455.00	325.40	330	2,500
June 5	Daily sales	1,225	347.25	466.65	220	0
June 6	Daily sales	665	348.50	207.65	55	0
June 7	Daily sales	235	473.90	768.45	2,300	0
Week total		4,645	2,435.43	2,299.55	3,070	13,500

TABLE 19-5 *Disbursement journal*

Date	Payee or account	Check no.	Amount of check ($)	Vendor inventory ($)	Advertising ($)	Payroll ($)	Food and beverages ($)
June 1	T. Jones, Mgr.	1010	987.43	0	0	987.43	0
June 1	A. Stone, Mgr.	1011	632.76	0	0	632.76	0
June 1	Philadelphia Beverage	1012	98.10	0	0	0	148.10
June 2	Spalding Golf Distribution	1013	887.66	887.66	0	0	0
June 2	WMMR Radio	1014	350.00	0	350.00	0	0
June 4	MaxFli Golf Supplies	1015	544.78	544.78	0	0	0
June 5	Pennsylvania Liquor Authority	1016	99.75	0	0	0	249.75
	Total distribution	—	3,603.48	1,432.44	350.00	1620.19	397.85

types of vendor purchases (e.g., merchandise, food, beverages), advertising, and insurance. The income statement and cash flow analysis documents should use the same terminology (see table 19-5).

The columns of the disbursement journal are usually totaled at the end of the month, although some businesses choose to do it more often. The uses of this information are numerous. For example, the columns that coincide to the items on the income statement can be used to formulate that finan-cial document, and the total amount for checks writ-ten can help the manager check bank statements.

A more detailed explanation of how to set up journals can be found in many small-business man-agement courses and textbooks.

SUMMARY OF ACCOUNTING

Accounting practices vary with the form of business ownership, but the three most commonly used financial statements are the balance sheet, the income statement, and the cash flow analysis. All three financial statements serve a different purpose and should be used together. Journals are used to record all sales and disbursements, whether either cash or accrual accounting methods are used.

The intention of the previous section was to prepare the sport management student with a working knowledge of accounting practices. More in-depth knowledge should be obtained in a small-business management or accounting and finance course.

CONCEPT CHECK

The three financial statements used to manage the financial aspects of a business are the balance sheet, income statement, and the cash flow analysis. The balance sheet shows the financial condition of the business; the income statement shows profit or loss in the business operations; and cash flow analysis shows cash sales and disbursements records.

ACCOUNTING FOR PUBLIC/NONPROFIT ORGANIZATIONS—BUDGETING

Most organizations that operate as a nonprofit enterprise (e.g., private universities or nonprofit clubs that are supported by voluntary contributions and other sources) or that are organized as a part of a governmental agency (municipalities and state-owned universities that are tax supported) receive allocations from the general fund of the overall unit. These entities are established under specific regulations and restrictions, by law, to operate on a nonprofit basis. Therefore, they are not subject to income tax laws. In sport management, examples of these types of operations are school athletic programs, community youth sport programs, club sport programs, and municipal golf courses.

Each year, a public/nonprofit organization submits a budget request to its superior body (e.g., city council budget review committee, university financial officer, board of directors). A sport manager will be competing for funds with many other groups within the organization (unless it is an athletic department that is expected to be self-sufficient). Over the past decade, traditional sources of revenue, including tax support, broadcast revenues, and gate receipts, have not kept up with rapidly escalating costs (Masteralexis, Barr, and Hums, 1998, p. 67). The way in which the budget is presented, the selection process for the items included on the budget, and the related justifications are three extremely important tasks required of a management team. Remember that a sport or athletic program is only one part of a large picture, and the preparation and administration of an effective budget is probably one of the best public relations tools a manager can use, internally and externally. On the other hand, the mishandling of funds, when other constituencies are vying for a "share of the same pot," can be professional suicide. The purpose of the budgetary process is to facilitate the realization of the organization's goals and objectives through fiscal responsibility, sound business practices, effective decision-making, and prudent financial management (Stier, 1999 p. 158).

Types of budgets

By definition, a **budget** is a statement of financial position based on estimates of expenditures and suggested proposals for financing them—in other words, a management plan for revenue and expenses of an organization for a period of time (usually 1 year). Some of the criteria to consider when establishing a budget are past revenues generated, changes in prices or fees, marketing research predictions, the current promotion and advertising strategies, and the economic environment of the general public and the institution (Bendit and Koehler, 1991). The following list includes practical advantages of budgeting:

1. It substitutes a plan for "chance" in fiscal operations; foresees expenditure needs; and organizes staff, along with the work that needs to be accomplished.
2. It requires a review of the entire operation (all divisions and subdivisions) in terms of funds available and revenue needs; it prevents over-budgeting (padding).
3. It promotes standardization and simplification of operation by establishing priorities and objectives, and it eliminates inefficient operations.
4. It provides guidelines for a staff to follow.
5. It provides the governing body with factual data for evaluating the efficiency of the operation.

6. It helps the taxpaying public (contributors) to see where revenues are coming from and what expenditures are for.
7. It acts as an instrument for fiscal control.

Object classification budget. The **object classification budget** is one of the most traditional types of budgets and one of the easiest to understand. To conceptualize an object classification budget, one must understand the basic premise of structure that the budget uses: It is established using an object classification that defines the areas of expense in a uniform grouping of categories. The following is a typical classification system:

1000 Services: Personnel
   1100 Salaries, regular
   1200 Salaries, temporary
   1300 Wages, regular
   1400 Wages, temporary
   1500 Other compensations
2000 Services: Contractual
   2100 Communication and transportation
   2200 Subsistence, care, and support
   2300 Printing, binding, and advertising
   2400 Utilities
   2500 Repairs
   2600 Janitorial
3000 Commodities
   3100 Supplies
   3200 Materials
4000 Current charges
   4100 Rents
   4200 Insurance
   4300 Refunds, awards, and indemnities
   4400 Registrations and memberships
5000 Current obligations
   5100 Interest
   5200 Pensions and retirement
   5300 Grants and subsidies
   5400 Taxes
6000 Properties
   6100 Equipment
   6200 Buildings and improvements
   6300 Land
7000 Debt obligations

The advantage of this budget's classification is the uniformity of the numbering system and the ease in setting up the budget. The clarity among similar organizations can be very helpful to the sport manager for the purpose of making comparisons.

Line item budget. The **line item budget** is very similar to the object classification budget, and these two budgeting systems are the most often used in the public sector. The term *line* refers to the listing of each item on a line in the budget; the items are not defined by a numbering system, they are simply listed by name. This allows for more flexibility than the object classification budget. See table 19-6 for more details on setting up a line item budget.

In the early 1900s, line item budgets listed every single cost item—for example, each employee's name was listed under the salary/wage category. The complexity of this method is obvious. Now a budget includes expenditure categories in an effort to simplify the system (Deppe, 1993).

Increment-decrement budget. This type of budget is considered an extension of the object classification and line item budgets. The increment budget consists of adding or deleting a certain percentage to the current budget. The increases or decreases can be attributed to specific line items or object classifications or the overall budget will reflect equal adjustments based on the percentage. The purpose of the **increment-decrement budget** is to provide a predictable growth or decline over a period of time, which allows for planning, especially long-range planning (Kelsey and Gray, 1986).

Program budget. The **program budget,** unlike the three previous budgets, separates an organization by unique units. A program budget could easily be adopted by an athletic department. Each sport would develop a separate budget, with a narrative description of the sport's goals and those features of its program that are deemed to be the most important. This allows the athletic director to compare the various budget requests and make decisions based on a fuller understanding of their needs instead of simply looking at lines and numbers. The three components of a program budget are (1) agency goals, (2) program goals, and (3) unique features of the program. This process is then followed by a line item or object classification budget.

TABLE 19-6   *Line item budget for XYZ Swim Pool and Club*

	Current budget	Proposed budget
Personnel		
Manager	$ 4,000	$ 4,500
Guards	6,300	6,700
Instructors	2,800	3,000
Coaches	1,200	1,500
Maintenance	1,000	1,200
	15,300	16,900
Supplies		
Office supplies	350	450
Operating supplies	4,600	5,000
Repair and maintenance supplies	3,500	3,900
Miscellaneous	500	600
	8,950	9,950
Operations		
Utilities	4,200	4,500
Telephone	400	500
Insurance	1,300	1,400
Printing and advertising	600	700
Security	500	650
	7,000	7,750
Capital expenditure		
Equipment	3,500	4,000
	3,500	4,000
	$34,750	$38,600

Performance budget. The difference between a program budget and a performance budget is minute. The purpose of a **performance budget** is to explain what services are being provided by the institution rather than just how much money is being spent. The budget is broken into categories or service activities. Each category is defined by the amount of time that is involved to perform the activity. Then a cost can be attributed to each activity. The manager has a great deal of financial control and can be precise when using this type of budget (Kelsey and Gray, 1986).

Planning programming budget system (PPBS). The focus of this type of budget is on the end product of the service provided rather than the actual cost. One of the purposes of the **planning programming budget system (PPBS)** is to provide a rationale for each of the competing budget units within an agency or department. The budget provides a narrative picture of the expenditures rather than simply listing the amount of money spent. When resources are scarce, this budget type can be a useful management tool (Kelsey and Gray, 1986).

Zero-based budget. A **zero-based budget** is based on the premise that an organization begins each year with no money. This type of budget was designed to stop basing the current budget on last year's budget (Rue and Byars, 1995). From that point, a budget is prepared by justifying each expenditure as if it were a new expense. The purpose of this type of budget is to control overbudgeting and waste. The manager has to scrutinize the reasonableness of every budget request in relationship to the whole department.

This method is a radical departure from traditional methods that look at past costs, add an increment for projected expenses, and continue to operate in the same manner year after year (Deppe, 1993).

Capital budget. A **capital budget** describes capital expenses that include long-range budget items. A capital budget usually covers a number of years—as many as ten years. It includes major purchases, such as new buildings and equipment, that are not found in operating budgets that only cover one year. Capital budgets, like program budgets, require a narrative explanation or justification for each expense.

Enterprise funds

A newer method of financial management that is being implemented in many public/nonprofit organizations is called the **enterprise fund system.** The premise that this system works on is that every individual program of operation is viewed as a separate enterprise. The revenue generated by the enterprise is then used to finance the enterprise's operation.

Originally, the enterprise fund system expected the operation to break even, which meant that the enterprise needed to generate at least as much income as was budgeted for expenses. But it is more common today to expect a profit. In a municipal setting, this could mean that the profit generated by a financially successful enterprise, such as the community golf course, could be used to fund another program, such as the "latch-key program" for underprivileged youth, which is known to lose money.

Fund accounting

Fund accounting is a standard method of accounting used by many government operations (Rossman, 1984). A fund is defined as a fiscal and accounting entity with a self-balancing set of accounts recording cash and financial resources, with liabilities and equity. The format of the financial document is very similar to the balance sheet. The accounts are separate operations (programs or activities) within the organization, and they include funds that aren't necessarily reflected in day-to-day operations, such as capital funds, benefits funds, or retirement funds. The segregation of the fund accounts usually has been specified by external sources, such as the board of directors (Rossman, 1984). Sometimes these funds are referred to as cost or revenue centers.

Annual reviews of the accounts will be used to evaluate the activities that took place within the segregated fund. Decisions will be made on the fund account's future, based on the growth or decline in the financial picture of the account. Getz (1997) describes cost-revenue management as an important process of reviewing and identifying all cost and revenue centers to ensure financial health (p. 230).

BUDGET PROCESS

It is important to follow a systematic process when it comes to developing or reviewing a budget. Ten steps have been identified as a comprehensive approach to the budget process. Keep in mind that the budget should be completed and approved months in advance of the organization's financial calender year.

Step one—Examine the organization's mission, goals, and objectives.

Step two—Research the organization's strengths and resources relative to the future needs.

Step three—Include all key players in the budget process. The knowledge and expertise of others should be included in the data-gathering step, as well as the actual construction of the budget.

Step four—Review the information and data gathered. Include a past, present, and future analysis.

Step five—Prepare the budget by using the budget type, as well as the criteria set forth by the organization's executives.

Step six—Examine the budget for accuracy, feasibility, and reality.

Step seven—Submit the budget to a few key people for additional critical analyses.

Step eight—Prepare and execute a formal budget presentation. Anticipate questions and timely responses.

Step nine—Implement the budget.

Step ten—Audit the budget. This should be done as the cyclical budget process begins for the next year (modified from Stier, 1999).

SUMMARY OF ACCOUNTING FOR PUBLIC/NONPROFIT ORGANIZATIONS

Separate budgets can be written for expenditures and revenues, or the projected revenue should be included in the expense budget. Most departments or programs have some method for generating income. Projected revenues should be estimated in the same way expected expenses are. Whether it be in ticket sales, user fees, or memberships, the amount of income required to operate the programs should be projected. This can be very useful in getting approval of the budget from the financial director, because it shows potential. In the book, *The Ultimate Guide to Sport Event Management & Marketing,* the authors describe the "Elements of a Successful Sport Event Business." One of those elements states that a successful plan will explain how you will amortize this capital investment and repay the loan or provide profits for your shareholders (Graham, Goldblatt, and Delpy, 1995, p. 193). The type of budget chosen will be decided upon by the institution or the department, so the sport manager should become familiar with a variety of methods.

The sport manager will have two important functions when it comes to dealing with the financial affairs of the department. The first is to oversee disbursements made by each unit, making sure that budgets are not overspent. The second is to develop a budget that will make it possible for the institution to realize the highest possible return on its investment (Lewis and Appenzeller, 1985).

Enterprise funds and fund accounting are two terms the sport manager should be familiar with because of their implications for public/nonprofit financial accounting.

CONCEPT CHECK

The two most important tasks a sport manager will have to master when it comes to budgets is to (1) prepare and justify the annual budget and (2) control the expenses and disbursements once the budget has been approved.

CRITICAL THINKING EXERCISES

1. You are the new athletic director of an athletic department that has a national reputation as a financial success story. What part will you play in financial decisions?
2. As the executive director of a major sport event that is seeking corporate sponsorship, which financial statements will you prepare for potential sponsors? This event has been estimated to bring 30,000 visitors and $10 million to your community.

SUMMARY

Sport managers, regardless of their specific job function within the organization, will have a critical role in the management of capital revenue and expenditures. The understanding of accounting and finance cannot be understated. Every sport business needs to be concerned with fiscal responsibility and sound business practices. This is true for both profit and nonprofit businesses and organizations. The need to develop and follow a sound budget and to make effective and efficient fiscal decisions is essential for every business and organization (Steir, 1999).

The $152 billion estimate of sport product and services spending based strictly on spectator sport and sport participation, ranks the industry as the eleventh largest industry in the United States (Hiestand, 1997). This figure should have all potential sport managers extremely sensitive to financial issues. This chapter is truly the first education in a series of educational experiences that a sport management student should encounter during their academic curriculum.

CASE STUDY I: PREPARING THE INCOME AND EXPENSE STATEMENT

The statement of income and expense (profit and loss statement) covering the past fiscal year for the athletic department must be submitted to the university accounting office in one month. As the director of athletics, you are responsible for several programs. One is varsity sports, which include football, women's basketball, men's basketball, women's volleyball, and men's baseball as revenue-producing sports. Non–revenue-producing sports in your program are track, wrestling, swimming, tennis, and field hockey. In addition, there are several club sports under your direction. These are soccer, rugby, lacrosse, water polo, and crew. Finally, your department oversees a fitness program offered to faculty, their partners, retirees, and students.

1. *What are some typical accounts you would use for each program?*
2. *What special income and expense accounts are you likely to encounter for each program?*
3. *Into what major categories would the income and expense statement be divided?*
4. *What types of indirect overhead would you have for each program?*
5. *How would indirect overhead expenses affect your figures?*

CASE STUDY II: PREPARING THE BUDGET

As manager of a corporate fitness program, it is your responsibility to submit a budget for the next fiscal year to the director of human resources and development. The fitness program, which employs two fitness specialists and you, has operated for three years and has consistently lost money. The director of human resources and development has agreed to subsidize the program with an additional $10,000 with the understanding that a portion of the funds will be allocated to a marketing and advertising campaign.

1. *What steps would you take in planning and preparing your budget?*

2. *From whom would you solicit information?*
3. *What options do you have when allocating funds?*
4. *What changes in the budget would you propose?*
5. *Would the process of forecasting be helpful to you? If so, how?*
6. *How might asking "what if" questions be useful?*

REVIEW QUESTIONS AND ISSUES

1. What is accounting, and what is the difference between cash accounting and accrual accounting?
2. What are the three financial statements most often used in business, and what is the major purpose of each?
3. What are assets, liabilities, and equity in reference to a business? How is each used on a balance sheet? What is depreciation?
4. What is the difference between gross sales, net sales, gross profit, and net profit?
5. How does one calculate the cost of goods sold?
6. What are some examples of operating expenses?
7. What are sales and disbursement journals, and how are they used?
8. How does accounting differ in a private business operation versus a public/nonprofit organization? Give examples of each type of business operation.
9. What are the most commonly used types of budgets? Describe how each type is set up.
10. What are enterprise funds, and how are they being used in public operations?
11. What is fund accounting, and who would be most likely to use it?

SOLUTIONS TO CRITICAL THINKING EXERCISES

1. All financial decisions ultimately rest on your shoulders. Never take the position that, "if it isn't broken, don't fix it." The type of budget used will be a university decision, but the budgetary process, the contents of the budget, and the implementation of the budget will be your responsibility. So include all the steps of the budget process and surround yourself by the key individuals who will give you the best advice and support before you make the required presentation to the board of trustees.

2. Most communities are frantically looking for ways to bring outside revenue into their cities. Sport events have been identified as attractive ways to do this. Before corporate sponsors are going to support your efforts, they will expect to see all of your financial statements. This is especially true if this event has been produced in the past. If other communities have sponsored this event in the past, if available, their financial records would be a tremendous help. In any event be prepared to distribute a complete event plan, which among other things must have a detailed and clear financial report. Even if the event has the status as a nonprofit, a pro forma balance sheet and income statement are essential.

REFERENCES

Bendit, O. G., and Koehler, L. S. (1991). Accounting and budgeting. In Parkhouse, B. L., *The management of sport: Its foundation and application.* St. Louis: Mosby Year Book.

Crossley, J. C., and Jamieson, L. M. (1997). *Introduction to commercial and entrepreneurial recreation.* Champaign, IL: Sagamore.

Deppe, T. R. (1993). *Management strategies in financing parks and recreation.* New York: Wiley.

Ellis, T., and Norton, R. L. (1998). *Commercial recreation.* St. Louis: Times Mirror/Mosby.

Getz, D. (1997). *Event management and event tourism.* Elmsford, NY: Cognizant Communication Offices.

Graham, S., Goldblatt, J. J., and Delpy, L. (1995). *The ultimate guide to sport event management & marketing.* Chicago: Irwin.

Hiestand, M. (1997). How big's the big? *USA Today,* Feb. 14, 2C.

Kelsey, C., and Gray, H. (1986). *The budget process in parks and recreation.* Reston, VA: AAHPERD.

Lewis, G., and Appenzeller, H. (1985). *Successful sport management.* Charlottesville, VA: Miche.

Masteralexis, L. P., Barr, C. A., and Hums, M. A. (1998). *Principles and practice of sport management.* Gaithersburg, MD: Aspen.

Pickle, H. B., and Abrahamson, R. L. (1986). *Small business management.* New York: Wiley.

Rossman, J. R. (1984). Fund accounting: A management accounting strategy. In Bannon, J. J., ed., *Administrative practice of park, recreation and leisure services.* Champaign, IL: Management Learning Laboratories.

Rue, L. W., and Byars, L. L. (1995). *Management skills and application.* 7th ed. Chicago: Irwin.

Siropolis, N. (1984). *Small business management: A guide to entrepreneurship.* Boston: Houghton Mifflin.

Stier, W. F. (1999). *Managing sport, fitness and recreation programs.* Needham Heights, NJ: Allyn & Bacon.

WEBSITES

Resnick, Amersterdam, Leshner P.C. CPA
www.ral-cpa.com/ralsports.htm
Building Sports and Entertainment Businesses
The accounting/consulting firm Resnick, Amersterdam, Leshner P.C. has served over thirty professional sports franchises or entertainment businesses since 1986. The firm helps organizations grow their revenues, control cash flow, and manage investments. They also provide tax and financial planning for professional athletes and entertainers.

Team Marketing Report Inc.
www.teammarketing.com/io.htm
Team Marketing Report Inc. specializes in developing a complete directory of the ownership and financial structure of pro sports. TMR has joined forces with Houlihan Lokey Howard & Zukin, (www.hlhz.com), the specialty banking firm and advisor to over thirty sport franchises. The result is the most complete source of sports business data and analysis around, including inside details on every MLB, NBA, NFL, and NHL franchise, broadcast deals, revenue figures, lease arrangements, sponsorships, and more.

CHAPTER 20

Financing Sport

Tom H. Regan

In this chapter, you will become familiar with the following terms:

Financing sport
Cash flow
Exemption
Municipal securities (munis)

Revenue bonds
Investing activities
Financing activities
Operating activities

Cash inflows
Cash outflows

Overview

Professional, collegiate and interscholastic organizations require financing options and opportunities to compete in the business of sport. Leagues, teams, and communities are challenged to maintain and support adequate facilities and teams for sport organizations.

Financing sport related facilities often requires public, private and joint public/private financing. The financial arrangements surrounding sport may be the most creative area of business outside the playing field. Financing sport business is a simple enough concept: You must have adequate funds to enable the landlord, tenant, and team owner to start, expand, and continue operations.

The purpose of this chapter on **financing sport** is to explain a few of the various types of financing needed for different sport organizations and establish the need for cash flow management. The fact that funds are needed is the simple part. Where they come from is another matter. We will identify the sources of different financing options. **Cash flow** is essential to a successful sports enterprise. Sport is

seasonal in nature; the teams play specific schedules during assigned times. The management of cash flow requires a knowledge of finance, accounting, and basic business principles such as the *time value of money* and *discounted cash flow.* The list is by no means exhaustive, but a strong foundation for the sport business manager.

THE PUBLIC NEED

It is important for government leaders to attract professional teams to their region or city. In the United States, cities compete to attract and retain professional sports franchises. Federal, state, and local governments subsidize the financing of sports facilities. Financing arrangements are a key element to attract teams and investors. A key element of the funding plans is the **exemption** from federal and most state and local income tax on the interest earned on qualified **municipal securities (munis)** that could be issued to finance these stadiums. The borrower can then sell bonds at a lower interest rate than if the interest was taxed.

Government authorities are usually proponents of stadiums. They claim that without the necessary local support, teams might choose to relocate and the cities would lose employment, tax revenues, and other indirect benefits. Government opponents claim that benefits are probably overstated and likely future costs understated, making probable the need for even more public support in the future.

Sport facility financing

"If you build it, they will come," is the familiar passage from the hit movie *Field of Dreams*. Professional, collegiate, interscholastic, and touring sports require adequate facilities to practice and play the game, in addition to attracting fans. The United States has great athletic facilities throughout the country. Often stadiums become a source of regional community pride, for example, Oriole Park at Camden Yards in Baltimore, Maryland, and The Ballpark, in Arlington, Texas.

The majority of professional and university sport facilities have traditionally been financed by municipal debt, with annual debt service funded from the municipality's general fund or from one of several other revenue sources. In recent years, due to the recession, an increase in construction costs, and municipality budget constraints have resulted in various private-sector financial participation. Private-sector participation in financing facilities is primarily due to the increase in available revenues generated by the facility. These public, private, and joint public/private financing arrangements are necessary for sport facility construction today.

Public facility financing

Sport arenas, stadiums, and multipurpose facilities are large capital projects for municipalities. Several mechanisms are used in structuring public-sector participation in sports facility development, expansion and renovation. Among the most common public-financing instruments are bond issues backed by general obligations and/or dedicated revenues, lease appropriations bonds (certificates of participation), and tax increment bond financing. For a breakdown of public-financing instruments, see the following box.

> ### Public-financing instruments
>
> * General-obligation bonds
> * Revenue bonds
> * Certificates of participation
> * Tax increment bonds

State and local governments issue bonds in the capital market to finance their capital spending programs: construction of arenas, stadiums, parking lots and infrastructure upgrades. Infrastructure improvements include roads, water/sewer, and other utility needs. Investors call these bond issues *municipals* because they are issued by municipalities, subdivisions of states; they are also called *tax-exempts* because the interest investors receive is exempt from federal taxation. Most states exempt state income tax as well on the interest earned from their bonds. Each state differs on how interest earned on bonds is taxed on a state basis. For example, in South Carolina citizens do not pay state income tax on bonds issued by a state municipality; however, bond interest earned from out-of-state bonds is subject to South Carolina income tax.

General obligation bonds. General obligation bonds, backed by the full faith and credit of the issuing body (state, local or regional government), generally require the use of ad valorem taxes. *Ad valorem* taxes are property taxes. This means taxes are levied according to the value of one's property; the more valuable the property, the higher the tax, and vice versa. The underlying theory of ad valorem taxation is that those owning the more valuable properties are wealthier and hence able to pay more taxes. General obligation (GO) bonds typically result in lower costs of issuance and higher credit ratings and the bond size is often reduced because a debt reserve fund is not always required. However, in some cases, the bonding capacity of the municipal unit for other capital needs can be reduced.

Revenue Bonds are special obligations in public financing which are payable solely from a particular source of funds, which may include tax/surcharge revenues from hotel/motel, restaurant, sales, liquor/beer, cigarettes, rental cars, and other sources. For a list of public-facility funding sources, see the box on the next page.

Public-facility funding sources

- Hotel tax
- Meals tax
- Liquor tax
- Sales tax
  - Auto rental tax
  - Property tax
  - TIFF Districts
  - Business license tax
- Utility tax
- Road tax
- Public and private grants
- State appropriation
- Taxi tax
- Team tax

No pledge of state, regional, or local ad valorem tax revenues is required; however, the typical revenue bond does carry a higher interest rate and require a higher debt service coverage ratio as well as debt service reserve.

Certificates of participation (COPs). This public-financing mechanism involves the governmental entity creating a corporation to buy or build a public facility, such as an arena or convention and visitors' center. The corporation then issues certificates of participation to raise money to buy (build) the public facility. The government leases back the building, and the lease payments build pay back the bonds. All this happens without a public vote.

Though certificates of participation (COPs) seem like traditional bonds, they are *not* backed by the full faith and credit of the government entity that issues the bonds. In a recession-hammered environment, Certificates of Participation and lease appropriation financing become popular with local governments looking to fund projects as real estate values decline, and with them property tax collections. These securities are not backed by the full faith and credit of a municipality; therefore, they are a greater risk than a general-obligation bond and rated a full step lower.

Tax increment financing (TIF)

Tax increment financing transactions are based on the incremental property tax value of the ancillary economic development projects that are triggered by a major new facility. The tax base of a defined area identified as the tax increment financial (TIF) district surrounding the capital project is frozen and any increases in the tax base are used to repay tax increment financing bonds. The area surrounding the facility may be one county/parish or several counties/parishes.

The economics of any tax increment financing district are highly dependent on the development potential of a chosen site and its surrounding land. It is essential to anticipate future revenues on increases in ad valorem taxes or funding sources, described in the box shown on the left.

Other public-sector contributions

The general public indirectly subsidize sport organizations in other ways. There are a number of ways facilities have obtained additional public funding or government has directly reduced interest costs or borrowing requirements. A few of these mechanisms include the purchase or donation of land; funding of site improvements, parking garages, or surrounding infrastructure; direct equity investments or construction of related facilities, either directly or through an independent authority and lending the government's credit by guaranteeing payment on new debt. Public-sector financing is extensive in professional sport franchises. Cities, states, and regional communities have financed the construction of major arenas, stadiums and related convention centers for the benefit of the economic community. A recent trend is a joint financial arrangement, described in the next section.

CONCEPT CHECK

Facility construction often requires public-financing instruments. General-obligation bonds, revenue bonds, certificates of participation, and tax increment bonds are the primary financial mechanisms used by municipalities to develop, expand, and renovate facilities. Each public-financing instrument has advantages and disadvantages ,-depending on the financial situation of the community and the issuer.

Private and joint public/private financing

The trend seems to be leaning toward joint public/private partnerships. Public/private partnerships have been utilized for the financing of major public-assembly projects, particularly sports facilities. Typically, the public sector utilizes its authority to implement project funding mechanisms, with the private sector contributing project-related or other venue sources. The expanded revenues generated by the facilities and their tenants have resulted in increases in the level of private participation in facility financing. Several of the private-sector revenue streams, which have been utilized in structuring facility financing include the items in the box on the right.

Recent examples of joint public/private participation are illustrated in Table 20-1. It is clear that there has been extensive state and local government interest in the development of sports and other

---

Private-sector revenue streams

- Premium seating
- Building rent
- Corporate sponsorship
- Lease payments
- Vendor/contractor equity
- Parking fees
- Merchandise revenues
- Advertising rights
- Concession revenue
- Naming rights
- Food and beverage serving rights

---

public-assembly facilities in recent years, and there are a variety of means with which to structure the financing for those facilities. Expanding building

TABLE 20-1   *Financing participation for public/private facilities*

Arena	Public	Private
Alamodome	City revenue bond backed by 0–5% sales tax	Arena revenues
America West Arena	City revenue bonds backed by excise taxes	Naming rights
		Arena revenues
Bradley Center Arena	Land donation purchased with general bond issue	Local family donation
Charlotte Stadium (proposed)	Land donation	Naming rights
		Arena revenue
		Premium seating deposits
		Luxury suite revenue
Coors Stadium	Special tax district revenue bond secured by sales tax increase (1/10) of 1%	Naming rights
		Arena revenues
Delta Center Arena	City tax increment financing bonds	Private loan secured by building revenue
		Naming rights
Cleveland Cavaliers Arena	County general-obligation bonds	Private donations and foundation contributions
	Luxury tax allocation	Premium seat deposits and revenue
Target Center Arena	Tax increment financing bonds	Loan secured by arena and health club revenues
		Naming rights
Ballpark in Arlington	City revenue bond secured by sales tax increase	Luxury suite revenues
	Infrastructure improvements	Ticket surcharge
		Seat options
		Concessionaire payment

operating and tenant revenue streams have encouraged a public/private partnership whereby public-sector financing vehicles (various bonding techniques) are supplemented with private-sector revenue streams. Creative financial arrangements allow communities to benefit economically and create a lifestyle conducive to public opinion. Table 20-1 provides examples of how communities created a financial vehicle to build sport and entertainment facilities.

Examples of financing new stadiums include the following: The Alamodome in San Antonio, Texas, is a 77,000 seat domed arena. The Alamodome was completely funded by an additional 0.5 percent sales tax on all retail sales. The $170 million project was completed in 1993 and is now debt free. Therefore, the facility only has to cover operational expenses, not bond premium and interest expense.

Another example concerns the Colorado Rockies, the newest member of the National League and Major League Baseball. The Rockies attracted over four million six hundred thousand fans during the 1993 season. Coors Stadium was completed for the 1995 season opener in Denver. The new stadium did cost $179,803,016 to complete. Financing the stadium required a vote by the public to collect 0.1 percent sales tax upon all taxable retail sales within the jurisdiction of a special tax district. The special tax district includes six Colorado counties, Adams, Arapahoe, Denver, Jefferson, Boulder, and Douglas. Colorado state legislators allowed the special tax district to be created in H.B. 90-1172, therefore, creating a financial mechanism to provide a sales tax revenue stream to finance the $158 million in revenue bonds necessary to build Coors Stadium.

A key element in financing sport-related facilities is the relationship between government and entrepreneurial sport owners. A public/private partnership exists between the parties to create an entertainment and economic opportunity for the regional economy. Without this relationship, few professional or collegiate programs could financially exist. Financing facilities and the revenue streams shared between the tenant and the municipality are essential for retaining and attracting sport franchises, special events, and fans.

The proper financial team needs to be assembled in order to design, organize, and finance a public, private, or public/private facility. Components of a successful team should include the following members:

- Issuer/owner
- Facility management
- Feasibility consultant
- Examination accountant
- Business plan consultant
- Financial advisor
- Architect
- Cost estimator
- Design builder
- Construction manager
- Senior underwriter
- Co-underwriter
- Bond council
- Issuer's council

The financing team must work together to obtain the goal and objectives of the community or owner. Each facility scenario is different and requires study and analysis. Successful facility financing is a partnership between the regional community, the owner/tenant, government, and the financial institutions (Figure 20–1).

The next section focuses on the revenue streams in sport and the importance of cash flow management.

CASH FLOW IN SPORT

All good business requires the proper utilization of cash. Sport is a seasonal business that requires careful cash management. Professional sport franchises cost hundreds of millions; to purchase existing teams and expansion franchises require tens of millions. For example, the Baltimore Orioles were recently purchased for an estimated $173 million, and the Philadelphia Eagles are expected to receive approximately $185 million. Major League Baseball expansion teams in 1993 were required to pay $95 million for the privilege of joining the league. National Football League owners required a franchise fee projected at $140 million and the National Hockey League expansion franchise fee was $50 million.

Major collegiate athletic departments have budgets in excess of $20 million. The athletic director must be a fund-raiser, budget director, and professional manager. The college athletic department requires proper use of cash flow to help finance and schedule stadium maintenance, sport expansion, or post season play.

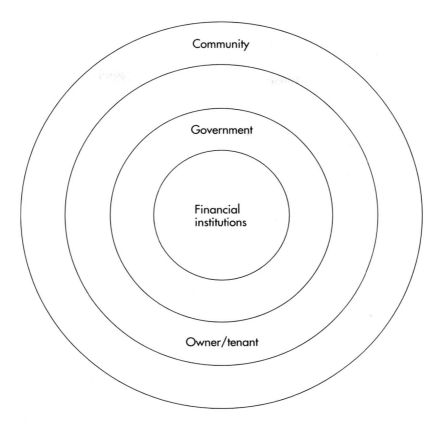

FIGURE 20–1   Community partnership for facility success.

Revenue streams

Sports create revenue streams and produce cash very quickly. The major revenue producers are ticket sales, concessions, advertising, broadcasting (local radio, local television, national media), parking, preferred seating, and licensing agreements, along with other miscellaneous revenue. Professional sport organizations negotiate a contract with the, municipalities. For example, the Colorado Rockies lease includes the following terms with the Special Tax District and the city and county of Denver. Table 20-2 identifies the sharing of revenue in a publicly financed stadium.

The Colorado Rockies' stadium agreement is beneficial to the team, as Table 20-2 indicates. The public officials must consider the overall business relationship between the owners, other Major League Baseball owners, and the subsidizing public. Each must feel the new franchise in Colorado has a reasonable opportunity to be economically successful. Leagues, teams, cities, and businesses need cash flow to successfully operate.

Cash flow is defined as reported net income plus amounts charged off for depreciation, depletion, amortization, extraordinary charges to reserves that

---

TABLE 20-2   *Colorado Rockies Stadium agreement summary*

Date of agreement	March 14, 1991
Term	17 years, with option to renew for 5-year term

Sharing of revenue

Admissions	Starting in 2000, team pays $2\frac{1}{2}$% of net taxable income, provided partners of team have received distributions equal to 5% of contributions
Concessions	Team keeps all revenue
Parking	Team keeps all revenue
Advertising	Team keeps all revenue
Other events	Team keeps all revenue
Television revenue	Team keeps all revenue
Stadium club	Team keeps all revenue
Set fees	—
Reimbursements	Starting in 1995, team pays city up to $150,000 a year for operating costs if city's costs exceed revenues
Miscellaneous	—

Sharing of costs

Field maintenance	Team
Stadium maintenance	Team

Game day

Ushers, etc.	Team
Security	Team
Cleaning	Team
Utilities	Team
Field equipment	Team
Concession equipment	Team

Data from Hurt, Richardson, Garner, Todd, and Cadenhead: Stadium lease arrangements. In International City Managers Associations, Sports and Special Events Conference, San Antonio, Texas, 1993.

---

are bookkeeping deductions, and not paid out in actual dollars and cents. The primary purpose of a cash flow statement is to provide relevant information about cash receipts and cash disbursements of an enterprise during a particular period. This will help investors (partners), creditors, and others to:

1. Assess the team's ability to generate a positive future net cash flow
2. Assess the sport enterprise's ability to meet its obligations
3. Assess the difference between net income and cash receipts and disbursements
4. Assess the effects of both cash and noncash investing and financing during a period

The term *cash* in FASB 95 refers to cash in the bank and all short-term liquid investments that can be readily converted to cash. Examples of items considered to be cash equivalents are marketable securities with less than three months maturity, treasury bills, commercial paper, and money market funds.

Cash receipts and cash disbursements are classified as operating, investing, or financing activities. In sport organizations it is often difficult to compare teams, and the statement of cash flows provides an opportunity to compare similar enterprises. **Investing activities** include the purchase or sale of securities or other entities, the sale or purchase of fixed assets, and loans made or payments on loans received. **Financing activities** include issuing securities, borrowing, paying of dividends, buying treasury stock (the company's own stock), and repaying debt.

The cash flows from the investing and financing activities are usually balance sheet items. The final section of the statement of cash flows is the **operating-activities** section. This activities section covers everything that is not investing or financing activities. Daily sport business activity generates operating funds as do most business organizations on interest or dividends earned. Accounts receivable and accounts payable are generally operating activities. Cash flow derived from operating activities typically applies to the cash effects of transactions entering into profit computations. **Cash inflows** from operating activities include:

1. Cash sales or collections on ticket receivables
2. Cash sales or collections on licensed merchandise
3. Cash receipts from returns on loans (interest income) or dividend income
4. Cash received from licensees and lessee

TABLE 20-3   *Sports Enterprises, Inc. balance sheet years ending 19×8 and 19×9 (thousands of dollars)*

Assets	19×8	19×9	Cash increase (decrease)
Current assets			
Cash	$280	$230	ignore
Accounts receivable	340	380	($40)
Inventory	210	260	(50)
Total current assets	$830	$870	
Property, plant and equipment	500	525	(25)
Less accumulated depreciation	(110)	(125)	15
Net fixed assets	$390	$400	
Total assets	$1,220	$1,270	
Liabilities & stockholders equity			
Current liabilities			
Accounts payable	$220	$220	0
Taxes payable	80	110	$30
Total current liabilities	$300	$330	
Long-term liabilities—bonds	432	240	(192)
Total liabilities	$732	$570	
Stockholders equity			
Common stock	280	290	10
Paid-in-capital	40	50	10
Retained earnings	168	360	192
Total shareholders equity	$488	$700	
Total liabilities and equity	$1,220	$1,270	

5. Receipt of a litigation settlement (i.e., between city, team, owner and players)
6. Reimbursement under an insurance policy (strike insurance, etc.)

Cash outflows for operating activities include:

1. Cash paid for raw materials and merchandise for resale
2. Principal payments on accounts payable arising from purchase of goods
3. Payments to suppliers of operating-expense items (insurance, advertising, supplies)
4. Player and personnel salaries/wages
5. Payment of taxes
6. Payment of interest expense (bonds or loans)

7. Lawsuit payment (collusion settlement)
8. Charitable contributions
9. Cash refunds to customers for merchandise, ticket sales or service

Current profitability is only one important factor for success in sport. It is essential that current and future cash flows are positive. In fact, a profitable sport franchise may have a cash crisis. Inadequate cash flow has possible serious implications since it may lead to declining profitability, greater financial risk, and even bankruptcy. Teams are sold because of franchise market value increases and cash flow decreases. To demonstrate how important cash flow is to a sport manager, review the following financial statements in Table 20-3.

The balance sheet indicates all the information needed to calculate the statement of cash flows for Sport Enterprises, Inc. for the year ended 19×9. Additional information is helpful to clearly understand the cash flow statement. Earnings after taxes (net income) was $202,000; depreciation expense was $15,000 and common stock was issued.

Table 20-3 enables us to prepare a statement of cash flows as seen in Table 20-4. It is important to note that preparing a statement of cash flows involves calculating the dollar change in each of the balance sheet items *other than cash.*

It is important to note that Sport Enterprises, Inc. had $202,000 in earnings after taxes; however produced a $50,000 decrease in cash flow for the year ended 19×9.

The sport manager needs to understand why cash decreased by $50,000. This is accomplished by careful examination of the statement of cash flows in Table 20-4. Cash was primarily decreased by the retirement of $192,000 in bonds. The answer to a cash flow problem is always the change in cash. The difference between 19×8 cash $280,000 and 19×9 cash of $230,000 equals a ($50,000) decrease in cash for the period ending 19×9.

Managing cash flow is essential for the sport administration professional. Cash flow will assist in determining future expansion of facilities, players' salaries, bonuses and investment opportunities, to mention only a few essential components. The sport business game is managing cash flow. **You must win!!!**

CRITICAL THINKING EXERCISES

The Houston NFL franchise will require a record $700 million dollar franchise fee from Robert McNair. Houston was able to outbid the Los Angeles ownership group for the new franchise. You are the Chief Financial Officer (CFO) for the Houston franchise. What other financial issues must be considered for football to begin in the 2002 NFL football season?

The Philips Arena in Atlanta, Georgia, cost an estimated $213 million to build. It was a public/private partnership between the area taxpayers ($62.5 million) and private ownership. The new arena is home to the Atlanta Thrashers and the Atlanta Hawks and has ninety luxury suites and 1,800 club seats. Philips Corporation paid a record $185 million over twenty years for naming rights at the facility. What financial information is necessary to negotiate a naming rights deal of this magnitude? Consider tangible and intangible benefits from the perspective of Philips Corporation and the potential trend this may create for other new arenas.

SUMMARY

1. Financing sport-related facilities usually requires public, private, and joint public/private financing. New construction, expansion, and maintenance of stadiums, arenas,

---

TABLE 20-4 *Sports Enterprises, Inc. statement of cash flows for period ended 19×9*

Operating activities	
Earnings after tax	$202,000
Add depreciation expense	15,000
Increase in accounts receivable	(40,000)
Increase in inventories	(50,000)
Increase in taxes payable	30,000
Net cash flow from operating activities	**$157,000**
Investing activities	
Increase in plant and equipment	($25,000)
Other	0
Net cash used by investing activities	**($25,000)**
Financing activities	
Payment of dividends	($10,000)
Issue of common stock	20,000
Retirement of bonds	(192,000)
Net cash used by financing activities	**($182,000)**
Net increase (decrease) in cash	**($50,000)**

and practice facilities are assets needed to attract and retain professional teams.

2. Professional, collegiate and interscholastic sport facilities are usually built using public financing instruments such as: general-obligation bonds, revenue bonds, certificates of participation, and tax increment bonds.
3. Investors call these bond issues municipal securities (munis) because they are issued by municipalities, subdivisions of states; they are tax-exempt investment instruments and appeal to high-income investors.
4. Private-sector sport organizations are creating public/private partnerships to finance a few major sport facilities. The financing arrangement must be negotiated between the governmental unit and team ownership. Financing a public/private sport facility provides an opportunity for creative financial agreements between communities and sport owners.
5. The proper financial team should be assembled in order to design, organize, and finance a public, private, or public/private facility. A successful financial team should include: owner, facility manager, feasibility consultant, accountant, financial advisor, underwriters, bond council, and issuer's council.
6. Sport is seasonal and requires proper cash flow analysis. Season tickets may be sold six to eight months before the season opens and the business manager or controller needs to utilize proper cash flow techniques.
7. Cash flow involves knowledge of the balance sheet and income statement. FASB 95 requires a statement of cash flow to be a required financial statement for organizations. Cash flow involves inflows and outflows of cash related to operating activities.
8. Sport business managers must be aware of financial arrangements available for facility construction and how to analyze and manage cash flow.

REVIEW QUESTIONS AND ISSUES

1. Identify and discuss facilities recently constructed for sport organizations in the United States.
2. What public-financing options are available for constructing a stadium or arena?
3. Describe and identify public/private and private financing options available for construction of major sport facilities.
4. What is the difference between cash flow and cash?
5. Describe how sport is seasonal and the effect this has on cash inflows and outflows.
6. Public-financing instruments are usually tax free. What is the benefit to the investor? The benefit to the community?
7. Why do communities build stadiums for sport organizations?
8. Give examples of private financing of sport facilities.
9. Cash flow requires revenue streams. Discuss and identify the major revenue streams produced by sport enterprises.

CASE STUDY 1

Scenario

You are interested in purchasing a minor league AAA baseball team. The team is located in Colorado and requires an infusion of capital. In order to consider the purchase price you need to create financial statements, amortization, and depreciation schedules. The financial information is very poor, but what is available follows:

1. *No balance sheet, income statement, or cash flow statement exists.*
2. *The team was created in 1999 and uses the accrual basis of accounting.*
3. *The Colorado team was capitalized as follows (in 1999):*
   a. *Sold 100,000 shares of common stock for $10 per share.*
   b. *Borrowed $1,000,000 at 8 percent interest for seven years.*
4. *The team incurred certain costs and expenditures in 1999:*

a. Equipment	$ 250,000
b. Building	$1,000,000
c. Land	$ 100,000
d. Inventory (year end)	$ 20,000
e. Player salaries	$3,000,000
f. Baseball operations expense	$ 820,000
g. General and admin. expense	$ 310,000
h. Utilities	$ 100,000
i. Maintenance	$ 125,000
j. Bad-debt expense	$ 12,000
k. Insurance expense	$ 100,000
l. Miscellaneous	$ 115,000

5. *The team generated revenue in 1999 as follows:*
   a. *Ticket sales: 1,000,000 fans at $5/ticket.*

b. Stadium concessions: 1,000,000 fans at $1 per fan.

c. Parking $100,000 per year.

6. Depreciation information:

a. Building: thirty year life using straight-line method.

b. All other long-term assets over a five year life and straight-line method of depreciation.

7. Other information:

a. The baseball team must pay the city **10 percent for each ticket sold.** This is called a license fee.

b. The team invested in a **certificate of deposit (CD)** on January 1, 1999 for **twenty-four months at 10 percent compounded daily.** The CD had a **face value of $200,000** and interest income is recorded at year-end.

c. Prepaid insurance was $20,000.

d. Accounts receivable balance is **$80,000 at year-end.**

e. Accounts payable **$75,000 at year-end.**

8. Accrual basis of accounting is observed.

9. Income tax rate is 34 percent.

10. Dividend paid: $5 per share of common stock at year-end December 31. Dividend is paid each year.

11. **2000 Information: December 31, 2000**

		Balances
a.	Inventory	$ 40,000
b.	Prepaid insurance	$ 20,000
c.	Accounts receivable	$ 60,000
d.	Equipment	$300,000
e.	Accounts payable	$100,000

12. **Revenue: 2000**

Tickets, concessions, and parking same as previous year. **Don't forget interest income.**
Expenses: 2000
All 2000 expenses are the same except **depreciation expense.**

REQUIREMENTS FOR CASE STUDY:

1. Prepare financial statements for Sports Properties, Inc:

a. Balance sheets for 1999 and 2000

b. Income statements 1999 and 2000

c. Statements of cash flows for 2000

2. Prepare corresponding schedules:

a. Loan amortization

b. Depreciation

c. Cash balance "T" account schedule for 1999 and 2000

3. Do an analysis of the financial statements and indicate strengths and weaknesses of **Sports Properties, Inc. (Be specific)**

CASE STUDY 2

Scenario

The University of the South wants to increase revenue streams inside the stadium. They have decided to build luxury boxes in the stadium. They are in the process of evaluating alternative financing arrangements to fund the construction of the boxes. They need $2.5 million dollars for construction and operation. The project includes building 28 corporate boxes with 24 seats per box. Compare financing arrangements and discuss the advantages and disadvantages of each.

SOLUTIONS TO CRITICAL THINKING EXERCISES

1. The franchise must pay $700 million in cash to the current NFL owners. This fee will have to be borrowed or paid from earnings from the McNair ownership group. The ownership group must now obtain a stadium to play the football schedule—estimated cost of $300 million. The ownership group must organize an administrative staff and coaches—estimated cost of $5 million, and then draft players to compete in the NFL—estimated cost of $30 million. This must be completed before one fan has entered the proposed new facility to watch a NFL game. The essential element to plan for an expansion franchise is cash flow. The Houston organization must formulate a plan to borrow money through bank loans, public or private bonds, and equity investors to accomplish this task. The task will involve partnerships with interested corporate investors, public governmental support, and community taxpayers. The business plan has to include an anticipated rate of return for the ownership group.

2. The financial information necessary to negotiate a naming rights deal of this magnitude must include the tangible monetary benefits for Philips Corporation. You must be able to demonstrate that the naming of Philips Arena will provide $185 million of tangible and intangible exposure. The Atlanta Hawks and Thrashers will be the major tenants promoting

fan attendance. However, the concerts, road shows, and other touring entertainment will provide potentially greater attendance than the team sports. A breakdown of naming rights costs per fan per year and over the life of the twenty-year contract should be developed.

A recall survey should be developed to highlight the media exposure for the Philips Arena. The number of times the arena's name is used on national television, newspapers, and other media outlets should be recorded. The media exposure has a monetary value that can be determined by developing a schedule indicating what it would cost to advertise the brand name in the various media. The Philips Arena will be the site of future NBA and NHL all-star games and hopefully playoff games. These events will focus national and international attention on the Philips Arena.

The naming rights deal is a trendsetter for new arenas looking to subsidize public facilities that host private sport enterprises. Philips Arena's naming rights will now be the baseline for larger media markets to negotiate new naming rights agreements. It appears like a great marketing scheme, but it is really a financial arrangement between the arena and private corporations to build new multi-purpose facilities throughout the nation.

REFERENCES

Hurt, Richardson, Garner, Todd, and Cadenhead, (1993). *Stadium lease arrangements*. San Antonio, Texas. International City Managers Association, Sports and special events conference.

WEBSITES

www.heartland.org/sprtstad.htm
This website offers solutions to many public policy problems.
www.wwcd.com/stadiums/home.html
The website for dealers in the collectibles community. This website contains links to live sport scores and has a listing of stadium's and arena's seating charts.
www.sun-sentinel.com/money/details.htm
This website contains information about sports, entertainment, and news covering southern Florida.

Index

Page numbers in italic type refer to figures. Tables are indicated by "t" following the page number.